MINNESOTA HERITAGE

II

MINNESOTA HERITAGE

A Panoramic Narrative of the Historical Development

of the North Star State

Editor-in-Chief, LAWRENCE M. BRINGS

Research Editor, TRULY LATCHAW

Art Design Editors, EDWARD OLDEREN
HOWARD LINDBERG

Publishers

T. S. DENISON & COMPANY, INC.

Minneapolis

Printed in the U. S. A.
By THE BRINGS PRESS

International Copyright Secured
Library of Congress Catalog Card Number: 58-9508

IV

CONTENTS

Foreword

How can we meet the ancient admonition to "Know Thyself" except as we know whence we came, the generations of forebears who gave us life and inspiration—awareness of the ongoing stream of history in which we, too, have our being?

All this needed knowledge begins, like charity, at home—our Minnesota home. Whether native-born in this state or not, our lives and work here are bound up in the Minnesota heritage—and meaningful in some measure to Minnesota in the time to come, let us hope.

To see things in perspective is difficult but infinitely rewarding. That is the gift of this volume by eminent authors possessed of insight and experience, of rich lore and learning. To read and enjoy it is more deeply to appreciate our Minnesota heritage and thereby better to know ourselves.

J. L. MORRILL, *Former President*
The University of Minnesota

What's Past
Is Prologue

by THEODORE C. BLEGEN

In an age of anxiety it is fair to look at our past and examine our traditions, not in a mood of defeatism, but in one of courage and intelligent anticipation. Are there not poles of confidence and stability by which we can steady ourselves for ordeals of the future? Can we not gain buoyancy by viewing ourselves with historical perspective? It may be useful to recall that perspective means to look or see through, and that is one of the basic purposes of history.

In this volume a panorama is presented of Minnesota's past from geological ages and the days of native Indian nations to the coming of the white man, from explorers to modern scenes, from pioneering to the far-flung business and industry of today, from the frontier mingling of peoples to the complexities of life in the twentieth century. Here are recorded the resources of the Minnesota earth, the early trade in furs, the farming story, the building and development of schools in full range, the role of churches, and the transforming changes in transportation and communication. Government and politics, the crises of war, and the multiform aspects of peace and growth all play their significant parts; and alongside the progress of agricul-

ture and the fast pace of industrialization, one finds records of professionalization of talent and function and of institutionalizing of many forms of service. The blossoming of men's minds in science and the arts contributes to the flavor and to the substance of the story; and in every period and activity one finds, on the one hand, the impact of personality and leadership and, on the other, the aggregate of the contributions of the people in the grass-roots ranks of society—those from whom, as a statesman once said, a nation draws "its power of renewal and enterprise."

As the panorama unfolds from one stage to another, the reader is aware not only of a pervading and mounting interest, but also of sequence in events and of human forces and state-wide trends that invite a broader interpretation than particular topics reveal; and it is in this setting that perspective comes quickly to one's aid. The problem of disentangling what is unique for this one state from what is common to section or nation is baffling enough but such disentanglement is less important than it is to know what is true, whether unique or shared.

One general interpretation of Minnesota is so

simple that, perversely, we sometimes fail to see it. It is that the past of the state reveals a story of curiosity, of a stubborn and courageous will to find answers to problems—to open new paths or widen old ones to trade, agriculture, industry, education, and human welfare.

In this tradition we can view a long line of explorers who faced nearly every hazard in their stubborn effort to reduce European and American ignorance of the good earth of this region. Radisson, a seventeenth-century fur trader, fighter, woodsman, and adventurer who was among the first Europeans to see the region, was driven by curiosity and eagerness to know. A self-styled caesar of the wilderness, he came to a tangle of lands and streams and lakes, with no map to guide him. He looked and observed—and then he had a dream of what this area, "so pleasant, so beautiful and fruitful," might mean to an Old World which, as he said, started wars over some "sterile rock" in the sea. But it was less his dream than his curiosity and willingness to face peril among people who had never before seen a white face that explains his historical importance.

And so with scores of other explorers who were determined to know and understand a physical world not yet mapped by man. Their minds buzzed with questions that no encyclopedia could answer. What were those vast inland fresh-water lakes of America—that closely linked chain from Ontario to Superior? Where did the country's great river, the very father of waters, take its rise? Could paths be marked out to the "shining sea" of the West and to the domain of the Great Khan of Cathay, whose fabulous riches had been seen by Ser Marco Polo in the era of the Mongol Kublai Khan? How chart this western region, with its meandering streams and its myriad lakes? And what could the "fruitful" acres that Radisson saw mean to the war-ridden and land-hungry peoples of the Old World?

The company of explorers did the job they set for themselves—Radisson and Groseilliers, Hennepin and Duluth, Le Sueur, La Vérendrye, Jonathan Carver, David Thompson, Lieutenant Pike, Cass, Schoolcraft, Nicollet, Beltrami, and others whose names enter this book of history. For them all, a

motion picture would have lines running here, there, and everywhere through the western country, each representing the will and curiosity and courage of a man, or group of men. So the map took shape, and gradually the age-long curtain of mystery was lifted. The kind of ignorance that caused our American diplomats in 1783 to try to run a boundary west from Lake of the Woods in a futile quest to intersect the Mississippi was replaced by accurate knowledge based upon observation. The explorers and map makers could say, "Yes, we were there. We know."

All this took time. Minnesota had the flags of France and England, of Spain, and the United States over its lands in whole or in part, but for more than a hundred years the search for specific information went on. Marco Polo's Cathay proved to be very far away. The French explorers, landing on the shores of Michigan or Superior, quickly understood that they had not reached the empire of the Far East, but men of will and curiosity broke through the continent to the Pacific Coast. In doing so, they found and told the world about an inland empire better for their time and needs than Cathay. They had the precious sense of wonder. Is it transmitted to us of the twentieth century when we speculate about space travel and space men? Sometimes they soared into prophecies that have come true with time, as when Jonathan Carver, after seeing Minnesota before the American Revolution, wrote, "There is no doubt that at some future period, mighty kingdoms will emerge from these wildernesses, and stately and solemn temples, with gilded spires reaching the sky, supplant the Indian huts, whose only decorations are the barbarous trophies of their vanquished enemies." Close onto two centuries have gone by since Carver saw the Falls of St. Anthony in the 1760's and rhapsodied about the future of a Minnesota as then unnamed, but today hundreds of spires, some gilded, reach the sky, and the mighty kingdom of which he dreamed (though not a kingdom but a state) has risen out of the wilds he saw.

As the decades went by, the traits of curiosity and the will to solve problems found outlets in many areas other than the physical world, but before following these into other fields, it may be enlightening to look at some other traditions that time and human effort wove into the fabric of Minnesota life.

European history has three ages: ancient, medieval, and modern, and their span runs across all the centuries that have elapsed since the emergence of civilized man in the western world. American history has likewise had its ages, but the speed of western life has outrun the time span of its ancestral lands. Minnesota too has its ancient, medieval, and modern ages. Its ancient era reaches far into the Indian past and merges with the period of white explorers and the early fur traders. The medieval era is that of settlement and the pioneer and the modern that of the state's growing up—its advance from youth to maturity. In many aspects, as in transportation, these ages overlap, but by and large they are identifiable. We may talk about ages in an impersonal way, but when we probe into their meaning and character, we come to people. For every age catches its character from the people who did its thinking and work in every rank, who met its problems, who held and expounded its philosophies and faiths.

Much has been said and written about the second of our ages, that of settlement and the pioneer, and here we note scores of forces and actions and achievements. The lumber industry, following the trade in furs and pelts, helped to build the Middle West. Land takers arrived in steadily increasing numbers in the spirit of the Yankee ballad:

We'll cross the prairies as of old
The Pilgrims crossed the sea,
And make the West, as they the East,
The homestead of the Free!

Farms were plowed and cultivated towns and cities were laid out (some only on paper, others in reality), industry got its start, institutions were established, the land was dotted with churches and schools (many of them unpretentious at the beginning), government took form (first the territory, then the state, everywhere the local), steamboats and sleds and carts were early acts in a drama that eventuated in networks of highways, railroads, and airlanes. People overcame the earlier loneliness, took hard work in stride, met the ordeals involved in transforming a wilderness into a nineteenth-century garden.

All this, in section after section, is reviewed in this book, but certain things of enduring interest for the interpretation of the state's history need to be said in addition, not in adulation of pioneer courage, but in simple appraisal. Some people buckled under as they faced loneliness and ordeal. Some gave up and returned to New England or New York or elsewhere. The bad in society came along with the good. There were dark and ignoble as well as bright and noble sides in the pioneer experience, as in our later history. But we indulge in no idealizing of our past when we point out a few traits or characteristics or traditions that constitute a part of the pioneering heritage of Minnesota, alongside the material achievements that customarily and properly are chronicled.

One is the tradition of work. Minnesota, like Rome, was not built in a day. Nor was it built by lazy people. This fact needs emphasis, for, like the barn on the landscape, it often goes unseen. The American, in European eyes, is strenuous, and strenuosity is an American tradition, rooted in the pioneer experience from early Colonial times onward as the frontier moved westward. Theodore Roosevelt, advocating the strenuous, rather than the reflective life, voiced American habit and made it into a doctrine. The simple truth is that there was so incredibly much to do in telescoping into decades, a building job that the Old World spent centuries doing, that Americans had to be strenuous. Historians have not given sufficient attention to this tradition of strenuosity in American life or to the contributions made to it, not by Rooseveltian spokesmen, but by millions of people whose names are not in the textbooks. These millions have been both men and women—and any interpretation of Minnesota history must give a place of honor to women. Elsewhere I have spoken of the important role of "the wilderness Marthas who sustained the men of the frontier—the farmers and workers who did the jobs of their day quietly and efficiently, the men of trades and professions and business and enterprise, the men of faith and dreams, the builders of homes and of the web of our social life, the sustaining folk at the roots of our existence."

One can argue that there was not enough leisure in the past or that leisure was much too restricted to a Veblenian privileged class; and one can differentiate kinds of work done—unskilled, skilled, professional. But whatever the lines of differentiation, the unspecialized pioneer age was an age of hard work. It deepened the tradition of determination to get jobs done, big or little. The vocal enthusiasts about the "good old days" often bewail what they call laziness or lack of moral fiber in the present age — or whatever new age they are talking about, and the theme has been repeated in every generation—but usually each age measures up to the tradition of work and enterprise that is part of its heritage.

Allied with the tradition of work is that of hope and opportunity. The pioneers had a lively awareness of the potentiality of "better days." Work may have had a certain satisfaction and solace, but it was a means, not an end. The people who built Minnesota and other states of the Midwest knew that they were erecting the foundations of great states and societies to come. They saw state and society as widened opportunities for their children—as doorways to economic advantage, education, and a more rewarding kind of life than they themselves had lived. This fundamental widens into the larger American trait of optimism, which so often has interested Europeans. The optimism looked beyond triumph to the future, and it would not ordinarily settle for defeat, though setbacks were often discouraging. I have seen this spirit reflected in hundreds of immigrant pioneer letters—a kind of patience and underlying purpose that could meet just about every kind of ordeal—loneliness, back-bending work, privation, suffering, losses of land and money, even the disaster of Indian wars—always with patient hope for the future buoying up courage.

In our own day terrible world wars, a long-continuing depression, and the anxieties of a divided world, with an even worse war as a possibility for the future, have made some thinkers skeptical about progress. Down underneath the optimism of the pioneer people was a conviction that people were building a good future. There were doorways to that future if only one had the will to go through them—land, work, opportunity, education, freedom. Whatever the skepticism of today, people still regard these as portals to advancement, even though the frontiers of today are unlike those of the untamed West. Such a regard is a clue to the democratic concept of western and American life, and few today will accept the notion that progress itself is a shibboleth or a myth. Recently a historian, reviewing the belief in progress, wrote that during the middle of the twentieth century America "was not yet prepared to reject as no longer relevant or viable the belief in progress, rooted as that faith was in the experience of generations. Continuity of thought and hope survived the discontinuities posed in an age of anxiety."

Yet other writers have suggested that the American frontier, in terms of fulfillment of hopes, was a myth, but this is a transfer to history of the dreams, hopes, and frustrations of fiction. It represents a failure to grasp the realities of American life in the span of more than one generation, or even one. There were individual disappointments, frustrations, failures, problems. There were exaggerated claims. There were blasted speculations. But no one can survey the broad story that includes native Americans and Europeans alike without understanding that the pioneer hopes were substantially realized. Myths sprang up in the literature of the West, but the frontier as a fulfillment of hope was no more a myth than America itself is a myth.

Some years ago, while exploring the beginnings of the University of Minnesota, I came upon the report of a territorial legislative committee in 1851 calling for the establishment of a university. The territory was then only two years old, its population only a few thousand, and yet the legislature took action to found a university. The committee said that "the cause of education in the territory demands the early establishment of an institution of learning, which shall afford to the youth of the territory an opportunity of obtaining a liberal, scientific and classical education. . . . Men do not 'gather grapes of thorns, or figs of thistles,' neither does society grow virtuous citizens from the haunts of vice, or exalted minds from the abodes of ignorance and stupidity." The committee offered the opinion that "to govern and restrain the ignorant is far more difficult than to educate and fit men to govern themselves," and it went on to say that the children of that pioneer day were "the citizens and rulers of the future," upon whose education depended the "character and destiny" of the infant commonwealth. The mass immigration of people to Minnesota had not then taken place, but the leaders who wrote that document spoke the faith and standards of thousands to come. They illustrated the trait of frontier hope coupled with planning and work. They also blended into Minnesota thinking other traditions that went back to seventeenth-century New England and merged with the drive for enlightenment and the fight against ignorance.

The episode from the birth of the university could be accompanied by illustrations touching all the colleges and the schools of the state as well as the many churches of different, but usually related, faiths—and indeed all our institutions which began with the hope of service through an expanding future. The founding of the Minnesota Historical Society in 1849 was less a bow to what Governor Ramsey called "History in a land of yesterday" than it was a confident approach to the land of tomorrow. The pioneers created a society of history because they believed in the promise of Minnesota. They believed that the state would have a great history, the records of which would deserve to be preserved and cherished. So a society of history was an act of faith harmonizing with that of Minnesotans in their future.

Today we are apprehensive and hard hit by war—war of the past and war as a dread possibility for the future—and our thoughts are centered in the problems of an atomic age. Talk about faith may fall upon frightened or even cynical ears, but there is such a thing as faith in good purpose and in the integrity underlying such purpose. It may be helpful, therefore, to recall some of our sturdy traditions. The absence of faith girded by resoluteness of purpose might mean a static society inspired by fear instead of confidence.

Mighty forces in agriculture, industry, and the transition from a general to a specialized society compelled Minnesota to adapt its ways and methods as it moved into the machine age—the age in which we live. Transfers of ideas from the East and from Europe had gone hand in hand with experiment in the pioneering days, but as the need for transition came with all its urgency, our people developed more and more the practice of experimentation, coupled with research as specialization equipped itself to solve new problems. Many things happened as we grew from the pioneering age to maturity. Our population jumped from some 6,000 at mid-century to 1,750,000 in 1900. The frontier pushed westward toward the Pacific. The railroad age came, with giants like James J. Hill; and lumbering, with other giants like Frederick Weyerhaeuser, came into its golden age and helped to build Minnesota and the Middle West. Minneapolis emerged as the milling center of the world; St. Paul as a trading mart and capital; Duluth as a port fronting upon the world. Seven iron men (the clan of Merritts) roused the giant Mesabi from its age-long sleep, and Minnesota became a producing partner in the American steel age. Articulate labor lengthened its stride, while agriculture, after serving the mandate of King Wheat, struggled with the transition to new and diversified crops. At the same time its protests gave vigor to political reform movements in a consistent and persevering "agrarian crusade" that has marked Minnesota politics in singular fashion. State government expanded its interests and activities and moved toward the complex, wide-spreading, and expensive range of its present scope.

In all this change, things did not just happen. Minnesota did not just grow, like Topsy in *Uncle Tom's Cabin*. There was leadership. There was planning. There was experiment—and there was courage. People leagued themselves with the future in the Ibsenian sense. Business and industry had an eye to new needs and opportunities, adapting its techniques and operations, sometimes with great efficiency. Education met with imaginative vigor new needs in an age of specialization and research and embarked upon the overwhelming task of universal education of our people, with opportunities for the many and also the gifted to carry their training to a very high level. The state proved that it was not afraid of widened responsibility, though often it was conservative and slow in turning ideas and proposals into constructive action.

In modern pioneering, individual persons occupy the stage — the whole people in a general sense, but also leaders of intelligence, will, and courage. Conservation, once a dim idea, grew into a movement, and its prophet and explorer bore the fitting name of Christopher Columbus Andrews. But we were slow to act. Andrews preached his doctrines for two decades until they were re-enforced by calamity—the tragic Hinckley Fire of 1894—and then we took action. Sometimes, outside governmental action, results flowed from the ideas and will of men of "hope and forward-looking minds," to use a phrase applied to the Doctors Mayo, father and sons. Theirs is one of the great sagas of the state—that of surgeons who kept pace, and more than pace, with the age of scientific transition, pioneering medical cooperation and a vast medical practice, employing research in every part of their enterprise, and blazing trails to high training in clinical medicine. In public health, Dr. Charles N. Hewitt of Red Wing was a quarter century ahead of his time, but his ideas gradually took hold. A village minister, Hastings H. Hart, laid the foundations of our advances in social welfare and public institutions, while a social pioneer, LeGrand Powers, stirred the people, with his painstaking reports, to use state intervention in behalf of better conditions for labor and industry. So also there were leaders in parks and playgrounds, the cooperative movement, state regulation of railroads and warehouses, education, and many other fields, rallying people to achieve better conditions of life.

Minnesota has also a tradition of research and experiment. In scores of fields the people know well that research is no remote ivory tower, isolated from everyday life, but a dedicated and often applied service, as is most recently illustrated in the story of a scientific explorer named E. W. Davis, who, like Radisson, wanted to know. His researches helped to open up the new taconite industry of the north country. And these researches typify hun-

dreds of studies in medicine, agriculture, and the various sciences and the arts, which have advanced man's knowledge of nature and of human beings— studies that have reached out to the world in impact and benefit, with university scholars in the van.

When the state saga is written in amplitude, it will interpret such factors as our mobility, our age-long interrelations with nation and world, and the special flavor of a people who have interwoven diverse cultural and national strands and combined transfers from Europe and the American East with the newer ways and ideas that are distinctively Midwestern and Minnesotan.

Each of these themes is an unwritten book of interpretation. Historians are often chary of interpretation, but we need it as an instrument of understanding. In our mobility, we share in and reflect the national character. An essayist has described our people as "the moving Americans." We played leap-frog with our lands, even in Colonial times. We moved from frontier to frontier, from country to town. We moved from crop to crop, job to job, level to level. We moved from cabin to house and house to apartment — and "development." Our story is migration, a hunt for freedom, an indefatigable pursuit of happiness. Land frontiers disappeared, but we continued to move socially, economically, politically. Henry Ford widened our front yard; and if we couldn't go away on wheels, we moved vicariously with the strident aid of radio and television and the impressively expanding arts of communication. The reflective life may have suffered in the process, and it is unquestionably true that we gained in stability as the frontier ended, but we have never stayed put. So a poet, Archibald MacLeish, tells us that "America is west and the winds blowing," and another sings about Americans always moving on. The tradition of migration finds a thousand and one illustrations in Minnesota. We move from somewhere or something to somewhere to something else. The tradition merges with those of space and freedom, of opportunity and free choice.

We cannot understand Minnesota unless we understand that from the dim days when the flags of France and England and Spain figuratively flew over our lands, we have been part of the currents of world history. We have never been an isolated island, cut off from the world, as some commentators on isolationism have assumed. The wars and turbulence, ambitions and hopes, ideas and aims of nation and world have, through all our history, left their marks upon this state and people. Frenchmen sang their ballads on our rivers; Scotsmen ran our fur-trading posts; our furs in early times went out to London and Leipzig and Russia and even to Canton, China; our northern boundary was set by international treaties; we have been caught up in national and international wars; and our people, only a generation after the state itself was founded, were two thirds of European blood in the first and second generations. We have known a good deal about our involvement with the world —and our once extensive immigrant press gave a better and more detailed picture of the affairs of the European world than did our English-language newspapers. We had a better schooling in international relations than some critics have realized, though we shared the traditional American skepticism about foreign entanglements as expounded by the fathers of the country.

We have been a merging cosmopolitan people, with bridges facing not only New England and the East but the many cultures of the Old World. A scholar of medieval history once suggested that if Desiderius Erasmus of Rotterdam, whose life touched the fifteenth and sixteenth centuries, came alive and visited Minnesota, he would find many things here that would be quite familiar to him. We have had and still have pulsating links with the Old World from which we sprang. In the long historical run the Zangwill melting-pot theory may come true, but it represented wishful thinking and the processes are slower than people once thought. No one traveling about the state or studying its history can fail to realize that cultural streams, slowly merging as the decades pass by, have identity enough to stamp Minnesota with a marked and colorful individuality. One sees its signs everywhere—the leadership of New England in the

launching of our professional life, our newspapers and banks and schools and commerce—the tough strain that Oscar Firkins caught when he praised a teacher, Maria Sanford, "travel-soiled and dusty . . . vehement and gusty . . . kinked and knurled and crusty . . . leonine and hale and lusty . . . oaken-ribbed and trusty." Alongside this wiry heritage, many other elements in the making of the state have left their impress on leadership and everyday life.

Minnesota history must take account of a host of institutions, traditions, and practices that are suggested by recalling our schools and colleges, Catholic and Protestant; the churches that enfold age-old faiths; the St. Olaf Choir and the sacred songs of hundreds of congregations; the sokol of the Bohemians; the kantele and sauna of the Finns; the Scandinavian and German singing and other musical societies; skiing and other sports, the German Turners; the Danish cooperatives and folk schools; our symphony orchestra and institutes of arts; our creative literature and arts in wide range; and newer streams of trained and imaginative leadership. As Esther Jerabek has truly written, "Each nationality, bearing with it its own special heritage, has woven strands in the web of Minnesota's cultural life, helping to make a rich fabric of unique design." So we have had background and schooling in tolerance and the amenities of intercultural living as well as in the spirit of the frontier, in which a man's demonstration of worth, not his pedigree or claims, gave him status. This twin schooling has helped Minnesota to weather with balance and sense sundry storms of intolerance, of hate, and the fears and suspicions that feed greedily on ignorance—though its record is not without blemish.

It is characteristic of maturity and the tradition of curiosity that Minnesota is in a period of self appraisal. Lengthening perspective and a sense of significant decisions to come contribute to this scrutiny. Much remains to be done, but historians are supplementing the earlier work of Dr. William W. Folwell and others. Novelists are going on from where Sinclair Lewis, Scott Fitzgerald, and O. E. Rölvaag left off. Appraisals are being made of education as well as of banks, mills, the iron industry, and other business organizations and forces. Leadership in the past is being recognized through biographies of Minnesota men and women. Artists are interpreting Minnesota life and scenes. Musicians, sculptors, poets, dancers are enriching the state's cultural life. The drive for appraisal has reached into state government. How far it will go in social, cultural, intellectual, educational, and political affairs one cannot say, but the impulse to know ourselves springs from tradition and fits in with the spirit of an adult state that has now celebrated its one-hundredth birthday. The centenary itself, with its many-angled emphases, did much to provoke thought about Minnesota's heritage and about the second century of statehood upon which it embarked in 1958.

Deep as is our concern with problems of the future, we should not fail to recall some imponderables that are difficult to phrase in precise words. The people of Minnesota have an affection for the state which, if not so vocal as the rhapsodies of a Texan, still has substance. Who can analyze the deeper sources of state affection and pride? Perhaps they are related to the sum total of our heritage. Perhaps they are rooted in an awareness of things done—things that have made this portion of the earth a good place in which to live, notwithstanding the many anxieties of passing times. In part affection flows from the fact that, with all the work and problems and crises and troubles and battles of people, they have been human and resilient enough to find joy and happiness, reward,

recreation, and fun here. This is of course not unique to the North Star State, but it is true that the harshness of struggle has been abated by the genialities of community living and by a sense of advance toward better days.

The setting has been and is a state not denied a beauty and charm of its own, alongside resources developed from earth and water and human effort. If we are moving Americans, we can move out from the confines of towns to areas that still have a touch of the wilderness Radisson once saw. There are lakes of beauty; there are rivers that bend to sea, including the one the Indians termed the "Great River"; and there are waterfalls that inspired legends among aboriginal redmen. There are cherished valleys and hills, deep woods and wide prairies, and red earth and black earth, all encrusted with natural and historic lore. And there are the material monuments of man's dreaming and industry.

Only to superficial eyes are the Gopher Prairies alike. There is natural and man-created diversity in the state. For local and state scenes, as indeed for the nation, we need to remember that we are not just land and people and buildings and institutions. These, plus a myriad of ideas and practices, are bound together and given meaning by a past that stretches through all our ages and comes up to the evershifting line of the present. All who stand on that line could deepen their wisdom by recalling with Shakespeare that "What's past is prologue." The prologue merges into the ongoing drama of life in which they are both inheritors and actors.

CHAPTER ONE

Minnesota Heritage In the Making

By J. MERLE HARRIS

This volume holds many interesting facets of Minnesota's past which form the backdrop and set the stage for her interesting present. As each of these facets is brought into view, scene by scene, on the pages that follow we shall see at what price our heritage has been bought and become better acquainted with our benefactors. We shall see varied aspects of the human drama as they reacted upon one another during, and even before, her hundred-year history as a state—the 32nd state in the Union.

We all realize, however, that neither Minnesota's history, her present abundance nor her future potential can be explained by human activity alone. Man is surrounded by an all-important environment which provides the base for his operations—the stage for his work and his play. Minnesota's history could have been enacted in just one place, and that place is Minnesota. It is within the framework of her unique array of natural resources that her history has been, and her future will be, written.

Before turning to the dramatic interplay between man and man, let us look far behind those scenes to earlier scenes, just as dramatic in character, long before the Age of Man. Many of these extend so remotely into the past as to stagger the imagination, but they were packed with events of such lasting importance that they influence or provide a livelihood for virtually the entire population of our state today.

Northern Pike takes to the air

Grain binder in action

We may find our antiquity easier to grasp if we do not attempt to grasp it all at once. Let us begin with familiar scenes and look for their explanations in terms of preceding events. In this way the great age of Minnesota, and of the Earth, will impress itself upon us more gradually and more understandably.

Before launching our trip backward in time it may be well to consider what we may and may not expect to find along the way. A geologic maxim says that "the Earth writes its own history." We must be warned, however, that even at the time of "writing" it was not all recorded at the same place. And, as surely as certain geologic processes work to record Earth history, still others work to erase it—some of the pages have been torn out. Moreover, the language is obscure. We have on any portion of the globe only a fragmentary record at best —to decipher it is a difficult, but exciting, challenge. Few places on Earth present the geologist

Geologist at work

with greater problems than Minnesota because in few places do the known rocks represent so great a span of time—few places where so many pages have been torn out. Nevertheless, certain outstanding events in Minnesota's geologic history are still intact—written in the rocks and glacial deposits beneath our feet. These we shall examine, as far as we may, on the following pages.

OUR PRESENT HERITAGE

If we are to explain our heritage, let us take a moment to see what this heritage is. Some of us are familiar with one aspect of it, others of us with other aspects, but few of us take the time to contemplate the whole of it. None of us can do this fully but our vision will be broader for trying to see this heritage in panoramic view: waters, hills, prairies, soils, forests, minerals and climate . . .

Perhaps the most outstanding geographical characteristic of Minnesota is its water—its lakes, streams and marshlands. It has a larger water area than any other state—even if we do not count its share of Lake Superior. But why should we not count it? Who can forget the rocky, rugged, picturesque North Shore of Lake Superior once he has experienced it? Our more than 10,000 lakes are of virtually all sizes, shapes and depths. Lake Superior is over 1,300 feet deep while many others, even of quite a large area, are less than 20 feet deep.

Lakes due to glacial scooping

DRAINAGE TO THE ARCTIC OCEAN

DRAINAGE TO THE
ATLANTIC OCEAN

DRAINAGE TO THE
GULF OF MEXICO

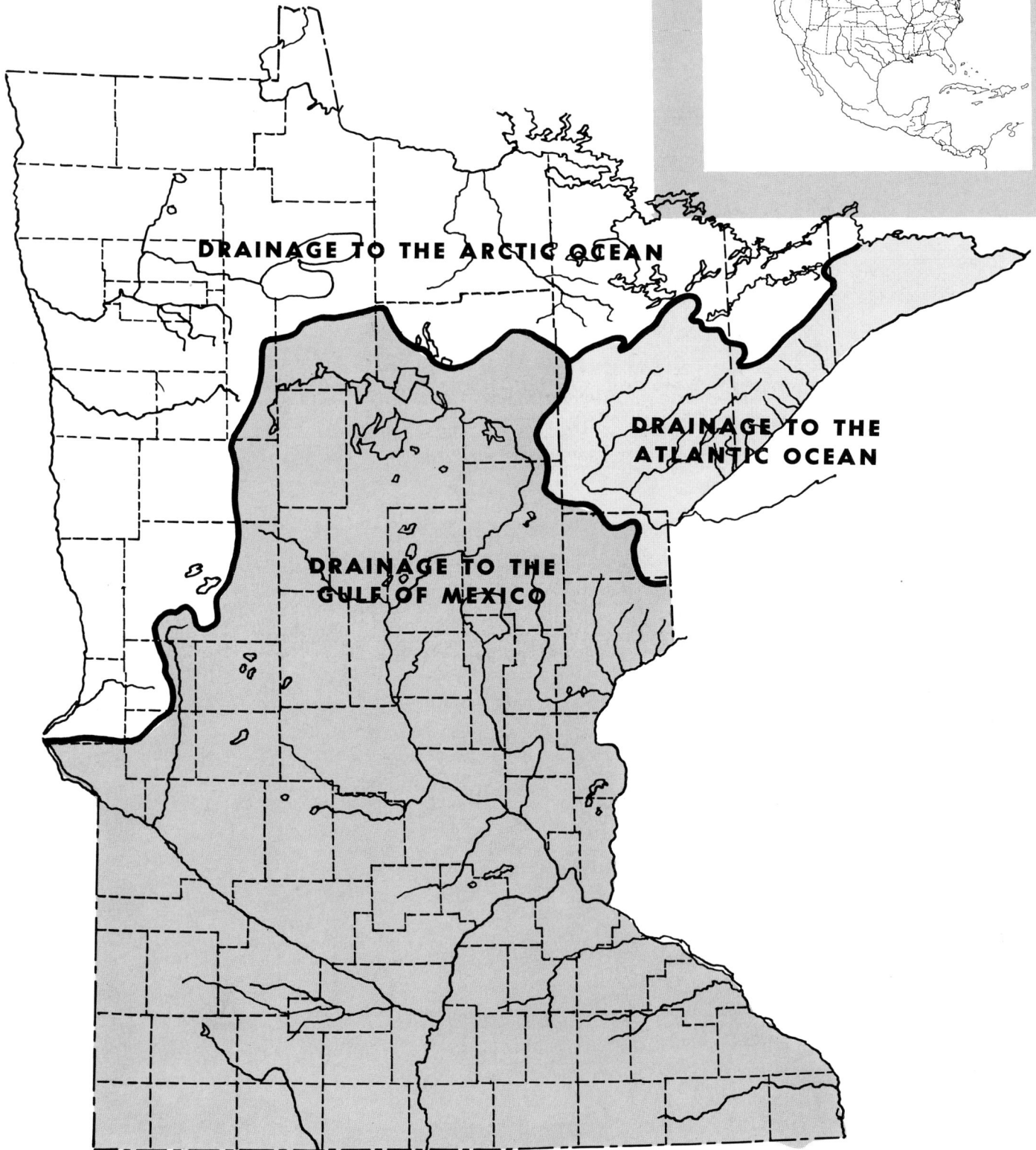

Three continental divides meet in Minnesota

If we note the position of Minnesota on a map of North America we see that it is near the center of the continent. It is not surprising then to find that water flows outward from here to the oceans in three different directions. This means that three gigantic watersheds come together corner to corner within its boundaries—this point being at the intersection of three continental divides near Hibbing. The western and northern border drainage is to Lake Winnipeg and finally to the Arctic Ocean. The area immediately surrounding Lake Superior drains into it and, by way of the other Great Lakes and the St. Lawrence River, to the Atlantic Ocean. The remainder of the state, which includes much of northern and all of the central and southern parts, belongs to the enormous drainage basin of the Mississippi River, which finds its way to the Gulf of Mexico. No comparable drainage pattern exists in North America—except for one in Glacier National Park. But in spite of having three great drainage basins within its borders, Minnesota remains one of the most poorly drained states of all. But in this we are fortunate. Our poor drainage allows us our many lakes. Minnesota has the equipment, in the form of lake basins, for catching and holding for a time much of the precipitation that falls within its borders. The water, thus caught, eventually overflows into streams, soaks into the rocks and soil or evaporates, but it is conserved long enough for greater use. than if it drained quickly to the oceans. It is as if Minnesota had a finer sieve than most states in which to catch its water so that it drains through more slowly. Why does Minnesota have a finer sieve—a surface so pock-marked? For the answer we must look back to the time when nature employed one of her most dramatic sculptoring agents—the glaciers. This will be the subject of a later part of our story.

The story of Minnesota's hills and prairies commands our interest next. In broad view, the surface of the state is probably best described as a gently rolling prairie. In closer view, we see the prairie surface dented in places, bumpy in others.

Flat-topped hill

Rolling hills

Glacier

Sawtooth hills

The dents are the lakes and the bumps are the hills. But the bumps are not all alike—they have personalities of their own. Looking through the lower part of our bifocals we notice some family resemblances between certain groups of them. They group themselves by areas more or less. Those of the central part of Minnesota, while differing greatly in size, are mostly round-topped hills with gently sloping sides. They are composed of loose material—a mixture of clay, sand, pebbles and boulders—not of bedrock. No two of them seem to be of the same height. They seem to have been deposited from above. But what natural agency can deposit material from above in an area where there are no mountains? Again we shall call on the glaciers for our explanation. But this is not the whole story. In some areas, particularly in the eastern and southeastern portions, there are hills that are flat-topped, steep-sided, exposing bedrock layers in their flanks. In the northeastern part of Minnesota we may find rock hills that are sharp and angular on top. And there are still other areas, particularly in the northern and western parts, where there are virtually no hills at all. What of these?

Soils, vegetation and climate are inseparably connected. Soil is the result of the interaction of parent rock substance of the earth, chemical and physical processes induced by the climate and organic remains of life supported by it. The parent rock substance may be derived from the bedrock directly beneath it. If so, the soil is called a residual soil. If the rock material has been brought in by water, wind or glaciers, the soil is a transported soil. Since nearly all of Minnesota has been glaciated, nearly all of Minnesota's soil is of the latter type. Along the bottom lands near streams and on the floors of extinct lakes we find alluvial soils— also transported. Even in the uplands of the southeastern part of the state — the only part not glaciated—we find still another type of transported soil. It is a fine clay soil derived from wind-borne dust called "loess." Very little residual soil is to be found in the state and most of this is in northern Minnesota where the glaciers dropped little or no material on the bedrock—though scraping it clean as they passed over. Transported soils are generally rich since they normally contain mixtures of different minerals from many sources. Minnesota's position as one of the leaders in helping to fill the nation's food basket may be largely attributed to the beneficial effects of the glaciers of long ago. Although Minnesota is eleventh among the states in land area it is second in number of acres of excellent and good agricultural land.

Minnesota's mineral resources, particularly its iron ores, are well-known throughout the nation. Its iron ore is the most important source of iron in the United States. This was true even before the utilization of the low-grade ore called taconite.

Iron mine at Hibbing

Other mineral products of great commercial importance are: building stone, sand and gravel, clay and shale, limestone and marl. Still other minerals found in Minnesota but not developed commercially as yet are: gold, copper, nickel, lead, zinc, manganese, aluminum, magnesium, cobalt, vanadium and titanium. For most of these the reason for their lack of commercial development is, of course, their scarcity. However, in some cases the quantity may be large but a profitable method of extraction has not been found. Since the age of most of these minerals is far greater than that of the glaciers we must seek their origin in much older events. The distribution of some of them may be accounted for by the glaciers, however.

Climate as a natural resource may be a new idea to us, but it is now so considered—and with good reason. Although we cannot undertake a thorough discussion of climatic influence and values we can note one or two. The dependence of agriculture on precipitation is too well-known to require discussion. Many also appreciate the dependence of our "10,000 lakes" on this same factor. During a dry year, or series of years, lake levels fall enough to keep most of us reminded of this. Studies have shown that under the conditions of temperature and humidity of central Minnesota about 30 inches of water evaporate from open lake surfaces annually. This is an amount approximately equal to the average precipitation (about 25 inches) for the same period. Lakes are recharged, of course, not only from direct precipitation into the lake basin but principally from ground water seepage, inflowing streams and springs. Each of these ways, however, originally acquires its water from precipitation. Minnesota's enviable water wealth, both surface and underground, depends on our climate as surely as upon the fact that the land surface is pock-marked with lake basins. It may be well to recall this while leaning on the snow shovel handle in winter or when a well-planned picnic is "rained out" in summer.

Let us now look backward to our yesterdays to see something about "how come?"

BACKWARD THROUGH TIME

The First Yesterday

Glacial History—Our Geography in the Making

Our first "yesterday" may go back as much as a million years and include events up until about 10,000 years ago. This was the time of the glaciers. Glaciers did not exist continuously all of this time. Very probably their actual duration was less than half of this time but they did recur during four different periods over a span of a million years, as presently estimated. These periods have been named, beginning with the earliest: Nebraskan, Kansan, Illinoian and Wisconsin for well-developed deposits in those states. Interglacial periods, believed to have lasted hundreds of thousands of years, apparently with climates as warm or warmer than ours, existed between them. Vegetation of types requiring warmer climates are often found where they grew on the surface of one glacial deposit and buried by the next one. For example,

beech trees apparently grew in Lyon County during one of these interglacial periods. None grows in Minnesota today. So, although the entire period is often called the "glacial period," part of the time it was warmer than our present climate.

Whence came these glaciers? Apparently they were largely Canadian products — but northern United States, including Minnesota, made their contributions as well. For long periods of time in certain areas especially around Hudson Bay, more snow fell during the winters than melted during the summers—the formation of glaciers is no more mysterious than that. The mystery that remains is only why the climates of those periods were enough different from those of the present as to produce this effect. Was it because of different patterns of ocean and wind currents; different composition of the earth's atmosphere, or of volcanic or meteoric dust in it; changes in position of the earth's axis; shifts in the position of the continents on the globe; changes in elevation of the continents; differences in the heat given out by the sun; changes in shape of the earth's orbit; or wobbling of the earth's axis? All these possible causes, and more, have been suggested. Whether one of these, or some combination of them, or a cause not yet imagined, is the real answer is unknown at the present time. Overwhelming evidence forces the fact upon us but withholds its explanation. Climatologists tell us that as small a temperature change as 10° Fahrenheit might produce a glacier—but what would cause even that?

The first two of these glaciers came into Minnesota from the northwest—from a center west of Hudson Bay. The glaciers moved out from this center in all directions, like pancake batter in a skillet, but it is the part of the movement toward the southeast into Minnesota that concerns us. As it moved in our direction it crossed areas underlain by gray limestones and shales. Some of these rock materials were scraped up and carried long distances. Some were dropped nearby. This material gave us the "old gray drift," noted by early geologists, that is rather deeply buried under later drifts in most of the state. It is occasionally seen exposed in southern Minnesota as well as in states farther south. These two glaciers are believed to have covered all of Minnesota except the eastern parts of Houston and Winona counties. The next, or Illinoian, glacier apparently came into Minnesota from the northeast—from a center in Labrador. Entering the state from this direction it rode over a very different assortment of bedrock from that crossed by the previous two glaciers. The bedrock of the Lake Superior area consists largely of igneous and metamorphic rocks, many of them having a high iron content. Consequently, the rock debris, especially upon weathering, shows red and yellow colors characteristic of iron rust. This glacier apparently did not go much farther south than the Twin Cities, nor much farther west than central Minnesota. Therefore, the "old red drift" may be seen only in the northern and eastern portion of Minnesota, but especially in Dakota and Washington counties where it "peeps out" from under later deposits. The next and last glacial stage was the Wisconsin. Since it was comparatively recent and no later glaciers disturbed its deposits, a wealth of evidence and clues concerning this period present themselves. It does not follow, however, that the Wisconsin glacial stage is perfectly understood. Such a variety and distribution of glacial evidence exists as to become somewhat overwhelming. The picture does not appear simple. Suffice it to say here that this stage consisted of probably no less than four substages—that is, times of resurgence and partial withdrawal of the ice at comparatively short intervals—and that the advances were from different centers, all at the same time in some cases. This is believed to be so because of the discovery of many examples of complicated overlapping and interfingering of differently colored layers of these deposits. As one comparatively simple example, doubtless many readers have observed that the uppermost drift (beneath the topsoil) in St. Paul is generally red. On the contrary, in Minneapolis the red layer is generally not encountered until after penetrating a few feet of gray (or slightly tan) drift. This is explained by the fact that the most recent glacial activity in the Twin Cities area was the invasion by a lobe, originating in the northwest, whose gray blanket covered most of Minneapolis but not St. Paul. The familiar hill and lake country over most of Minnesota is due largely to the deposits and other glacial activity during the Wisconsin stage—deposits so recent that erosion has had time to erase but little of them.

In what ways did the coming of the glaciers change the face of Minnesota? The first effects must have been upon living things. Virtually all life must have been either pushed southward or ridden over and buried by the glaciers at each advance. As we have seen there was sufficient time and favorable conditions for life to re-establish itself between at least some of the glacial advances. The forces that pushed life southward were not all mechanical; some were climatic. The existence of a climate in Minnesota favorable enough to glaciers to permit their entry must have been a cold climate indeed—especially during the summers. We must conclude, therefore, that long before the actual arrival of the glaciers their cold breath had driven out all but the most hardy—of both plants and animals. Perhaps our best clues as to the kinds of life that remained to put up stubborn resistance to the glacial advances lie in their remains found buried between layers of glacial deposits. Among the animals are found a surprisingly large number, both large and small. Everyone has heard of the woolly mammoth and the mastodon, cousins of our present-day elephants. But remains also of elk, bison,

Mastodon

musk ox, moose, reindeer and rarely of the horse, as well as of smaller animals such as the badger, beaver, rabbit and skunk have been found. Not all of the beavers were of "our kind," however. Some were giant beavers as large as black bears. Hundreds of plant specimens have been found in all parts of the state, many of them in buried peat bogs. Specimens representing all four of the major

Mammoth tooth

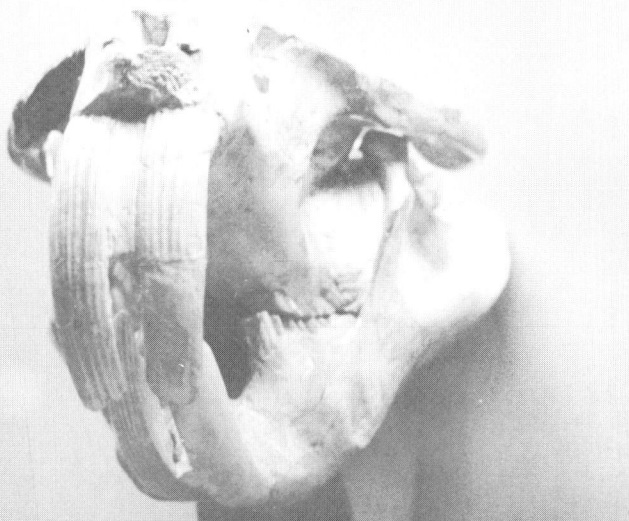

Skull of giant beaver, twice the size of present-day beaver

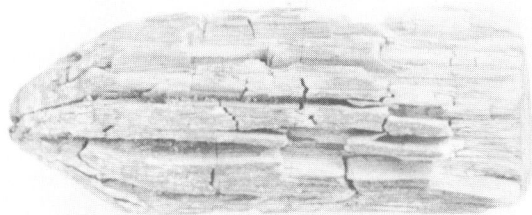

This piece of white oak was found near Taylor's Falls buried under 6-8 feet of marl in a bog on glacial drift of middle-Wisconsin (Cary) age. One end was clearly cut by a beaver whose teeth marks are much larger than those of present-day species. It is probable that it was cut by a giant beaver such as the one pictured above.

plant groups have been identified. They range all the way from the lowly algæ, fungi and mosses to trees such as willow, poplar, birch, beech, oak, elm, maple, fir, tamarack and spruce. Only three species of mosses and three of fungi are extinct. The remainder have all been identified with living forms found here or near here today. White spruce was predominate over all other forms both in quantity and in distribution.

Another obvious effect of the glaciers was that of rubbing out or subduing the existing relief features. Hilltops were scraped off, valleys filled in, drainage patterns destroyed. Just how rugged the terrain was before the glaciers is not easy to discern. Even if all the glacial drift were cleared away we would get only an inadequate idea of pre-glacial topography. If a hill were found beneath the drift we would have no idea how high it was originally. We would see only what remained after the glaciers, possibly several of them, had taken their tolls. The Iron Range and the Giant's Range just north of it are relatively high today, but how much were they reduced by the grinding and scraping of sheets of ice a mile or more in thickness? In a few places we do catch some glimpses of an answer, however. Into a small portion of eastern Houston and Winona counties, as well as a much larger adjacent area in Wisconsin, the glaciers apparently did not spread. This area is known as the "Driftless Area." Those familiar with it know the ruggedness, the depth of the valleys, such as those of the Root River and Beaver Creek, the steepness of the hills. True, some of this has been the result of erosion since the glaciers but presumably only a small amount. It seems probable that this area now is fairly representative of the surrounding area before the glacial invasions. Clues are to be found also from well-drilling records, provided enough of them exist in a particular area to yield an adequate picture. Old drainage lines may be reconstructed in this way. Well drillers often discover that the bedrock is missing, beneath the glacial drift, in such a pattern as to suggest strongly that pre-glacial streams have removed it. If enough deep wells are drilled in an area the width and depth of the old, buried valleys may be determined. An area in which a wealth of such information is available is the Twin Cities.

17

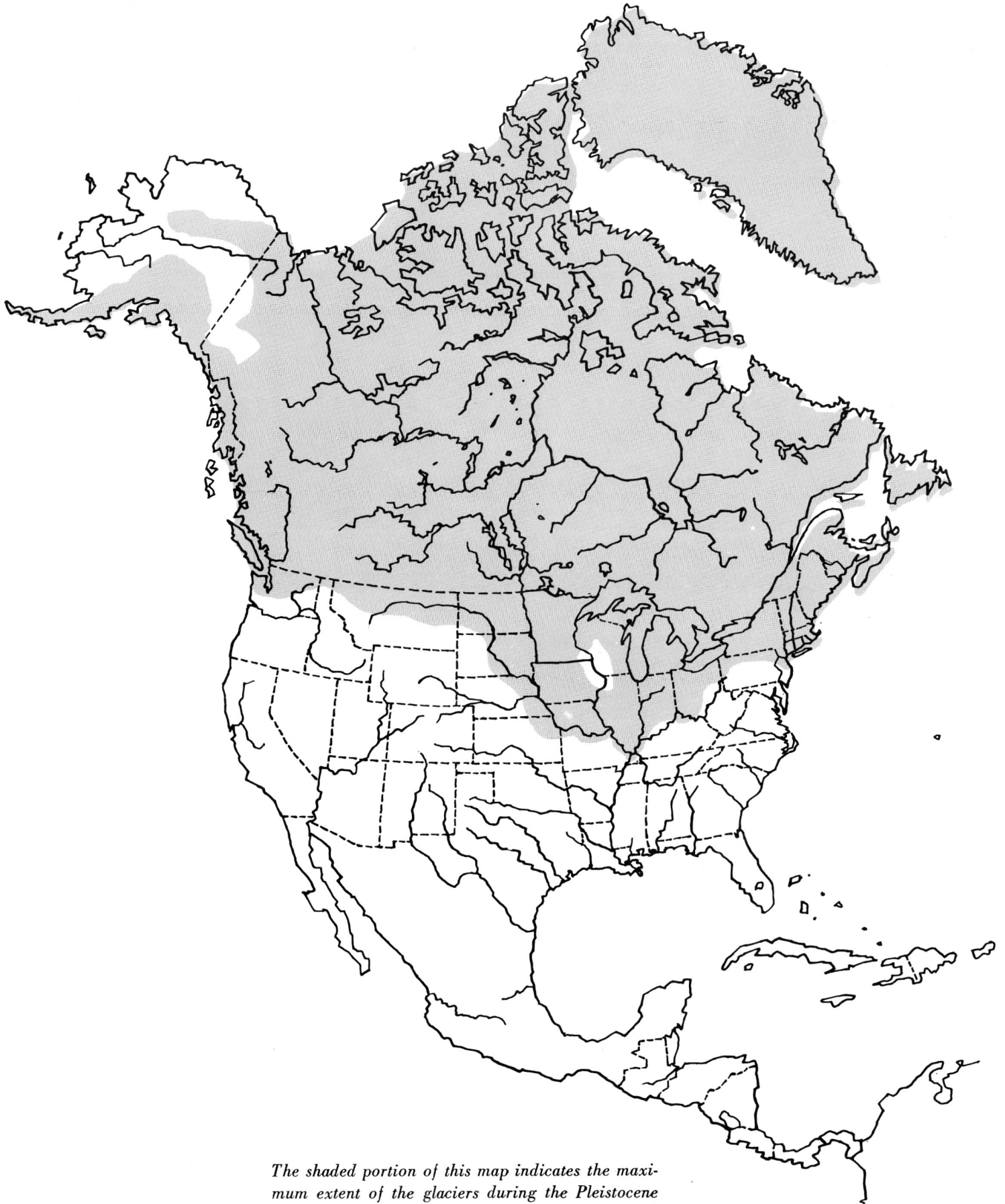

The shaded portion of this map indicates the maximum extent of the glaciers during the Pleistocene Ice Age and the relatively small "Driftless Area" which was surrounded, but not covered, by them.

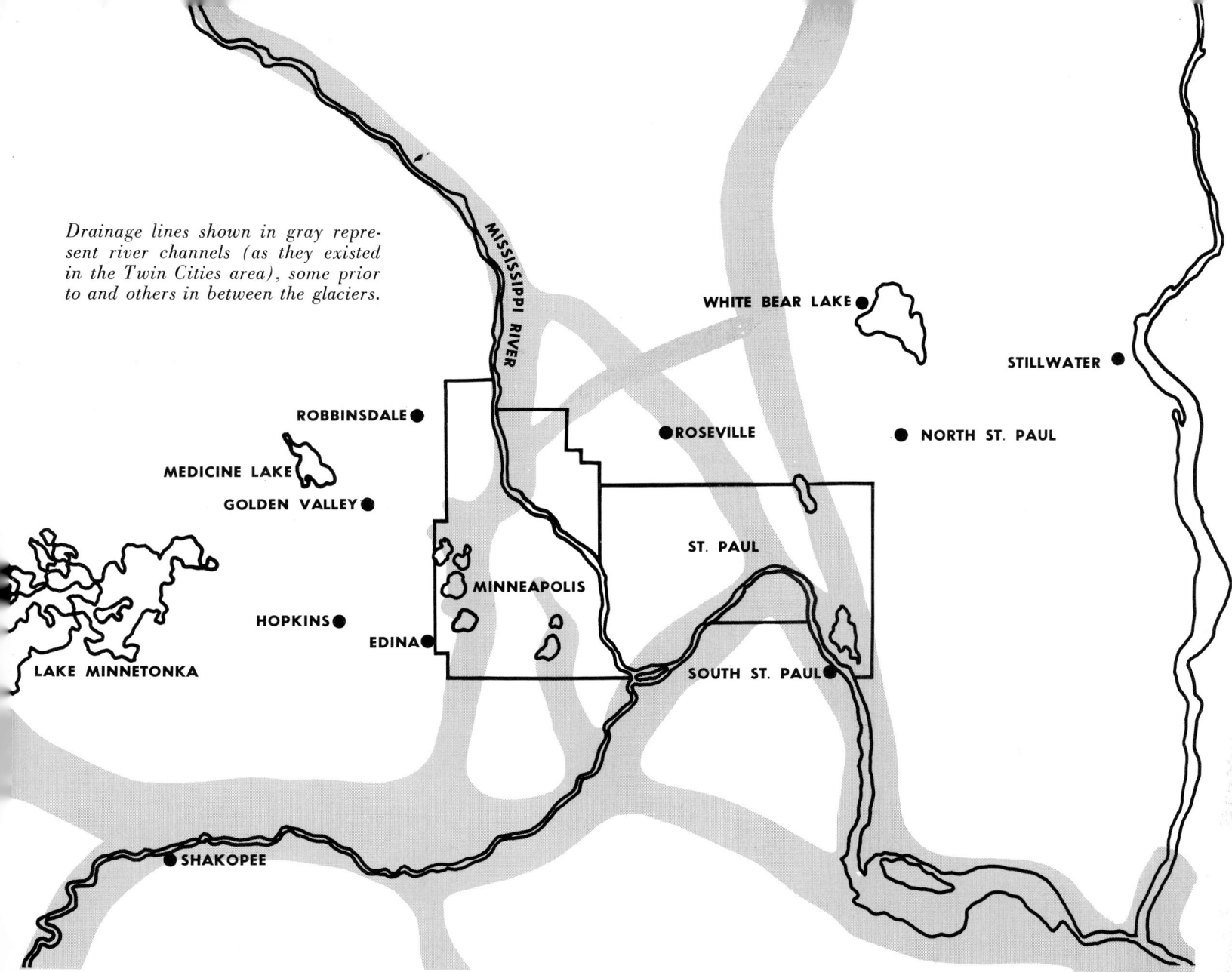

MISSISSIPPI RIVER

WHITE BEAR LAKE ●

STILLWATER ●

ROBBINSDALE ●

● ROSEVILLE

● NORTH ST. PAUL

MEDICINE LAKE

GOLDEN VALLEY ●

ST. PAUL

MINNEAPOLIS

HOPKINS ●

EDINA ●

LAKE MINNETONKA

SOUTH ST. PAUL ●

● SHAKOPEE

Adapted from G. M. Schwartz, Minnesota Geological Survey

Hundreds of deep industrial wells have been drilled here—and the records made available. The reconstructed drainage pattern indicates that the Minnesota, the Mississippi and the St. Croix rivers all had very different channels before and between the glaciers than now, and most of the former channels were much wider and deeper than the present ones.

The glacial effects we have thus far spoken of might be regarded as active effects—those produced while the glaciers were advancing. The effects of greatest value to Minnesota, however, may have been those produced in the more passive stage —as the glaciers were melting. At least it was at this time that the groundwork was laid for Minnesota's most distinctive characteristic—her 10,000 lakes. The vast quantities of rocks and soil scraped and torn from her previously rugged features, and

much that came all the way from Canada, was dropped irregularly over most of Minnesota and surrounding states. Although glaciers usually leave an area much smoother than they find it, it is neither perfectly smooth nor level. The materials dropped directly by glaciers are called moraines. If the rate of melting at the glacial margin is about equal to the forward motion of the ice the margin is essentially stationary.

Under these conditions rock material is fed toward and squeezed out along the margin to form irregular ridges called "end moraines." When the margin itself recedes more or less uniformly, due to more rapid melting, the rock debris is dropped as an irregular blanket over the area of retreat and is then called a "ground moraine." Minnesota is virtually covered by ground moraines upon which there are also many end moraines. The re-

19

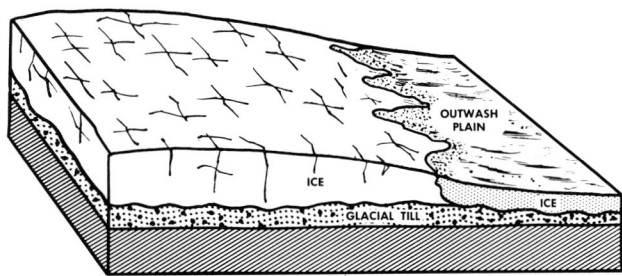

End Moraine

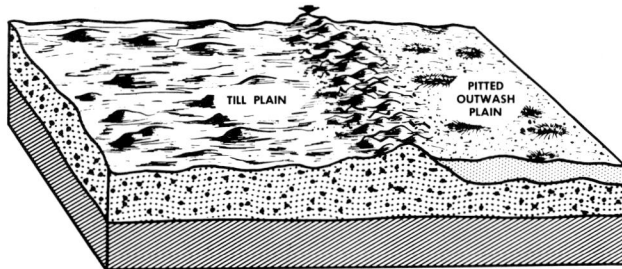

sulting hills and depressions, often called "knobs and kettles," form a large proportion of our lake basins. And, as the glaciers began to fall apart, many blocks of ice remained here and there, buried or half-buried, to melt at a later time. When they finally did melt, depressions formed which gave us another large share of lake basins. While many other lake-producing processes have been studied it was by these two processes that the great majority of Minnesota's lakes were born.

Thus, even in their retreat, the glaciers performed valuable service. In many places, oddly enough, they modified their own previous deposits by the action of temporarily ponded water. Wherever the slope of the ground beneath the glacier was to the north, meltwater was ponded against the slowly retreating ice wall, and a temporary lake was formed. We say "temporary" because as soon as the ice wall melted the lake disappeared for lack of a northern rim. But in some cases the ice wall retreated so slowly that the lake lasted hundreds, or even thousands, of years. While they lasted, these lakes were the scene of activity—some of it quiet, some of it thunderous. In two ways this action greatly modified the lake bottom—later to become the land surface. Small streamlets brought in silt from the surrounding land and the melting glacier furnished more. Thus a blanket of relatively fine material was laid down over the irregular de-

posits of the glacier. The settling of these fine sediments undoubtedly smoothed out some of the small wrinkles in the lake bottom, but the real leveling action came from the pounding of the waves and their swash on the beaches. Most of these lakes probably dwindled in size rather slowly and we may picture their shrinking shore lines as gigantic chains that were slowly dragged in, thus leveling virtually the entire area of the lake by the time it became extinct. Some of the larger of these glacial lakes are shown on the accompanying map. King of them all was Glacial Lake Agassiz that occupied all of the present Red River Valley (in North Dakota as well as Minnesota), most of the counties in northern Minnesota west of Lake Vermilion and a vast area in Canada. It was larger than all the present Great Lakes combined. The present Red Lake, Rainy Lake, Lake of the Woods, and Lake Winnipeg are remnants of this once vast lake in the sense that they represent the largest depressions on the old lake floor that did not yield

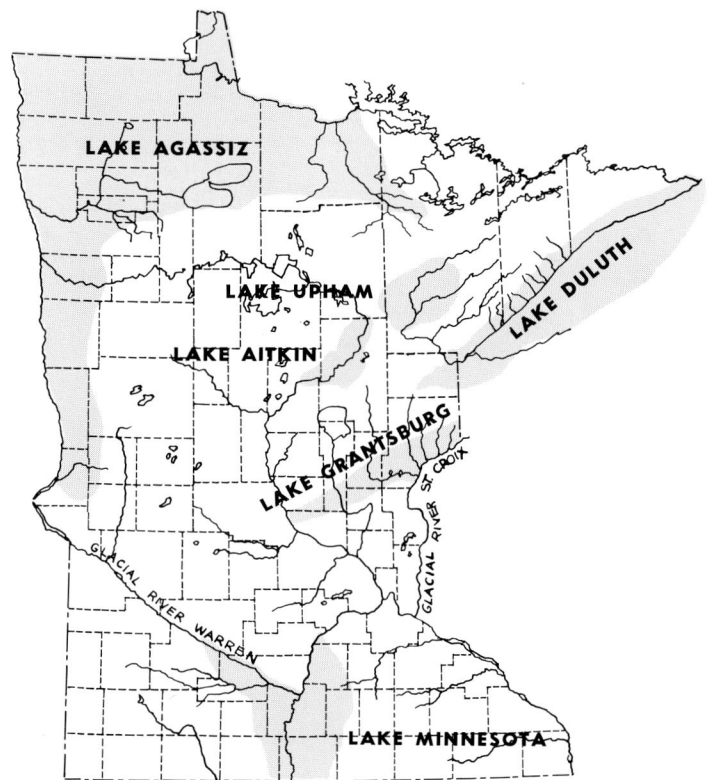

Adapted from Various Sources

20

Red River Valley

to the leveling forces. When the parent lake finally subsided it left one of the most fabulous areas of rich, level agricultural land in the world.

When we consider the great benefits derived from the glaciers: leveling effects, soils, vast supplies of sand and gravel, our "10,000 lakes," greater conservation of water and the creation of waterfalls by forcing streams into more youthful channels, we may get the idea that everything the glaciers did for us was good. This is not quite true. In some areas the glacial boulders on the surface are so numerous as to interfere seriously with agriculture. Then, too, the iron-mining industry has some cause for complaint—but also some cause for appreciation. Prior to the glaciers the iron formations were doubtless exposed prominently at the surface—perhaps as much or more than Jasper Peak, near Tower, is today. The glaciers played no favorites. Iron-bearing hills were scraped away as blithely as any other. Scrapings from these iron-bearing deposits are partially responsible for the "red drifts" farther south. Then, too, when the glaciers melted they buried the iron formation under 50 to 200 feet of drift. This retarded discovery, made exploration difficult and adds to the cost of strip-mining operations. But, as if to compensate the mining companies for these losses, the glaciers from the northeast scooped out the connecting chain of Great Lakes, without whose cheap transportation to eastern furnaces the companies would be seriously handicapped and taconite development would doubtless have been ruled out.

The portion of Minnesota's heritage discussed above was created during the geologic epoch called the Pleistocene, meaning "newest." Except for the Recent (present) epoch, the Pleistocene is the most recent portion of geologic time. Both the Recent and Pleistocene epochs belong to the most recent era, called the Cenozoic. For the reader who wishes to keep in perspective the stretch of geologic time and the events as they are discussed, a brief chart of geologic history, with special reference to Minnesota, will be found on the last page of this chapter. For lack of space the reader is referred to this chart and to references mentioned in the bibliography for the explanation of certain geologic terms he finds not adequately explained here.

The Day Before Yesterday

(The Era of Minnesota Seas)

Our plan of going backward in time suggests that in imagination we should peel off the layers of the earth's crust one at a time to see what lies beneath. Let us strip off the glacial deposits just discussed. We would then find that they rest on bedrock of many types, varying greatly in age, in different parts of the state. In southern and western Minnesota they rest on "middle-aged," sedimentary (layered) rocks, while in central and northern Minnesota they rest on vastly older rocks which are mostly igneous or metamorphic in character. These terms will be explained as the different rock types are discussed.

21

Sedimentary rocks are those whose parent materials were at one time layers of sediment, deposited almost always in water. Thus the story of our southern and western rocks is in terms of invasions of the sea rather than by invasions of ice. The time span was much greater also—being a matter of several hundred million years rather than a million or so for the glaciers. The story of the still older rocks of central and northern Minnesota is reserved until later.

The rocks described above as "middle-aged" are actually very old, and some are much older than others. There are two distinct age groups: one 70-100 million and the other perhaps 350-550 million years old. The younger ones were formed during the Cretaceous period of the Mesozoic era. The older group came into being during the Cambrian, Ordovician and Devonian periods of the Paleozoic era. The Cretaceous rocks cover large areas in southwestern and western Minnesota while those of the earlier periods are found principally in the southeastern part of Minnesota.

It has doubtless occurred to the reader that quite a large slice of geologic time is apparently being studiously ignored—namely, the time from the oldest glaciers we discussed, back to the youngest bedrock, apparently about 70 million years! But this is as it must be since the geologic story is one whose pages are the rocks themselves and in Minnesota no rocks representing these intervening years have been found. If there ever were any rocks here representing this (the Tertiary) period presumably they were eroded away before, or perhaps partially by, the glaciers. Here we have the first of the "torn-out pages" referred to earlier.

During the Cretaceous period an arm of the sea extended itself into Minnesota apparently from the west and south. This was an eastward extension of a very large sea that extended all the way from the Arctic Ocean to the Gulf of Mexico, across what are now the High Plains and Rocky Mountain states. At that time this area was a very broad, low trough—the Rocky Mountains had not yet been born (though the end of the period did see their beginnings). Whether the ocean level rose, the land sank, or both, we cannot be sure. Neither do we know just how far east the sea extended. The general method of determining the extent of an ancient sea is to map the existing sedimentary rocks of that age. The large connected area of Cretaceous rocks in Minnesota lies in the southwestern and western parts of the state. They are continuous with much thicker layers in the Dakotas and Nebraska. (See page 38.) But there are also isolated patches of these rocks, too small to be shown on this map, scattered as far east as Fillmore and Goodhue counties in the southern part of Minnesota and St. Louis County in the northern part. From the nature of the sediments and the fossils found in them it seems that these patches too must represent deposits in the same sea. Their isolation may easily be understood by supposing that these near-shore deposits were never very thick and that pre-glacial erosion, assisted by the glaciers themselves, removed all but these remnants. They are vestiges of the past that add clues to the story. Many authorities feel, therefore, that the Cretaceous sea at its greatest advance may have covered all of Minnesota except possibly the northeastern corner.

The Cretaceous rocks, hardened sediments of the Cretaceous sea, vary considerably from place to place in Minnesota. The word Cretaceous means "chalky" and was chosen as the name of this period because in many places in America and in Europe its rocks are chalky. In very few places in Minnesota, however, would they be so described. They are mainly sandstones, shales and some conglomerates. These rocks are not very thick generally, but they do attain a thickness of more than 400 feet in Lyon and Redwood counties.

The reader will probably be more interested in the fossils found in the rocks than in the rocks themselves. Looking back 70 million years, what does the life record show? Were there any resemblances between the life of that day and this? Our first thought probably is that there could be no resemblances because these fossils would be those of sea life—not of the landlubbers of today. This thought, however, is only partially correct. The earlier Cretaceous deposits in Minnesota apparently were made in a shallow inland sea—possibly with irregular shore line and numerous islands. This thought stems from the fact that there are many fossils of land plants, mainly leaves, in these earlier deposits. And, surprisingly enough, many of them closely resemble forms familiar to us to-day. None of the present-day species had emerged at that time but the ancestors of many of them had, namely cottonwood, elm, sassafras, maple, poplar, willow, oak and numerous others. Indeed, one of the remarkable life phenomena of this period was the great variety and extensive growth of flowering plants (angiosperms). The clay (shale) pit at Springfield, Brown County, has a layer a few inches thick containing fossil leaves.

The Mesozoic era, of which the Cretaceous period is a part, is far better known for its remarkable animal life than for its plants. This was the "Age of Reptiles"—so named because of the dominance of reptiles, especially dinosaurs, over other kinds of animal life. Although no dinosaur bones have ever been found in Minnesota there is some reason to believe that some of them did inhabit the area because of the "gizzard stones" that have been found. Mighty and numerous as some of the dinosaurs were, for some unknown reason they all died out at the end of the Cretaceous period. Why so powerful a group of animals, after dominating the scene for 60 million years or so, should so suddenly (geologically speaking) vanish is not clear. Imagination enters into all such scientific mysteries and several clever suggestions have been made. One has it that change to a colder climate (which doubtless did accompany the uplift forming the Rocky

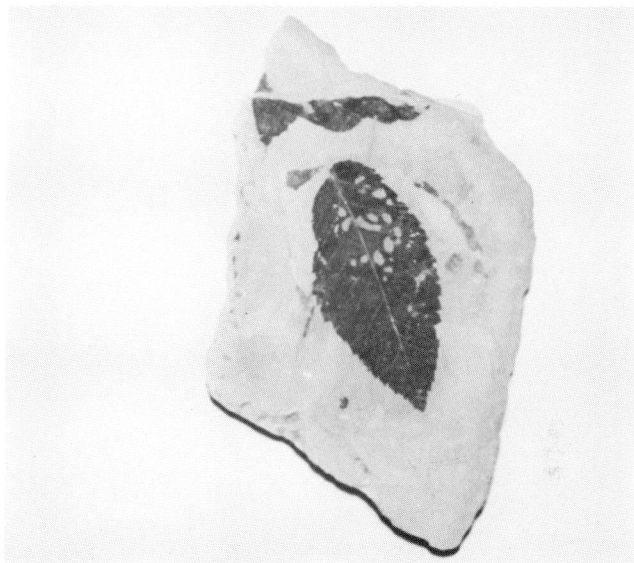

Cretaceous elm leaf

Dinosaur

Chicago Natural History Museum

Mountains) and unfriendly neighbors were responsible. Reptiles are cold-blooded and as such it is well-known that they are relatively inactive in cold weather. Colder winters may have rendered the dinosaurs defenseless against the much smaller, but warm-blooded mammals that were multiplying rapidly at this time. Another factor may have been simply the "war of nerves"—dinosaurs vs. mammals—which the dinosaurs would surely lose in view of their small capsule of brains. Perhaps this

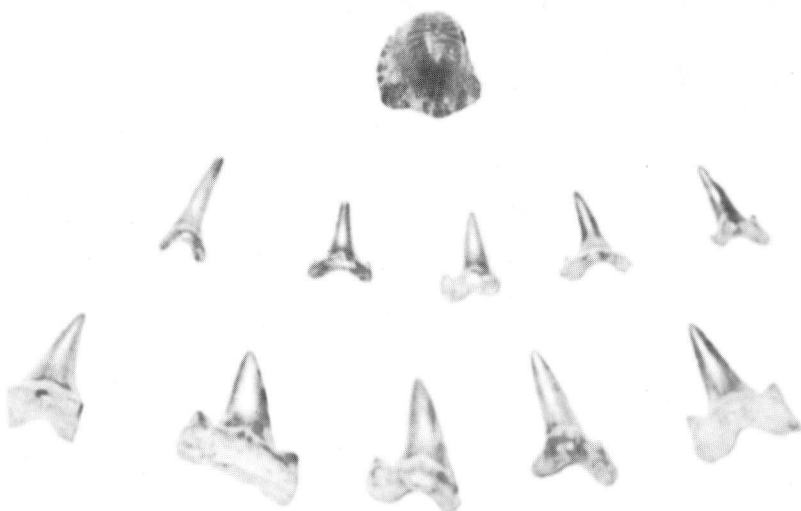

Cretaceous shark teeth

Snail

was an early example of the common phrase "there is no substitute for brains." Or again, it may be that some new disease—perhaps the common cold —was responsible. Imagine a dinosaur with a sore throat! Although certain of these ideas have some degree of plausibility, real evidence for any of them is difficult to find. All we know is that evidence in the rocks of dinosaurs more recent than the

Cretaceous period is lacking. From the terrifying appearances of many of them this is a comforting thought — to be 70 million years removed from them seems quite close enough!

Several other kinds of animal fossils of this period have been found in Minnesota. Shark's teeth and several kinds of fish teeth and bones have been found in the western part of Minnesota, especially in Big Stone County. Scattered outcrops on the Mesabi Range also yield shark's teeth as well as several types of marine mollusks: oysters, snail-like forms and ammonites (a coiled type related to the present-day chambered nautilus). Ammonites, too, became extinct at the close of the Cretaceous.

In summing up the life of the Cretaceous with respect to its influence on the present, it seems fair to say that interesting and spectacular as some of the animals were the plants were much more important to us—at least in one sense. Although the animals of today are just as truly the products of their Cretaceous ancestors as are the plants, nevertheless the plants advanced during the Cretaceous period much closer to present forms than did the animals. To put it another way, if we could be transported back to the Cretaceous period the plants of that time would appear much more familiar to us than the animals.

Economic products derived from Cretaceous rocks in Minnesota are not very impressive. The greatest contribution is from shales and clays used in the ceramic industries. The pottery at Red Wing is an example of such use. As building stone Cretaceous rocks are without sufficient crushing strength for building purposes. Salt is found in certain Cretaceous layers, especially in the Red River Valley. The amount is great enough in some instances to make the water from these horizons unfit for use but it is not great enough to support commercial salt production now. One well in Kittson County was used for salt production for a time in the 1880's. Perhaps the Cretaceous period should be given credit ("A" for effort if not for achievement) for its attempt to correct Minnesota's fuel shortage. Lignite ("brown coal") in small amounts is found occasionally. One occurrence of about one foot in thickness is reported from Brown County. But nowhere is the amount great enough nor the quality high enough to render it worth mining. This feeble attempt at fuel-making is the only one in Minnesota's past of which we have evidence—except, of course, the more or less recent peat deposits in northern Minnesota. But despite the Cretaceous "effort," Minnesota is fuel-less so far as the so-called "fossil fuels" are concerned.

Iron ore of some importance occurs in southeastern Minnesota, especially in Fillmore County, often associated with Cretaceous rocks but apparently not as part of them. What sometimes appears as basal Cretaceous is in reality a residue on an old erosion surface resulting from certain physical and chemical activity prior to submergence beneath the

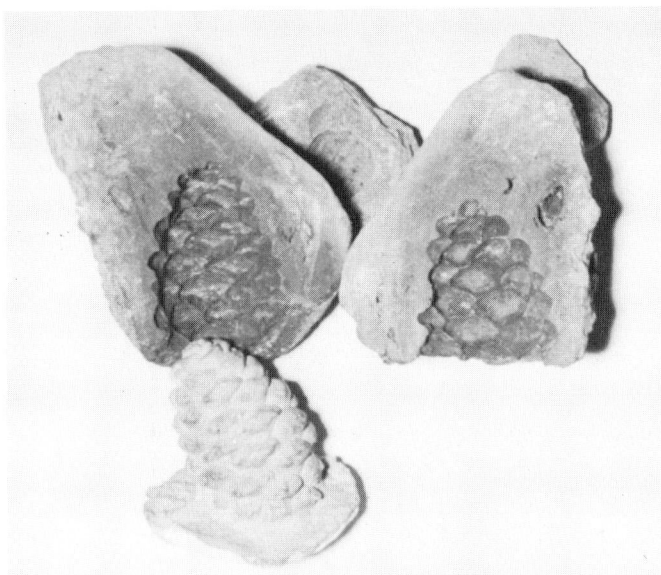

Cretaceous pine cone

Cretaceous sea. It occurs in "lenses" or "pods" of relatively small size, which are, therefore, slightly older than Cretaceous.

Let us now consider the older (that is, the Paleozoic) group of Minnesota's "middle-aged" rocks. In order to see these we might expect to have to peel off the Cretaceous rocks, just discussed. This turns out to be largely unnecessary, however, since the two groups overlap in a relatively narrow band in the central counties of southern Minnesota. All we would need to do would be to lift up the edge of the Cretaceous rocks and peer under a short way. (The reader will remember that we have al-

ready cleared away all glacial deposits.) From the fact that the Paleozoic rocks are beneath those of the Cretaceous, in this zone of overlap, we might suppose that the Paleozoic rocks are only a little older than the Cretaceous ones. Comparisons with the rock record elsewhere, however, indicate that between them there is a lapse of 180-200 million years! This represents, not just a few missing pages, but large parts of two volumes are gone—the last part of the Paleozoic and the first of the Mesozoic.

This matter of "torn-out pages" (the geologist calls them "unconformities") has such significance and recurs so often in our story as to deserve a brief glance at how they become torn out. Let us begin with a basic idea in geology that is only slightly exaggerated by the brief statement: "If (at any particular place) erosion is not taking place deposition is." The meaning is that on land erosion is continuously occurring while silt is continually being deposited in ocean basins. If, through warping of the earth's crust, a part of the ocean floor becomes uplifted enough to drain the water away, what was the ocean becomes dry land. Immediately upon pushing its head above water the erosive forces begin to chisel and carry away the upper layers—back to the ocean. Carrying away the upper layers is the "tearing out" of some of the "pages," spoken of. If and when the area is submerged beneath the sea again, erosion ceases but deposition begins again. There are several kinds of unconformities based principally on the kind of evidence that exists. The accompanying sketch shows what is perhaps the simplest kind, an "angular unconformity."

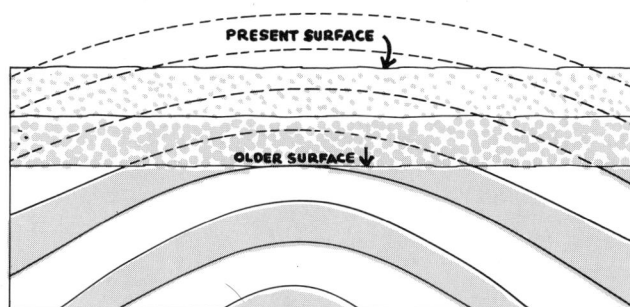

Angular Unconformity
(Dotted lines indicate eroded portions)

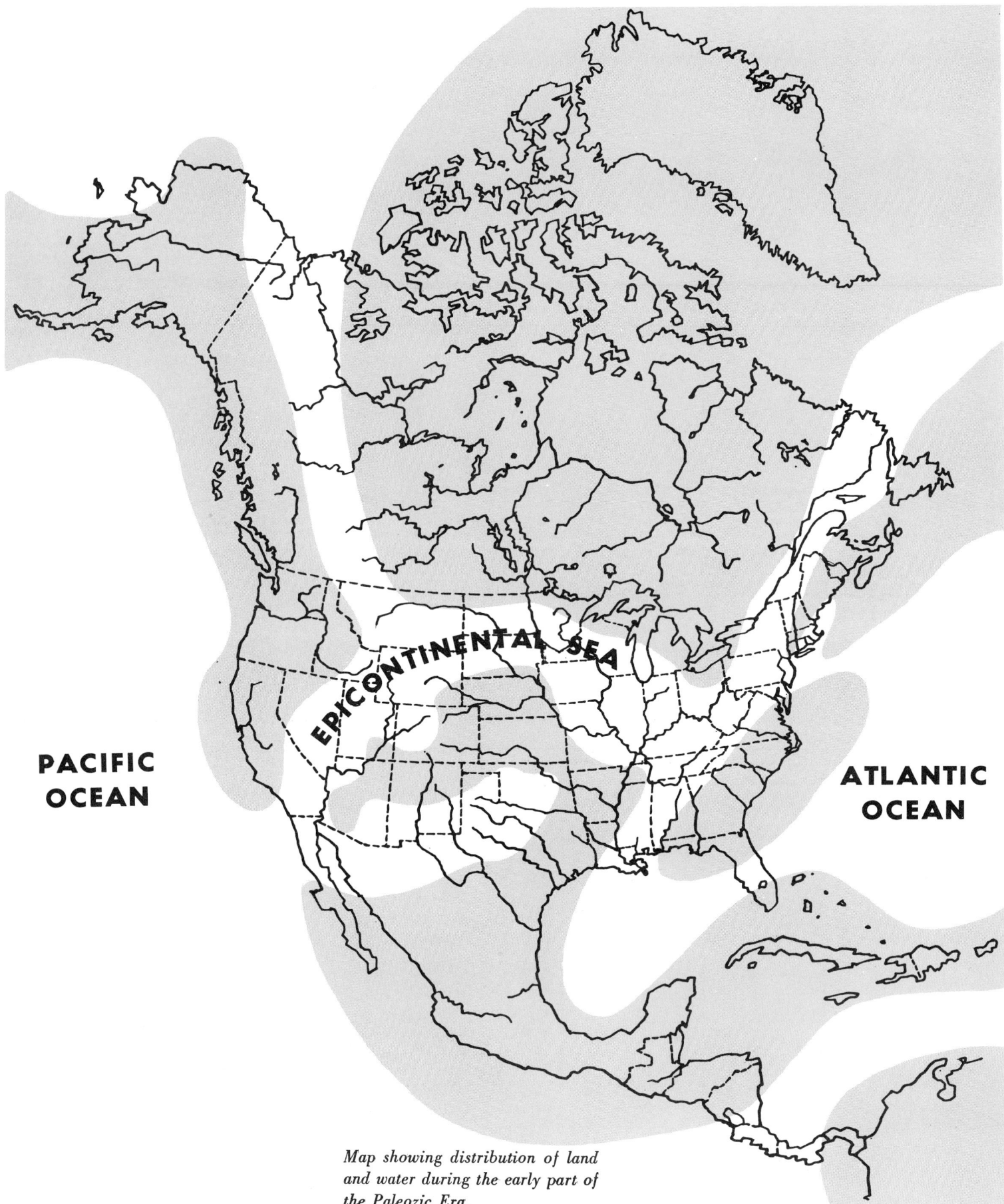

PACIFIC
OCEAN

EPICONTINENTAL SEA

ATLANTIC
OCEAN

*Map showing distribution of land
and water during the early part of
the Paleozic Era.*

Here we see clearly two sets of layers. The lower (folded) one was deposited during one period of submergence. Then the area was folded and uplifted above the sea and erosion removed parts of the (then exposed) upper layers. Later the sea encroached upon the land again and the upper (nearly horizontal) layers were laid down. The degree of flatness of the surface of contact between the two sets of unconformable beds is an indication of the length of the erosion interval—the flatter the longer. To apply this to our Minnesota situation, the gap in time from the Mesozoic rocks back to the Paleozoic rocks is believed to have been 180-200 million years. If so, it means that for this enormous length of time Minnesota presumably kept her head above water—and all this time erosive forces were chiseling away at her exposed countenance. The time estimate is made by finding the missing rocks elsewhere (some of them farther down the Mississippi River) and determining, as accurately as possible, the time required for their deposition. These rocks include those of the Jurassic, Triassic, Permian, Pennsylvanian and Mississippian periods. Were they, or some of them, present at one time here in Minnesota, only to be completely removed during the long erosion interval? Informed speculation suggests that they may have been—and speculation is encouraged in science, provided it is in keeping with known facts and provided it is admitted to be speculation. It may lead to fruitful new knowledge. In this case, however, the prospects are not bright that we shall ever know.

Space does not allow us to give consideration to all of the periods of the Paleozoic era—not even to all of those represented in Minnesota. It is inferred that the Paleozoic seas entered Minnesota from the south, coming up what is now the Mississippi River Valley. This is believed to be so because deposits representing these periods are found on both sides of the river, and the Minnesota rocks are continuous with those in several states to the south —but not to the north. Just how far north and west these seas extended is a matter of conjecture. We may be sure that part of the time at least they came somewhat north of the Twin Cities and nearly as far west as central Minnesota. The rocks existing

Barn Bluff, Red Wing

today assure us of this. For example, Cambrian rocks (the oldest and lowest) are found near the surface about halfway between the Twin Cities and Duluth and are exposed along the St. Croix River both above and below Taylor's Falls (though not at the falls). But these are only the rocks that remain after hundreds of millions of years of erosion. Perhaps they once extended all the way to Duluth, or even farther. Devonian rocks (the youngest and uppermost of the group) occur in Minnesota only along the Iowa border and are almost entirely confined to Fillmore, Mower and Freeborn counties. The indication is, therefore, that

Mississippi River

the Devonian sea was less extensive in Minnesota than that of the Cambrian and Ordovician periods. There are no known Silurian rocks in Minnesota —though they do occur in Iowa.

The Paleozoic rocks in Minnesota consist of all the common types of sedimentary rocks: sandstone and conglomerate, limestone and dolomite, shale and siltstone. The total of the average thicknesses is about 1,600 feet, although not all of the layers are present at any one place. Several of the sandstones are quite porous and have high permeability, hence they are excellent water-bearing layers, notably the Jordan sandstone. The slope of the beds is such as to produce two artesian basins— that is, areas where water encountered at depth is under sufficient pressure to rise an appreciable distance in the well and may overflow. One of these, the so-called Twin Cities artesian basin, could hardly have been more centrally located beneath Minneapolis and St. Paul so that each city shares in its advantages. It is about 40 miles in diameter and as such has meant a great saving in water costs for a vast number of industries and commercial concerns. The other is an enormously larger basin involving most of southeastern Minnesota and extending into Iowa. Its lowest portion in Minnesota is between Albert Lea and Austin with rocks sloping toward this region from as far away as Wisconsin. Though much larger than the former basin it is doubtful whether it has been of as great economic value due to the heavy concentration of industry and people in the Twin Cities area. The best opportunity to view Cambrian and Ordovician rocks is along the walls of the valleys of the Mississippi, Minnesota and St. Croix Rivers where erosion has laid them open—like a slice through a layered cake. Nearly 600 feet of them are exposed south of Winona. If we could have seen this part of the valley at its deepest, some 200 feet more of rock would have been exposed. Since the glaciers, when the carrying power of the river has been reduced, approximately this thickness of sand and gravel has been laid down on the valley floor in southern Minnesota. Sometimes we are able also to see these rocks in the flanks of scattered, butte-type hills, referred to earlier, which occur along, or not far "inland" from, these major rivers. Their

flat tops are usually controlled by one layer or another of these Cambrian or Ordovician rocks, with only a thin cover of glacial drift and soil. Small ones occur east of St. Paul and larger ones farther south, such as Barn Bluff at Red Wing.

We find, just as we should expect, that the life of Paleozoic times was greatly different from that of the Mesozoic. We also find great differences within the Paleozoic since its duration was a matter of hundreds of millions of years. We must omit all but the most general discussion, however. Paleozoic rocks in Minnesota are all marine and as such give us no clues as to the land-life of the times. Evidence from elsewhere indicates that there were little, if any, land plants or animals until Silurian and Devonian times, at the end of which there were abundant forests of primitive trees and ferns. Land animals were probably non-existent until near the end of the Devonian and only then if we wish to call a certain primitive type of primitive lungfish a "land animal." Its use of the "lung" was probably about as limited as that of the present-day lungfishes, that is, as an aid to survival until it could get back into the water. Sea-life was abundant even in the Cambrian seas. The fossil evidence is mostly of animals in this early period, but the dependence of animals upon plants for food argues for an abundance in quantity, if not in variety, of plants. Lime-secreting algæ (seaweeds) are among the oldest known fossils — older even than the Cambrian. By Ordovician times they occurred in great profusion as may be seen in many of our Minnesota rocks. The ornamental stone sold under the trade-name "Winona Travertine" probably owes the ropy appearance of its surfaces to these organisms. Evidence of a host of marine animals representing Cambrian, Ordovician and Devonian times are known from rocks in Minnesota. Chief among these in Cambrian rocks are the trilobites (three-lobed creatures), brachiopods ("lamp shells") together with some snail-like forms and worms. To this company were added corals, bryozoans, crinoids clams and cephalopods during the Ordovician period. The last-named were cigar-shaped ancestors of our present-day squids. Some have been found in the Twin Cities area and at Faribault that were five or six feet long and six or

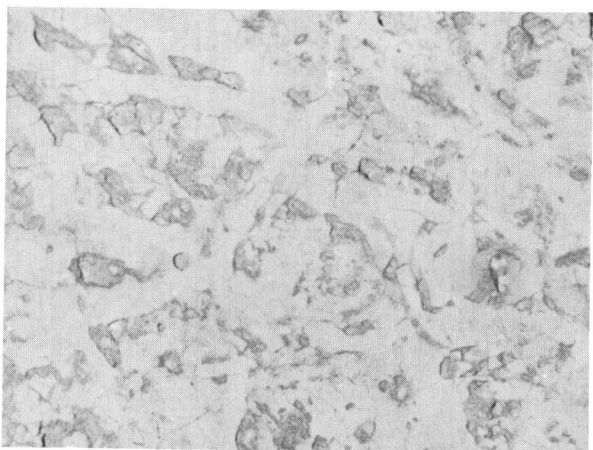

Winona Travertine

eight inches in diameter. The Devonian period is sometimes called the "Age of Fishes" because of their abundance in the fossil record. Devonian rocks in Minnesota have yielded only a few identifiable fragments but enough to prove their presence. Thus Minnesota (to be) had an imposing array of Paleozoic, marine citizenry.

The Paleozoic era gave much more to our present economy than did the Mesozoic. At the head of the list we should put building stones. Those of this era commercially produced in Minnesota are various varieties of Ordovician limestones and dolomites—most of these in the Mankato-Kasota and Winona districts. Several layers are particularly prized for their pleasing colors and their attractive ornamental effect. The sandstones are too poorly cemented, except in rare instances for use as building stone. Other rock products of importance are: agricultural and chemical lime, crushed rock, rock wool, natural or "hydraulic" cement, shales for brick making. The St. Peter sandstone which crops out here and there over a wide area in the Middle West is a celebrated formation for glassmaking. It is one of the purest sands known having a silica content of well over 99% in many places. Until recently it was mined beneath the Ford Motor Company plant in St. Paul and used for the manufacture of automobile glass. It is very poorly cemented and is therefore easily quarried or mined.

The Day of the Beginning
(The Story of the Ancestral Rocks—Minnesota's Real "Old-timers.")

We hope that the reader has not been too staggered by the haste with which we have reviewed vast stretches of time on the previous pages. Whatever our speed has been in millions of years per page, now we shall have to slip into overdrive and go several times faster. Though we have sped through some 500 million years or more, more than three fourths of all geologic time still lies before us—in our backward flight through time. We must speak now, not in millions of years but in billions. Rather than rock formations a few hundred or a few thousand feet thick we must speak of some that are four or five miles thick. And all of this must be done in the next few pages!

In keeping with our practice it would seem that we should begin by stripping off all Mesozoic and Paleozoic rocks and view what lies beneath. We would learn very much that the geologist would like to know if we were able to do this but, in one sense, this is unnecessary. We can keep ourselves very busy for a long time trying to decipher the rocks of central and northern Minnesota which are covered only by glacial deposits—and the reader will remember that we stripped them off several pages ago.

These "old-timers" of northern Minnesota belong to the portion of geologic time called the "Precambrian." This obviously means the time before the Cambrian. We may be curious as to why the Cambrian period has been singled out as such a significant signpost or "time post." There are excellent reasons for this. In the first place, rocks of Cambrian age and younger are more or less well-supplied with fossils—giving us ample evidence that the Cambrian seas, and those that followed, were teeming with life. Rocks older than Cambrian age contain almost no fossils. We should not conclude from this, however, that Precambrian seas were necessarily lifeless. But whatever life there was—and it may have been abundant—failed to be preserved in the rocks, except in rare instances. It may be that these primordial forms of life had no hard parts, and therefore, there was little that could be preserved. Or it may be that certain violent chemical or mechanical processes prevailed, which destroyed even the hard parts—dissolved or pulverized them. Whatever the reason, the fossil hunter's "happy hunting ground" is not in the Precambrian. A few rare examples of lime-secreting

"Black Granite" (Gabbro)

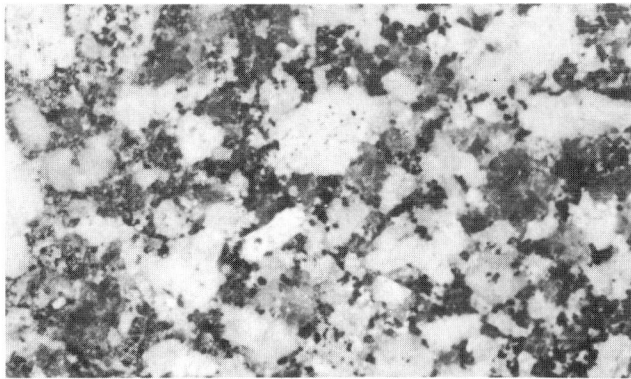

Rockville Granite

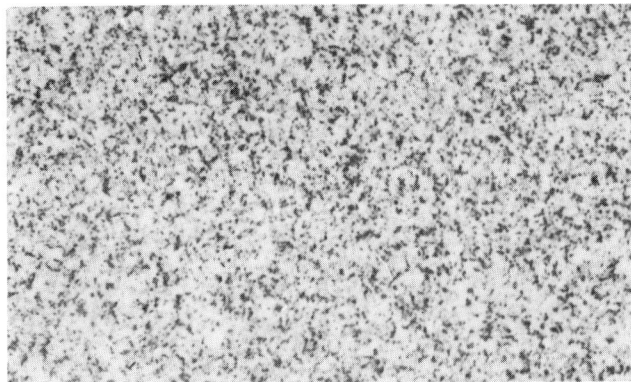

Isle Granite

algæ, iron bacteria and worm burrows are about "the crop" to date. Another good reason for considering the Cambrian as a reference point in the geologic time scale lies in the nature of the rocks themselves. Most rocks Cambrian and younger constitute an orderly, layer on layer, sequence of sedimentary rocks, more or less horizontal except near mountains, and extending over fairly large areas. As such, relationships and relative ages are fairly easy to decipher. On the other hand, rocks older than Cambrian, in many portions of the world, are found to consist of all manner of igneous and meta-

morphic types which often appear as if they had been thrown together in a heap after a prolonged period of torture. They are generally better described as "masses" rather than layers. Occasionally, sedimentary rocks do occur among them but these are to be regarded as unusual. Igneous rocks, as the reader may know already, are those whose parent materials were molten at one time. Granite is the best known example.

Metamorphic rocks are those whose parent materials were still older rocks which have been recast (transformed by heat and/or pressure) into their present condition. Despite their rugged experience they usually bear sufficient clues to reveal the fact that they have had a previous existence either as an igneous or as a sedimentary rock. Slate (from shale) and marble (from limestone) are well-known examples, although marble is a very scarce item in Minnesota. Thus our story of the Precambrian will have little to do with glacial invasions (through glaciers are believed to have occurred amidst all the turmoil of this remote era), and not especially with invasions of the sea—although the seas did play their part. Rather it will be in terms of the pouring forth of lavas, cooling of the surface, buckling of the earth's crust, the formation of mountains, erosion—enormously long periods of erosion—and then more lava flows, more buckling and more . . .

The Precambrian rocks found in the northern part of Minnesota form the southwestern corner of a much larger area of similarly old and contorted rocks of central and eastern Canada centered around Hudson Bay. This assemblage of ancient rocks is known as the "Canadian (or sometimes as the Laurentian) Shield"—a kind of core of the North American continent around which the other rocks have been laid down. Most other continents likewise have their "shield areas." It is often said that they have kept their "heads" above water for a greater share of geologic time than other portions of the continents and because of this these areas were the sources of much of the sediment that later formed the surrounding sedimentary rocks. But when the geologist goes to northern Minnesota to study the rocks of the Canadian Shield, especially during a wet season, he may be tempted to ask whether the Canadian Shield indeed has its head above water now! And, although in imagination we may have done a neat job of "stripping off the glacial drift to view what lies beneath," the reader realizes that the geologist must rely on something more substantial than such an imaginary trick. Actually, both the glacial drift and the swamps are tremendous handicaps. When rocks are not exposed at the surface, either naturally or artificially, the geologist is usually not too perplexed if sufficient contact can be made with them through well drilling. But in northern Minnesota the sparsity of population, with little need for deep well drilling —except notably on the Iron Ranges, has withheld much badly needed data. Consequently the reader will see on the "Geologic Map of Minnesota" (see page 38) a very large portion of this part of the state marked "Formations Not Determined." Thus we are compelled, partly from lack of knowledge and partly because we must soon bring our story to a close, to choose for discussion only a few outstanding rock formations of this era. We shall choose those whose "heads" are the highest—actually high enough to be above the glacial drift or the swamps, or important enough economically to have had these handicaps removed.

Since the Precambrian is so very long it is convenient to subdivide it. Just how most properly to divide it, in different areas of the world, has long been a subject for debate. Since, as we have said, these rocks are highly contorted and "thrown together," lacking in fossils, and further because their exposures are generally far apart, their connections and relationships are almost impossible to determine. This has led to doubt about the relative age of the Precambrian rocks and events in one part of the world, or continent, and those of another. More or less traditionally, the Precambrian has been divided into two parts, the Proterozoic and Archeozoic eras. Rather recently it has been decided that for Minnesota (as well as for some other places) a three-part division is more meaningful. Consequently, we have the Late or Upper, the Middle, and the Early or Lower Precambrian. Each

of these is separated from the others by enormous unconformities. Moreover, the beginning of each of the erosional periods associated with the unconformity saw the formation of high mountains— either in Minnesota or nearby (Canada and/or Wisconsin). These events constitute excellent natural breaks in the geologic time scale. In fact, an era is often defined as the time *between* periods of major mountain building activity.

The most recent mountains of the Precambrian, of which we have some evidence in Minnesota, are called the Killarney Mountains. These mountains now long extinct, whose high portions were principally in Wisconsin and Canada, only touched Minnesota's northern border. However, reverberations of these violent upheavals are believed to have brought a corresponding downwarping of the earth's crust to form a gigantic trough, the central portion of which after glacial scooping is now Lake Superior. Prior to the downwarping, this area was the scene of hundreds of lava flows over a prolonged period. They issued from cracks and fissures presumed to have been about parallel to the long axis of Lake Superior. Their edges may be seen today as the dark-colored basaltic rocks that slope into the waters of Lake Superior for nearly all of the 150-mile stretch of Minnesota's famous North Shore. Measurements indicate that these flows may have totalled 30,000 feet! They are believed to extend completely beneath Lake Superior since they are known to outcrop in northern Wisconsin —though not along the lake shore. How extensive these flows were on the old surface of Minnesota is problematical. They are seen at Taylor's Falls (at the falls and for a short way below) and are known from a deep well at Stillwater to be about 3,000 below the surface there. Until recently this was the farthest south that they were known to occur. But recently they have been encountered in a few wells near Montgomery about 40 miles southwest of the Twin Cities—though they apparently do not occur beneath the Twin Cities themselves. In the trough formed by the downwarped lava flows great thicknesses of sandy sediments accumulated and later hardened to form standstones, in some places more than a thousand feet thick. The best known portion of this series is the upper part called the Hinckley or Kettle River sandstone for outcrops in that vicinity. It is quarried at Sandstone and used extensively for building purposes. It is virtually the only sandstone in Minnesota that is well-enough cemented for this purpose. It occurs about 900 feet below the surface at the Twin Cities and is even deeper in the southern counties. The Hinckley is a good water-bearing layer—its water being softer and a few degrees warmer than that of the Jordan sandstone. The Hinckley is an exception to our general statement about the usual topsy-turvy condition of Precambrian rocks. Partly because of its uniformity over wide areas and because there is no well-marked unconformity between it and the rocks overlying it, known to be Cambrian, the age of the Hinckley itself was at one time regarded as

North Shore of Lake Superior

probably Cambrian. But because of relationships established between it and other sandstones in Wisconsin and because it is devoid of fossils the Hinckley sandstone is now regarded as the uppermost and youngest of Precambrian rocks in Minnesota. Its age? Perhaps 600-700 million years.

Another rock formation closely associated with the lava flows, which is geologically very impor-

Geologists examining Duluth gabbro

tant, is the Duluth gabbro. It is a dark-colored, coarse-grained igneous rock, chemically very similar to the lava flows but differing from them in the coarseness of its crystals. Some are one-half to three-fourths of an inch in length while those in the lava flows are too small to be seen by the unaided eye. This speaks of very slow cooling (cooling at great depth) of the gabbro. It is found wedged between lava flows very near the bottom of the stack. Presumably it represents molten rock material that "tried" to make its way to the surface. Had it done so it would have become more lava flows. But it was apparently easier to wedge the lava flows apart than to break through them—so this it did. This

formation is approximately 15,000 feet thick. Whether it entered the lava flows at one big "squeeze" or by several stages is not known. In Duluth the heavy dark cliffs on the west edge of the city and along Superior Street as far east as Mesaba Avenue are composed of this massive formation. Though covered with glacial drift most of the way, this formation extends from Duluth northward nearly to the Iron Range, close to Aurora, bends northeastward missing Ely by 10 or 12 miles and finally eastward until it returns to Lake Superior near Hovland. It forms a gigantic crescent-shaped area which is one of the world's largest examples of this type of rock. It is believed by some, to extend completely beneath Lake Superior since, like the lava flows, it also is found in northern Wisconsin. There has been a growing demand for this rock as a building stone because of its strength and attractive appearance when polished. It is often sold under the name "Black Granite" to distinguish it from true granite which is light colored. Quarries have been opened north of Duluth and along the Ely-Finland road which passes over this formation for 20 miles or more.

An adequate discussion of Minnesota's world-renowned iron "ranges" is clearly out of the question here and will not be attempted. Nevertheless, the time is right for a few brief remarks about them for we are now passing the "time post" that says, "Early part of the Late Precambrian." These iron-bearing formations occur in three main belts or "ranges": the Mesabi, the Cuyuna and the Vermilion. There seems to be little doubt that the Mesabi and the Cuyuna are both of the age stated, though there are no known connections across the 40-mile gap between them. The Vermilion Range is much older and discussion of it will be held till later. The rocks of the Mesabi and Cuyuna ranges apparently started their existence as sedimentary layers of gravel, sand and mud on the floor of a shallow sea that flooded an old erosion surface atop a great variety of very old rocks.

For a reason that remains obscure after many years of study by able geologists, unusually large amounts of iron oxides and silica were deposited along with the sediments. These materials may have had a volcanic origin—for some lava flows occur

33

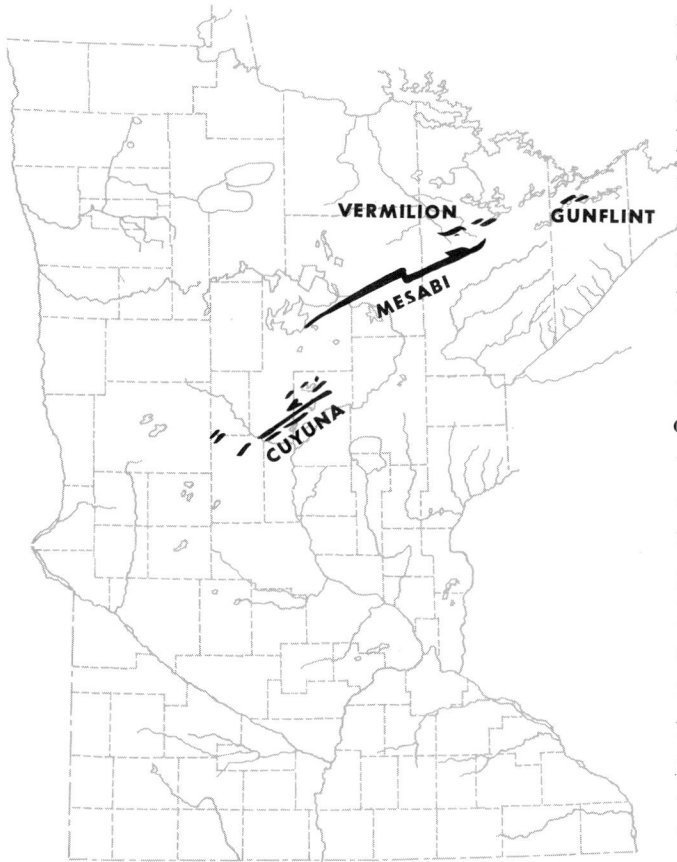

Iron ranges in Northern Minnesota

the world's largest source of iron for many years. The Mesabi Range alone has supplied about one third of the world demand! But now the end of the high-grade ore is in sight and we must turn to the use of lower-grade "taconite." We must, by costly, artificial means, bring about the enrichment that nature did for us free of charge over millions of years.

Although correlation is very uncertain there is some belief that the reddish or purplish Sioux quartzite rock that forms prominently in the southwestern counties especially near Pipestone, Jasper and Luverne may have been deposited at about the same time and under somewhat similar circumstances as the iron formations just described. It began its existence as a sandy sediment in a shallow sea in which some iron was present—just enough to give color to the rocks but not enough for commercial use. The resulting red sandstone was later transformed into a quartzite by the cementing action of silica deposited between the sand grains. This formed the very hard, resistant rock which is

among the sediments—or they may have been derived from the weathering of previous rocks that contained them. Whatever the source, it contributed iron to the formation until it was built up to a thickness of 500-700 feet. Thereafter deposition of mud continued but without the iron. Then strong forces went to work—some chemical, some physical. In the vicinity of the Mesabi Range the sea floor was tilted gently toward the southeast. Near the Cuyuna Range conditions were more violent. The formation was crumpled and thrown into tight folds. When the tops of the folds were eroded later several essentially parallel belts of outcrops resulted. Heat altered the sediments in places to rock forms now described as "cherty" and "slaty" and in some cases made them magnetic. The magnetic forms are found principally on the South Cuyuna Range and on the east end of the Mesabi. In isolated patches, a further process, believed to have been leaching by hot percolating waters, removed much of the silica but left most of the iron. About ten percent of the Mesabi iron formation was thus enriched to high-grade ore through the removal of the unwanted silica. These enriched ores have been

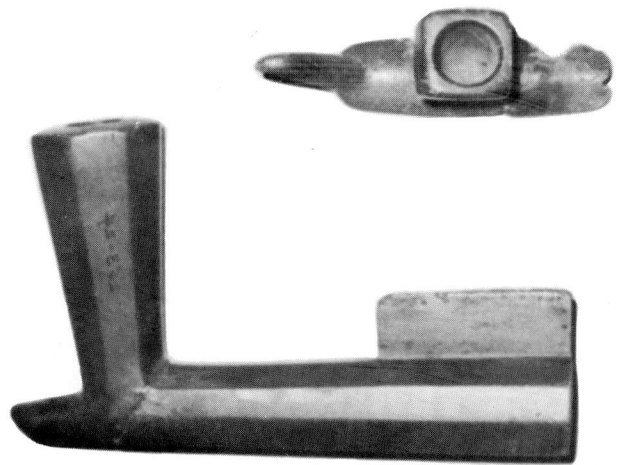

Pipestone Pipes

quarried and used extensively for building and other purposes. The famous "pipestone," used by the Indians in making pipes and other artifacts, is a thin layer of very uniform, red shale enclosed between layers of the quarzite at Pipestone.

We are now crossing the boundary between the Late Precambrian and the Middle Precambrian.

34

The outstanding event marking this time division was a gigantic uplift and folding that produced a high mountain range which probably ran from north central Minnesota in a northeasterly direction into Canada. These are called the "Algoman Mountains." Their eroded "stumps" still remain as a granite ridge about 100 miles long running just north of the Mesabi Range from near Grand Rapids to Birch Lake near Ely. This ridge rises as much as 500 feet in places above the surrounding terrain. A granite ridge convinces a geologist of a previous mountain range as surely as a tree stump is witness to the existence of a former tree. Similar granite is found beneath thin glacial drift in St. Louis County north of Lake Vermilion. The Algoman Mountains were presumably mostly eroded away by the time the iron formations were deposited against their flanks but further uplift of the same region likely produced the tilt of the Mesabi iron-bearing rocks previously mentioned.

Most commercial granites, for which Minnesota is well-known, are quarried from granite masses underlying large areas of the state, especially in the St. Cloud area, near Mille Lacs Lake, and in the Minnesota River Valley. Most of these granites are believed to have moved into Minnesota's "basement" during Middle Precambrian time. We should point out that granite is not the result of lava flows but, like its cousin gabbro, cooled far below the surface of that time. This we know because of its large crystals. These granites

Drilling granite

Granite quarry at Cold Springs

35

are variously colored: gray, pink, or even reddish —but generally light colored, in contrast with gabbros which are dark.

We can spare no more time in the Middle Precambrian but must race across the boundary into the Early Precambrian in order to have a view of the most remote, ancestral rocks of Minnesota, which may well be as old as any in the world. We do take notice of the nature of the boundary, however. It is another mountain range—this time extending entirely across Minnesota from the southwest corner near Pipestone to Saganaga Lake in the northeastern corner, and on into Canada. This is our oldest known mountain range with only traces left here and there as evidence. These are sometimes called the Laurentian Mountains. We are now in the land of the real "old-timers"—the primordial stuff out of which the earth took shape—in search of the oldest rock. But how shall we recognize the oldest old-timer? We must remember that in this time of old-timers there was much igneous

activity—of molten rock material making its way toward the surface, working its way into cracks and crevices, some of it reaching the surface and some not. An important clue is found in the simple statement: "An intrusive rock is younger than the rock that it intrudes"—simple, that is, after a little explanation. An intrusive rock is one that, while molten, squeezes in between layers of rocks already present. Clearly, the rocks already there are older —and the ones that enter are younger (since the age of an igneous rock dates from the time that it solidifies). In principle then, our search is as simple as this: Find the kind of rock that has been entered by other rocks but which has entered none itself. This will be the ancestor of them all—all, that is, that are known to date. Years of searching have led to the kind of rock found at the surface in and near the town of Ely. It is found also in places on the south shore of Lake Vermilion and underlies the glacial drift in a rather large area in Itasca County north of Grand Rapids. This rock is called the "Ely Greenstone" because of its greenish color. What kind of a rock is "greenstone"? From several clues in the rock itself there is no doubt that it was a lava flow poured out beneath, or that flowed quickly into, a sea. The evidence for the latter point

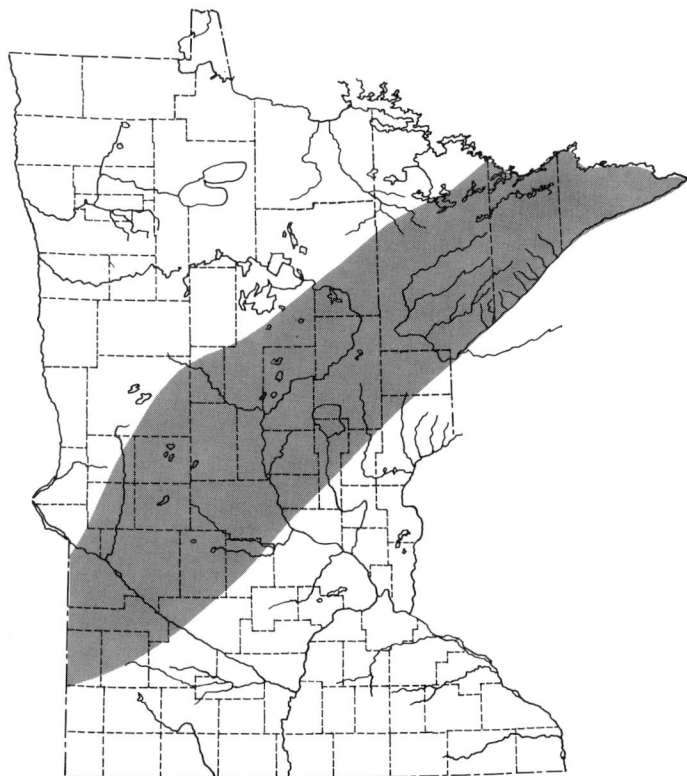

Laurentian Mountain Region of Minnesota

Ely greenstone

36

lies in the pillow-shaped masses contained in it which are believed to represent separate "lumps" that cooled under water. This rock is no ordinary basaltic lava—and this is no surprise considering all the "ups and downs" through which this ancient rock has "lived." It is now a metamorphic rock which the geologist calls a "chlorite schist." It has been crumpled and folded and in many places contains the Soudan iron formation within its folds. It is in this situation that the iron mines operate at Ely and Tower—pulling iron from deep folds in the Ely greenstone. This indicates that the Soudan iron formation (which is also a metamorphic rock called

jaspilite) is the second oldest rock in Minnesota. Long searching has not dislodged the Ely greenstone from the head of the procession of "old-timers." How old is it? Radioactive determinations, believed to give us more accurate answers to such questions than any other method, place its age between two and three billion years! Almost immediately comes the question: Might there be an even older rock, not yet discovered? We remember that the greenstone was a lava flow—and it must have flowed out upon some kind of surface, whether it was land or a sea floor. It would be older. Where is it? The search goes on.

EPILOGUE

We have come to the end of our flight backward in time. We have seen much—and missed much. We have found in Minnesota earth fragments as old as any known to man—molded by the same timeless forces that are at work today. We have seen the vast stretches of time that wrought our heritage. Rooted thus deeply in the past as our inheritance is we may be tempted to think of it as endless—yet we know it is not so. Vast, but finite, it will not be given a second time.

Let us return now to our point of departure—to the time when Man began to stir upon the Earth. We approach the epic of Man with new perspective —new awareness of our past. It is almost as if the forces of Nature had said to Man, "Long ages have been spent investing your inheritance. It is given to you now to use as you will—wisely or foolishly. The stage is set for a multitude of enterprises. Scatter your cities, farms and mines along the rivers, on the plains, among the hills. You are ready now to make history."

SUGGESTIONS FOR FURTHER READING

(Special Reference to Minnesota)

POWELL, LOUIS H.
The Giant Beaver in Minnesota, Science Museum, (St Paul) Bulletin No. 2, 1948.

ROSENDAHL, C. O.
A Contribution to the Knowledge of the Pleistocene Flora of Minnesota (Reprinted from Ecology, Vol. 29, No. 3, July 1948).

SCHWARTZ, G. M.
Geology of the Minneapolis-St. Paul Metropolitan Area, University of Minnesota Press 1936 (Minnesota Geological Survey Bulletin No. 27).

SCHWARTZ, G. M. and THIEL, G. A.
Minnesota's Rocks and Waters, University of Minnesota Press 1954 (Minnesota Geological Survey Bulletin No. 37)

THIEL, G. A.
Minnesota's Mineral Heritage, Conservation Bulletin No. 12, Minnesota Department of Conservation, 1947.

WILLARD, D. E.
The Story of the North Star State, Webb Publishing Company, St. Paul, Minnesota, 1922.

ZUMBERGE, J. H.
The Lakes of Minnesota, University of Minnesota Press, 1952 (Minnesota Geological Survey Bulletin No. 35)

(GENERAL)

EMMONS, W. H.; THIEL, G. A.; STAUFFER, C. R.; ALLISON, I. S.
Geology, Principles and Processes, McGraw-Hill, 1955.

GARRELS, R. M.
A Textbook of Geology, Harper and Brothers, 1951.

LEET. L. D. and JUDSON, S
Physical Geology, Prentice Hall, 1954.

MOORE, R. C.
Introduction to Historical Geology, McGraw-Hill, 1949.

STOVALL, J. W. and BROWN, H. E.
The Principles of Historical Geology, Ginn and Company, 1954.

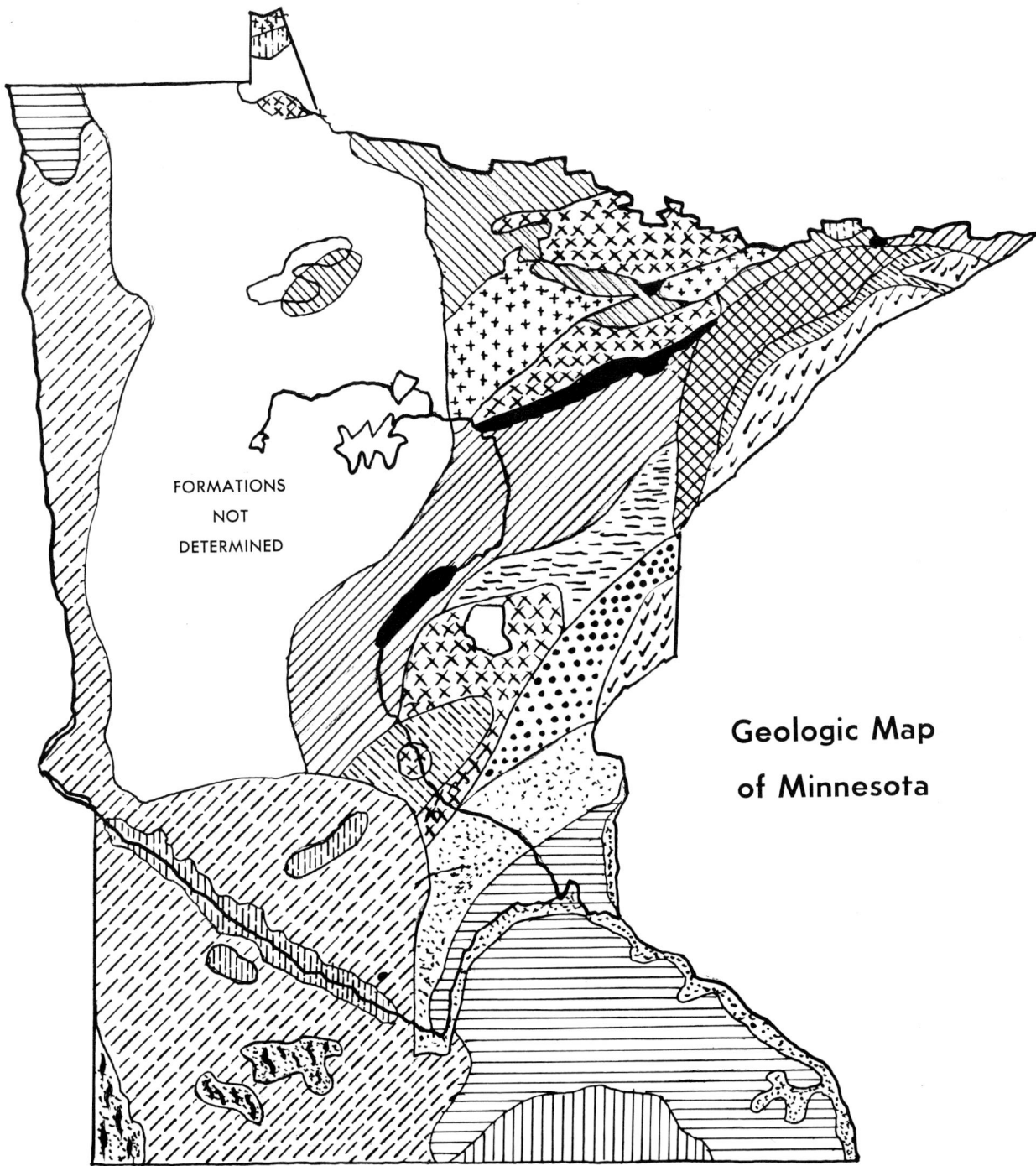

Geologic Map
of Minnesota

FORMATIONS
NOT
DETERMINED

Upper Pre-Cambrian
8. Sioux quartzite___
7. Virginia slate____
6. Iron fm _____

Middle Pre-Cambrian
5. Algoman granite_
4. Knife Lake slate _
3. Thompson slate___

Lower Pre-Cambrian
2. Granite _____
1. Ely Greenstone___

Mesozoic Era
16. Cretaceous sh, ss___

Paleozoic Era
15. Devonian ls _____
14. Ordovician ls, sh, ss
13. Cambrian ss, dol___
12. Hinckley ss _____
11. Red granite_____
10. Duluth gabbro____
9. Lava flows_____

The oldest rock is #1; the youngest is #16

Adapted from the Geologic Map of the State of Minnesota 1932

BRIEF CHART OF MINNESOTA'S GEOLOGIC HISTORY

ERAS	PERIOD (OR EPOCH*)	MILLIONS OF YEARS SINCE BEGINNING (APPROXIMATE)	REPRESENTATIVE DEPOSITS IN STATE	WHERE OBSERVED
CENOZOIC	Recent		Alluvial Deposits	River Valleys
	Pleistocene	1	Glacial Deposits	Most of State
	Tertiary	60	(None)	

~~~~ **FORMATION OF ROCKY AND ANDES MOUNTAIN SYSTEMS** ~~~~

MESOZOIC	Cretaceous	120	Sandstone and Shales	Southwestern Minnesota
	Jurassic		(None)	
	Triassic	180	(None)	

~~~~ **FORMATION OF APPALACHIAN AND URAL MOUNTAIN SYSTEMS** ~~~~

PALEOZOIC	Permian		(None)	
	Pennsylvania		(None)	
	Mississippian		(None)	
	Devonian	350	Limestone	Freeborn, Mower Co.
	Silurian		(None)	
	Ordovician	450	Sandstones, limestones, and shales	Southeastern Minnesota
	Cambrian	520	Sandstones, shales	Southeastern Minnesota

~~~~ **FORMATION OF KILLARNEY MOUNTAINS — CANADA (Extinct)** ~~~~

PRE-CAMBRIAN	Late Or Upper		Sandstone	Pine County
			Gabbro	Duluth
			Lava Flows	North Shore Lake Superior and Taylor's Falls
		+2000	Mesabi Iron Ore	Mesabi Range

~~~~ **FORMATION OF ALGOMAN MOUNTAINS — MINNESOTA, CANADA (Extinct)** ~~~~

	Middle		Granites	North of Mesabi Range / St. Cloud
		+2500	Slates	Rainy River, Rainy Lake

~~~~ **FORMATION OF LAURENTIAN MOUNTAINS — MINNESOTA, CANADA (Extinct)** ~~~~

	Early or Lower		Granite	Saganaga Lake
			Soudan Iron Ore	Soudan, Tower
		+3000	Ely Greenstone	Ely

* These values approximate

CHAPTER TWO

The First Minnesotans

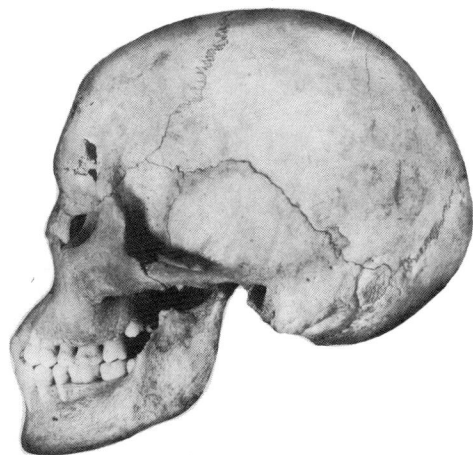

By LLOYD WILFORD

Part I

NEW HUNTING LANDS FOR
OLD WORLD PEOPLE

In the seemingly inevitable spread of man to all parts of the earth, the last large area to be reached and settled by him was the Western Hemisphere. He and his nearest kin, the anthropoid apes and the Old World monkeys, had evolved in the tropical and subtropical portions of Asia and Africa and were acclimated to the warmth of their original habitat. The apes and monkeys have never been able to adapt themselves to the cold regions of the North Temperate Zone, an adaptation which would require significant changes in their physical traits. The two land hemispheres are separated by oceans except in the Bering Strait area, and during much of Earth's history Asia and North America have actually been joined there by a broad isthmus rather than separated by a strait. The apes and Old World monkeys were barred from reaching the isthmus by their inability to penetrate the cold barrier to its approaches. The monkeys living today in Middle America and South America, the New World monkeys, are descendants of primitive primates who lived here sixty million years ago.

Man, too, has been unable to adapt himself to live in cold regions by physical change alone. But his vastly superior intelligence and ingenuity eventually led him to discoveries and inventions which permitted him to move out of his ancient environment if he chose to do so. Most important of these were clothing, first made from the skins of animals, and fire, which he first learned to con-

trol, and then to kindle by the invention of the fire drill. The European record tells us at about what time he had achieved these triumphs. In the past million years the Northern Hemisphere has experienced four prolonged glaciations separated by warm interglacial periods. Men were certainly living in Europe in the second and third interglacial periods and probably the first, but there is no evidence of their presence there during the first three glaciations. Presumably the onset of a cold cycle drove them back to Africa. At the end of the third interglacial period, however, men of the Neanderthal race remained in Europe, south of the ice sheet, for the first half of the last glaciation. They lived in caves, built fires, and used a scraper-like tool for working hides and skins for clothing. This tool was a rather thick flint flake, with a flat lower surface and with a sharp, bevelled edge on one side. For half a million years before this time men had been making use of flint for tools and had been steadily improving in their techniques of flint chipping and in the refinement of the finished products. But the earlier stone tools had been principally axes and knives for hunting, fighting, and cutting up meat.

Near the middle of the fourth glaciation the Neanderthal men were replaced by men of our own species, homo sapiens. The earliest of these had a type of scraper that also was flat on the lower surface, but was of a blade-like form, smaller and thinner than the Neanderthal scraper, and with its cutting edge at one end rather than at one side.

This is called an end scraper and its general type endured for millennia. End scrapers were still being made in Minnesota in Father Hennepin's time.

The last Europeans of the Old Stone Age used the first long distance weapon, the spear-thrower, best known in America by its American Indian name "atl-atl." The atl-atl resembled a lath with a hand hold at the forward end and a hook or projection at the rear to engage the projectile. The projectile it hurled resembled an arrow, but its head, usually of stone, was larger than an arrowhead, and the butt of the shaft was notched or hollowed to engage the atl-atl. Such projectiles are sometimes spoken of as javelins, though the true javelin is longer and is usually hurled by motion of the arm alone. America is full of large projectile points often mistakenly called arrowheads. But the bow was not to be invented for a long time yet, and the atl-atl was the principal weapon of the Indian for most of the time he lived in America.

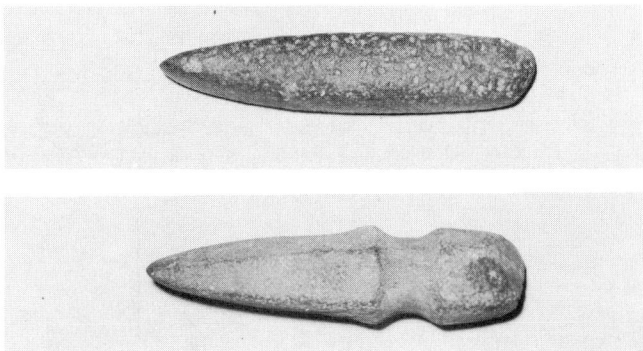

Atl-atl points

Equipped with the atl-atl, clothing, scrapers, and probably fishhooks, and with a knowledge of fire-making, homo sapiens was well prepared to spread into the cold regions of the world. His northward migration was not due to a desire to move to a colder climate, but was the outcome of his way of living. People who depend upon hunting as a principal source of food require large hunting territories. As the population increases the food supply dwindles and groups move on into uninhabited areas where there has been no depletion of the game animals. In this manner men had ultimately reached the northeastern limits of Asia at a time when the climate had ameliorated and the last great continental glacial of North America

was slowly shrinking. Part of the world's water was still contained in the ice sheets on the continents and the level of the oceans was lower than at present, so it is probable that at this time the old land bridge between Asia and America was again well above water. Men pressing onward to new hunting territories may have crossed the land bridge and not have been aware that they had entered a new continent.

The animals they saw in the New World would not have seemed strange to them, for the fauna of northern Asia and North America is much alike, due to the long periods when the land bridge was in existence. On both sides were the musk oxen, the wolves, and the bears, venerated by men on each side of the Pacific. The American caribou is closely related to the Siberian reindeer. But most spectacular of the mammals common to both was the woolly mammoth, a true elephant. Men of the ice age in Europe painted his likeness on the walls of caves, and his bones and tusks have been found in Siberia, Alaska, and south through the Great Plains and Minnesota as far as the Valley of Mexico. Pursuing the large game animals, men gradually crossed Alaska and turned south through an open corridor between the glaciers of the Rocky Mountains on the west and the great continental ice sheet, covering eastern Canada, on the east. Arriving at the southern ends of the glaciers, some spread out to the east and west while others continued on to the south, and eventually the southern tip of South America was reached.

Who were these first inhabitants of the New World? The area from which they came is today inhabited by peoples of the Mongoloid race. The American Indian of today is predominantly Mongoloid also. He shares with eastern Asiatics the yellow-brown skin color, the straight black hair, dark brown eyes, a lack of body hair, and prominent cheek bones. But he is not wholly Mongoloid. He differs from them in having heavier jaws, prominent ridges above the eyes, and high, even beaky, noses; and Indian males lack the fatty eyelid and the Mongoloid fold, often spoken of as a slant-eye, so characteristic of the Asiatics. Prominent brow ridges and high-bridged noses are characteristic of the white race. Does the Indian vary from the Mon-

Mastodon

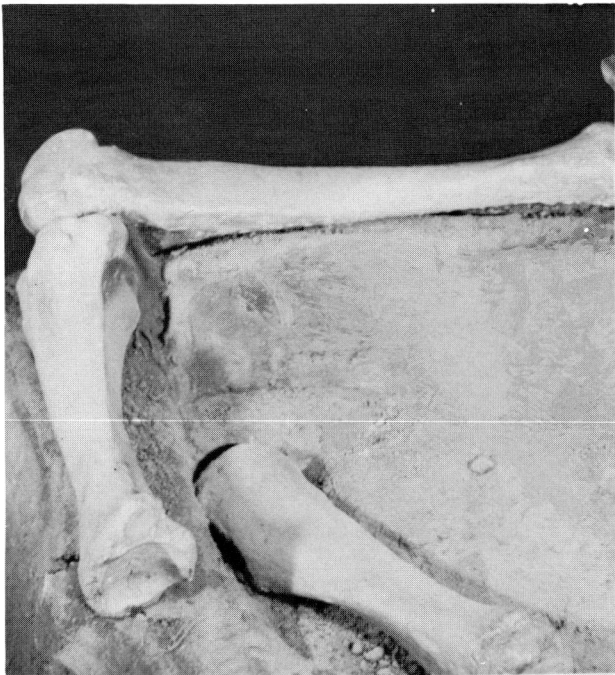

Mammoth bones

goloid because he had some white admixture before he left Asia, or is it because during the long separation, each has changed from the original type? Probably both. Today in Asia there are small groups that are not typically Mongoloid. Such a group is the Ainu of northern Japan, whom the late Professor Hooton of Harvard classed as belonging to the white race, a sort of remnant from a much earlier period. Peoples of the Ainu type might well have formed part of the ancestry of the Indians. Changes have undoubtedly taken place since the separation. Today eastern Asia has a higher incidence of type B blood than any other part of the world, but it is virtually absent among Indians. The mutations or events that gave the Asiatics so much B blood must have occurred after the departure of the Indians from Asia, and the time elapsed since their departure must be con-

Indian from Asia

siderable. The Eskimo is much more Mongoloid than the Indian and probably reached America much later. Hunting on the water from his efficient skin-covered boat, he needed no land bridge to the New World.

The question most often asked regarding the coming of man to the New World is not how, or why, but when. It is not at this time possible to give an exact answer. Sandals from an Oregon cave have been dated as more than 9,000 years old by the Carbon-14 method, which determines age by measuring the loss of radioactivity in the carbon component of organic materials such as plant fibres, charcoal, and shells. There is no reason to believe that the rope sandals were made by the very first immigrants, and many students of the problem are willing to accept a date of 15,000 to 20,000 years ago as very probable.

The first people in America that archaeologists have been able to single out as distinct from others were the makers of an unusual type of atl-atl point. The point has no stem and its base is concave. On each face a broad flake is struck from the base, leaving a wide groove or channel running part of the way toward the tip. The general name for points of this type is "fluted points," and the oldest form is called the Clovis Fluted point. The makers of the Clovis points were mammoth hunters and their points have been found among the bones of the mammoths they have killed.

Later the fluted points were improved. The base was more deeply concave and the ends of the base projected backward forming "ears." The channel flake was more cleverly struck off and the resulting groove reached two-thirds or more of the distance from base to tip. This type is known as the Folsom Fluted point. Both Clovis and Folsom points have the base, and the sides near the base, ground smooth to prevent cutting of the strings which fastened the stone point to the wooden shaft. Folsom points have never been found in direct association with mammoth bones, so probably the mammoth had become extinct in America by this time. They have been found with the glacial age bison, Bison Taylori, which was larger than the modern bison, and had longer, flatter horns.

Many mammoth bones and tusks have been found in Minnesota and are still being found. Bison Taylori lived in Minnesota too, but fewer finds of this animal's bones have been reported, probably because they have not been recognized as different

Bison

from the bones of the modern bison, which are so plentiful in Minnesota. Three skeletons were found on the Cuyuna Range near Crosby, several years ago, and more recently the bones of many ancient bison were found at Itasca Park. Several fluted points have been found in Minnesota, but none has been found associated with the bones of either mammoth or the Bison Taylori.

The skeletal remains of men who may have lived during the era of the fluted points are very rare. Part of a human skull was found near Mid-

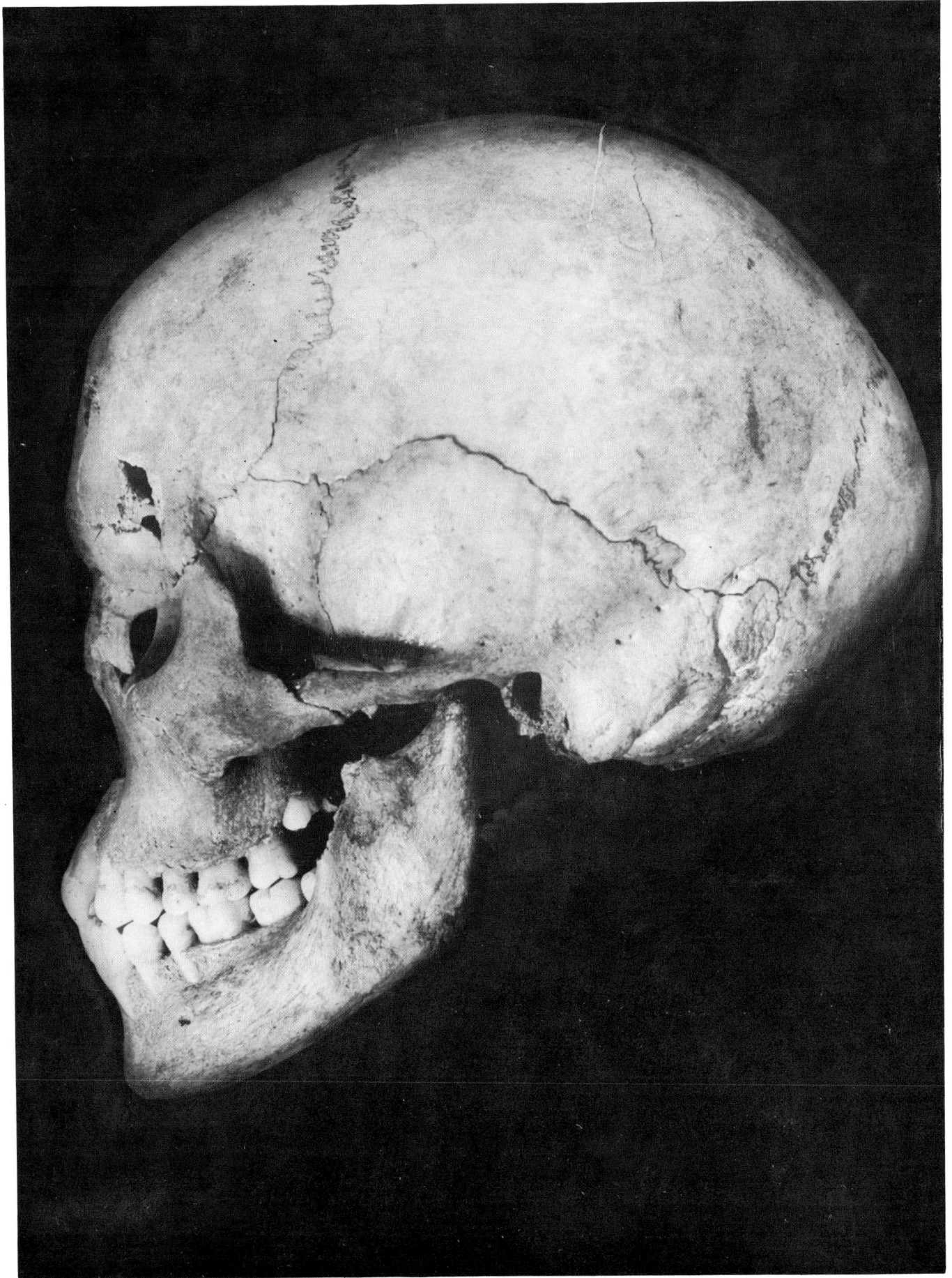

Skull of the first Minnesotan

land, Texas, in 1953, in a sandy deposit in which fluted points occurred. Other human bones for which a high antiquity has been claimed have not been in association with fluted points, and for none of them is there clear proof of great age. The skeleton accepted by most geologists as contemporary with the Glacial Age mammals is a Minnesotan, for it was found on the east shore of Prairie Lake about three miles north of Pelican Rapids in Ottertail County. The skeleton is that of a fifteen-year-old girl found nine to ten feet below the surface in what is known as a varved deposit. A varved deposit is one in which there are silts in regular horizontal layers that were formed at the bottom of a glacial lake not far from the ice front. The glacial lake in which this particular deposit was formed has been named Glacial Lake Pelican, and it was a little earlier than huge Glacial Lake Agassiz, which later filled the valley of the Red River in the United States and Canada. With the young lady were found a dagger made from an elk antler and an ornament made of conch shell. The latter is most interesting because the nearest source of conch shells is the Gulf of Mexico, and a conch shell in Minnesota indicates that the area from Minnesota to the gulf was inhabited, and that the trade in shells had already begun.

The large Glacial Age bison and the fluted points seem to have disappeared at about the same time. In their places were the smaller, modern bison and a new kind of atl-atl point, called the parallel flaked point. Like the fluted points the new points had smoothed basal edges and were without stems, except for some that had stems only a little narrower than the blade. They were characterized by the excellence of the flaking across both faces. Narrow parallel flakes were detached side by side from the edges to the middle of the blade, giving a sort of ripple effect, sometimes horizontal and sometimes oblique. Parallel flaked points have been found associated with animal bones, but only with those of animals of modern types.

The most complete human skeleton of this period is again a Minnesotan, the Browns Valley Man. He had been buried at the eastern edge of Browns Valley in Traverse County. With him were

four projectile points and two knives, all made of brown chalcedony, as well as two fragments of sandstone abraders. The two finest points are beautiful examples of parallel flaked points, but as they are wider than most such points they have been given a name to denote their special type — "Browns Valley Points." The skeleton of this early man is interesting because it combines a long head with a short, broad face in which the lower jaw is very wide. He is much more recent than the Minnesota girl, for the gravel pit in which he was buried was deposited as a gravel bar in the floor of Glacial River Warren, the great river which drained Glacial Lake Agassiz. The gravel bar was formed in a late stage of the lake, whereas the Minnesota girl was in a deposit that was made before the beginning of Lake Agassiz, a difference of several thousand years.

Part II

THE ARCHAIC PERIOD

About 7,000 years ago the cool climate associated with the final retreat of the glacier was succeeded by a warm dry period, known as the altithermal. The large game animals seem to have disappeared from the prairies of Minnesota and from the Great Plains to the west. Perhaps the growth of prairie grass was too poor to sustain them. The people were forced to turn to other means of subsistence, and developed many ingenious devices to exploit the food resources of their territories. The men hunted small game, fished, and learned to build fish traps. The women gathered nuts and berries, and preserved such fruits as cherries by drying them. They found that the roots of several plants were edible and dug them up with pointed sticks. They searched the shores and shallow waters of lakes and streams for clams. They gathered seeds and ground them to flour on a flat milling stone with a small flat stone held in the hand, or placed them in a depression in a rock and crushed them by pounding with a smaller rock.

It is probable, but not proven, that during this difficult period two great new sources of food were utilized in Minnesota's wooded area—wild rice and maple sugar. One of the stages in curing wild rice is parching by stirring in a container over a fire.

45

Harvesting Wild Rice

Lacking pottery it is not certain that the Indians of this period had containers suitable for this purpose, but almost certainly some method of preparing wild rice was used. Maple syrup and sugar also need heating over a fire, but this could be done by the method of stone boiling, using a hide, bladder, or other pouch to contain the sap into which the hot rocks were dropped. Some sort of water craft is almost indispensable to wild rice gathering, but the raft is a simple invention where wood is plentiful. There are no remains to tell us when the dugout canoe and eventually the beautiful birch bark canoe developed, but it may well have been during this time.

Food gatherers learn a great deal about their natural environment and pass this information on to their children. They know where the blueberry patches are and when the berries ripen; where the maple sugar trees are plentiful; where the best rice lakes are. Their life is necessarily a nomadic one, moving with the seasons—to the sugar bush in spring, to the blueberries in midsummer, to the rice lakes in late summer, to a sheltered wooded area in winter. At times they lived in small groups, but at the sugar bush and the rice lakes they could congregate in larger numbers.

Big game hunting did not become a lost art in Minnesota. The caribou and moose probably moved northward, not to return until the close of the warm period, but there were deer, bears, and other game in our wooded areas. One of the markers for this period is a new type of atl-atl point. The older non-stemmed varieties gave way to stemmed and notched points, the types most common in collections and in illustrations of arrowheads. Stems are now definitely narrower than the blades and occur in three main varieties, parallel-sided stems, stems which contract from blade to base, and stems which expand from blade to base. Notched points have a notch on each side near the base and the base may be as wide as the blade. If the base is narrower than the blade it is sometimes difficult to decide whether a point should be classed as a notched point or as a point with expanding stem. Some archaeologists use a somewhat arbitrary rule in the matter and class a point as notched if the base of the stem is more than two-thirds the width of the blade. Some points are corner notched and therefore have barbed shoulders and expanding stems.

At a time about coincident with the close of the altithermal, estimated at about 4,500 years ago, a new technique of working stone arose in both the Old World and the New. Men learned that some stones could be shaped by grinding and polishing with another stone. Perhaps they learned this by observing how the milling stones were hallowed out when rubbed with another stone. They also learned that the grinding process could be speeded up by pecking—battering with another stone to roughly the shape desired, and then finishing by grinding with rough-textured stone such as sand stone. By the chipping method, up to now the only method

axes which are called celts. The age which saw the introduction of ground stone tools is called the Neolithic (New Stone) Age in Europe, and the celts which the ancestors of white Minnesotans used in Europe are very like the celts their Indian contemporaries were making here. Mauls are stone heads for sledge hammers. They are blunt and rounded at both ends and grooved around the middle. Axes are common in Minnesota and in the woodlands to the east of us. Mauls are common in Minnesota and in the prairies to the west.

The polishing and grinding techniques were used not only on the hard rocks but also on the softer rocks such as soapstone (steatite), red pipestone (catlinite), slates and others. Some of these were made into ornaments, such as pendants and

Maul

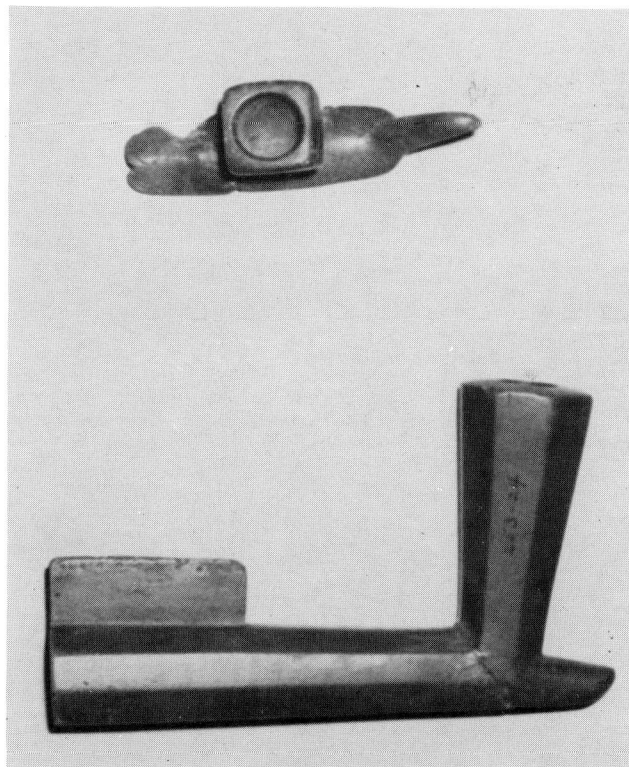

Indian Pipes

known, only a few kinds of stone could be used, principally the flints and the quartzites, but now many more varieties of stone could be used. Such hard rocks as granite and greenstone were shaped into axes, adzes and mauls. Axes were of two main varieties, the grooved axes in which a groove was pecked and then polished either three-fourths or all of the way around the axe, and the ungrooved

gorgets. Knives and gouges, as well as ornaments, were made of slate. The adze and the gouge would both be very useful in hollowing a tree trunk for a canoe. Among the more interesting objects of polished stone were the banner stone, the bird-stone, the boat-stone, and the bar amulet. Only recently it has been discovered that these objects (formerly called the problematicals) were used as weights fastened to the under side of the atl-atl to give it proper balance. The banner stones have holes drilled through the middle and some apparently were drilled by a core drilling process, in which a hollow stick or reed is twirled in the hands, using sand with water as a cutting agent.

Our Minnesota Indians and their neighbors on the south shore of Lake Superior discovered still a third method of working stone—by the pounding process alone. They found a variety of rock that could be hammered into the desired shape without breaking, and which could be flattened out into thin sheets for ornaments or even wires. This, of course, was copper. They shaped it into the forms of their stone tools such as knives, celts, and gouges, and added some new forms such as the heavy chisel, and the spud used in cutting birch bark from the tree. They worked the veins on Isle Royale, just off the North Shore, so zealously that they had exhausted its copper before the coming of

Indian knives

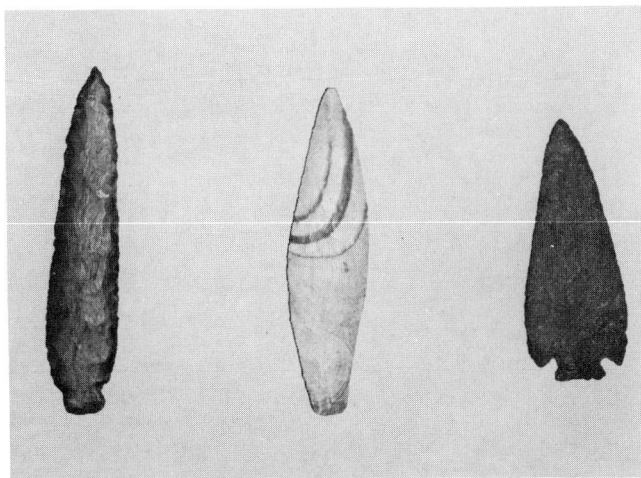

Indian arrows

the Whites. They found in copper a very valuable commodity for barter with peoples to the south and southeast of Minnesota.

Part III
THE EARLY WOODLAND PERIOD

The Early Woodland period is a relatively short time span extending from 1000 B.C. to 300 B.C. Its beginning is marked by the introduction of two important culture traits—agriculture and pottery making. During the preceding period the Indians living in the Middle American area from central Mexico to southern Peru had been making much faster progress toward civilization than had the Indians of other areas. Most important of all, they had learned to domesticate certain plants native to their areas, such as corn, beans, squash, tobacco and cotton. Population increased and towns and villages grew up near the cultivated fields. They apparently invented pottery and made other ceramic objects such as human figurines.

The idea of agriculture spread slowly northward, reaching Minnesota about 1000 B.C. The Minnesota Indians were not too much impressed with the idea of farming. It didn't fit their nomadic type of existence, as it interfered with their seasonal movements. They saw no good reason to undertake the task of planting and weeding corn, when nature had supplied them with another cereal, the wild rice, which required only the harvesting. Two thousand years were to elapse before farming was to be seriously pursued, and it never became important in the favored wild rice areas.

The one agricultural product that appealed to Minnesotans was tobacco, which they first smoked in simple tubular pipes made of stone or clay. The pipe was smoked much like a cigar, with the tobacco at one end and the other end held in the mouth. The best evidence we have of the existence of incipient agriculture in this period is the finding of these simple pipes. Tobacco and the pipe came to be held in very high esteem and the smoking of the calumet became an important ritual in social and even religious gatherings.

Minnesota's earliest pottery is believed not to have come as an idea from Mexico but rather from the Old World, where pottery had been invented in southwestern Asia by 5,000 B.C. Pottery is probably more important to the present-day archaeologist than it was to the Indian of 3,000 years ago, for pottery has such a wide range in shapes and varieties of decoration, and fashions in pottery change so rapidly, that it is the archaeologist's most sensitive tool for showing relationships of cultures in space and in time. This first pottery was tempered with grit, which is crushed rock, usually granite, or sometimes with sand. The temper was added to the clay to prevent the pot from cracking when drying. The vessels were elongated, cone-shaped jars with pointed or nearly pointed bottoms, and with wide mouths as wide or nearly as wide as the greatest width of the jars. They were not used by suspension over the fire, but the pointed base was set in the fire hearth and the fire built around the pot.

The outer surfaces of some pots were plain or smoothed, but others bore the impressions of cords that had been wound around the wooden paddle that had been used in shaping the pots. Pots of the latter type are spoken of as having cord-wrapped paddle surfaces. Decoration, if present, was confined to a narrow band of impressions at the rim, made by impressing objects into the clay while it was still soft, and before the pot was fired. There were only five principal types of impressions. A short length of twig, or very slender rod, wound with a cord and used as a stamp in parallel lines or end-to-end lines, is called a cord-wrapped stick. A narrow stick with notches across one edge, and used in the same manner, is called the dentate stamp. A row, or rows, of separate depressions made by the end of a stick or similar object is known as punctate. The stick might be pushed against the inner wall to form a row of bumps or nodes on the outside, which are known as bosses. Finally, lines of varying widths were drawn in the soft clay, and these are called incised lines or trailed lines.

The two common surface treatments and the five main types of decorative impressions are characteristics of the Asiatic-derived pottery to which the name "Woodland" pottery has been given (though not exclusively). All cultures characterized by the use of Woodland pottery are placed in

a super-grouping named the "Woodland Pattern." Woodland pottery was made in Minnesota from the first introduction of pottery until historic times, when the Indians finally gave up the manufacture of clay vessels for the copper and iron kettles of the French traders. The pottery from any Woodland Pattern village or campsite can be classified as to the presence or absence of any of the seven traits listed above, the combination of traits, and the emphasis on one or another type of decoration as shown by percentages of occurrences. As illustration, two styles of pottery are found in the Rainy River area, and are made by people of different

Early woodland pottery

49

cultures. The vessels of the earlier group have plain surfaces, and dentate stamps and bosses are common decorations, but cord-wrapped stick stamps were not used. The vessels of the later group have cord-wrapped stick stamp and punctates. There are some minor types of surface treatment and decoration, in addition to the seven types emphasized above, and because they are unusual they stand out and help to distinguish the pottery complex in which they occur.

An example of an Early Woodland site in Minnesota is a small cave fronting the Mississippi River south of La Moille in Winona County. The people living in the cave had left a deposit 15 feet deep which was a solid mass of firehearths, charcoal, ashes, animal bones, particularly fish bones, and clam shells. No pottery was found in the lower levels, which may therefore be considered as belonging within the Archaic period. In the upper levels were parts of two thick pottery vessels, representing the Early Woodland period. There were enough sherds (pieces of a broken vessel) of one pot to permit its reconstruction. It is 12½ inches high and 10¾ inches wide at the mouth. It is cone shaped, tapering toward a point, but the base is flattened rather than a true point. The exterior has cord-wrapped paddle impressions, but no decoration. The second vessel is decorated at the rim by straight lines drawn over cord-wrapped paddle markings. The projectile points are of the large stemmed and notched types of the Archaic, though one is non-stemmed with a concave base, which is more characteristic of the period preceding the Archaic.

THE MIDDLE WOODLAND PERIOD

The Middle Woodland Period extending from 300 B.C. to 1000 A.D. is dominated in the Mississippi Valley by a brilliant culture, the Hopewell Phase of the Woodland Pattern, which developed out of the cultures of the Early Woodland period. The outstanding features of Hopewell is the attention devoted to burial practices, with the erection of huge burial mounds and associated earthworks at community centers. Associated with mound building was great activity in the making of beau-

Knives

tiful and artistic objects to be placed with the dead. In the making of these gifts materials were gathered by trade from much of the area of the eastern United States. From the Rocky Mountains came obsidian which was chipped into knives, daggers, and projectile points. From the Gulf Coast came conch shells and other varieties of shell to be made into beads and other ornaments. From the rivers of the southeast came bushels of fresh water pearls to be made into necklaces, and from sheets of mica from the Carolinas were cut ornaments with geometric and realistic designs. Among the more spectacular objects were those made of the copper from the Lake Superior area. Although some of the copper objects were of the types that had been made in Minnesota since the Archaic period, more commonly the copper was pounded into thin sheets. It might be cut into ornaments as was done with mica sheets, or used to cover wooden cores for gorgets or earplugs, or made into beads, breastplates and headdresses.

Several modes of burial were practiced. Primary burial, interment of a complete body, in an extended position with the legs straight out, or in a flexed position with the legs doubled up, was a holdover from the Archaic. Secondary burial, in which only the bones were buried some time after the death of the individual, was practiced also, and often the bones of a secondary burial were placed with a primary burial. But the mode of burial to which the Hopewellians gave increased attention was cremation. Buildings were erected with several rooms, in one of which may have been a crematory

50

basin, in another tombs or vaults in which the ashes were deposited, and in the third shelves on which were placed the gifts to the dead. The gifts were often broken or "killed," and some gifts were destroyed by placing them with the body at the time of the cremation. Primary burials were placed in log-walled tombs, containing one or several bodies. A small mound was placed over each tomb and later a single large mound was erected covering the small mounds and the crematory building.

The widespread trade engenderd by the activities of the Hopewellian people served to spread traits of their culture to most of the area of the Mississippi Valley. The most brilliant center was southern Ohio, but an important secondary center developed in central Illinois. In general as one moves out from these centers the Hopewellian traits fade out, and Minnesota is peripheral in that many of the more exotic traits never reached it. Never-

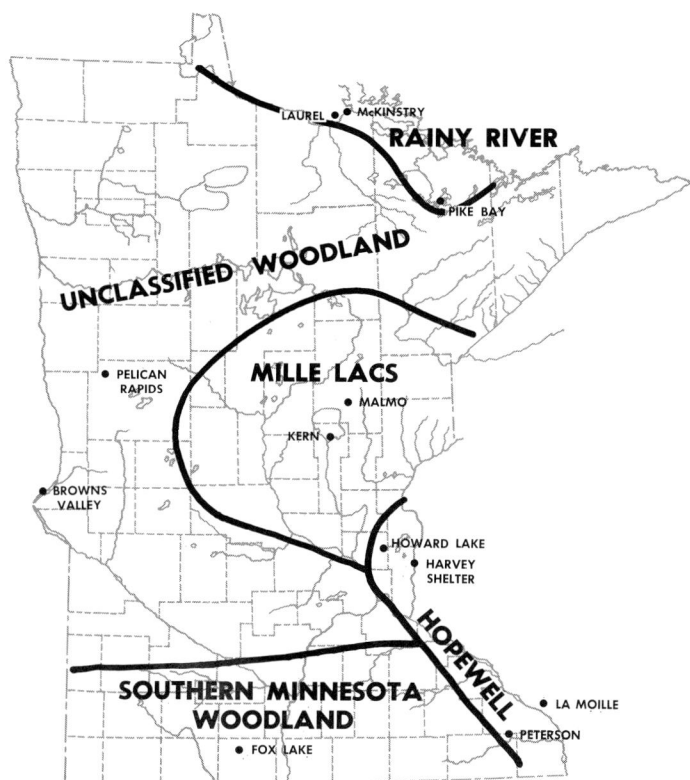

Laurel mound

51

theless, Hopewell influences played an important role in Minnesota throughout the Middle Woodland period. There is little doubt that the chief source of these influences is the Illinois Hopewell.

Most important of the new traits was the construction of burial mounds, a trait which spread over the state. The largest known mound is the Grand Mound at Laurel on the Canadian border. Minnesota is estimated to have had at least 10,000 mounds, which may be more than any other state had. They were not all built in the Middle Woodland period, however, for they continued to be built in the following Late Woodland period. Indeed, if the artist, Catlin, is correct, a mound was built at Pipestone as late as about 1830.

Another Hopewellian trait was the platform pipe. A platform pipe looks like a spool sitting at the center of a ruler four or five inches long, with a hole leading from one end of the platform to the bowl. In Ohio the base is often curved by being raised at the center, and the bowl is often beautifully carved in the form of a bird or other animal. The few platform pipes found in Minnesota are of the plain variety with flat bases.

A third Hopewellian trait found in Minnesota is a particular variety of pottery traits, that in Minnesota is little more than a new combination of Woodland decorations on the old jar shape. For the most part, Minnesota cultures of this period are essentially Woodland cultures with burial mounds added, and are classed as Woodland rather than Hopewell. Some sites, confined to the southeastern part of the state, that have the distinctive Hopewellian pottery, are classed as Hopewell.

An important trait entering Minnesota at about the beginning of this period is the bow and arrow. This did not come from the Hopewell centers, but is derived from Asiatic sources. The atl-atl did not disappear all at once, but during the early part of the period the large atl-atl points were gradually replaced by the smaller arrowheads.

Five distinct cultures can be recognized in Minnesota in this period. In the southeast are a few mounds and village sites with pottery resembling Hopewell types; the Effigy Mound culture is found in the same general area; throughout southern Min-

nesota is found the culture designated as Southern Minnesota Woodland; in the center of the state is the Malmo Focus of the Mille Lacs Aspect; and in the north is the Rainy River Aspect.

The Hopewell Phase

Best known of the Hopewellian sites is the village and the Mound Group at Howard Lake in southeastern Anoka County. The village is on the south shore of the lake. A very small part of it was dug and yielded a quantity of potsherds, 44 stemmed or notched arrowheads, scrapers, four copper gorges, which look like thick toothpicks and were used as fishhooks, and the bowl of an elbow pipe of clay. The mound group is on the northeast shore of the lake and consists of three large mounds. Only the smallest one has been excavated. The mound fill contained the same types of pottery and arrowheads as were found in the village and it is certain that the mounds were the burial place of the village people. Below the mound a rectangular grave had been dug, and in it were the very badly decayed bones of at least 21 people. The burials were secondary, that is the individuals had died some time earlier, and had been kept at the village, probably on platforms made for the purpose, for a period of months or years. At the time of burial all of the bones were gathered and placed in the common grave. An attempt was made to place the bones of each individual in a separate bundle, with the long bones (arm and leg bones) in a neat pile, and with the skull at one side or one end. The bones of one individual were charred. Either his body or his bones had been cremated elsewhere, and the charred bones brought to the grave.

Bundle burial is by far the most common form of burial in Minnesota mounds, and has persisted from the beginning of mound building until very recent times. When the Reverend Samuel Pond was living at the village of Chief Shakopee in the 1840's and 1850's, the platforms for the dead were on the south side of the village. The bodies on the platforms were considered to be village residents, and were given gifts and told the news, and even the scalp dances were held in their vicinity so they might share in the glory of the victories.

Cremation has never been practiced in Minnesota to the extent that it was in the Ohio Hopewell. But it, too, has persisted through the years as a minor burial type. Where charred bones are found under circumstances in which it is clear that the cremation took place elsewhere, it may be that the individual died or was killed away from home, and the cremation was the simplest means of returning his remains. But several Minnesota mounds are built over the area in which the acutal cremation of one or more bodies occurred.

No gifts accompanied the Howard Lake burials, though red ochre was sprinkled on some of the bundles. The lack of funerary gifts, so different from the rich offerings of the Ohio Hopewell, and the use of red ochre are characteristic traits of Minnesota mound burials.

The Howard Lake potters used both types of surface treatment and all five types of decorative impressions. Their pottery is distinctive because of the decorative pattern. They used what is called the alternate area plan; in which decorative bands, usually horizontal, are separated from one another by plain bands. The decorated bands usually consist of a pair of parallel incised lines with dentate stamping filling the space between them. There is often a row of bosses in the plain band, and sometimes the bosses have punctates between them. Very characteristic is a band of incised lines just below the lip, in which one set of parallel diagonal lines is crossed by another set in the opposite direction to form a crisscross that archæologists call crosshatching. The lip, too, is unique, for very commonly the inner edge of the lip is lower than the outer edge, forming an interior bevel which is often crossed by dentate lines.

Southern Minnesota Woodland

Peoples of the culture known as the Southern Minnesota Aspect lived in the southern third of the state and left many campsites and mounds. One of their largest known villages was on an island in Fox Lake in Martin County. The arrowheads were of the common stemmed and notched varieties, and the culture is distinguished primarily by the pottery. The pots normally have cord-wrapped paddle impressions on the surface, though plain surfaces do occur. All of the five common decorative impres-

sions are used, but there is no alternate area design, no crosshatching at the rim, and no pots with bevelled lips. The design is usually bands of cord-wrapped stick stamp or dentate stamp (never both) accompanied by punctates or bosses. In addition there is some use of impressions of single-twisted cords, and of incised lines drawn over the cord-wrapped paddle impressions. The use of the single cord never became popular in Minnesota though it recurs at a later period as a minor element, but it spread westward to the Great Plains and became one of the most common decorative devices of the Mandan Indians in the historic period. The incised lines over cord-wrapped paddle surfaces are interesting because they relate this culture to the La Moille cave and to the oldest pottery of Illinois.

Mounds of the culture are essentially the same as those of Howard Lake—multiple burials (more than one person) in shallow graves covered by a mound. There is one difference in that some of the graves contain primary burials. A typical mound group is at the mouth of High Island Creek in Sibley County. It is on the high ridge between the creek and the Minnesota River, and one imaginative writer called it the Black Tortoise Group. One of the largest mounds of the group was dug in 1955. Under the mound was a shallow rectangular grave with multiple bundle burials, the bones of which were very poorly preserved. A cover of logs had been laid across the top of the grave, and traces of the logs were still visible.

The Effigy Mound Aspect

The Hopewellian culture that had once flourished so brilliantly began to disintegrate and decay. The widespread trade in the raw materials needed by the Hopewell artisans declined, and Hopewell traits no longer spread out to the north and west. In the Ohio and Illinois centers the culture was reverting to the simpler Woodland Pattern from which it had emerged. During the hey-day of Hopewell a few mounds had been built to represent animal figures, of which the great Serpent mound of Ohio is the most famous. In the latter part of the Middle Woodland period there was a revival of the building of animal mounds, called effigy mounds, that centered in southern Wisconsin and spread into Minnesota.

The Minnesota Historical Society, under the leadership of Mr. Alfred Hill, undertook the project of surveying Minnesota's mounds in the years from 1880 to 1896. Mr. Theodore Lewis, who was the field surveyor, located thirteen mound groups containing effigies and an additional single effigy. All were close to the Mississippi River from Goodhue County south, except for one group at Prior Lake in Scott County. It is very fortunate that the survey was made early, for all of the effigy mounds,

the middle third of Minnesota and centering around Mille Lacs Lake. Malmo vessels are jars with shapes typical of the Middle Woodland period. All five types of rim decoration are found, and they are used in much the same frequencies as they are on Southern Minnesota Woodland vessels. Malmo pots differ from Southern Minnesota pots in that surfaces are plain rather than cord-wrapped paddled; the single-twisted cord is not used, and several vessels are decorated with what has been

Effigy mounds

like most of Minnesota's mounds, have since been destroyed. The last one, in the park at Hokah in Houston County, was destroyed when a skating rink was constructed there as a WPA project in the 1930's.

Effigy mounds have been excavated in Wisconsin and Iowa. They have shown some Hopewellian remnants in the character of the pottery, but lack the fine art objects. In Minnesota they probably occupied an intermediate position between Hopewell and Southern Minnesota Woodland.

The Malmo Focus

The area of the Malmo Focus may be thought of as a broad band from east to west comprising

termed "push-and-pull" bands. These are made with either a short length of dentate stamp, or a straight-edged stamp. Instead of using the stamp to make a row of distinct impressions side by side, it is pressed in and then dragged, then pressed, then dragged to make a continuous depression. Malmo burials are often simple bundle burials placed on the surface with a mound erected over them. Sometimes the bones were placed in shallow graves under mounds, and occasionally logs were placed over the graves. In a rather large mound at Lake Onamia, which is close to Mille Lacs Lake, a layer of logs had been laid parallel to one another on the original ground level, with a second layer above at right angles to the lower logs. On this cribwork human bones, not bodies, had been placed and the logs set afire. Many of the logs were present as charcoal and many of the bones were not completely burned, so it is believed that dirt had been thrown on the fire and the mound started before the fire had burned out.

Malmo arrowheads are of the notched and stemmed types, but they are small. It would seem that Malmo people had discarded the atl-atl and used only the bow.

The Rainy River Aspect

Mounds of the Rainy River Aspect are found along the Rainy River, which flows between Minnesota and Canada, and at Lake Vermilion. The burials have two outstanding characteristics. At the time of death the bodies were disarticulated, the back of the skull was cut out to remove the brain, and in most of the long bones a hole was punched into the marrow chamber and the marrow removed by heating. The bones were then exposed until the time of burial, at which time they were placed on the ground in bundles and a mound heaped over them. A second characteristic is the practice of placing the bundles on top of an existing mound and adding dirt above them. Some mounds have several layers of bones, and it is this practice of building cumulative mounds that makes some of them so large. The Grand Mound previously mentioned is of this type. It is one of a group at the mouth of the Big Fork River in Koochiching County.

Although mortuary gifts seldom accompany the bundles, the mound fills often contain many objects. The mounds were built in the midst of the villages or campsites and a great deal of village debris went into the mounds with the earth. The Rainy River is one of the main routes to Isle Royale and copper objects such as bracelets, beads, and thin knife blades are found. Stone arrowheads are stemmed and notched like those of the Malmo Focus, but more numerous were projectile points made of antler tips with sockets at the base. These may have been used for spearing fish, as many fish bones, especially sturgeon, are found. Another common object is a beaver tooth cut diagonally across at the biting edge.

The pottery is called the Laurel type and it is more like Malmo pottery than any other type. Both have plain surfaces and use dentate stamps, bosses, punctates, incised lines, and push-and-pull bands for decoration. There are two traits that distinguish them. Laurel pottery does not have the cord-wrapped stick impression, and the dentate stamp is different. Instead of cutting parallel notches across the stamp, they are cut into the edges of the stamp and alternate from side to side. The result-

Laurel pottery

ing impression in the clay is of ridges projecting from the edges around which is a continuous depression in a meander line. This has been called the meander variant of dentate, and is also found, though not common, in Howard Lake sherds.

Part V
THE LATE WOODLAND PERIOD

The Late Woodland Period, from 1000 A.D. to 1700 A.D. is dominated by the rise of another brilliant cultural center, this time the lower Mississippi Valley. Like the Hopewell culture it had important ceremonial and esthetic elements, but it had a much better economic basis, for it was based on developed agriculture. Agriculture, originally derived from Mexico, had been known for several centuries, but only now does it become important as a primary source of food. The ceremonial and esthetic traits are seen as a combination of holdovers from the Hopewell with new traits coming into the area from Mexico.

One of the conspicuous traits derived from Mexico was the temple mound, a flat-topped pyramid of earth at the top of which was a small temple, which had a framework of wood plastered over with mud, and a thatched roof. Early Mexican pyramids were of earth and stone and the oldest is dated at about 500 B.C. In a later period in Mexico stone construction was highly developed and the huge Pyramid of the Sun in the Valley of Mexico was built about 500 A.D. The oldest dated pyramid in the United States is the Davis Mound of Texas, dated about 400 A.D. Pyramidal mounds spread eastward, northeastward and up the Mississippi Valley, but only as earthen mounds. The largest of these mounds is at Cahokia, Illinois, opposite St. Louis. The most northern pyramids are found at a site called Aztalan, a few miles east of Madison in southern Wisconsin. Aztalan is considered as an outpost or colony of the Cahokia people.

The general term used to designate the cultures east of the Rocky Mountains in which developed agriculture was as an outstanding trait is the "Mississippi Pattern." Traits of the Mississippi Pattern reached Minnesota in a rather dilute form, expressed largely in agricultural practices, pottery, arrowheads, and certain burial practices. These traits reached as far north as the Minnesota River, which remained their northern limit. North of the river the peoples retained their older Woodland cultures, with some modifications due to contacts with their southern neighbors. The cultures of the Mississippi Pattern in Minnesota fall into two divisions called the Upper Mississippi and the Plains Mississippi respectively. In the Upper Mississippi are three named cultures, Cambria, Silvernale, and Oneota. They are related to the Cahokia-Aztalan cultures. The Plains Mississippi is represented in Minnesota by a single culture, the Great Oasis, which is related to cultures to the westward on the Great Plains.

THE UPPER MISSISSIPPI PHASE

The Cambria Focus

The Cambria Focus is best known from a large village site on the south bank of the Minnesota River between Cambria and Judson in Blue Earth County. The chief feature of the site is the great number of pits dug into the subsoil for the storage of corn. Charred corn and corncobs have been found in the pits, but in general they are full of trash and ashes. Apparently the pits became unsuitable for storage after a time, so new ones were dug and the old ones used as dumps. This practice has proven very valuable to the archæologist for the pits have yielded quantities of potsherds and other objects.

Further evidence of the importance of agriculture is the number of hoes recovered. The hoes are the shoulder blades of bison. A shoulder blade was made into a hoe by cutting away the prominent spine from the outer face, and by sharpening the flat broad edge opposite the head. There is no evidence that handles were used, so apparently the women held them in their hands and worked in a crouched posture.

There are new types of arrowheads. They are small triangles, some of which have side notches near the base, and infrequently a basal notch (a notch in the middle of the base) as well. A common object is the arrowshaft polisher, a small rectangular block of red standstone with a groove in its upper face in which arrowshafts were smoothed. The shaft polishers and the arrowheads tell us that hunting was still important, and that corn was an addition to the older varieties of food rather than a substitute for them.

The pottery is very different from the older Woodland wares. The jars are shorter, with round bottoms and definite necks, and often with paired handles at the rim, indicating that they were suspended over the fire rather than set in the ground. Both plain surfaces and cord-roughened surfaces are still present, but the former often have a degree of polish, and the cord-wrapped paddle marks are made with finer cords. The use of cord-wrapped stick, dentate stamp and bosses as decoration has disappeared, and decoration is by means of drawn lines, often broad, which are usually straight lines. Much more of the pot is decorated, for the decoration commonly covers the area from the shoulder to the neck. Most of the vessels have straight or flaring necks. One variety has no true neck, but around the edge of the opening the clay has been rolled back and down to form a coil at the top of the vessel. This variety is called the rolled rim type and it commonly has a sharply angular shoulder. The space between rim and shoulder is decorated with broad curved lines forming plain scrolls and interlocking scrolls. The shape and decoration are typical of vessels from Cahokia and Aztalan, though there is one difference. The clay of the Cahokia-Aztalan vessels is tempered with crushed shell rather than grit. Shell-tempering is a characteristic Mississippi trait. Cambria vessels have the grit-tempering typical of Woodland wares. A third and very minor type of vessel at Cambria has an S-shaped rim and is decorated with single twisted cords. Both the shape and the decoration are more at home in the Plains Mississippi cultures than in the Upper Mississippi.

Cambria burials are not well known. Mississippi peoples practiced primary burial, usually extended and often accompanied by a small pot, probably made especially for a burial offering. A mound near Cambria and four mounds on Big Stone Lake are believed to belong to the Cambria culture. Burials were on the floor of the mound or in shallow pits beneath it. They were primary, one extended, the others flexed, and three were accompanied by small mortuary pots of the Cambria type.

Only three Cambria village sites are known. All three are on the Minnesota River with the steep river bank at the front. Two have ravines on two sides and the third has a moat on three sides. The sites are adapted to defense. They give the impression that they are the homes of farmers moving up from the south, who have settled among strangers whom they fear.

The Silvernale Focus

Villages of the Silvernale focus are known from only one area in Minnesota, the mouth of the Cannon River west of Red Wing. The first village studied was at the point where the valley of the Cannon River joins the valley of the Mississippi River, and has been named the Silvernale site. Here were found the usual storage pits, bison scapula hoes, triangular arrowheads with side notches, and

arrowshaft polishers of red sandstone. It is the pottery which differentiates the Silvernale Focus from the Cambria Focus, for the former has the shell-tempering characteristic of Mississippi sites with pyramids. Vessels with rolled-rims, angular shoulders, and curved line decoration comprised only a small percentage of Cambria types, but at the Silvernale site are the major type. Some of these vessels are indistinguishable from vessels from Cahokia or Aztalan.

A question which has not yet been solved is whether the Cambria people were in Minnesota earlier than the Silvernale people. Their grit-tempered pottery would seem to represent an earlier type than the shell-tempered pottery of the Silvernale people. But at the Silvernale site about 15% of all the pottery was of Cambria types, indicating close contacts between the two groups.

Another village is the Bryan site about two miles up the Cannon River from the Silvernale site. This village was inhabited later than the Silvernale village. At the older village the shell particles in the pottery had nearly all been dissolved out of the clay by the mild acids in the subsoil water. At the Bryan site the shell particles are still present. Modifications in the pottery have taken place. Rolled rims are now in the minority, and vessels with outward flaring necks are the dominant type. Burials were found in two of the storage pits. They were primary burials, doubled up to fit into the pits, and each accompanied by a large pottery vessel. Two houses were also found. They had been dug down into the subsoil and were squarish with rounded corners, but were only eight feet square. One had a fireplace at the center. The second had been destroyed by fire, and two charred skulls were found in one corner. They were evidently trophy skulls, for one had had a circular area cut out of the top of the skull, and then set back in like a lid on a cooky jar.

The Oneota Aspect

Sites of the Oneota Aspect, both burial sites and villages, are much more numerous than those of any other division of the Mississippi Pattern. They are found in three main areas: the Root River valley of southeastern Minnesota, the area around

Winnebago on the Blue Earth River south of Mankato, and the Mississippi River near Red Wing.

The Bartron site is on the southern end of Prairie Island, a large island in the Mississippi River between Hastings and Red Wing. The site is only three miles from the Silvernale and Bryan sites, in a straight line, though farther by land or water. It has so many traits in common with the Silvernale culture that it is regarded as a lineal descendant of the latter. It has the storage pits, scapula hoes, arrowshaft polishers and triangular arrowheads, but the arrowheads are simple triangles without side notches. The principal difference is in the pottery. The vessels have round bodies without angular shoulders. The rolled rims have disappeared and all vessels have flaring rims. Decoration is by means of straight lines, though a few curved lines are found. By far the most common design is the chevron, which is drawn on the upper body. The pottery is clearly more like the pottery from the Bryan site than that of the Silvernale site, so the Bryan site is regarded as transitional bewteen Silvernale and Oneota.

An interesting site is the Sheffield site on the St. Croix River, three miles south of Marine-on-St. Croix in Washington County. Unlike other Oneota sites, it has no storage pits and no hoes. It has a great number of arrowheads and arrowshaft polishers and some fine bone fishhooks. Present were many mammal and fish bones, turtle carapaces and clam shells. This was no farming village, but a hunting and fishing camp of people who farmed farther down the Mississippi River, and returned to this camp annually to fish and hunt. The pottery and arrowheads are like those of the Bartron site. The great accumulation of village debris indicates that the camp was used a long time.

The group of sites around Winnebago are typical Oneota sites with storage pits, hoes, non-notched triangular arrowheads, and shell-tempered pottery. There are a few pottery traits that distinguish this group, particularly the type of handle. The Bartron and Silvernale handles resemble a curved little finger in size and shape and are called loop handles. The sites on the Blue Earth River have broad flat handles, one to two inches wide, that are known as strap handles. There are minor differences in treatment of the lips and in frequency of decoration on the inside of the necks. These differences are recognized by naming the culture of this group the Blue Earth Focus of the Oneota Aspect.

To the sites in the Root River Valley and the southeastern corner of Minnesota the name "Orr Focus" of the Oneota Aspect has been given. No extensive village site of the focus has yet been dug, and it is known primarily from burial sites. These are of two kinds — mounds and cemeteries. The mounds are on top of the bluffs which are usually 400 to 500 feet above the river. Burials are in individual graves dug into the subsoil, and bodies were placed on the back with legs fully extended. Flat slab rocks were placed on the body to the top of the pit. An earth mound was then constructed over the grave or graves, and a covering of slab rocks was placed over the mound. Most of the burials are found in the cemeteries, which are on low ridges extending from the foot of the bluff out into the valley. Burials are primary in the extended position, as in the mounds, and slab rocks were often used to form a box around the body, or to cover the body. Grave goods, particularly ornaments and small mortuary vessels, are common in both mound and cemetery burials.

The vessels are often placed at the shoulder of the body. They vary greatly in size. The largest is 8 inches in diameter and 5½ inches high; the smallest is the size of a teacup. Some vessels are round, but more are elliptical in cross section. The latter have handles at each end; the former may have four handles. Handles are of a narrow strap type.

Copper ornaments are usually coils of thin copper wire or tubular beads. Pipes are distinctive. They are made of catlinite, the red pipestone from the famous quarry at Pipestone, Minnesota. They are called disc pipes from the wide flange or disc at the top of the bowl. The use of catlinite first becomes common in the Orr Focus and indicates that the quarry was discovered and mined relatively late. Arrowheads are the small triangles found at all Oneota sites.

The most informative objects with Orr burials are glass beads, obtained from French traders.

Catlinite pipes

Burials with glass beads can be dated as from 1650 to 1700 A.D.

THE PLAINS MISSISSIPPI PHASE

The Great Oasis Focus

The only extensive site of the Great Oasis Focus discovered to date is on the bank of former Great Oasis Lake, now drained, in Murray County, nine miles west of Lake Shetek. That the inhabitants engaged in farming is attested by the numerous storage pits. Hoes have not been found, but the site yielded two sickles made of bison shoulder blades. Arrowheads include stemmed types, simple triangles, and triangles notched either at the sides or at the corners.

The most distinctive trait is the pottery. A typical vessel has a globular body with a short flaring neck. The body is marked with cord-wrapped paddle impressions, but the neck is smoothed and covered with horizontal incised lines, across which are drawn oblique lines to form triangles and lozenges (diamonds). The lines are very neatly drawn and the effect is very pleasing. The ware is grit-tempered and there are no handles.

Great Oasis pottery is found at a few small sites in the southwestern corner of Minnesota. It is also found at sites in eastern Nebraska and resembles some of the pottery found in prehistoric sites in South Dakota. There is evidence that the culture is older than Oneota in Minnesota, and that the people had moved west and southwest before the end of the Late Woodland period.

The Woodland Pattern in the Late Woodland Period

As previously stated, developed agriculture, which characterizes the cultures of the Mississippi Pattern, did not spread north of the Minnesota River, so in the greater part of Minnesota there is a continuation of the Woodland Pattern with its hunting and gathering economy. The presence of the farmers in the south affected the northern Indians in minor ways only. There is evidence of contacts between them through trade and probably through intermarriage. Oneota pottery, for instance, is found as far north as Leech Lake and Breckenridge, and occurs as mortuary furniture in Woodland mounds. The most obvious influence is seen in the arrowheads, for the northerners adopted the simple triangular point of the Oneota people, and the presence of triangular arrowheads becomes a marker for the period. Another custom that was taken over was the placing of mortuary pottery and other offerings with the dead, though this practice was more common with some groups than with others. A third influence is seen in a limited substitution of shell for grit as pottery temper. Otherwise typical Woodland pottery with shell-temper is not uncommon at Mille Lacs Lake, Leech Lake, and Height of Land Lake.

In general, the activities of the people continued much as in the Middle Woodland period. Campsites contain the bones of all the mammals, game birds, and fish native to the region. At the wild rice lakes are extensive deposits of ashes and broken pottery. The birch bark canoe was clearly perfected by this time, and is probably much older. Mound building continued to be practiced.

Toward the end of the period there is an expansion of Woodland cultures to the south, and by 1700 they had replaced Mississippi cultures everywhere in the state.

The Arvilla Focus

The area of the Arvilla culture is the Red River Valley throughout its length from Browns Valley at the head of Lake Traverse to the Canadian boundary. The culture is known from a single cemetery site, and a large number of mound groups that were usually built on the sand beaches of former glacial Lake Agassiz. It is characterized by a variety of burial types, and a general custom of placing gifts with the dead, especially objects of shell, bone, antler, and teeth, and occasionally objects of copper and mortuary vessels.

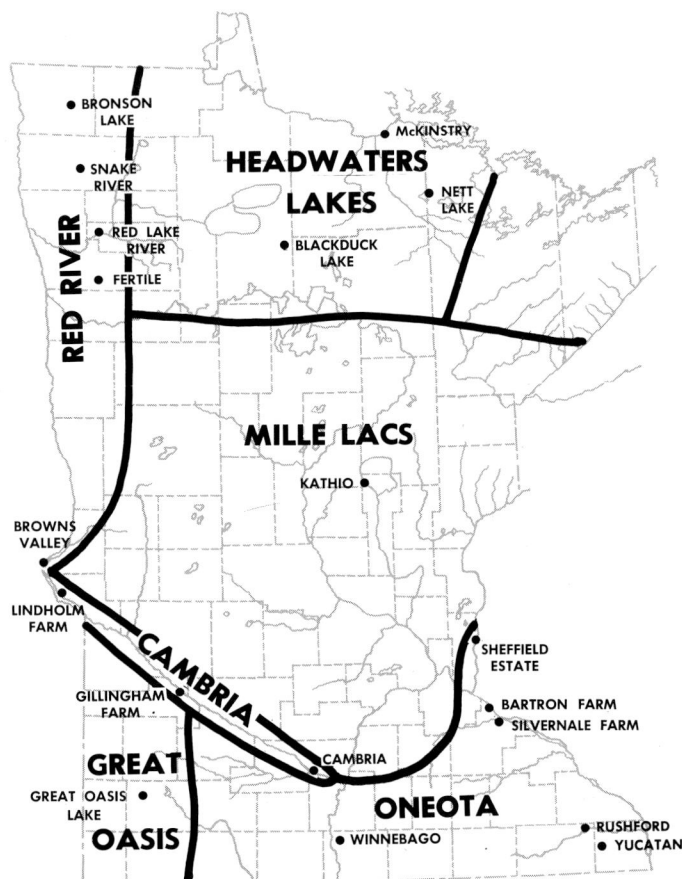

The cemetery site at Browns Valley was a series of rather deep pits each containing one or more burials. Some pits contained only skulls and arm bones, in others were the bones of the torso and legs interred as a primary burial. The gifts were usually placed with the disarticulated skulls and arm bones, and not with the bodies.

Mounds are of two types, circular and linear, both of which may be found at a single site. At Arvilla, North Dakota, there was a series of pits in line, with a single long low mound covering all of them. A large pit was under a circular mound. In the pit were several skeletons interred as pri-

mary burials in the sitting position, one primary burial at full length, and a burial of arms only. A second circular mound covered two pits.

At Lake Bronson was a series of six linear mounds in a north-south line extending one-fourth mile. They were from 150 feet to 200 feet long, about 20 feet wide and 6 inches high. A circular

Interior of Arvilla burial mound

mound at Fertile covered a grave in which there was a primary burial, the bones of a secondary burial, and four extra skulls with cuts across the forehead, believed due to scalping. At Red Lake Falls one grave included a mass of bones interred as secondary burials and not arranged in bundles. Another had primary burials, and across one of the skeletons were rows of small snail shell beads that had probably been the decoration on a dress.

Objects of shell placed with the dead included whole clam shells, geometric shapes cut from clam shell and perforated for suspension, and washer-shaped disc beads of clam shell. More interesting were thick barrel-shaped beads cut from the columella (the inner whorl) of a conch shell, for the nearest source of conch shells is the Gulf of Mexico. The columella beads were found in nearly every mound and were a great aid in distinguishing Arvilla mounds from other mounds of the area.

Bone objects included awls, long pins, arm bands, tubular beads and whistles, and harpoons with several barbs on one side only. With one important individual was a bell-shaped tubular pipe of polished antler. As a breastplate he wore two

60

Breastplate Ornaments

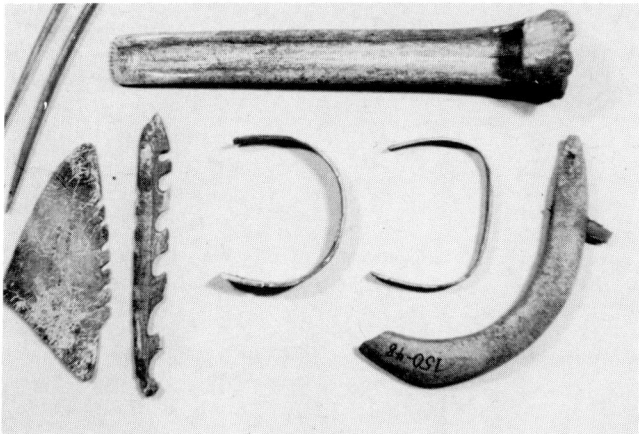

Ornaments

large crescent-shaped ornaments of copper with two grooved bear canines below, which were attached to an imitation clam shell of copper. Interesting were deer antler tines perforated at the middle, with beaver teeth wedged into the perforation. Perforated bear teeth were used as pendants, and claws and teeth were used as necklaces. One necklace consisted of a large number of the canine teeth of dogs or wolves.

The pottery is known mostly from the small mortuary vessels. The same old Woodland decorations were still being used, and body surfaces were treated with the cord-wrapped paddle. Plain surfaces had gone out of style in all the Woodland cultures of this period.

The Arvilla culture did not persist until the end

of the period, for it was superseded by the Kathio culture moving in from the east.

The Kathio Focus

The area of the Kathio focus is most of Minnesota except for the area north of the Mississippi River. It centers around Lake Mille Lacs and is a continuation of the Malmo Focus. Both of these foci have been grouped in the Mille Lacs Aspect to show this relationship. The differences are relatively minor. Arrowheads are predominantly triangular in the Kathio Focus. The use of catlinite for pipes has become common and the typical pipe is an elbow pipe with a relatively long stem which projects behind the bowl. Pottery vessels often are wide-mouthed but some contract to definite necks. Shell-tempering is used sporadically. Plain surfaces have given way to cord-wrapped paddle markings. Dentate stamp and cord-wrapped stick stamp are still used, but bosses and push-and-pull bands have gone out of fashion and incised lines are rare.

Burials are commonly secondary burials as simple bundles on the surface of the ground under a mound. Fairly often the bones of bodies or parts of bodies are found in proper anatomical position. From this it is believed that at a given time all of the bones of the deceased were taken from their platforms and placed on the ground to be covered by a mound, and that some of the individuals were so recently dead that all or some of their bones were still held together by other tissues. The Huron tribe held such a ceremony every seven years, known as "The Feast of the Dead." But other forms, such as pit burials and cremations, were also practiced. The Kathio people rarely placed funerary gifts with the dead and in the absence of pottery and arrowheads it is often impossible to determine whether a mound represents the Malmo Focus or the Kathio. Among unusual practices were placing the body of a dog, or parts of the carcasses of bison in the mound, probably a food offering, or the building of a small pile or cairn of rocks near the burials, or covering the bones with small logs.

The Blackduck Focus

The area of the Blackduck manifestations is north central Minnesota between the headwaters of the Mississippi and the Rainy River. Blackduck pottery varies from Kathio wares in that vessels nearly always have definite necks and commonly have flat, thickened lips. Dentate stamping is never used, so decoration is solely by use of the cord-wrapped stick stamp and punctates. Like Kathio pottery, only the necks are decorated. The necks of some of the vessels are smoothed before stamping, but about as many were covered with fine vertical combed lines which formed the background for the stamp. The stamp was also applied across the flat lips. The Blackduck potters produced vessels that are among the most handsome Woodland wares.

Burials were primary and bodies were often placed in a sitting position. Small mortuary pots were common gifts to the dead, but other objects were rare. Some burials are found shallowly buried in village sites, but most interments were in mounds. Burials occur singly in pits under the mounds, or on the floor of the mound, or in the mound fill. Those in pits are almost invariably in the sitting position, the others are flexed, in a sitting position, or on the back or side.

Projectile points are triangular, or triangular with side notches, rarely stemmed. Harpoons with barbs on one side only, were made of bone, as were awls and spatulate-shaped objects which are believed to be quill flatteners. Sharpened antler tips were used in flint chipping.

The Blackduck people were apparently moving northward in Minnesota. In the Rainy River area they seldom built mounds of their own, but either buried their dead in an old mound built by the people of the Rainy River Aspect, or enlarged one of the old mounds. One of their most spectacular mounds is at the mouth of the Littlefork River west of International Falls. Here there had been a small mound erected by the Rainy River people. The Blackduck people dug a pit in the north edge of the mound, placed a man's body in it, and built the mound a little higher. Just north of the edge of the new mound they then dug a very shallow grave and in it buried the bodies or bones of thirty people, placing with them fifteen pottery vessels and some other artifacts, and sprinkling them with red ochre. The bodies were covered with earth and a

fire was built on top of the earth at the south end of the group, charring or partly charring eight of the skeletons at that end. Later a floor of small poles placed side by side from east to west was placed on the earth above the thirty skeletons. On this floor were placed thirty-six bodies, together with twelve mortuary pots, some copper beads, and much red ochre. The mound was then built higher above them to include the south side in a single elongated mound. Later at the south side of the mound a small pit was dug and five bodies placed in it. Then a huge fire was built on the southern half of the mound. The heat was so intense that the clayey earth beneath was burned brick red to a depth of one and one-half feet, and the bones were charred, some being reduced to a white powder. Two pits were later dug to the base of the red burned clay. Five bodies were placed in one pit and six in the other. Once again a fire was built above the graves, but it was not as intense as the first one had been, and the bones were only partially charred. Finally two more pits were dug in the south half, one for seven and one for eleven bodies. No fire was kindled above them.

A total of ninety-six bodies was buried in the mound, of which 43 were adults, 12 were adolescents, 18 were children aged 6 to 12, 14 were young children aged 2 to 6, and 9 were infants. The 55 adults and adolescents included 21 men, 21 women, and 13 individuals whose sex could not be ascertained. With one of the women was the skeleton of an unborn child.

No objects of European manufacture have been found in any of the Blackduck villages or mounds, so they had left Minnesota before the coming of the French traders.

Part VI

THE HISTORIC PERIOD

As the history of Minnesota is for the most part the history of the people who live or have lived in the state, it is well at this point to anticipate a little and to identify the various Minnesota Indians and their relationships to one another. The relationships are based on language affinities, and were not fully worked out until studied by linguists in the 19th century. The linguists have identified more than fifty language families in North America, north of Mexico. Minnesota Indians, and most of the Indians with whom they had contacts by way of trade or warfare, belonged to one or the other of two large language families, the Siouan and the Algonkian. The following list includes all tribes known to have lived in Minnesota, some tribes who may have lived here, and some who did not live here except as visitors, invading enemies, traders, etc.

THE ALGONKIAN FAMILY:

1. Chippewa (Ojibwa, Saulteur)
2. Ottawa
3. Potawatomi
4. Cree
5. Menominee (from Mahnomen, meaning wild rice)
6. Sauk
7. Fox
8. Cheyenne

THE SIOUAN FAMILY:

A. The Dakota group (the Sioux proper):

9. Mdewakanton
10. Wahpekute
11. Wahpeton
12. Sisseton
13. Yankton
14. Yanktonai
15. Teton

B. Speaking the Dakota language but not a member of the group:

16. Assiniboine

C. The Chiwere Group:

17. Winnebago
18. Iowa
19. Oto
20. Missouri

D. The Dhegiha Group:

21. Omaha (there were four other Dhegiha tribes)

E. Tribes not grouped linguistically:

22. Mandan
23. Hidatsa (lived with Mandan; speech most like Dakota)

Speech differences were not as great among the Algonkian tribes as among the Siouan tribes. The Chippewa, Ottawa, and Potawatomi languages are so close that the differences are merely dialectic. The Cree, Menominee, Sauk and Fox constitute a second group. The Cheyenne language is the most unlike the others. The Chippewa were, and still are, one of the largest tribes in America, and the Algonkian family was the largest linguistic family. Algonkians once held the entire Atlantic Coast from North Carolina to Labrador, and some were as far west as Montana.

The seven Dakota tribes divide into three dialectic groups. The Mdewakanton, Wahpekute, Wahpeton and Sisseton speak one dialect and are often included under the term Santee or Eastern Sioux. The Yankton-Yanktonai group constitutes a second division, and the Teton tribe the third. The dialectic difference is shown in their name for the whole seven tribes, which the first group pronounces Dakota, the second group Nakota, and the third group Lakota. The word means "the allies."

The Teton was much the largest of the tribes and comprised about half the nation. It was so large that it was divided into bands, many of which are more often called by the band name than by the tribal name. The name "Mdewakanton" is unfamiliar to most Minnesotans, but it is the tribe the oldest white settlers knew best; and their tribal chieftains, such as Little Crow, Wabasha, and Shakopee, are probably better known than any other Sioux except possibly Sitting Bull and Crazy Horse of the Tetons. There is some evidence that the Mdewakantons held a very special place among the Dakota. The word "wakan" in the middle of their name is the Dakota word for supernatural power. Its Algonkian equivalent is "manitou." The whole name means "the people of the spirit lake" or can even be translated as "the people of the holy lake." The "Spirit Lake" was Mille Lacs, which may be thought of as the center of the Dakota world. An observer who participated at a meeting at Lake Traverse attended by representatives from all the Dakota tribes reported that they all addressed Little Crow as "father." It may be inferred that they regarded the Mdewakanton as the origi-

Little Crow

Hole in the Sky, Indian chief

Water color sketch of Indians

nal nucleus of the Dakota, and that the band headed by Little Crow was ranked at the top of the Mdewakanton bands.

A custom found among the Mdewakanton in the 19th Century was the assumption of the father's name by the eldest son when he inherited an important chieftainship. Thus there were three Wabashas, three Little Crows, and two or three Shakopees. The custom prevailed to some extent among the Chippewa also, for there were three Hole-in-the-days. The custom may have been aboriginal, but may have risen after white contacts from the practices of bestowing of medals by government agents as recognition of chiefly status.

The Assiniboine speak the Yanktonai dialect of the Dakota language. They had quarreled with their Yanktonai brothers and moved northward. After the quarrel they were bitter enemies of all the Dakota. Assiniboine is a Chippewa word meaning "stone-boilers, or those who cook with stones."

The Chiwere group are recognized as relatives by the Dakota. Traditionally the Winnebago were the parent tribe, who remained behind in eastern Wisconsin when the three others moved westward to the Mississippi and beyond.

The Dakota-Assiniboine, the Chippewa, and Iowa-Oto are the three Indian groups most closely associated with Minnesota, and are the most important in the historic and late prehistoric periods.

History begins in Minnesota with the early reports of literate Frenchmen. Perhaps the first report alluding to Minnesota is that of Nicolet, who is said to have visited Green Bay in 1634. Both the date and the place are uncertain, but it is probable that he visited either Lake Superior or Lake Michigan at some time in the 1630's. He stated that in the neighborhood were the "Naduessiu" and the "Assinipour." The word Naduessiu in the Algonkian tongue means the snakes or the enemy. It was the Chippewa name for the people who called themselves Dakota, and, shortened to Sioux, is probably used more today than is Dakota. The Assinipour of Nicollet is the tribe now known as Assiniboine. It is obvious that the Assiniboine had split from the Dakota before Nicolet's time, for his statement implies that he heard of the Assiniboine as a tribe distinct from the Sioux rather than as a tribal division of the Sioux.

In 1641 the Jesuits, Joques and Raymbault, visited Sault Sainte Marie, which was then the principal village of the Chippewa. Besides Chippewa they found a number of Potawatomi there, who were apparently only visiting their kinsmen. The Sault was famous for its whitefish, the principal food of its inhabitants. The French usually called the Chippewa the Saulteur, the people of the Sault. Chippewa and Ojibwa are the same word. They are two attempts to represent phonetically the name as the Chippewa themselves pronounce it. Neither spelling correctly duplicates the native sound, though the latter is a little closer. The missionaries were told that the Nadouessis were situated eighteen days journey west or nothwest of the Sault; the first nine days occupied in crossing another great lake (Lake Superior) that commences above the Sault, the second nine days in ascending the river that traverses their lands.

In the 1640's and 1650's French traders and missionaries became familiar with Lake Superior and we learn that the people inhabiting the north shore of the lake in Minnesota were the Cree. The Cree were enemies of the Dakota and therefore allied with the Assiniboine.

The fur trade was a monopoly of the Canadian government which granted licenses to individuals or companies to operate in a specified territory. Many of the early traders were unlicensed and could not openly report their activities. Radisson was an exception, but he reported his journeys after he had left Canada. His route and dates cannot be determined with any certainty, but it is clear that he saw much of the area around the upper end of Lake Superior in the latter half of the 1650's; and he is given the honor of being the first white man in Minnesota. He describes a meeting he held that was attended by both Dakota and Cree. This meeting would logically have taken place in Minnesota, the only place where the two groups had a common boundary. He said that the Indians had a drum that was made by stretching a skin over an earthen vessel, but unfortunately did not mention which of the two tribes had the vessel.

Early mission

In 1665 the Jesuits, with Allouez and later Marquette as priests, established a mission at La Pointe, the name used as a general designation for the area of Chequamegon Bay, on which Ashland and Bayfield, Wisconsin, are located. The Indians at La Pointe at this time were Hurons, an Iroquois tribe formerly living on the eastern shore of Lake Huron, and the Ottawa, who had been living on the north shore of Lake Huron, east of their Chippewa kinsmen. They told Allouez that they had been attacked and defeated by the powerful Iroquois League of New York in 1650, and were so terrified that they had fled in panic into Lake Michigan, across Wisconsin, and across the Mississippi River into northeastern Iowa and southeastern Minnesota. They had been well received by the Indians they met there, and spent some time at

Prairie Island in the Mississippi River between Red Wing and Hastings. They outwore their welcome there, and incurred the ill will of the Sioux, so they moved north, reaching La Pointe on Lake Superior in the early 1860's.

At this mission outpost near the western end of Lake Superior the priests met some of the Sioux and learned about others. They reported that the Sioux had little canoes, and had no guns but were expert bowmen. They cultivated fields but raised only tobacco, and "principally used the calumet." They raised no corn, but had false oats (wild rice) which they prepared so well that it was highly appetizing and very nutritious. They learned that some Sioux lived on the prairies, and that some of their cabins were covered with deer skins carefully dressed and skillfully sewed together. These would be the tepees probably used by all the Sioux at times, though primarily by the prairie tribes.

The La Pointe mission was abandoned in 1671 when the Huron and Ottawa moved east to the region of Mackinac Island. Marquette accompanied them, but soon left with Joliet on their voyage of discovery down the Mississippi in 1673. They used the Fox-Wisconsin portage so they did not enter Minnesota, but on their map they showed Iowa, Oto, and Omaha tribes in a region that could be equated with southern Minnesota.

In 1679 La Salle was establishing a station near Peoria, Illinois, as an advanced base for his voyage of the next year in which he was to discover the mouth of the Mississippi. In that year an unlicensed trader, Du Luth, journeyed to Mille Lacs Lake from Lake Superior and visited the Sioux at their great village of "Izatys." He also visited the Songaskicons (Sisseton) and Houetbatons (Wahpetons) twenty-six leagues from Izatys. This is the first mention of the tribal divisions of the Sioux. Unfortunately, Du Luth was a poor penman, and his "Iz" of Izatys was mistaken for a "k," and his "s" for an "o" so the word was reported as "Kathio." Izatys is seen to be a version of Issati, Isanti, and Santee, terms used to designate the Eastern Sioux or more narrowly, the Mdewakanton. But the word Kathio has remained in the literature also.

The next year Du Luth returned to Kathio and found Hennepin there. La Salle's plan was to have his main party descend the Mississippi to its mouth, while he sent a smaller group under Accault to explore the upper reaches of the river. Hennepin was chosen to accompany Accault, but is much better known than Accault because he published an account of the voyage. His account contains obvious untruths, and withholds information as to the activities of the other members of the party, yet it is of great value. He introduces us to the first native Minnesotan to stand out as an individual, Chief Aquipaguetin. This chief met the party on the river somewhere below Lake Pepin and took them to his village at Mille Lacs. On this trip the party left the river at St. Paul and walked by land to the lake, so Hennepin did not see St. Anthony Falls until his return trip. Also important is his description of Lake Pepin which he called the "Lake of Tears," because it was there that the chief opened a bag containing his father's bones and wept over them. At Mille Lacs, Hennepin was given an earthen pot in which to cook his food. These facts are important in showing that the Sioux had pottery, and that they presumably practiced secondary burial, after keeping bodies and bones for some time after death. Hennepin also adds to Du Luth's list of tribes the names of Hanctons (Yanktons) and "Tinthona or prairie-men" (the Tetons).

Among the Indians who visited La Salle's fort was a group reported as the Chaa, who said they lived at the headwaters of the Mississippi. They are believed to be the Cheyenne, but no one at that time knew where the headwaters of the river were. The Cheyenne are believed to have lived on a western branch of the Red River at that time, but may have been on the Minnesota.

In 1685 a licensed fur trader, in the person of Nicholas Perrot, finally reached the Mississippi River area. Perrot was a high-pressure salesman and has left us an account of one of his sales talks which had proved to be highly effective in inducing the Indians to buy European trade goods to replace their stone age weapons and utensils. He built a trading post at Trempealeau, where he was visited by Iowas, whose village was nine leagues away. His map shows a river, which probably represents the Root River, on which he shows the Iowa to be living.

Our next important informant on the location of Indian groups is Le Sueur. In 1693 he built a post at La Pointe among the Chippewa. After the Hurons and Ottawa had abandoned the area in 1671 the Chippewa had been moving westward, and with the establishment of Le Sueur's post made a permanent settlement there, which soon became one of the most important Chippewa villages. Le Sueur then turned his attention to the south and in 1694 built a post on Prairie Island among the Sioux. In 1700 he brought a ship from France via Louisiana and ascended the Mississippi and Minnesota rivers to Mankato. He built a post, called Fort L'Huillier on the Blue Earth River a few miles south of Mankato. He was told by Indian inform-

Summer village of the Sioux

ants that this was the country of the Iowa and Oto and the Sioux of the West. He sent messengers to the Iowa and Oto to invite them to live at the fort, because he wanted farming Indians at the settlement. The messengers returned to report that the Iowa and Oto had left Minnesota and had gone westward to establish themselves near Omaha in eastern Nebraska. Iowa and Oto are never again reported in Minnesota. It is believed that they had moved across the Missouri River to avoid raids by the Sauk and Fox of Wisconsin.

Our last important direct informant is La Verendreye, who, starting in 1731, established a trade route from Lake Superior to Lake Winnipeg via Pigeon River, the boundary lakes, Rainy River, Lake of the Woods, and the Winnipeg River. He met Monsony Indians at Rainy Lake and Crees at Lake Winnipeg and Lake of the Woods. The Monsony are believed to have been a division of the Cree. He reports the Assiniboine as living on the Assiniboine River, which flows from the west to join the Red River of the North at Winnipeg. From Winnipeg the Red River flows north into Lake Winnipeg. In 1742 Verendreye's sons met "Prairie Sioux" on the Missouri River somewhere near the present boundary between North and South Dakota.

In 1736 occurred an event so important that it serves to terminate the first phase of the history of the Minnesota Indians, a period of about a century's duration. This was the famous massacre of a group of La Verendreye's men on an island in the Lake of the Woods. The attackers included both eastern and western Sioux, and there is evidence that some Chippewa were also among them. The French believed, or chose to believe, that only Sioux were involved. They armed the Chippewa and induced them to attack the Sioux, starting a war that was to continue for more than a hundred years.

The information received from French traders and missionaries by 1736 enables us to locate and identify most of the Indian groups of Minnesota of the first period, and permits us to relate some of the late archæological manifestations with known Indian tribes. We know that in 1736 all of Minnesota, except the far northern portion was held by the Dakota, and the northern portion was held by the Cree. Immediately prior to 1700 the Iowa had lived in the southeastern corner, and earlier both Iowa and Oto were in the Blue Earth Valley. The Dakota told the Reverend Riggs that at one time the Iowa and Oto held most of Minnesota south of the Minnesota River. Early maps show Omaha Indians in the southwest corner, though we have no reports of Frenchmen actually finding Omaha there. The Dakota told Reverend Riggs that they learned of the famous pipestone quarry from the Omaha, so it is clear that at one time the southwest corner was Omaha territory.

No Assiniboine were met in Minnesota, but early maps show Lake of the Woods as "Lake of the Assiniboines." They had separated from the Yanktonai before 1634 and had lived in north central Minnesota between the Mississippi River and the northern boundary, gradually moving to the northwest. The Cheyennes were living not far west of the Red River Valley in 1736 and may well have been in the valley at an earlier time.

As to archæological connections, it is safe to conclude that the Mille Lacs Aspect is the prehistoric culture of the Dakota. The Jesuits' reports that the Dakota were non-agricultural, and Hennepin's evidence of pottery and secondary burial, fits the archaeological evidence. This being so, it is seen that Mille Lacs had been a Dakota center for a long period of time, including both the Malmo and Kathio foci.

The Blackduck culture is found in the area where the Assiniboine are known to have lived. The practice of primary burial in sitting position is at variance with the secondary burial of other Dakota groups, yet an observer, Alexander Henry the Elder, who visited the Assiniboine soon after the British took possession of Canada, describes just such a burial. At historically known Assiniboine sites in Canada the Blackduck types of burial and pottery are found. Blackduck culture can be equated with the Assiniboine.

In the southeast the Orr focus of the Oneota culture is found where the Iowas lived at the time of Perrot. Cultures of the Oneota Aspect, to which the Orr focus belongs, are found in Wisconsin, Iowa, Nebraska, and Missouri where Chiwere Siouan peoples are known to have lived. The Orr Focus is equated with the Iowas of the 17th Century, and the Oneota Aspect with the Chiwere Siouan group. Finally, it is believed that the Great Oasis culture of southwestern Minnesota can be equated with the Omaha tribe. The culture is found in that part of Minnesota where the Omaha once lived, and the Great Oasis pottery type is found in eastern Nebraska where they lived in historic times.

The Silvernale culture is believed to be a predecessor of Oneota in Minnesota, in which case it could represent an earlier variant of the culture of the Iowa and Oto tribes. There is insufficient evidence to connect the Cambria culture and the Arvilla culture with any historically known tribes.

The first historic period, 1634 to 1736, in terms of tribal movements can be seen as an expansion of the Dakota to the west and southwest, with the vanguard already at the Missouri River. The westward movement apparently included withdrawal from parts of northwestern Wisconsin, formerly inhabited, or at least claimed as hunting territory, by them. At the end of the period, the Sioux held all of Minnesota, except for the northern border, as well as most of the eastern half of the Dakotas.

In terms of culture change, contact with French traders, at first in the Lake Superior region, and later on the Mississippi River, was beginning to effect important changes in the Indian way of life. From the first, the superiority of steel knives, scrapers, needles, and awls over stone tools, of guns over bows and arrows, and of kettles of copper or iron over clay vessels, was obvious to the Indians, and they were anxious to obtain them. Glass beads for trimming garments and for ornaments were eagerly sought by women as a substitute for dyed porcupine quills, which required so much labor

The trading store

to produce. Blankets and woven cloth began to take the place of skin clothing. New tastes were acquired for exotic drinks such as tea and coffee, but especially for rum and whiskey. The Indians north of Mexico had never known any form of alcoholic drink, but they took to it avidly, and rum was a "must" item in every trader's stock of goods. Probably more than anything else it contributed to the breakdown of Indian cultures.

The coming of the trader worked a revolution in the Indian way of life. The trader's goods could be had in exchange for furs and pelts, so trapping and hunting for hides and furs increasingly occupied the Indians' time formerly given to hunting for food. They tended to congregate around the trading posts in new villages, and vied with one another to induce the traders to settle among them. Some of these rivalries erupted into warfare. More and more the Indian was losing his former self-sufficiency.

The French installed missionary priests in the more important posts. The priests had success in introducing the Christian religion among the Chippewa and Cree, and made converts. An important influence was exerted by the custom of taking Indian boys and girls to Canada for education in Catholic schools. But among the Sioux the priests seem to have met with little success.

The second phase of the historic period may be included within the dates 1736, which marks the beginning of the Chippewa-Dakota war, and 1825, which marks the limit of Chippewa expansion in Minnesota. The most important feature of this period is the Chippewa invasion of Minnesota, resulting in the conquest of the northeastern and northern half of the state. At the beginning of the war the Chippewa scored tremendous successes over their new enemy. As enemies of the Dakota, the Chippewa found themselves allied with the Cree and Assiniboine, and the old balance of power in the north was upset. The Chippewa expanded rapidly along the Verendrye trade route, though in doing so they displaced their Cree allies who withdrew to the north. In 1736 Verendreye's men met Chippewa at the mouth of the Vermilion River, and in 1737 they were established at Rainy Lake with the Monsony. At some time in the 1750's they were

reported at Pembina on the Red River in the northeast corner of North Dakota, so by that time they held all of the northern border. The movement along the border was not in territory claimed by the Sioux and apparently involved no important battles. The real fighting occurred farther south, spearheaded by Chippewa moving westward from La Pointe to Fond du Lac at the west end of Lake Superior, where they established a village soon after 1736. In this movement the Chippewa were aided by the weakness of their old enemies, the Sauk and Fox, who had suffered disastrous defeats in two wars with the French, and were in no position to oppose them.

From Fond du Lac the Chippewa launched an attack on the Mdewakanton villages at Mille Lacs. Armed with guns, and probably led by Frenchmen, they dealt the Sioux a crushing defeat and successively destroyed their three great villages. The survivors fled south and never again returned to Mille Lacs to live. This event is called the Battle of Kathio and occurred about 1745. It was the most decisive battle of the war.

Three or four years later the Chippewa gathered another large war party at Fond du Lac and marched west to attack the large Sioux village (believed to be Wahpeton and Sisseton) at Sandy Lake. The attack was successful, the Sioux withdrew, and shortly after the Chippewa established a large village there. As Sandy Lake is almost on the Mississippi River, the Chippewa had cut the most important route between the Sioux of the upper Mississippi and the Sioux on the lower Minnesota.

The powerful Yanktonai, living on the Upper Mississippi in the vicinity of Cass and Leach lakes, was now threatened by encirclement by the Chippewa on the northern border and the aggressive Sandy Lake group. About 1760 they organized a counter-offensive and assembled a large war party at Leech Lake. The party was split into three groups to attack the Chippewa at Sandy Lake, Rainy Lake and Pembina. None was victorious and the Yanktonai retreated to the Red River Valley, though part of them stayed for a time on Thief River. The Sisseton and Wahpeton withdrew toward the Minnesota River, where most of the Mdewakanton and Wahpekute had already gone. The Yankton and

Teton tribes probably played no part in the war as they had already moved out of Minnesota, except that some Yanktons were in the southwest corner.

Fort Beauharnois, the post at Frontenac, was abandoned by the French in 1756 shortly after the outbreak of the French and Indian War. By this time the Mdewakantons had purchased some guns from the French, and were recovering somewhat from the Kathio disaster. About 1765 they felt strong enough to attempt to regain their ancient lands and sent a strong war party up the Mississippi River. They were badly defeated in a battle at the mouth of Crow Wing River, west of Mille Lacs. Following this disaster the Mdewakanton and Wahpekute moved the rest of their villages south of the Minnesota, one band under Wabasha, moving all the way down to Winona. The victorious Chippewa moved south into the St. Croix Valley and also established a village at Mille Lacs. The area above Sandy Lake abandoned by the Yanktonai was also occupied and an aggressive Chippewa band known as the Pillagers was settled at Leech Lake, where they were visited by Alexander Henry the Elder in 1775.

A final attempt to oust the Chippewa was made by the Mdewakanton about 1773. This time they enlisted the aid of the Foxes and the combined armies marched north up the St. Croix River. The Chippewa met them at St. Croix Falls and defeated them, though this battle was much less one-sided than the earlier Chippewa victories.

During the Revolutionary War both Sioux and Chippewa were allied with the British against the Americans and Spanish and there was an interval of peace that terminated the rapid phase of Chippewa conquest. The French had always favored the Chippewa over the Sioux in the sale of guns, and the expulsion of the French was now beginning to be felt as the Dakota obtained arms from British and Spanish traders. The western Sioux tribes, Sisseton, Wahpeton, Yankton, and Yanktonai, were acquiring horses from the west, and the earlier Chippewa superiority in arms was nearly gone. During the interval of peace the Chippewa from the northern border moved south unopposed to establish themselves at Lake Vermilion, Nett Lake and Red Lake. From Red Lake they moved on to Thief River, ousting the last remnants of Yanktonai, and had a village at Red Lake Falls by 1784. The Dakota still held all of the Red River Valley above Pembina. In eastern Minnesota the Chippewa were as far south as southern Pine County.

Between the Dakota villages in the south and west and the Chippewa settlements in the northeast was a wide strip of territory that constituted a sort of neutral ground. Truces were arranged permitting hunting parties from either side to hunt here without meeting one another. Even third parties were permitted, for the Menominees of northeastern Wisconsin were reported hunting here by the trader, Perrault, in 1786-87, and by Zebulon Pike in 1805. This arrangement lasted until 1797, when a band of Sissetons and Wahpetons at Cross Lake attacked and nearly annihilated the Sandy Lake and Mille Lacs Chippewa who had been hunting on Long Prairie River. After this disaster the Chippewa determined to seize this debatable hunting ground. A band drawn from the bravest warriors and hunters of the Mississippi Chippewa established a settlement at Gull Lake under Chief Curly Head. In 1805 this band attacked and severely defeated an encampment of Sisseton and Wahpeton on the Long Prairie River, capturing thirty-six horses. After this event the Sioux tribes made a few attempts to return in force to hunt, but suffered so much at the hands of the Chippewa that they soon gave up all claim to the valley. The area around Little Falls, to the east of the Long Prairie Valley, now outflanked on the west, also became undisputed Chippewa country.

In the next twenty years no major changes occurred, except that the Chippewa moved nearer Ottertail Lake, and occupied a little more of the Red River Valley above (south of) Pembina. The period was marked by mutual raids for scalps across the neutral territory, many of which have been reported as battles.

In 1825 the United States Government succeeded in getting the Dakota and Chippewa to agree on a definite boundary line dividing their territories. The line passed through the neutral belt, beginning at the St. Croix River about on the boundary between Washington and Chisago coun-

Mississippi scenery between Lake Pepin and St. Croix River

Mouth of the St. Croix River

Indian teepees and squaw—Mille Lacs Lake

74

ties. It crossed the Mississippi at Sartell, north of St. Cloud, then to Lake Carlos near Alexandria, to Ottertail Lake, and to the Red River at the mouth of the Buffalo River north of Moorhead. The treaty by which this line was established provided for a cessation of warfare between the two peoples, but the peace was soon broken and the mutual raiding was resumed, not to terminate until the Sioux were eventually expelled from Minnesota. The importance of the line is that it became the basis on which the ownership of the land was determined in all future treaties between the government and the two Indian groups. The Chippewa invasion was finally halted, and they were in possession of the larger part of the state.

Until 1765 all of Minnesota was French territory and after 1818 it was all American. Between these dates various areas had been divided between British, Spanish, French, and Americans. The changes in sovereignty had no important effect on the Indians, whose chief contacts were with the fur traders. The backbone of the fur trade remained the French-Canadian voyageurs, no matter whether they worked for French, English or American owners. Trading posts were much more numerous than in the earlier period, and the Indians' dependence on the European trader increased. The acculturative process was steadily at work, and was speeded up by frequent intermarriages between Europeans and Indians. During the period there was little organized missionary effort, but contact with the French Catholic voyageurs was advancing the Catholic religion, especially among the Chippewa.

Indian history after 1825 is marked by the treaties between the government and the Indians in which the latter ceded much of their lands, which were then opened to white settlement. It is also marked by missionary efforts, a continuing loss of Indian culture, and by one outstanding event—the great Sioux outbreak of 1862.

The land cessions began in 1837 when the land east of the Mississippi River as far north as the east-west line, drawn from the mouth of the Crow Wing River to the Wisconsin border, was ceded.

The portion north of the Sioux-Chippewa line of 1825 was ceded by the Chippewa; the southern and smaller portion by the Sioux. The treaties pro-

vided for payments of money, payments in goods, and payments to traders to whom the Indians owed money. Provision was made to supply the Indians with tools and implements, blacksmiths and farmers. Unlike most of the later treaties there was no provision prohibiting the sale of spirituous liquors in the ceded territory, and no lands were reserved for the Indians, though the Chippewas were to be allowed to hunt in the lands ceded by them until further notice. Later some small reservations were created in the tract ceded by the Chippewa.

In 1847 the Chippewas ceded their lands south of a line from Ottertail Lake to the mouth of the Crow Wing. The government wanted this as a reservation for the Winnebago Indians, whom they were planning to move from Wisconsin. The southern boundary of the Chippewa territory after this cession was a fairly straight east-west line from the Wisconsin boundary through the mouth of the Crow Wing River to Ottertail Lake, thence northwest along the treaty line of 1825. In 1854 they ceded their lands east of a line running approximately south from the mouth of the Vermilion River to the east-west line of 1837. Some small areas, including the Pigeon River Reserve, were held out as reservations.

A year later they ceded lands east and south of a line running approximately from Loman, on the Rainy River, to Turtle Lake, just north of Bemidji, to Halstad, on the Red River. However, the area between the Big Fork and Vermilion rivers, including Nett Lake, was not included in the cession. Eleven years later, in 1866, a reservation was created at Nett Lake and the rest of the tract was ceded.

The last important Chippewa cession was made in 1863 by a treaty known as the "Old Crossing Treaty," in which they ceded the northwestern corner of the state, west of a line running southwest from the intersection of the Canadian boundary and the west shore of the Lake of the Woods, to Thief River Falls, then southeast to the 1855 line near Bagley. This left a large unceded area, including Red Lake, whose northern boundary was Lake of the Woods and the Rainy River below Loman, and whose southern boundary was the Thief River Falls-Bagley line. When later the large Red Lake

Reservation was created, the balance of this tract was opened to white settlement.

For a period of years after the five principal cessions, the boundary lines of reservations were shifted by treaties, Acts of Congress, Presidential Executive Orders, and by better surveys. In 1864 an attempt was made to eliminate some of the smaller reservations by creating the White Earth Reservation and moving the smaller bands there. Many of them found themselves uncomfortable on the new reservation and found their way back to their old areas.

By 1889 all of the reservations, except White Earth and Red Lake had been allotted. Instead of a band owning an entire tract in common, specific pieces of land were given to individual Indians, and the excess opened to white homesteaders. As of now, only Red Lake is not allotted, and it is the only true reservation. Much has been written on the effects of reservation life on the Chippewa. The system developed in an attempt to open the land to white homesteaders with a minimum of friction, taking most but not all of the land from the Indians, with compensation for the part taken. The reservation formed a segregated area, which protected the Indian from the full impact of the still alien Western civilization. It slowed down the acculturation process and permitted him to retain a part of his ancestral culture. The value of the system is debatable, and it is in large part responsible for the so-called "Indian Problem" of today. It is clear that as time passes, it becomes more and more an anachronism doomed to eventual extinction.

In the meantime, the tide of white settlement had reached the Mississippi River from Sartell, south to the Iowa border, and there was a steadily rising demand that the rich agricultural lands of

Buffalo hunt

Group of Sioux Indians who went to Washington in 1858

the Sioux be opened to homesteaders. After the creation of Minnesota territory in 1849, Governor Ramsey took the lead, and in 1851, induced the Mdewakanton and Wahpekute to sign a treaty at Mendota, and the Sisseton and Wahpeton another at Traverse des Sioux. By the treaties, all the Sioux lands in Minnesota were ceded except for a strip twenty miles wide on both sides of the Minnesota River from just above New Ulm to Lake Traverse. The portion below the mouth of the Yellow Medicine was the reservation of the Mdewakanton and Wahpekute; the upper portion was the reservation for the Sisseton and Wahpeton. Though a large sum of money was to be paid the Indians, much of it went to satisfy the claims, often dubious or highly padded, of the traders. From the payment were also deducted fat commissions paid to various individuals who had helped persuade the reluctant chiefs to sign the treaties.

From the first, the Sioux were very unhappy in their limited area, particularly the lower tribes who were far from their old hunting grounds. As settlers moved in, all game moved out, and the Indians became dependent for food on the traders. Soon squatters began to move into the reservation itself, and neither the Federal government nor the Territorial government made any attempt to live up to the treaties by expelling them. The Indians realized that any attempt on their part to forcibly remove the squatters would meet with grave reprisals. In 1858 a delegation was sent to Washington to petition Congress for aid in this situation. The result was a farce. The north half of the reservation was taken from them and they were allowed thirty cents an acre for it. After the usual payment of traders' claims, nothing of this payment was left for the two lower tribes and very little for the upper tribes. The squatters south of the river were given title to their lands for a payment to the government but nothing to the Indians. The latter were resentful and bitter in the face of their hopeless situation, and the knowledge that the government had no intention of honoring its treaties with them.

Even so, the majority, including the principal

Battle of New Ulm, 1862

Fort Ridgely in 1862

chiefs, was not inclined to resort to warfare. But a hot-headed minority was able to force the issue. In 1857 had occurred the famous Spirit Lake Massacre of some white settlers by a band of Wahpekute under Inkpaduta, an action which most of the Dakota deplored. The governor's insistence that the tribal leaders would be held accountable for any such occurrence in the future gave the hotheads a lever of which they took advantage. They staged the raid at Acton in 1862 and returned to the reservation to inform Little Crow and Shakopee that they now had no choice but to call a general uprising.

The events of the uprising, the wanton slaughter of over five hundred scattered homesteaders, the looting and acts of cruelty, the attacks on Fort Ridgely and New Ulm, the pursuit by Sibley's troops, the Battle of Wood Lake, and the surrender of the white captives at Camp Release have been told many times. The Indians who surrendered to Sibley were not the ringleaders, for the latter fled to the westward, many reaching a haven in Canada, where their descendants still are. Of the more peacefully inclined group who surrendered, thirty-eight were hung at Mankato, with the balance enduring the horrible ordeal of the concentration camp at Fort Snelling the next winter, and final removal to Dakota territory in the spring.

The story of the Sioux from 1825 to 1863 is tied up with the activities of the American Fur Company, the soldiers at Fort Snelling and Fort Ridgely, the missionaries, particularly Williamson, Riggs and the Pond brothers, and the missions at Lake Calhoun and Lac Qui Parle. But this story is part of the history of the white pioneers of Minnesota.

Many of the early settlers in southern Minnesota recall Indians in that area after the final expulsion of the Sioux in 1863. These were Winnebagoes. In 1848 the government had brought them from Wisconsin and given them a reservation on the Long Prairie River on the land ceded by the Chippewa a year earlier. They were dissatisfied with the reservation, and in 1855 they were moved to a small area at St. Clair, near Mankato, on lands ceded by the Sioux four years earlier. Although they took no part in the Sioux uprising, their removal was demanded by the white settlers of the area, and in 1863 they were moved to South Dakota and two years later to eastern Nebraska where they still are. For years after that, individual families moved back and forth between their old homes in Wisconsin and Minnesota and their new home in Nebraska, and a few families have homes here now.

After the Sioux outbreak, two small Mdewakanton groups were allowed to return to Minnesota, one to Prairie Island and one to the Episcopalian Mission near Morton. More recently some Sisseton families have been placed on federal lands below Granite Falls.

Fort Snelling

CHAPTER THREE

The Indian Nations of Minnesota

The Sioux Uprising

By MR. AND MRS. HARRY LAWRENCE

Edited by Eugene T. Newhall

Little Crow.

The Sioux uprising of 1862, last big Indian challenge in Minnesota, has been told and retold for most of the century of Minnesota's history as a state. Here is the tale from an Indian point of view, as passed down through a niece of Chief Little Crow, and her husband. The modern tellers of this ancient tale, in Indian cadence, are Harry Lawrence, known to his tribe as Scarlet Boy, and Mrs. Harry Lawrence, Morning Star. The story was tape-transcribed in 1958, much of the direct detail as told to Mrs. Lawrence by her mother, Mrs. John Wakeman, who was Little Crow's sister-in-law and 17 at the time of the outbreak.

The Indians, by this account, had been seething with mounting grievances in the decade since signing of the treaties of Traverse des Sioux and Mendota in 1851. Some felt their chiefs were tricked into signing traders' papers to pay private debts, in the guise of treaty papers.

Little Crow, a Sioux chief, has often been blamed for his part in the uprising. His descendants tell of some of the complex pressures working upon him after what are described as four "renegade" Indians precipitated the outbreak by stalking into a store and opening fire.

"Little Crow had put away his Indian dress, and now dressed in the style of the white man. Some of the people were angry with him because he followed some of the white man's ways. He attended the mission on Sundays. He lived in a frame house while a brick house was being built

for him near the agency. Only three months before the outbreak of the war, Little Crow had been voted out of office as the head chief of his people. His opponent had been backed by the Indian Agency.

"I was seventeen and had two children," Chief Little Crow's sister-in-law continues. "My brother and my husband worked at the agency.

"On that fateful morning in August, 1862, Little Crow had gone hunting to get some fresh meat for breakfast. I went to the corn field to chase the crows away from the corn. I heard voices and I climbed up on the protection that had been built to protect the corn.

"Men were coming from the direction of Redwood. I heard one of them say, 'If we do this, we will not have to worry for at least two years.' I jumped down from the protection so that I would not be seen, and a little later I heard shooting.

"Frightened, I ran to the house. Little Crow had just come back from hunting. He had some catfish and ducks. When I told him of the shooting, he did not say a word.

"I was worried about my husband and brothers, so I ran to the agency. Two men were coming from the agency, supporting my brother between them. I was told that they had been eating breakfast when Ta-wa-su-ota suddenly appeared in the room and shot the storekeeper. My brother who was sitting next to the storekeeper became covered with blood and fainted.

"I continued to the agency and ran through the rooms. The place had been ransacked. It was horrible. Someone spoke to me: I turned my head and saw a white man hiding. He said, 'Don't speak to me.' Ta-wa-su-ota appeared in the doorway and shot at him. He escaped through the window.

"I could not find my husband. When I saw him again, he told me he had escorted two white women to a ravine and told them to follow it, traveling by night only to New Ulm. One of them offered him her wedding ring. He answered, 'No, no! I don't want your ring. Just look at my face and if anything happens, remember it.'

"Like a destructive storm, the war struck suddenly and spread rapidly. Everything was confusion. It was difficult to know who was friend and who was foe.

"Little Crow divided some white women and children who found it difficult to escape among his friends to protect them from the renegades. The Indians raided farms to get food for the refugees. One day a large group of soldiers attacked them and they were forced to fight.

"Little Crow wanted to make peace, but the majority of the people wanted him to lead them in a war. At a council meeting, they threatened him and called him a coward until he in anger agreed to lead them in war.

"During the war, my husband and I fled to Canada. When we returned we were imprisoned for three years. Our treatment was terrible. All the food was mixed in one big pot and it wasn't fit to eat. Three of my brothers died of smallpox while in prison."

Little Crow, whose Indian name was Ta-O-yah-te-Doota, though described as "something of a playboy when young, after he became chief he tried to stop whiskey drinking in his band and encouraged them to become industrious and thrifty," the Indian account relates.

"He applied to the Sioux agent at Fort Snelling and asked that a missionary be sent to establish a mission and reside in the Kaposia village. In November, 1846, Dr. Williamson came; after his arrival, and Ta-O-yah-te-Doota's coming to the chieftaincy, both the white men and red men's conditions improved."

"Mr. A. W. Daniels of St. Peter, who was physician at the lower agency for a number of years and intimately acquainted with Little Crow, in his article on him in Minnesota History, Vol. XII, pays him this tribute: "Little Crow was a man of good habits. I never knew him to use intoxicating liquors. He was truthful and strictly honorable in his dealings with the government.""

But in the spring of 1862, when the Sioux nation met to elect a head speaker, "Little Crow was defeated by Traveling Hail, the candidate of the progressive white man's party," the Indian account continues.

"When the four renegades committed the act of murders and plunged the Sioux nation into war, they realized that Traveling Hail was not the person to lead them. Little Crow was not altogether to their liking, being tinted with ideas of progress and civilization, but he was by far the strongest man available and known to have ambition for power. The forces hostile to the whites combined in their demand that he lead them in war.

"At first he declined. It was only when the crowd became threatening and called him a coward that he was persuaded, after making the following speech which was obtained from the chief's son, who had a wonderful memory.

"Little Crow sprang to his feet, snatched the eagle feathers from the head of his insulter and flung them to the ground. Then, stretching himself to his full height, his eyes flashing fire, and in a voice trembling with rage, he exclaimed:

" 'Ta-O-yah-te-Doota is not a coward! He is not a fool! When did he run from his enemies? When did he leave his braves behind him on the warpath and turn to his teepee? When you retreated from your enemies, he walked behind you on your trail with his face to the Ojibways, and covered your backs as a she-bear covers her cubs. Is Ta-O-yah-te-Doota without scalps? Look at his war feathers! Behold the scalp locks of his enemies hanging there on his lodge poles! Do they call him a coward? Ta-O-yah-te-Doota is not a coward! He is not a fool! Braves, you are like little children. You know not what you are doing. You are full of the white man's devilwater. You are like dogs in the hot moon, when they run mad and snap at their shadows. We are only little herds of buffalo left scattered; the great herds that once covered the prairies are no more. The white men are like the locusts when they fly so thick that the whole sky is a snowstorm. You may kill one, two, ten; and ten times ten will come to kill you. Count your fingers all day long, and white men with guns in their hands will come faster than you can count. Yes, they fight among themselves away off (Civil War). Do you hear the thunder of their big guns? No! It will take you two moons to run down to where they are fighting, and all the way your path would be among

white soldiers as thick as the tamaracks in the swamps of the Ojibways. Yes, they fight among themselves, but if you strike one of them, they will turn on you and devour you, your women and your little children, just as the locusts in their time devour the leaves on the trees in one day. You are fools. You will die like rabbits when the hungry wolves hunt them in the hard moon (January). Ta-O-yah-te-Doota is not a coward—he will die with you.' "

"After the massacre began and before he was drafted into the war by the angered people," the Indian account concludes, "Little Crow did not permit a single woman or child to be killed or injured at the lower agency, but permitted 32 of them, mostly adults, to escape to Fort Ridgley."

Our Ojibway or Chippeway Neighbors

By WILLIAM MADISON and MRS. WINIFRED JOURDAIN
William Madison (May-zhuc-ke-ge-shig) is Hereditary Chief Clearing Sky

It was in the unrecorded ages that the Great Mon-ne-do gave to his red children the forests, the waters and the plains. All of Ge-shay-mon-ne-do's gifts were sacred to the Indian. Each had a "soul" to be freely given to nourish and strengthen—the deer, the buffalo and beaver, the fowls and the fishes, the medicinal herbs and the berries. Hence, solemn ceremonies opened each season of the year.

Nor did the Ojibways interfere with the plans of the Good Spirit but, accepting their gifts with grateful hearts, they evidenced their gratitude by frugality and caution. They refused to touch lest they might harm, until the sign was given them and thereafter they touched only as the wise men of their Ancients had instructed them.

Everything that the Great Mon-ne-do had given had a spirit within. Way-na-bo-shew was sent to earth to help the red men to transform their everyday living. Evil had crept in. Way-na-bo-shew was

given the power to understand and work with the animals and all spirits of Nature. Tradition informs us he founded the twelve clans which had to do with the governing powers of the people. Each clan had its leader. An insignia illustrating the animal or bird for which the clan was named identified each. The clan had a certain duty to fulfill towards the tribe. For instance, the Bear Clan (O-do-day-me-win) governed the marriage law. The other clans had jurisdiction over the business affairs. Unwritten laws governed the rule of the clans.

Grand Medicine Lodge

According to tradition, Way-na-bo-shew founded the Mid-da-wi-win, the Grand Medicine Lodge or Society, which was the center of spiritual and physical healing. Herbs were used for the healing of the body, and the medicine men and women appealed to the Great Spirit to aid the soul. The

Nett Lake Grand Medicine Lodge.

May-day-we-jig Grand Medicine Society burial ground.

medicine bag was made of some part of the bird or animal for which the clan was named. The Indian was taught that all that was put on earth was for a purpose and, being given by the kind Monne-do, was only good. There was no evil taught, but later a belief in evil spirits and witchcraft developed. The man-from-God (Way-na-bo-shew) had been sent to earth to help the red man overcome the evil that had arisen. But he was rejected by them and ridiculed, so at last he went sorrowfully away. He left only the Grand Medicine Lodge to remind the earth of his healing power and mighty works.

The Ancient Sacred Spiritual Order, (Mid-da-wi-win) or Grand Medicine Lodge, has always been held in high esteem by all tribes, which also had to do with blood relationship towards one another. Only the worthy young people were permitted to take the sacred oaths for the degrees offered by the order. The gift they acquired through the Grand Medicine belief was their own and could be used only by them in administering the medicine herb to the sick. When a medicine

man or woman passed to the happy hunting ground, the gift died with them.

Division

As the ages wore on, the Indian tribes began warring against each other. The Ojibways or Chippeways, one of the largest of the North American Indian tribes, covered at one time over 1,000 miles of territory from East to West, mainly along the Great Lakes region. They scattered along the shores and spread westward across the intervening country into the Dakotas. It is difficult to define accurately the Ojibway's country as this tribe blended readily in the course of many years with members of the other tribes of Algonquin stock of which they are a part. Among these are the Potawatomi, Ottawa, Miami, Delaware, Sauk, Fox, Wyandot, Iowa, Menominee, Pembina, Cree, Tamas-Mus-qua-keeg, (names as spelled in Charles J. Kappler, L.L.M. Indian Laws and Treaties Vol. II). Moreover, they frequently changed their habitat, because of the long and tedious warfare with the Sioux, which lasted approximately two hundred years.

Food

According to native tradition, the Ojibways have lived along the Great Lakes ever since the beginning of the race. At the time of their discovery they were cultivating their crops of corn, squash and other plants, drying wild berries and meat, and smoking the fish. They were making sugar and syrup from maple trees in the spring, and harvesting wild rice in the fall. Wild Rice (Mah-no-min), the Ojibway's native food, resembles wild oats and grows for the most part in lakes and rivers in Minnesota and Wisconsin. Wild rice does not ripen as other grains do. Its process is nature's own style, there is no cost for seeding nor for cultivating. Nature does the rest until time to harvest. Its ripening

Cass Lake Chippewas at work parching wild rice.

Ojibway woman boiling sap tapped from maple trees.

process starts from the top of the stock. It requires skill to knock and handle the rice from start to the finish. It requires a special kind of flail. The wild rice field should be worked with tender handling as this process in ripening requires at least three weeks. It is necessary to go over the same place several times. Wild rice is a delicate grain until it has been properly dried and parched. The process in finishing requires scientific handling.

Birch Bark Canoes

The birch bark canoes were most important in the harvesting of wild rice which grew in lakes and rivers. Therefore, transportation was necessary for the Ojibways (Chippeways). It takes skill to make a birch bark canoe, as well as skill to paddle one. The canoes are usually made for two. The frame work of canoes was made out of white cedar, or basswood, and covered by the inner layer of the birch bark trees. It was as important for the women to take part in the construction of birch canoes as the men. Their ability was needed to help select the best kind of bark, prepare the sinew, or strips of inner bark from basswood trees, to be used in sewing the layers of bark, and they also cooked pine pitch to be used for joining and sealing all cracks to keep the canoe from leaking.

Hunting

The Ojibways (Chippeways) were expert hunters and trappers and practiced true conservation, being taught to kill only as there was a need, a custom which they still follow. Their bows were made from seasoned white oak, and the arrows from different kinds of wood, tipped with colorful bird-feathers which were tied on with sinew. Sinew was most durable for bowstring, and also was used for fine thread in sewing.

84

Wigwams

The Ojibways used to live in wigwams the year round. The wigwam was made of small poles about one inch and a half in diameter, arched from about eighteen inches to twenty inches apart, thus forming a round roof. The studs or ribs were about eighteen inches apart, with crossbars about the same distance. Instead of using nails each crossbar was tied with an inner bark of basswood, which was stripped like fine cord or rope. They wet the bark and when it dried it tightened. Then the frame was covered with birch bark or flat rushes from lake shores. This type of wigwam was used long before the white man came.

Appearance

When white civilization came into the forest and lakes and rivers of the west the Ojibway Indian was a free child of nature, enjoying and accustomed to life in the open. The ways of civilization were strange to him. This new life was contrary to his nature. When the white man first came into the Great Lakes territory, he found a strong and handsome race, the copper-skinned Ojibway. The men were from five to six feet in height, from 150 to 200 pounds, of stocky build, with black, straight, shiny hair and dark brown eyes. There were no beards. The hair on the head was parted in the center making two long braids over the shoulders, hanging in front. Earrings made out of small shells, or metal, were worn only by men. The warrior's headdress was made of several eagle feathers. It was not made into a bonnet, as were the Sioux headdresses.

The Ojibway headdress is made out of deer tail, using porcupine quills to make the hair stand. Only the highest rank of warriors can wear three eagle feathers which is the maximum worn.

The women braided their hair in one or two braids, which hung down the back. The women did not wear ornaments and had no right to wear a headdress or feathers. The men wore leggings and a breechcloth, held up by a belt, with buckskin fringe hanging from the side. The buckskin apron was worn over the breechcloth. The women wore dresses of buckskin, about four inches below the knees in length, and they also wore leggings and moccasins.

Group of Minnesota Chippewa Indian Chiefs called to Washington, D. C. in 1890

Episcopal Church at White Earth. Chippewa Indian Reservation.

Equipment for making and storing maple sugar.

Articles used in gathering, processing and storing wild rice.

Men's Dance (Pow-Wow) being performed on special occasion at Cass Lake, Minnesota.

The Coming of The White Man

When the French explorers, missionaries, voyageurs and traders came to Minnesota, the Indians accepted them as friends. There were many intermarriages between the dashing voyageurs and the beautiful Indian maidens. The French were friendly and fair in their dealings with the Ojibway. They traded iron and steel weapons, trinkets and utensils for furs.

But the newcomers from the eastern shores of the United States and from England found the Indians an obstacle in settling the areas, which the Indians themselves had cleared. They pushed the Sioux and Ojibway farther and farther West. According to former treaties with other tribes the Government had to recognize the natives as owners. In order to get the land from the Indians without declaring war, the usual pattern was to call the head men or Chiefs together to make treaties. This led to more broken promises. These treaties have been called "Legal Fiction." The treaties were one-sided, because interpreters had to be used, and because of the Indian's complete unfamiliarity with the trade method of the newcomers. The Indian lacked capital, and some of the traders were dishonest. The Indian was at a great disadvantage: his native art was stifled, his ambitions almost totally wrecked. Yet withal, he still stands forth as a tradition of a noble race and he can still play the part for which nature equipped him. Even today his art has a very special appeal to people of all lands and his handicraft catches the eye of all who see it. It will indeed be unfortunate if we are unable to restore the ancient arts of the Indian crafts before they are lost entirely.

Sorrowfully and regretfully the Indian race has been reduced to a beggarly status, a condition against which the native Indian pride rebels. They did not bring about this condition themselves.

The Indian of Today

What are the living conditions of the Indian today? He has been deprived of his hereditary birthright. He has seen the beautiful land of the cloud-tinted waters acquired by the white man through broken promises. The fur-bearing animals from which he gained his livelihood have been

86

wantonly destroyed. His timber rights were taken either by enactment of law contrary to treaty agreements, or the timber was burned purposely to classify it as down and dead timber, contrary to treaty agreement; his mineral lands were used by the white man for their own gain. The Indian is even now being denied the right to fish on lakes without a license, in spite of treaties reserving the right to hunt and fish, even in the ceded territory. One of the treaties had promised that the Indian would be allowed to fish and hunt forever. The Indians understood that only the top soil of four inches was to be sold, hence the mineral rights would belong to them.

The Indian tribes were considered nations because of their distinct independent political communities. They retained their original communal rights and were possessors of the land until Congress passed a law in 1801. The land ownership of the Indians in the United States cannot be disputed or denied. The statutes of the United States and the Supreme Court rulings recognize the Indians as owners.

The Ojibway's first agreement with the United States was the treaty of January 21, 1785, at Greenville, Ohio. The territory and lands now included within the states of Ohio, Indiana, Illinois, Michigan, Wisconsin and Minnesota, were occupied by the Ojibways and other tribes of Indians. In Minnesota alone, 43,877,000 acres of land were ceded by the Ojibways by nine treaties at various times. The government agreed to pay for the land and the Indians accepted it in good faith. Unfortunately payment is still due. By virtue of treaties, orders, rulings and Acts of Congress the United

Running Elk and Morning Bird (Sioux Indians) working pipestone.

Indian Church at Pine Bend, White Earth, Reservation. Built of logs by Indians.

Beaded bandolier bag.

Sweet Grass Basket—making equipment, shown on a bulrush mat.

States of America, constituted and assumed itself to be, a guardian of the Ojibways and all Indians. The Indian is still a ward of Uncle Sam, and his property is held in trust. In Minnesota about half of the Indian (Ojibway) population are living off the reservation. Tribal funds for schools were taken. Indians do pay taxes contrary to popular belief.

The power of Congress over the Indians is found in Section 8, article I. Congress was given authority to "regulate commerce with foreign nations and among the several states and the Indian tribes"; Corpus Juris, page 329 says:

Under the constitution of the United States, Congress has the exclusive and unfettered power to regulate commerce with the Indian tribes and to extend that regulation to the individual members of the tribe, not only in the Indian Country but through the States themselves wherever the Indians who belong to any tribal organization may be found, and to say with whom and on what terms they shall deal.

The Indians and the territory which may have been specially set apart for their use are subject to the jurisdiction of the United States, and the power of Congress to deal with Indians and their property is of the most sweeping character. It may pass such laws as it sees fit, prescribing the rules governing the intercourse of the Indians one with another and with citizens of the United States, also the courts in which all controversies to which an Indian may be part shall be submitted. It has likewise power to punish all offences committed against or by Indians within their reservation.

The Power of Congress is superior and paramount to the authority of State whose limits are Indian tribes. Such power does not cease when the Indians become citizens of the United States, when they become electors under State laws or when their lands are alloted in severalty.

The Indians have no constitutional rights; but they pay taxes; they are governed by the legislative and executive departments of the Government. The Indian has no appeal and must ask Congress even to go to court.

The framers of the Constitution never contemplated that Congress would presume to legislate for the Indian tribes, any more than it would for foreign powers; neither foreign nations nor Indian tribes were included in Sec. 2, article III of the Constitution which confers judicial jurisdiction on the Supreme Court. Because of this, the Supreme Court has no authority over any legislation which Congress may enact concerning the Indian tribes. No Congress is bound by the action of a prior Congress. The good intention of one Congress can be utterly destroyed by a subsequent Congress.

From the sunny side of the problem, some progress was registered by the 83d congress. The Indians are thankful for public law 568, transferring all Indian hospitals to the United States Public Health Service, and for public law 280, conferring jurisdiction on the several States with respect to criminal offenses and civil actions committed on Indian reservations.

There is still much to be done to solve the Indian problem. After the Federal Government has settled its obligations to the Indians, then Minnesota's solution would be to have her own state program, satisfactory to the Ojibways' needs. We know our own peculiar circumstances in our state, and can work with the state representatives in Washington.

All the Indian wants is an equal chance to live as a human being. Pay the Indian the treaty obligations, give him his rightful heirship for the land, timber and mineral rights which he has coming to him by written agreements for years, loosen the shackles that bind him from progress, show him the path of a full citizenship and he'll stand and walk like other men.

Living conditions on the reservations are pitiful. Most of the Indians live in tar paper shacks where they cook, eat and sleep in one room for a family of from four to ten. The water is from impure water holes; there is no plumbing. Now that the Public Health Service has taken charge, they report that these conditions have been responsible for the Indians' poor health.

Many of the Indians are on public relief, because their income is so small from insufficient work on the reservation. Although there are good state schools available for them, the little money the Indians earn cannot adequately clothe school children, so they will feel accepted, especially when they go into the towns to the high schools.

Those who have ventured away from the reservation, (they are many living in cities in all parts of the United States) have found much better living conditions. The Indians who have left the reservations have proved that, given a chance, they can make an adequate living, keep their homes up in excellent condition, live happy and useful lives as American citizens. The working conditions in the cities for the Indian are gradually improving, but the Indian lacks education and training in skills. He needs a special trade, in many cases. In the cities, Indians are employed in a good many different capacities—as salespeople, nurses, doctors, lawyers, merchants, judges, teachers, and business men, supervisors in various trades and manufacturing establishments. This seems to point out that, off the reservations, given the education, there is no height an Indian cannot reach. The future holds great promise. The problems are not insurmountable. This great State of Minnesota, a true melting-pot of all races, can fulfill the Declaration of Independence which says:

We hold these truths to be self-evident, that all men are created equal, that they are endowed by their Creator with certain unalienable rights, that among these are life, liberty, and the pursuit of happiness.

CHAPTER FOUR

By Minnesota Waters

"The Kensington Runestone"

By GRACE LEE NUTE

Waterways have played a conspicuous role in Minnesota history. Without them it is unlikely that a region so deep in the heart of the North American continent could have been visited by Europeans as early as the opening years of the seventeenth century. Since it is believed by some persons that, even earlier than that century, Europeans from the Scandinavian countries were here and left their record chiseled on the so-called Kensington Runestone, we must suppose that they are believed to have reached the region by water. There was no other avenue of approach at that time.

Indeed, it was not until roads and railroads were built that explorers, fur traders, missionaries, and adventurers could reach the area now known as Minnesota by any other means of transportation. Up the Mississippi and through the Great Lakes and streams entering those huge inland seas came the men who opened the Minnesota country to trade, Christianity, and general civilization. They were intrepid souls, who deserve all the acclaim that later generations have given them.

The first European visitors of whom we have reasonably exact information appear to have been Etienne Brulé and another Frenchman named Grenoble, companions of Jesuit missionaries on the lower Great Lakes. These two men are believed to have ventured into Lake Superior about the year 1618. Our sources of information about them are vague, but one permanent reminder of their journey may well be the Brulé River in northwestern Wisconsin close to the Minnesota border. This stream became one of the major waterways leading into the Minnesota country in the seventeenth and eighteenth centuries by way of the St. Croix River, and may conceivably have been used by Brulé on his exploration voyage. It was customary among French explorers to attach their own names to streams and lakes of importance as soon as they were discovered. Early French maps show the Brulé River, just as they also show other waterways named for the first men to use them: the Groseilliers (Gooseberry), St. Louis, St. Pierre, and St. Croix rivers and Lake Pepin, among others.

Next along our fluid highways, as far as extant records of Minnesota explorations are informative, came Médard Chouart, Sieur des Groseilliers, and his youthful brother-in-law, Pierre Esprit Radisson. Unlike Brulé they left written accounts of their trips, some of which have been published in the *Voyages of Peter Esprit Radisson, Being An Account of His Travels and Experiences Among the North American Indians, From 1652 to 1684.* This book tells, among other exploits of the two men, of two trips by Des Groseilliers and one by Radisson into the general region of Lake Superior, and constitutes our earliest available, eye-witness account of our countryside.

The explorations of these two adventurous Frenchmen resulted in a great influx of fur traders and explorers into the Minnesota country after 1660, the year in which the brothers-in-law returned to Quebec and told their countrymen what they had seen and heard, and showed the great

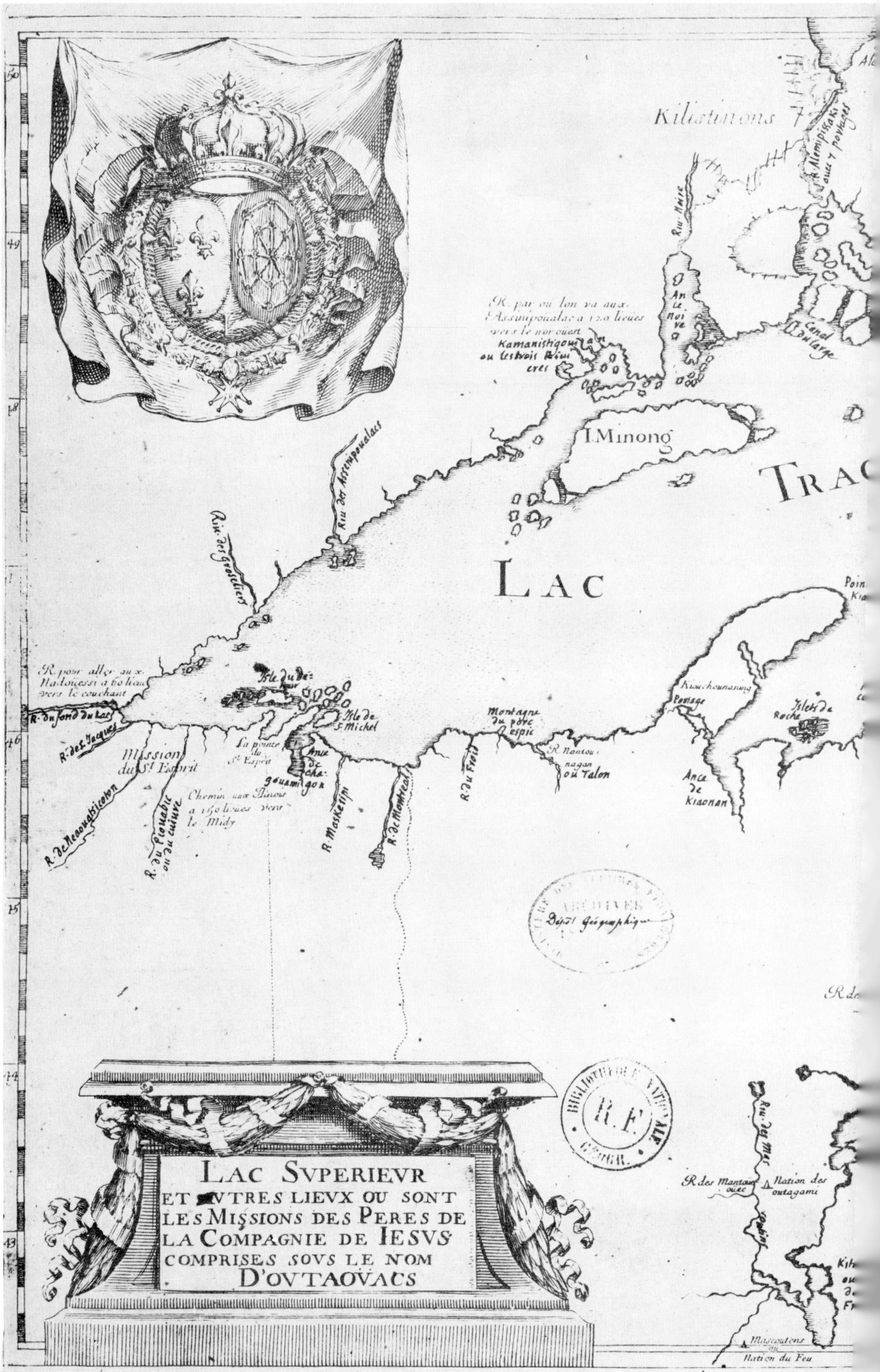

Kilistinons

R. par ou lon va aux
Assinipoualac a 120. lieües
vers le nor ouest
Kamanistigoua
ou les trois Riui
eres

I. Minong

TRAC

LAC

R. pour aller aux
Nadouessi a 60. lieües
vers le couchant

R. du fond du lac

R. des Jacques

MISSION
du St Esprit

R. de Nesouakitchon

R. du Piouabic
ou du cuiure

Isle du Rei

La pointe
du St Esprit

Chemin aux Ilinois
a 150. lieües vers
le Midy

Isle de S. Michel

Anse
de cha.
goüamigon

R. Masketyn

R. de Montreal

R. du Froit

Montagne
du perc
d'espic

R. Nantou
nagan
ou Talon

Kiouchonaning
Portage

Anse
de
Kiaonan

Islets de
Roche

ARCHIVES
Dépôt Géographique

BIBLIOTHEQUE NATIONALE
R.F.

R. des Mantou
oüec

Nation des
outagami

LAC SVPERIEVR
ET AVTRES LIEVX OV SONT
LES MISSIONS DES PERES DE
LA COMPAGNIE DE IESVS
COMPRISES SOVS LE NOM
D'OVTAOVACS

Mascoutens
ou
Nation du Feu

90

Jesuit Map of Lake Superior, 1670.

47.6 x 35.8
MS. additions par D'Anville

Gens des Terres

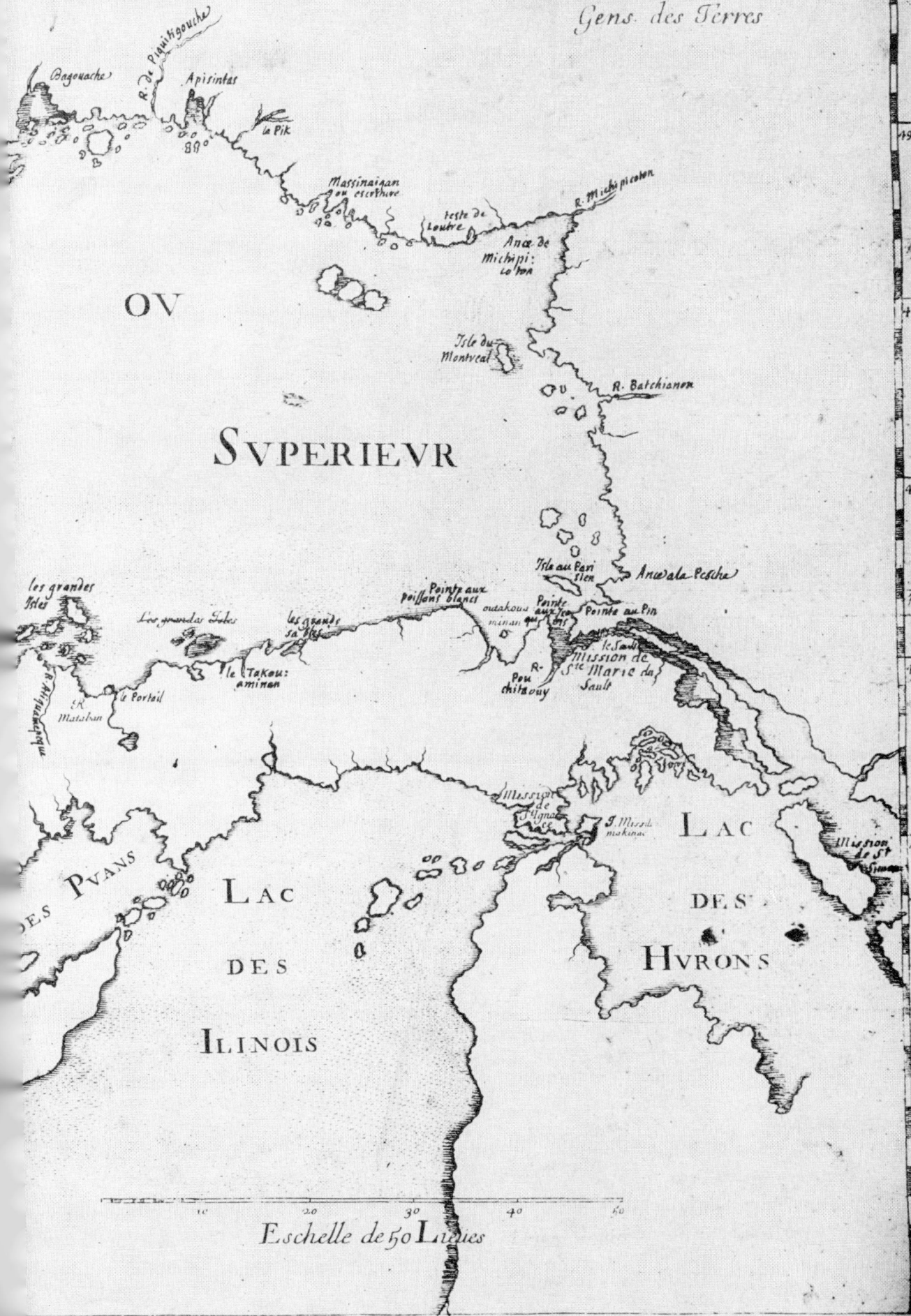

Gens des Terres

Bagouache
R. de Piquitigouche
Apisintas
la Pik

Massinaïgan
ou escriture
teste de
Loutre
R. Michipicoten
Ana de
Michipi:
coton

OV

Isle du
Montreal

SVPERIEVR

V.
R. Batchianon

Isle au Pari
sien
Anwala Pesche

les grandes
Isles

Pointe aux
poisson blanc

Les grandes Isles

les grands
sa Isle

outakous
minan
Pointe
aux Ico
ons
Pointe au Pin

le Takou:
aminan

le Portail

R.
Pou
chitaouy
le Sault
Mission de
Ste Marie du
Sault

R. Matabau

R. Alimabanika

Mission
de
St Ignace
I. Missili
makinac

LAC

DES PVANS

LAC

DES

DES

HVRONS

Mission
de St

ILINOIS

Eschelle de 50 Lieues
10   20   30   40   50

91

piles of beaver skins they had obtained in the far West of that day. Other results were the establishment of a Catholic mission near the site of Ashland, Wisconsin, the circumnavigating and charting of Lake Superior, the naming of the Mississippi River (after an Indian word) by the missionary, Claude Allouez, and the establishment and chartering of the Hudson's Bay Company in 1670.

In addition, the advice of the two explorers was heeded as to the best route into the interior of North America, which they insisted was through Hudson Bay. Thereafter—except for some years between 1682 and 1713—the Hudson's Bay Company monopolized the shorter, cheaper, and time-saving route. Consequently, the French from Canada had small choice but to use the old canoe route through the Great Lakes. This meant that they also had to develop a superb class of voyageurs, or canoemen, who became the mainstay of the French fur trade. Without these hardy, diligent, resourceful, and meek subordinates the explorers and fur traders of Canada could not have competed successfully with their rivals, the English traders using the sailing-vessel route into Hudson Bay.

For about a century, however, the English did not establish posts in the interior, but induced the Indians over a very large part of inland North America to take their furs to Hudson's Bay Company forts on the shores of Hudson Bay. It was only after the Conquest of Canada by the British in the last of the French and Indian wars, that the London corporation encountered such stiff competition from Canadians of their own nationality, that they were forced to establish posts in the interior. The most aggressive of these rivals formed themselves into the North West Company, which was the heir, so to speak, of the French traders' route up the Ottawa River, through Lake Huron and Lake Superior, over the Grand Portage, along the waterways now forming the boundary between Minnesota and Ontario, down the Winnipeg River into Lake Winnipeg, and west across the continent by means of the Saskatchewan, Assiniboine, and other streams. This long and difficult transportation line has come to be called the Voyageur's Highway.

The French were almost incredibly active and hardy in their western trade and explorations as long as New France existed, that is, until 1763. In the century and more that spanned this period, some of the world's best known explorers set foot on Minnesota soil or reached the general region of our state. One has only to mention the names of La Salle, Hennepin, Jolliet, and Duluth to confirm that statement.

Besides sending to the Sioux country in 1680 the expedition of which Father Hennepin was a member, La Salle is thought by some very able historians to have been on Lake Superior even earlier. As for Jolliet, modern scholarship has restored him to his proper and very high place in the annals of North American discoveries. It used to be thought that a Jesuit priest, Father Jacques Marquette, accompanied him on his trip in 1673-4, when he explored the middle reaches of the Mississippi River. Today's most advanced scholarship rejects the idea that the priest, if priest he really was (there is considerable question about this), should share honors with Jolliet.

Who accompanied Jolliet is still not clear, but from the time of his expedition, the Fox-Wisconsin river route between Lake Michigan and the Mississippi became one of the chief avenues of approach to the Minnesota country. At the junction of the Wisconsin and the Mississippi, as well as south along the Father of Waters, Frenchmen began to settle. One of those early Illinois pioneers, Michel Accault, was the leader of the so-called Hennepin expedition, which La Salle sent up the Mississippi in 1680.

Just how much credit for that expedition should go to Hennepin is a question. In one of his last published books the Recollect grey robe makes clear that he knew Des Groseilliers and had conversed with him about the Sioux country of the Upper Mississippi. Whether the friar convinced La Salle of the wisdom of trying to explore that area, or whether La Salle already knew something of the region from personal experience, we may never know. In any event, the decision was made to send an expedition up the great river, and within three years an account of what was seen and what happened on that journey appeared in Paris as a thick little book in mottled boards, printed exqui-

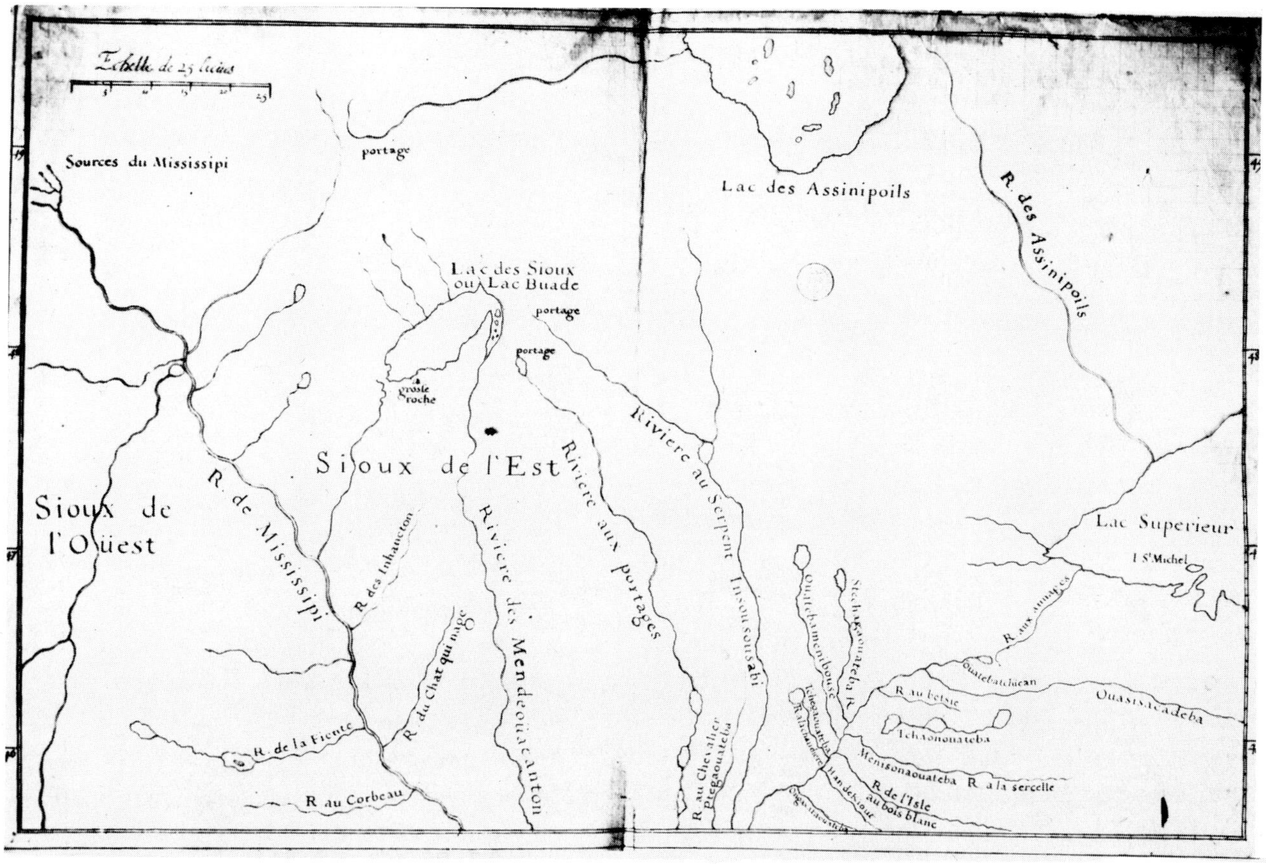

Le Sueur's Map. About 1702.

near Mille Lacs Lake. On this map Sioux names for certain rivers are given, and words like Yankton and Mdewakanton appear, designating the habitat of those Indians. Snake River is so named in both French and Sioux, but the Wisconsin branches of the St. Croix are mainly designated only by Indian words. The "Sources of the Mississippi" are shown relatively correctly.

The conjectured author of this map, Pierre Le Sueur, must have drawn it about 1700, though he had been in the Minnesota country for some years prior to that time. He is best known for his associations with Nicholas Perrot and the Sioux of the West, but his first contacts with Minnesota Indians were in the territory of the Sioux of the East, that is, between the St. Croix and the Mississippi rivers.

He seems to have reached the Upper Mississippi with Perrot in 1685 by way of Jolliet's old route, the Fox-Wisconsin canoe waterway. Perrot established Fort St. Antoine—probably the following year—on the Wisconsin side of Lake Pepin, and appears to have become acquainted with a

large part of the territory of the Sioux on the Upper Mississippi. He is generally credited with having been one of the earliert traders on Lake Superior and with having established the first trading post on Minnesota soil, variously called Fort Bonsecours, Fort Le Sueur, and Fort Perrot. According to a map of 1700, it stood just above the entrance of Lake Pepin.

In 1689 Perrot took formal possession of the Upper Mississippi for the French king in a colorful ceremony at Fort St. Antoine, at which Le Sueur was also present. In the document there read and then sent to France, Perrot mentioned that he had just visited the region about the mouth of the St. Croix and the St. Peter (now the Minnesota) rivers, and listed some of the Sioux of the area by tribal names. According to some historians, the St. Peter River was named for Le Sueur, who may have been on it as early as 1682.

In 1693 Le Sueur built a post on Madeline Island on the south shore of Lake Superior not far from the mouth of the Brulé River. Between his two posts he maintained an important trade route via

97

the Brulé-St. Croix waterway. In 1700 he established an important post on the St. Peter River not far from the mouth of the Blue Earth River, approximately the site of the city of Mankato. To reach it he came up the Mississippi from the Gulf of Mexico in a sailing vessel, ostensibly to locate a copper mine on the St. Peter River. As fur traders had just been prohibited by royal order from going into the fur country, it is supposed that Le Sueur made his copper venture an excuse for getting back to his old haunts. Fort L'Huillier, as this new post on the St. Peter was named, lasted only a few years, but long enough for one of Le Sueur's men, named Alexandre Turpin, to get to the source of the St. Peter River from it.

Thus by 1700, or thereabout, Minnesota's waters had been explored from north to south and from east to west. Besides the forts on Lake Pepin, the Mississippi, and the fully explored St. Peter River, Duluth had established a post at the mouth of the Kaministiquia River and one on Lake Nipigon, a man named De Noyons is reported to have journeyed westward from Lake Superior to Lake of the Woods and beyond, and there was an establishment on Madeline Island in Lake Superior.

Meantime the first two known explorers on Minnesota soil, Radisson and Des Groseilliers, had spent considerable time in Hudson Bay, first for the Hudson's Bay Company, then for the French. In 1682 their activities there precipitated a minor war between English and French subjects, which continued until King William's War between France and England commenced in 1689. Then it was merged in that conflict, which persisted until the Peace of Ryswick in 1697. By the treaty that ended the war, the French gained control of most of Hudson Bay and its posts and kept them until the end of Queen Anne's War (1702-1713). As a result of the treaty ending that conflict, the entire picture changed.

This Treaty of Utrecht in 1713 gave back the Bay to the English. Therefore, the French had to return to their old, long, tedious, and expensive canoe route along Minnesota's present northern boundary waters. In 1717 a Frenchman prominent in the early French capture of Hudson's Bay Company posts during the wars, Zacherie Robutel,

Sieur de la Noue, was ordered to establish a post at the outlet of Rainy Lake. Recently investigated records of the Hudson's Bay Company report Frenchmen on that lake just before 1720. From that time until the close of the French regime in North America there was also a French garrison on western Lake Superior.

La Noue and his successors at the Kaministiquia post, where Fort William, Ontario, now stands, undoubtedly did a considerable amount of exploring in the general area of northeastern Minnesota, but it is not until La Vérendrye's time that anything definite is learned of the terrain west of Lake Superior. In 1726 Pierre Gaultier de Varennes, Sieur de la Vérendrye, a trader on Lake Nipigon, learned from trading Indians of a route to the Sea of the West that was not the Kaministiquia route of earlier explorers. Thinking the sea was much closer to Lake Superior than it actually was, he got permission to establish forts on that water route which began at the Grand Portage and joined the Kaministiquia route at Lac La Croix. Grand Portage was a carrying place of some eight miles, which avoided waterfalls and other obstructions in the last stretch of the Pigeon River before it empties into Lake Superior some forty miles southwest of the Kaministiquia fort. Using that route in 1731 some of La Vérendrye's men established Fort St. Pierre at the outlet of Rainy Lake. The next year

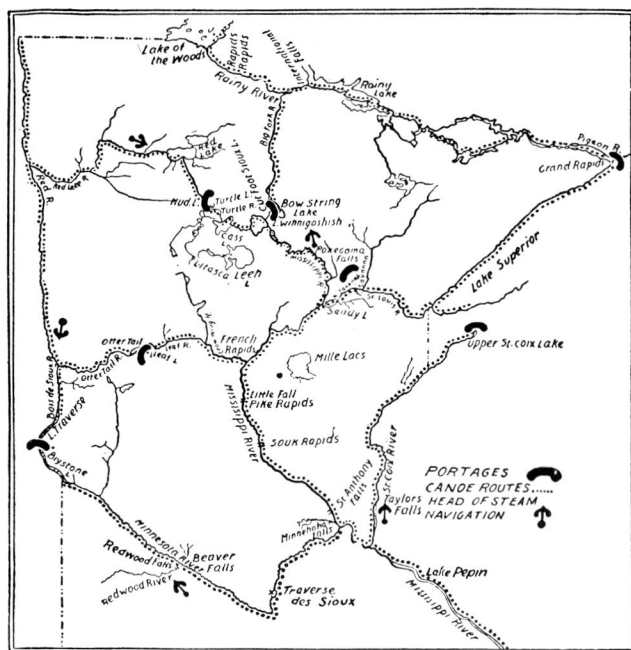

Water routes of Minnesota according to Edward Robinson's "Early Economic Conditions" and "The Development of Agriculture in Minnesota."

La Vérendrye and his men went on to the Lake of the Woods. There they built Fort St. Charles on an island in the area known today as the Northwest Angle, the northernmost piece of ground in Minnesota and the United States.

In preparation for the establishment of this post among the Cree and Assiniboin Indians—for the Chippewa, or Ojibway Indians had not yet entered the Minnesota country from their "home" on Madeline Island on the south shore of Lake Superior—the French government had already provided a protection in the shape of a post on the west side of Lake Pepin among the Sioux. This was established in 1727 as Fort Beauharnois, probably not far from the site of Frontenac, Minnesota. Fox Indians in the Wisconsin and Illinois country were waging war on French traders and on Indian allies of the French and were trying to win the Sioux to an alliance against the white men.

In part, Fort Beauharnois fulfilled its mission, but only in part; for Sioux Indians in 1736 ambushed a party from Fort St. Charles on its way to Lake Superior, killed all twenty-one members of the group, including a La Vérendrye son and a Jesuit missionary, and soon thereafter showed the grisly trophies of their deed to the garrison at Fort Beauharnois. The commandant of that fort, realizing that the Sioux could no longer be counted upon as friends, abandoned the post in 1737.

La Vérendrye, however, continued to maintain his station on Lake of the Woods and the other forts that he built from time to time on the Rainy, Winnipeg, Red, and Assiniboine rivers and neighboring waterways. He even went on an exploring expedition to the Mandans of the Upper Missouri in 1738; and he sent out an expedition, which included two of his sons, on the western plains in 1742-3. Just where they went is uncertain, except that we know that in the spring of 1743 they must have been near the site of Pierre, South Dakota. There in 1913 one of the inscribed lead plates deposited by the La Vérendrye party was found and recognized. Whether the explorers included any of the Minnesota country in their journeying is unknown but quite possible. At all events, the area of exploration had now passed beyond Lake of the Woods and the Red River of the North, and the Minnesota stage was being set for the final act of the French drama, that is, occupation.

This was accomplished — insofar as it was achieved by the French — by another father - son team, the Marins. In 1729 the elder Marin (Paul de la Margue) was sent to the Upper Mississippi to complete the subjugation of the western tribes at the close of one of the Fox Wars. In 1749 his son, Joseph, was sent to Madeline Island to make peace among the Chippewa and other tribes of that region. Two years later Joseph was told to relieve his father on the Upper Mississippi, in order "to make discoveries among the nations yet unknown." Later he reported that "during two years" he did so, "covering on foot more than two thousand leagues, sometimes in snow." He listed among the tribes that he "conquered" the Foxes, Sauk, Winnebagoes, Sioux of the Lakes, Sioux of the Prairies, the Menominee, and the Illinois.

Meantime, in 1750, his father built a post in the Sioux country, probably the one whose remains were found in 1885 near the site of Frontenac and old Fort Beauharnois. From a diary kept by his son during the winter of 1753-4, after he had succeeded his father on the Upper Mississippi, it is possible to watch the younger Marin building several other posts. To them and to his father's post he gave such names as Fort Duquesne (near the site of Brainerd), Fort La Jonquière (near the site of Frontenac), and Fort Vaudreuil (just below the mouth of the Wisconsin River, on the Iowa side of the Mississippi). There were also lesser posts of which little is known. One seems to have been on the St. Croix River and another near the junction of the St. Peter and the Mississippi, close to or on the site of the Twin Cities.

During the winter of 1753-54 Marin's men came into competition with the youngest La Vérendrye, who, after his father's death in 1749, had been assigned the post on Madeline Island. Both Marin and Louis Joseph La Vérendrye claimed the right to trade with the Indians of the Upper Mississippi and in the valley of the St. Croix. For the moment La Vérendrye seems to have gained the upper hand. Marin's diary shows that his own efforts kept peace between the Sioux and La Vérendrye's invading Chippewa, but it also makes clear that only a temporary truce was effected. Soon the Chippewa advanced into the northern Minnesota country, driving the Sioux before them with French guns and ammunition.

In recounting the struggle with La Vérendrye in his diary and letters, Marin reveals much of Indian life, personalities, habitat, and culture in the Minnesota country. Then the curtain goes down on the French regime in the Minnesota country, as the Seven Years' War drained all possible French traders, including both Marin and La Vérendrye, into the armies struggling against British encroachment in the Ohio country and throughout the Great Lakes—St. Lawrence region.

Even before peace had been made with Great Britain, traders of the conquering empire began to advance through the Great Lakes and beyond. During the long period of negotiations leading up to the Treaty of Paris in 1763, which turned Canada over to Great Britain, several Canadian, British, and colonial traders got into the Minnesota country. The first adventurer inland from Lake Superior may have been James Finlay, or, more likely, Thomas Corry. Whoever he was, Benjamin and Joseph Frobisher, in a letter to the governor of Canada, October 4, 1784, state that he went from Michillimackinac in 1765 and that his canoes were plundered at Rainy Lake by the Indians, who would not let him and his men proceed farther. François Le Blanc, Maurice Blondeau, and others of whom we know little must also have reached their posts in the Saskatchewan country by way of northern Minnesota waterways at this time. Then came Alexander Henry the Elder.

Since Henry wrote his reminiscences later, we are able to watch him and his associates overspread the West, as the French regime became more or less a dim memory after 1760. Yet French traders at first accompanied most of the English traders, for the latter had slight knowledge of the countryside, its inhabitants, or the Indian languages. At first Henry's activities in the Minnesota countryside were confined pretty largely to Lake Superior. He probably did not penetrate beyond Grand Portage on Lake Superior until the period of the American Revolution. Meantime Grand Portage had been occupied as a rendezvous of traders. Ground for a

fort had been cleared and an English post had been established there about 1768.

The next person in the Minnesota country of whom we know was of outstanding importance, for he left behind him a published book telling a vast amount about the area as he saw it in 1766 and 1767. This was Jonathan Carver, a New Englander who had seen service in the French and Indian war that ended in 1763. Besides his book, published in his lifetime, he left behind him—buried in archives in London, where they were found and copied some thirty-five years ago—three original diaries telling of his journeying in the Minnesota country. They have never been published.

Portrait of Jonathan Carver.

Carver's book (1778) was the first one in English to give an account of the Minnesota country from personal experience. Most of his first winter was spent in the valley of the St. Peter River. In the spring he held a conference with certain Sioux bands in a cave on the site of St. Paul, which is called to this day Carver's Cave. In an edition of his book that appeared after his death, a land transaction with certain Sioux chiefs in the cave was described and a document was produced, on which many later claims to ownership of a vast territory in Minnesota and Wisconsin were based. The document has been proved a forgery and the claim has been disallowed by Congress, on the principle that the Royal Proclamation of 1763 prohibiting such land transactions west of the Appalachian Mountains was in effect in Carver's time. There is no reference to the land transaction in the original diaries, and it is believed that Carver knew nothing about the claim.

Carver's book became very popular and appeared in many editions and languages. It gives no hint, however, as his diaries do, that he was not the head but merely the draftsman, of an expedition sent out from Michillimackinac by Robert Rogers. This founder of the famed Rogers Rangers of New Hampshire in the Seven Years' War had been made commandant at Fort Michillimackinac immediately after Pontiac's uprising.

Rogers had plans to find the mouth of the "Oregon River" by way of the Upper Mississippi and streams farther northwest, but he made some unwise decisions as head of an army post in Indian country and was court-martialed. Consequently, the men of his expedition got no farther than Grand Portage, where they were to find supplies from Michillimackinac. They advanced by way of the Upper Mississippi and the valley of the St. Croix River, and reached the post on Lake Superior only to find no supplies from Rogers' post, so they turned back.

Immediately after Carver's visit in the Minnesota country, a still more colorful character put in an appearance in the valley of the St. Peter. This was an illiterate but very intelligent Connecticut Yankee, Peter Pond, whose reminiscences were rescued dramatically from a descendant's kitchen stove at a much later time. They tell us of two winters spent by Pond in the valley of the St. Peter, 1773-4 and 1774-5, among several bands of Sioux, one of whom came from the vast plains beyond and had never traded before with white men. Pond's reminiscences are as unique as his personality, and just as forceful. His spelling is highly phonetic, as can be seen from the following excerpt describing the Minnesota Valley: "The intervale of the river St. Peter is exsalant and sum good timber—the intervels are high and the soile thin and lite. The river is destatute of fish but the wood and meadows abundans of annamels Sum turkeas, buffeloes are verey plenty, the read and moose deare are plentey hear, espeasaley the former. I have seen fortey kild in one day by surrounding a drove on a low spot by the river side in the winter season. Raccoons are verey large. No snakes but small ones which are not pisenes. Wolves are plentey—thay follow the buffeloes and often de-

The Falls of St. Anthony in the River Mississippi. From Carver's Travels.

stroy thare young and olde ones. The natives near the mouth of the river rase plenty of corn for thare one concumtion."

Pond did not return to the Minnesota country in 1775, but went to the north and became one of the great names in Canadian Northwest history, as the maker of maps of international importance, the explorer of the Athabasca and Mackenzie River region, and one of the principal founders of the North West Company, the chief rival of the Hudson's Bay Company.

That group of Montreal outfitters and traders had vastly more to do with the exploration and development of the Minnesota country than did the century-old corporation founded by Radisson and Des Groseilliers. It came into gradual being between 1768 and 1800 and was at the peak of its success about 1790. Its chief station in 1793 was at Grand Portage, where it had sixteen buildings within a stockade, a canoe yard, a sailing vessel on Lake Superior, and other facilities.

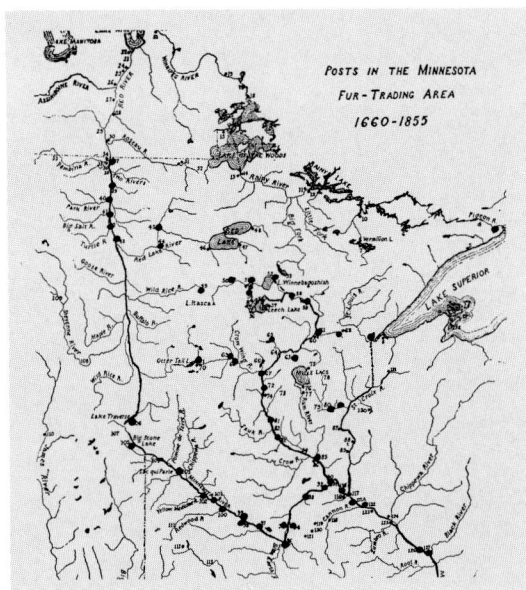

POSTS IN THE MINNESOTA
FUR-TRADING AREA
1660-1855

Drawn by Warren Upham.

On Minnesota soil were scores of its lesser posts: Fond du Lac, Lake Vermilion, Sandy Lake, Red Lake and River, Lake of the Woods, the Red River of the North, Lac Qui Parle on the St. Peter River, Mendota at the mouth of the St. Peter, several forts in the valley of the St. Croix, and many other stations. Some of its outstanding traders besides Pond were the Frobisher brothers, James

McGill, Charles Paterson, Jean Baptiste Cadotte, Alexander Henry the Younger, Michel Curot, Joseph Renville, Jacques Porlier, Hugh McGillis, Jean Baptiste Perrault, and many others. There is hardly a region of any size in Minnesota that does not bear evidence of the presence of North West Company traders at some time between 1768 and 1821, when the company was absorbed by the Hudson's Bay Company. Remains of posts, inscriptions on cliffs, names of topographic interest (Paterson's Rapids on the Minnesota River, for instance), nuclei of cities or villages (Mendota, St. Paul, Crow Wing, Fond du Lac, International Falls, Grand Portage, etc.) all testify to the influence of this company's traders on Minnesota history. In addition, they left important records, such as letters, diaries, account books, reminiscences, and personal narratives.

This company also brought to its highest usefulness and importance the class of men known in the fur trade as voyageurs. These were the singing, bright-sashed, red-capped canoemen, who every summer brought to Grand Portage enormous birchbark canoes laden with trade goods from Montreal or furs from inland posts. Canadian French in origin and speaking little if any English, the voyageurs gave a special vocabulary to their English, Scotch, and American superiors, or *bourgeois.* Their language prevailed in the North West Company's posts dotting the Minnesota landscape. They also established certain customs, some of which persist to this day in Minnesota canoeing. They had their own speech, their own voyaging and fort customs, and their own type of dress.

After reaching Grand Portage, some voyageurs went to winter in the fur country. They became known as "winterers" *(hivernants),* whereas their companions who returned to Montreal the same season were known as "pork-eaters" *(mangeurs du lard).* Those who passed over the height of land beyond Lake Superior en route to distant posts became "Northwesters," the élite of the class. They were entitled to wear plumes in their hats and to initiate novices in the so-called baptism ceremony at the height of land. It was a landlubber version of the well-known Neptune ceremony of baptism on ships crossing the tropics.

Three oils by Frances Hopkins. Courtesy Public Archives of Canada.

Top: "Camping on Lake Superior."

Middle: Canoe Trip on Lake Superior.

Bottom Left: "Mending a Canoe."

Bottom Right: Portaging Scene by C. Bertsch.

Hundreds of these voyageurs passed yearly into or through the Minnesota country or along its borders during fur-trade days. A converging of travel routes between Grand Portage and Lake Winnipeg into a bottleneck of canoe waters meant that nearly all *bourgeois*, clerks, and voyageurs for posts as far distant as the Columbia River and Lake Athabasca, used Minnesota waters in traveling to their stations. Therefore, Grand Portage was inland headquarters of great significance in the fur trade.

At that place occurred a complete change in food supplies and travel facilities. Pemmican— dried, pressed buffalo meat and grease—was obtained by brigades of canoes to take the place of their provisions, exhausted between Montreal and Grand Portage: dried whole peas and fat between Montreal and Michillimackinac; and hulled corn between Michillimackinac and Grand Portage. Buffalo herds in the plains adjacent to a certain North West Company post on the Assiniboine River, west of the site of Winnipeg, provided the buffalo-hide bags of pemmican stored at Grand Portage. These were furnished to brigades of canoes traveling still farther west and southwest, and were stowed away in canoes a little more than half as big as the forty-foot Montreal canoes. These so-called North canoes were supplied by the canoe yard at Grand Portage.

The voyageurs, their speech for the most part, their posts, and their customs have vanished, but their songs remain. They were a part of the repertoire of old Loire Valley folk songs and *chansons* of *trouvères* of the Middle Ages brought to Canadian shores before 1680 by the men and women who settled New France and became known as *habitants*. Cherished through the century that has elapsed since the fur trade waned and disappeared, these haunting melodies can still be heard, frequently in French Canada, occasionally in Minnesota among descendants of the voyageurs. Wherever the voyageur passed or lived, his songs rang out: in summer from birchbark canoes as he glided over lakes and rivers; in winter from his log fort or his dog team expeditions, while tramping the snow-covered countryside on snowshoes as he guided his huskies from trading post to trading post or from Indian wigwam to Indian wigwam.

LA ROSE BLANCHE

Par un ma-tin je me suis le-vé
Dans mon jar-din je m'en suis all-é

Par un ma-tin je me suis le-vé, Plus
Dans mon jar-din je m'en suis all-é Cueil-

ma-tin que ma tan-te Plus
-lip la po-se blan-che Cueil-

ma-tin que ma tan-te
lip la po-se blan-che

A favorite Voyageur Song about a white rose.

One other remnant of this vanished era in Minnesota history can be seen occasionally. This is the voyageur's sash. No proper voyageur ever was seen without a yards-long sash *(ceinture fléchée)* which was his badge of office, so to speak. Braided

Voyageur Sashes from Quebec. Courtesy Marius Barbeau and National Museum of Canada.

in a special manner at L'Orignal near Montreal by Norman women practicing a household industry inherited from their Norse ancestors, this sash was worn in place of a belt for the voyageur's trousers or his blanket coat *(capote)*. The sash was worn properly when wound several times around the waist and tied on the left side, so that its long, bright fringes fell gracefully to the knees or below.

When the North West Company reached the peak of its activities about 1790, it competed so successfully with the Hudson's Bay Company, that the London corporation was obliged to abandon its century-old practice of having the Indians take their pelts to posts on Hudson Bay. About the time of the American Revolution the older company began to build posts in the interior, and by 1793 it was establishing forts on Lake Superior and along Minnesota's border waters, especially at the outlet of Rainy Lake, where Fort Frances is today, and along the north shore of Lake Superior. Therefore, it can be seen that Hudson's Bay Company posts on Minnesota soil did not appear until late in the development of the fur trade of our region. were never numerous, and were, in general, relatively insignificant. When one hears of remains of "Hudson's Bay posts" being found, one can safely assume in most instances, that they were either North West Company or American Fur Company forts.

The American company came into being even later than the North West Company, and unlike that "gentlemen's agreement," was an incorporated entity like the Hudson's Bay Company. John Jacob Astor incorporated it in 1808 under New York law for twenty-five years. At the end of its term, one of its departments or branches took the name in 1834, and confined its attention to a much smaller area than the parent organization had monopolized, namely, the region of the Upper Great Lakes and the Upper Mississippi River. It lasted for less than a decade before going into bankruptcy.

After 1816 an act of Congress made it illegal for foreign fur traders to operate within the United States, ending a privilege permitted by Jay's Treaty with Great Britain in 1794. Before the close of the War of 1812, therefore, North West Company traders had things pretty much their own way in the Minnesota country, and the American Fur Company made little headway. The act of 1816, a rejuvenated Hudson's Bay Company, extermination of the beaver, and other factors spelled doom for the North West Company after 1815, and in 1821 it passed out of existence through absorption by the Hudson's Bay Company. For half a century it had been the most important single influence in the Minnesota country. Thereafter for a generation the American Fur Company monopolized the Minnesota fur trade.

Sibley House, Mendota.

One of the posts that became important in this period was the St. Peter's, or Mendota establishment, at the junction of the Mississippi and the St. Peter rivers. After a long period of incumbency there, Alexis Bailly left in 1834 and a promising young man, Henry Hastings Sibley, took charge of the Sioux trade. He was to remain there, a figure of increasing importance, as the fur trade ended and settlement began. In 1858 he became the first governor of the state of Minnesota. His stone house at Mendota remains as the earliest surviving residence in Minnesota, maintained by the D.A.R.

During the British regime in the Minnesota country little formal exploration occurred other than that of the two colonials, Carver and Pond. It was not until the opening years of the nineteenth century that exploratory expeditions occurred once more. The first of these was a military operation under the command of Lieutenant Zebulon Montgomery Pike, which traveled up the Mississippi and located sites for military posts. One of these was occupied fifteen years later by Fort St. Anthony, renamed Fort Snelling in the early 1820's. Pike's main party spent the winter near the Little Falls on the Upper Mississippi, while he and a picked company of men advanced to the North West Company forts at Sandy Lake and Leech Lake. A British flag flying over the latter post was shot down and the Stars and Stripes run up, but we may be sure that the American flag did not remain aloft long after Pike began his return journey. Until 1816, as already related, North West Company men had control of the fur trade throughout the Minnesota country.

Round Tower, Fort Snelling.

Hexagonal Tower, Fort Snelling.

So much so, in fact, that their highhanded treatment of Hudson's Bay Company traders and the latters' recriminatory deeds of violence became the occasion for another United States military expedition and the actual establishment of a garrisoned fort on one of the sites chosen by Pike. After Hudson's Bay Company men seized the Fond du Lac fort of the North West Company in retaliation for some acts of violence along border waters and across the northern Minnesota country, Astor recommended to the American government that garrisoned forts be established to control the situation. As a result, Major Stephen H. Long was sent to the Upper Mississippi in 1817 to make prepara-

tions for establishing one or more of them, and in 1819 his recommendations were carried out by the establishment of Fort St. Anthony.

Six years after his first trip, Long was sent again to the Minnesota country with a military expedition. In the meantime a treaty had been arranged between Great Britain and the United States which ended the uncertainty, hitherto prevalent, as to the exact location of the boundary line between the Lake of the Woods and the crest of the Rocky Mountains. By the so-called Convention of 1818 this was recognized by both countries to be the forty-ninth parallel. Long was sent to observe where that line lay in the Red River Valley and eastward, and to determine whether British subjects from Lord Selkirk's settlements were infringing on American territory. Those settlements had been made by Thomas, Fifth Earl of Selkirk—one of the largest shareholders in the Hudson's Bay Company—at the outbreak of the War of 1812, and in time were to become Winnipeg, St. Boniface, Pembina (N. D.), and neighboring places.

Long had as a companion on the outward journey up the valley of the St. Peter River and north through the Red River Valley, an Italian gentleman named Giacomo Beltrami. Before passing the newly established boundary line, Beltrami left Long's party and started southward, at first up the valley of the Red Lake River and southeastwardly thereafter, to find the source of the Mississippi. He came to believe that he had discovered it in a little lake to which he gave the name of Julia. After his return to civilization, Beltrami published an account of his journey in book form, first in French and later in English. Today we know that Lake Julia empties its waters into the basin of the Red River and not into the Mississippi.

Long's party meantime traveled on to the Red River Settlements, finding some evidence of British encroachment south of the forty-ninth parallel. Then he returned to the boundary line by descending the Red River of the North to Lake Winnipeg, ascending the Winnipeg River, and reaching Lake of the Woods. From that lake he went eastward up Rainy River to Rainy Lake on the boundary line agreed upon by Great Britain and the United States four years later.

East of Rainy Lake the boundary line was not agreed upon until 1842. It is interesting that Long chose to reach Lake Superior by the northernmost route of fur traders, that is, the old French canoe route from Lac La Croix to the Kaministiquia River and down that stream to Fort William. Boundary commissioners for both the United States and Great Britain were operating on border waters that very summer of 1823 and were in touch with Long. The chief American commissioner was claiming the Kaministiquia River as the usual waterway route between Lake Superior and Rainy Lake during the fur-trade days, whereas the British surveyor was claiming that fur traders of 1783 used the St.

Louis River. The Treaty of Paris of 1783, it will be recalled, specified that the boundary west of Lake Superior should follow the traders' water route. Ambiguity in the wording of the treaty kept the boundary question open until 1842, when the Webster-Ashburton Treaty decided that the boundary line should lie along the Grand Portage canoe route of the fur traders.

At Fort William, which had superseded Grand Portage as inland headquarters of the North West Company in the opening years of the nineteenth century, Long found an important post of the Hudson's Bay Company. A recently discovered journal of the fort reveals the fact that at Fort William Long also found the schooner "Recovery" in process of building. In it Lieutenant (later Admiral) Henry Bayfield explored and charted Lake Superior. His explorations included the north shore,

Lac La Croix in 1823.

Basswood Lake in 1823.

107

Duluth harbor, Bayfield harbor, and the Apostle Islands. Bayfield's chart was the only reliable guide to the treacherous inland sea until General George H. Meade's survey in the early 1860's.

Meantime, other official American expeditions found their way into the Minnesota country. One of these, in 1820, was led by Governor Lewis Cass of Michigan Territory, of which the Minnesota country was then a part. The expedition entered from Lake Superior by way of the St. Louis River-Sandy Lake canoe route to the Mississippi, journeyed up that river to Upper Red Cedar Lake, thereafter named Cassina, or Cass Lake, and returned to Michigan via the newly established Fort St. Anthony and the Mississippi River to Prairie du Chien. Cass believed that the lake named after him was the source of the Mississippi River.

One of the men of his party, Henry R. Schoolcraft, was not convinced that the true source of the great river had been found. Therefore in 1832 he headed still another official expedition sent out from Michigan Territory to find the "true head" of the Father of Waters. Following his earlier route from Lake Superior, he passed beyond the limits of the 1820 expedition and found Lac La Biche (Elk Lake), so-called by North West Company traders, and renamed it Lake Itasca.

This was a concocted name, composed of the remnants of two Latin words supplied Schoolcraft by the Reverend William Thurston Boutwell of the expedition. "Caput" and "veritas," supposedly meaning "true head," were written on a piece of paper by the missionary. Schoolcraft left off the first syllable of "veritas" and the last of "caput," combined the remaining syllables, and produced the exotic word, "Itasca." In some of his published works of a much later period he explained the origin of the word by saying that it was an Indian term, and told a romantic legend to explain why he chose it. Apparently he relied upon his belief that an account from his own pen in 1832 would never be found and read by historians. Almost exactly a century later, however, a scholar chanced to go through the files of a Galena newspaper of 1832 and found therein Schoolcraft's own version of the naming of Lake Itasca. It corresponded exactly with the account given above, which had always

been maintained by Boutwell to be the origin of the word.

With the finding of the true head of the Mississippi the main explorations of Minnesota may be said to end, though details about small areas continued to be added to the body of knowledge of the area. These were supplied by such travelers as the artist, George Catlin, the engineer, George Featherstonhaugh, and the Italian count, Francesco Arese, all of whom published books about their Minnesota travels. Reports of certain members of the corps of topographical engineers and of the dragoons, including Lieutenant Albert Miller Lea, Captain Edwin V. Sumner, and Major Samuel Woods, appeared in the 1830's and the 1840's in government publications. The records of botanists like the German Karl Geyer in 1838 and the Frenchman Auguste Lamare-Picquot in 1846 and

Augustin Christophe Lamare—Picquot, 1832. Courtesy of Centre Nationale de la Recherche Scientifique, Paris, France.

1848 remain unpublished, but recently the activities of these men have been recognized as typical of the general exploratory work so characteristic of men of their profession. In addition to all these men, there were the missionaries, both men and women, scores of whom appeared in the Minnesota country during the 1830's and 1840's. Their printed reports in church periodicals and elsewhere present facts about the Minnesota country available from no other source.

Before telling the story of these highly intelli-

Battle between Sac and Fox Indians on the upper Mississippi about 1848. By George Catlin. Courtesy Smithsonian Institute.

Sioux Braves Dance. Fort Snelling, 1848. By George Catlin. Courtesy Smithsonian Institute.

gent and articulate teachers and preachers, we should consider the two chief mapmakers of the Minnesota country during the British and American periods of exploration—David Thompson and Joseph N. Nicollet. Thompson was primarily a fur trader, but his enduring fame rests upon the maps he made for the North West Company and for the British members of the boundary commission of 1817-27; and upon the diaries he kept meticulously throughout his long and active career in most parts of British North America and in certain northern parts of the United States.

Slightly educated in a large charity school in London, young Thompson came out to the bleak shores of Hudson Bay in 1784 as an apprentice of the Hudson's Bay Company. His scientific interests seem to have been nurtured and guided by a famous Canadian explorer, Samuel Hearne, and if so, the pupil was worthy of his teacher. After fourteen years of service, Thompson left the Hudson's Bay Company and journeyed to Grand Portage to join the ranks of the Nor'Westers.

At that time Alexander Mackenzie (soon to be Sir Alexander) was a very powerful figure in the fur-trading world. He was anxious to change the boundary between British North America and the United States, as ambiguously laid down in the Treaty of Paris of 1783, and to place it much farther south. Indeed, he wanted to include most of the Minnesota country in British North America, partly in order that the North West Company might retain Grand Portage, its great inland headquarters, and partly that the company might utilize the Mississippi in shipping its furs.

To effect these changes, Mackenzie's company needed to know the terrain under consideration. Thompson was chosen to explore and map it. In 1797-8 he journeyed as far west as the Mandan villages on the Upper Missouri and returned via the Red River Valley, Red Lake, the Upper Mississippi, Sandy Lake, and Fond du Lac on Lake Superior. In the early years of the century he completed an enormous map of the company's domain, which hung for years in the great salon of the North West Company's fort at the mouth of the Kaministiquia River, Fort William. It contains the earliest accurate delineation of northern Minnesota.

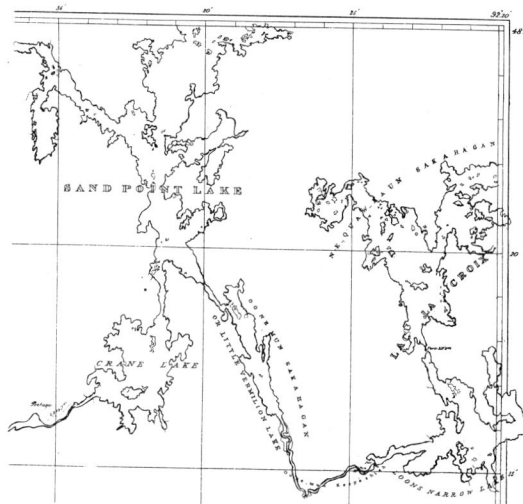

One of David Thompson's manuscript maps of border lakes.

Later — when Mackenzie's schemes had been thwarted by the purchase of Louisiana, by the astuteness of Secretary of State James Madison, and by the War of 1812—the Treaty of Ghent provided for a boundary commission to examine the disputed boundary region and to recommend a boundary line. For the British survey party, Thompson was made the astronomer and surveyor. In 1822, 1823, and 1824 he was a member of exploring parties in canoes, which journeyed up the three streams claimed as the dividing line intended by the negotiators of the treaty of 1783: the Kaministiquia, the Pigeon, and the St. Louis rivers. As already mentioned, Thompson claimed that the treaty meant the St. Louis River to be the boundary line, whereas the American commissioner claimed that the Kaministiquia was intended. Thompson's diaries and maps of these boundary waters have been preserved, and afford minute details about the Minnesota country. His maps were printed by the United States government in 1898.

Thompson is remembered not only as a careful scientist, but also as a fairminded man, of great probity, courage, and justice, who would not cheat his Indian customers, sell them spirituous liquors, or allow his voyageurs to maltreat them. Every Sunday he assembled his men and solemnly read to them from the Bible in a French that would have elicited smiles, if not jeers, had the voyageurs not held him in great respect. Gradually the other documents that he compiled over a long lifetime are

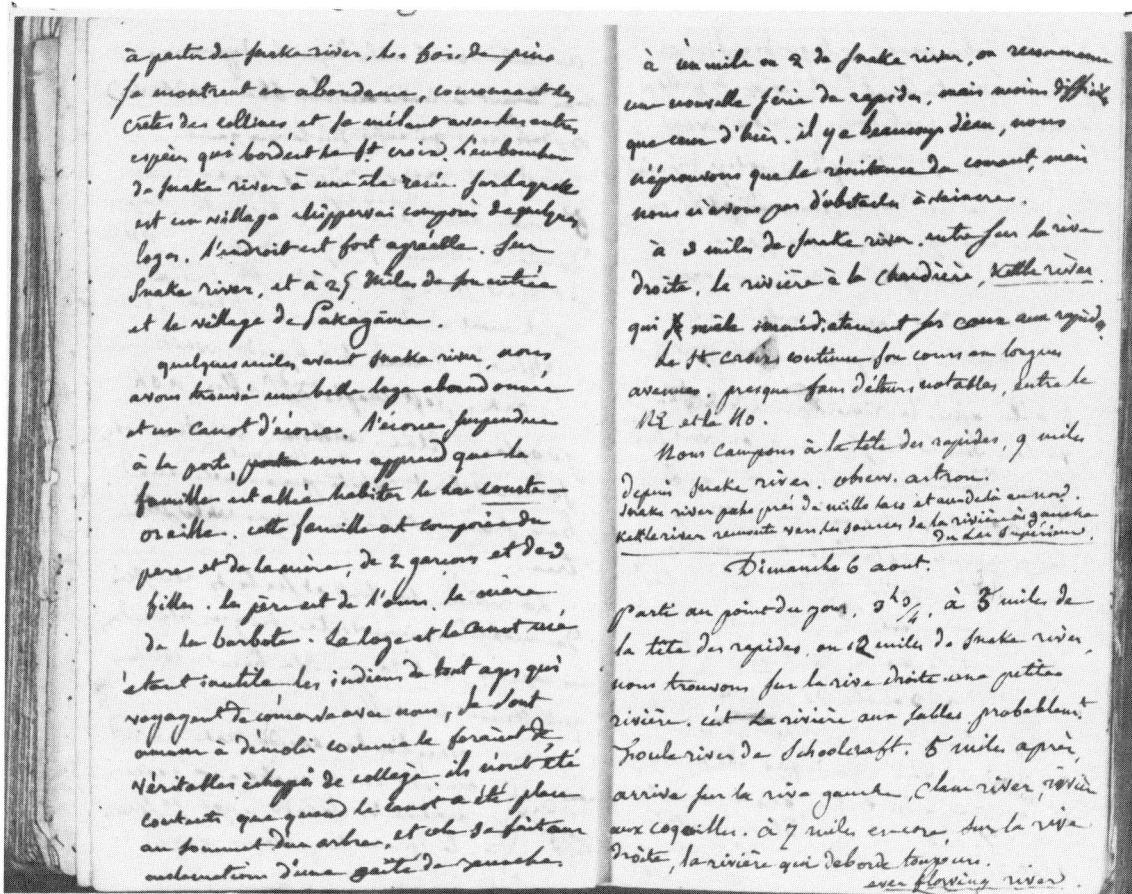

Two pages from Joseph N. Nicollet's diary of a St. Croix River journey.

appearing in print, and reveal him as one of the most brilliant stars in the firmament of Canadian and Minnesota exploration.

The other cartographer, Joseph N. Nicollet, had many of the same characteristics as Thompson—personal integrity, courage both physical and moral, and a meticulous scholarship. He, too, was greatly respected by his voyageurs, not alone for these qualities, but also for his playfulness and good fellowship. During the middle and later 1830's he made several expeditions in the Minnesota country—up the St. Croix River, to the source of the Mississippi, across the prairies, and into the southwestern corner of the present state. As he went, he journalized, partly in English and partly in his native French; and he was as careful as Long had been to illustrate his diaries with maps. The printed results of his travels and studies appeared as a government document in 1843. It consisted of a report and a map of great size and remarkable detail covering the region between the Mississippi and the Missouri rivers.

Lost for many years, his manuscript remains were discovered in forgotten files in the State Department in Washington, D. C. during World War I. A biography of this remarkable man is badly needed, especially as a rich new collection of his papers has just been discovered. His map is especially valuable for recording the original Indian and French names of the Minnesota country. Besides his cartographical and exploratory services, he is remembered as an astronomer who discovered a comet, as one of the founders of modern scientific life insurance calculations, and as a member of the French Legion of Honor.

Nicollet's personality and services were recognized immediately by such men as Henry H. Sibley and the missionaries. Both entertained him during his sojourns in the Minnesota country and wrote of him at the time. Indeed, the letters and reports of the numerous missionaries to the Minnesota Indians cannot be equalled for wealth of detail on practically every subject of the day in their region. They kept diaries, wrote reports and letters, and published books, so that their literary remains are profuse.

Unfortunately, there was little missionary activity among Minnesota Indians before 1830. After that time it increased steadily year by year, until most denominations were represented. During the French regime, only the Jesuits and the Recollects made any serious effort to convert the local Indians. Father Claude Allouez of the La Pointe mission in the 1660's, Fathers Michel Guignas and Nicholas de Gonnor of the Fort Beauharnois mission, and Fathers Claude Godefroy Coquart and Jean Pierre Aulneau of the Fort Charles mission, as well as the Franciscan Louis Hennepin, touched the lives of Minnesota Indians briefly in their short periods of residence in the region. Thereafter, throughout the British regime, practically no Christianizing influence was felt.

Concern began to be expressed once more in Washington's administration, and a slight provision by the United States government was made for the civilization of the native tribes. Jefferson, ever interested in Indians, added slightly to that provision, but it was not until John C. Calhoun's term of office as Secretary of War under President Monroe, that a real step forward was made. Then funds were made available to such organizations as provided schools for the natives, and rate of payment was based primarily upon the number of pupils in those schools. Accordingly, it was mission boards, by and large, that founded Indian schools; for education in that day, even among white people, was almost solely the work of religious denominations.

The first resident missionaries came to the region under the aegis of the American Board of Commissioners for Foreign Mission, a Boston organization composed mostly of Congregationalists and Presbyterians. Several years earlier, it is true, a Catholic mission had been established on the fringes of the Minnesota country, by the diocese of Quebec. This was at Pembina in Lord Selkirk's colony, now in the northwest corner of North Dakota on the Red River of the North. It lasted only about five years under the guidance of its founder, young Sévère Dumoulin; later, in 1831, Father Georges Belcourt resumed ministrations to the

Church of the Assumption, Pembina, N. D. From "George Anthony Belcourt" by Monsignor James M. Reardon. Courtesy, North Central Publishing Company.

same bands, but in other places until 1848. Then he re-established the Pembina mission, this time under an American bishop, and remained south of the border, at Pembina and later (after 1853) in the Turtle Mountains. Some of this time he also maintained an itinerant mission at Wabassimong on Winnipeg River just north of Lake of the Woods, and on Rainy Lake.

These Canadian missions played only a small part in beginning the Christianizing of Minnesota Indians. It was not until the early 1830's that there were actual mission stations on Minnesota soil. In 1830 the American Board sent Frederick Ayer to open a mission school on Madeline Island at La Pointe, a gathering place for Chippewa Indians and the center of American Fur Company activities among Upper Michigan, Wisconsin, and Minnesota natives. In 1831 Ayer began a school at Sandy Lake on the Upper Mississippi, and Sherman Hall reached La Pointe to take charge of all the American Board's missionaries in the region.

Besides Ayer at Sandy Lake and later at Yellow Lake and Pokegama Lake in the St. Croix Valley, Hall's subordinates were Boutwell at Leech Lake and later at Fond du Lac, Edmund F. Ely at Sandy Lake and Fond du Lac, and some others. At the Pokegama mission, near the site of Pine City, Minnesota, a very promising beginning was made.

The Islington Mission near Rat Portage. (from Hind's "Red River Expedition.")

Agriculture was taught a willing and intelligent group of Chippewa until their enemies, the Sioux, attacked and frightened them away in 1841 as part of a general outburst of warfare between the two rival tribes. Nevertheless, the Chippewa mission was maintained for some years and even extended to Red Lake, but at the end of the 1840's the American Board practically abandoned its work among the Minnesota Chippewa, leaving them generally to the care of the American Missionary Association.

Among the Sioux, the American Board in the late 1820's seems to have had some part, at least, in sending two young men, Alvan Coe and Jedediah Stevens, on a reconnaissance trip to Fort Snelling. Stevens, however, spent the winter of 1829-30 in the Chippewa country, mostly at a trader's post on Yellow Lake. Probably his reports of the great desire for religious training on the part of the trader and some of his associates occasioned the beginning of the Yellow Lake and Pokegama missions, and possibly even of the La Pointe mission. Stevens did not remain longer than one season among the Chippewa, but in 1835 he was sent by the American Board to the site of Minneapolis. There he started and maintained for some time a mission school for little Sioux Indians and half-breeds. Thus he has the distinction of being the only white missionary to serve both the great rival tribes in Minnesota.

Before Stevens opened his school on Lake Harriet, two stalwart young brothers from Connecticut, Samuel and Gideon Pond, came without sponsors of any kind to Fort Snelling and began missionary work among the Sioux in 1834. Soon, however, they found it politic to be taken under the wing of the American Board, and were joined by regularly appointed missionaries of that organization, Dr. Thomas S. Williamson and the Reverend Stephen R. Riggs. Though the last two established a station at Lac Qui Parle on the upper St. Peter River, the Ponds and Stevens remained in the vicinity of Fort Snelling. The same warfare of the late 1830's which caused the abandonment of the Pokegama mission in 1841 also led to the flight of the Sioux from Lake Calhoun and Lake Harriet. Some of them settled at Oak Grove on the St. Peter River, and there Gideon Pond made his home. Samuel established his mission eight miles farther upstream on the site of Shakopee.

A score or so of American Board men and women ministered to the Sioux between 1834 and the removal of the tribe from Minnesota in 1863 after its great uprising against the white people of the region. During almost three decades the missionaries taught schools, established churches, printed many books and a newspaper in the Sioux language, and published the dictionary and grammar that are still the standard works in the field.

113

A Lake Calhoun Village, 1848. By George Catlin. Courtesy Smithsonian Institute.

View on St. Peter (Minnesota) River, 1848. By George Catlin. Courtesy Smithsonian Institute.

Indeed, it was these missionaries who reduced the Sioux, or Dakota, speech to a written language.

Closely associated with the American Board missionaries was a group of young men from the Protestant church of Switzerland. Letters and reports preserved in that country, from the pens of the Reverend Daniel Gavin and the Reverend Samuel Dentan, tell how they and a few others were sent by their mission board to the Sioux of the Upper Mississippi in the middle 1830's, how they settled first at Trempealeau on the east shore of the Mississippi with the Wabasha band of Sioux, then moved a year or so later to the site of Red Wing. Here they and their wives—Gavin married a niece of Jedediah Stevens skilled in the Sioux language, and Dentan married a member of the Mackinac mission—worked in close cooperation with the Ponds, Riggs, Williamson, and others of the American Board mission. Gavin spent a winter at the Lac Qui Parle mission and was very helpful with the missionaries' translation, partly because of his intimate knowledge of the French language.

Since the 1700's French had been the language of the voyageurs and half-breeds, one of whom, Joseph Renville, had persuaded Williamson to place his mission at Lac Qui Parle. There Renville lived in barbaric splendor like an ancient Saxon chieftain, supported by Indian and half-breed relatives and retainers, yet deeply interested in educating and civilizing them. Though he could not read nor write, he had a phenomenal memory for words and was of inestimable value in translating the Scriptures into Sioux through the medium of a French Protestant Bible.

Other close associates of American Board missionaries were the so-called Oberlin Band. After the first, rather unsuccessful venture among the Chippewa, the board suffered a dearth of interest in those Indians. Ayer and his wife persisted, however, and in 1843 they established a mission on Red Lake, where Ely joined them. They and others petitioned the board to resume its efforts in the Chippewa country, and partly at least, as a result of their entreaties, a group of energetic young men and women came out that year and the following one from Oberlin College under the direction of the American Missionary Association.

Alonzo Barnard and his wife, D. B. Spencer, and Sela G. Wright occupied Red Lake alongside the Ayers. Dr. and Mrs. William Lewis and P. O. Johnson went to Leach Lake. In 1847 a mission was established on Cass Lake, where Barnard and

Mt. Trempealeau on Lake Pepin. Early Steel Engraving by J. C. Ward.

Spencer went and were joined by A. B. Adams and his wife. Others joined them later and a very successful mission was operated for a time, with a church building and society, and houses for Indian converts testifying to the energy of the missionaries.

About 1849 another mission was established in the Chippewa country, this time on Lake Winnebagoshish, and before the end of something more than a decade and a half of labor in this northern field, other missions and missionary schools—boarding schools in at least two instances—had been founded as far south as Belle Prairie near Fort Ripley and as far northwest as Pembina. In 1852 the number of missionaries was twenty-one. This was the peak of activity. In 1856 there were only four stations and seventeen missionaries, and in 1859 work was discontinued. Yet as late as 1878 Wright, now a government teacher, could write that the harvest of the seed sown in earlier years was being gathered. At least forty converts had been made over the years, there were "good and very attentive congregations," and there was "no time when there was not considerable religious interest."

Thus one of the large religious boards—the American Board of Cimmissioners for Foreign Missions—operated for well over a generation among the Chippewa, and, until the Sioux Uprising, among the Sioux as well. After that tragedy, several of these missionaries and some of their children, continued their ministrations among the exiled Sioux.

Though the Ponds and Stevens abandoned the red mission field relatively early to take up home mission tasks, the Lac Qui Parle Mission persisted, and expanded at times to take in Traverse des Sioux, the site of South St. Paul, the site of Red Wing after its abandonment by the Swiss mission in the middle 1840's, and the Yellow Medicine River. When the Sioux sold their land west of the Mississippi to the federal government in 1851, the Red Wing, Kaposia, Traverse des Sioux, and Oak Grove missions had to be abandoned, of course, for the natives were moved onto reservations on the Upper Minnesota River.

In 1854, after the Lac Qui Parle mission house had been lost in a conflagration, that mission was also moved—to the Yellow Medicine area—and the new station was named Hazelwood. It was often called the Hazelwood Republic because of the training in local government that it afforded the natives. It was reaping the fruit of long years of toil and devotion on the part of the missionaries, when the Sioux Outbreak occurred in the summer of 1862. This was a true trial by fire for the converts, but almost to an individual they stood the test. Like the early Christians they suffered for their faith but proved their allegiance by their deeds.

Some forty or so missionaries and members of their families were taken to safety by Indian converts. John Otherday led sixty-two white persons to safety. Peter-Big-Fire slyly led the war party of his tribe away from the trail of the escaping missionaries. Lorenzo Lawrence took two canoeloads of white women, children, and others to the safety of Fort Ridgely. John B. Renville and his able wife and other converts worked in the hostile camp to bring about a counter revolution, got the white captives into their possession, and delivered them up to a rescuing army under General Henry H. Sibley after the battle of Wood Lake, the final engagement in the outbreak. All in all, the missionary effort had borne rich fruit.

Another denomination that was not far behind the Presbyterians and Congregationalists of the American Board in an early establishment of missions among Minnesota Indians was the Methodists. Though their stations did not last long in most instances, the consecrated men and women in them made their mark on the region. They began with three natives, Peter Marksman, John Johnson, and George Copway, Chippewa under the superintendency of the Reverend John Clark of Sault Ste. Marie.

Through the efforts of the Reverend Alfred Brunson of the Pittsburgh Conference—a celebrated circuit rider, who visited the Upper Mississippi in 1837—a site was chosen at Kaposia (South St. Paul), where a mission was begun. Despite the fact that the newcomers were Chippewa, the Sioux received them well. David King was brought to take charge of the school. Unlike the American Board schools, this one used only the English language. The Reverend W. W. Pope and the Reverend James G. Whitford were added later to the mission staff. Still later the Reverend B. T. Kavanaugh took Pope's place, when his health failed in 1839.

Meantime a mission destined to outlast the Kaposia effort had been established by the Methodists among the Chippewa. At first it was located on Elk River, on the east bank of the Mississippi. In 1840 its location was changed to Sandy Lake, where Samuel Spates took charge. Still later branches were founded at White Fish Lake, Rabbit Lake, and Fond du Lac. A number of able men and women served in these short-lived branches. Spates' mission, however, continued into the middle 1850's.

Sioux worshipping at Red Boulders, Southwestern Minnesota, 1848. By George Catlin. Courtesy Smithsonian Institute.

The Sioux mission of the Methodists did not prosper and the school was soon moved to Red Rock prairie on the east bank of the Mississippi. There work among the Sioux quickly ended because of the sale of land in that area by the Indians in 1837. Instead, the station served pioneer white settlers as they began to appear in the early 1840's and built their homes between the Mississippi and the lower reaches of the St. Croix River. Meantime the American Board took over the mission on the site of South St. Paul and continued it until the Sioux lands on the west side of the Mississippi were sold in 1851. It was Williamson at Kaposia, preaching occasionally to the few white persons in a little settlement called St. Paul's across the river, who helped secure the first schoolteacher, Miss Harriet Bishop, for the future capital of Minnesota.

A Methodist missionary operation totally unassociated with those already described, began about the same time along the Canadian border under the direction of Wesleyans in England and Canada. James Evans, known especially as the apostle to the Cree of western Canada and the first missionary in the Rocky Mountain area of Canada, made some heroic missionary journeys along the north shore of Lake Superior in 1838 and 1839 and established several stations. From them he proceeded inland to found a renowned mission at the upper end of

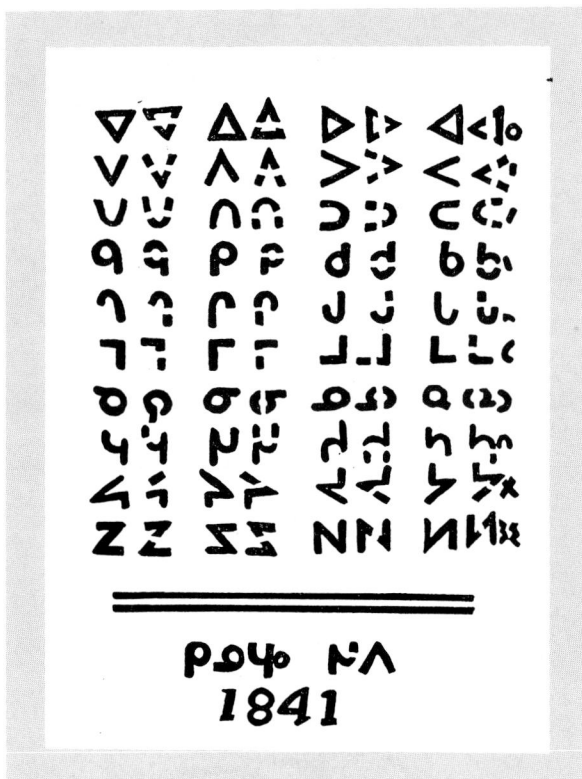

▽ ⩗ △ ⩒ ▷ ⊳ ◁ ◁ lo
∨ ⩔ ∧ ∧ ⋗ ⋗ ≺ ≺ ⸾
∪ � ∩ ∩ ⊃ ⊃⸾ ⊂ ⊂⸾
ᖯ ᖰ ᑭ ᑭ ᗡ ᗡ ᖯ ᖯ'
ᐱ ᐱ ᒄ ᒄ ᑌ ᑌ ᑌ ᑌ'
⅂⅂' ᒥ ᒥ ⅃⅃ ᒪ ᒪ⸾
ᐁ ᑫ ᓀ ᓂ ᓄ ᓇ⸼ ᖴ ⟨⟩
ᕤ ᕤ' ᑯ ᑮ ᔑ ᔑ ᖽ ᖾ
ᐊ ᐃ ᐴ ᐻ ⋖ ⋖⸾ ᕝ ᕟ
Z Z ᔓ ᔓ ᐤᐤ ᐃ ᐁ ᕼ

═══════
═══════

ᑭᐅᒡ ᑑᐱ
1841

Page from James Evans' Cree Spelling Book. He invented the Cree alphabet.

Lake Winnipeg—Rossville—close to the Hudson's Bay Company post of Norway House. En route there he left several missionaries—including William Mason and the native pastor, author, and European lecturer, Peter Jacobs, at a Rainy River mission. There a school and mission were maintained until 1846; later, in 1853, the mission was re-established under Allen Salt and supported until 1858.

Catholic missions in northern Minnesota also stemmed from activities on Lake Superior. In the middle 1830's came Frederick Baraga, a scholarly Slovene, who later became the first bishop of Sault Ste. Marie and Marquette. He and two other well-known Slovenian missionaries on the Minnesota stage, Francis Pierz and Otto Skolla, were dispatched under the ægis of a Vienna board of missions, the Leopoldine Society. Its special care in the years immediately after its founding in 1829 and for a considerable period thereafter, was the North American Indians. Another European society that helped support the Minnesota Indian missions of the Catholic Church was the Society for the Propagation of the Faith with headquarters in Lyons and Paris, France.

With help from these organizations Baraga, Pierz, and Skolla saw missionary service at La Pointe, Fond du Lac, and Grand Portage in the Minnesota country. Only the first station survived for any considerable period. The letters, reports, a Chippewa dictionary, a Chippewa grammar, many doctrinal works, and other products of Baraga's pen, made Europeans acutely aware of Catholic Indian missions, and large sums were bestowed on the parent organizations to aid the work of the missionaries. Except for two short-lived resident missions at Grand Portage and near by, the work in Minnesota was itinerant at this time; but much later, in 1852, Pierz became a resident of Minnesota Territory on the Upper Mississippi and ministered for many years to white settlers, half-breeds, and some Indians. By his works published in Europe he was especially instrumental in causing Stearns County to be settled in the 1850's and 1860's, largely by German Catholic immigrants.

Among the Sioux there was less Catholic interest and success. Bishop Loras of Dubuque visited the vicinity of Fort Snelling by steamboat in 1839 and immediately thereafter sent a missionary to Mendota. This priest's work, however, seems to have been confined to the whites and half-breeds at that place and its vicinity. Ministering to settlers across the river, he established a chapel there dedicated to St. Paul, from which the name was transferred also to the locality. Thus the capital of Min-

Bishop Frederick Baraga.

nesota received its name indirectly from Lucien Galtier, the missionary priest.

His successor in 1844 was Father Augustin Ravoux, who had reached the Minnesota country in 1841 and had done mission work among the Sioux of Traverse des Sioux and Lac Qui Parle that year and the next, even going eventually across the prairies to the Missouri River. After Galtier removed to Keokuk, Ravoux had little time for Indian work, since settlers were flocking into the Minnesota country and demanding most of his attention. He did establish a chapel and a school on the site of Chaska, but work there ended for the most part in 1844, and finally in 1846.

Episcopal and Lutheran work began late among the Minnesota Indians. There was also a little Baptist missionary work. John Johnson (Enmegabowh), after the abandonment of the Methodist mission among the Sioux, persuaded the Reverend James Lloyd Breck, of the Protestant Episcopal Church in St. Paul, to enter the Chippewa field in 1852. In this way the Gull Lake Mission on the Upper Mississippi was established under tall pines. Here St. Columba mission and school arose. Enmegabowh was the interpreter and eventually the priest there. Breck also established a mission and school at Leech Lake in the summer of 1856. The Reverend E. Steele Peake succeeded him at the Gull Lake mission. When opposition from the natives forced the abandonment of most of this mission work in the late 1850's, Breck established a mission school for Indians at Faribault, the headquarters of his church in Minnesota. Here twenty to thirty Sioux and Chippewa children were instructed and lived in peace together. In the summer of 1859 Peake established a mission at Crow Wing.

For some years in the period of the Sioux Outbreak, practically all of the missions in northern Minnesota were given up, including re-established missions of the American Board and the American Missionary Association. Then, about 1870, came a turn in the tide. The first Episcopal bishop of Minnesota, Henry B. Whipple, became a tireless proponent of work among Indians as soon as he reached Minnesota in 1859. His courageous stand for the condemned Sioux, after the Outbreak of 1862, led to acts of mercy by President Lincoln in releasing over two hundred and fifty natives from the death sentence. Thereafter Whipple was partly instrumental in forcing a new Indian policy on Washington leaders of government. He also prosecuted vigorously the Indian missions in his own diocese, especially in northern Minnesota. The field had been sowed by earlier men and women and he reaped the harvest, but he did so with unusual courage and tireless industry.

All too little is known of an early Baptist missionary effort in the Pembina area; and of the only Lutheran mission among Minnesota Indians before the Civil War, the Rabbit Lake station on the Upper Mississippi. Under the direction of the Reverend Ottomar Cloeter, it was supported by a Lutheran missionary organization in Germany, but did not last long.

* * * * * * *

Minnesota waters played a major part in the history of the region from about 1620 until modern methods of transportation took away some of the importance of our streams and lakes in state development. Explorers, fur traders, and missionaries preceded pioneer settlers on the Mississippi, on Lake Superior, and on the thousands of lesser streams and lakes that are Minnesota's glory today. Indians of several great tribes, Frenchmen, Englishmen, Scotsmen, colonials, and Americans paddled their canoes during two centuries and more of recorded history over our waterways. They opened the area, appreciated its beauties, and even fought for it. Their part in our annals should not be minimized.

CHAPTER FIVE

The World Comes to Minnesota

Part 1   Minnesota Melting Pot

by VAL BJORNSON

The Indians were here first, wherever they came from. The French were next—first among white men, as Jesuit priests, voyageurs, explorers carried their widespread wanderings inland across the Great Lakes, penetrating deeper, into the Mississippi valley and beyond it.

What a heritage of place-names the two have left. Fleeting trips by French explorers are still memorable in names of streets, cities and counties —Hennepin, Nicollet, LaSalle and DuLuht, to mention but a few. And how fortunate Minnesota is that its real "first settlers," the Indians who roamed the area for centuries, made their impact permanent not alone in the state's musically meaningful name, but in countless others which stud its map.

Mud Lake, Sand Lake and Elbow Lake may be accurately descriptive designations. But there's a lilt and a distinction to Minnewaska, and Kabetogama, and Winnibigoshish. There are other, later names, tracing migration's course as they emerge. There is no mistaking the origin of settlers who founded New Ulm in Brown County, any more than that of those who established New Germany in Carver, or New Munich in Stearns. Hanover in Wright County and Hamburg in Carver bear an equally German imprint.

Svea in Kandiyohi County and Vasa in Goodhue transplant Sweden just as certainly as Oslo in Marshall County and Torfin in Roseau reflect their Norwegian backgrounds. Askov in Pine County perpetuates a familiar Danish name here in Minnesota in the same manner as Kalevala in Carlton County transfers to our map the title of Finland's classic ballad. Ghent is as Belgian in Lyon County as it is on Belgium's map, and the same goes for Czechoslovakia—or Bohemia—with reference to New Prague in Le Sueur County.

Reliance can't be complete, though, on the transfer of place-names from other parts of the globe to Minnesota's map. No one came from India to help found Delhi in Redwood County, nor does a lake's name in Hungary have any particular significance for Balaton in Lyon County—there isn't a Hungarian in the place! Yet Holland in Pipestone County and Hollandale in Freeborn are named with complete accuracy as to immigrant background. Kilkenny is Irish in Le Sueur County, as Dundas is Scotch in Rice. Berne is Swiss in Dodge County— but so is Pine Island in Goodhue.

Taunton in Lyon County hasn't much of a link with Taunton, England, or Taunton, Massachusetts. Its name provides no more of a key to its Polish population than does Ivanhoe's, in Lincoln County. Fairmont, in Martin County, was originally an English colony—but descendants of the British Isles, from Maine down through New England, did more than give place names to many a Minnesota village. They made Minnesota a state. They formed its institutions and ran its government until the Scandinavians and the Germans began to "take over," in the nineties and since.

To continue relating Minnesota's map to its "United Nations" make-up, names in the rural areas, out in the townships, are often most revealing. Thus, one could properly expect the Archbishop Ireland colonies in Swift County to turn up township names there such as Tara, Kildare, Dublin and Cashel. It is not surprising to find Toivala township in the Finnish region of St. Louis County or to discover names such as Terrebonne and Gervais on the roster in heavily French-populated Red Lake County. Cambria in Blue Earth County is appropriate, where Mapleton is Scotch enough to make Bobbie Burns Day an annual event. Sibley County remembers Prussian military leaders in such township names as Bismarck and Moltke, while Luxemburg is, very properly, found in Stearns County.

If there is anything more Norwegian than Sverdrup, Tordenskjold and Trondhjem townships in Otter Tail County, Normania, Sandnes and Wergeland in Yellow Medicine might provide their match. There are Anglicized versions too, which are unmistakable—Swede Grove in Meeker, Swede Prairie in Yellow Medicine, Swedes Forest in Red-

If close study of the map isn't convincing enough in proof of Minnesota's cosmopolitan aspect, a survey of telephone books and tax rolls is conclusive. Our state personifies the motto marking coins we use—"E Pluribus Unum," "out of many, one." We have built gradually toward a mounting national unity, but we aren't doing it at the price of uniformity. We differ in nationality background, but with each varying group there is the common hope that worth-while features of a well guarded heritage may be made contributions toward the evolving composite. Learning from one another, the opportunity is one for enrichment and broadened tolerance, not provincialism and conflict.

There was conflict with the Indians first, in the white man's gradual, relentless advance. The Chippewa and the Sioux who roamed the region uncounted and unhindered are few, indeed, as Minnesota turns the century mark—18,000 Indians in all in the state, according to a 1957 survey, with a significant shift from the reservations noted

Norwegian Immigrant Sod Home, Canby, Minn.

wood, and New Sweden in Nicollet County. The precise part of northern Norway from which early settlers came is obvious in Nordland township, a name found both in Aitkin and Lyon counties. Sweden's southern tip is transplanted in Kittson County's Skaane township, and Westerheim in Lyon County isn't hard to decipher, from the Icelandic Vesturheim, meaning "western home."

in the fact that about 8,000 of them make their home in the Twin Cities.

Missionaries, explorers, fur traders, were the real frontiersmen among the whites, French, French-Canadian, and a few of them, English. From scattered fur-trading posts and river-front villages built to handle their "harvest," the shift to exploitation of timber resources came next.

Maine lumberjacks and sawmill operators came to Minnesota in generous number then, the vanguard of a still larger number of New England "Yankees" who dominated the state in its formative stages, establishing the flour milling industry, building up towns and cities, launching and expanding business enterprises of every sort.

Deliberate promotion of immigration to Minnesota came at the earliest stages, and took varying forms. There was the era of advertising the area's salubrious climate, bringing victims of tuberculosis to a degree that gave a 1949 study its title, "Invited and Conquered."

Theodore C. Blegen, dean of the University's Graduate School, one of the state's greatest historians, an expert on Scandinavian mass movements generally and Norwegian migration in particular, says: "Minnesota, newly created a territory, was trumpeting in newspapers and other unofficial forms of printed matter its advantages for prospective settlers, and in 1855 it sent a commissioner of emigration to New York, where for two years he represented the territory officially, advertised its resources, refuted unpleasant charges about Minnesota's climate, and gave practical aid to newly arrived immigrants. The commissioner's efforts were only one among many causes that account for Minnesota's phenomenal increase in population in the fifties, but they are an index to the popular point of view in Minnesota. The increase itself is a matter of statistical record: less than 5,000 people in 1849; more than 172,000 in 1860; 12 Scandinavians in 1850; nearly 12,000 ten years later; 147 Germans in 1850; 18,400 in 1860."

Although the post of Commissioner of Immigration was added to the roster of Minnesota officialdom by the mid-sixties, the promotion of settlement was by no means an exclusive government function. Blegen has noted how the "America letters" sent from immigrants here to kinfolk in the homelands, produced a veritable migratory fever in Norway and Sweden. Then came a great colonizer such as Bishop John Ireland, who joined forces with another of Minnesota's early "giants in the earth," James J. Hill, and other railroad executives—buying up railroad land for pre-planned Catholic colonies. His work is described in the im-

pressive 1957 volume by James P. Shannon, "Catholic Colonization on the Western Frontier." Father Shannon, now president of St. Thomas College in St. Paul, who earned his doctor's degree at Yale on this exhaustive and interesting immigration study, says flatly: "The largest and most successful Catholic colonization program ever undertaken in the United States was that sponsored by Bishop John Ireland in Minnesota between 1876 and 1881."

German Catholics had been coming into Brown County long before Ireland's big effort, centering about New Ulm by the mid-fifties. The Benedictine monks who founded St. John's Abbey had helped start the stream of German Catholic migration to Stearns County in the same period, as recounted in the monumental 1957 volume, "Work and Worship," by Father Colman J. Barry, O.S.B.

The Archbishop Ireland colonies drew recruits from Ireland, England, Belgium, Germany, French Canada, and from states east of Minnesota. They include ten villages with their surrounding areas in five western and southwestern counties, Swift, Big Stone, Lyon, Murray and Nobles.

There have been other colonies with organized church sponsorship—German Mennonites whose ancestors had fled to Russia in the first place, coming in 1873 and soon thereafter to settle on Cottonwood county farms and establish the village of Mountain Lake; Danish Seventh Day Adventists in the Hutchinson community of McLeod county; and the early Dutch colony at Greenleafton in Fillmore county among them. The first sizeable number of Jews to come to Minnesota had fled the pogroms of Czars Alexander II and III in Russia in the eighties. Others had come here from Germany earlier in mass migrations to America that had extended from the forties into the eighties.

Some of Minnesota's most recent immigrants came in flight from persecution, as did many of our nation's earliest, along the Atlantic seaboard. Armenian arrivals here in the nineties had made their escape from Turkish misrule. Refugees coming since World War II have been fairly numerous, mainly from the Baltic countries, torn for a time between Nazi and Communist onslaught, swallowed up by the Soviet Union—Estonia, Latvia and Lithuania. Ukrainians in Minnesota had left their country long before it became a province in the Soviet Communist empire. Jewish refugees from Nazi persecution came in the war and postwar period, and the most recent of all arrivals are those who came in flight from Hungary after the 1956 Soviet suppression of their own nation's revolt against Communist dominance.

The centennial version of the Festival of Nations, that inspiring event arranged once every three years by the International Institute in St. Paul, provided once more a dramatization of what it is that has made Minnesota and the nation truly unique in the world. Forty ethnic or nationality groups took part, portraying the tremendous diversity of backgrounds going to make up modern Minnesota. The elaborately printed program's alphabetical roster of participants, from American Indians to Yugoslavs, provides something of a skeleton summary of the state's immigration record.

After the obvious "first settlers" — the Indians who were here when others came — Arabic-speaking groups are listed next. Syrians were the first of such arrivals, in the nineties, Lebanese coming shortly after them. Members of both groups scattered, settling in four or five of the state's larger cities and towns. They began as peddlers, selling fabrics and smaller merchandise items. They entered more stable pursuits in smaller business establishments, while children and grandchildren have continued in trade or gone into the professions.

Austrians came early—860 of them were here the year statehood was attained, with expanded

New Ulm Post Office

settlements since concentrated mainly in Hennepin, Ramsey and Stearns counties. From Belgium, there were fewer than a hundred in territorial days, and the major colony became Archbishop Ireland's at Ghent, founded by Angelus Van Hee in 1880. There has been expansion through a goodly section of southwestern Minnesota since, with Belgian immigrants coming in considerable numbers even after the first World War.

The fur-trade attracted French-Canadians in large numbers in earliest days, a fairly easy flow of population back and forth across the border continuing for a long time. St. Paul had such a heavy concentration that papers in the capital city

Harvesting Scene, German Immigrant Farmers Near St. John's, Stearns County

printed advertisements in French through the fifties, as well as in English. Unquestionably the best known Canadian immigrant to Minnesota was James Jerome Hill from New Brunswick. Arriving at the St. Paul levee in 1856, when 33 years old, he remained until his death at 93, in 1916, and had well earned the title of "Empire Builder" in those 60 intervening years. He did more than build railroads. He helped bring immigrants to Minnesota, improved cattle breeding and soil tillage, and helped promote success for settlements along his rail lines.

Chinese numbered 166 in the state in 1900, rose to a peak of about 800 some 30 years later, leveling off now at about 500. Restaurants and business enterprises in the Twin Cities have been major fields of activity for the group.

Czechoslovakians have been in Minnesota for a long time. Czechs, or Bohemians, began to arrive in 1857 from earlier settlements in Wisconsin and Illinois; Slovaks, from the eastern province, came after 1880 and later, many of them to work in mines on the Mesabi range. Many of the state's 8,000 Czechs live in St. Paul, but there are sizeable settlements at New Prague, Montgomery and Hopkins.

There were fewer than 200 Danes in Minnesota before 1860, the very first arrival evidently having been Charles Borup, who came to St. Paul shortly after 1848. The first settlement was at Clarks Grove, near Albert Lea, in Freeborn County, begun during the Civil War; the largest is at Tyler in Lincoln County, founded nearly 20 years later, while another major center for this Scandinavian group is the Askov community in Pine County.

England, while represented mainly by "Yankees" whose ancestors had come to the eastern seaboard much earlier, nevertheless provided the first Minnesota immigrant to whom naturalization papers were issued. William Willim, born in England, became a citizen of the United States at Stillwater in 1847. He was a building contractor there and, among other things, built the first lime kiln in the state. Earliest English settlers came as managers of fur-trading posts. Certainly the most memorable name among those of English birth is that of Dr. William Worrall Mayo, born in Manchester

in 1819, coming to St. Paul in 1854 and to Rochester in 1883—father of the world renowned Doctor "Will" and Doctor "Charley," builders of the Mayo Clinic.

Linking the Baltic lands, Estonia, Latvia and Lithuania, one finds few who came here early. There were some Estonians in the state as far back as 1905, but most of the 500 living here now, mainly in the Twin Cities, came after 1948 as refugees following Russian conquest of their homeland. Latvians came in largest numbers—2,500 of them after the Soviet occupation in World War II, the largest number professional people and skilled artisans. Lithuania sent its first group of emigrants to the Twin Cities in 1901, but by far the larger number—200 families— to the same metropolitan area some time after World War II's "double invasion" by Nazi and Soviet troops.

Finns were numerous enough in Minnesota by the early eighties to have their own newspaper, and they have had several of them since, the most widely circulated still being published, thrice weekly, at New York Mills, in Otter Tail County. Germans remain the largest single national group in Minnesota's melting pot; Swedes, second; Norwegians, third. But Finns are in fourth place. Their first colony was in the Cokato area in Wright County, immediately after the Civil War. A few went to Franklin in Renville County. Thereafter the course was northward—into Otter Tail, Becker and Carlton counties, and in most sizeable numbers to St. Louis County. Working first as miners on the Mesabi range, Finns moved increasingly into areas most closely resembling their homeland—lake-studded, pine-forested regions, where dairy farming and the operation of timber tracts are major occupations. Among other distinguishing features have been the building of strong consumers' cooperatives, and the most stubborn loyalty to a linguistic heritage found among any immigrants to Minnesota.

French influence, so obvious from earliest times, is typified by Father Lucien Galtier's role, arriving in 1840 to minister to 185 Catholics in the Fort Snelling area, remaining to build the frontier church of St. Paul's, from which the state's capital city took its name. Indicating the large proportion

Pioneer family

Icelanders, from the smallest nation in the Scandinavian family, put in their first appearance in Minnesota in 1875 when one of their number, already an immigrant to Wisconsin, took his family along, joining Norwegian neighbors in a covered wagon trek from Dane County, near that state's eastern edge, to the banks of the Yellow Medicine River, northeast of Minneota. The colony expanded through the seventies and into the nineties, with about a thousand descendants of that ancient republic in the state today. A Duluth colony developed in the nineties, and so did another in Roseau County, but southwestern Minnesota, and now the Twin Cities, count the largest number.

Apart from Archbishop Ireland's Irish colonies, already briefly traced, it should be noted that the state had Irish immigrants as early as 1841—and enough of them to celebrate St. Patrick's Day by 1851.

With their backgrounds as European nationals varying, Jewish participants in the centennial Festival of Nations chose the re-established "homeland" of Israel as their rallying designation. Jewish history in Minnesota antedates statehood. In January of 1851, Julius Austrian, who died in St. Paul 40 years later, first made his appearance in the capital city, driving two dog-trains down from Duluth, loaded for trading. He and his Austrian bride were among the first white people in the north country, and when they moved to St. Paul permanently in 1860, they found the Mount Zion Hebrew Association, already a four-year-old religious congregation. Metropolitan centers have remained most attractive to those of Jewish background, though many are now located widely about the state.

There were 59 Italians in Minnesota in the 1860 census count, joined by many more, coming as railroad workers in the nineties, mainly to St. Paul. Sizeable groups came shortly afterward to the Iron Range area as well.

From the turn of the century on, just 51 Japanese had lived in Minnesota until 1942, when establishment of the large military intelligence school at Fort Snelling brought a larger number, mainly from earlier West Coast locations, with Minneapolis the principal center now for some 750 descendants of Japan.

of French Canadians in the group, one finds that while the 1860 census showed more than 800 Minnesotans born in France, there were 8,000 from "British America," most of them of French descent.

One of the most famous of early German arrivals was Wendelin Grimm, settling in Carver County in 1857—the man who developed Grimm's alfalfa. Countrymen of his had begun settling further up the Minnesota River valley before that time, and the Stearns County settlement dates from that same period. It is still possible to drive in a southwesterly direction out of the Twin Cities today, a distance of 160 miles, without ever leaving "German territory," so great is the area covered by settlers who ultimately made up the state's largest single nationality group.

Greeks have had no sizeable out-state settlement, first immigrants coming to the Twin Cities in the nineties, with Minnesota's 1,700 people of Greek descent still living in urban centers. Many worked on the railroads first, but many became businessmen—restaurant operators, candy-makers and florists prominent among them.

There were some 200 Hungarians in Minnesota by 1870, more than 5,500 natives of that country in the state by 1910. They have located mainly in the urban centers, and their ranks had conspicuous recruits among the "freedom fighters" who came, mainly to the Twin Cities, after the uprising against Soviet Communist rule in 1956.

Latin Americans, the product of migratory waves themselves from the fifteenth century onward, haven't shifted in sizeable number to North America, but Mexicans have come to Minnesota to stay in increasing numbers. The first among many migratory workers to remain here were those employed in the Chaska beetfields during the World War I period. The Twin Cities colony from Mexico counts about 4,000 members now.

Negroes, with just one from Africa listed in the 1860 census, have grown in number to 18,000 in the state now, almost wholly in the Twin Cities. "First settlers" were mainly freed slaves. The Supreme Court's Dred Scott decision, it should be recalled, helping draw more sharply the lines of cleavage that led to Civil War, was a Minnesota case, originating through a fugitive slave brought to Fort Snelling from the South.

Far removed from a foreign background through their long-standing American residence, the northward movement of Negroes in the country has brought Minnesota a growing group of citizens whose position has become steadily more secure and whose contributions to every facet of the state's life has seen steady expansion.

The Netherlands are represented by first settlers in the mid-fifties in Wright County, and by the largest early colony at Greenleafton in Fillmore County, beginning with 320 arrivals in 1856. Dutch settlers in sizeable concentration are scattered from the southeast area of Hollandale in Freeborn County westward to Renville County, and southwestward to Edgerton and Holland in Pipestone County.

Norwegians, making up, along with the Swedes, the overwhelmingly dominant Scandinavian population of Minnesota, began to arrive in largest numbers after the Civil War. They were here in earliest days, however. The first known resident of Norwegian birth was a woman who came to do housework in St. Paul in territorial days. There were under ten natives of Norway in Minnesota when the 1850 census was taken; more than 8,000 of them ten years later. Apart from the few early arrivals, the first approach to large-scale permanent settlement was a modest start made in Red Wing in 1850. Goodhue, Fillmore and Houston counties became the "gateway" for Norwegian settlement, transplanted first from Wisconsin, but moving in in waves direct from Norway after the homestead act of 1862. Paul Hjelm-Hansen blazed the trail into the Red River valley a bit later, until that region, extending over to the North Dakota side, became the largest concentration of Norwegian population outside Norway itself.

Permanent immigration from the Philippines was never a reality until legal changes made it possible in 1946, but student contacts with the University and with St. Thomas, Macalester and Hamline in St. Paul had become numerous by the twenties. More than 300 Filipinos now live in the state, most

Early house

of them students who decided to stay on—and most of them in the Twin Cities, except for about fifteen who farm near Albert Lea.

Immigrants from Poland have a long and impressive record in the state. There were 127 of them here by 1858. Many came to acquire free land; many to do railroad work. Shortly after the turn of the century, a total of 60 Polish settlements had been established in various parts of the state, one of the earliest and most sizeable among them being in Winona.

Romanian migration to this country began fairly late in the last century, but by 1904 there were only about twelve families from that country, living in South St. Paul. Growth was rapid the next few years, a total of 300 in St. Paul and South St. Paul by 1907. Some 120 families in the metropolitan area now have St. Mary's Romanian Orthodox church in St. Paul as their community center.

Russians have been here, to an extent, since statehood. Fifty-nine of them were counted in the 1860 census. St. Mary's Russian Orthodox Church in Minneapolis dates back to 1887. Migration from Russia reached its peak in 1913, many going to the Mesabi range.

Scotsmen, coming mainly from Canada in earliest days, numbered more than a thousand by the time the 1860 census was taken. Martin McLeod outstripped nearly all of them, entering the fur trade at Lac qui Parle in 1837, founding the Glencoe settlement later and giving McLeod County his name. He was territorial legislator, active particularly in connection with the federal land grant laying the University's groundwork.

Swedes have remained Minnesota's second largest nationality group, outnumbered only by the Germans. They started early, with more than 3,000 of them here by 1858. Jacob Falstrom was the first settler. Coming to Canada as a mere boy, he was in the employ of the American Fur company in 1819, in the Lake Superior region. He took an Indian wife, lived for a time in Pembina, and settled in what is now Washington County in 1837.

Swedish settlement had its actual start in Washington County in 1850, extending to Chisago County in the following year. Goodhue County was "in-

vaded" through the Vasa settlement in 1853, with Hans Mattson one of its leaders—the first Scandinavian elected to state office, as Secretary of State in 1870, having earlier served in the appointive post of Commissioner of Immigration. Frederika Bremer, Swedish novelist who visited Minnesota in 1850, was prophetic when she observed: "The climate, the situation, the character of the scenery, agrees with our people better than that of any other of the American states."

The first settler of Swiss origin came from the Lord Selkirk colony at what is now Winnipeg, in 1823, to Fort Snelling, having come down from Hudson Bay, and by 1858 there were more than a thousand Swiss in Minnesota. Fairly sizeable colonies are found, mainly in the southeastern section, where dairying and cheese-making were, logically, their earliest pursuits.

Immigrants from the Ukraine began to come in the early eighties, to the Iron Range, to the upper Red River Valley, and to Minneapolis.

Yugoslavia is a comparatively new name on Europe's map, and when immigrants from there came, shortly after the turn of the century, they were listed as Serbs, Croats and Slovenes. Most of them established homes in the Iron Range area, where they entered the mines, though one of the oldest colonies dating back to 1866, is in a farming region near St. Cloud, with another colony of farmers in Itasca County. Welsh, scattered throughout Minnesota in somewhat limited number, have their only colony of sizeable proportions in the Minnesota river valley, northwest of Mankato.

Homogeneity has been regarded an asset with close-knit countries abroad — a common background, a single language, often limited area. The complete opposite has stimulated and strengthened Minnesota and the nation. Foreign languages were widely preserved here well beyond the turn of the century, and some are still spoken. The carry-over of cultural heritages has been strong, and it has given strength and variety to the Minnesota fabric. United in the basic principles that constitute true Americanism, we differ as to ethnic background, religious affiliation and political conviction—but we do so as friends and neighbors, and our stature has grown in the process.

Part 2

Archbishop Ireland Colonizes

By JAMES P. SHANNON

At the time of the great migrations to the United States during the 19th century people of good will on both sides of the Atlantic, aware that the migrants were undergoing hardship both in transit and after their arrival, were prompted to formulate plans to alleviate their suffering. Among the leaders of these humanitarians were Catholics in England and Ireland and on the Continent who attempted to provide not only transportation but large tracts of land for the establishment of farming communities in America. In this way a considerable number of Catholic colonies were established. Unfortunately, many of them failed to survive.

One of the important reasons for their failure was that closely ruled, paternalistic communities, whether patterned after the 17th-century Jesuit model in Paraguay or the 19th-century Mormon model in Utah, were hardly suited to the twin standards of democracy and individualism which ruled the American West. Disillusioned Catholic leaders soon found that the religious bond was not enough: immigrants could practice their religion just as well in the cities as on farms or in small villages; some prominent churchmen, such as the Archbishop of New York, even went so far as to warn that in moving to western colonies, Catholics ran the risk of losing their faith, since, he assured them, they would have no priests on the frontier to minister to their spiritual needs.

Into this hostile atmosphere in 1876 moved a man with enough idealism to render him impervious to the previous failures and enough realism to enable him to find a way for industrious immigrants to earn a fair living from the hard ground of the West. John Ireland, Coadjutor Bishop of St. Paul, who never tired of reminding urban Catholics that "man made the city but God made the country," successfully established between 1876 and 1881 ten rural villages and farming communities (De Graff, Clontarf, Graceville, Minneota, Ghent, Currie, Avoca, Iona, Fulda, and Adrian) in five

counties (Swift, Big Stone, Lyon, Murray, Nobles) of western Minnesota. In most of these colonies the land was furnished by land-grant railroads; in all of them the settlers were Catholics—recruited partly from Ireland, England, Belgium, Germany, and French Canada, partly from the states east of Minnesota. This article undertakes to analyze the distinctive features of these religious settlements, the history of their founding, their significant role as archetypes in a projected national colonization association, and the reasons for their growth or decline.

During the years that Bishop Ireland was most active, the Church, the state, and the railroads were all equally anxious to secure settlers for the newly

128

Oxcarts in St. Paul

opened western lands; and since it was possible for good citizens to be at the same time good Church members and frequent railroad patrons, a common interest shared by these three agencies worked toward the rapid population of Minnesota and often toward jointly sponsored programs of colonization. Ireland was named a land agent by five different railroads, and the layman he selected to direct Catholic settlement was named by the governor to the State Board of Immigration. The distinctive conditions accompanying the settlement of Minnesota offer unusually clear illustrations of the dual role played by the Catholic Church in America as an agency of Americanization and as custodian of the Faith.

As late as 1870, twelve years after Minnesota entered the Union and five years after the Civil War, the Red River trail was still the only major trace through the western part of the state. At this

date a huge triangle of fertile farmland—bounded roughly by the present-day cities of St. Paul in Minnesota, Fargo in North Dakota, and Sioux City in Iowa—remained for the most part unsettled and uncultivated.

This vast tract still lay open, waiting for settlers; but before the settlers would farm it, they had to have assurance that they could transport their grain to market. It was small consolation to the Red River farmer to have his land yield twenty-five bushels of wheat to the acre if he had no means of getting the bumper crop to a market. In the columns of Horace Greeley's New York *Tribune* one pioneer Minnesota farmer eloquently described the plight of the land-locked settlers in an open letter to President James Buchanan:

"We came to this part of the country with the hope that by a few years of labor, economy, prudence, and deprivation, we could pay for enough land to make homes for ourselves, and our families. In this we have been disappointed. Many of us have raised enough produce and stock, which, if they could have been sold . . . at fair prices, would enable us to pay for our lands; but we have no market at home, and no railroads to carry it abroad. If we wish to exchange our produce for necessary articles,

Minnesota Valley Railroad Passenger Train

129

we must carry it from five to fifteen miles to find a store, and when there, we must give ten bushels of wheat to buy a pair of boots, and four bushels of corn to buy a yard of coarse woolen cloth."

The barriers which held back settlement were the lack of transportation, fear of Indian uprisings and the absence of a major grain market near the good land of western Minnesota. However, between 1870 and 1876 the railroads entered this portion of the trans-Mississippi West and the gold rush to the Black Hills pushed the Indians farther west and opened this fertile region to settlement.

Now the western triangle of Minnesota was no longer virgin land. Each day hordes of prospectors took the Winona and St. Peter to Lake Kampeska in Dakota Territory, or the Northern Pacific to Bismarck, en route to the Hills. And with the creation of a new and daring frontier to the West, Minnesota's western lands changed with incredible speed from buffalo grazing sites to tidy farmsteads. The rails had come from the East and the Sioux had departed into the West; the barriers that had held back the tide of settlers fell away. After this it was never difficult to attract new homemakers to the region, and during the decade ending in 1880 the state's population rose from 439,706 to 780,773, an increase of 77.6 per cent. The acreage of farm lands increased 107 per cent and that of improved lands 212 per cent. It should have been obvious to any observer of that day that the cheap lands of the western part of the state would soon be filled. Actually, the frontier was to pass beyond Minnesota even before 1890!

John Ireland was consecrated coadjutor Bishop of St. Paul in 1875. From 1876 to 1881 he engaged in colonization projects in western Minnesota. Previous to this time, colonization planned and stimulated by railroads had proved feasible, (I.C. after 1854; NP, 1872-1873), but these plans had been hard hit in the Panic of 1873. The railroads were willing listeners to a plan put before them by Bishop Ireland in 1876.

The colonization plan of Ireland and his chief aide, Dillon O'Brien, was developed with knowledge of these railroad experiences and with awareness, also, of the successful Mormon colonization in Utah. But, although Ireland's plan drew upon these earlier efforts, it was basically a variation of a plan tried by Daniel O'Connell in Ireland, 1841-1845, and proposed again by Thomas D'Arcy McGee in the United States in 1856-1857.

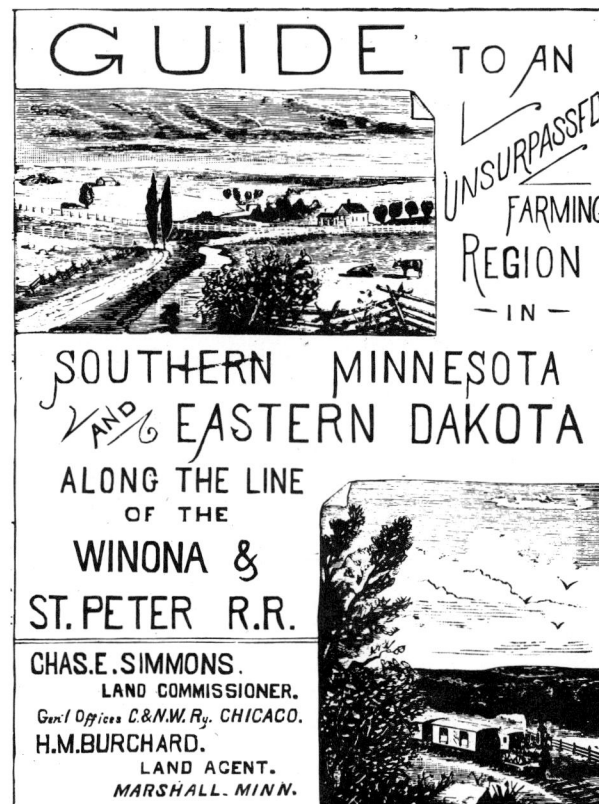

Cover of an Immigrant Guidebook

Unlike many such proposals emanating from Europe, this settlement plan did not try to regulate completely the lives of the emigrants. It was concerned only with the major problems of selection of land, creation of capital, spiritual guidance, and reasonable direction.

Between the death of O'Connell and the rise of Michael Davitt and Charles Stewart Parnell three decades intervened; and during this period the colonization program of Daniel O'Connell was given one more chance through the efforts of Thomas D'Arcy McGee. Within a year after the death of O'Connell, McGee's facile tongue and prolific pen had convinced the police authorities in Ireland that his continued freedom was a threat to civil order. They were perfectly correct, but before they could arrest him he managed, with the help of the Bishop of Derry, to disguise himself as a priest and sail for the freedom of America.

In Philadelphia, New York, and Buffalo, McGee carried on his journalistic campaign to free Ireland, though during the passage a sea change had come over him. After O'Connell's death, he had thrown in his lot with the fiery Young Irelanders who frowned on emigration and opposed any scheme of colonization as a means of curing Ireland's economic ills. According to their plan for a cultural restoration every Irishman was expected to stay in the land of his birth to suffer and work for the awaited renaissance. True to the Irish pattern of assimilation, however, McGee quickly became an American of the Americans, regularly proclaiming to his Irish readers the advantages of settlement in the United States and Canada.

The O'Connell-McGee plan failed owing considerably to 1) Irish opposition to emigration, 2) the plan's aim of financing the colonization, and 3) the opposition of Bishop Hughes of New York. Involved, also, was the peculiar nature of Irish nationalism.

Ireland's variation of the O'Connell-McGee plan was the elimination of the financial burden placed on the colonizer. Ireland limited his financial action to that of land agent, bringing the colonist and the railroad together, without acquiring title to the land himself or ever becoming responsible for periodic payments on it.

In the period, 1876-1880, Ireland formed eleven contracts with five railroads for land in five counties of western Minnesota. The contracts covered 369,000 acres and resulted in the formation of nine colonies: DeGraff, Clontarf, Adrian, Avoca, Iona, Fulda, Graceville, Minneota, and Ghent. A tenth colony of 10,000 acres, Currie, was founded by a wealthy Irishman, John Sweetman, of County Meath, a venture in which Bishop Ireland participated.

In 1880, late in John Ireland's colonizing period, and in response to pleas from an English priest, the bishop completely financed and subsidized the movement of twenty-four families of impoverished, undernourished Connemara fishermen and garden farmers from Galway to Graceville in Big Stone County. At the same time, John Sweetman in his Currie colony undertook somewhat the same type of "assisted," subsidized migration of destitute people from County Meath. Both of these efforts were miserable failures which cast a shadow on the whole colonization effort and brought deep sorrow to John Ireland.

Unfortunately, the dramatic overtones of the Connemara and Sweetman failures have proved too great a temptation to many popular historians. There is something peculiarly attractive about the narration of misfortune. When it is used in the writing of history, this human fascination for calamity has often produced dramatic but distorted and inaccurate portrayals. One recent specimen of this type of history cites the Connemara incident as typical of the "failure" which marked the Minnesota colonies, but it does not indicate that the twenty-four families from Connemara and the handful of early Sweetman settlers were only a tiny fraction of the larger numbers who came to the Catholic colonies of Minnesota and stayed to become successful farmers. The work dismisses the entire Minnesota project of Bishop Ireland in three sentences. "John Ireland . . . did not get very far (in the work of colonization), because by then it was too late . . . . In 1880 . . . he induced three hundred fishermen from Donegal to migrate to Minnesota . . . (and) it is hardly surprising that they proved failures as farmers. What should have been done was not to bring over more immigrants from Ireland but to induce those already in the great cities to settle on the land."

Since the majority of American immigrants came from the traditionally stable society of western Europe, it might have been expected that the new social order which they created would reflect the established pattern of the lands from which they came. On the contrary, the great shock which was necessary to uproot the European peasant from his native land continued to influence his life in the New World and made subsequent shifts in space and residence relatively easy, after the initial painful break with his fatherland. "Americans are always moving on."

Among the thousands of farmers and prospective farmers in New York, Ohio, and Illinois during the last quarter of the 19th century there were many successful operators of small farms who recognized the greater opportunities offered by the newly opened wheat lands of Minnesota. These men knew what they wanted: rich land, lying level, serviced by railroads, and available in large tracts at a low price per acre. They were the men who settled rural western Minnesota after 1875; and the Catholic members of this tide were the men who settled John Ireland's colonies. Again and again their letters of inquiry to Bishop Ireland, Bishop O'Connor of Omaha, or to the Irish Catholic Benevolent Union in Philadelphia asked whether or not the colonies could offer good land near a Catholic church and school. The warning against western settlement originally sounded by Bishop Hughes and often echoed by other eastern clergymen in these years had reached the Catholic immigrants in the middle states. To go west without the assurance of a resident priest was tantamount to risking the loss of their Faith. This the Catholic immigrants were not willing to do.

These same people, however, in addition to being Catholics were often reasonably successful farmers or small businessmen and were shrewd enough to realize that the wheat lands of Minnesota offered unusual opportunities to those who would claim them. The weekly market reports, listing Minnesota hard wheat at a premium price of $1.00 a bushel, together with the railroad land booklets quoting farmlands at prices from $1.50 to $5.00 per acre, were compelling inducements to any farmer who wished to improve his fortune.

And once Bishop Ireland announced to Catholic settlers that they could be assured a local priest and a church in every colony, the Catholic portion of the westward tide moved more and more toward Minnesota. Ireland had warned that he did not want farmers in other states to sell their farms to come to Minnesota for better ones. He hoped to recruit laborers from the industrial centers of the East. But while these laborers remained at their jobs, either through choice or necessity, thousands of small businessmen and farmers from New England to Wisconsin sold their business or their land and headed for Minnesota.

During his eastern speaking tour of 1879 Ireland delivered a series of six lectures on western colonization to the Catholics in Marlboro, Massachusetts. From this urban parish he recruited six families for the Graceville colony. The father of one such family, Maurice Greene, was an Irish-born immigrant who had been in this country long enough to have established a modest business of his own as a shoemaker. Impressed by the future described by the bishop, Greene sold his house and shop and moved to Graceville, where he was able on arrival to buy outright 100 acres of land at $5.00 an acre. In company with Greene at this time were five other families from Marlboro and seven whom Ireland had recruited in Philadelphia.

A few years later one Daniel J. Walsh wrote from Philadelphia to Bishop O'Connor in Nebraska inquiring about the conditions for settling in one of the new western colonies of the Irish Catholic Colonization Association. The letter, written on his own business stationery, reveals that he was the proprietor of a wholesale woolen and cotton rag warehouse: "I write to you to ascertain in what manner I can join your colony opened some two years ago. . . . I am as you see by my letter heading in business here and just about making a living and I have a wife and 4 children. I am 33 years old, my oldest child, a boy, 10 years. I have had a desire for some years to take up a farm when lands are cheap and growing in value and I write you for advice. . . . I presume I could bring with me nearly four thousand dollars." Walsh was no illiterate. He wrote a fine Spencerian hand,

No. 107 North — **DAN'L J. WALSH & CO.** — **Front Street.**

WHOLESALE

Woolen and Cotton Rag Warehouse,

SHODDY MATERIAL, ETC.

Philadelphia, June 14 187

At Rec'd Dear Sir.

I write you to ascertain in what manner I can join your colony opened some two years ago. I understand the land are very good and climate mild. If it would not be too much trouble I would feel greatly obliged if you would give me full particulars in regard to the farming it. What the best quality and best located lands can be had for on time and also for cash. How near to a Rail Road and if streams are plenty on the Colony Lands. I am as you see by my letter heading in business here and I wish about making a living and I have a Wife + 4 Children. I am 38 Years old. My oldest is a boy 10 years. I have had a desire for some years to take up a farm where lands are cheap and growing in value and I write you for your advice as I have heard of your kind heartedness from some parties here who met you when you were here on a visit ten years ago. Hoping to hear from you at your earliest convenience. Remain,

D. J. Walsh

I presume I could bring with me nearly four thousand dollars.

Letter from Prospective Colonist

owned his own business, and could bring "four thousand dollars." He and Maurice Greene are typical of hundreds of farmers and small businessmen from the East who came to John Ireland's Minnesota colonies. The rising price of western lands, contrasted with the uncertainties of business competition in the East, convinced them that a better economic future awaited them in the West.

On January 25, 1879, an unemployed miner in Brady's Bend, Pennsylvania, wrote to Dillon O'Brien, "This place, once famous for its iron works, (is) now abandoned by every body that can leave. . . . Brady's Bend once had the largest blast furnaces and rolling-mill in Pennsylvania, giving employment to five or six thousand men, but, through the incompetence and mismanagement of its officers, it has gone under, never to rise again, leaving a debt of $75,000 due the poor workingmen employed in and around here." The writer assured O'Brien that several of the unemployed steel workers were anxious to come to the Minnesota colonies, if some means could be pro-

vided for their transportation and subsidization. As in so many similar instances, O'Brien most likely extended his sympathy and explained that his bureau still lacked sufficient funds to underwrite such worthy pleas.

In contrast to the plight of the steel worker in Brady's Bend is the story of John Gorman, the boss puddler in a steel mill at Oxford, Warren County, New Jersey. Gorman was told by his doctor that the intense heat of the blast furnaces had injured his lungs so much that it was imperative for him to change to some kind of job that would keep him out in the fresh air. The doctor had read some of the railroad publicity recommending the "salubrity" of the climate in Minnesota for any persons suffering from respiratory illnesses. He suggested that Gorman write to Bishop Ireland in St. Paul. On his foreman's salary, Gorman had saved a sufficient sum to enable him to buy outright three forty-acre tracts near Sweetman's Currie settlement in Minnesota. In 1883 he brought his family to Murray County, Minnesota, and his great-grandchildren still live in the Currie settlement.

During the first year of operations in Bishop Ireland's Swift County colony, Ignatius Donnelly reported in his *Anti-Monopolist* that several delegations "from the workshops of Boston and the coal and iron mines of Pennsylvania have visited Swift County and secured land. They will be followed by others. If the stream of idle mechanics and miners of the East, many of whom have considerable sums in savings banks, can be turned to the fertile plains of Minnesota, the welfare of the immigrants and the growth of the state will both be secured in an eminent degree. Success to the great and charitable enterprise." Many of the settlers who first came to the colony in Swift County were precisely men of this category, miners or shop workers who had sufficient savings to move west and buy their own land. They were enterprising fellows who recognized the limitations of their positions in the East and who grasped at the same time the opportunities to be found on farms in the West.

That these particular instances are typical of the status of settlers coming to western Minnesota

133

in these years is demonstrated by Secretary Young's report to the Minnesota State Board of Immigration for 1879. During eight months of that year 40,000 immigrants had entered the state and had brought with them a sum exceeding $4,000,000. "Those with most means were the German and French; less, English; least, Irish. Many had from $1,000 to $10,000. Seven from Germany arrived at one time with drafts of $20,-000; one came with $9,000, and possessed property in Germany; it was common for them to have $500-$8,000 with them."

Patrick Donohue, Secretary of the Irish Catholic Benevolent Union National Colonization Board, reported to the members of the Union in March 1876 that most of the inquiries about colonization came from Catholic farmers and small-town residents in New England, and he added, "Most of the correspondents represent themselves as possessing 'some means.'" A few years later Martin Griffin mentioned in an editorial in his Journal, "Very few correspondents of the Philadelphia Colonization Society are from the large cities, but nearly all are from the small towns and villages of the country."

Eighteen months after the opening of the colony at Adrian, Minnesota, a settler named O'Hearn wrote to the *Northwestern Chronicle* that all the government land and all but a few parcels of railroad (colony) lands had been sold in Nobles County and that most of the new residents had come to that colony from other farms in eastern Minnesota. "Nearly all the colony land that has been bought here is (sic) by farmers from the eastern and northern parts of Minnesota, generally old Minnesotans, most of them pretty comfortable, many of them buying half-sections, and several of them buying more." O'Hearn explicitly stated in this letter that the great attraction in Nobles County was the bumper crops of flax and wheat that had been harvested during the three previous seasons. The harvest of 1878 had in some parts of the colony yielded forty bushels of wheat to the acre, and the average had been from 25 to 30 bushels. Given these facts, the migration within Minnesota in these years can be explained primarily by the greater economic advantages to

be found in the West. Men who knew farm values moved into the areas of agricultural opportunity, and of these men, the Catholic members settled in the townships which had a church and school. Even to the present day the parish of St. Adrian, with its parochial elementary and high school, has the largest enrollment of Catholic students in Nobles County. Men who came West for realistic reasons found what they wanted, and the subsequent history of their settlement has been characterized by great stability. For the most part the residents in Nobles County today are essentially the same kind of people who came when the land there was first opened for settlement.

Bishop Ireland had warned Minnesota farmers that he would sell his colony lands only to persons coming from out of the state. He had been disturbed to read in his own diocesan paper an account of three farmers from Watertown (eastern Minnesota) who had arranged to sell their eighty-acre farms (with log houses and thirty acres under the plow) for $1,600 each, with the intention of moving into his Swift County colony (western Minnesota), where this sum would purchase four times as much land. His stern warning against this practice had little effect; there were too many ways of getting around his regulations.

It was always to be a disappointment to John Ireland that he never succeeded in bringing poor people into his colonies; but by the very nature of the enterprise, and especially because of its timing, capital was a necessary part of its success. By this time the design of bonanza-type farm machinery had advanced sufficiently to enable one farmer and his family to cultivate huge tracts of land which formerly could have been worked only by several farmers.

The Minnesota settlers of this period were far from impecunious pioneers. Just a few months after the opening of Ireland's first colony in Swift County, a farm machinery distributor in Benson reported that the larger areas of these western farm lands made the new type of machinery imperative for the settlers. "The farmer who would stop to sow his wheat broadcast, or to reap it with a cradle, would be laughed at by his neighbors."

Such elaborate machinery, however, required a considerable investment from the prairie farmers. That they were for the most part prepared to meet such an outlay would appear from such notices as that printed in the *Benson Times* for June 5, 1876: "There are some 35,000 bushels of wheat in our elevators, mostly owned by the farmers in the vicinity of Morris who are not disposed to part with it at the present prices. They are rich enough to pay storage and wait for a rise in the market. Not so bad for a frontier community."

In an era of industrial growth, American agriculture, while it became increasingly lucrative, resembled the rest of American business in that it demanded ever increasing amounts of capital. The family of one M. Daly, after arriving in Bishop Ireland's De Graff colony, found to its dismay that this was no place for poor people. Being unable to find open government land near the railroad, they all packed up and returned to their home in Buffalo, New York. Even on this new frontier a modicum of capital was necessary for success. Payments on the land, seed, livestock, and farm machinery of recent design, not to mention cash reserves sufficient to supply a family with food and clothing for at least two years, effectively limited the number of persons who were in a position to take up colony lands.

It is more difficult to determine the political sympathies of the new colonists than to describe their economic status, although the two factors were certainly not unrelated. It is clear, as might have been expected, that many of the incoming settlers voted the straight Democratic ticket. However, there is good reason for believing that the financial position of many of the colonists influenced their political allegiance and inclined them to share their episcopal patron's loyalty to the Republican party.

In these years John Ireland was already becoming famous as one of Minnesota's leading Republicans. His party ties, which were to bring him international prominence under the Republican administrations of McKinley, Roosevelt, and Taft, were already widely known; and although he did not openly campaign in Minnesota for Republican candidates, he was able to write to one Angela Ewing on March 26, 1885, that he was confident the Irish vote in Minnesota had supported James G. Blaine against Grover Cleveland.

It may have been that some Catholics—normally Democrats—voted for the Republican Blaine, prompted by the knowledge that Blaine had at one time practiced the Catholic Faith. In a private letter to Austin Ford, editor of the New York *Irish World*, Ireland spoke of having tried to bring Blaine back to the practice of his religion. Whatever the motives behind the vote of 1884, the bishop was satisfied that the Irish Catholics in Minnesota had voted for the Republican candidate. On the other hand, Dillon O'Brien, who was in more immediate contact with the Catholic settlers on the land, was an equally loyal member of the Democratic party all the years he lived in Minnesota. As often as he was called on, though, to address political and civic gatherings, O'Brien "gave little attention to politics." Certainly in comparison to the acknowledged Republican sympathies of Bishop Ireland, O'Brien's quiet and enduring loyalty to the Democratic party was not likely to influence the Catholic vote in Minnesota substantially.

Exactly what part the Catholic vote played in the western counties at this period remains uncertain. No candidate received a landslide vote from the Catholics of western Minnesota. On the basis of such limited evidence it can only be said that there was no discernible Catholic bloc of votes among the colonists. Apparently, immigrants who had been assimilated to American ways were already beginning to vote according to their economic interests and not primarily according to their religious or Old World ties.

When the first colony opened in Swift County in 1876, most of the settlers who came to it were Irish-born or the children of parents born in Ireland. With the passage of time Irish names became less and less numerous in the various colonies. It would be a serious mistake, however, to assume that even in the beginning these colonies were exclusively Irish settlements. In some instances, as at Ghent, they were from the start almost entirely non-Irish. So much has been written on the Irish portion of this westward movement that the non-Irish element (which eventually inherited at least the earth in western Minnesota) has been greatly neglected.

Many French, Belgian, German, and English —and a few Polish—Catholics answered Bishop Ireland's invitation to Minnesota. In every colony there were representatives of each of these national groups, although each colony had its own dominant national strain. In De Graff, Clontarf, Graceville, Avoca, Currie, and Adrian, Irish names predominated on the parish rosters. From the beginning until now the names in Ghent have been almost exclusively Belgian; and in Fulda, German. A significant, if not dominant, number of French families came early and are still prominent in the vicinity of Clontarf. The large numbers of French who came to Ghent and Currie have for the most part sold their lands and moved to the city. The English who came to Minneota, Adrian, and Swift County have demonstrated the "staying power" that has been traditional with the colonial representatives of their nation.

For several reasons German settlers were never numerous in John Ireland's colonies. Long before the bishop announced his first colony, German Catholic settlers had established their own thriving rural centers at New Ulm in Brown County and at St. Cloud in Stearns County. These centers continued to grow throughout the years of his episcopate, although they were in no sense part of his colonization endeavor. There were, of course, many settlers of German origin who finally settled on his lands, although there was never anything like a mass movement of German settlers to his western colony sites.

If the work of John Ireland, Dillon O'Brien, and John Sweetman in settling western Minnesota demonstrates conclusively any single axiom for future colonizers, it is that contained in John Sweetman's discerning remark: "Men taken at haphazard will not succeed in Western farming." Of all who came to the Catholic settlements in Minnesota between 1875 and 1881, the Belgians have been the most successful colonizers, because they were farmers when they left home. They knew the science of agriculture, and they wanted to continue as farmers. The only reason for their leaving home was a desire to find more and better land than was then available to them in Belgium and Holland.

Conversely, the Irish settlers who were brought to Minnesota by various forms of "assisted emigration" were almost universally unsuccessful. These were men, to use Sweetman's term, "taken at haphazard." Almost without exception they left the land as soon as they could. This should not surprise anyone who will consider their previous training and qualification. Few of them had ever farmed before; none had money at stake in the farming venture and hence risked no loss by giving up the land. Probably of even more significance, they had not been tested by the rigors of independent farming on any earlier frontiers in states lying east of Minnesota.

The Irish-American farmers who came to Minnesota by stages are the ones who have persevered. These are the farmers with Irish names who now farm the land at De Graff, Clontarf, Graceville, Avoca, Currie, Adrian, Lismore, and Iona. The stages of their respective treks westward can be followed in the pages of the unpublished state and federal census reports for the years the colonies were getting started. These census schedules indicate the place of birth for every child and adult listed. Such listings make it possible to check the various stages in the movement of a family. For example, the Irish-American settlers who made up the bulk of the De Graff and Clontarf settlements in 1876 had already moved at least twice before coming to Minnesota. Often the head of the family is listed as having been born in Ireland, his wife in New York or Massachusetts, his first two children in Pennsylvania or Ohio, and his last two or three in Indiana or Illinois. The evidence is overwhelming that the actual process of migration, through various stages, conditioned the Irish-American farmer. At home he had not learned the science of agriculture, because that science was then neither widely known nor carefully practiced in Ireland. Settlers coming from farms in Belgium or Germany or Quebec had a tremendous initial advantage over the Irish farmer brought directly from his native land to the American West. The European farmers knew the value and importance of fertilizer, and the necessity for crop rotation, and they knew from experience the bountiful rewards the earth would yield to those who tended it wisely and with perseverance. These important truths the Irish-American farmer had to learn by trial and error on small farms in the East before he could succeed on a large farm in the West.

This interpretation does not imply or assume any kind of national genius on the part of either European settlers or native Americans. It is based simply upon a recognition of the vital importance of the cultural heritage and previous training brought to the western frontier by new settlers. Free land did not make these settlers over; it merely challenged them to apply the talents and training and knowledge they brought with them. By and large, the European settlers (from Belgium, Holland and Germany) came with superior training and knowledge in . agriculture. Other Europeans and many Irish immigrants who came to Minnesota by progressive stages had learned on

various eastern "frontiers" the new skills necessary for western farming. And what is just as important, they had learned to appreciate the demands and the rewards of the farming life. The immigrant newly arrived from Galway, with his memories of farm life, its insecurity, its poverty, and its intolerable injustice did not plunge joyously into the life of a western farmer.

Ole Rolvaag's hero, Per Hansa, conversely, is very much a farmer in the European tradition. As he awoke at dawn on his first day on the Dakota prairie, he dressed quickly and hurried out to yoke his sleepy oxen. Long before breakfast he had plowed several furrows in the rich prairie loam. This was his own, his very own land; and it promised him wealth, social position, and honor. In Norway his father had labored a lifetime but had never been rich enough to own eighty acres of such soil as this.

Similarly, after Kirtland, Ohio, Nauvoo, Illinois, and Council Bluffs, Iowa, Brigham Young knew when he saw the Great Basin in Utah that this was "the place." European, French Canadian,

Early threshing rig

Lake Benton

and Irish-American farmers who knew what they wanted when they left home recognized it when they found it in western Minnesota. Others who came and saw that vast prairie, stretching for miles to the western sky, were only repelled by its loneliness. They moved back to the cities in search of another kind of opportunity.

The largest and most successful Catholic colonization program ever undertaken in the United States was that sponsored by Bishop John Ireland in Minnesota between 1876 and 1881. In subsequent years the specific virtues of this local western project have regularly been overlooked by historians who were interested only in describing the national scene. Most often Ireland's work as a colonizer has been lumped with that of the unsuccessful stock companies and pronounced a failure. This article, it is hoped, has at least established the unfairness of this judgment and has demonstrated that Ireland's settlement program was unique and that it therefore merits separate consideration as a significant chapter in the history of the upper Mississippi Valley and as an illustration of that rare phenomenon in American history—successful colony settlement.

The besetting evil of most colonies throughout history has been the inflexibility of the plan on which they were established, usually with preconceived notions as to the type of settlers to be accepted, the economic basis to be adopted, and the social organization to be enforced. Such dogmatic bases have imparted to most colony settlements an internal rigidity and a degree of social isolation which separated them from the surrounding society. Religious colonies especially have been characterized by such singularity. Quite properly, histories of these settlements have most often been studies of the peculiar features of these "islands" in American society.

In contrast to this traditional pattern of exclusiveness in colonization programs, the Catholic colonies in Minnesota were organized according to an unusually flexible plan. They avoided both the fixity of a preconceived program of activity and the rigor of an imposed regime. Although they were designed primarily but not exclusively for people of Irish stock and Catholic faith, these were virtually the only *a priori* decisions made by their founders. The test for the type of settlers was a pragmatic one: Ireland wanted colonists who were qualified to succeed in a western agricultural enterprise. As to the financial basis, it was a very permissive one in which the colonizing agent held no permanent control but simply served to bring the colonist and the land owner (in this instance the railroad) into a productive relationship with each other (again the criterion was success). Socially, no regime was imposed and no exclusiveness was attempted—the only social policy was to provide churches under the guidance of well chosen priests— and the influence which the Church exercised was no different from that which it exercised over its members in other parts of the world. Social relations were worked out on a pragmatic basis. As new situations arose demanding changes in colony affairs, these settlements were able to adjust to the new status without the convulsions which occurred in earlier rigidly controlled communities. Also, the Minnesota colonies fitted into the society around them and did not become set-apart villages. The fact that they have been somewhat less distinctive than earlier similar foundations has possibly made them less appealing as a subject for writers who are in search of the unusual and the extreme. This same lack of singularity, however, makes them especially noteworthy in the history of the western settlement in America. They represent a successful fusion of the group-settlement plan tried by so many utopian communities and the far more common pattern of westward migration by individual families.

In the pragmatic character of the Minnesota colony plan, in its voluntaristic or permissive conditions, in its emphasis upon success, and in the willingness to seek its objectives (the extension of Catholicism and the attainment of financial security) through competitive trials rather than through protection, there is something markedly American. Archbishop John Ireland is known in history as a prelate who did much to adjust Catholic beliefs to American attitudes, and the character of his colonial settlements furnishes a striking illustration of one way in which he succeeded.

CHAPTER SIX

The Church
in Minnesota

by DANIEL J. HAFREY

The frail canoes which carried the first white explorers and fur traders over the perilous waters of Lake Superior into what later became Minnesota often as not also held a priest or friar. For next to the quest for furs and riches, and the search for the Northwest passage, the desire to spread the word of God was among the most powerful motives sending forth the men of New France into the wilderness of the Sioux and Chippewa. Hennepin, Marquette, Galtier, Cretin, Pierz and Baraga are just a few of the numerous place names in the state which attest to the early activities of the Catholic church in this area.

If men of the church were important in the opening of the Minnesota territory, religion also played a vital role in the settlement of the state some two centuries later. The tens of thousands of pioneers who streamed into the territory from Germany, Scandinavia and other parts of Europe were looking for a better living as well as for escape from the confining rigidities of Old World institutions, including their churches. Family devotions, prayer meetings and the building of primitive churches were high on the priority list of these pioneers.

Thus, from the day Father Louis Hennepin, the Belgian Recollect Franciscan, first set eyes on St. Anthony Falls, religion and the church have been an essential part of the Minnesota scene. Minnesota history, its past and present, have been closely joined to the life of the church, first to missionaries and frontier priests, now to some of the sturdiest, most solidly grounded church organizations in the nation.

Minnesotans always have taken their religion seriously, even in what some call the "Godless days" when American church membership fell low and lower before the current religious revival. Church membership in Minnesota has been, and is today, high. Most recent figures (1957) list 61.5 per cent of all Minnesotans as belonging to a church.

Nationwide figure for 1957, according to the National Council of Churches, was 49 per cent. Among all states, Minnesota ranked seventh highest in church membership. It was exceeded significantly only by Rhode Island, with 75.5 per cent, and Utah, with 73.6 per cent. Both of these states are typical in the sense that their religious scene is overwhelmingly dominated by one strong church, the Roman Catholic in Rhode Island, the Mormons in Utah.

Speak to an Easterner of Minnesota and the things that come to his mind are the Mississippi, Indians and Lutherans. And to be sure, Minnesota fully deserves its title of "Lutherland of America." The sons and daughters of the monk of Wittenberg make up 42.5 per cent of all church members in the state. Lutherans make up the single largest denomination in the state and their number is more than double that of all other Protestant groups combined.

Using the last official census figure—1950—of 2,982,483 for the state's total population, the

1957 National Council of Churches survey found 794,445 Lutherans, organized in 1,996 congregations. At the rate new congregations and churches are springing up, their number had gone over the 2,000 mark by the time the results of the survey were in print. One Lutheran synod alone, the Evangelical Lutheran Church, reports setting up a new congregation every ten days over the past several years. A good share of those new congregations are in Minnesota, the synod's home state.

But the Lutherans are not alone in the state, nor were they the first. Probably the first house of worship, expressly built for that purpose, in Minnesota territory was put up by Radisson and Groseilliers, both good Catholics, on Prairie Island in 1655. The first mass on Minnesota soil was said at the French Catholic mission of St. Michael the Archangel, part of Fort Beauharnois on the western shore of Lake Pepin, in 1727. Until then, and for another century to come, the men of the church of Rome had the Minnesota territory exclusively to themselves. Plans now are under way to restore the historic Lake Pepin site with the creation of Frontenac State Park. Catholics hope to recreate the fort and chapel as part of it.

The first Protestant church in the territory was what later became First Presbyterian in Minneapolis, founded in 1835 at Fort Snelling. Presbyterians today still are the fourth largest religious group in the state. Again, as in the case of Catholic expansion in this part of the country, Protestant missionaries came to the northern part before they moved into today's centers of population. The first Protestant mission to serve this territory was opened in 1830 at LaPointe on Lake Superior's Madeline Island, one of the main centers of the fur trade in the Northwest Territory. An attractive, recently-opened historical museum at LaPointe, now part of Wisconsin, gives graphic illustrations of the activities of these pioneer missionaries among the Ojibway.

Roman Catholics today are the second largest religious group in Minnesota, although a variety of figures is given for their strength. Current figures from Catholic sources put them at 790,400. The 1957 National Council of Churches survey,

whose figures usually are on the conservative side, places them at 690,807.

Still using National Council figures, total Protestant strength in Minnesota is 37.1 per cent of the population, with Lutherans followed in terms of membership by Methodists, Presbyterians and Congregational Christians. Catholics make up some 23 per cent of the population. This is the highest percentage in any state west of the Mississippi, except for the old Catholic states of Louisiana and New Mexico. There also are 37,872 Jews, a smaller number of Eastern Orthodox church members— such as the Greek, Ukrainian and Russian Orthodox—and a small handful of Moslems and members of Far Eastern religions, in addition to the less numerous Protestant denominations.

Protestants have the majority of church members in all but 15 of the state's 87 counties. Their majority includes the most populous, Hennepin. Catholics outnumber Protestants in the remaining counties, which include Ramsey and St. Louis, the second and third most populous.

While the Lutherans were comparative latecomers to Minnesota soil — they didn't start to arrive in any appreciable numbers until the middle of the last century—there is one main feature that set them apart from the others. The other churches in the state started out largely as missions. Catholic churches, for instance, were supported financially and with manpower through the Leopoldine Society of Austria and the Jesuits of France. Methodists, Presbyterians, Congregationalists and Episcopalians sent out missionaries and funds from the East through such organizations as the American Board of Commissioners for Foreign Missions.

But the Lutherans were on their own the moment they left home. The clergy of Lutheran state churches in Germany and Scandinavia had little in common with the ordinary folk and showed little interest in the emigrants streaming to the American Midwest. In a number of cases, the clergy even put obstacles in the way of these emigrants. Hence they had to fend for themselves from the time they came to this country. This partly explains the vigor of the budding Lutheran congregations which either

Central Lutheran Church

had to overcome fearful odds or go under. Hence, also the vast multiplicity of the Lutheran church as it developed in America. Today all sixteen of the major Lutheran synods are represented in Minnesota. At one time there were more.

This immediate need to fight for material survival, plus the often critical shortage of pastors, combined with that peculiarly American flair for pragmatic practicality to create a condition which persists somewhat until today. American Lutherans, compared with their brethren elsewhere, have been short on theology and long on organization and practical deeds. The system of lay administration of a congregation, and lay responsibility for its financial condition, has led to the unique stewardship program which has flourished so prodigiously in this country.

Old World Lutherans may have looked down a bit on their Midwestern cousins in the past for their not too impressive showing in the field of profound religious thought. But this feeling soon was overshadowed by gratitude and admiration when American Lutherans came to their assistance after two devastating world wars. Scores of Minnesota Lutheran leaders were active in the relief and reconstruction work of Lutheran World Relief which poured millions upon millions of dollars into impoverished European churches. And Minnesotans also are leading among the American

Lutherans who have gone abroad to teach their brethren the American concept of voluntary stewardship responsibility to replace the impersonal, chill state support of established churches.

If the conditions which 19th century Lutheran immigrants found in Minnesota led to separatism and isolation, the churches they founded also were responsive to the challenges of the American melting pot and its great unifying force. Separated by language, geographic origin and liturgical tradition the Danes, Norwegians, Swedes, Germans and Finns first set up their distinct churches and synods.

But as American Lutherans grew into the second and third generation—and especially as the flood of immigrants dried up after World War I— they soon came to appreciate the injunction of 18th century Melchior Muhlenberg of Pennsylvania, the grand old man of American Lutheranism: to exist successfully in this country it isn't enough for a church to preserve the purity of its old country beliefs and traditions; rather it has to move along with the stream of American development and thought.

Minnesota's Norwegian Lutherans, under the leadership of venerable Dr. J. A. Aasgaard and like-minded men of firm convictions and even firmer will, for instance, have been in the forefront of the merger movement to draw together a multitude of groups into stronger, more efficiently organized and better administered synods. The Evangelical Lutheran Church, with 1,083,007 members, the third largest Lutheran synod in the country, is the result of these repeated mergers.

For the past several years the Evangelical Lutheran Church also has been engaged in negotiations which will culminate in an even bigger step soon— merger with the German-origin American Lutheran Church and the Danish United Evangelical Lutheran Church. The leaders of the Evangelical Lutheran Church, along with those of the United Lutheran Church in America, have been among the first to discard the idea of a national-origin church and think in the framework of a country-wide church. Thus these two churches—the United Lutheran Church, though relatively weak in Minnesota, is the largest Lutheran synod in America and especially strong in the East—were pioneers in seeking converts among national groups to whom Lutheranism is foreign and in setting up congregations in parts of the country without a Lutheran tradition.

Just as the Norwegian Evangelical Lutheran Church is promoting its three-way merger, the Swedes' Augustana synod is an active participant in a movement which will result in the merger of Augustana with the United Lutheran Church in America (largely of German origin), the Finns' Suomi synod and the Danes' American Evangelical Lutheran Church.

The American need for unity, plus the realization that only by joining forces could Lutherans hope to do an effective job of charity and welfare work at home and relief and mission work abroad, also has placed Minnesota Lutheran leaders in the van of the movement for even broader co-operation. They were active in setting up the National Lutheran Council representing five of this country's seven million Lutherans. And they were equally active in setting up the Lutheran World Federation and its predecessor organization.

The role that has come to Minnesota because of all this is shown by the fact that three of the sixteen synods have their national headquarters in Minneapolis. They are the Evangelical Lutheran Church, Augustana Lutheran Church and Lutheran Free Church. When the Evangelical Lutheran

Church's merger with its two partners goes through in 1961, the headquarters of the mammoth new church will be in Minneapolis still. Well over two million of America's Lutherans will look to Minneapolis then.

While there is less room in the centralized Roman Catholic Church for independent development than in the individualistic Protestant denominations, Minnesota Catholics, too, have made a significant contribution to their church's life in this country. It was St. Paul's Archbishop John Ireland who never tired of impressing on the Catholics of his day that it was not enough to be good Catholics but that they had to be good Americans, too. It was Ireland who pulled the underprivileged, hesitant Irish and German Catholics of the late 19th and early 20th century into ever deeper involvement in all aspects of the American scene—economic, cultural and civic as well as religious.

It was the same towering figure brimming over with purposeful energy who helped bring thousands of European Catholic farmers to the rich land of southwestern Minnesota, where settlements such as Ghent, Currie, Avoca, Fulda, Iona and Adrian bespeak the Irish, Belgian, German, English and French-Canadian origins of these settlers. In this enterprise, as in many others, Ireland was greatly aided by his friend James J. Hill of St. Paul, the "Empire Builder." Finally, it was the same Archbishop Ireland who fought the successful fight for establishment of Catholic University in Washington run by the secular clergy, who founded St. Thomas college and St. Paul Seminary and who built the St. Paul Cathedral.

Ireland's successors in the metropolitan see of St. Paul and its bishoprices diligently continued his efforts to correct the imbalance between large

St. Mark's Cathedral

142

urban and weak rural Catholic populations. The St. Paul Province has provided some of the strongest backing for organization of the Catholic Rural Life Conference. To this day the Province—and more particularly the Diocese of St. Cloud, that solid center of German Catholicism in this country —is among the strongholds of this organization dedicated to keeping Catholic families on the farm and enriching their spiritual and secular lives.

One of the major developments in American Catholic thought, the Liturgical movement, is centered in the ivied walls of Minnesota's St. John's University at Collegeville. St. John's Dom Virgil Michel, son of an immigrant German family of St. Paul, was among the very first Americans to be caught up in the Liturgical movement during a study tour of Europe in the early 1920s which took him to Mont César Abbey in Belgium and Maria Laach Abbey in Germany where the doctrine of the movement was being developed. Returning to St. John's to teach, and with the active approval of Abbot Alcuin Deutsch, he threw himself into the work of spreading the movement in this country. A major liturgical publication is edited at St. John's now. And North American Liturgical Conferences have been held repeatedly on the quiet, graceful St. John's campus.

Recognition of Minnesota's role in religious affairs also has come in the gathering of other national and world religious events in the state. In the summer of 1957 the Lutheran World Assembly, representing some 50 million faithful in 29 countries, met in Minneapolis. The World Anglican Conference of 1954 was an equal tribute to the state's Episcopal Diocese and the late Bishop Stephen E. Keeler.

Minnesota churches and religious leaders have had a distinguished part in the development in this country of what has been described as the "three major faiths concept." It is the idea that America is based on the Judeo-Christian tradition as expressed today by Catholicism, Protestantism and Judaism. And it is the thought that, while not numerically equal, all three major faiths have an equally important role to play in shaping the course of this nation and are entitled to the same rights and consideration. A practical illustration of this

Cathedral of St. Paul

St. Paul Chapel

concept is the presence at all major gatherings or ceremonies of a priest, minister and rabbi.

Such equal standing, and the growing respect that has come from greater familiarity gained in joint civic and charitable enterprises, also have contributed to better understanding among differing religious groups and have tended to increase tolerance and reduce religious prejudice of the kind against which John Ireland was struggling for the Catholics of 60 and 70 years ago. One practical expression is the spreading idea of the interfaith Thanksgiving service pioneered in Minneapolis by Grace Presbyterian, Trinity Community

143

(Baptist) and St. Paul Episcopal churches and Temple Israel and Adath Jeshurun synagogue.

Finally, clergymen of all faiths have been pioneer members of inter-racial councils, human rights commissions, fair employment practices commissions and the like.

But services, churches and church organizations are only the beginning of the religious picture in Minnesota. Education, too, from the very start has been a vital concern of the church in Minnesota. The first schools of the territory were conducted by Catholic fathers and Baptist and Episcopal women missionaries. Today, no less than in the early days, church-connected institutions play a decisive role in keeping the state's educational standards among the highest in the country.

Thriving seminaries supply the needs of churches in the state and beyond for young pastors. Leading among them are the seminary of the Catholic Archdiocese of St. Paul and Luther Theological Seminary in St. Paul. St. John's was founded to meet the shortage of priests on the western frontier. Today, operated by the largest Benedictine abbey in the world, it shares with a string of Catholic colleges the burden of providing a general education with a Catholic bent for the state's youth. With a grant from St. Paul's Hamm Foundation, St. John's also has added another pioneering first —it has set up a summer institute on pastoral psychology for the clergy of all faiths. Within a stone's throw of St. John's, at St. Joseph, also stands the world's largest Benedictine convent for women— St. Benedict's.

The Methodists' Hamline, Augustana's Gustavus Adolphus, the Lutheran Free Church's Augsburg, the Presbyterians' Macalester, the Evangelical Lutheran Church's St. Olaf, the Catholics' St. Mary's, St. Teresa's and St. Catherine's and Carleton College founded jointly by the Episcopalians, Baptists and Congregationalists—all these are just a random few of the many contributing so mightily to the moral and intellectual fiber of state and nation.

Northwestern Bible College in Minneapolis, founded by First Baptist Church's fiery William B. Riley, is one of the mainstays of fundamentalist religious education in America. Billy Graham went on from the school to world fame as an evangelist. The headquarters of his far-flung organization still is in Minneapolis.

Several of the Lutheran bodies maintain parochial schools. The Synodical Conference—made up of conservative Lutherans led by the Lutheran church-Missouri synod—is planning a high school in Minneapolis. So is the Wisconsin synod. Breck, Pillsbury, Shattuck, De La Salle, Villa Maria Academy, St. Mary's Hall and others—all founded and maintained by the churches—continue to provide high class elementary and secondary education. Three hundred eighty-four parochial schools are teaching 120,222 of the state's Catholic youngsters. And the archdiocese just has embarked on a 10-million-dollar program of expanding Catholic school facilities in the Twin Cities.

In the mushrooming suburbs whose explosive growth is close to bursting the public school systems, churches and synagogues again lend a helping hand. Where public schools can't provide kindergartens, such as for instance in Bloomington, the churches take over. Hebrew schools, too, shoulder a share of educating the state's Jewish children.

Every Sunday morning hundreds of thousands of more and less attentive youngsters throng Sunday schools up and down the state. If anybody feels the baby boom more than the public schools it is the churches, pleading almost desperately for more Sunday school teachers, doubling and tripling up to make enough room and launching crash programs to build more facilities.

With man's spiritual and educational needs served, the churches also busily minister to the needs of the flesh. Just as they pioneered in the schools they also were the first to build hospitals. Church connection in many cases is evident from a first glance at a hospital's name—such as Asbury Methodist, Lutheran Deaconess, Mount Sinai and the St. Mary's, St. Joseph's and St. Luke's across the state. In others the connection is just beneath the surface—as in the case of St. Barnabas and Sheltering Arms, both of whom owe their existence to Gethsemane Episcopal Church; Abbott, founded by Westminster Presbyterian Church, and the Evangelical Lutheran Church's Fairview Hospital, all in Minneapolis.

Father Hennepin at the Falls of St. Anthony

Confirmation of Sioux Indians at Fort Snelling, April, 1863 by Bishop Whipple

Christ Lutheran Church

Mt. Zion Synagogue In St. Paul

A unique chapter in the medical history of Minnesota was written by the Franciscan Sisters of the Congregation of Our Lady of Lourdes. Following the devastating Rochester cyclone of 1883 the sisters, under Mother Alfred Moes, offered to build a hospital if the Doctors Mayo would agree to direct it. St. Mary's Hospital was built and has contributed importantly to making Rochester one of the world's great medical centers. Today, with more than 1,000 beds, St. Mary's is one of the world's largest privately operated hospitals and a vital part of the Rochester team operation.

The churches' charitable and welfare work also has grown to the point where there is no problem, no need or difficulty they cannot meet. Among the most novel is the work of Dr. John B. Oman of Wesley Methodist Church in Minneapolis, a doctor both of divinity and psychiatry, who has started group therapy sessions for inmates of the Minneapolis workhouse. Incidentally, too, Dr. Oman is among the first pastors to give communion to shut-ins by means of television broadcasts.

In the field of welfare work, Catholic Charities was largely instrumental in bringing victims of Hungarian Communist terror to the state. Lutheran Refugee Service has brought over enough Latvian and Estonian displaced persons to make Minnesota one of the major Baltic settlements in America.

Protestant, Catholic and Jewish appeals channel tens of millions of dollars into overseas relief and rehabilitation.

The Lutheran Welfare Society of Minnesota, representing 1,103 National Lutheran Council congregations in the state, is the largest of its kind in the nation. The number of children it places for adoption—about 200 a year—is the largest of any private agency in the country. About one-third of all the unmarried mothers in the state use the services of Lutheran Welfare. Nor does the society limit its services to Lutherans. Finally, the society has become a valuable training ground for some of the nation's top welfare administrators. A former society executive, Jay L. Roney, was in charge of all public assistance programs in the United States Department of Health, Education and Welfare. Another, Dr. Henry J. Whiting, now is executive director of the welfare division of the National Lutheran Council.

Churches and synagogues have been pioneers in the care of children, from Duluth's Bethany to Minneapolis' Catholic Boys' Home. The nationally-known North Shore Cathedral in the Pines of Mount Olivet Lutheran—largest Lutheran congregation in the nation—is one of a legion of church-connected summer camps in the state. Now Mount Olivet is showing the broad range of its concern by blazing new trails in the care for the nation's growing senior citizen population with its projected million-dollar residence for older people.

The Evangelical Lutheran Church, too, with its string of old-age residences across the country, is in the van of forward-looking thought in the field. Walker Methodist Home for older people, located in Minneapolis and serving the entire state, is considered one of the finest in the nation.

Brick and mortar don't make a church and religious leaders through the years have put spiritual values first. Yet the physical plant to house them has grown to impressive proportions since the days of St. Columba's Mission on Gull lake and the Mission of St. Michael the Archangel. Figures for 1957 listed 4,399 church buildings in the state, from the modest wooden rural church to the unique St. Mary's of Warroad, probably the largest log church in the country, to architectural masterpieces such as stately St. Mark's Episcopal Cathedral in Minneapolis, the classical archdiocesan Catholic Cathedral in St. Paul or the homespun Gothic Cathedral of the Holy Trinity in the newly-created Catholic Diocese of New Ulm.

Some of the finest examples of contemporary church architecture can be found in First Christian, St. Olaf's Catholic and Christ Lutheran in Minneapolis and Mount Zion Synagogue in St. Paul. The Missouri synod's brand-new St. Peter's Church on the line between Minneapolis and Edina, designed by Ralph Rapson, is a revolutionary departure in church building with its central altar surrounded by pews and its glass roof. Equally revolutionary is the design of the new St. John's abbey church by Marcel Breuer, on which work started in the summer of 1958.

CHAPTER SEVEN

From Furs to Farming

By THEODORE FENSKE

"It is for our cool healthful climate that braces up the human frames for vigorous exertion, physical and mental, that we regard Minnesota incomparably superior to any other new state or territory in North America. They may raise more corn in Illinois, more wool in Ohio, more pork in Iowa, more cotton in Mississippi, but Minnesota can beat them all in raising men." So said an enthusiastic writer about Minnesota in a book published in 1853.

In another paragraph he points out that on the headwaters of the Mississippi, Rum River, and the St. Croix are extensive pine and hardwood forests, apparently inexhaustible for centuries. The logging, lumbering and the manufacturing of wood products have been important in Minnesota since the very early days up to the present time. Modern conservation practices have now insured that we probably will have forest resources far into the future, but the virgin pine and hardwood did not last for the centuries the writer spoke about. In parts of Minnesota much of the forest land has now become farm land.

Minnesota still has the reputation of producing healthy, strong and vigorous citizens. In the past one hundred years it has also become one of the leading agricultural states in the nation.

The products of Minnesota farms now help to feed the United States and the world. In the early years of statehood, with few exceptions, most of the farm products produced were consumed within the state, and in many instances, it was necessary to import food into the state. Horace Greely, editor of the powerful New York Tribune, had some rather caustic things to say about the failure of Minnesota to feed herself. He said that the worthlessness of the territory was proven by the fact that it could not feed itself and then went on to say, "it imported loafers, the bread that they ate . . ."

Now Minnesota farmers sell more than a billion and a quarter dollars worth of agricultural products each year. Truly, this is a far cry from the days of 1858 when the territory became a state.

Up to 1840 the fur trade was the economic basis of Minnesota's development. Lumbering was still in its infancy in 1850 but was fast becoming the leading industry. By the close of the 1850-60 decade, agriculture had established itself in the new state, and has continued to develop ever since.

The change from furs to timber to agriculture is a thrilling story and will be told briefly in the following pages.

The Indians were the first farmers in what is now the United States. History records that on more than one occasion the early colonists owed their existence to the fact that they were able to secure food, notably corn, from the Indians. Captain John Smith and his colony are said to have benefited this way. The Pilgrim fathers and their group were able to survive only because of the food they secured from the friendly Indians of the area. Indeed, they learned some primitive but very useful lessons in agriculture from the Indians—for example, the practice of fertilizing the crop by placing fish in a hole, covering it with dirt, and then planting the corn above the fish, which served to provide plant food in the same way that commercial fertilizer does today.

The first agricultural efforts in Minnesota, if they could be called that, were undertaken by the Indians. As a matter of record, twenty-eight definite farm practices have been credited to the American Indians north of Mexico, and it is likely that many of these were practiced by those tribes that inhabited what is now Minnesota.

The Indian's supply of foods from cultivated plants, however, was limited and varied in quantity from year to year. Samuel W. Pond, one of the early missionaries in the state, said in commenting on the Dakotas or Sioux in Minnesota as they were in 1834:

"At most of the (Indian) villages a very little corn was raised by some of the families, but only enough to supply them with food for a few days. Before 1834, no land had been plowed by or for them except a little at Lake Calhoun. Mr. Renville's relatives raised a little corn at Lac qui Parle, but only a little. More corn was raised at that time at Lake Traverse than anywhere else among the Dakotas. Mr. Mooers, who had been there many years, had persuaded the Indians to plant corn. Major Long found him at Lake Traverse, and mentions the cornfields which he saw."

Major Stephen H. Long, referred to by Pond, conducted an expedition up the Mississippi and down the Red River in the summer of 1823. On this trip he visited Lake Traverse, and, no doubt, this is the reason for the reference made by Pond. Incidentally, Major Long, in his report of that trip, mentioned the fact that the Red River Valley was, in places, extremely fertile. In this observation he was entirely correct as later developments in that famous valley have shown.

Henry Schoolcraft, in his Journal of Travels, described a corn festival in August of 1820, at Little Crow's village below Fort Snelling on the Mississippi. Apparently, the harvesting of corn was a cause for celebration and festivity. Schoolcraft concludes his description of this particular festival with these words, "From all that could be learned, it was a feast in honor of the cereal goddess or Manito of the Indians which is annually held when the corn first becomes suitable for boiling in the ear."

The white man began farming in Minnesota around trading posts, military posts and missions. Early accounts of traders in this area mention food products which were produced in their gardens and small fields nearby.

For example, an account written in 1807 concerning the Northwest Company's post at Fond du Lac says, "Here are two horses, a cow, a bull, and a few pigs; with the manure of these animals a garden of 3 acres is cultivated which produces about 220 bushels of potatoes."

This same writer also describes the garden at the Sandy Lake post which produced about 1,000 bushels of potatoes, some beans and peas, and mentions also the Northeast Company's post at the west end of Leech Lake with its garden providing 1,000 bushels of potatoes, and other garden products.

Lieutenant Zebulan M. Pike of the United States Army visited Minnesota in 1805-06 and in his journal wrote of the Northwest Company's post at Sandy Lake, mentioning a protected inclosure of about four acres in which Irish potatoes were produced. He also described the Northeast Company's fort at Leech Lake with its inclosed garden of about five acres.

Henry Schoolcraft in 1820 visited the military post, then known as Fort St. Anthony, later Fort Snelling, and wrote as follows:

"Since its arrival the garrison has cleared and put under cultivation about ninety acres of the choicest bottom and prairie lands which are chiefly planted with Indian corn and potatoes; besides a large hospital, a regimental and several company and private gardens which supply vegetables in great abundances for all the men. Here we were first presented with green corn, pease, beans, cucumbers, beets, radishes, lettuce, etc. The first green pease were eaten here on the 15th of June and the first green corn on the 20th of July. Much of the corn is already too hard to be boiled for the table, and some ears can be selected which are ripe enough for seed corn. We found the wheat nearly ripe, and melons nearly so. These are the best commentaries that can be offered on the soil and climate. To ascertain, however, that the former is of the richest quality, a cursory examination is only required. It presents all the peculiar appearances which characterize the fertile Alluvians of the valley of the Ohio. In favor of the climate all the officers of the garrison speak in terms of highest admiration."

In these early years there was no land legally available for settlement. This was all "Indian country." Lieutenant Pike had made a purchase from the Indians in 1807, but this was for military purposes only. In 1837 treaties were made with the Indians whereby certain lands were ceded to the white man, thus opening land for settlement. In 1838 congress ratified the treaty, but survey of the land was delayed. It was not until August 14, 1848, that title could be obtained to any land in Minnesota. The townsites of St. Paul, Stillwater, and St. Anthony were included in a sale held at the land office at St. Croix Falls. The price was $1.25 per acre.

It is interesting to note that Minnesota's first farmers came from the north rather than from the south and east as would naturally be supposed. In 1811 Lord Selkirk, who had secured a controlling interest in the Hudson's Bay Company, acquired a tract of land of 116,000 square miles west and south of Lake Winnipeg. This was roughly the area of the province of Manitoba and the northern parts of North Dakota and Minnesota. Selkirk intended to establish Scotch peasants on farms in his domain.

In 1821 a group of Swiss merchants and tradesmen came to the Selkirk settlement. They found that Selkirk's agent had painted a much rosier picture of conditions than actually existed. Five of the Swiss families decided not to stay and migrated south to the "States," and were permitted to squat near Fort Snelling. In 1823, thirteen other Swiss families left the colony in Canada and some of these came on down to Fort Snelling. Again, in 1826, over two hundred people, mostly Swiss, left Pembina and came to Fort Snelling. Some stayed, others went on down the river.

Farms were cultivated on the military tract at Fort Snelling. There was some question as to whether they should be permitted and there was some resistance to them, until 1837 when the Indian treaty was ratified.

At that time (1837) there were reported 82 persons in the settlement on the Fort Snelling reservation. They had about 200 head of horses and cattle. In addition, there were 25 persons at Mendota and 50 at other trading posts immediately surrounding the vicinity. Most of these people were Swiss and had come from the Selkirk settlement in Canada. Some two years after the legal opening of the territory east of the Mississippi to settlement, that is on May 6, 1840, all squatters were removed from the Fort Snelling reservation. Some of them moved to what is now St. Paul, and one, Gervais by name, founded an agricultural colony about nine miles north of St. Paul in what is now known as Little Canada.

Actually, in 1840, Minnesota was pretty much of a fur state. In the years 1850 to 1860 agriculture began to be established. From 1860 to 1885 was the period of extensive wheat and small grain farming. Next came the period, 1885 to 1905, when the livestock system of farming became fairly well established. Farming has always been a way of life, but in recent years it has taken on more aspects of business than in the earlier years when the pioneer farmer was more or less self-sufficient. The period after World War II has seen more rapid development of machinery, use of fertilizers and chemicals, and other changes than has been true at any other time in history.

To return to the first farmers, one who is sometimes given credit for being the territory's pioneer farmer was Joseph R. Brown for whom one of Minnesota's counties was named. Primarily a trader and early lumberman, he is said to have broken up a piece of prairie near Minnehaha Falls and in 1829 to have raised a crop there. Actually, as we have already seen, other traders and soldiers at military posts had raised garden and other farm products before this date.

Most agricultural historians are agreed that the first real agricultural locality to be settled was in southern Washington county. The first farmers were Joseph Haskell and James S. Norris who settled near Afton about 1839. Later, in 1841, Norris moved to a new claim in Cottage Grove. The first field of three acres of broken sod was planted to corn and potatoes. This is said to be the first farm north of Prairie du Chien.

Sod House

Farming in those early days was very much different than it is at the present time. Most of it was of the self-sufficient type. Early diaries indicate that the farmer's wife made her own soap and did many other things which now the farmer's wife would never think of doing. The farmer dressed pork and prepared beef for his own use. In the woods country buildings were built out of the native logs at hand. Later, as farming spread into the prairie acres, the sod house and barn were often the first buildings on the farm.

Early farm implements were crude, and often home built. A sharp axe and a set of carpenter's tools were a very useful and necessary part of the settler's equipment.

William Watts Folwell makes this comment about the early settlement of Minnesota:

"As we reach 1849, the close of the period under present observation, we find the major part of the white population on Minnesota soil in the villages of St. Paul, Stillwater and St. Anthony—the first a commercial river port, the other two lumbering towns. Other aggregations, mostly of transient persons, were at minor points in the St. Croix, at Fort Snelling and Fort Gaines, at Mendota and other trading ports. To these must be added the bois brullis at Pembina, residents more or less permanently on the American side of the international line. Of rural settlement there was but a bare beginning on the beautiful prairie land abutting on Lake St. Croix in Washington County. With the exception of the trifling amount of produce from these farms and a few gardens and of wild game, the whole substenance of the white population was brought up from below by steamboats. Whole cargoes of pork and flour were discharged at St. Paul and Mendota for distribution. Even forage for animals was thus imported."

The organization of the Minnesota territory was formally proclaimed on June 1, 1849. In order to comply with the provisions of the territorial constitution, a census was ordered to be taken as of June 11, 1849. It should be kept in mind that the territory then included the present state of Minnesota, and the Dakotas east of the Missouri and the White Earth Rivers. The only organized county in the whole territory was known as St. Croix County and the sheriff was the officer empowered to take the census. Indians were excluded, but half breeds were to be included in the census.

The official reports of this census shows that there were 3,067 males and 1,713 females or a total of 4,780 people in the territory. Some historians doubt that figure, feeling that it was higher than the actual number of people.

The census of 1850 reported 6,077 persons. The number of men reported as farmers was 340 including 77 in St. Paul, and probably also included others elsewhere who were not actually farming. Total land in farms was 28,881 acres, improved land 5,035 acres, and the number of separate farms 157. Some of these farms, however, were only garden plots.

The largest farms were in three counties: Ramsey, Benton and Washington and the honor of having the largest farms went to Washington County with one of 339 acres.

By way of comparison, the Agricultural Census of 1954 lists 165,225 separate farms with 165,324 farm operators. There were 32,284,539 acres in farm land. What a remarkable change in the short space of 104 years!

The early settlers in Minnesota faced a problem which we scarcely think about today. During the interval between actual settlement and government registration, the question of obtaining legal title to his land was uppermost in the settler's mind. In 1841, Congress passed a comprehensive preemption bill, which in effect made it possible for the settler to obtain title to the land on which he may have settled.

However, in some cases there was no machinery for determining who was the rightful preemptor or settler on a specific piece of land. Without a government survey, description of tracts of land was impossible. Blazed or marked trees, stakes, or stones, all of which could be readily changed, invited claim jumping. The settler might leave his claim for a time only to come back and find that someone else with little regard for temporary markers had taken over in his absence. To meet the

problem, the pioneer settlers devised what they called land claim associations.

Some nine of these associations existed at one time or another. Three were along the Mississippi River, one at Brownsville in Houston County, two near what is now Winona at Wabasha Prairie and Rollingstone. There were four near the Twin Cities, one at Mendota, one east of Fort Snelling in what is now St. Paul, one in the area of what is now downtown Minneapolis, and one near Lake Calhoun. There was also one in what is now Nicollet County and another in Benton County.

The purpose of the claim association was to insure that the rightful claimant would not lose title to his claim through the action of someone who had no scruples as to how he obtained a piece of land claimed by another.

In 1847, government surveys extended into sections between the Mississippi and St. Croix Rivers. In 1848, Henry H. Sibley, acting as agent for the claimants of lots totaling 90 acres that had been surveyed, bid for all of these lots and secured them at a land sale at St. Croix Falls. In this instance, there was no formal claim association, but the strategy was the same, namely, the claimants came in a body and watched to see that no outsider made a bid. What would have happened if one were so bold as to do that can only be speculated upon, but it is a safe guess to say he would have received rough treatment. Presumably, the threat of this kept the unscrupulous claim jumpers away.

An interesting sidelight to the acquisition of claims is given by Elder Ely who is quoted in the Winona Republican of June 11, 1867 as saying:

"It is said that there are tricks in every trade but ours. Claim making was a peculiar science and could only be learned by residence in a claim country. First, when you measure a claim you must look out that there are 320 acres instead of 160 which the law allows. You must claim for yourself and some brother, father, cousin, or friend that you expect will come soon so as to be your neighbor. You must claim so that you can sell a claim and have one more left."

In the early eighteen fifties treaties made with the Indians opened Minnesota to settlement on a wide scale. The movement of settlers into the area, which was small in the beginning, became a regular flood. Naturally, most of the settlement was in the river valleys, or adjacent to them, where water made transportation available. Later, as the railroads came, the settlers moved into lands away from the river, and gradually the whole state was opened up.

Transportation to the region was at first difficult. In most instances, settlers were short of money and household goods and utensils were not easy to acquire. The settlers brought such things with them as they actually needed. These items were carefully packed in boxes made of inch thick lumber. The packing boxes and nails later could be used to make temporary cupboards and other items of furniture.

Diaries and other sources of information about early settlers indicate that in the wooded sections they lived in log houses. However, along the St. Croix River where early lumber mills were established some of the pioneers in Washington County found it possible to build frame houses.

Early Farm Home

Sod houses and dugouts were used when the lack of timber prevented the construction of anything more elaborate. Pieces of sod a foot wide, a foot and a half long and four inches thick were dug on the prairie. These were placed in somewhat the same manner as bricks or cement blocks are used today, and in some cases were fastened together

with a mortar of clay mixed with buffalo grass. A roof formed of poles and covered with sod, and rough windows and doors cut in the sod walls completed the structure. Sometimes the floors were covered with rough boards; otherwise, the hard-packed dirt formed the floor. One can readily imagine the feelings of joy and satisfaction that came when the family was at last able to build a frame house, or even a log house.

Barns were built of logs, or in some cases of straw. Corner posts were set in the ground, a lattice work of poles put over the top and wheat straw was threshed on top of the structure. The straw, of course, had to be renewed from time to time.

One writer points out that frame houses, barns, granaries and drilled wells were not available in many parts of Minnesota until the seventies.

The very first method of getting about exclusive of the river was, of course, on the old Indian trails, which are said to have given general direction to most of the early roads.

The first form of land transportation in Minnesota was by sled in winter and by Red River Ox

Red River cart

Cart in summer. The first of these Red River Ox Carts were said to have been made in 1801, and perhaps were brought into Minnesota as early as 1821. By 1839 they were familiar objects at Fort Snelling.

In 1844 regular trains of Red River Carts began to reach St. Paul. The chief articles transported, however, related to the fur trade and not to agriculture.

The first wagon roads in Minnesota were laid out from St. Paul to Fort Snelling, Mendota, Stillwater and what is now Hudson, Wisconsin. Other roads ran from St. Paul to St. Anthony (Minneapolis) then to Sauk Rapids and Crow Wing along the Mississippi. In January, 1850, a winter road was opened along the Mississippi from Galena, Illinois to Prairie du Chien, Wisconsin to St. Paul. This gave Minnesota access to the outside world during the season of closed navigation.

Rapid agricultural development, however, did not take place until the railroads spread out over the state. In the early days of statehood the legislature tried to stimulate interest in railroad building ahead of population growth by lavish land grants and bonuses, including state bonds. These were for the most part failures.

The first pieces of railroad in Minnesota were built from St. Paul to St. Anthony and from Winona westward about ten miles. Both of these were built in 1862. During the next few years eight roads or portions of roads were completed prior to 1869. For the next five years, until about 1873, railroad building progressed rapidly. 1871 saw completion of a main line to Breckenridge, and the Northern Pacific building west from Duluth reached Moorhead. Direct rail connection was established with Chicago by way of Tomah, Wisconsin. In 1872 a railroad reached Sioux City, Iowa and the Winona road (Northwestern) arrived at the western boundary of the state. The St. Paul and Pacific (later a part of the Great Northern) united the upper Red River Valley with Minneapolis and St. Paul. Other important branch lines were built. All of this opened the way for the development of agriculture, and year by year farming spread over the state. In these days of good roads, trains and air transportation, this fact is often forgotten. One should recognize that the railroads did and still continue to play an important part in the history of Minnesota agriculture.

During the Civil War, Congress passed the Homestead Act of 1862. Under its terms a citizen or one who had applied for citizenship, who was twenty-one years of age, or who was the head of

Early railroad

a family and who had never borne arms against the United States or given aid or comfort to its enemies was allowed to secure land at a very low cost. Entry was allowed on 160 acres or use of government land which was open to preemption. After five years of occupying, the claimant was entitled to a deed from the United States government.

The original act of 1862 was amended from time to time to provide, among other things, additional benefits for honorably discharged soldiers and sailors.

There were those who filed on homesteads who were not bona fide settlers, but who were looking for an easy way to make a few extra dollars. However, most of the homesteads were taken by those who were really seeking to establish new homes that would better their living conditions.

Between May, 1862, and June 30, 1880, some seven million acres were filed under the Homestead Act.

The early settlers had little in the way of farm machinery. Hand labor was used in cutting hay with a scythe, planting, picking, husking and shelling corn, building homes, fences, and the like. In fact, the early pioneer used methods that an Egyptian farmer of two thousand years ago would have found quite familiar.

The first mechanical reaper came into Minnesota not later than 1854. This was a McCormick,

155

Threshing grain with flails in early days

Automatic self-rake reaper invented in 1858

156

a name that is still known in the agricultural implement business. During the 1850's other agricultural implements came into the state. These included steel plows, mechanical threshers and well drilling machines. The threshers were horse driven, and with the early machines, the straw had to be pitched on a stack with forks, and the grain cleaned with a fanning mill.

During the Civil War the scarcity of labor accelerated the use of machinery. There were many improvements in farm machines in the 1860's. One of these was the self-raking reaper. This made it unnecessary to have a man on the machine to rake the grain onto the ground. Esterley and Dorsey were two of the names attached to this type of machine. McCormick also entered the field in 1861.

Each company producing reapers claimed that its machine was the best. In that respect the companies of those days were no different than they are today. However, it was suggested that there be a trial of the machines of all companies that wished to enter to determine their real merit. Such a trial was held on the fair grounds of the Minnesota State Agriculture Society (State Fair) in 1867. A Manney machine won first place for the reapers, the combined self-raking reaper and mower was awarded to a Kirby machine and the sweepstakes were given to the Wood combined reaper and mower. These names, unfamiliar today, are just typical of the literally hundreds of industries and companies that have engaged in the manufacture of farm equipment and machinery over the past one hundred years.

Steam threshers came in about 1867. Various types of grain drills were offered for sale. Other implements in use by 1860 were horse hay rakes, wheat field gleaners, potato diggers, harrows, straw cutters, iron corn shellers, and fanning mills.

Old steam threshing rig

Six-horse outfit pulling plow

157

To trace the development of farm machinery from those early days to the present would require a volume in itself.

The advent of the railroad and the introduction of machinery combined to bring about a period of extensive wheat and small grain farming. J. J. Hill reported that the first wheat he knew to have been shipped from Minnesota was in 1857 and was raised on the Le Seuer prairie. He also said that in 1859 there were a few thousand bushels of wheat raised principally about Le Seuer and St. Peter. This was shipped to St. Louis by boat. The fall of that year saw the beginnings of an important export movement in farm products. Wheat first became the leading crop in the southeastern part of the state along the Mississippi River, and then spread to the north and west. With the opening of the fabulous Red River Valley in the 1870's, wheat production gradually moved principally to that area, and the older area of the state began to diversify and go more into livestock and dairy production.

The great flour milling industry of the state began as early as 1823 with a government grist mill at St. Anthony Falls. Local grist mills sprang up and, for a time, were important to the local communities. Gradually, however, the center of the milling industry shifted to Minneapolis where it is today.

One of the interesting developments which now has largely passed out of the picture was the so-called bonanza farm. This was farming on a very large scale, and demonstrated for a time, at least, the possibility of mass production of wheat in the Red River Valley region at a profit.

In 1873 the failure of the Northern Pacific Railroad left many people holding bonds, which in 1875 were worth ten cents on the dollar. In that year some of the bond holders exchanged their bonds for lands held by the railroad. Among the best known of the bonanza farm operators was Oliver Dalyrymple who contracted to take charge of large blocks of land. In 1875 he broke 1,280 acres which in 1876 produced a crop of 32,000 bushels of wheat. In 1877 he had 4,500 acres which produced 25 bushels of wheat to the acre. By 1880 there were 82 farms in the Red River valley that had more than 1,000 acres per farm. Most of these were on the North Dakota side, but some were in Minnesota.

It is said that a typical threshing crew, and there were many such on the larger farms, included twenty-three men, and a foreman, and ten teams of horses. They could clear fifty acres a day. Labor, of course, was one of the problems of such farms. Many of the workers came from the small farms in the east and south and from the Woods Country of

Grain binder of early '20s

158

the north, also laboring men from the large cities who came West for the harvest.

By 1890 the outlook for the large wheat farms was not as bright as it had been in previous years. There was a drouth in 1889. An increase in the price of land also decreased the profits. The Panic of 1893 was disastrous to many. As a result, there was a gradual shift from wheat to diversified farming.

Wheat is still one of the important crops of the state. Hard red spring wheat grown in the Red River Valley is a high quality milling wheat. Rust epidemics, grasshoppers and various other natural enemies have failed to reduce the desire of many farmers to grow wheat which, in their opinion, is the king of crops. In recent years wheat acreage has been controlled by government allotments.

It has been mentioned earlier that the coming of the railroads was one of the forces responsible for the spread of agriculture in the state.

After the railroads came, however, there was a feeling, on the part of many farmers that the freight rates were too high, and that favoritism was shown to certain shippers, or to certain cities where competition existed. Farmers also felt that the prices they received for their wheat and other products were too low and reflected, in part, the high freight rates and also the natural desire of the middlemen or the marketing agency to get more than their fair share of the consumer's dollar. Such a state of affairs brought about the organization of the Grange, the Anti-Monopoly Party, the Greenback party, the Farmers' Alliance and the Populist Party.

The story of the farmer's crusade in Minnesota has been well told by Dr. Theodore C. Blegen in an article which appeared in a University of Minnesota Alumni publication in 1933. With his consent we reproduce, in part, the interesting story he has told.

"As settlers pushed the American frontier westward after the Civil War a farmers' paradise seemed in prospect. Tracks of steel were flung out toward the Pacific; thousands of people responded to the magic of free land; the click and whirr of improved farm machines sounded on the prairies.

Crop acreage and specialized production expanded on a gigantic scale. The agrarian paradise did not materialize, however. Instead, markets were soon glutted, grain prices fell, farm mortgages mounted, and pioneer optimism waned.

"A Minnesota pioneer farmer, Oliver H. Kelley, was chiefly responsible for founding the Grange. A native of Boston, he took up a claim in 1849 in what became Elk River township in Sherburne County. He was early interested in agricultural organization, was one of the founders in 1852 of the first county agricultural society in Minnesota, and took part in the founding of the Minnesota Territorial Agricultural Society two years later. In 1864 Senator Ramsey obtained a clerkship for him in the Bureau of Agriculture at Washington. A tour of the South in 1866 convinced Kelley of the need for cooperative action among farmers, and the next year, with six associates, he founded the National Grange, or the Patrons of Husbandry, a secret order of farmers. Its object was the "advancement of agriculture" by educational processes. The plan was to enrich the social and intellectual life of the farmers; and the local granges, open to both men and women, were to function as clubs, with specially prepared programs for their meetings. It is of interest to know that as early as 1865 a "Farmers' Association", primarily a mutual insurance project, was started in Minnesota, and that two years later this "Farmers' Union" as it was then called, launched a campaign for the organization of farmers' social clubs. In 1868 Kelley set out for St. Paul, and there, on September 2, with Colonel Daniel A. Robertson, founder of the Minnesota Horticultural Society, he established the North Star Grange. A practical tone was given the project by including among its objects the protection of members against corporations and the establishment of depots for cooperative buying and selling. The Farmers' Union approved heartily of the new plan of agricultural organization. Early in 1869 eleven local granges united to form the Minnesota State Grange, the first state federation of its kind. By the close of that year Minnesota had forty out of forty-nine local granges in the United States. The movement spread vigorously, and by 1874 Minnesota alone had 538 granges.

"Though the Grange itself was non-political, its members throughout the Middle West agitated for reasonable railroad rates, against discriminations, and for regulation through state laws; and legislatures took action. Thus Minnesota in 1871, under Governor Horace Austin, prescribed maximum fares and rates and set up the office of railroad commissioner; and three years later he created a board of railroad commissioners with power to establish a schedule of fares and rates. The early regulatory legislation of the Middle West was in most instances hastily framed and did not last; the problem proved more complex than was at first realized; but the Granger legislation established the principle that railroads and other corporations 'clothed with public interest' were properly subject to public regulations, a principle set forth by the Supreme Court in 1876 in its decision in Munn vs. Illinois and other Granger cases. Private property, Chief Justice Waite announced, 'does become clothed with a public interest when used in a manner to make it of public consequence, and affect the community at large.' And it must submit 'to be controlled by the public for common good.' Thus a legal foundation was laid for later and more carefully devised regulations.

"Meanwhile, the farmers in many states had plunged into partisan politics by establishing independent third parties. In Minnesota the versatile Ignatius Donnelly lent his pen and fiery eloquence to the Granger movement, published his 'Facts for the Granges,' lectured up and down the state, and took the lead in forming the Anti-Monopoly Party in 1873, a short-lived reform party demanding subjection of corporations to the state and governmental economy. Some attempt was made to unite farmers and laborers. Thus Donnelly in the first issue of his newspaper, The Anti-Monopolist, wrote that 'the true interests of the country are the true interests of the city,' declared that there was 'no real antagonism between the farmer and the mechanic,' and promised as full a hearing to the workingmen's societies as to the Granges.

"The Panic of 1873, the bankruptcy of various railroads, the repeal of Granger legislation, and the difficulties of the Grange in its cooperative enterprises help to explain the decline of the order that came in the middle seventies. The Grange had about twenty thousand local chapters in the United States in 1874, but by 1880 this number had dwindled to four thousand. An interesting revival of the organization was to come in the twentieth century. In its earlier phase the Grange had stimulated the interest of the farmer, stirred his class consciousness, added something to his social life, given him experience in cooperation, and established a legal basis for the public regulation of corporations. The farmers had also set a precedent for independent political action.

"The Greenback Party, voicing the debtor sentiment of the West, attracted considerable agrarian support, but it was the Farmers' Alliance that represented the next great stage in the agrarian crusade. The Granger movement had scarcely slackened when the Northwestern Alliance was launched at Chicago in 1880 in a new attempt to unite the farmers. The Movement quickly took root, and before the end of 1881 Minnesota had eighty local alliances and a state organization. Like the Grange, the Alliance, north and south, emphasized the social and educational side. It sponsored neighborhood gatherings, picnics, rallies; conducted an annual farmers' congress; launched newspapers; promoted reading circles and set up cooperative elevators and marketing projects.

"The one-crop system, booms, over-expansion, and world competition were important factors in the distress of the farmer, but he had many specific grievances. Though he raised bumper crops, he said, the price that he got for his grain was so low that he was in distress. If wheat sold for eighty-five cents in New York, the Minnesota producer received only fifty, the balance going to railways, warehouse companies, and commission merchants. He was especially bitter about the impositions of local roads. He pointed out that it cost nearly twice as much to send a bushel of wheat from Fargo to Duluth as from Minneapolis to Chicago. Moreover, he alleged that the roads discriminated between the small and the large shipper; and he charged that elevator companies fixed prices to suit themselves and took advantage of the farmer in grading his wheat.

Country grain elevator

"Remedial legislation in Minnesota was brought about in 1885, during the governorship of Lucius F. Hubbard, as a consequence of the popular agitation. A railroad and warehouse commission of three members to be appointed by the governor was created; and a grain bill providing for uniform grading and weighing of grain at terminal points was passed. In 1886 the powers and duties of the Commission were enlarged and it received virtually full rate-making authority, enforceable through the courts; but this provision was later held unconstitutional. Not until 1893 were country elevators brought under the supervision of the commission.

"The Alliance thus far had cooperated with one or the other of the older parties. In 1886 it held a joint state convention with the Knights of Labor at which a platform embodying both the farmers' and the workingmen's demands was adopted. This convention named a committee of thirty, with Donnelly at its head, to go before the old parties with its demands. The Republicans gave the committee members seats at their convention and wrote into their own platform most of the farmer-labor demands. In 1889, however, the Farmers' Alliance, dissatisfied with the policy of nonpartisan politics, took on the character of an independent political party and elected thirty-three representatives to the Minnesota House. By 1890 it had decided upon full third-party action; and it nominated Sidney M. Owen of Minneapolis, the editor of Farm, Stock and Home, as its candidate for Governor. That the attempts at farmer-labor cohesion were continued is evidenced by the presence in this nominating convention of fifty-three representatives of trade-unions. It may be added that the Farmers' Alliance, in turn, was well represented at the organization, also in 1890, of the Minnesota State Federation of Labor.

"Owen, as the Farmers' Alliance candidate, polled nearly sixty thousand votes, but ran far behind both the Republican and Democratic nominees. The Alliance, jointly with the Democrats, elected its candidates for state auditor; it sent two men to Congress; and it obtained the balance of power in both houses of the state legislature, where Donnelly directed the Alliance delegation as a bloc.

"The desire to accomplish nationally what the Alliance was doing in Minnesota and other states led in 1891 to the formation of the People's Party at Cincinnati, where Donnelly headed the Minnesota delegation and emerged as one of the national leaders of Populism. Upon his return to Minnesota he persuaded the state alliance to enter into the new movement; and in 1892 the Minnesota Populists named an entire state ticket, headed by Donnelly. A spectacular campaign followed. One of Donnelly's broadsides read: "From Forge and Farm; from Shop and Counter; from Highways and Firesides come and hear the 'Great Commoner' on the mighty issues which are moving mankind to the ballot box in the great struggle for their rights." In the election the Populists won one seat in Congress and twenty-four in the state legislature, but Donnelly was snowed under by Knute Nelson, western Minnesota Republican, Civil War veteran, farmer, and lawyer. As Governor, Nelson supported the measure of 1893 subjecting local elevators to state inspection; and he signed an act making the creation of pools and trusts illegal. A law providing for the erection of a state elevator at Duluth was later declared unconstitutional.

"The third party now turned in the main to issues of a national character. In 1894 it advocated free silver, government savings banks, government ownership of public utilities, income and inheritance taxes, equal suffrage for men and women, and other reforms then considered radical. In the Minnesota election of 1894 Owen again ran for Governor but was decisively defeated by Governor Nelson. The Republicans elected their entire state ticket and sent an undivided delegation to Congress.

"In 1896 the Democrats came out for free silver, following the leadership of the silver-tongued Bryan; and the national People's Party gave him its support, though it nominated its own candidate for the vice presidency. A fusion policy was also decided upon in state politics. A single Democratic-Populist-Silver Republican ticket was put in the Minnesota field, with John Lind a Silver Republican, as its head. Even fusion failed to bring victory for the reformers, though Lind polled a vote of over 162,000 and came very near winning the election. Two years later, again as a fusion candidate, he was carried into the governorship.

"Gradually the Populists were absorbed by the older parties, as these parties adopted many of the reforms for which the agrarian forces had stood. The 'pioneers of an earlier age,' writes a recent historian, 'had barely tolerated government as a necessary evil, but these farmers of the last American frontier could see no other way to check the aggressive tendencies of those who opposed their interests than the interposition of the power of the state. No little redress of grievance was won at the time. Many reforms, rejected then, were later substantially adopted, especially in the fields of political democracy, currency and credit, railroad and trust control, and conservation. Political independency was stimulated. Rural living was brightened socially. The farmers learned the value of organization, and it was certain that they would be heard from again. Meanwhile, they were coping with basic problems of a non-political character, such as agricultural diversifications and adjustment to changing conditions as American agriculture faced the industrial twentieth century.' "

Thus Dr. Blegen tells the story of the farmer's crusade in the earlier years. In more recent years the Farmer-Labor party carried on this crusade. With the combination of the Farmer-Labor party, with the Democratic party in Minnesota, the state again reverted to the two-party system which seems to be most characteristic of political action in American government.

Early in the history of the state, farmers began thinking about specialized education for the farm youth and the need for research in agriculture. In 1858, the same year that Minnesota became a state, the legislature established an experimental farm and agricultural college at Glencoe. Colonel John H. Stevens along with others brought to the West the New England idea of public institutions. Upon election to the legislature in 1857, he began to work for legislation that would provide for agricultural education.

Legislation establishing the college was passed in 1858, but, unfortunately, no funds were provided for the new institution. Stevens, himself, donated some land, and a public subscription of $10,000 provided some funds.

The Civil War came on and actually the college at Glencoe never got underway. In 1865 a grant of land became available to the college under the Morrill Act of 1862. In 1868 the University of Minnesota was reorganized and the land grant of 1862, for the encouragement of agricultural education, which had been made to the Agricultural College at Glencoe in 1865, was given to the University on the condition that it provide for a college of agriculture, a college of mechanical arts, and an experimental farm.

The development of a college course in agriculture did not proceed smoothly. Space does not permit a discussion of the many changes in ideas, and personnel that took place in the years following 1868. Looking back at that period, one is forced to conclude that the subject matter available for teaching agriculture at that time was not too extensive. Furthermore, the ideas of what a college of agriculture ought to teach were many and somewhat confused. Gradually, there developed what is today known as the College of Agriculture, Forestry and Home Economics. In 1947 the legislature established a School of Veterinary Medicine. This was a part of the College of Agriculture, Forestry, Home Economics and Veterinary Medicine until July 1, 1957 when it became a separate college.

To go back again to the matter of agricultural research, the University was obligated to establish an agricultural experiment station under terms of the agreement reached in 1868 when the interests of the College of Agriculture at Glencoe in the lands provided by the Land Grant Act of 1862 were merged with the University. The first agricultural experiment station was established near the present site of the Minneapolis Campus of the University. In 1882 this land was sold by the Board of Regents of the University and under legislative authority the proceeds from the sale were to be used for the purchase of a new farm at St. Anthony Park, St. Paul.

In 1884 Experiment Station buildings were erected on the new farm, which for many years was known as the University Farm and which now, by the Board of Regents' action, is known as the St. Paul Campus of the University of Minnesota.

The School of Agriculture (non-degree) opened at St. Paul in October of 1888. Later Schools of Agriculture were opened at Crookston (1906), Morris (1910), Grand Rapids (1926) and Waseca (1952).

The teaching of agriculture was established in the public high schools of the state in the early years of the 1900's. The Smith-Hughes Act passed by congress in 1917 stimulated this development until today there are almost three hundred high schools in the state offering courses in vocational agriculture.

The development of the Agricultural Extension Service also began in the early 1900's. Again federal legislation in the form of the Smith Lever Act of 1914 stimulated this development. Today there are County Agricultural Agents in every one of the eighty-seven counties, Home Demonstrations Agents in most of them, and temporary or full time 4-H Club Agents in a majority of the counties. All of this is a part of the present Institute of Agriculture of the University of Minnesota and is often spoken of as the off-campus teaching arm of the University on the farms and in the homes of the people of the state.

Earlier it has been mentioned that wheat and small grains became important in the economy of Minnesota. The period of specialized wheat farming for the state roughly covered the years 1860-1885. Actually, the high point in this period came in 1878. Other crops such as potatoes, flax and some of the other small grains, and hay began to assume more importance. Attention began to be focused upon the improvement of livestock.

In the period 1890-1900 the use of a mechanical separator to separate butterfat from milk quickly and easily came into general use. The Babcock test for a quick and easy method of determining the butterfat content of milk came in 1890. These inventions tended to put dairying on a more scientific basis.

The introduction of the cooperative creamery also stimulated dairying. What is generally recognized as the first cooperative creamery was established at Clarks Grove in Freeborn County by a group of Danish farmers in May, 1890. From this humble beginning has sprung the great cooperative dairy products marketing organizations in the state today.

A good summary of the development of agriculture in the state up to 1900 is given by Edward Van Dyke Robinson in a bulletin of the University of Minnesota published in 1915. Dr. Robinson said:

"The immense expansion of agriculture from 1890 to 1900 compared to earlier decades is nowhere more clearly apparent than in the distribution of the value of products. The entire southern section, and also the Red River Valley, now belonged to the agricultural zone, while the northeastern two fifths of the state still remained almost untouched by the plow. In spite of the rapid spread of agriculture toward the west and northwest the value of products per square mile was greatest in the older section south and east of Stearns County. The fresh soils of the newer counties were then more than offset, so far as concerned the financial return per acre, by greater labor applied to the land in the older counties. It should be noted, however, that while this more intensive use of the soil naturally gave larger returns per acre the returns per man and per team were frequently larger on the new lands, owing to the increasing cost of production per unit of output under intensive cultivation.

"In 1900 the center of density of population

was in the counties adjacent to the two great lakes, and in the Minnesota Valley counties below the big bend. Settlement had continued to spread in the Red River Valley, occupying the last of the prairie townships, and from there had begun to work eastward into the brush prairies. Except for the strip adjacent to this valley, most of the hardwood belt of the State was in farms, though woodlots still occupied a considerable area. East of the Mississippi scattered clearings appeared along the railroads, even in the cut-over and largely burned over coniferous zone especially between St. Paul and Duluth. This decade was also reached by the development of the Mesabi iron range and, therefore, by the appearance of a considerable population, for the most part, residents in St. Louis County.

"If all incorporated places be eliminated, most of the apparent settlement in the northeastern region disappears. The coniferous zone stood in 1900 as a great island of wilderness, thickly sprinkled with logging and mining camps and towns, but barely touched as yet by agricultural settlement. On the other hand, the remainder of the state, aside from the density west and southwest of the Twin Cities, showed a surprising evenness of settlement. Evidently, a dominant type of agriculture, based on substantial equality of soil, had worked itself out in an approximate equal spread of population over the land."

One of the striking things that has taken place since 1900 is the slowing up of the movement of land into farm use. In the early years prairie homesteads could be had for the taking, but by 1900 most of the prairie land was occupied or at least in private hands. Making a farm out of the forested areas was a much harder job. Unwise settlement projects were sometimes carried out which put settlers on land which later experience showed might best have been left for the growth of forests.

In 1850 there were 28,881 acres in farms in the state of which 5,035 acres (or 17.4%) were improved land. In 1900 there were 26,248,498 acres (or 69.9%) were improved land. Today there are approximately 32,234,539 acres in farm land.

The first half of the one hundred years of Minnesota's statehood saw an expansion of acres in

Modern rubber-tired farm equipment

Steel wheel tractor forerunner of modern day rubber-tired tractor

Modern farming

farms; the last half has seen a tremendous expansion in number of acres farmed.

Up until World War I most of the power used on farms was horse power. Then came the introduction of gasoline tractors. The first of these machines was mounted on steel wheels, and was heavy and clumsy. They were patterned somewhat after the steam tractors which were used a great deal prior to World War I for the operation of threshing machines, and to some extent on larger farms for plowing.

Gradually, however, the machinery manufacturers built light and more competent tractors. Rubber tires for tractors and complementary machines were introduced in the early 1930's, and from that time on the use of tractors increased by leaps and bounds and the faithful old horse gradually faded out of the picture. For example, the census for 1920 lists 943,032 horses and mules in Minnesota. Today this number has dwindled to 107,923 and many of these are of the light variety used for riding.

The real push in the use of mechanized implements drawn by tractor or powered in one way or another came during and after World War II. One may get some idea of the rapid growth in the field of mechanization by comparison of the following figures from the Agricultural Census figures for Minnesota.

	1930	1940	1954
Tractors in Minnesota	48,457	105,075	255,431
Trucks	36,557	38,617	90,295
Automobiles	185,717	208,693	192,877
Grain Combines	not reported	not reported	61,331
Milking Machines	not reported	not reported	73,989
Electricity — Farms reporting	23,342	80,220	155,530

The modern farm in the centennial year is a far cry from the early farm. The farmer has as much money invested in the machinery on one typical farm than the cost of all implements in the entire territory in 1840. The cash cost of operation has increased tremendously. The modern farmer can make money faster, but he also runs the chance of going bankrupt faster than his predecessors. The farmer of today must be a good manager or expensive machinery can mean his downfall.

The period from about 1897 to World War I is said to have been the best in agricultural history in the United States up to that time. Commodity prices, although subject to ups and downs, were slowly rising. There was a large export market for farm products in foreign countries. The exploration of virgin land resources had leveled off. Minnesota farmers shared in this period of relative prosperity.

166

Then came World War I with its slogan of "Food Will Win The War". Minnesota farmers responded as did their counterparts over the entire nation. Production was pushed upward. The United States entered the war in April, 1917. A Food and Fuel Control Act was passed by Congress on August 10, 1917. This act guaranteed a minimum of $2.00 per bushel for the wheat crop of 1918. On August 30, the President fixed a minimum price of $2.20 per bushel for No. 1 Northern at Chicago. An executive order on June 21, 1918, raised that to $2.26. There was a substantial wheat acreage increase in the United States, and the spring wheat region of Minnesota participated in this increase. The states of Minnesota, North Dakota, South Dakota and Montana accounted for about 4,150,000 acres of the spring wheat increase. This crop expansion in Minnesota was brought about by plowing up some pastures and meadowland.

Livestock and livestock products increased. Prices went up, also. Prices of all farm products rose until they were more than double the prewar

Dairy cows grazing

Typical Minnesota farm

figures. Farm products, as a whole, had a moderately favorable exchange value in terms of non-agricultural commodities, especially during the latter years of the war period.

Then came the end of the war. For a year or two the war-torn countries took a great deal of the United States food production. By 1920, however, they were beginning to produce for themselves. Average prices of corn in the United States fell from $1.86 in July 1920 to 41c in November of 1921; potatoes dropped from $4.21 a bushel in June, 1920 to 67c in June, 1921; and sheep dropped from $10.66 in April, 1920 to $3.84 in November, 1921. Other farm prices dropped correspondingly. Minnesota farmers were hit hard by the falling prices. The price of things they had to buy did not fall off as fast and they were caught in the middle. There was some recovery in the latter part of the 1920's, but then came the great depression beginning in 1929. By 1932 average farm prices in Minnesota read something like this:

Corn	26c per bushel
Oats	16c per bushel
Spring Wheat	45c per bushel
Barley	27c per bushel
Rye	36c per bushel
Flaxseed	$1.00 per bushel
Potatoes	28c per bushel
Butterfat	18c per pound
Wool	9c per pound
Cattle & Calves (Choice)	$6.78 per hundred
Hogs	$3.70 per hundred

There are many farmers living today who can report sales at even lower prices. Farm mortgages were being foreclosed. This was a period when such organizations as the Farm Holiday Association flourished. Forced sales of property often did not take place because of the threat of violence that might occur if someone attempted to make capitol of the misery of a farmer who could not pay his interest or principal due on the mortgage.

Gradually, however, prices began to improve. The government entered the picture with such things as the Agricultural Adjusted Administration with its ever normal granary and an executive order of 1933 which created the Farm Credit System.

Then came World War II and again the demand for expanded production. The farmers of Minnesota responded although short handed. Production increased. Special price incentives were offered to stimulate production of needed crops. Prices of the goods and services the farmers bought were somewhat controlled with the result that for a time, at least, there was a period of relative agricultural prosperity.

After the war was over, demand again fell off and prices were kept up in some major areas only by a price support program. Space does not permit a review of the arguments for and against this phase of government in agriculture. There are those who think this is the only way to maintain prosperity, and there are others equally vociferous who say that farm prices should be allowed to drop to the world market level as once was true. This argument will, perhaps, continue for many years in the future, or until population and demand again catch up with production.

No history of agriculture in Minnesota would be complete without mention of three major farm organizations in the state. Following are statements prepared by representatives of these organizations which outline briefly their history, and their present-day objectives.

The oldest of these is the State Grange of Minnesota or Patrons of Husbandry as they are sometimes called. This is what the Master of the State Grange had to say about this organization:

"Homesteads free for the taking was the driving force that urged the more hardy people from the eastern states to migrate west, for larger opportunities and wider horizons. These New England and New York migrants stopped in Ohio, later moving on to Illinois and Iowa—some of them coming to Minnesota. Not a few followed the trails to the Pacific Coast. Their motive force to propel the wagon trains was oxen, horses and even cows were used to do double duty as beasts of burden, and producers of milk for their owner. Many came by boat up the Mississippi River taking land and making their homes on the banks of the Father of Waters. Among these pilgrims was a man named Oliver Hudson Kelley. He was Boston bred and educated and worked his way as a salesman in

Farm Home and Buildings

The old Chatfield creamery

Farm scene

Dairy cattle grazing

Grain Elevator at Duluth

Cattle Ranch

Chatfield Co-op Creamery

171

Ohio, later in Chicago as a journalist and later in Davenport, Iowa, as a telegraph operator.

"Evidently, these vocations were not to his liking as he voyaged north to what was then Itaska Landing and later became Elk River, Minnesota. Here on the east bank of the Mississippi River he realized his vision for a home and here he settled and carved out his farm from the Minnesota wilderness. This was in 1849. Here he worked, played and dreamed till 1866 when he was sent to the southern states with a commission from President Andrew Johnson to investigate and report to him the true condition of the Southern Planter. After an extended inspection, he found the condition in such a chaotic state that it aroused in his humanitarian heart a deep desire to do something that would be of lasting benefit to the American Farmer. His vision took the form of a Farm Fraternity that would know no boundary, creed or political division. His sole purpose being to be of service to the farmer.

"Following the suggestions of his niece, Caroline Hall, also Boston bred and educated, that women be admitted on an equal footing with men, he began to unfold his vision and put his cherished dream on paper in a workable form. Enlisting the help and advice of friends in Washington, D. C., he laid his plans before them and with their help, The National Grange was born in our capitol city on December 4, 1867. He was elected secretary and made his office on this farm. From this farm he went forth to organize the Grange in Minnesota as well as in other states. Organized Agriculture, then, has as its birthplace this farm in Minnesota.

"From this beginning the Grange has grown so that there are Granges in 37 states extending from coast to coast and from border to border. Our state Grange is a potent force in forming laws and policies favorably affecting farmers of Minnesota.

"Among its present goals are: A revision of our present farm program so that a desirable relationship shall exist between producers of food and others in the national economy. We believe that self-help programs controlled by producers should be developed for individual commodities through studies made by qualified groups.

"We favor adequate appropriations for the Soil Conservation Service, Agricultural Stabilization and Conservation Service, and for the Agricultural Extension Service to the end that our soil may be kept fertile to produce food for generations yet unborn.

"The Grange as a farm organization may seem to go to the right. Its record shows no tendency to go to the left and it usually goes down the center when considering what is good for rural America. All questions are considered with open minds and an inborn desire to do the greatest service possible for the rural people."

The next of the three organizations to be formed in Minnesota was the Minnesota Farm Bureau Federation. This is what its President had to say about it:

"The Farm Bureau did not come out full grown and fully developed from the thinking of any man or the plans of any group of men. It is the product of evolution, growing out of the rich experience and background of many earlier farm organizations. Farm clubs and later 'Farm Bureaus' developed from small groups of farm people who started working together on economic problems common to their communities.

"Farm Bureau and county agents work has developed together through the years. Farm advisors, or county agents, were first hired in Minnesota in 1912. Traverse County was the first county in Minnesota to have a county agent.

"The Smith-Lever Act, which was passed by Congress on May 8, 1914, gave the Extension program a big boost all over the nation. It provided federal funds for county agent and Extension work. The county Farm Bureaus developed from the need of a local organization to serve as a vehicle to bring Extension to the farmer.

"The pattern developed was that before a county agent would be assigned or approved by a county board of commissioners, a county Farm Bureau must be formed on a membership dues gasis to pledge a certain amount of financial support, assist the county agent in working out a program of work and, in general, help him in every way possible to promote the welfare of farmers.

172

Miller's row in Minneapolis

Country elevator at Pipestone, Minnesota

173

"This idea was written into a law in Minnesota in 1923 after most of the county Farm Bureaus had been formed and that law tied county Extension work and county Farm Bureaus very closely together. This tie was loosened in 1953 when Extension and Farm Bureau people, through mutual agreement, supported a separation bill through the state legislature.

"Realizing the need of an organization that would represent agriculture in an effective statewide manner, 62 county Farm Bureau associations united in 1919 to form the Minnesota Farm Bureau Federation. Today 86 county Farm Bureaus make up the state organization.

"The Farm Bureau is national in scope. At the same time it is "grassroots" in character. Its policies are developed and it is directed from the local level where individual farm families, through study and discussion, evolve the policies and programs through local, county, state and national steps through a unique resolutions process.

"In latter years Farm Bureau has expanded into a five-point program: Education, Legislation, Rural Living, Commodities and Service.

"Close working relations are still kept in agricultural education fields through agricultural extension, 4-H activities, young people's programs, women's committee work, and many other educational activities."

The last of the three organizations to enter the picture in Minnesota's agriculture is the Minnesota Farmers Union. Its President supplied the following information:

"The first record of organization of Farmers Union Locals in Minnesota goes back to about 1920. The organization had its ups and downs membership-wise in the early years, and, in fact, the Farmers Union in those years was mainly recognized for its active work in formation of farm marketing co-operatives and for its attempts at mass buying of food and supplies for its members.

"Farmers Union placed basic emphasis on the importance of co-operative marketing and was one of the pioneer organizations in this field.

"Perhaps the chief distinction of the Farmers Union in this field was its leadership in developing a further step in co-operation—the establishment of regional co-operatives and the gaining of a place for them on terminal and wholesale markets.

"Historians have noted the importance of the early efforts of Farmers Union to establish co-operatives on the livestock markets and later attempts to gain a place for co-operatives on the terminal grain markets.

"Today, Farmers Union co-operatives in Minnesota include two nationally recognized regional co-operatives—Farmers Union Grain Terminal Association, the nation's largest grain co-op marketing firm, and the Farmers Union Central Exchange, one of the leading farm supply wholesale co-ops in the nation.

"The policy of the organization is written by the membership, with the process beginning with resolutions adopted at Local Union meetings and sent to the state convention for the consideration of delegates elected to the convention from the Local Unions.

"As a rule, Farmers Union throughout its history has been known as a liberal group, seeking measures through co-operatives and through state and federal legislation to counteract the lack of bargaining power which farmers have in selling their products."

There are many forces which have helped to change the course of agriculture in the one hundred years since Minnesota became a state. Some of these have already been mentioned such as the mechanization of most farm operations, the development of general farm organizations, the founding of educational institutions, and the spread of railroads throughout the state.

Others which can only be mentioned without discussion would include such things as the introduction of electricity on a broad scale to most farms in the state, the development of new knowledge and techniques for the farmer by the Agricultural Experiment Station, the cooperative movement in Agriculture, and the organization of the Soil Conservation Farm, and Soil Conservation districts.

Farm youth of the state have been influenced by the 4-H Club Movement and its counterpart in

Concrete storage bins

the public high schools, the Future Farmers of America. In fact, many youths of high school age are members of both organizations.

What of the future for the Minnesota farmer? Farms are becoming larger, more machinery and equipment is required for effective operation, operating expenses are higher. There will, no doubt, continue to be ups and downs in prosperity as there has been in the past. Farm life will always hold a certain attraction for some people. Those who operate efficiently will, no doubt, continue to make a satisfactory living. The next hundred years will see developments unheard of today. And finally, farm life today is much improved over that of the first farmers. The modern generation of farmer has much to be thankful for, and not a little is owed to those who have gone before. The challenge of tomorrow is to so live to pay in part that debt to the past, so that those who come after may look at what men of today are doing and be satisfied with what has been done.

Calling quotations at Minneapolis Grain Exchange

175

CHAPTER EIGHT

Education
in Minnesota

By GRACE ORR ARMSTRONG
and
BERNICE DAINARD GESTIE

Education in Minnesota is a many faceted endeavor, yet the parts, when seen in proper perspective and setting, blend together to make a design. Public supported education extends from the elementary school to the state colleges and university, by way of the secondary school and junior college. It reaches out to the handicapped and atypical, to youth seeking vocational training, and to the adult whose days of formal schooling may be past. It is augmented by non-public educational facilities. It began when the territory of Minnesota was created and has grown slowly, sometimes painfully and blunderingly, to its present status. Glimpses of some of the facets may help the reader to understand the scope and significance of education in Minnesota and to realize that ceaseless effort will be the price of improvement.

ELEMENTARY

A decayed log hut with a bark roof housed the first regular English school in Minnesota. Seven pupils came that first day in July, 1847, two of them white; their teacher was Miss Harriet E. Bishop, a native of Vermont who had answered the call of the national board of popular education to meet the needs of the people of the new territory bordering the Mississippi River.

The first territorial superintendent of common schools, Edward D. Neill, in 1853 said the first school of any description was taught at a trading house at Sandy Lake in 1832. He cited other loca-

tions and teachers of what were undoubtedly mission schools.

Miss Bishop's school in St. Paul was followed by others at Stillwater and St. Anthony. "Every new settlement is soon christened with a schoolhouse," reported Governor Willis A. Gorman in 1854. By 1861 there were at least 456 schoolhouses in the state, seven of stone, four brick, 220 frame, and 235 log.

B. F. Crary, superintendent of public instruction at that time, was none too happy about some of the buildings, for he wrote, "It would be an abuse of the term architecture to apply it to most of the schoolhouses. One room, one door, two airtight windows, no anteroom, no outhouses, no fences, no trees, no paint, no one happy conceit or slightly beautiful thing in sight, except as God made . . . "

In 1862 the state superintendent set forth specifications for several models of the small box-type school that dotted the countryside for many years thereafter. Larger brick or frame structures began to appear in the more populous centers. Some of them outlived their time, wars and depressions being effective deterrents to the building of new schoolhouses. Then the nineteen forties and fifties brought a new era in school architecture and construction, for the increased birthrate and the reorganization of districts made new buildings imperative.

First superintendent, Edward Duffield Neill

Curriculum

At no time in the history of the territory or state did the chief school officers intend the curriculum of the elementary school to be limited to the Three R's. In 1852 Superintendent Neill listed what he considered suitable textbooks in geography, reading, spelling, arithmetic, history, grammar, and natural philosophy for the common schools — textbooks determining the curriculum at this time.

Courses of study began to appear as early as 1872 when Superintendent H. B. Wilson included in his annual report a course of study recommended for district schools. It was not until shortly before World War I, however, that a course of study to be used in all elementary schools, both rural and urban, was planned.

In 1946 the first of a completely new series of *Guides to Instruction* was introduced. Subsequent

Harriet Bishop's School
(Kozlak, artist)

Gradually the box-type one-teacher school and the two-story frame or brick building are disappearing from the Minnesota scene. Taking their place are comfortable, attractive, efficient buildings located in selected attendance centers. School transportation is big business these days. Throughout the state the school bus is rapidly consigning the traditional concept of the youth of the land "creeping slow to school" to the realm of nostalgic memories.

guides for social studies; arithmetic; language arts; science and conservation; music; art; health, physical education, and safety followed. Procedures used in developing courses of study have changed from the days when the administrator or a recognized authority designed all courses to the present time when the development of guides is a statewide, cooperative, and continuous undertaking. Local teachers and administrators adapt them to the local school.

178

Horse-drawn busses

Motor-operated busses

Early school without materials

The elementary school today has access to a wealth of research nonexistent in 1902. State curriculum bulletins incorporate the valid research findings of the past prolific years — findings related to child growth and development, to individual differences, to the selection and organization of curriculum materials, and to teaching procedures.

School Law

The state legislature has made few stipulations as to what shall be taught in the schools. The first general legislation relating to curriculum was passed in 1881. This law authorized all school officers to make provision for daily instruction in the elements of social and moral science, including industry, order, economy, punctuality, patience, self-denial, health, purity, temperance, cleanliness, honesty, truth, justice, politeness, peace, fidelity, philanthropy, patriotism, self respect, hope, perseverance, cheerfulness, courage, reflection, self reliance, gratitude, pity, mercy, kindness, conscience, and the will!

In the early history of the state, religion was frequently taught in the public schools, for many foreign-born patrons were accustomed to this practice in their homelands. In 1877 a state constitutional amendment forbade the teaching of religion in the public schools.

179

Kindergarten teacher with pupils drinking milk

In 1887 it was made mandatory to give instruction in physiology and hygiene with special attention to the effects of narcotics upon the human system. Other laws require the public schools to teach the Declaration of Independence and the United States Constitution; to use the English language in all instruction except in courses specifically teaching other languages; to give physical education and to provide for temperance education.

Criticism

A survey of the reports of state inspectors makes the reader realize that "the good old days" of education frequently referred to by modern critics never existed. In 1902 the inspector of state graded schools evaluated the work done in various subjects of the elementary school curriculum.

Of reading, " . . . the importance of mechanics of reading was overestimated;" of language: "The child is allowed to form habits of spelling incorrectly . . . He is allowed to sprawl all over the page in penmanship;" of grammar: " . . . technical grammar . . . begun too early . . . the poorer the school the earlier grammar is taken up!" in general: "The formality, the rigid seating, the bookishness are barriers to progress in the present school system."

He deplored the inaccuracy of geography textbooks; the reaction against vertical handwriting gave him some concern for he feared that legibility would be sacrificed in favor of slant. A tendency to force children to master abstraction in arithmetic at too early an age was noted.

It is often said that it takes at least twenty-five years for the findings of educational research to reach widespread practice in the school. Relatively

Field trip on airplane

little research in elementary school education was done in the early part of the present century, but much has been done since the first world war. The inspector would surely have to agree that textbooks are vastly improved. In reading alone, the interesting content contrasts sharply with selections of the caliber of the following:

> See the pot of jam,
> Yes, I see it.
> Jack is in the van. See him.
> Yes, I see him.

. . . an absurd little number appearing in an earlier primer. Modern pupils and teachers have the benefit of colorful illustrations, vocabularies selected to harmonize mastery of mechanics and pleasure in reading and sheer abundance of materials.

Today's geographies and histories are more easily read, better organized, and designed to bring about insight and understanding rather than memorization of unrelated facts. Since 1900 books in science, health, safety, the wider area of social studies, written for children and understandable to them, make possible a breadth of experience unheard of in 1902.

Let us trust the inspector would rejoice in the substitution of a functional type of composition for the technical grammar of yesterday. His gloomy outlook on the spelling situation ought to be cheered by improvements in methods of teaching that sub-

ject, a subject both enriched and complicated by the fascinating additions of recent years—radar, television, supersonic, nuclear power, automation, sputnik—to mention a few.

As for drawing and music, they are considered today to be among the fundamentals. If abstractions in arithmetic are still presented too early it is not the fault of the modern arithmetic textbooks.

The inspector does not mention special services, for there were few at the time, but surely he would approve the hot lunch, the many health and recreational facilities provided by the present day school. He might even approve such enriching activities as field trips and science experiments.

School Year

The first compulsory attendance law and the free text book law, both passed in the 80's had a marked effect on attendance. Terms of three months or shorter were common at one time. In 1900 the average length of the school term in ungraded schools was 7.2 months. It took nearly fifty years and considerable state-aid therapy, but a minimum of nine months has finally been achieved by all elementary schools in the state.

The holding power of the elementary school through the eighth grade is remarkable, the percentage of children enrolled in the fifth grade who complete the eighth grade ranging between 95 and 99 percent.

New materials—tapes, tape recorder, film, etc.

Expanding School

The state of Minnesota insists that all children of school age attend school if they are able, and if they are not, the school goes to the child, providing instruction for the homebound. All public schools must now provide for the education of handicapped children, the crippled, the slow learning, those with speech difficulties, and those visually handicapped. State schools for such children have long been a part of the educational program, and some districts have had special departments for several years, but near-at-home education is now possible for all.

Kindergartens have increased substantially in number in recent years, but are not yet found in all districts even though they are state-aided. The private kindergarten had an early start in Minnesota, but public kindergartens lagged until the normal schools began preparing teachers for them. District reorganization may speed their development.

The education of Indian children has been a responsible undertaking of the Federal government and the state. The account of their schools is a long and important one.

Then there are the non-public schools. Privately supported, they, too, have made their contribution to Minnesota education, stemming principally from religious groups.

And so we must leave the elementary school and hasten on with our story. We have had no glimpse of sunbonnets and dinner pails, no time to share in corn husking, potato harvesting, and "mud" vacations. There has been no opportunity to listen in while the non-English-speaking youngster struggled with *bu, cu,* or *mu* as his teacher attempted to teach him phonics, no chance to read the records of district clerks with their unconventional spellings—*schrubin,* and *clining, teatching, fier insurans, oil bookit, mappes,* and *diconery.* There is time only to label what has been written "continued story" and proceed with the next installment.

SECONDARY SCHOOLS

There seem to have been three ventures into secondary school work during the territorial and early statehood period, one of which led to the public high school as we know it today. The first was the extension of the common school curriculum to include certain secondary school subjects for more advanced pupils; the second, the founding of a number of private academies, seminaries, and colleges, modeled on those of older states; and the third, the gradual development of public high schools.

Legislation and Support

In 1860 the legislature authorized the city of St. Anthony, now a part of Minneapolis, to establish a high school. In 1870 only 17 cities reported high schools, although a few more may have been in existence. Reports were not wholly reliable at the time, and there was some confusion over the difference between a high school and advanced classes in the common school.

The first general high school law was passed in 1878. It was in effect but one year, the legislature failing to make an additional appropriation to pay the state aid. Nevertheless, in that year 42 schools received state aid, and state inspection was begun.

During the legislative session of 1881 another law was passed, which, with two amendments, one in 1883 and the other in 1891, laid the foundation of the secondary school system that developed rapidly thereafter. Free tuition, state aid, and state inspection were the triumvirate that stimulated the development of the high school and the maintenance of sound educational practices.

By the time the first general high school law was passed there were only a few struggling private academies left. However, the public high schools were not strong. Of the 117 graduates reported in 1877, authorities estimate that not 20 of them could have entered the freshman class of a reputable college.

William Watts Folwell, appointed president of the university in 1869, state superintendent Burt, and the State Teachers Association worked diligently to get the needed school legislation. In 1876 the university refused admission to its preparatory department to students who could get the equivalent instruction in their local schools.

Citizenship training—polls

Scope of Instruction

To make sure that the instruction was equivalent, committees of educators were appointed to outline courses of study for the high schools. In 1896 three courses were recommended, the classical, the literary, and the scientific. Algebra, geometry, English, and physics were common to all courses. The courses proposed were definitely geared to university entrance requirements and in competition with liberalizing trends could not long survive as the total high school offering. Elective

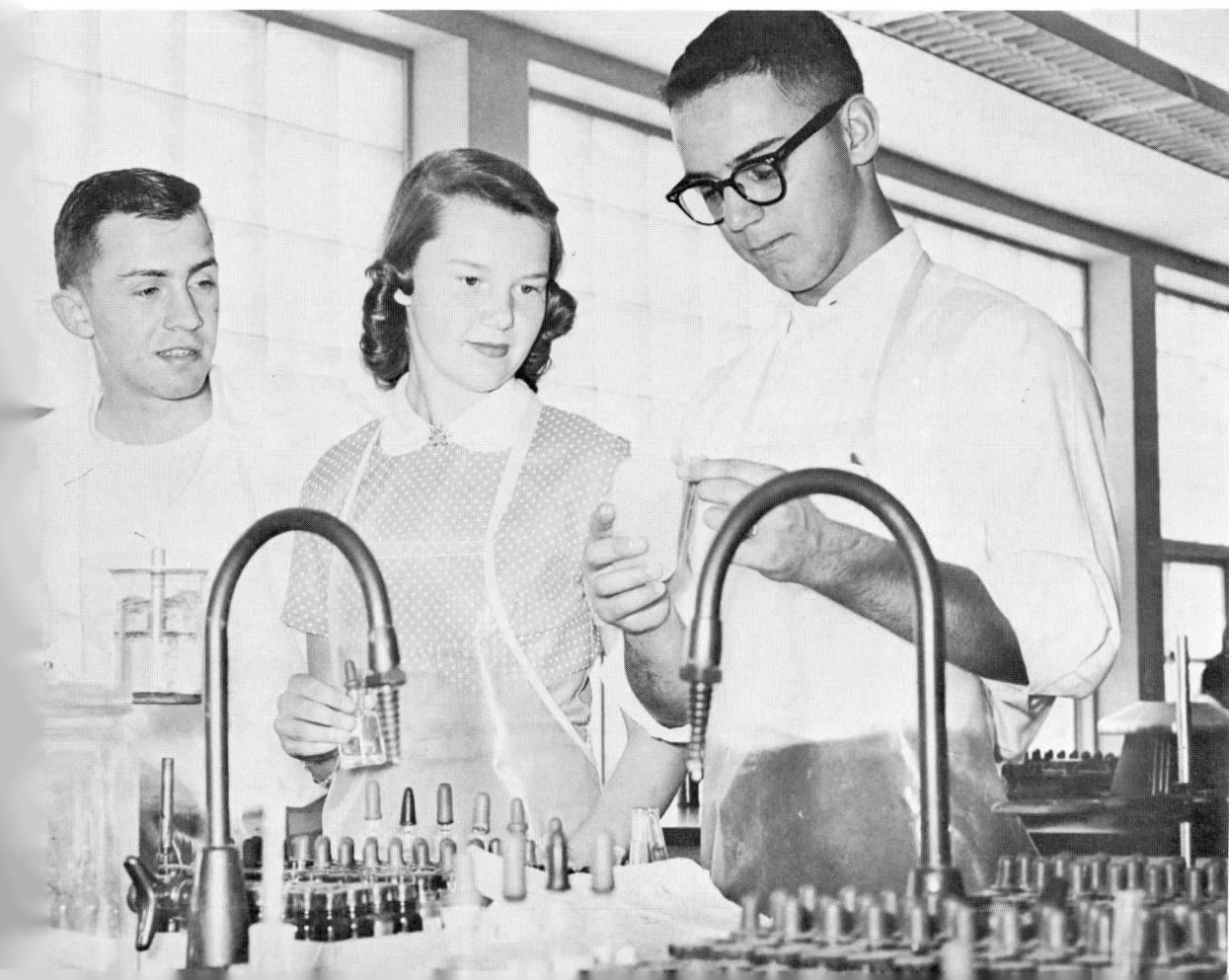

183

courses increased in number. Interest in vocational education developed. Between 1909 and 1915 state aid was provided for instruction in agriculture, home economics, industrial arts, and business subjects.

The junior high school, which began to get well under way between 1916 and 1921, offered generalized, exploratory, and practical arts courses, modifying still further the academic tradition. The state university liberalized its entrance requirements and began to accept graduates of approved high schools regardless of the specific nature of the high school course pursued.

The high school curriculum has been further enriched and diversified by the addition of art, music, health and physical education courses, on-the-job work programs, and various extra-class activities. Experiments have been made in reorganizing subject matter to relate it with problems of living. Guidance programs assist high school youth in planning their future and in selecting courses contributing to their plans. Area vocational schools are maintained in a number of centers throughout the state.

In Minnesota today, close to 80 percent of the boys and girls enrolled in the fifth grade can be expected to complete the twelfth grade; 97 percent will enroll in the ninth grade. In 1937 the percentages were 48 and 76, respectively. The tremendous importance of the high school in the lives of Minnesota youth may be inferred from these figures.

Organizational Developments

The high school was proposed as the "people's college" by a curriculum committee reporting in 1872. This committee, writing today, might include the junior college (where local young people may take two years of terminal job-preparing courses or college preparatory work.) In 1925 the first enabling legislation for public junior colleges was enacted, although several had been established before that time. State aid was granted these institutions by legislative enactment in 1957; this may be expected to give impetus to their growth.

Whatever the upper reaches of the public common school, may it reaffirm the sentiment expressed in 1862 by David Blakely who served both as sec-retary of state and superintendent of common schools: "Let the Free School then continue as a perpetual and untarnished memorial of the intelligence and liberality of a free people."

FROM HICKORY STICK TO PROFESSIONAL KNOW-HOW
or
PREPARATION OF TEACHERS

Early reports of school officials made frequent reference to problems of discipline but at the same time spoke of the low standards of teacher qualifications. The successful pioneer teacher was, indeed, one who succeeded in the face of great odds. He had to possess considerable natural talent and deep devotion to the cause of education. If these were lacking, he made frequent recourse to the hickory stick.

For several years following the opening of Miss Bishop's school in 1847, Minnesota relied on the older states for teachers. (Miss Bishop came from Vermont.) The facilities for preparing them locally were limited. Miss Bishop, herself, with the help of a friend from Ohio, established a seminary and boarding school in St. Paul in 1850 for that purpose.

Teaching as a Profession

In 1851, according to Edward D. Neill, "the legislature of the territory of Minnesota recognized teaching as a profession and in the charter of the university . . . created . . . the department of the theory and practice of instruction." However, "friends of education, unaware of this feature, moved in the year 1858 for the establishment of normal schools."

Although soon after Minnesota became a state the legislature passed an act reaffirming the action of the territorial government for the education of teachers the university did not open a normal department during its early history. It is probable that the establishment of normal schools was one reason for the delay. At any rate, the normal schools began their history with the preparation of elementary school teachers.

When the normal schools became teachers colleges, by legislative action in 1921, they were authorized to offer the bachelor's degree, and it was then that four-year curriculums for the preparation of both elementary and secondary school teachers were introduced. In 1953 these institutions were authorized to offer a fifth year of work.

In 1892 the university established a department of education and a two-year normal curriculum for high school teachers, which was extended to four years in 1899. In 1905 the legislature passed a bill creating the college of education, a professional school for the preparation of teachers, both elementary and secondary.

Along the Way

Teacher examinations (discontinued in 1929) were the order of an earlier day, administered in territorial times by district trustees, later by town superintendents, still later by examiners appointed by county commissioners, and, after 1864, by county superintendents of schools. Incidentally, educational requirements for county superintendents were defined in 1873, but the law passed in 1877 making the office elective failed to set forth any qualifications other than that the candidate must be entitled to vote. From that time to the present all efforts to establish educational requirements for county superintendents have failed.

As a way of getting an increased supply of teachers for rural districts, county superintendents urged the establishment of normal departments in high schools, and these departments spread over the state. Eventually, a two-year normal course became the minimum requirement for initial teaching in a graded school, but the one-year standard for rural schools continued.

Institutes, authorized by law in 1868, were a means of helping teachers review the common school subjects and become acquainted with improved methods of teaching. They are still used as an inservice and supervisory medium by the state department of education. Summer schools, authorized late in the past century, continue to be an important agency in the education of teachers.

Certification

In 1949, legislation was enacted which gave to the state board of education the authority to set up and administer certification regulations. Steps were immediately taken to raise standards for the preparation of elementary teachers, the process to be gradual until March 1, 1961, after which teachers new to the profession will be required to have four years of preparation beyond high school.

In the development of standards of teacher preparation the secondary schools have progressed more rapidly than the elementary, for in 1913 the high school board set as a requirement for high school teaching the bachelor's degree, with professional as well as academic background included. Before this time it had been possible for teachers with less than this amount of education to secure high school positions, although the action of the university in 1899 and the development of four-year private colleges tended to stabilize the four-year pattern.

Improved Standards

Throughout the years there have been several movements that have influenced the supply of teachers, their qualifications, and the quality of the work done. For example, state funds have been used as a leverage to raise educational standards.

In 1851, according to Edward Neill, the legislature of the territory of Minnesota recognized teaching as a profession. Today, more than 100 years later, it can be said that the confidence expressed by the legislature was justified, for teaching *is* a profession in Minnesota. At least ninety-eight percent of the secondary teachers in the public schools of the state have had more than four years of preparation—22 percent of them, five. More than a third of the elementary teachers have four or more years of preparation and the number is increasing rapidly. Inservice activities—additional schooling, travel, workshops—are helping them to keep abreast of the educational times. Research is continually disclosing better ways of teaching and learning.

Edward Neill once said that the duties of a teacher were such as to require an angel's wisdom. Today, Minnesota teachers find this wisdom in professional competence developed through thorough preparation and continued growth in service.

The Educational Timeline
in Minnesota

Pre-Territorial Time

1832 — First school of any description taught in trading house of Mr. Aitkin at Sandy Lake by F. Ayer; 1847 — First regular public school taught by Miss Harriet E. Bishop at St. Paul.

Territorial Days 1840 - 1857

1849 — Law passed by territorial assembly for common schools — Minnesota Historical Society chartered by territorial assembly — first institution in Minnesota; 1851 — First superintendent of common schools appointed — County commissioners authorized to set up school districts; 1854 — University campus purchased — Hamline University organized at Red Wing.

First Decade of Statehood 1858 - 1867

1858 — Permanent school fund created by act of state constitutional convention — Normal school board created by first legislature; 1860 — First superintendent of public instruction appointed — Board of regents appointed for university — First normal school established at Winona; 1864 — First provision for handicapped in school for blind and deaf children at Faribault.

Second Decade of Statehood 1868 - 1877

1868 — Second normal school established at Mankato; 1869 — Third normal school established at St. Cloud — First university president named — First university students enroll; 1877 — Women given right to vote on school matters.

Third Decade of Statehood 1878 - 1887

1878 — First legislative grants for schools from state funds; 1878 — State high school board created; 1885 — First compulsory school attendance law; 1885 — First regular course in teaching at university.

Fourth Decade of Statehood 1888 - 1897

1888 — Fourth normal school established at Moorhead; 1893 — First high school inspector appointed; 1895 — High school training departments authorized for rural teachers.

Fifth Decade of Statehood 1898 - 1907

1902 — Fifth normal school established at Duluth; 1905 — College of education established at the university.

Sixth Decade of Statehood 1908 - 1917

1911 — Consolidated districts authorized; 1915 — First junior college established at Rochester; 1917 — First federal aid for vocational education.

Seventh Decade of Statehood 1918 - 1927

1919 — State board of education and state board for vocational education formed — First commissioner of education appointed — Sixth normal school established at Bemidji; 1921 — Normal schools become teachers colleges.

Eighth Decade of Statehood 1928 - 1937

1933 — State income tax law assigns funds thus received to schools.

Ninth Decade of Statehood 1938 - 1947

1947 — Reorganization law passed for reduction of school districts — First area vocational school established at Mankato — Duluth teachers college becomes branch of university.

Tenth Decade of Statehood 1948 - 1957

1955 — Law on compulsory school attendance changed to 7-16 years or completion of ninth grade; 1957 — Special instruction for handicapped required in all school districts — State teachers colleges become state colleges — State aid given to junior colleges.

Private Liberal Arts Colleges

By LEAL A. HEADLEY

Minnesota in 1858, when it became one of the United States, already had three institutions of higher learning. The Territorial Legislature established the University of Minnesota in 1851 and granted charters to Hamline University in 1854 and to St. John's University in 1857. The University of Minnesota, as recorded in the first scene of this chapter, has grown into a typical and an outstanding American university with its college of liberal arts and its separate faculties devoted to instruction and research in the areas of various practical arts. In the universities of the United States, less than ten per cent of the students are in non-technical work. The two other institutions, though nominally chartered as universities, have followed the pattern of the private college whose primary concern is liberal education.

The goal of liberal education, in contrast to that of technical training, is conceived by its exponents as the development of what Greek philosophers called the "complete" human being. For many centuries the chief formal means employed in trying to reach this goal has been a study of the "humanities." During the Middle Ages humanities were specifically catalogued as grammar, rhetoric, philosophy, arithmetic, geometry, astronomy, and music. And so essentially stood the list, except for the addition of ancient Greek and Latin, up to our

focal year of 1858. In the remaining years of that century natural and social sciences were added. More recently, as everyone knows, the liberal arts program has been tremendously enlarged and enriched. In some areas the line which separates practice from theory becomes increasingly tenuous. Still, strictly speaking, the immediate concern of the liberal arts college is not with vocational preparation whether that be training for skill in artisanship or acquiring information requisite for practicing a profession. The underlying premise of liberal education is that those who best understand life in its larger and more intricate aspects have the best chance, other things being equal, of meeting with satisfaction to themselves and to others the complex problems which confront every alert individual.

In America the private college has had a unique place. Between 1636, when Harvard College was founded, and 1755, when the College of Philadelphia was chartered, all institutions of higher learning were private. The private liberal arts college is the most distinctively American feature of our ramified system of education. Its influence has been felt at every level and phase of our scheme of education. In our religious, social, economic and political life graduates from liberal arts colleges have exercised an influence far out of proportion to their number. This is evident in almost any community; and it is supported by biographical studies. Persons of eminence in the United States are largely college educated. For convenience, consider an eminent person as the one in a group of 10,000 persons, picked at random, who is most distinguished in one or more fields of socially useful endeavor. Then it may be said that, whereas 3% of those who make up the national population are college graduates, upward of 85% of eminent citizens are college graduates.

In this tradition are the private liberal arts colleges of Minnesota which are accredited by the authoritative North Central Association of Colleges and Secondary Schools. While charter dates for these fourteen colleges run from 1854 to 1915, the launching of each college has been, within its geographic and social environment, a pioneer venture. In many respects the story of each is the story of all—invariably a saga of almost unbelievable devotion, sacrifice, and unremitting effort. Each had its modest beginning—usually as a secondary school of doubtful scholastic standing. Though no two of the colleges are alike, all have common characteristics. No one of them is subsidized by public appropriation, except that such of its properties as are devoted to educational work are freed from state and federal tax levies. No civic authority exercises more control over any one of them than it does over any other corporate entity. No one is operated for profit; most of them incur sizable annual operating deficits which are made up, in last analysis, by private philanthropy. Each college has its own campus, plant, teaching faculty and core of resident students. As a rule, each admits only students who have completed a preparatory course with a pattern of subjects studied and a record of scholastic achievement which the college announces as acceptable. Each typically grants a baccalaureate degree upon completion of a four-year course of rather closely prescribed academic work. Each college has been founded by some ecclesiastical body. Of these fourteen Minnesota colleges, half are Catholic; three being for men, four for women. The seven other colleges are coeducational.

The fourteen colleges are somewhat scattered, although all of them fall within a central area that covers only a third of the state. Five are in the Twin Cities. Improvements in transportation naturally have made location decreasingly important. At present no college in the group is narrowly regional; some are almost national in their reach.

Although each college functions separately, it may be of interest to note a few instances of what their combined count means to Minnesota. Their plants represent an investment of $65,000,000. In ten years after the war $25,000,000 went into construction. The book value of their endowment funds exceeds $21,000,000, translated into current market value by adding $8,000,000. Together they number more than 800 faculty members and 300 part-time teachers, 15,000 students including 250 foreign students, and 50,000 living alumni.

While each college is autonomous, except for varying degrees of church control, members of the group work together in various ways. Since 1935 a conference made up of the presidents and other representatives of the fourteen member institutions, now known as the Private College Council, has given solidarity to the group. Eight of the colleges belong to a Minnesota Intercollegiate Athletic Conference. Cultural programs are interchanged. The Hill Foundation program, which enables each of five colleges to invite a distinguished scholar to its campus for one semester of each year, has had a unifying influence. Recent Ford grants, totaling $4,162,500 for the fourteen colleges, even if not a result of cooperative effort, have made for a mutual strengthening of members of the group. For some years the four St. Paul colleges have offered a "series of integrated area studies." The fourteen colleges have organized the "Minnesota Private College Fund" through which Minnesota industries have contributed more than a million dollars which have been prorated to the individual colleges. The most recent cooperative adventure is the "Minnesota Private College Hour" on the non-commercial educational television station KTCA-TV. Here the fourteen colleges share responsibility, during five evenings between eight and nine o'clock each week of the college year, for two half-hour programs devoted to topics from various academic fields. The audience for these programs averages somewhat more than 22,000 listeners.

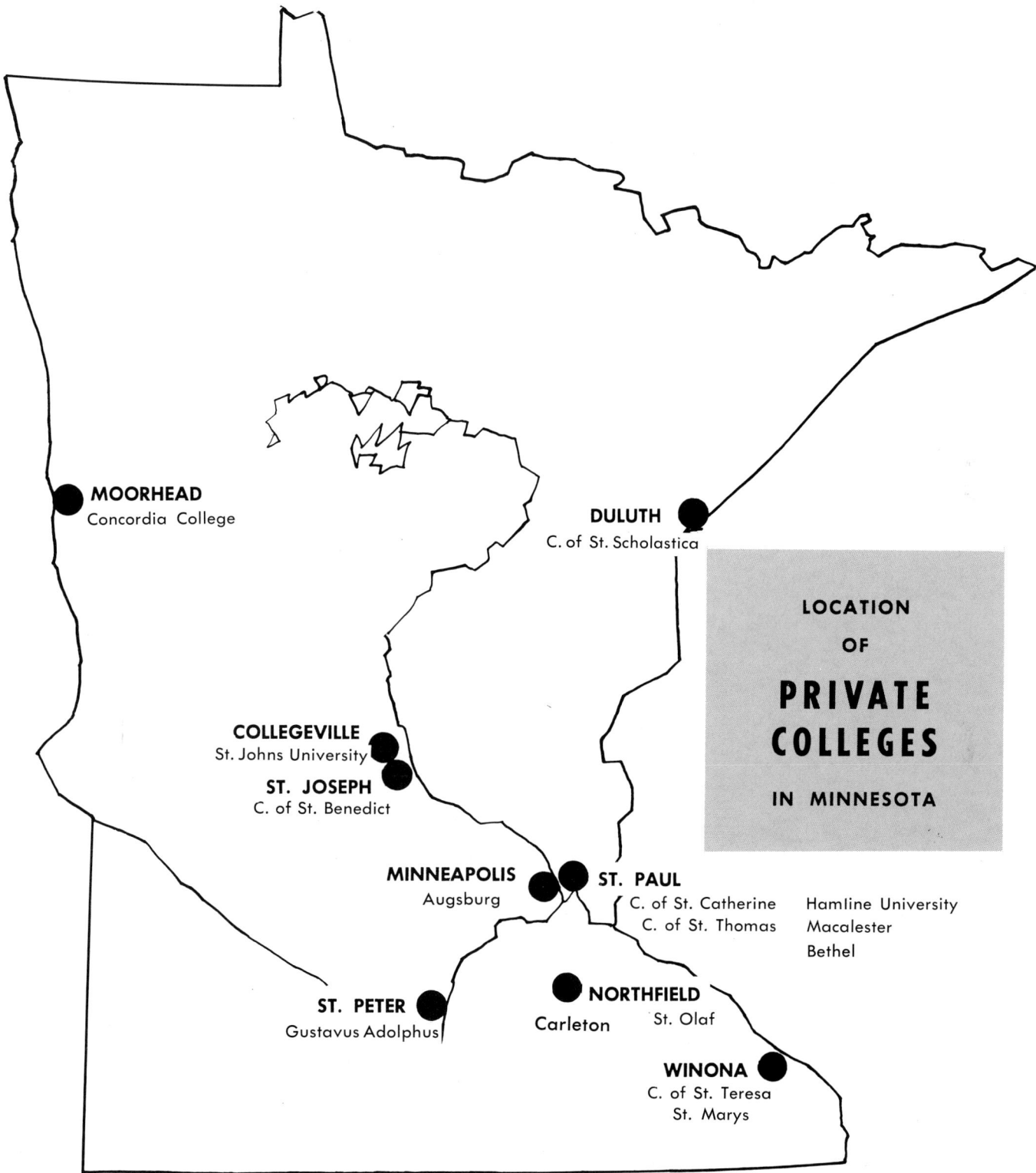

MOORHEAD
Concordia College

DULUTH
C. of St. Scholastica

LOCATION
OF
**PRIVATE
COLLEGES**
IN MINNESOTA

COLLEGEVILLE
St. Johns University

ST. JOSEPH
C. of St. Benedict

MINNEAPOLIS
Augsburg

ST. PAUL
C. of St. Catherine
C. of St. Thomas

Hamline University
Macalester
Bethel

ST. PETER
Gustavus Adolphus

NORTHFIELD
St. Olaf
Carleton

WINONA
C. of St. Teresa
St. Marys

Augsburg College

Because of involvement in shifting synodical relations among Scandinavian Lutheran churches the line of descent of Augsburg College is somewhat complicated. Its immediate antecedent was Augsburg Seminary. This was the earliest Norwegian Lutheran seminary in America. It was founded in 1869 at Marshall Academy, in Wisconsin, whose humble abode it at first shared. In 1872 the Seminary was moved to Minneapolis where a new building awaited it. In the same year it was incorporated under the laws of Minnesota and started academic work.

But the significance of Augsburg is in its fruits rather than its roots. In 1874 a college curriculum was offered and the first college students were enrolled. The five members of the first college class were graduated in 1879. The preparatory course, developed by 1910 into a full four-year offering, was discontinued in 1933. Both the preparatory and the college departments were organized primarily to afford adequate preparation for seminary students. Originally the College offered a "scientific" course along with the "classical" or pre-theological course but the former did not elicit sufficient interest to warrant its continuation at that time.

The relation of the college to the seminary has gradually changed until, at least by numerical count, the former appendage now vigorously wags its one-time master. Augsburg has become essentially a liberal arts college. For its geographical and socio-denominational area it is a highly influential college. It is, in fact, the only institution of collegiate rank sponsored by the Lutheran Free Church. Of the nearly one thousand students enrolled in what is still officially known as *Augsburg College and Theological Seminary*, scarcely more than a score in any recent year have been in the Seminary. But graduates of the College are now found in many theological seminaries. It is doubtful whether any other college in its area has so large a proportion of alumni who undertake theological studies.

Religious emphasis in the College is strong. The dominating architectural feature of its campus is a cross of bold proportions high on the wall of a focal shaft. On the fourth floor of this shaft is the "Tower Prayer Chapel." Most Augsburg students are from Lutheran families. Incoming students are invited, in the words of the college catalog, "to take up their college work with the distinct understanding that the Christian spirit is determining in all things." All students are expected to attend a daily worship service conducted by different members of the faculty. Twice each year a period of institutional life is designated as "Spiritual Emphasis Week." Credit for sixteen hours of courses in religion, two hours of which must be earned each semester, is required for graduation. And beyond campus confines college authorities have been religious leaders and builders of the Christian Congregation.

But with all of its emphasis on spiritual values, Augsburg has not lost sight of the intellectual aspects of a liberal arts program. Neither does it neglect the practical and vocational interests of its students. Specified sequences of courses, selected from regular academic offerings, or carried in addition to them, enable the student to prepare himself for any one of a variety of occupations including religious and social work, secretarial service, home economics, medical technology,

Tower of Prayer, Science Hall

First Minneapolis Building

business administration, and education. In recent decades secondary-school teaching, mostly in Minnesota high schools, has claimed more of Augsburg's graduates than has any other calling. Likewise the majority of graduates who, in increasing numbers, enter the fields of business and social work establish themselves in Minnesota. Other sequences of courses prepare students for further vocational study in the fields of dentistry, engineering, law, and medicine. Among the Augsburg students is a group of about 150 young women who are studying in two of the large hospitals of Minneapolis to become registered nurses. In another arrangement with two hospitals in the city, the College offers a course which combines three years of work on the campus with a twelve-month period of practical hospital laboratory experience, enabling the students to become qualified medical technicians.

Augsburg is the only one of Minnesota's fourteen fully accredited four-year liberal arts colleges which is located in Minneapolis. It is in the Riverside Park area within a twenty-minute walk of the metropolitan business and cultural centers. The main campus of the University of Minnesota, when it is extended to the west bank of the Mississippi, will be almost adjacent to Augsburg. As might be expected the College derives rich cultural and intellectual benefits, through both formal arrangements and informal contacts, from the great city in the heart of which it lies.

Naturally a metropolitan setting is not an unalloyed blessing. Eight acres do not afford the free environs and the open quadrangles which characterize the popular concept of a campus. Most of the six buildings which constitute the Augsburg physical plant lie in one city block. Careful planning, however, has in considerable measure compensated for limitations of space. Buildings are set near enough to streets to allow an open quadrangle in the center of the block. This landscape effect is enhanced by the fact that one side of the quadrangle opens onto a city park beyond which are additional college buildings. Psychologically and artistically, if not legally, the College has incorporated the park. The two chief college buildings, each extending for the best part of a city block, are joined in a massive tower at the corner of Seventh Street and Twenty-first Avenue South. In one of them is a well-appointed modern library.

Augsburg was started as a college for men, but opened its doors to women in 1921. It still enrolls more men than women though its resident dormitories accommodate about 180 women and 170 men. More than seven out of nine of its students are from Minnesota homes. Forty-eight percent of them live in the Twin Cities. More than 1500 Augsburg alumni and former students are residents of the Twin Cities. All of this means, of course, that Augsburg makes a contribution to its local community which is quite out of proportion to its size.

191

Carleton College

Carleton is an independent college. It is loyal to the state which chartered it and to the church which founded it; but all responsibility for it and all authority over it rest with its board of trustees. It began when the Annual Meeting of the Congregational Churches of Minnesota, held in Faribault in 1866, voted "the acceptance of the offers of Northfield, and the adoption of that place as the location of the college." The offers were 20 acres of land and 21,029 of the hard dollars of that day. Articles of incorporation for Northfield College provided that three-fourths of the initial trustees be Congregationalists and that thereafter the board be self-perpetuating. And so it has been; but through the years Minnesota Congregationalists and the College have cooperated in many ways. Cooperative relations have been established also with the American Baptist Convention in 1916; and with the Episcopal Diocese of Minnesota in 1923.

At an early meeting, trustees authorized the employment of a teacher and bought, for temporary occupancy, the American House—a hotel too ambitious for its time, built by John W. North, founder of Northfield. By June of 1870, the College had started a permanent building, had a preparatory department with an average yearly enrollment of "41 1/3 gentlemen and 12 ladies," and a faculty of four, counting the "acting financial agent." But it did not have a president until September when James W. Strong, pastor of the Congregational Church in Faribault, was persuaded to take the thankless job. While in New England, soliciting funds, he suffered an all but fatal accident. The tragedy moved a newly acquired friend, at whose home near Boston he had been staying, to contribute $50,000 to Northfield College. This was the largest gift any western college had then

received. The name of the donor was William Carleton; the name of the college henceforth was Carleton College.

The development of Carleton has been steady, but never spectacular. Of its 92 years, 70 have been spanned by two phenomenal administrations. The Strong period (1870-1903) brought to the college recognition as a Minnesota institution; the Cowling period (1909-1945) brought to it a degree of national recognition. Total assets—divided almost evenly between plant and endowment—have grown to $12,500,000. Annual academic operations require approximately $1,346,000. Student fees provide 46% of these instructional costs. Endowment income and yearly gifts from almost 3000 contributors keep the budget in balance.

To the original 20 acres, 70 have been added to form the central campus. Repeated additions have brought the total acreage to 900. Nearly half this area is devoted to a dairy farm. The remainder makes possible a hundred acres of lawn and shrubbery, a riding field with stable, an athletic field and stadium, a women's athletic field, a stream spanned ten times by foot bridges, artificial lakes with their May-fete island, eight miles of bridle path, six miles of nature trail along two sides of the Cannon River, a lilac garden, and an arboretum in which may be studied almost every variety of woody growth suited to this climate.

On the campus 22 permanent buildings have appeared in fairly regular succession. Two are for the arts; three are for the sciences. A building which served as library from 1896 to 1956 has been superseded by one with desks for 460 readers and shelves for 370,000 volumes. The present book collection comprises 156,000 bound volumes. In the library are continuing microfilm records of

42 scholarly journals and a complete film file of the New York Times. An accumulated library endowment now totaling $1,350,000 helps defray expenses for maintenance and book purchases.

Students now number 975; with 528 men and 447 women. They come from 42 states and seven foreign countries. Minnesota supplies 295 students; Illinois, 211. Living accommodations on the campus have been available to women since 1882; to men, since 1916. There are now eight dormitories. Inasmuch as Carleton is a residence college, the size of its student body is conditioned by its dormitory space. Admission to college is determined by a formula for evaluating scholastic records and by College Entrance Examination Board tests.

Carleton students represent 25 religious denominations. The largest group is Presbyterian; though the Congregational, Episcopal, Methodist and Lutheran groups number more than a hundred each. But all join once a week for a chapel period, for a convocation hour, and for a Sunday vesper service.

With the closing of its Academy in 1907, and with the changing of its School of Music into a collegiate department of music in 1925, Carleton has limited its work, except for a few courses in secondary education, to the four-year liberal arts program. It was recognized in 1913 by Phi Beta Kappa and in 1935 by Sigma Xi. Through the years student choice of academic studies has varied. In the 1880's class rooms for Greek required extra chairs. Since then preferences have shifted through philosophy, science, English, and the social

sciences. At present the largest number of students choose English as their major subject.

Carleton has graduated 6977 of its students; according to latest count 6250 of these are living. During the last score of years research work has earned the Ph.D. degree for 158 of them. Nine alumni have gone to Oxford as Rhodes Scholars. The names of 96 graduates now living have appeared in *Who's Who in America*. Of those who were seniors last year 45% are engaged in graduate studies. For the last five years the average is 41%. Alumni and former students maintain 40 Carleton clubs. Some 2600 of them contribute annually more than $75,000 to the support of their college.

Equated in terms of full-time service, Carleton has a teaching faculty of 90 persons who have been educated at 102 different colleges and universities. Three of these, as an average, are on sabbatical leave each semester. Of the total group 24 are professors. The Ph.D. degree is held by 67. The constancy of this ratio is suggested by noting that of twenty living retired faculty members fifteen have this degree. During the past twelve years Carleton teachers have published 23 full-length books.

Miscellany *re* Carleton: Its long-time tolerance for divergence of opinion is illustrated by the fact that in the 1880's it graduated both Thorstein Veblen and Pierce Butler. . . . One family, within four generations, has supplied a trustee during 71 years; during half of these years this trustee has served as Chairman of the Board. . . . Between 1903 and 1951 students and alumni contributed funds and staff to a hospital and school unit known as "Carleton in China"—temporarily their contributions find other outlets, especially in Japan. . . . In behalf of salary schedules private contributions are being solicited to match the recent Ford grants. . . . Two-thirds of those who enter Carleton as freshmen are graduated from Carleton. . . . Few, if any, other colleges receive so much financial aid from parents of students. . . . Doubtless Carleton is the only college to have its affairs administered intermittently from the South Pole.

View from the East

College of Saint Benedict

The College of St. Benedict is the baby sister in the family of Minnesota colleges. All of its students and all of its teachers except two are of feminine persuasion; and it is smaller and younger than any of its thirteen siblings.

Measured by enrollment figures of nowadays, St. Benedict's is distinctly small; in this dimension it is determined not to become large. Its 360 students are served by 45 instructors. The resulting quotient is enviable: one teacher to every eight students. Seldom are so few students inspired by so many dedicated teachers. The College is well described as a community of living and learning.

Even in youthful Minnesota the College of St. Benedict seems young. It was not incorporated until 1913; but its history antedates its existence. In 1857 Sisters of the Order of St. Benedict, by dint of arduous journey down the Ohio and up the Mississippi, came from Pennsylvania and settled in St. Cloud.

The following year, contemporaneously with Minnesota becoming a state, they opened a boarding school for girls. This school stood where the St. Cloud post office now stands. After five years the Sisters again moved westward. This trek, however, was short. It was halted eight miles west of St. Cloud in the village of St. Joseph. The locality was known for its healthfulness. Doubtless a factor which favored this location even more than its salubrity was its national and religious heritage. For St. Joseph nestles congenially in Stearns County which is the most German and the most Catholic of any county west of Pennsylvania.

In this tiny community, in 1863, were embedded the roots of the Convent of St. Benedict. The roots sank deep. And in good time they yielded fruit. In the Convent were blended the mellowed culture of Bavarian hills and the adventuresome spirit of Minnesota prairies. It became the largest community of Benedictine women in the world, numbering nearly a thousand sisters. It became also a mother house from which the Sisters of the Order, for nearly a century now, have initiated and conducted their good works in priories and schools and hospitals throughout a wide area between Lake Michigan and Puget Sound, and in Puerto Rico and the Orient. Among its offspring is the Villa Sancta Scholastica in Duluth, which in turn mothers the College of St. Scholastica.

But the Convent has not limited its pioneer efforts to distant places. Within its own precincts St. Benedict's Academy was incorporated in 1887. In language which did not then sound quaint this school assayed instruction in "every useful and ornamental branch of education suitable for young ladies." In 1913 courses of junior-college level were added to those of the secondary school and the corporate name of the institution became *Saint Benedict's College and Academy*. The final two years of collegiate program were added in 1915 and academic degrees have been granted since 1917. In 1932, it was accredited by the North Central Association of Colleges and Secondary Schools.

St. Benedict's is primarily a liberal arts college but it offers a number of courses which assist students in adjusting themselves to the work-a-day world. A Bachelor of Arts degree may be earned in any one of twelve major fields including elementary education. Students in education do their practice teaching in the public and parochial schools of nearby communities. A Bachelor of Science degree may be earned in business education, in dietetics, or in home economics. The three

194

Mary Hall

most largely elected majors are Elementary Education, Home Economics, and English. Required of all students for graduation are ten semester hours of work in philosophy. Catholic students must carry an additional twelve hours of work in theology. A minimum of one year of residence is needed for graduation.

Because most of the teachers contribute their time, as is true in so many Catholic colleges, student expenses are moderate at St. Benedict's. Basic fees for day students are $525 a year; total costs for resident students average a little more than $900 a year. An unusual but palpably fair arrangement reduces by ten percent basic costs for two or more members of one family who are simultaneously full-time students.

Though the Convent has its own square mile—denominated by surveyors as a section or 640 acres—most of it is woodland. Its buildings, both ecclesiastical and educational, are clustered on a hundred acres near the village. They form a compact functional unit, and an unusually picturesque unit, but scarcely an architectural unit. The Dean of the College unofficially describes their architecture as "American Chaotic," a term which might fairly be applied to many an American campus, were all

college officers equally forthright. It is hard to assimilate into one context the Roman renaissance style of the Sacred Heart Chapel (1914), with its high dome and its Baroque ornamentation, and the ultra-modern design and trappings of Mary Hall (1957) where more than three hundred women reside. But he would be a hardy critic indeed who, within the gracious walls of Mary Hall, whose every stone echoes a final word of charm and comfort, could quibble about intramural consistency in design.

Like most colleges St. Benedict's has its customs and traditions. One of these is unique. It is a "commencement exercise" which marks the beginning—not the conclusion—of one's college days. It is, in fact, a pageant for the initiation of freshmen. Presented on a Sunday night each October for more than twenty years, it has come to attract thousands of spectators. Initiates both witness and participate in it. The central theme of spreading, in varied settings, the light of prayer and work which was kindled by St. Benedict is presented with superb artistry by dancing maidens who symbolize the hallowed flame. The pageant is known as *So Let Your Light Shine* and enacts the contributions to civilization made by the Benedictines during the fourteen centuries of their existence.

Pageant, "So let your light shine."

College of Saint Catherine

Paradoxically the College of St. Catherine, in St. Paul, was founded by the Sisters of St. Joseph of Carondelet. The congregation of St. Joseph was established in 1650 in the old lace city of Le Puy in southern France. Its convent was commonly referred to as the "poor little institute." Sisters of the institute had such aversion to ostentation that they shunned as pedantic any suggestion of scholarly attainment. In 1863 Sisters from this Congregation came to America and established themselves in Carondelet near St. Louis. Then in 1854 Sisters from Carondelet came to Minnesota and established themselves at Pig's Eye near the foot of what is now Robert Street in St. Paul.

It was by this congregation, and out of this background, that the College of St. Catherine came into being. First there was St. Joseph's Academy. Almost at the beginning of the century Mother Seraphine Ireland, Provincial of the Congregation of St. Joseph—upon the insistence of her renowned brother Archbishop John Ireland—undertook to improve the educational background of the Sisters. As early as 1902 students wearing the black habit of the Congregation appeared on the campus of the University of Chicago. Within a few years their silhouettes against those gray walls became a familiar sight. As if by overcompensation, St. Joseph's Academy attained a degree of urbanity which prompted General C. C. Andrews in his *History of St. Paul* (1910) to refer to it as one which is "exclusively for young ladies, who are given instruction in every branch of learning and in every accomplishment."

The paradox is that descendants of the Sisters of "the poor little institute"—too humble to aspire to learning—should have developed a college in which scholarship is esteemed so highly. Recognition for sound scholarship came early to the College of St. Catherine. Eleven years after its founding it was admitted to the North Central Association of Colleges and Secondary Schools. It is now approved by the National Catholic Educational Association and The Association of American Universities. Its standing is recognized by the American Association of University Women. In 1937 the United Chapters of Phi Beta Kappa established on its campus the Gamma Chapter of Minnesota. St. Catherine's is the only Catholic college for women to have membership in this venerated honor society. More recently trustees of the Ford Foundation have recognized the College by including it in a limited list of 126 American colleges to which a supplementary "accomplishment grant" has been made.

Among the factors which warrant such recognition capable teaching is central. The faculty of St. Catherine's includes the equivalent of 71 full-time instructors of all ranks. This number provides an average of one teacher for each fourteen students. Of these instructors 25 hold the Ph.D. degree; another 25 have professional degrees or have had specialized training; most of them are members of learned societies; seven have enjoyed Fulbright, Danforth, or Ford appointments; four have received significant prizes, some being notable ones, for creative work in art; and eight are known as authors of books.

The core of the academic program is the liberal arts course. In addition to meeting requirements for English, mathematics, and foreign language,

196

Chapel of Our Lady of Victory

St. Joseph Hall

however, each graduating student must have studied philosophy and theology during four years. Aside from the more usual curriculum divisions of humanities, natural science, philosophy, psychology and religion, and social science, the College has a division designated as community services which includes the areas of education, home economics, nursing, occupational therapy, physical education, and secretarial work.

The College currently enrolls 972 students of whom about half live in the Twin Cities and 350 live on the campus. Of the total group, 882 live in Minnesota and 18 are from foreign countries. All students, whether or not they reside on the campus, participate in a full program of social and recreational activities. Varying with the time of year are receptions, mixers, picnics, dinners, buffet suppers, teas, and dances both formal and informal, not forgetting stated occasions such as the Winter Carnival, the May Fete, and the Senior-Junior Prom.

The baccalaureate degree of St. Catherine is held by 3945 living women. Of these 2105 are married and 883 devote their lives to religious service. Even so, the vocational roster covers some 60 different occupations and includes names which are widely known in fields as varied as art, opera, psychology, and business. While 1100 alumnae live in the Twin Cities they live also in nearly every state of the union and, scattered across the country, they have 24 chapters which are affiliates of the Alumnae Association.

The College of St. Catherine is an independent corporation, chartered by the state of Minnesota, but belongs to the Sisters of St. Joseph of Carondelet of the Province of St. Paul. It was founded

by these Sisters under the patronage of the Archbishop of St. Paul. Its name, suggested by Archbishop Ireland, acknowledges as its patron the early philosopher and saint of Alexandria in Egypt.

The College occupies its original hundred acres facing Randolph Street and sloping south and west toward the Mississippi River a mile away. The southern portion of the area is open except for a wide border of a woodland. On the northern part, within a dignified wall of stone and wrought iron, are nine substantial buildings each with its own character. The most recent of these is the distinctively mid-twentieth-century St. Joseph Hall whose rectangular proportions bespeak the practical service rendered by its every nook. One and a half million is a tidy investment; but it pays large dividends to students and instructors in the service and comfort rendered by its commodious common rooms and in the educative influences which its dignity must exert on every student.

To step from St. Joseph Hall to the Chapel of Our Lady of Victory requires a scant minute; but architecturally the two are seven centuries apart. The motif for the Chapel, built in 1924, is the great French cathedral of Arles. Resemblances to its prototype are especially marked in the many stone carvings about its central portal which depict, among a multitude of items, incidents from the legend of St. Catherine. Within the Chapel candle holders of wrought iron, confessional stalls of carved wood, tiles of many colors, Byzantine pillars and vaulted roof suggest the peace and mystery of ages past. All who live in Minnesota should be grateful to the College of St. Catherine for placing in their midst a structure which has elicited almost universal acclaim.

College of Saint Scholastica

"Bernard likes the valleys, Benedict likes the hills." If there be warrant for this saying, the Benedictine College of St. Scholastica, itself named for the sister of St. Benedict, is true to an ancient tradition. The College occupies an eminence 680 feet above the level of Lake Superior which is scarcely two miles distant. Its sweep to the south and east includes, in addition to the ever-shifting shades and hues of the world's largest surface of unsalted water, many an intriguing glimpse of those twenty-six metropolitan miles whose name perpetuates the memory of their earliest white explorer. It was in 1679 that Sieur du Lhut first visited this north shore.

To this strategic spot the Sisters of St. Benedict moved the Institute of Sacred Heart which, under one name or another, they had conducted in Duluth since 1892. In that year Mother Scholastica and eight other Sisters from the Convent of St. Benedict in St. Joseph, Minnesota, opened a convent and an academy in the newly established Diocese of Duluth.

A group of buildings in native stone, which later became a wing of the college plant, was completed and occupied in 1909. This was called Villa Sancta Scholastica—a name which the people of Duluth now easily apply to the whole institution including the secondary school and the college and which tradespeople quite naturally shorten to *the Villa*. This designation had a certain aptness for, especially prior to the encroachment of real estate subdivisions, the setting was rural. As years passed the appropriateness of the Latin designation was reinforced by the gradual appearance in the center of the area of a massive pile of many-towered Tudor-Gothic buildings and by the development of landscape features such as groves, both deciduous

and evergreen, a stream which cuts through the 160 acres of campus, extensive gardens, and several shrines.

Growing through the stages of academy and junior college, St. Scholastica matured into a fully accredited college of liberal arts in 1932. During its short life it has done much to maintain and improve its academic excellence. One evidence of this is the trenchant study of its instructional program which it made in 1947—fifteen years after attaining legal status. The study was based largely on an evaluation of replies to a detailed questionnaire addressed to all its living graduates. Because the results of this study were of more than local interest, they were presented in a book entitled *The First Fifteen Years of the College of St. Scholastica* (1947)—"A Report on the Effectiveness of Catholic Education for Women." This was followed by a companion volume studying graduates from 1941-1951 and entitled *A Second Look* (1955). Typical also of St. Scholastica's intellectual initiative is the maintenance of a cancer research laboratory, the reception of several faculty awards for pioneer work in the field of educational television, and the fact that the Department of English has sponsored a state-wide conference of students and teachers of English from the private liberal arts colleges in Minnesota. The organization rotates its annual meetings among the fourteen institutions represented.

The atmosphere of St. Scholastica is definitely religious. And its religious life is exceedingly rich in symbolism. This is evident in the basic architecture and in the extensive ornamentation of both buildings and grounds. The focal and dominating structure of its plant is an early Christian and Romanesque Church—the Chapel of Our Lady

Queen of Peace. Almost everything about it is symbolic even to the design and grouping of its eighty-three windows which were made by leading thousands of fragments of imported glass.

In discussing the artistic appurtenances of the College, Sister M. Agnes, O.S.B., in *All Her Ways*, explains the symbolic significance of more than a hundred from the almost countless complex objects of art which are so vital a part of St. Scholastica. Likewise the emphasis on liturgical practices in music is strong. Every day the official prayer of the Church, known among Benedictines as the *Opus Dei*, is chanted in full, some of the "hours" now being sung in English. Students are trained in congregational singing of the traditional Gregorian chant. Large numbers of them join voluntarily in

Our Lady Queen of Peace Chapel

the daily noon Mass. Religious symbolism is marked even in many student customs, such as the Rose Procession on the Feast of Christ the King, the solemnizing of engagements, and the use of the Advent wreath.

In addition to the more typical divisions of a liberal arts curriculum, St. Scholastica has a "Division of Service Arts." In this division are listed courses with content designed to be vocationally serviceable to students preparing for teaching, nursing, or work in social service and allied fields. Unique is the course in Medical Record Library Science. The most largely elected field of professional work at St. Scholastica is teaching. Next in order, and elected by about equal numbers, are the fields of nursing, sociology, and medical records. To be graduated, however, any student, no matter how professional may be her approach to life after graduation, must have earned credits in general education centering around those in religion and philosophy, which amount to about 60% of her total credit hours.

Of the 346 students now enrolled in St. Scholastica, about 60% are from Minnesota. Many are from Wisconsin and Michigan. Nearly all are Catholic. The startlingly low tuition rate is $200 a year. This covers only about 47% of what ordinarily would be required to provide the quality of instruction which the student receives. The unusual ratio is made possible, of course, only by the generosity of the forty devoted sisters who, in keeping with their vows of poverty, seek compensation not in money, but in a satisfaction which money cannot buy.

College of Saint Teresa

The College of Saint Teresa is set in the midst of one of Minnesota's most spectacular panoramas. Not far to its east are the eddies and islands of the slow-moving Mississippi backed by the haze-ridden highlands of Wisconsin. To its west, towering four hundred feet above the river, is a bank of sandstone bluffs overlaid with dolomite and topped by that hardy survivor of milleniums of erosive onslaught and decades of quarrying, known to everyone in the valley as Sugar Loaf. It is difficult to realize that the college premises once were part of the swampy terrain which rimmed the north edge of the city of Winona.

Eleven acres of this area were purchased in 1884 by the Milwaukee School Sisters of Saint Francis who erected thereon a substantial building named Saint Mary Hall. For nearly a decade this building housed first an academy and then a hospital. Earlier the Sisters of Saint Francis of the Congregation of Our Lady of Lourdes had established a Motherhouse in Rochester, Minnesota, where in 1877 they had opened an academy for girls. In 1894 this Congregation, with the help of Bishop Cotter of the Diocese of Winona, purchased the Winona property including Saint Mary Hall. An index of their faith is the fact that the transaction left them with a mortgage of twenty-nine thousand dollars and assets of a horse and buggy. Staff and pupils transferred from the Rochester academy and became the nucleus of a school—the Winona Seminary for Ladies—from which developed the College of Saint Teresa.

College courses were organized in 1907. These were tutorial sessions for a small group of Franciscan Sisters. Learning was the order of the day. Subject matter was at once substantial and extensive. A routine schedule claimed the hours from eight-thirty to noon each morning, from one to five each afternoon, and from six to nine each evening. In 1909 lay students were admitted to college classes and tutorial procedures gave way to more conventional methods of instruction.

St. Teresa of Avila in Assisi Court

The name *College of Saint Teresa* was adopted in 1911. The first class of lay students, consisting of three members, was graduated in 1914. Between 1911 and 1914, however, baccaleaurate degrees had been granted to several sisters without benefit of commencement exercises. The College was accredited by the North Central Association of Colleges and Secondary Schools in 1917 and by the Association of American Universities in 1918. Since then the academic stature of its faculty has grown steadily; of the fifty-four members of its present teaching staff, nineteen hold the doctorate degree. The consistently high quality of its academic work at the start and during subsequent years has earned for the College of Saint Teresa a recognized place among the women's colleges of the United States.

The College now occupies a hundred acres in the heart of one of Winona's best residence areas. Its plant, being developed according to a fifty-year plan, is inspiring. Though not uniform in design its nine buildings present an artistically satisfying harmony. The Chapel of Saint Mary of the Angels, completed in 1925, unifies the surrounding buildings. In 1956 the college alumnae, through gifts exceeding a hundred thousand dollars, completed the decoration of its interior. For this work mosaics and stained glass were brought from various countries in Europe. The original structure and particularly the more recent interior ingeniously blend touches of modernity with a dominant mood of early Christian art.

A typical but an especially pleasant aspect of the campus is Lourdes Hall—largest of three dormitories. It accommodates five hundred students. Inviting porticoes paved with tiles burned in Italy and screened by multiple-arched walls, a spacious dining hall flanked by a mezzanine gallery, a wide sun porch overlooking the athletic field, a large and well-proportioned swimming pool, and numerous lesser features lend both grace and comfort to the building.

On the campus, in Assisi Court, is an arresting statue of Saint Teresa of Avila which seems to symbolize the quiet yet alert reserve that pervades the atmosphere of the college which bears her name. This spirit is always evident, but is especially manifest at the beginning of Holy Week when students observe a three-day period of silence. As if to galvanize the spirit, walls of corridors are hung with crisp aphorisms such as : "The voice so sweet, the words so fair, as some soft chime that stroked the air." "The student at the College of Saint Teresa," proclaims the college bulletin, "is educated in the Franciscan spirit of looking on all

that she has as possessed for the glory of God and the good of her neighbor."

It would be a mistake, however, to infer that the social atmosphere is oppressive. Students of Saint Teresa have many recreational facilities and opportunities. In addition to their varied campus events they enjoy social relations with the "Redmen" of nearby Saint Mary's College.

Recent benefactions from two Minnesota families have made possible at Saint Teresa's two significant educational experiments. One is a cooperative language center devoted particularly to the learning of foreign language. The other is a mental health program conducted by some of the leading psychiatrists in Minnesota and pointed particularly to the responsibility of teachers in building healthy personalities. More than three hundred sisters from thirteen religious communities attended these meetings during the college summer session of 1957.

Among the many claims which the college of Saint Teresa might make to distinction are these. It is one of five Catholic women's colleges in the United States to have been conceived as a full four-year liberal arts institution. Its resident enrollment is the largest of any women's liberal arts college in Minnesota. The homes of more than half of its seven hundred students are outside Minnesota. It has graduated 2,500 women. In proportion to its size it has more foreign students than has any other liberal arts college in the state. Continuously since the close of the First World War goodly numbers— as many as thirty-five some years—of these harbingers of international friendship have been on this Winona campus.

Lourdes Hall

College of Saint Thomas

In 1853 Joseph Cretin, first Bishop of St. Paul, bade Godspeed to two young voyagers to France on study bent. He was not destined to welcome their return. But they were destined to return; and to become chief instruments in realizing his fondest dream. The dream was of a theological seminary supported by a classical academy. It would prepare leaders, both priests and laymen, for the people of Minnesota; people whose number was multiplied nearly thirtyfold in that one decade. The two voyagers were John Ireland who in 1885, shortly after he had become the third Bishop of St. Paul, founded St. Thomas Aquinas Seminary, and Thomas O'Gorman who became first Rector of the Seminary.

A prime essential for a college is a home site. And what site could have been better than Finn's Farm on the east bank of the Mississippi River? It lay almost midway between St. Paul and Minneapolis. Its 60 acres, sloping gently to the river brink, its meadows and streams, its rocky knolls and standing timber, were accented by a miniature canyon with its Shadow Falls, and by Lake Mennith whose desiccating basin was finally filled in 1911. On the shore of this lake was a building designed as living quarters for a boys' industrial school. Built in 1878, it had long since been surrendered to nature and to vandals. This building was patched and extended and sheathed in brick and in it, on September 8, 1885, the Seminary was opened.

With lessening responsibility for preparatory courses, especially during the early years of the twentieth century, the College assumed the stature of a mature liberal arts institution. Its first baccalaureate degrees, as distinguished from former certificates for completing a six-year program of study, were awarded to two students in 1910.

After holding tenaciously for a generation to the classical pattern of liberal education, the College in the 1920's broadened radically its concept of education and also its curricular offerings. The avowed purpose of the College, as officially stated that same year, is to produce "men who are masters of life's situations."

Changes in the theory and content of education are difficult to evaluate. Growth is more obvious in realms where counting is possible. Since 1885 Finn's Farm and adjacent farms have become one of the fine resident areas of the Twin Cities. In the midst of this area the College of St. Thomas occupies eight city blocks bounded by Selby, Cleveland, Summit, and Cretin Avenues. In place of the original building—familiarly called the "Old Ad Building"—which was torn down in 1931, the College now has nine well-equipped buildings. These stand in two groups. On higher ground to the north are the older buildings. This group is dominated by a Romanesque and Byzantine chapel, built in 1917, which seats 800 students. On the lower ground to the south is an almost solid facade of softly textured Mankato stone which, when the library is completed, will extend for nearly two city blocks along the north side of the extreme west end of Summit Avenue. It adds much to the stateliness of this historic street. Doubtless the building in this group which is enjoyed most by students is O'Shaughnessy Hall built in 1939 and devoted to health, recreation and physical education.

Persons too can be counted. Associated with Rector O'Gorman in 1885 were four priests and four laymen who served as a faculty of instruction for preparatory, college and seminary students. Through the years this number has increased until now, for the college alone, there are 17 priests and 73 laymen. Of these 34 hold Ph.D. degrees from recognized universities. In 1885 nearly all of the 39 students in the classical department of the seminary were enrolled in preparatory courses. Now nearly 1400 students are doing exclusively college work. Of these about 1200 are from Minnesota homes.

From the College of St. Thomas and the Classical Department of the Seminary, out of which the College grew, more than 12,000 students have been graduated. Of the living members of this group 50% reside in the Twin Cities and 75% in Minnesota. The chief occupations of the alumni, listed in order of number in each category, are business, medicine, education and clergy. Perhaps because of its proximity in the early days to Fort Snelling, and perhaps because of the extensive officer-training programs conducted on its campus, St. Thomas alumni have distinguished themselves in military life, more than 300 of them having become ranking officers.

Campus life at St. Thomas is wholesome. Its academic activities are supplemented by carefully developed extra curricular programs.

"Old Ad Building"

The men have full schedules of both intramural and intercollegiate athletic contests. These include nearly every competitive college sport. In the Minnesota Intercollegiate Athletic Conference their record is enviable. Interest in both forensic and dramatic activities runs high. For some time the College has sponsored the Northwest Debate Tournament.

This diversity of interests and activities does not mean that St. Thomas has lost the touch of its ecclesiastic heritage. As a diocesan institution, it is under the control and guidance of the Archbishop of St. Paul and is directed by priests of the Archdiocese. Although there is no element of coercion in religious matters, the liturgical program is a regular part of campus life. For all its modernity, St. Thomas continues much of the flavor of the early fathers.

Concordia College

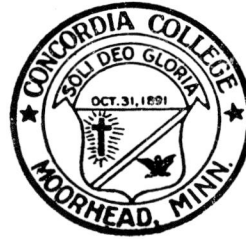

The forerunner of Concordia College was the Red River ox cart—pictured in 1949 on the 3¢ postage stamp commemorating Minnesota's territorial centenary—which carried freight between St. Paul and Winnipeg via the Red River valley. Following the middle of the last century, the prairie schooner brought hundreds of persons to the valley. After 1871 railroads assisted oxen in bringing thousands more. Most of the newcomers were emigrants from sections of Europe where Scandinavian, German, and English languages were spoken.

Almost as soon as their farms and homes and churches and schools were established forward-looking pioneers began to think of the future of their children. Their thinking crystallized into the Northwestern Lutheran College Association which founded Concordia College in 1891. It was named *Concordia* in recognition of the harmony which it symbolized; it was to be the college of the United Lutheran Church which had been formed a year earlier by uniting three competing Norwegian Lutheran bodies. Although the tide of immigration was ebbing, the institution within a few years enrolled 400 students.

Of all Minnesota colleges, Concordia is farthest west. By a small margin it is also farthest north. Its postal address is Moorhead but it belongs to the metropolitan center of Fargo-Moorhead. These cities, separated only by an unruly stream, constitute the second largest metropolis between the Twin Cities and the Pacific coast. Together they are the cultural as well as the commercial capital of a vast empire bounded on the west by the high-flung continental divide and on the east by the low-flung valley of the Red River.

Concordia looks to the west. It is owned and operated by the congregations of three Districts of the Evangelical Lutheran Church. The three Districts are Northern Minnesota, North Dakota, and Montana East of the Continental Divide. In them are 989 congregations, only 379 of which are in Minnesota. Within this area Lutherans outnumber all other Protestants; in most of its counties more than half of the Protestants are Evangelical Lutherans. In all this area no one of the scattered few colleges is comparable with Concordia in stature or prestige. Concordia enrolls nearly as many students from the area west of Minnesota as it does from Minnesota. Doubtless the ratio will become larger as the northern plains attain social maturity. Already there are about five hundred Concordia alumni in North Dakota as against one thousand in Minnesota.

Class work was started at Concordia in 1891. For some years instruction was mostly at the high school level. Transition to college work was gradual. A complete college course was not offered

until 1913. The first baccalaureate degrees were granted to six students in 1917; though Park Region College of Fergus Falls, which in that same year was united with Concordia, had granted this degree as early as 1912. The academy department was discontinued in 1927.

Since its opening the College has occupied twelve city blocks in a pleasant district not far to the south of the business section of Moorhead. A nearby athletic field of 65 acres has been acquired recently. The plant includes seven academic buildings and four modern attractive dormitories accommodating nearly a thousand students. A relatively new field house designed with such ingenuity as to include a gymnasium and an auditorium—capacity 6000—is used temporarily on five mornings each week as a chapel. The new Ylvisaker Library building is one which might be taken as a model for any college the size of Concordia.

Lying as it does on the level floor of the geologically famous Lake Agassiz the campus offers no opportunity for terraced slopes and contoured lanes. But even to its two-dimensional topography imaginative planning has given a happy diversity in the arrangement of buildings and landscape materials.

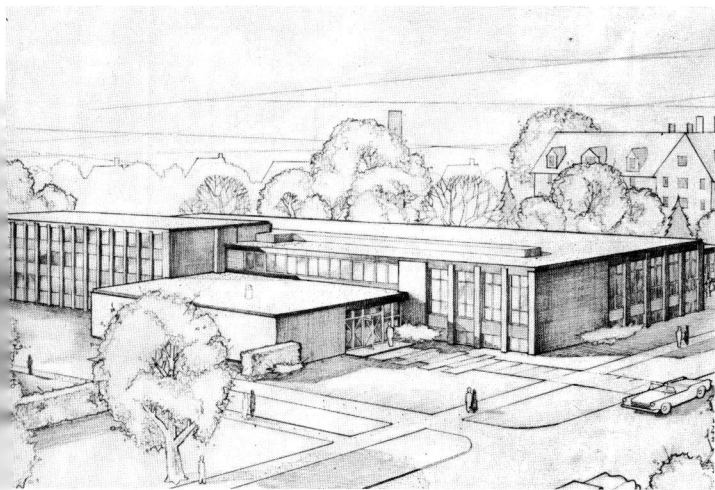

Carl B. Ylvisaker Library

Today Concordia has about 1500 students, aside from those enrolled in the conservatory of music, in nursing courses and in summer sessions. Of these, 94% are Lutherans. They represent twenty states and sixteen foreign lands. To be graduated a Lutheran student must earn fourteen credit hours in religion. Upper classmen, in about equal numbers, choose their major courses from the fields of history and political science, elementary education, and psychology. The College was founded for the purpose of training ministers, teachers, and leaders in the church. Nor has it deviated far from this purpose. About half of its graduates become teachers and many undertake theological study.

At Concordia artistic interests are pronounced. The Berg Art Center provides throughout the year a series of exhibits. The Concordia Theater presents both modern and classical plays. An artist course is arranged each year. The conservatory of music maintains a branch in Fargo. Since 1889 a concert band of 75 members has been welcomed by neighboring communities. Every spring is brightened by a May Day Festival. A program of Christmas music is presented on three consecutive nights to a capacity audience of 12,000 persons. The Concordia choir of 60 voices is known to audiences in the midwest, in eastern states, and abroad. Its current itinerary includes 39 European cities. Perhaps it would not stretch the aesthetic category too much to include forensic expression among artistic interests. Every year beginning with 1934 Concordia has sponsored an Intercollegiate Debate Tournament. The first year invitations were sent to seven colleges and universities. The invitation list now includes 163 institutions in 18 states and one Canadian province.

In terms of institutional longevity Concordia has survived the perils of infancy and is enjoying a robust childhood. It is growing more rapidly than any other college in Minnesota. While experiencing some growing pains, its health is sound. Its plant is being developed realistically; balanced courses of study are being organized; campus life is wholesome. Among the symptoms of basic health are the fact that an unusually large portion of students continue in college until graduation, and the fact that most members of the faculty are building their lives into the College. Many stay at the post of their choice, decade after decade, declining invitations whose social and financial rewards would entice many a less devoted servant.

Gustavus Adolphus College

Gustavus Adolphus College was started almost by accident. In May of 1862 members of a small church in Red Wing—oldest Swedish Lutheran church in Minnesota—were voting whether to appropriate twenty dollars toward outfitting their tiny building for parochial teaching. As if by way of rhetorical flourish, the enabling resolution carried the further suggestion "that older persons from other places might attend, receive instruction and prepare themselves for higher studies elsewhere." The motion was carried and a college was conceived.

Pastor Erik Norelius

Pastor Erik Norelius, without modification of pastoral duties or perquisites, assumed all offices of the new institution. Autumn brought one student, Jonas Magnuson—whose name was later changed by him to Magny, and by his children to Magney.

Despite these vicissitudes the name has been respected by the people of Minnesota through three generations in the realms of religion, jurisprudence, and architecture respectively. The pastor's study served as lecture hall; the hospitable parsonage as dormitory. Curriculum: Swedish and English grammar and spelling, arithmetic, geography, penmanship, singing and Christianity. Fees: Room, one dollar per month; Board, seventy-five cents per week; Tuition, gratis.

The following year the school, augmented by ten students, was recognized by the Augustana Synod of the Lutheran Minnesota Conference and was moved to the rural Swedish community of East Union. Here—as Saint Ansgar's Academy, it existed until 1876. Meantime citizens of St. Peter offered the Conference ten acres and pledged $10,000 if it would bring its college to them. Their offer was accepted forthwith. The new institution was legally entitled *The Swedish Lutheran Board of Education of Minnesota*. In spite of the fact that it rhymed with *Rah, Rah, Rah,* the name never took. Gustavus Adolphus lent itself better to endearing strains of a college song.

The St. Peter site was on a table-land overlooking the wide valley of the Minnesota River. It was hard by the spot where 26 years earlier was signed the Treaty of Traverse des Sioux which enabled legal pundits to assure Governor Sibley that his government held firm title to some twenty million of nature's choicest acres. Of these acres the College now has 246.

Here was built a proud structure of stone which in 1876 dominated the countryside. Then grasshoppers took over and money became scarce. Even though the good people of St. Peter paid their pledges, $10,000 could not remove a mortgage on the $25,000 building. Alas! Pictures of endowment funds, with which it had been hoped the College might open, turned out to be negatives.

But the Lord has been good to Gustavus; and those who have served it have done so with wisdom, determination, and zeal. Deficits have been replaced by a plant valued at $3,500,000 and an endowment of $1,256,000. Old Main is now surrounded by eighteen other college buildings. Replacing the hospitable parsonage, six modern dormitories now accommodate 1073 students. Instead of a pastor-teacher, there is now a staff of 78 competent instructors. Since Red Wing days annual fees have increased from $9 to $200 for room, from $27 to $360 for board, and from nothing to $750 for tuition. A curriculum of some half-dozen elementary-school subjects has been expanded to include the offerings of 24 departments each with its quota of courses. A course in arithmetic has been supplanted by 16 courses in mathematics. The Academy, which had been synonymous with St. Ansgar's, was discontinued in 1931.

A class of four members was graduated from the College in 1890. The number of living alumni is 4040. Many of these are well-known in Minnesota. St. Peter is often referred to as the home of governors. Five of its citizens, and an additional three graduates of Gustavus, have become chief executives of Minnesota. Two-thirds of the alumni live in Minnesota. About 20% of the men graduates go into religious work and an equal number become teachers. Business claims nearly half of them. The relation between alumni and their *alma mater* is close. For them each year, just before

Folke Bernadotte Memorial Library

commencement, the College arranges an Institute of World Affairs. As one indication of interest in their College about 1600 alumni contribute annually to its support.

Nowhere are temporal contrasts more marked than between the study of Pastor Norelius and the Folke Bernadotte Memorial Library. This handsome building was dedicated in 1950, in the presence of Countess Bernadotte, as a memorial to Sweden's martyred envoy of international amity. One unique feature of the library is the Pioneer Room for browsing with its 5000 not-too-academic volumes.

While contrasts with the past are encouraging, continuities are no less significant for Gustavus. From Old Main (1876) to the newest dormitory (1956) campus walls betray harmony in texture, if not in design, for nearly all of them are of limestone from the same quarry. The College still holds its charter of 1863. It is still owned, operated and supported by the Minnesota Conference which endorsed the Red Wing school. The first teacher and the first pupil from Red Wing have both rendered active service to Gustavus Adolphus of St. Peter. Pastor Norelius is still listed as the first president of Gustavus. Of its students, 90% continue to come from Minnesota and 83% are Lutheran. Six courses in Swedish language and literature are currently offered. The curriculum still emphasizes the study of Christianity—though course titles have multiplied from one to thirty-two. Daily prayers are still part of the College program. Nor have fundamental ideals been altered. Basic throughout 97 years have been the purpose to "impart knowledge of the background, faith and ideals of Christianity to all students" and the purpose to "foster a discerning appreciation of and devotion to the teachings and practices of the Lutheran Church."

Continuity is evident, once more, in human traits. In the center of the campus is a heroic bust of Gustavus II, known as Adolphus. The statue of this hero king of Sweden, without suggesting either hauteur or defiance, seems to embody unflinching resolution. Perhaps it is not fantastic to see something of this same sturdy quality also in those who have felt the imprint of the college which bears the name of this hero.

207

Hamline University

Hamline University is revered as the eldest member of the Minnesota College family. It belongs to this family even though it does not bear the family name. *University*—a childhood appelation, continued into adult life—represents a somewhat confused dream of its founding fathers. Despite this slight awkwardness in nomenclature, Hamline always has been faithful to the traditions of the liberal arts college.

Members of the Wisconsin Annual Conference of the Methodist Episcopal Church and friends in St. Paul founded Hamline in 1854. The breadth of their vision is indicated by charter provisions that no one should be barred from enrollment because of either sex or "religious tenet." At the time not more than four colleges in the country were coeducational. In the Minnesota Territory of that day neither colleges nor high schools existed, there was no public school system, and it was said that "teepees were more plentiful than houses." Bishop Leonidas Hamline gave to the new institution his name and a quarter of his $100,000 fortune. Because practically all traffic then moved on waterways, Hamline's charter stipulated that the University should be located "on the Mississippi, between St. Paul and Lake Pepin." When the "town proprietors" of Red Wing—population 300—made available a city block the issue of locus was closed. Here a building of brick served all college purposes for fifteen years. A preparatory school was opened at once. This was not discontinued until 1912. The first college class was graduated in 1859. Its members were the sisters, Emily and Elizabeth Sorin.

Ten years later, in March of 1869, while alumni from fifteen states and territories gathered in Red Wing to celebrate the anniversary and

to pledge unending devotion to their *alma mater*, the Board of Trustees reached a decision to suspend classes. In spite of progress made, and in spite of having weathered the strains of the Civil War period, odds were too great. Quite different was a festive scene in July of 1880 when the dedication of University Hall marked the reopening of the University. This capacious structure stood about midway between St. Paul and Minneapolis. Its site—now within the city of St. Paul—is the one occupied by Hamline today, except for the unfortunate circumstance that its area has since been reduced from 50 to 20 acres. Here University Hall stood for three years; then it burned to ashes. If the fateful year of 1883 snuffed from the campus its entire academic plant—leaving only "Ladies Happ"—it brought to the campus President Bridgman whose leadership initiated the building of modern Hamline.

The present plant, with its twelve buildings, has a book value of almost $5,000,000. The annual academic budget exceeds $1,400,000—less than a fourth of this amount is provided by an endowment of $5,411,000. Academic fees cover about 59% of the cost of instruction. Not counting a school of nursing with its 284 students and 28 in-

Hamline University at Red Wing, 1854-1869

New Women's Residence Hall

structors, Hamline's liberal arts college has a faculty of 80 members. It enrolls 946 undergraduates most of whom are from Minnesota. More men than women are regularly enrolled, though the campus dormitories house 150 men and 335 women.

All college men participate in intramural sports. In intercollegiate athletics Hamline is especially known for its basketball. It has won 268 and lost 38 games in the Minnesota Intercollegiate Conference; it has won, or tied for, the annual state championship 18 times in 24 years; it is the only member of the National Association of Intercollegiate Athletics to have won the championship in basketball as many as three times. But Hamline students do not live for basketball alone. They are quite alive to the cultural advantages with which their Twin Cities surround them. While their academic interests range widely, the three most common areas for concentration are economics, the sciences, and sociology. Among the organizations which elicit student interest are a concert choir, three undergraduate publications, fraternal organizations, seven honorary academic groups, and eighteen special-interest clubs.

The college calendar includes many activities. This sampling may suggest their diversity. Each November students and invited guests meet on the campus for "A World Affairs Institute." Hamline cooperates with three other St. Paul colleges in providing an "area studies" program in which some currently challenging portion of the globe is studied intensively. It is one of the sponsors of the Washington Seminar at American University in Washington, D.C. During the summer several Hamline students join in pilgrimages to Europe known as the "Student Project for Amity Among Nations." A grant from the Falk Foundation makes possible student participation in field projects involving local political activities. An annual competitive examination for scholarships is arranged on the campus for top-ranking high school students.

In the United States 74 senior colleges are officially related to the Methodist Church. Hamline is one of these. Its 21 trustees are nominated by its Board but are elected by the Minnesota Conference. Also elected by the Conference are seven visitors who meet and vote regularly with the Board. Though not pledged to specific financial support, the Church makes an annual appropriation to its College. About half of the students and faculty members are Methodists. Hamline has granted 5110 baccalaureate degrees. As part of its Centennial Program in 1954 it polled those who were graduated between 1888 and 1954. Nearly equal numbers of men and women responded. Replies from 2304 alumni indicate, among other things, that slightly more than half live in Minnesota, that more than half are members of the Methodist Church, that 71% are active in church work, and that 46% participate in community affairs. It is not surprising to learn that most women graduates are homemakers. Of all graduates 22% hold administrative positions, 21% are employed in business and industry, 26% are in education, about 9% are in some form of religious work, and 8% are in government service. There are other items of interest about Hamline alumni. Since 1917 four of them have been selected as Rhodes Scholars. The current volume of *Who's Who in America* lists 49 Hamline alumni. Between the years of 1936-1950, 72 graduates earned Ph.D. degrees. One alumnus is the Director of Research in the Naval Research Laboratory in Washington, D.C. Another is Secretary General of the John Simon Guggenheim Memorial Foundation. Many alumni have attained distinction in various fields of scholarship; but the list of notables includes also a star actress and a five-star general. Scattered over the country are 44 alumni clubs most of which keep in regular touch with their College.

No college can have a better index of effectiveness than the stature of its alumni. Would that each of the liberal arts colleges, of which Minnesota is proud, might have for *its* centennial year a testimony as assuring as that afforded by the Hamline roll-call.

Macalester College

Enshrined in an open belfry near the library of Macalester College is an old bell which, if it could recount events that it has heralded, might reveal much as to the complex origins of the college whose campus it graces. It once tolled scholars to a school which stood where the Federal Courts Building of St. Paul now stands.

This school was established in 1853 by Dr. Edward D. Neill, missionary, builder of schools and churches, army chaplain, diplomatist, historian, early chancellor of the University of Minnesota, and founder of Minnesota's public school system. In recognition of benefactions from M. W. Baldwin, of locomotive fame, it was called the Baldwin School. In 1857 Dr. Neill established the St. Paul College for men which was merged with the Baldwin School to become Baldwin University. After a ten-year period of government service Dr. Neill returned to Minnesota and established Jesus College, with the Baldwin School as a preparatory department, in the Winslow house overlooking the Falls of St. Anthony. The house had been a hotel, once patronized by southern planters; but, after the outbreak of the Civil War, patronized by almost no one. By benefit of mortgage foreclosure, title to the property passed to Charles Macalester of Philadelphia and from him, upon suggestion by Dr. Neill, to the incipient school which became, by due enactment of the legislature in 1874, Macalester College.

Financial stringency prompted the new institution to seek denominational backing. Conversely, Presbyterians in Minnesota were feeling the need for a college which would provide them with ministers and lay leaders. Here was a college seeking a church, and a church seeking a college. Two problems were solved with one vote. The vote was cast by the Presbyterian Synod of Minnesota at its annual meeting held at St. Peter in 1880. It was not until 1885, however, that a charter by-law provided that two-thirds of the college trustees be Presbyterians.

In the early eighties industry began to encroach upon the Winslow location. A group of Macalester trustees purchased the Holyoke farm in St. Paul and in 1883 gave the eastern quarter of it to Macalester. This was ideal for a campus. The forty acres stretched for a half-mile—now five city blocks—south from Summit Avenue along the west side of Snelling Avenue.

The birthday of Macalester College is September 6, 1885. This day marks both the occupancy of its present campus and initiation of its collegiate program. Since that date the College has known reverses; but, on the whole, has grown consistently. During three-score and twelve years its endowment has waxed from $25,000 to nearly $5,000,000; its enrollment has grown from six freshmen (along with thirty "prep boys") to 1341 fully qualified college students; the instructional staff has increased from four to the equivalent of 105 teachers. Generous friends have added a degree of stability and dignity to teaching at Macalester by endowing professorial chairs in departments as varied as Religious Education, English Bible, History, Economics, and Natural Science.

Women were not admitted to Macalester until 1893, though in its entire history the College has matriculated more women than men. In the first fifteen years, beginning with a class of ten in 1889, one hundred men received degrees. Of Macalester's nearly six thousand graduates about 40% now live in the Twin Cities. In recent years 20% have undertaken graduate work in various universities. The

Bell Tower and Library

Dr. Edward D. Neill

names of 23 are listed in *Who's Who in America*. Nearly half of Macalester's graduates enter the field of education; somewhat more than a quarter engage in business.

While the campus is still limited to its forty acres, it has undergone great change. During the early years most of the tract was claimed by fields of corn. Today the whole area appears as a well groomed park set in the midst of what has come to be one of the choicest resident areas in the Twin Cities. The original building, later incorporated into Old Main, is now surrounded by fourteen neighbors. Ten buildings are devoted to academic life; five are dormitories which house 275 men and 425 women. The recent buildings, all in red brick, present a harmonious colonial pattern.

"Macalester College offers to the serious student a balanced integration of education in the liberal arts, training for civic responsibility, preparation for specific vocations, and growth in religious life." So concludes a recent affirmation by the faculty. The liberal arts course, leading to the B.A. degree, is the core of the program. A more immediately functional B.S. degree may be earned in the vocational areas of business, elementary education, art education, medical technology, and

in work related to nursing. The degree of M.Ed. is given for advanced work in education. The three most largely elected majors are elementary education, economics and business, and English. Doubtless there is a relation between the first two choices and incorporation into the college in 1950 of Miss Wood's Kindergarten and Primary Training School and the establishment also in 1950 of the Bureau of Economic Research. Aside from its regular college program Macalester conducts an evening college in which more than a thousand adults are enrolled. A summer session provides accelerated courses for about 600 adults and undergraduates.

Aside from the usual athletic, forensic and social program a number of aspects of its life make Macalester interesting. It has a bag-pipe band and a choral reading group, its choir each year presents a concert jointly with the Minneapolis Symphony Orchestra, its library has two unique collections: the largest hymnology collection in the country and the Neill—none other than the versatile Dr. Edward D. Neill introduced at the opening of this sketch—collection of historical documents especially rich in materials concerning early Minnesota.

At Macalester interest in international understanding is especially keen. Every day on the campus flagpole, below the stars and stripes, floats the United Nations flag. The college joins other colleges of St. Paul in sponsoring each year a course devoted to some particular geographical or political area. The student body usually includes some 60 students from other lands. There is a chapter of the Minnesota SPAN (Student Project for Amity Among Nations) involving a number of students in study abroad. The students maintain Cosmopolitan and International Relations Clubs. A summer Caravan has travelled to Mexico each summer since 1946. An annual visit to the United Nations headquarters has been organized. Unique among its instruments for fostering international understanding is the Canadian-American Conference held each year since 1941. Twenty-four students from Macalester and an equal number from United College in Winnipeg meet on their respective campuses in alternate years for a two-day discussion of understanding between their two lands.

Saint John's University

Deep in the center of Minnesota is a monastery —St. John's Abbey—where Black Monks have prayed and labored, studied and taught, for nearly a century. Nowhere else is there so large a Benedictine order of men. The abbey quadrangle is joined with arterial lanes of traffic by a pleasant drive which winds through a mile of native wood.

Federal land grants dated 1856 conveyed to the monks much of their present lovely setting of meadow, water, thicket, and woodland. Early white men called the region "Indianbush." Its indigenous woody growth has been supplemented by thousands of transplantations.

A compact group of buildings rises between the shores of beautiful Lake Sagatagan and the banks of the artificially widened stream of the Watab. The earliest building in the group is the "Old Stone House" (1856) whose basic structure is granite; the most recent is the "New Monastic Wing" (1956) whose basic structure is iron and concrete. Each in its own way embodies a highly functional design. All other buildings are of clay which monks have dug, pressed, and burned on the premises.

Its institutional descent is not complex. In 529 Benedict of Nursia founded an abbey at Mount Cassino midway between Naples and Rome. In 792 Cassinese monks established the Bavarian Abbey of Metten on the banks of the Danube. Ten stormy centuries later, in 1846, representatives of Metten founded St. Vincent Abbey in western Pennsylvania. A new world spelled a new tempo. Presently the newcomers received, via Bavaria, an invitation from Joseph Cretin, first Bishop of St. Paul, to extend their work to the German Catholic families who were then pouring into central Minnesota. The response was a band of five Benedictines who, in 1855, arrived in the neighborhood of St. Cloud— identified by one house and four substandard shacks. Next fall one room of the house was serving as a school. This was the beginning of St. John's University. In March of 1857 the Territorial Legislature of Minnesota authorized the Order of St. Benedict "to establish and erect an institution, or seminary, in Stearns County" which should be known "by the name and style of St. John's Seminary."

At Indianbush the work of building a monastery and maintaining monastic life was combined, in true Benedictine fashion, with fostering missions, priories, hospitals, orphanages, convents, schools and churches in an ever widening neighborhood. At present some fifty Fathers of the Abbey are assigned to posts as widely flung as Puerto Rico, the Bahama Islands, Mexico City, and Tokyo; and to Kentucky where in 1948 they established the only interracial monastery in the United States.

But nearer, and perhaps dearer, to the Abbey than any of these projects is St. John's University within its walls. This consists of a theological seminary, a liberal arts college, and a preparatory school. Only the College falls within the scope of this sketch. The preceding story has been related only to suggest the setting of the College.

Devoted wholly or in large part to the College

Old Stone House (1866-1893)

Between the lakes

are fourteen buildings. They are well equipped. Most of them are modern, though the 98,000 bound volumes of an excellent library deserve better housing. Of 87 faculty members, 29 hold doctoral degrees and 20 have studied in European Universities. The approximately 8000 alumni of the College are widely dispersed both geographically and occupationally. Undergraduates number about a thousand. Of these 585 live on the campus, 680 are from Minnesota, upward of 40 are from foreign lands. Students have a varied athletic program with emphasis on such outdoor sports as the unusual environs make possible. Membership is held in the Minnesota Intercollegiate Athletic Conference. Among its musical organizations the College maintains a full symphony orchestra.

An announced purpose of St. John's University is "to make the study of religion and spiritual formation of the student the heart of its program." In keeping with this aim curriculum offerings are unusually rich in areas such as the classics, philosophy, religion, and theology. They include courses in Sacred Art, Liturgical Music, Scholastic Philosophy for the Laity and Theology for the Laity. A major in theology is possible. This does not mean, however, that areas of current interest are ignored. A qualified student might carry simultaneously one course in ancient Greek entitled *The*

Apostolic Fathers and another in economics entitled *Income Tax Accounting*. Still, the major elected by the largest number of students is philosophy.

St. John's Abbey and University makes contributions to its Church and to society beyond the realm of its routine work. Military training is directed by nine instructors of the ROTC. St. John's, together with St. Benedict's, maintains an adult night school in St. Cloud for 335 students. It conducts a summer school for the advancement of the Gregorian Chant. The Abbey is perhaps more liturgically minded than any other of its generation. Perhaps its most distinctive service is the sponsoring on its campus each summer of a four-week pastoral psychology workshop. Clergymen, whether of Catholic or Protestant faith, meet with outstanding psychologists and psychiatrists, invited from many parts of the country, to discuss problems of pastoral care.

Having completed one century of its work St. John's looks with confidence to a second. For its physical development a hundred-year plan already is on the drafting board of an architect whose concepts are embodied in public buildings on two sides of the Atlantic. May this plan for temporal growth be emblematic of plans which God is unfolding for St. John's Abbey and University.

213

Saint Mary's College

"Would it be a wrong to desire a spot so beautiful?" This inquiry was addressed to the President of St. Mary's College by one of the Christian Brothers who in 1932 were attending a retreat at St. Mary's. The "spot" was none other than the campus of St. Mary's on Terrace Heights at the edge of Winona.

All who travel U.S. Highway 14 between Winona and Rochester must agree that this spot is indeed beautiful. Upon leaving the Mississippi flats, the road wriggles westward and upward through the bluffs which almost encase the city. After a short ascent it levels off on a small plateau as if to catch its breath before attempting the sharper and more tortuous grade beyond. On this plateau from early days stretched the sixty acres of the Beck Farm.

In 1912 this farm was purchased by a group of Winona businessmen. No analysis of the complex of motives which may have prompted this real-estate venture is here in order. But it is in order to surmise that for Patrick Heffron, then Bishop of Winona just returned from a visit to Rome, the transaction must have seemed a direct answer to prayer—prayer, perchance, supplemented by some prodding of fellow townsmen. Title to the farm was assigned forthwith to the Diocese of Winona. Building operations were started at once to house the college for which the Bishop had wished and worked and prayed and prodded.

The new institution was formally founded in 1913. From the start it has borne the name St. Mary's College. For twenty years it was the property of the Diocese and its work was conducted by diocesan clergy. In 1933 it became the property of the St. Louis Province of the Christian Brothers. In the final transaction pragmatic sanctions re-solved any question of covetousness. To carry a relatively new educational institution through the depression years of the early thirties had been a disheartening burden for the Diocese. On the other hand, St. Mary's College offered the Christian Brothers a long desired Scholasticate where their young religious students might receive their college education in one place. Heretofore their work had been done partly in Missouri and partly in two different institutions in Chicago.

Since 1933 the College has been owned and conducted by the St. Louis Province of the Christian Brothers. In 1943 it was incorporated in the state of Minnesota but its work has continued to be directed by the Brothers of the St. Louis Province. This religious order of men is somewhat unique in that its members are not priests. They are dedicated to the service of education.

As is true of most American colleges, the courses of the early years at St. Mary's were largely preparatory and somewhat miscellaneous. When the college opened in 1913, its 80 boys were enrolled in classes ranging from sixth-grade to college levels. Offerings included a two-year commercial course. Up to 1919 there was a subsidiary department of agriculture. Since 1925 a full liberal arts program has been maintained. Its program now includes a year of graduate work in education leading to a M.A. degree. The first college class was graduated in 1926. St. Mary's became an accredited member of the North Central Association of Colleges and Secondary Schools in 1937. It is now recognized by both Catholic and secular accrediting agencies as a fully qualified college of liberal arts.

Through the addition of adjacent meadows and wooded hills the campus of St. Mary's has been

St. Mary's Hall. Erected in 1913

Choral Ensemble

increased to 575 acres. On them, mostly near the highway, are eleven substantial college buildings. Six are devoted to academic life. The oldest is a large structure, erected in 1913, which contains chapel, library, auditorium, classrooms, and offices. The most recent academic building is a beautifully designed and highly functional science hall. Five buildings afford living quarters for instructors and students. Ninety per cent of St. Mary's students live on the campus.

The current enrollment at St. Mary's, exclusive of summer-school students, is nearly 800. Less than half of the students are from Minnesota. Nearly 350 are from Illinois. Practically all are Catholics. Included among the students are two religious groups known as the *Scholastics*, to which incidental reference has been made, and the *Seminarians*. Each group has its distinctive habit, occupies its own residence and leads its own monastic life. The Scholastics number about 110. They are Brothers of the Christian Schools who have completed their novitiate training and are engaged in a six-semester program preparing them primarily for teaching. The Seminarians number about 50. They are enrolled in a seminary which was established within the framework of St. Mary's College in

1948. Its building is on the campus. Despite differences in garb, in abode, and in personal dedication, all students enjoy a common academic life. Interspersed in any classroom are likely to be Scholastics, Seminarians and secular students.

At St. Mary's religious emphasis is paramount. All members of the faculty are Catholics and most of them are Christian Brothers or priests. Spiritual advisers are available for all students at all times. Assistance at Mass is required each Sunday and on holy days. Week-day Mass each morning at seven is encouraged but not required. Every year students participate in a three-day retreat. During each of his first four semesters each student must register for courses in religion. During his last two years he must earn credit for eight hours of course work in religion. Beyond meeting these requirements, students show much spontaneous interest in religion. Of 38 student campus organizations, ranging from a Philosophy Club to a Winter Sports Club, nine are religiously oriented.

Though it is a men's college, and though its campus is peripheral to the city, St. Mary's is not without wholesome social life. Proximity to the College of St. Teresa makes possible the statement that "while the college is not coeducational it is corecreational." Local topography invites outdoor activities both social and athletic. Participation in intramural and intercollegiate sports is virile; but the college does not schedule intercollegiate football games. Among the many campus organizations the college choral ensemble has attracted wide attention. It appears on radio and presents concerts throughout the midwest.

St. Mary's is distinguished for its counseling system. This is characterized not so much by novel devices as by the systematic way in which known techniques and procedures have been organized and made effective. Each student, at the beginning of his course is assigned to a counselor who, with assistance and information from many college sources, helps the student better to understand himself and thus to plan realistically his own future. The program evolved by St. Mary's has been taken by the Catholic University in Washington as a model and has been recommended by it to every Catholic college in the United States.

Saint Olaf College

Few institutions in America have done more than St. Olaf College to conserve and to translate the substance of an adventitious culture. To the best of their national and religious traditions the men and women of St. Olaf cling tenaciously; and from these traditions they give freely. Without being reclusive, St. Olaf is Norse and it is Lutheran to the core.

Pastor Bernt Julius Muus, of rural Goodhue County, noted that the youth of his parish tended to be isolated by location, custom, and language. That they might prepare themselves for sharing in the privileges and responsibilities of a maturing Minnesota, without forsaking the faith of their fathers, he established at Northfield in 1874 St. Olaf's School.

In 1878 it was moved into a new building—now "Old Main"—high on Manitou, one mile west of the Northfield shopping center. The name *St. Olaf College* was adopted in 1889; the first college class, three men, was graduated in 1890.

In students and in faculty, St. Olaf now outnumbers every other independent college in Minnesota. Its 1858 students are taught by the equivalent of 114 full-time instructors. A well-arranged campus includes 250 acres. The plant is appraised at over $10,000,000. From the annual budget of $2,200,000, $1,368,000 goes for academic work. Twenty-one buildings include eight dormitories.

Notwithstanding its robust adolescent growth, St. Olaf is still glad to be a ward of the Evangelical Lutheran Church of America who provide a spending allowance of $150,000 a year. And from its generous family come special gifts from sixty thousand contributing Lutherans.

The academic program of St. Olaf has merited recognition from agencies as varied as the North Central Association of Colleges and Secondary Schools, the American Association of University Women, etc. Beyond its academic work, the College assumes responsibility for forensic and athletic contests at many levels. Of its men, 90% are in intramural contests. The College sponsors an Air Force Reserve Officers Training Corps program. For a limited group, it conducts with its own staff a school of nursing.

The thesis that St. Olaf conserves and translates for others its own rich heritage brings into focus many seemingly disparate facts.

Beyond the 128 credits, stipulated by most colleges for graduation, St. Olaf requires of all upper classmen six credit hours which may be elected from a variety of courses in evident also in other scattered areas of religion. Outcroppings of the Norse heritage appear in the curriculum. Up to 1947 every student of Norwegian parentage was required to study the Norwegian language.

As if to keep vital its ancestral bond, St. Olaf serves as registration and alumni office for American students in the Summer Session of the University of Oslo. Upward of two hundred registrants each year are oriented, on high seas en route to Norway, by teachers from St. Olaf. Credits earned in the Session are transferable to any university in the United States.

Professor Rolvaag's *Giants in the Earth* and other tales of Norwegian pioneers were written at St. Olaf in Norwegian and then translated into English. Teachers and students from the Art department give lavishly of time and talent to artistic creation in several media—usually with a religious motif—on the campus, in various parts of the United States, and in Norway. Members of the faculty have writ-

Looking West

ten extensively about Scandinavian life in both this country and Europe.

In a Christmas concert, which each year on four consecutive nights attracts 10,000 reverent listeners, Norwegian songs, sometimes by St. Olaf composers, are interspersed. To the singing, even in Norwegian, the audience occasionally lends its voice. The St. Olaf a cappella Lutheran Choir during a half century has carried its message to nearly every city in the United States and to many cities in Europe.

A broadcasting station, established in 1918 and licensed as WCAL in 1922 (5000 watt; 770 kilocycles) is on the air about forty hours a week. The programs are entirely cultural, educational, and religious. The station has its own well-equipped broadcasting building. The building was constructed and the programs are sponsored by nearly fifty thousand listeners.

Within the student body of St. Olaf—it is about 90% Lutheran—is a congregation which arranges its own services, supports its pastor, and provides a parsonage. To its work students contribute some $14,000 annually—this aside from campus-chest contributions.

On the campus each May about 5000 visitors participate in a Fine Arts Festival. Its program includes the singing of many different choirs, exhibits by painters and sculptors of note, and Norwegian folk dancing.

Of 8776 St. Olaf graduates nearly 20% have engaged in religious work; another 20% have become educators. About 30% undertake graduate work. Two graduates have been Rhodes scholars. *Who's Who in America* lists the names of more graduates of St. Olaf than of any other Lutheran college in America.

As years pass the uniqueness of the contribution which St. Olaf College can make to our society inevitably will be less sharp. But if as of this day St. Olaf ceased to be, those who cherish the best for American life should be grateful for the Nordic tradition which this college has shared with others of its adopted homeland.

Old Main

Public Higher Education
in Minnesota

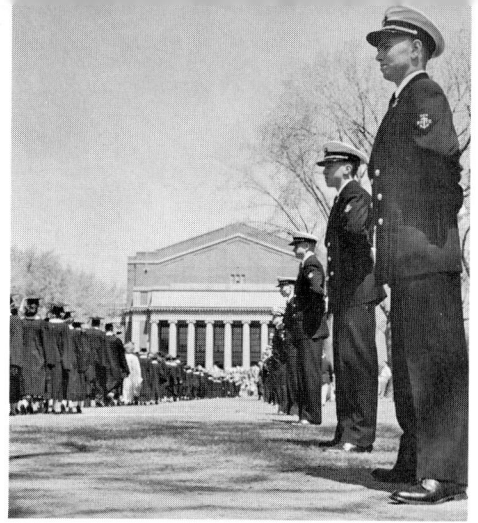

By RUTH E. ECKERT
and R. EDITH STEDMAN

Among Minnesota's rich educational resources are its thirty-two recognized colleges, fifteen of which are publicly controlled. The latter institutions, which include nine small junior or community colleges, five state colleges, and a nationally distinguished land-grant university, enroll more than 35,000 of the 50,000 full-time college students in Minnesota, as well as tens of thousands of adult students. Together with the private colleges, they constitute the top level of a long process by which the people of Minnesota prepare their youth for citizenship and job responsibilities in a complex, rapidly changing world. And through their programs of research and public services these institutions also keep adding constantly to our heritage, helping to make a better life possible for Minnesotans and people everywhere.

I. Relation to the Lower Schools

Historically, the people of Minnesota have always had a vital interest in education. Because the skills of the 3 R's were highly valued, the pioneers built elementary schools—hundreds of them—wherever there were children to be taught. Then as demands for further education multiplied, academies and high schools were built and more and more youngsters attended these institutions. In much the same way, Minnesota's public and private colleges were founded in response to the expanding needs for cultural and professional leadership.

Constituting the strong base for Minnesota's advanced program are 4,097 public elementary schools, which enroll about 80 per cent of the 507,-000 children attending elementary schools in this state. Their efforts are supplemented by 459 private and parochial schools, which enroll the remaining pupils. Upon this foundation rests the secondary structure of 661 public schools and 95

sponsored by other agencies, together enrolling about 180,000 students in grades nine to twelve, or roughly 80 per cent of the youth of high school age.

The success of the elementary and secondary schools vitally affects the role of Minnesota's colleges. Although these lower schools have made great strides in providing a good education, many elementary schools are still too small and too poorly staffed and housed to do the job they should be doing. A high school education is still out of reach of thousands of Minnesota youth, with one out of four fifth-graders leaving school before he finishes the twelfth grade. And many high school programs are still too limited to prepare students adequately for later studies or for life beyond the classroom. The stronger this foundational program becomes, the more effectively our higher institutions can contribute to the life of Minnesota and the nation at large.

II. The Historical Background of Minnesota's Higher Institutions

We should start with the determination that not a single youth of either sex should be permitted to leave the territory to acquire an education for want of an institution at home.—St. Anthony Messenger, 1851.

A dream came to Minnesota with the wagons and oxcarts of the pioneers, and that dream was to provide an education for each child. Even before there was a capitol or a territorial legislature, the farmers and tradesmen were earnestly discussing the schools they hoped to build and the colleges and university that might some day prepare leaders for the new land.

The First Colleges are Established. Public higher education is older than the State of Minne-

218

sota, with provisions for such schools anticipated in the Organic Act of Minnesota, passed March 3, 1849. In 1851, when Minnesota was still a territory and the largest community little more than a collection of shacks and wagons, the University of Minnesota was chartered. The new school, founded "at the Falls of St. Anthony," had modest beginnings. The first building, constructed in the same year, was a four-room preparatory school, paid for by individual subscription and run by a principal who was expected to pay costs from tuition fees. The financial crash of 1857 forced the school to close temporarily, and it was not until 1869, when William Watts Folwell was appointed its first president, that the University was launched on its distinguished career.

By the time Minnesota was received into the Union, three institutions of higher education were in existence, though on a very precarious basis. In addition to the University, two private colleges had been founded: Hamline University established by the Methodist Church in 1854 and St. John's University by the Roman Catholic Church in 1857.

The new state legislature, meeting in 1858, established a state normal school board and projected plans for three such schools to provide teachers for the common schools that were springing up everywhere, to serve the more than 130,000 persons who had settled in the new state.

During Minnesota's first decade of statehood normal schools were established at Winona and Mankato, and by the turn of the century nine church-related liberal arts colleges, four public normal schools, and an expanded University were serving the youth of Minnesota and neighboring states. This simultaneous founding and growth of public and private institutions of higher education is in the great American educational tradition, and accounts for much of the strength of Minnesota's present program.

The University Develops and Expands. Minnesota shares the distinction of being one of three states in which the legal basis for the state university was laid before the state itself was admitted to the Union. And certainly no institution has played a more important role in the subsequent development of the commonwealth.

Although the University had been conceived from the start to include instruction in the arts and sciences, engineering, architecture, agriculture, and education, it took many years to realize this dream. The earliest University division, which operated only a few years, offered a preparatory liberal arts program, and when the University re-opened in 1869 under President Folwell, with 13 students in its freshman class and 230 in its preparatory department, it still operated chiefly as a liberal arts division. In 1873, at the first University of Minnesota commencement, two students received bachelor of arts degrees.

Strengthened by the Morrill Act of 1862, which had provided financial support for more practical types of training, University officials gradually laid plans for a program of more distinctive design and outreach. Under the leadership of President Cyrus Northrop, who took office in 1884, the University added a law school, a medical school, and a college of agriculture, and by 1905 the University consisted of ten colleges, with 140 professors and 3,900 students. One of the newly established units was a College of Education, to provide professional direction for the education of teachers, which had been acknowledged in the state constitution as a major University responsibility. The School of Nursing, founded in 1909, became the earliest collegiate school of nursing in the country. After World War I the School of Business was added, followed a few years later by the Institute of Child Welfare, the University College, the General College, and the Schools of Journalism and Social Work. Within the past ten years the University Branch at Duluth and the College of Veterinary Medicine have been established, to enlarge still more the scope of the University's services.

The Graduate School, established in 1905, became the fitting capstone to the provisions Minnesotans were making for public higher education. The Mayo Foundation for Medical Education and Research, incorporated in 1914, greatly strengthened the new graduate school, and the University became the first institution in the world to award the Master of Science and Ph.D degrees for advanced work in medicine. As its graduate offerings became fully established and recognized, other colleges in the state concentrated their energies mainly on the development of superior undergraduate curricula.

The Normal Schools Are Launched. Designating the projected normal schools as the primary source for the education of candidates "for teaching in the Common Schools of the State," the legislature in 1858 took steps to establish one such school within five years, another within ten years, and the third within fifteen years. The act also specified that the communities involved should provide matching grants of $5,000 to help finance the initial buildings and equipment. By 1913 the number of normal schools authorized had been raised to six, to meet the ever-rising need for qualified teachers.

The settlement of Minnesota can be traced in the order of the opening of these institutions, for the settlers followed the state's great waterways. Authorized in 1858, the normal school at Winona opened in 1860 at a Mississippi River port that was a natural gateway to the Northwest. As the eleventh normal school in the United States and the first one west of the Mississippi River, it pioneered in the education of teachers. Though it had to be closed in 1862 when the principal and students joined in the disastrous Sioux Wars, it re-opened in 1864. Mankato was opened in 1868 to provide teachers for the Minnesota River Valley settlements, followed by St. Cloud in 1869 as the upper Mississippi Valley became populated. Similarly, Moorhead was established in 1887 to serve Minnesotans in the rich Red River Valley wheatlands, and Duluth in 1902 to meet the growing need for teachers as the great iron ore deposits of the Mesabi Range drew settlers into northern Minnesota. Bemidji, the youngest of the normal schools, was established in 1913 to serve the northwest tier of counties but, due to the war, did not open until 1919.

The new schools had to wage a vigorous and continuing fight for their existence. Many citizens seemed to be prejudiced against the new training programs, and some established colleges, viewing these schools as threats to their own academies, attempted to block their development. Yet despite cramping restrictions placed on their salary scales, buildings, and equipment, all six normal schools developed over the years from schools offering a bare start on a high school education into respected collegiate programs of teacher education. At first their students, coming from the limited "common schools" of the area, reviewed primary subjects for one year, and spent a second year on beginning high school subjects, including some pedagogy. By 1879 two more years of high school work were added, and a final year by 1881. After the first two years of college work had been authorized in 1882 and 1895, the normal schools began to raise their own entrance standards, and more and more candidates secured their high school education in their home communities. By 1919, high school graduation was required of all entrants, and a third year of college work was added to the curriculum. This gradual transition from high school to college status was recognized by a legislative act in 1921 which changed the names of these institutions to State Teachers Colleges, and granted them authority to confer the degree of Bachelor of Science in Education. By 1926 a full four-year program of college work was available to students, and by 1928 the state teachers colleges were authorized to prepare high school as well as elementary teachers. Tuition in these colleges remained free until 1934, so long as the individual pledged himself to teach at least two years in the schools of Minnesota.

In the quarter century that followed this change in name, the functions of the State Teachers Colleges steadily enlarged, and when veterans streamed back to college classrooms in 1946, the State Teacher's College Board authorized these institutions to grant the Bachelor of Arts degree. In 1947 the Duluth State Teachers College, through community initiative and legislature action, was made a branch of the University, leaving five institutions under the State Teachers College Board. Further steps were taken in 1953 to broaden the programs of these schools, including a legislative act that permitted them to initiate graduate programs leading to the Master of Science in Education degree. Mankato was also authorized to develop sequences that would qualify students for the Bachelor of Science degree in nursing. In recognition of these widened services, the legislature, in its 1957 session, appropriately changed the name of these institutions to State Colleges. Operating under the general direction of the State College Board, they constitute the state's second largest direct investment in higher education.

Junior Colleges Emerge. The junior or community college is the youngest member of the college family in Minnesota, as it is elsewhere. It is also a distinctively American form of higher education, for nowhere else in the world have higher institutions developed that are so closely related to the communities they serve.

The concept of a two-year program dates back to the middle of the last century, some two hundred years after the first liberal arts college in this country had been founded. William W. Folwell, the first president of the University of Minnesota and an early advocate of college re-organization, suggested in his inaugural speech in 1869 that "the body of work for the first two years in our ordinary American colleges" be assumed by the high schools. Although Folwell's plan was echoed in 1873 by Governor Austin of Minnesota and other leaders, no effort was made immediately to put this proposal into effect.

It was not until the turn of the century that the first public junior college was established in Illinois, as an extension of the public secondary school. In 1914 a similar institution, with a class of five students, was founded at Cloquet, Minnesota. The next year the cities of Faribault and Rochester also established junior colleges, but of these three only the one at Rochester has survived. By 1925 the legislature formally empowered communities to establish such units under conditions outlined by the State Department of Education.

Concordia College, founded in 1905 in St. Paul, was the first private college in the state to offer a program ending with the fourteenth grade. This was followed some years later by the establishment of Bethany Lutheran College at Mankato (1926) and Bethel College in St. Paul (1931), the latter of which has since become a four-year liberal arts college and Seminary.

During the twenty-five years that followed the first development of public junior colleges in Minnesota, more than a dozen Minnesota communities founded such units, most of which are still in existence. The junior college at Austin, established in 1940, constitutes the latest addition to Minnesota's growing college family. The purposes of these new types of colleges have expanded far beyond the role proposed a half-century ago. Not only do they provide the first two years of a regular college program inexpensively and conveniently, but they also offer a growing number of technical and semi-professional programs, combined with general education for citizenship. Reflecting and interpreting local conditions, they are becoming true community colleges, responsive to the particular economic and social needs of the youth and adults they serve.

Strength in Diversity. One great asset of Minnesota's program of higher education has been its richly textured pattern. Colleges developed along different lines and maintained under different auspices have offered the youth and older citizens of the state varied opportunities for personal and professional development, suited to the state's expanding needs for these services. In general, the differences among colleges in purposes and programs are a sign of healthy growth, reflecting the same sturdy sense of initiative and independence that Americans have valued in other areas of life. Alert to the possibility that some differences may be more accidental than deliberate, or may be resulting in unnecessary duplications of effort, the staffs of Minnesota colleges have been studying their programs cooperatively. In the context of concern for all, each institution has been trying to define its special traditions and goals and to project sound lines for its future advance. Minnesota institutions, both public and private, have wisely recognized that no one college, nor any one group of colleges, can or should live to itself alone. Only by working in close and productive partnership can they continue to pioneer in progress.

III. Current Enrollments and Programs

Minnesota enters its second hundred years with 32 recognized public and private colleges, the locations of which are shown on the accompanying map. There are also ten other higher institutions, chiefly professional schools or seminaries not affiliated with any college, which operate under private control and which are not part of the generally accepted pattern of collegiate education in this state.

FACILITIES FOR HIGHER EDUCATION
in Minnesota

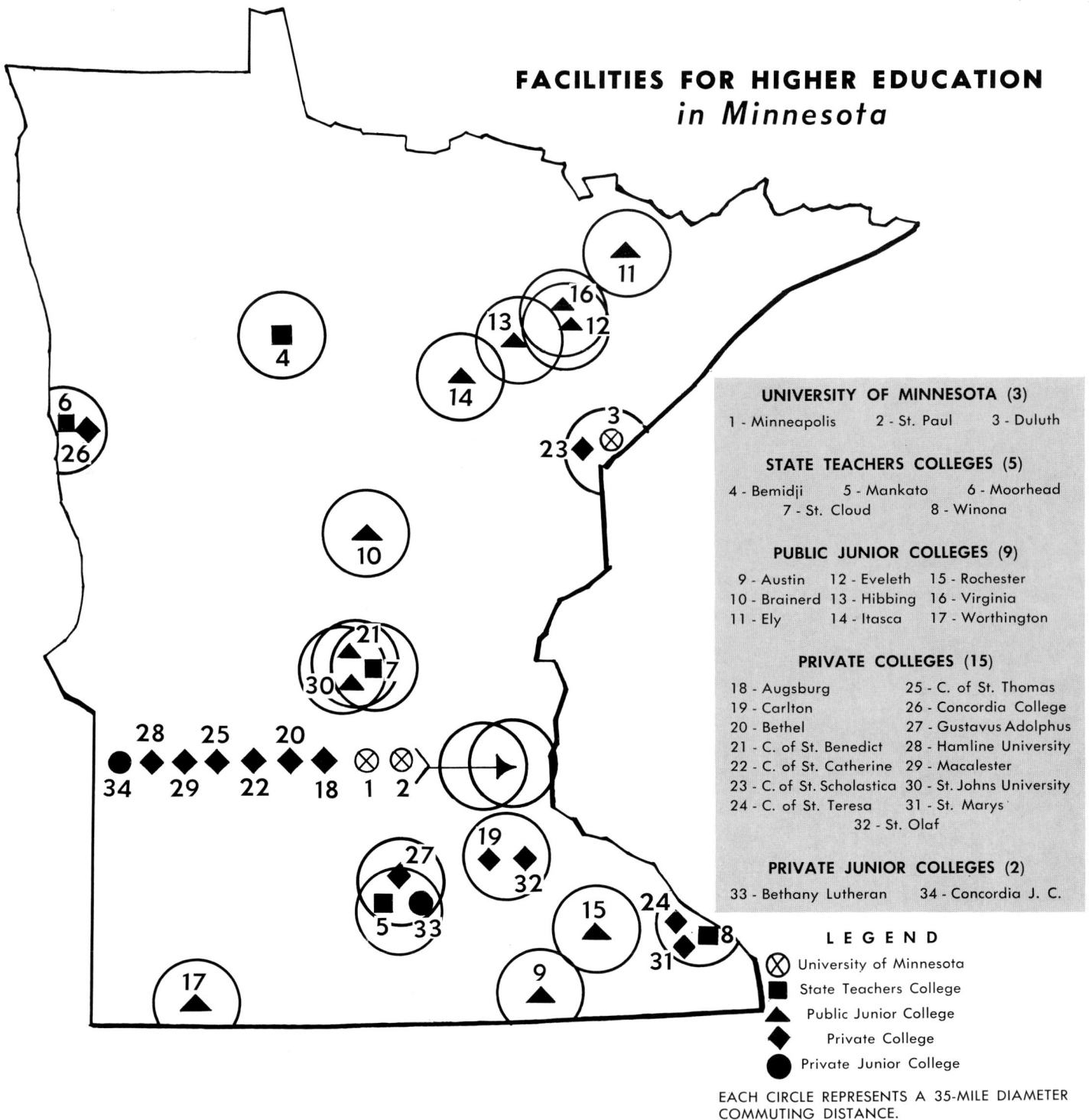

UNIVERSITY OF MINNESOTA (3)

1 - Minneapolis   2 - St. Paul   3 - Duluth

STATE TEACHERS COLLEGES (5)

4 - Bemidji   5 - Mankato   6 - Moorhead
7 - St. Cloud   8 - Winona

PUBLIC JUNIOR COLLEGES (9)

9 - Austin   12 - Eveleth   15 - Rochester
10 - Brainerd 13 - Hibbing   16 - Virginia
11 - Ely   14 - Itasca   17 - Worthington

PRIVATE COLLEGES (15)

18 - Augsburg   25 - C. of St. Thomas
19 - Carlton   26 - Concordia College
20 - Bethel   27 - Gustavus Adolphus
21 - C. of St. Benedict   28 - Hamline University
22 - C. of St. Catherine   29 - Macalester
23 - C. of St. Scholastica 30 - St. Johns University
24 - C. of St. Teresa   31 - St. Marys
                32 - St. Olaf

PRIVATE JUNIOR COLLEGES (2)

33 - Bethany Lutheran   34 - Concordia J. C.

L E G E N D

⊗ University of Minnesota
■ State Teachers College
▲ Public Junior College
♦ Private College
● Private Junior College

EACH CIRCLE REPRESENTS A 35-MILE DIAMETER
COMMUTING DISTANCE.

As a glance at the map shows, these facilities for higher education are quite unevenly distributed. Fourteen institutions, including four public junior colleges and the University, with its major campuses at Minneapolis, St. Paul, and Duluth, are concentrated in Hennepin, Ramsey, and St. Louis counties, all in the eastern half of the state. The eighteen remaining colleges are scattered among twelve counties. The entire western half of the state has only four colleges, two in the same city.

Growth in Enrollments. Minnesotans have reason to be proud of the expansion this state has achieved over the past decades in college opportunities. Since 1900 college enrollments in Minnesota have increased tenfold, or five times faster than the general population. After soaring to a record figure of 48,563 students in 1946, and then receding, during the Korean crisis, they have been moving steadily upward to reach a new high in 1956. The 50,106 regular day students who managed to gain admission to Minnesota colleges in the fall of 1957 represent about 28 per cent of the college-age group, and are actually a larger number than were enrolled in Minnesota high schools after World War I. And the enrollments now in prospect will far exceed the veterans' bulge of the 1940's, probably doubling that figure by the early 1970's. Despite wars, depressions and military "incidents," Minnesotans in unparalleled numbers have been seeking and obtaining a college education.

Enrollments of regular students in the fall of 1957 ranged from less than a hundred full-time students at Bethany Lutheran and Eveleth Junior Colleges to almost 26,000 at the University of Minnesota. The public higher institutions currently educate 70 per cent of those who attend colleges in this state—a figure that is significantly higher than for the United States as a whole (58 per cent). Minnesota's public institutions also seem destined to carry a still greater share of the load, for their full-time enrollments increased thirty-one per cent during the past three years, as compared with a fourteen per cent advance for the private colleges.

Types of Students. The students who attend Minnesota colleges come largely from this state. The fact that eight in nine of those enrolling in public colleges and two in three of those in private colleges choose Minnesota institutions shows how overwhelmingly popular these are with the people of the state. Although some young Minnesotans appropriately select colleges elsewhere, their number is more than balanced by persons from other states and foreign countries who seek admission to Minnesota programs, particularly at the professional and graduate levels.

Minnesota college students tend to be a rather select group academically, showing the talents, interests and motivations that justify considerable investment in their training. Some colleges screen

their entrants much more than others, but no type of college has any monopoly on talent. Some public junior colleges outrank many four-year colleges in this respect, and certain divisions of the University are also notably selective. The major aim in admissions, however, is not to outbid other institutions for talented students, but to attract those individuals who can best profit from a particular program. A society such as ours needs many kinds of giftedness, and different colleges play different roles in cultivating Minnesota's human resources.

Minnesota is also now doing a better job in getting its qualified students into college. The report issued by the Governor's Committee on Higher Education in 1956 shows, for example, that more than three-fifths of all students who rank in the top third of their high school graduating class are now going to college, as compared with only two-fifths a decade ago. But there is still too great an erosion of talent to permit any complacency. This is particularly true in the case of women students, who constitute only thirty per cent of the full-time enrollment in the public colleges and forty-five per cent in the private colleges, although as many girls as boys graduate from high school.

Present Types of Programs. Minnesotans can also take pride in the kinds of programs provided by the colleges of this state. Whether offered in public or private institutions, their common objective has been to cultivate the intellectual, moral and social qualities of our people, and to imbue all who attend or are reached by their services with a strong sense of public obligation. Studies show that practically all those who have attended Minnesota colleges would, if given a chance to remake their decision, return to some college, and overwhelmingly to the same institution. But the good of the persons so educated represents only a small part of the contribution that Minnesota's colleges make to the life of the state and nation. The fruits of these programs have also been public and social, benefiting the state and larger society beyond all calculation. It has been estimated, for example, that the value of the research done at the University alone has repaid many times all that Minnesota has spent on higher education.

The Public Junior Colleges

By RUTH E. ECKERT
and R. EDITH STEDMAN

Many young people in Minnesota who could not otherwise continue their education beyond the high school find encouragement and a chance to further their education inexpensively in a local junior college. In Virginia, Minnesota, for example, 75 per cent of the high school graduates continue their education in the local college. Minnesota junior colleges have thus helped to keep the door of opportunity open to qualified youth. Many freshman students also feel that they can make a better transition from high school to college in these institutions than in a larger college or university.

The Minnesota communities of Austin, Brainerd, Coleraine, Ely, Eveleth, Hibbing, Rochester, Virginia, and Worthington operate and control junior colleges under standards established by the State Department of Education. All these institutions are accredited by the University of Minnesota, and three also hold membership in the North Central Association of Colleges and Secondary Schools. Currently ranging in size from 86 regular daytime students at Eveleth in the fall of 1957 to 423 at Hibbing Junior College, these institutions operate under the direction of the local school boards, usually in the regular high school buildings. Grants of $200 per year for each student in average daily attendance, provided by the 1957 state legislature, now defray approximately forty per cent of operating expenses. A similar proportion of instructional costs and all capital expenses continue to be borne by the local communities. Student tuition and fees cover the remaining twenty per cent of operating expenses.

Enrollments. Minnesota's public junior colleges are now expanding, after a long period of public neglect in which four colleges discontinued operations and enrollments slipped dangerously in most

of the others. In fact, these institutions have just regained the number of regular students served in their previous high year (1940-41). The current enrollment of 1,968 regular students in the nine public junior colleges accounts for four percent of the state's total college enrollment, or ten percent of the freshman-sophomore enrollment. Although these figures are still far below the corresponding statistics nationally, the Minnesota public junior college enrollment has increased 43 per cent since 1954, and these colleges appear to be on the verge of filling a new role in the state's program of higher education. Rather significantly, the two colleges in the state that showed the greatest gains (more than 70 percent) during this period (1954-57) are both public junior colleges—Ely and Hibbing. The public junior colleges also enrolled 6,364 adults last year in part-time classes, or triple the number of their regular daytime students, showing the important community outreach of these programs.

Educational Services. The programs offered by Minnesota's public junior colleges are steadily broadening, to serve new groups of students and to provide new kinds of services.

They have long provided capable students with good preliminary college training. Although some junior colleges place greater emphasis on one type of preparatory curriculum than another, all offer sequences leading to advanced work in education, business, engineering, medicine, and liberal arts, and several provide preparatory courses in agriculture, home economics and social work. Rochester Junior College has recently completed installation of modern laboratory facilities for pre-professional courses in both the biological and physical sciences; Eveleth and Itasca have been significantly expanding their preparatory teaching program.

Typically, more than two-thirds of the students who graduate from Minnesota's junior colleges transfer to some four-year college or university. Studies dating back to 1929 of students who subsequently attended the University of Minnesota show that most transfers from Minnesota junior colleges make very creditable records, doing at least as well as University-trained students of comparable ability. Similarly, surveys made some years ago by the Minnesota Commission on Higher Education indicate that the later academic, occupational, and military records of junior college students compared favorably with those of students from other types of colleges.

All the public junior colleges of Minnesota also provide some terminal programs, which combine education for citizenship and personal living with training for various types of skilled and semi-professional jobs. In doing this, the junior colleges here and elsewhere are struggling to fill an impressive gap in our American system of education, namely, the dearth of programs planned for students who could profit from more than a high school education but do not necessarily require a full four-year program. From a sixth to a third of Minnesota's public junior college students now enroll in these terminal programs, chiefly in secretarial, business, and engineering fields.

Some illustrations may suggest the variety of training programs that are currently provided for technical and semi-professional positions. Austin Junior College and Austin Area Vocational School, for example, have recently developed a two-year program of training for engineering technicians, which combines practical experience in electronics and machines with training in drafting and foundational course work in physics, mathematics, and English. Similarly, students at Austin, Brainerd, Ely, Hibbing, and a number of other junior colleges can enter a Distributive Occupations Training Program, which combines on-the-job experience in retail sales with related class instruction. Rochester Junior College has pioneered in the development of a Medical Secretarial program, designed to prepare girls for employment in clinics, hospitals, and physicians' offices, and such a sequence is also now being offered at Hibbing. The new programs in

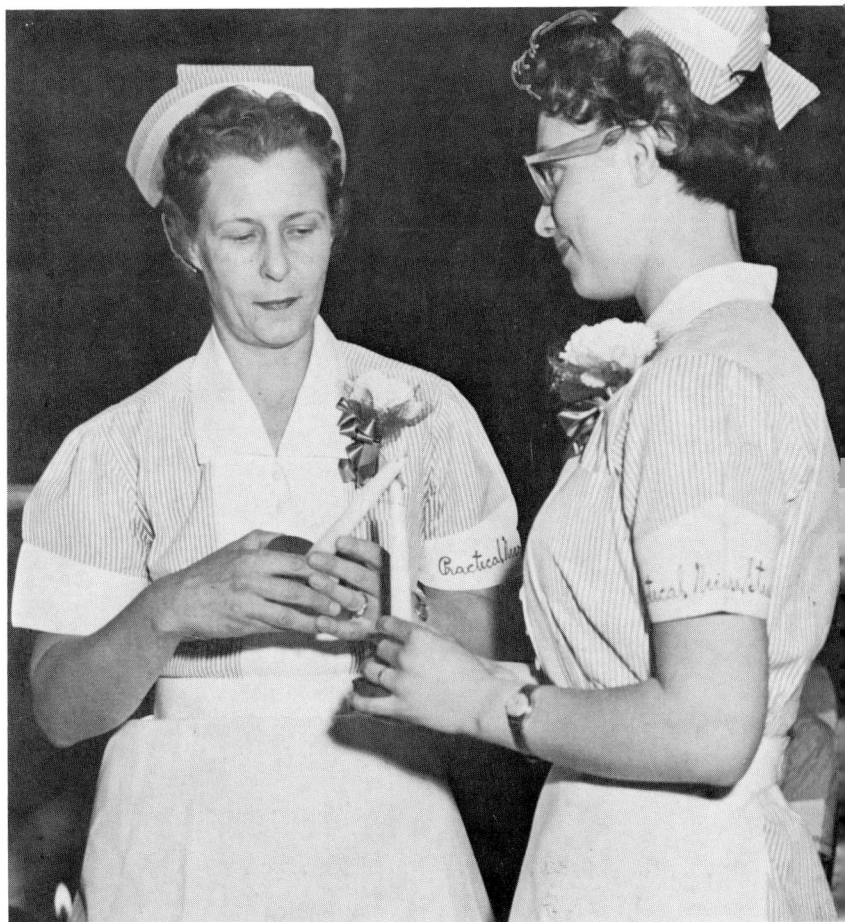

Practical Nursing Program, Virginia Jr. College

Medical Secretarial Training, Rochester Jr. College

Practical Nursing at Brainerd and Virginia Junior Colleges, the Agricultural and Farm Management course at Austin, and the sequence in Industrial Education at Eveleth are other examples of programs which prepare students for semi-professional

225

Library, Itasca Jr. College

Shop Work, Virginia Jr. College

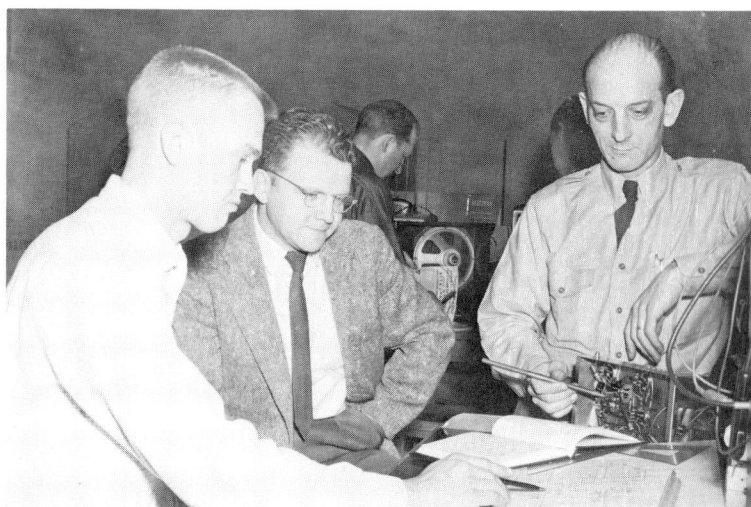
Engineering Technician Program at Austin Jr. College

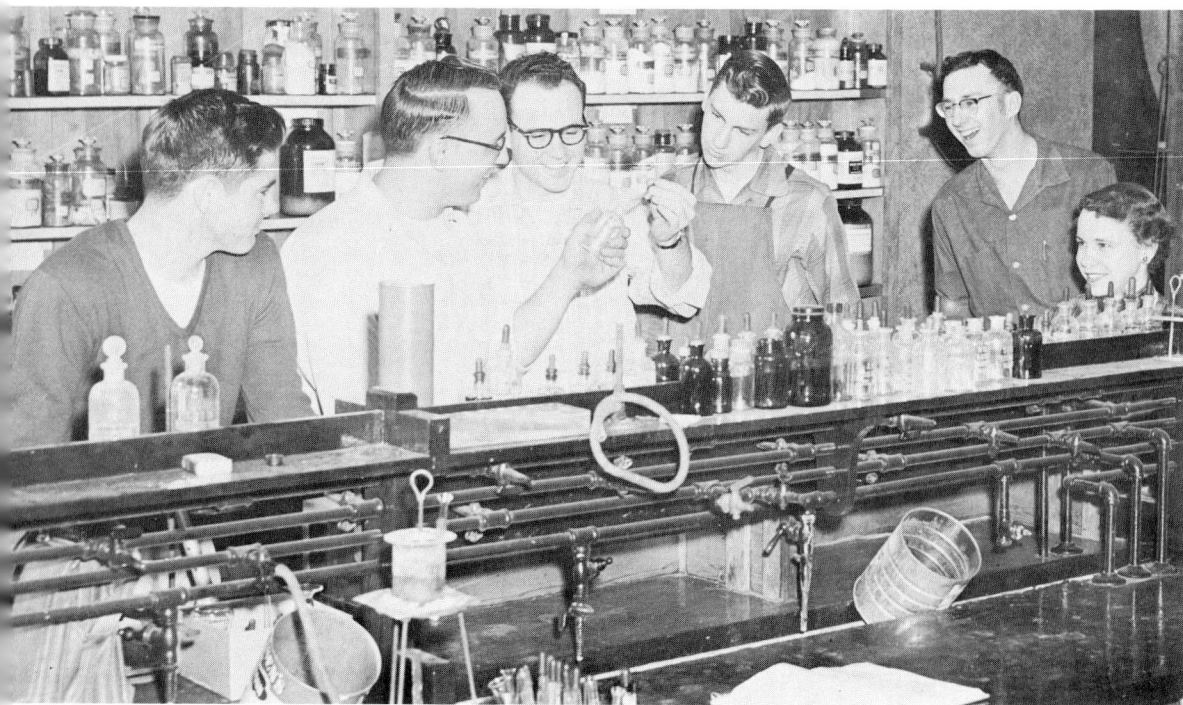
*Chemistry Laboratory,
Itasca Jr. College*

226

and technical jobs, and at the same time provide them with a good general education. Practically every junior college in the state is planning some additional courses and sequences, to serve students who will conclude their formal training at this level.

In addition to their class work, junior college students experience almost the full range of extra-curricular college life. Although most students continue to live at home, a carefully planned program of social activities enables them to explore a variety of avocational interests and to develop leadership skills. The *a Capella* Choir of 70 voices at Itasca Junior College, which has made numerous appearances throughout the community and on TV, suggests how musical groups help to develop talent, build aesthetic appreciations, and provide superior entertainment and cultural programs for the community. And this record can be duplicated for many other artistic, literary and dramatic groups. Some of the junior colleges have also developed good athletic programs, with the Ely basketball team recently chosen to participate in the National Junior College Basketball Tournament. Similarly honorary organizations give appropriate recognition to academic excellence, and help to nurture interests in continued study. Community responsibility

Adult Art Class Exhibit, Ely Jr. College

is also strongly emphasized, with a focus on projects likely to develop intelligent and responsible citizens. International Relations Clubs at Rochester and Worthington, for example, have powerfully reinforced instructors' efforts to stimulate discussion of vital national and international issues. Thus the social and educational parts of college life are joined to enable the student to profit as fully as possible from his college experience.

Finally, the public junior colleges afford facilities for continued education, on a part-time basis, for adults in the area. At Rochester and Austin, the number of adults enrolled each year has been close to 2,000, or about six times as many persons as attend the regular day sessions. Virginia Junior College, which now has the third largest adult program, attracts more than 1,000 students each year. The courses offered in these evening divisions range from the recreational or cultural type, such as Oil and Water Painting at Ely and the Great Books seminars now in their fifth year at Austin, through the usual freshman and sophomore collegiate courses, to vocational offerings, such as Virginia Junior College's courses in Machine Shop and Welding, and Worthington's special classes for young farmers. In collaboration with the daytime division staffs, many public forums, round-

Girls' Physical Education Class, Eveleth Jr. College

Dramatics, Rochester Jr. College

Agricultural Training at Austin Jr. College

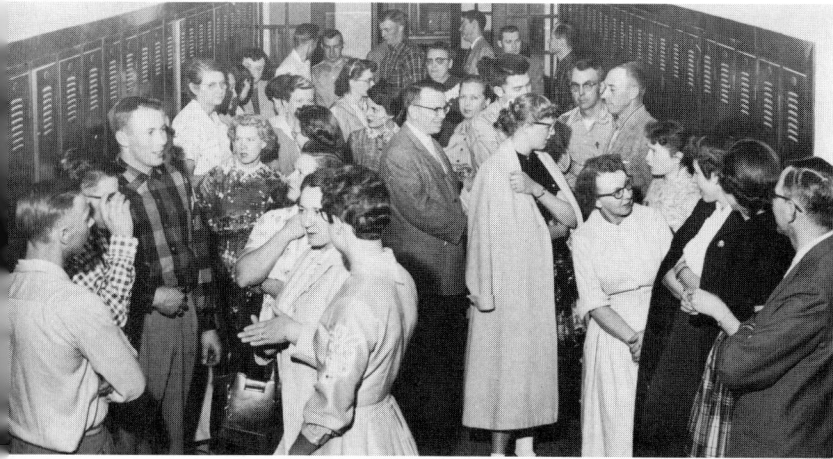

Visiting during break in classes. Adult Educational Program, Worthington Jr. College

Basketball Champions, Ely Jr. College

tables, and special institutes are also provided to enrich community living. Many instructors come from the regular day staffs; others are successful business, professional, or agricultural leaders or skilled workmen in the community. Although most of the work taken in these evening divisions is non-credit, Worthington reports enthusiastic response to its recent extension of degree-granting programs to the evening school, with some of the 180 students currently enrolled driving as far as fifty miles to attend these classes.

Because of all these developments the junior colleges are becoming significant intellectual and cultural centers for the community, as well as places where students can secure the earlier years of a college education and adults can acquire needed job skills, obtain help on their home-building, child-care, gardening, or dozens of other practical problems, or widen their outlook on national and world problems. In program, if not in name, Minnesota junior colleges seem well on their way to becoming genuine "community" or "people's" colleges.

Needs of Minnesota's Junior Colleges. Located in the midst of the people, responsive to their needs, and uniquely able to enlist and use local leadership, Minnesota's junior colleges have many distinctive and much-needed tasks to perform. But they must have help in several directions if they are to make their full contribution. Construction of separate buildings, financed in part by state monies, would greatly improve their prestige, administration, and educational services. So, too, would the development of a few new and strategically placed junior colleges, to serve educationally "barren" areas of the State and to relieve some of the pressure on four-year institutions in the metropolitan areas of Minnesota. Local or regional college boards, working under the guidance of the State Department of Education, might give more time than the present public school boards do to the special problems of these colleges. Similarly, the services of these colleges in counseling, testing and teaching need to be extended, and larger faculties recruited and encouraged to invest their professional careers in these institutions. Assured of such support, Minnesota's junior colleges will provide one promising answer to this state's expanding needs for education beyond the high school.

The State Colleges

By RUTH E. ECKERT
and R. EDITH STEDMAN

Kiehl Library, St. Cloud State College

Minnesota's centennial year had special meaning for the five State Colleges, since it also marked the one hundredth anniversary of the first normal school in this area. Just as the early normal schools evolved successively into teachers and state colleges as they discovered and met new educational needs, these "grass roots" colleges today continue to serve the people of Minnesota in unique and vital ways.

Located predominantly in the great agricultural areas of Minnesota, these colleges have attractive physical sites for their operations—Bemidji on the beautiful west shore of Lake Bemidji in Minnesota's famous northern recreational area, Mankato in the rich southern farmlands, St. Cloud on the northern bluffs of the Mississippi, Moorhead in the wide stretches of the Red River Valley, and Winona among the hills of the "Father of Waters" in southeastern Minnesota.

Currently these colleges provide for fifteen per cent of all full-time students enrolled in Minnesota colleges, and conduct the state's largest extension and institute programs for experienced teachers. Their chief mission continues to be that of teacher education, although they also afford general and specialized training to students entering a number of non-teaching fields. Yet critical shortages in physical facilities, staff, and general support funds jeopardize the future services of these colleges.

Enrollments. The State Colleges have recently experienced the greatest enrollment gains in their history, and the largest percentage increase of any type of institution in the state. The 7,382 full-time students who enrolled in these colleges in the fall of 1957 represent almost double the number in attendance in 1940, and 47 per cent more than these colleges enrolled just three years ago. This latter gain compares with a 25 per cent advance for Minnesota colleges as a whole during the same period. St. Cloud State College showed the largest full-time student growth (59 per cent for the past three years), followed by Mankato, with a 55 per cent gain. These two colleges, with current full-time enrollments of 2637 and 2315 respectively, are notably larger than their sister state colleges (Bemidji—813, Moorhead—810, and Winona—807).

Students Served. Since all graduates from accredited high schools are eligible for admission to these colleges, the freshman class includes students with an unusually wide range of abilities, interests, and social and economic backgrounds. In all these respects the State Colleges enroll a more representative cross-section of Minnesota high school graduates than do other colleges in the state. Although most of the entering students come from the top half of their high school graduating classes, those who did not achieve well in their earlier studies have another chance to prove themselves, and many have made good use of this second opportunity.

Nineteen students in twenty who attend these colleges are residents of Minnesota, and approximately a fourth come from the college's commuting area. More than half the students, except at Winona State College, grew up on farms or in towns of less than 2500 population, indicating how much these schools contribute to the advanced education of rural youth in Minnesota. In earlier years mainly women students enrolled, but more men have been steadily seeking admission, and they now make up about three-fifths of the regular daytime enrollment.

Educational Services. Preparation for teaching remains the prime objective of these colleges, and every phase of their programs has been designed

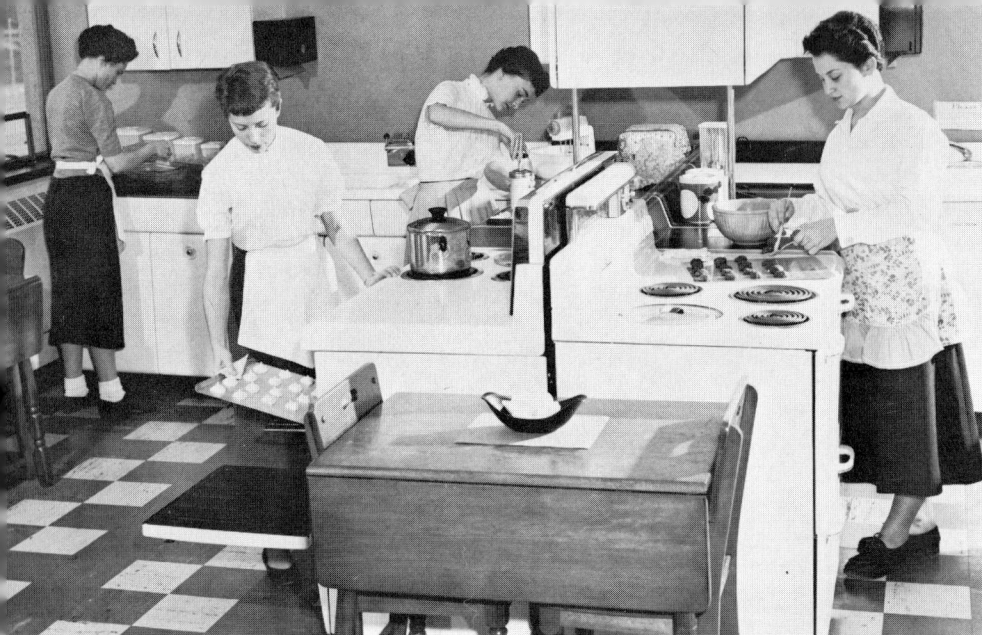

Home Economics Class, Mankato State College

Outdoor Art Class, Bemidji State College

to attract good students into teaching and to strengthen and support their professional training. The key role these schools hold in teacher education is shown by the fact that almost two-thirds of the new elementary teachers and more than a fourth of the new high school teachers in Minnesota come from these colleges, and that thousands of experienced teachers throughout the state secure their major professional stimulation and guidance from these colleges.

Programs through which candidates in the State Colleges are currently prepared include three- and four-year sequences for teaching in Minnesota's graded and ungraded elementary schools, four-year programs for prospective secondary school teachers, and a fifth-year professional sequence, leading to a Master of Science in Education degree. Planned for experienced teachers, the latter program is largely provided in summer term classes. Already four of the five colleges have been ap-

proved by the North-Central Association of Colleges and Secondary Schools for this advanced work.

Since certain training programs require highly specialized staff and equipment, preparation for these fields is limited to one or two State Colleges. For example, St. Cloud State College is currently preparing teachers for children with cerebral palsy, and Mankato and Moorhead are developing special training programs for teachers of handicapped children. Mankato is at present the only college providing full four-year programs in home economics education and nursing education.

The state colleges are also steadily improving the preparation given these future teachers. By 1961 all new elementary teachers graduating from these colleges will have had four years of training, and more and more high school teachers will be seeking fifth year professional certificates or degrees. Laboratory schools, offering instruction

230

from the kindergarten through the junior high school on four campuses and through the senior high school at Moorhead, help to make the professional courses more meaningful to students, and to develop valuable teaching materials and procedures. Other significant developments include the opening of the handsome Kiehl Library at St. Cloud, with its excellently-equipped Audio-Visual Center, the new Physical Education Building at Winona, the Library which is to be opened shortly at Mankato, the expanding dormitory developments on all five campuses, and large extensions planned in their library, laboratory and classroom facilities. Even more impressive has been the steady advance in the quality of the teaching staffs. At Bemidji College, for example, the full quota of sabbatical leaves for advanced study is filled every year, and an equal number of staff members take leaves without pay to advance themselves professionally. By emphasizing superior instruction, the staffs in these colleges have helped to raise the level of teaching practices throughout Minnesota and to induce many students who prepare for teaching to make it a lifelong career.

The State Colleges have also been continuously expanding their programs of resident and extension courses and other services to experienced teachers. Those working for their first degrees or seeking general professional improvement crowd the summer sessions on all five campuses, and former teachers who wish to return to the classroom find this a practical way to get the necessary "refresher" training. Services to teachers in the field have been multiplied through well-organized extension programs. In the 1951-55 period, for example, Mankato State College, which offers the largest program of off-campus courses, served 5,637 teachers through such instruction. This teaching takes some teachers throughout Minnesota, as in the 2600-mile "Know Your Minnesota Tour" sponsored by Mankato College, or to far parts of the country or world. In addition, the State Colleges provide a continuing succession of conferences and special institutes, aimed to improve education in Minnesota schools. Illustrative are the Fine Arts Festival at Mankato, the recent Science Fair at Moorhead, the Workshop in Conservation at Winona, and the nationally

known Band and Orchestra Clinic at Bemidji, which each August attracts some 500 high school musicians, band, and orchestra directors.

Now well into the second major cycle of their growth, the State Colleges also provide many services characteristic of general and liberal arts colleges, just as the normal schools had earlier made

Concert Rehearsal, St. Cloud State College

Business Administration, Moorhead State College

a high school education more widely available to students in their areas. At present roughly thirteen per cent of the students in the State Colleges enroll in the B.A. program and another eight per cent in terminal or pre-professional programs pointed toward some non-teaching goal. These percentages will likely increase as the State Colleges broaden their programs in response to steadily mounting needs for such training. Many students who complete the regular liberal arts program go later to professional or graduate schools, and others use this to enrich their subsequent careers as homemakers or in fields that do not require extended training.

Pre-professional students range, in these colleges, from those bound for agricultural or engineering programs to those headed for schools of journalism, medicine, pharmacy and social work. The normal spread in pre-professional offerings is supplemented, in some colleges, by more unusual sequences, such as those preparing for foreign service, government service, and meteorology at Moorhead, and the pre-fish and wildlife and pre-physical therapy programs at Winona State College. Students in some non-teaching fields secure their full training at the State Colleges, as, for example, in Nursing at Mankato and in Business Administration in all five colleges.

Terminal programs of one and two-year duration are now offered in four of the colleges, to provide for students who can give only two years to their college education. Commonly this leads to an Associate of Arts degree in general education, but Bemidji, St. Cloud, Winona, and Moorhead provide special sequences in Secretarial Training and General Business, St. Cloud in Retail Selling and Accounting, and Moorhead in Home Economics and Industrial Arts. Though these sequences do not yet attract many students, a promising beginning has been made in this direction, and the State Colleges may increasingly perform certain functions of two-year community colleges for students in their immediate area.

These institutions have also become important centers for lectures, dramatic and musical productions, athletic events, exhibits, and other means of intellectual and social enrichment for citizens of

Campus School Kindergarten, Winona State College

the area, as well as for the regular day and extension students. The Concert Choir at St. Cloud, which has become nationally famous for its excellence in the field of choral music, and the Warriorettes in Winona, who are widely known for their precision drill and dancing, are just two of the dozens of cultural projects encouraged by these colleges.

Needs of the State Colleges. Like Minnesota's other higher institutions, the State Colleges have been facing very great tasks with inadequate resources. Their plight is especially serious, since enrollments now far outstrip their physical and faculty resources, and only drastic improvements will enable these colleges to serve the predicted 17,000 students in 1970. Since none of these institutions has sufficient space for expansion, land acquisition must be an important next step for all five colleges. Old buildings must also be repaired, new ones built, and instructional equipment acquired on a scale to meet actual teaching needs. Student housing provisions are still inadequate, although the legislature took steps last year to improve this situation. Even more important, the teaching staffs must be increased in number and strengthened in quality, and administrative procedures and organizational patterns adjusted to the steadily widening sphere of State College services. As normal schools, then teachers colleges and now state colleges, these institutions have served well the people of Minnesota during the state's first hundred years. From attitudes of antagonism and indifference toward the little colleges with a normal school history, there has developed a strong sense of public appreciation, respect, and pride. The State Colleges must now be helped to plan the expansion and improvements necessary to serve even more effectively during Minnesota's second century of progress.

The University of Minnesota

By RUTH E. ECKERT
and R. EDITH STEDMAN

From a small preparatory school the University has grown into an institution of thirteen major schools and colleges, encompassing 136 separate departments of study. Main buildings on the Minneapolis campus now total 82, and 51 on the St. Paul campus. The Duluth Branch, with thirteen major buildings, is currently in the process of moving to its new upper campus, the land a gift from Duluth citizens and civic groups. In addition, the University maintains branch experiment stations at Crookston, Morris, Grand Rapids, Waseca, Itasca, Excelsior, Cloquet, Duluth and Rosemount. At the first four of these cities, as well as on the St. Paul campus, the University also conducts non-collegiate schools of agriculture. As the most complex unit in Minnesota's program of higher education, it has the largest, most varied and most difficult job to do.

Enrollment. In the fall of 1959 the University enrolled 26,538 full-time students, or 6,200 more than it had four years earlier. Of these 26,538 students, 2,428 were attending classes at Duluth Branch, and the others on the Minneapolis and St. Paul campuses. Together these students constituted half of all the full-time students in Minnesota's recognized colleges. The University also served some 50,882 additional persons through correspondence, sub-collegiate, short-course and extension programs offered last year. These figures suggest the dimensions of the task faced by the University in providing all these individuals with an appropriate education.

Selection and Guidance of Students. Beginning with the pioneering work of Dean J. B. Johnston in the College of Science, Literature and the Arts in the early 1920's, the University has been continuously seeking better methods of testing and guidance, aimed to help students select the right types of programs and to succeed in their chosen studies. Health services, carefully organized student activities, and programs sponsored by the various religious foundations provide additional resources for their development. Because the student is constantly thought of as a *person*—not merely a name on a class-list—many steps have been taken to promote his growth toward maturity and independence.

Provisions for General and Liberal Education. The University program aims, first of all, to develop men and women who will be responsible citizens and full-statured human beings. Education toward these ends, as distinguished from training for occupational skills, is known as general or liberal education, and is the special responsibility of three University divisions. The General College, established in 1932 to provide for students who might attend the University for only a year or two, pioneered both in Minnesota and the country at large in the development of new forms of general education. The College of Science, Literature and the Arts has long been known for its excellent program of liberal education, planned primarily for pre-professional students and for others who can give four years to these studies. The Duluth Branch, whose functions had earlier been limited to the preparation of teachers, has also been developing a broad and more functional program of general education, suited to students entering many different fields. Both the Minneapolis and Duluth divisions also offer an Associate in Liberal Arts degree to students who satisfactorily complete a two-year program of general education. As the importance of this type of education has been increasingly recognized, several of the professional schools have also added courses of a liberalizing character to

233

help students continue and extend their general education.

Opportunities for Specialized Training. Although some divisions of the University devote their primary energies to general and liberal education, they also provide opportunities for specialized study. Illustrative are the General College's sequences in retail sales, child care, and practical nursing, and the provisions that the College of Science, Literature and the Arts and the Duluth Branch make for pre-professional training and for majors in different academic fields, often with a vocational objective in view. In addition, a special division, known as the University College, administers individually designed programs, based on courses and seminars provided by two or more University divisions. In all these colleges an effort is made to provide a balanced education, combining expertness in a single field with alert competence in many others.

Most of Minnesota's doctors, dentists, lawyers, engineers, soils experts, and other professional men and women received their specialized training at the University. In addition, the University has supplied a great many teachers for Minnesota schools, with 28 per cent of the new elementary and 31 per cent of the new secondary teachers coming from University programs of teacher education. In order to insure instruction of a high quality, the faculties in these professional divisions are constantly studying the jobs that their students will be performing, and trying to find more effective ways of preparing for them. The purpose is not merely to prepare *more* engineers, nurses, teachers, social workers, foresters, and the hundreds of other specialists needed in American life, but to prepare *better* ones more quickly.

The Graduate School's Expanding Program. Enrollments in the Graduate School have soared in the past thirty years, paralleling a great expansion in the fields in which advanced instruction is provided. Its faculty of more than a thousand members, including hundreds of distinguished scholars and scientists, currently serves some 6,000 students, a fifth of whom are candidates for the Ph.D. or highest earned degree conferred by any university. Two-thirds of these graduate students are from

Coffman Memorial Auditorium

Johnston Hall, Minneapolis Campus

Minnesota or the adjacent economic area for which this state has special concern. The graduate program at the University Branch at Duluth was expanded in 1953 to permit qualified students to fulfill all requirements for a Master of Arts degree.

Interdepartmental programs, such as those in Cancer Biology, American Studies, the Behavioral Sciences, International Relations, and Nuclear Engineering are opening important new fields for scholarly study and research. The breadth and variety of the Graduate School's program is also illustrated by the Scandinavian Area Program, which makes effective use of the cultural resources of Minnesota's Scandinavian heritage, the training program for Vocational Rehabilitation Counselors, initiated with support from the United States Department of Health, Welfare, and Education, and Minnesota's world-renowned program of graduate medical instruction and research. Like other divisions of the University, the Graduate School is also constantly examining its program and exploring new possibilities for cultural and professional leadership.

Adult Education Services. Adults in all walks of life are confronted almost daily with problems that require new skills, new abilities, and new outlooks. Through its General Extension Division, its Agricultural Extension Division, and its other service programs, the University of Minnesota attempts to make its resources available to every citizen. The General Extension Division, established in 1909 and vigorously championed by President Vincent, first offered courses in business, economics, and education. Last year this one division of the University enrolled 11,852 persons in late afternoon and evening classes in the Twin Cities, 1,300 in Duluth, and 935 in other Minnesota communities, and provided opportunities for correspondence study for approximately 7,000 additional persons. Unique among its agencies for inservice training is the University's Center for Continuation Study. Since it was founded in 1936, 1,886 institutes have

been held there, ranging in length from two days to several weeks and enrolling some 109,510 adult students. Although four-fifths of these were Minnesotans, the registrations to date have included 23,264 persons from other parts of the United States, and 1,127 from foreign countries. The varied groups served—including surgeons, lawyers, bankers, teachers, foresters, policemen, and municipal finance officers, to cite but a few examples— reveal how responsive this program has been to needs for specialized training.

The General Extension Division also provides a number of other services for public enlightenment and public welfare. The Community Service Program, for example, offers concerts, lectures, assembly programs and maintains a play library. University Station KUOM brings the Minnesota University of the Air, the Minnesota School of the Air, and musical and other educational programs to the Upper Midwest. Since the fall of 1957, the University of Minnesota has launched an extended series of programs on the Twin Cities Educational Television Station, ranging from a telecourse on "Your Government," and "In Search of Science," to "At Home with Music," a program of informal concerts. The goal is to combine broad audience appeal with the integrity and high educational standards expected of a college or university. The Audio Visual Extension Service supplies sound motion pictures and slides to groups and individu-

View of Campus from the River

Research in Science and Technology

als. The Municipal Reference Bureau, the State Organization Service, and the Minnesota World Affairs Center similarly illustrate the Extension Division's central theme: "Learn for Living."

The Agricultural Extension Division contributes directly to economic and social progress in Minnesota's rural areas. Important research information reaches farm people through local demonstrations and farm visits, and through short courses on the St. Paul and Duluth campuses devoted to such topics as dairy herd improvement, farm electrification, soils and fertilizers, and pest control. About 12,000 people attend the more than fifty short courses given each year. Farmers throughout Minnesota also cooperate with the Agricultural Extension staff in studies of soil conservation, livestock and dairy production, farm management, and dozens of other problems of special concern to them. In addition, the activities of 4-H clubs and other groups directed by county agents afford rural youth important agricultural, social and civic training. Local communities supply a portion of the money required to hire these county and home demonstration agents, the rest being provided by the Federal and state governments.

Research Activities. Research is of fundamental importance in modern life, as witnessed by the vast sums that industry and government now invest in this effort to improve their services. It is no less important in a university, which remains the pre-eminent center for certain types of investigation. Some of the University of Minnesota's research is carried on solely to discover new knowledge, and thus to build the capital reserves from which future Minnesotans and others may draw in their efforts to insure the health, increase the wealth, and improve the living of all citizens. Other studies are aimed at applying known principles or techniques to current problems.

Illustrative of the University's current research projects is the new Gamma Radiation Facility, which provides the tools to explore the peaceful uses of atomic energy, and which will involve at least eleven University departments in studies on radiation. Sponsored by a number of state industries and the University, this project dramatizes the joint concern of industry and education for the welfare of the people of Minnesota. Similarly, the Social Science Research Center, founded in 1947, has been giving special attention, in a carefully planned series of studies, to the problems and needs of this general area.

Although these projects involve many scholars, significant research often results from the dedicated work of one man. Because of the persistence and ingenuity of one professor in mining engineering, for example, a huge new taconite industry is rising in the "worn-out" Mesabi Range. Another professor, this time in the Medical School, has devoted twenty years of painstaking research to brucellosis, and has become a world leader in the fight against this disease which has taken such a heavy toll of animal and human life.

The development of rust-resistant strains of wheat, diversified dairy products, new heart surgery techniques, better methods of coping with mental illness and juvenile delinquency, and striking advances in nuclear physics, such as the isolation of uranium 235, also show how diverse and significant is this constant search for new knowledge, new skill, and new applications. Creative work in literature, music, and the fine arts, though not measurable in the same terms, has helped to enrich our common life and make it an experience more truly worthy of man.

Some aspects of the University's wide-ranging research program are carried on in specialized research units, such as mines and agricultural experiment stations. The Minnesota Institute of Research, the Hormel Institute, the Dight Institute of Human Genetics, the Social Science Research Center, and the Mayo Foundation—all operating under the direction of the Graduate School—represent another form of research activity undertaken by the University. Still another is seen in the units established to study the state's and the University's educational problems. University nursery, kindergarten, elementary, and high schools, located on the Minneapolis campus, and an elementary and junior high school at Duluth provide training laboratories for prospective teachers and testing grounds for new teaching materials and procedures. Supported in part by a grant from the Ford Fund for the Advancement of Education, the Uni-

versity High School and the College of Education are currently experimenting with closed circuit television in classroom instruction. The University's five schools of agriculture likewise assist in studying problems of rural life education. Studies of school and college problems, by the Bureaus of Educational Research, Institutional Research, and Field Studies, also illustrate the University's unending search for more economical and effective programs of education.

Other Public Services. But the story of a great university is not told wholly in terms of its organized programs of study and research. Service, too, is a major purpose, and the sphere for this has been

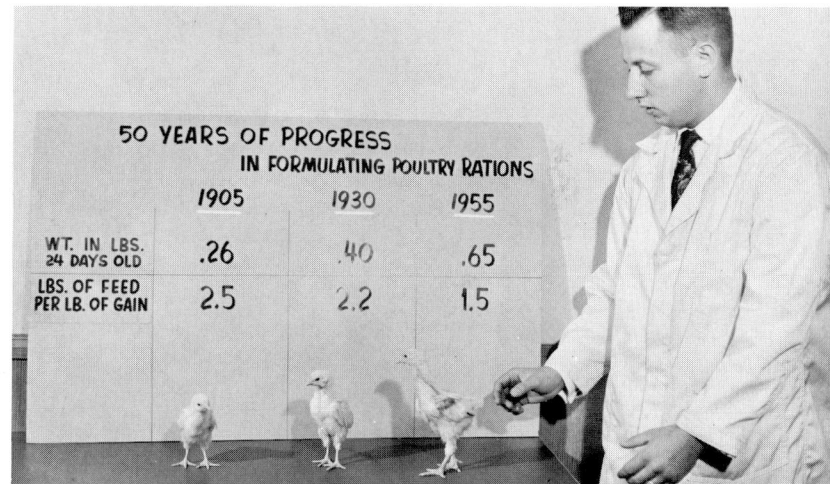

Agricultural Research

constantly widening. Three-fourths of the regular academic staff typically give some time to off-campus talks, conferences, consultative services, and other activities aimed at helping civic, business and professional groups find better answers to their problems. Service of this type is also a chief function of the Agricultural Extension Division. Similarly the influence of the University radio station (KUOM), the University television programs, the University Press, the University Library, the University News Service, and the University Theatre, as well as of convocations, lectures, art exhibits, symphony concerts and other musical programs, extends far beyond the campus, to benefit all Minnesotans and others within reach of the University's services. The University also contributes expertly trained persons to projects in all parts of the nation and world. This is well-illustrated by the University's cooperative program with Seoul National University, designed to help the latter institution rebuild after the ravages of the Korean War. The University of Minnesota provides a team in residence in Korea and also special short-term consultants; the University of Korea sends young, promising faculty members to Minnesota for advanced study; and the University of Minnesota advises and acts as procuring agent for equipment and supplies for the University at Seoul. Not all University service has such broad dramatic implications for international understanding, but each phase helps to assure a richer and better life for our own citizens, and often for people elsewhere.

Needs of the University. As the most complex form of higher education in the state, the University represents Minnesota's crowning effort to advance itself through education. Its needs are correspondingly great in terms of the recruitment of new staff to carry forward the University's far-flung program of teaching, research, and public service, the constant efforts that must be made to retain distinguished scholars and to provide them with suitable conditions of work, the never-ending tasks of improving the educational program, and the greatly extended physical facilities demanded by the University's soaring enrollments. The latter have been conservatively estimated as likely to climb to a total of 31,000 full-time students by 1960, 38,000 by

Science Laboratory, University of Minnesota Duluth Branch

Mall from the Southwest

Physical Education Building

1965, and 47,000 by 1970. As the barren areas of the state develop junior colleges and other Minnesota higher institutions are strengthened and enlarged, the desire for university-level education is bound to increase, and may result in an even greater flow of students into the University. And the better its own program becomes, the more will the University help to nourish interest in education and to build excellence in every school and college in the state. Constituting the vital energy-core—or "the thinking, philosophizing, and experimenting center of the commonwealth"—the University must be strengthened for its massive tasks.

A Look Ahead

"Going to college is no longer merely fashionable or simply a desirable, but optional, extension to one's training. Such education increasingly is becoming a necessity . . . An even larger portion of tomorrow's citizens will not be able to do their part with only a high school education . . ."

President J. L. Morrill

The task confronting Minnesota's higher institutions is so large that its dimensions cannot yet be laid out in detail. Local faculties and boards of trustees, councils of educational institutions, and citizens' and legislative committees must together develop the broad outlines of this program. It must also be left free to grow in the years ahead in ways that we cannot now chart.

It is no longer necessary, in 1959, to document the sharp upswing in the birthrate, which began in the early forties, and which will bring a great flood of students to Minnesota college campuses in the sixties and seventies. Were this "explosion in population" the only factor operating, there would still be 67 per cent more Minnesota college students in 1973 than there were in 1954. But both in Minnesota and the nation at large the demand

for a college education is also steadily mounting. Industry, government, and the professions are calling insistently for trained manpower, to provide the technical skill and understanding required to operate our vast economy and to protect the free world. As a result, the percentage of Minnesota students who go to college may be expected to advance, in the next ten to fifteen years, from the present 28 to 35 or even 40 per cent of all youth of college age, and adult programs will continue to grow and multiply. Unless this coming expansion is planned with wisdom and foresight, Minnesota colleges will not be ready for the estimated 95,000 students who will be beating at their gates by 1970.

Admitting more students to Minnesota colleges will not meet their needs or those of the state and nation unless the education they obtain is also of high quality. Men and women with intelligence, vision, and sound judgment are needed to plan and administer all aspects of government and industry, to provide medical, legal, educational, social, artistic and religious services, and to prepare others to succeed them, and each of these people must receive appropriate education for his tasks. The need to fortify and strengthen programs is fully as great as that of searching out qualified youth and removing financial barriers to their college attendance.

The largest problem facing higher education in this state, as in institutions elsewhere, will be to find and hold enough good teachers. Adequate physical facilities must also be provided, as well as support funds equal to the tasks facing Minnesota's public and private colleges. Although the Legislature and the people of the State have made great efforts to extend and improve college opportunities, Minnesota slipped between 1930 and 1950 from sixth to eighteenth place among the states in the per cent of its total income spent for higher education. As the Governor's Committee on Higher Education reported in 1956, only 42 per cent of the support for public higher education in this state now comes from public funds, as contrasted with 68 per cent in Illinois and 51 per cent for midwestern states as a whole. Minnesotans have enough money to provide excellent education from the kindergarten through the graduate school. The question is what they will choose to spend it for.

Model of University of Minnesota Campus showing proposed construction

The Challenge

Once Minnesotans saw little need to do research, to replant, to restock. The State's great resources of timber, iron ore, and rich topsoil seemed almost inexhaustible. Nor did the state recognize fully its need to develop its human resources. Although hundreds of public and private schools were established during Minnesota's first century of statehood, many youth failed to get a high school education; college opportunities were often restricted to those who could pay for them or who lived close to a public institution. Programs of continued adult education also lagged far behind the state's expanding need for them. Similarly, efforts in the fields of research and expert public services were often cramped by lack of funds. In all these respects can be discerned an important difference between Minnesota's yesterday and Minnesota's tomorrow.

Today we stand considerably taller in wisdom. Provident instead of wasteful, we have found new ways to conserve and create wealth. We have learned to protect and promote the common welfare through cooperative democratic action. Having made such strides, we stand on the threshold of the new challenges of the Space Age. Even our survival in this uneasy world may depend on the answers we develop, for the communist nations are making great use of the power of education. Constant extension and improvement of our educational program will be required to realize our democratic ideals and to promote better living for all.

The skill, knowledge, energy and ingenuity of our people now constitute Minnesota's greatest resource. Excellent school and college programs will help to refine and develop this potential and put it to productive use. But these institutions, as "the trustees of Minnesota's heritage," will require the dedicated support of all citizens, expressed in value judgments, in legal actions, and in financial deeds. What Minnesota hopes to become in its second hundred years, it must strive to be today—and nowhere with greater energy and imagination than in its schools and colleges.

The Minnesota Historical Society
The Oldest Institution in the State

By RUSSELL W. FRIDLEY

The Minnesota Historical Society is different from all other state historical societies, in that it is older than the state it serves. It was created, nine years before there was a state of Minnesota, by the fifth act of the territorial legislature. That was in 1849.

The men who founded the society and guided it during the first few decades of its life were the makers of Minnesota itself. Among them were Alexander Ramsey, the first governor of Minnesota Territory, and Henry H. Sibley, who became the first governor of the state. Some of the other organizers were: Charles K. Smith, Edward D. Neill, Martin McLeod, Aaron Goodrich, Henry M. Rice, and Franklin Steele. Governor Ramsey was the society's first president.

In 1849 the only part of Minnesota country that belonged to the settlers was the small wedge of land between the St. Croix and Mississippi rivers. The rest was still the home of the Indians. St. Paul was a village of fewer than a thousand people, and the total white population of the territory was perhaps five thousand.

Edward D. Neill, pioneer Minnesota educator, speaking at the first annual meeting of the society in 1850, described the scene: "Around us, the skin lodges of the Dakotas are still visible. Our nearest village is the residence of the band that was here a century ago. The scalp-dance is yet enacted within our hearing, and not a year rolls by, but the soil of Minnesota is reddened with Ojibway and Dakota blood."

The founders of the society knew that some day these conditions would be changed. Most of the Indians would be gone. The settlers would have cut down the forests, plowed up the prairie soil, and made farms and towns. Ramsey, Sibley, Neill, and the others wanted to establish a society that would record and save materials from this early period of Minnesota's development. They knew they were making history, and they wanted it perpetuated. Generations who came after them would then have a record of the state's beginnings and development.

As soon as the society was formed, the members began to gather material for it. They collected books, newspapers, maps, pictures, magazines, tools, and articles of everyday living. Sometimes the society advertised, asking people to bring contributions for the collections. One of these advertisements said: "The historical society wants journals, sketches, records, accounts of exploring or of pioneer life, Indian objects, and anything that shows the early settlement and progress of Minnesota and will be of value and interest to later generations."

At first the collection was so small that it could be kept in one basement room in the first capitol. As time passed, more was gathered, and the society had to move into larger quarters. Finally the historical material was divided into five collections, which are maintained to this day: books, newspapers, pictures, manuscripts (hand-written papers), and museum objects.

Since 1917 the Minnesota Historical Society has occupied a building of its own—the gray stone structure just east of the capitol in St. Paul. There the five collections are kept, and there the people of the state and other visitors may come to see and to study them.

The book collection of the society is now a library of two hundred thousand books, most of which have to do with Minnesota and the upper Midwest. Some are rare books printed long ago.

Minnesota Historical Society

Red Oxcart in MAS Museum

Dean Melva Lind with the Nicollet Barometer

Examples of these are Father Louis Hennepin's account of his explorations in this region, printed in 1663, and the *Travels* of the explorer Jonathan Carver, printed in 1778. The society's library also has many books on genealogy, used by people who want to learn about their ancestors.

The newspaper department of the society has the finest collection of Minnesota newspapers found anywhere, and includes copies of most of the papers published in the territory and the state. It begins with the first issue of the *Minnesota Pioneer*, printed on April 28, 1849, the first newspaper published in Minnesota. Every week five hundred and forty Minnesota newspapers are added to this collection.

In the picture department are nearly a million paintings, photographs, daguerreotypes, and other pictorial items. These include pictures of most of the important people who have had a part in making Minnesota. Many of the paintings were made before the days of photography, and show scenes of Indian life which no longer exist. There are paintings of early St. Paul and Fort Snelling made more than a century ago. Among the portraits are those of Harriet Bishop, Joe Rolette, James J. Hill, and Zebulon Pike.

The manuscripts department has more than four million hand-written documents telling about the history of the area. Some are letters of early settlers describing their experiences; some are accounts written by explorers, fur traders, and lumbermen. Some are reminiscences written by pioneer farmers, housewives, and tradesmen, telling how they went to Minnesota, and how they lived there. Besides this there are records of churches, schools, towns, clubs, and other groups. One of the treasures of the collection is Abraham Lincoln's Sioux War Order, ordering the execution of thirty-nine Indians who took part in the Sioux Uprising of 1862. Another is the daily journal of Lawrence Taliaferro, who was the Indian agent at Fort Snelling when it was first established. Among the famous Minnesotans whose papers form part of the collection are Alexander Ramsey, Henry H. Sibley, Franklin Steele, Ignatius Donnelly, Frank B. Kellogg, and Knute Nelson. Thousands of items are added to this collection each year. Whenever an important Minnesotan dies or retires from public life, the society makes an effort to obtain his papers.

The museum collection has more than a million objects, including such Indian artifacts as stone axes, hide scrapers, eagle feather war bonnets, peace pipes, and beaded moccasins. From the period of the fur trade there are guns, traps, beads, and other trade goods, sashes worn by the voyageurs, and a Red River oxcart. Objects from the early lumbering period include saws, axes, stamp hammers, pike poles, and peaveys of the lumberjacks. Probably the largest group of items in the museum is the collection of articles used by pioneers. Here are tools seldom seen any more—such as the broad ax, frow, and draw knife; also equipment used in early industries such as the blacksmith's six-foot bellows, and the wooden plow, flail, and ox yoke used by the frontier farmer. From the pioneer home are such articles as the candle mold and candle snuffer, warming pan, and spinning wheel. Would you like to see Minnesota's first

printing press or St. Paul's first automobile? These and many more interesting objects of the past may be found in the museum of the historical society.

The founders of the society wanted the materials of state history to be saved and taken care of. They also wanted the society to use these materials to take history to the people. This important task is carried out in several ways.

One way the society tells about Minnesota history is through its publications. The organization has issued dozens of books during its long history, including the annals of the society, printed in 1850, the first book published in Minnesota. It now also puts out two magazines: the popular *Gopher Historian*, used in most of the schools of the state, and the more scholarly quarterly *Minnesota History*.

Every year more than one hundred thousand people visit the historical building, seeking information on Minnesota. Authors and scholars wish to study in the library or to read newspapers and manuscripts in order to get facts for writing books. Lawyers go to search old newspapers for records of land sales or for other matters. Many people visit the historical building looking for records to establish the date and place of their birth so that they can draw an old age pension or get a passport. Thousands of school students, adult groups, and tourists go to see the museum displays. The picture department is visited by people who need historic Minnesota pictures to illustrate books or newspaper articles, or to use on television programs.

About ninety per cent of the income of the society comes from the state, the rest from private sources. At every session, the Minnesota legislature appropriates thousands of dollars for the support of the society. The state government recognizes that it is important to perpetuate the heritage of every Minnesotan by collecting and preserving many kinds of historical materials and making them available and useful to the public.

If Ramsey, Sibley, Neill, and the other founders of the historical society were to return, they would be pleased to see that the materials of Minnesota's past are being preserved, that the collections are increased each year, and that they are being used by great numbers of citizens.

Minnesota's

First Public Libraries

By GLENN M. LEWIS

Libraries for the use and enjoyment of the citizens of Minnesota were organized simultaneously with the creation of the territorial government. In 1849, during its first session, the territorial legislature established the Minnesota State Historical Society. Although no direct connection between the Society and the beginnings of local libraries can be traced, its origin implies that the legislature and the people it represented were aware of the advantages of a library and the preservation of historic materials. In various settled parts of the territory a number of local associations and informal groups organized libraries. The first of these, also created by enactment of the 1849 Legislature, was the St. Anthony Library Association which existed for about six years. By 1857 ten other library associations were in existence in St. Paul, St. Cloud, Mankato, Austin and other towns. Under their articles of incorporation these associations, all inspired and organized by male citizens, could hold property of a stated amount, sue and be sued, receive gifts, write constitutions, and have a corporate seal. Not much is known today about the size and composition of their book collections, but much of the time and zeal of the membership was spent in promoting lectures and debates. In other words, they took on the character of lyceums. The fact should not be overlooked that during this period certain individuals, apart from the associations, were often responsible for maintaining libraries from which books could be borrowed. Undoubtedly, many of the early association libraries were the heritages of the intellectual life of the Eastern states from whence many of our people came, or from the European homes of our early immigrant population, especially Germany.

During the early years of statehood it is a matter of record that 27 new library organizations were established. The census of 1860, however, is not adequate in its coverage of libraries. It does accredit 86 of all types, but it is not clear how many were actually town libraries.

Ten years later the United States Census gave Minnesota credit for 1412 libraries, containing 360,810 volumes. Since the total population of the state was now 439,706, the per capita ratio is encouraging, though it must be noted that not many of these were public libraries in the modern sense. More explicit than that of 1860, the Census of 1870 in classifying libraries indicates 587 of semi-public character with many of these related to churches and schools. The fifteen libraries actually typified as town libraries may seem small in number, but considering the size of our towns at that time, the coverage is significant. Among these fifteen were such towns as Austin, Duluth, Minneapolis, Rochester, St. Paul, St. Cloud, St. Peter, Stillwater, Winona, Mankato, New Ulm, Wabasha, and Zumbrota. These were all association libraries operating on a subscription basis. In other words, only subscribers or share holders could enjoy the reading room and book-borrowing privileges.

In the three large towns of St. Paul, Duluth and Minneapolis, the origin and function of the subscription libraries form a chapter in themselves. Space permits indicating only certain noteworthy facts in their respective evolutions. In St. Paul the Y.M.C.A. Library, closed by 1859 and reactivated in 1861, finally merged with the St. Paul Mercantile Library in 1863. The 2000 volumes collected by these organizations formed the nucleus of the St. Paul Public Library and have been in existence from that day. The result of the merger was still a subscription library governed by shareholders and used by readers who paid an annual or a semi-annual fee to borrow books or frequent its reading rooms, open from 2 to 9 every day except Sunday. By 1875 this collection of books had more than tripled in size and included many newspapers and periodicals.

In its outlines the Duluth Library Association was similar to St. Paul's. It was organized in 1869 by the Young Men's Literary and Library Association with a capital stock of 1,000 shares at $5.00 each and annual fees of $3.00 for subscribers. In 1870 this Library contained about 360 works of considerable variety including government documents, pamphlets, periodicals and newspapers. A full-time librarian was employed to check out books and to see that proper decorum was observed in the reading room. In the middle seventies, its status becomes rather obscure, but according to the Report of the Commissioner of Education for 1876 it was operating in 1875 and had a collection of 725 volumes. By 1884 it had apparently ceased to function.

Although the first library to be organized in the area that is now Minneapolis was that of the St. Anthony Association, the largest subscription library in Minnesota, was the Minneapolis Athenaeum. The Young Men's Library Association first met on May 16, 1859, completed their organization, and appointed a full-time male librarian. A short time later its name was changed to Minneapolis Athenaeum. In 1860 the Athenaeum was

Center block, Athenaeum building

incorporated, though the books numbered only 300. In 1863 subscriptions were invited toward purchase of a building site. In 1866 a library building was erected. Four years later there were 2,269 volumes in the library with a supporting stockholder membership of 200. The Athenaeum grew rapidly until in 1889, it had 20,932 volumes. To a great extent this rapid increase was due to a bequest left by Dr. Kirby Spencer, a pioneer dentist. In 1890 the gift provided $10,000 annual income. Substantial support by its stockholders and subscriber membership and strong direction by its board accounted for its successful development.

In a period of about twenty years after statehood twenty-four other association libraries came into being, under a variety of names such as Austin Circulating Library, Northfield Library Association, Rochester German Library Association, St. Cloud Union Library, Wabasha Ladies Library Association, and the New Ulm Turnverein. If the names varied, so did the sponsorship. Women were becoming increasingly active in promoting libraries, and many were supported by their study clubs, others by the local public school, the W.C.T.U., German physical education units and similar groups. In more than one case women were the reactivators of declining organizations started by men.

According to the State Bureau of Education figures for 1875, these libraries outside the larger towns were relatively small ranging from 384 volumes in Chatfield to 2,000 volumes in Winona.

Many collections were housed in stores, some in banks, a few in schools, still others in public buildings such as a post office or courthouse. They were thus subject to damage and sometimes complete loss. Usually, no regular librarians were employed, records were irregular if kept at all, but these organizations as impermanent as they were, besides serving a temporary need, provided the basis for implementing legislation and were the forerunners of many a public library now well established. Moreover, they served to make a community library conscious and aware of the benefits of libraries.

In 1879 the legislature passed a general law

Dr. Kirby Spencer Memorial

Herbert Putnam appointed Athenaeum librarian

246

providing that in incorporated cities and villages, the respective council "has power to establish and maintain a public library and reading room and may levy a tax not to exceed one mill on the dollar, except that in cities of over 30,000 inhabitants a tax not to exceed 1/2 mill may be levied." Other sections of the law provided for the appointment of nine library directors and outlined their powers. Less than three months after the passage of the law the first tax-supported library was established in Zumbrota. In the following twenty years several towns already enjoying the benefits of some kind of library service organized their public libraries with tax support. In the 80's eleven towns took advantage of the law, including Sauk Centre, St. Paul, Minneapolis, St. Cloud and Winona. In the '90's seventeen followed and in 1900 five more came into existence.

Although legislation provided three ways by which a tax-supported library might be established, most were put on tax support by vote of village or city councils. This was true of both St. Paul and Minneapolis. In St. Paul the volumes of the St. Paul Library Association were transferred to city control in 1882. It was a simple continuation of the organization with continuation of policy implied. In the same way the Minneapolis Athenaeum brought its book collection of 20,932 volumes into the new Minneapolis Public Library Building, completed in 1889, and contributed $8,000 toward its cost. The Athenaeum board continued its meetings in the new building, expended its funds, and appointed its assistant librarian. The Minneapolis Public Library Board agreed to insure the Athenaeum collection and properly maintain it. The contract between the two boards was drawn for 99 years and is, of course, still in effect though minor changes have been made.

With its new building, its excellent collection of books for a Western library, and strong leadership, Minneapolis in its first year issued 13,000 borrower's cards and purchased almost 9,000 city-owned books. In circulation of books it placed seventh among American libraries.

Often the newly organized tax-supported libraries in smaller towns were housed in rented quarters. Some occupied rooms in a city hall or high school. When the library had proved itself, usually public spirited citizens campaigned for a library building and invited subscriptions for at least part of the cost of construction. As in the case of Minneapolis, bonds were issued for a few new buildings. Any history of public library development in Minnesota would be deficient unless it recognized the contributions of Andrew Carnegie and many residents of the state for new buildings. By 1900 Carnegie had promised funds to Duluth and Mankato, and in the first ten years of the 20th century his gifts amounted to over $1,000,000 to 58 cities for 68 buildings. By 1919 the Carnegie grants had been discontinued. Eleven of the larger Minnesota towns by 1929 owed their buildings to outright gifts or bequests from residents of their communities.

Stack room

To supplement the service of local libraries and to reach areas without library service, traveling libraries came into being. Borrowed from Oxford, England, the idea seemed adaptable to our needs and rapidly spread across the United States. By 1899, through the efforts of the Minnesota Library Association, the Women's Federation of Clubs, the Women's Council of Minneapolis and women's or-

247

Delivery room

ganizations in other cities, several traveling libraries were collected and circulated, usually on a county-wide basis. So successful was the program and its acceptance that the State legislature in 1899 amended the law of 1879 in order to set up the State Library Commission of five members. The primary function of the Commission was to purchase books to form a circulating library from which any community in the state might borrow. The Commission was also authorized to aid and encourage the creation of free municipal libraries and to keep statistics and make reports to the Legislature. As soon as the State Library Commission was in operation, requests for traveling libraries poured in. By January 1901, nearly 150 applications had been received and 85 libraries were soon in circulation.

During its first fifty years Minnesota gave ample evidence that it really valued libraries. From the date of its organization as a territory people worked together in various communities and towns to build libraries. When the association library had served its day in a community and better cooperation was desired, the tax-supported library took its place. The traveling library was a natural reaching out to bring books to areas which could not afford their own libraries. A further application of the traveling library program is the prevalent use of book mobiles in our larger cities and for county-wide or regional service.

In the next 35 years came many changes in library legislation, organization, and general function. As examples may be cited the increases in millage for towns and counties, the reorganization of the State Library Commission from an independent status, to a division of the State Department of Education, and a greater emphasis on consolidation of two or more counties, or a town and a county, if such a merger was better economy. The foundations had been well laid and though the structure stood firm it was amenable to enlargement and improvement. That this state has done as well as it has is in no small part due to strong leadership in its formative years, and to the never ceasing efforts of the Minnesota Library Association from its founding to the present to create the proper atmosphere for the use and appreciation of libraries.

As vigorous and prevalent as library progress has been, Minnesota still has room for constructive effort. In the late '30's a statewide WPA project was organized under the direction of the State Library Division to demonstrate to communities with inadequate or no library service what a public library could mean in cultural, recreational and informational advantages. Though some communities benefitted and programs were continued by tax support, a few slipped back to their former condition. Today a bill enacted by Congress makes it possible for Minnesota to enjoy the benefits of $400,000 in federal funds on a matching basis for a new demonstration project more far reaching and effective than the earlier one. Under the guidance of the State Library Division the federal aid program, besides other benefits, serves as an incentive to neighboring counties to join together to provide a better library than any one of them could provide alone. Recent surveys show that some sparsely populated counties could provide no more than 25c per capita for library service while an amount from $1 to $1.25 is considered a very minimum per capita cost for bare essentials. Adequate service costs today about $2.50 to $2.75 per capita.

Since about twenty-six per cent of the people of Minnesota are without any library service, consolidation of funds in two or more counties to furnish a library, buy books, employ staff, and operate bookmobiles where necessary, would aid greatly in meeting this discrepancy.

Though Minnesota must still be characterized as chiefly agricultural, within the years since World War II it has become more industrialized with increasing urbanization. As the state changes character, so will its public libraries as they meet new needs and conditions. In the past, Minnesota has surmounted many difficulties. It will continue to progress.

PUBLIC LIBRARY STATISTICS 1957

Number of Libraries

Public libraries maintained by tax support or public funds 163

Libraries organized as separate county units 8

Public libraries maintained by associations 43

State Institution libraries 20

Total 234

Population of Minnesota (87 counties) with Public Library Service 2,982,483

Population served by public libraries 1,612,303

Population served through county service 575,962

Population served by Association libraries 26,760

Total population served (74%) 2,215,025

Without Public Library Service

Urban 19,985

Rural 747,473

767,458

Source: *Minnesota Libraries*, March 1958, Page 17

Total population not served (26%)

Rochester, Minnesota public library

St. Paul public library

CHAPTER NINE

Minnesota Business and Industry

By J. W. CLARK

FOREWORD

The shifting panorama of Minnesota life is nowhere more varied and appealing than when recording the changes and adaptations made in the occupations of its people and the growth of its economy. The last 150 years of the state's history has seen recorded much more of this change and growth than in all the centuries of human life in this area preceding 1857.

The works of man, by which he makes a livelihood and builds a social structure, is affected by many factors. Most important is the character of those who perform these works. With a high degree of validity it can be claimed that the citizens of Minnesota have displayed qualities of ambition, purpose, health, competence and intelligence which are not exceeded by any others anywhere.

As has been noted in previous pages, a process of selection took place in the establishment of our pioneer stock. Minnesota never held out an invitation to those who would like to enjoy an easy life, acquire a quick fortune, or be favored by an ever-smiling nature. Minnesota made its appeal to those who, from the ends of the earth, would come here to hew from the forests, harvest from the earth, and dig from the mine in ways which were hard but were rewarding. From the inheritance of this rugged stock has come, more than from any other factor, the economic achievements of the past and the potentials of the future.

A second factor which has made of Minnesota an area of expanding productivity is the nature of its natural resources. In comparison with other areas of the nation, Minnesota's resources are more remarkable for their size than their variety. The state possesses relatively few known minerals with no fuels of consequence. Her deposits of iron ores are, however, of immense proportions. So, too, is the fertility of her soil, the extent of her forest lands, and the beauties of her lakes and wildlife. The combination of the application of superior human aptitudes and interests upon these large resources makes for many pages of compelling history. From those pages a few are here extracted.

MINNESOTA AGRICULTURE

When Radisson and Father Hennepin and their associates and the early explorers who followed them penetrated Minnesota's forests and prairie by means of the waterways which opened up before them, they noted little evidence of human activity. The Sioux and Chippewa made but little impress on the land. Their numbers were small, probably less than 5,000 in all, and their known needs were usually easily satisfied from forests, streams, and those small portions of the good earth from which they extracted food.

It took hundreds of years for the tempo of economic activity to change to any great degree. The Minnesota panorama moved slowly during the 150 years from 1700 to 1850. As noted in earlier chapters, the fur traders established some more or less permanent posts as well as moving about to trade more directly with the various Indian groups by whom they were, on the whole, welcomed and appreciated. There was some lumbering, some farming, some river transportation, but previous to 1850 there was little industry in Minnesota, because there were so few living here to carry on such enterprise.

Immediately after the turn of the half century and the establishment of the Minnesota territorial government, the pace quickened. European nations were in ferment. The more ambitious of the youth of Scandinavia, Germany and New England were looking at and listening to pictures and stories of a new land where there were great undeveloped resources, healthy living conditions and where no compulsory military service was required. This nation and state held out welcoming arms, and transportation facilities became increasingly adaptable to their use. Minnesota began to grow with exceeding speed.

It was, of course, the land that called the loudest to these immigrants, whether they came from foreign lands or from neighboring states to the east. The land was never expensive, terms of purchase were made easy by those who had it to sell, and during the '60s the homestead laws which were passed made little more than residence on that land required for acquisition. It is not strange, therefore, that it seemed like floodgates had been opened and the best of Europe and the more settled regions of this nation came pouring in.

If one could go back and get a mental picture of a river port such as Red Wing or Reads Landing in the later fifties some such scene as this would be presented.

The ice has left the Mississippi River. The first steamboat from downriver is pushing its way toward the wharf. Lined along the bow of the boat are the men and women, bundles in hand, ready to seek their fortune in the new land they have spent weeks to reach.

The boat docks. A cry of welcome rises from those of the village who recognize friends and former neighbors. Some livestock is unloaded along with provisions for both the "old settlers" and the newcomers and the long awaited mail. Lodgings are found, sale signs are put up in store windows, directions given to those traveling west, and hurried trips made to the land office.

It was during this period that the commonly heard expression "doing a land office business" came into being. On an occasion such as that described, our Minnesota panorama would show a line of new arrivals standing before the door of the land office awaiting their turn to make application for a claim or a down payment of a few dollars on a purchase.

When this farmer started off to find and work his land, he carried with him something much more valuable than the pack on his back or his pair of oxen or whatever might show to the eye. He brought to Minnesota, and invested in the acres of land he acquired, a high degree of healthful energy, persistent courage and intelligent ambition. His purpose was to build a home, have a family, and give to that family those qualities of character and educational advantages which he felt were appropriate for the new state he was helping to build.

Then he found the land upon which he was to stake his claim. It was, in all probability, in one of two general areas—the prairie lands of the west and southwest or the forested lands of the north and east. Because the forested lands were, generally speaking, closer and the early settlers came in large part from forested areas, most of the early farm homes were made of logs. Those who were willing to go out where the only trees were the willows growing along the banks of the winding prairie streams, built many of their first homes from the tough sod they cut in squares of thickly matted prairie grass, roots and soil.

Whether in forest or prairie, the early pioneer home was distinguished for extreme simplicity, for only bare necessities, and few of them, were at first possible. Also there was, of course, considerable isolation. Neighbors were distant in point of miles, still more distant in point of transportation because roads were almost nonexistent. As a result, many of our early farmers, and more particularly their wives, have told those who followed them that the feature of the first few years they most remember was the deep silence. Whether living in forest or on the prairie, there was little in the way of sound reaching their ears. Birds were few, there were no machines, only a scattering of domestic livestock. As a result, the loneliness which was felt was accentuated by the silence which seemed to prevail except in times of storm.

There was much to do, however, and the typical

Minnesota pioneer started in to do it. In the forest, there were trees to cut, logs to haul, and stumps to get out. No present-day citizen can appreciate the handicap to farming those stumps provided. Without the explosives and power equipment of today, they hardened the hands and tired the muscles of the men who worked on them for year after year. They were much more an obstacle than were Indians or forest fires or even mosquitoes, which probably rated second in the way of physical difficulties. While the land was cheap in terms of dollars, it was tremendously expensive in terms of human toil.

Those who set their stake in the prairie had it somewhat easier, but the earlier settlers there had no easy road to fortune. For countless centuries the grass had grown tall and rank each year, then dried, fallen, and rotted to form a thick deep seed bed for the next year. As a result, the breaking plow of the prairie needed six oxen to pull it and six oxen were hard to come by. In addition there was, each fall, the threat of prairie fires and the difficulty of getting fuel. Either long trips to islands of forest growth were required or the burning of hay in the Sibley stoves. These stoves were somewhat like the airtight stove of a later date and required constant tending in the blizzard nights of winter.

Why did these first farmers of Minnesota endure such hardship and impose it on their families? Because they were confident that this was but a passing phase; that as Ohio and Illinois and Wisconsin had opened up before, so Minnesota too, would become a great agricultural state with many

Oxcart carrying supplies from railroad depot

more people, growing markets, and better prices. And they were right.

First along the streams and then the rapidly extending railway lines, villages came into being. Money for machinery and home equipment, always at a high rate of interest became available. A simple one-room school, used as a community center, was built by common effort on the part of neighbors. Church services were held upon occasion and there were even home talent plays given and debating societies established. Life came to have less austerity and a promise of the cultural.

Nothing, however, could subtract much from the job at hand which was to make the virgin soil blossom with the harvest it was able to produce. Letters sent to the homeland, wherever that might be, told of cabbages that would fill a bushel basket, wheat that produced fifty bushels to the acre, and potatoes several times that amount. Except when grasshopper plagues came, as they sometimes did, with all their destructiveness, prosperity seemed promised at least for "next year."

As a result, their numbers grew with speed and certainty. The state itself established its State Immigration Board, which sent emmissaries east and abroad. Minnesota had a multi-storied hotel in New York City where immigrants were housed until farms were located for them. The railways, hungry for return freight, helped by providing low-cost transportation for people and their possessions into the burgeoning West. One who had lived on his land for five years, or had what passed for a house and barn and a score of cultivated acres, was an old settler.

Agriculture thrived apace. Wheat became king because there was a growing world market for it; there were no rusts or blights to injure it then, and wheat was relatively easy to store and to transport. Acreage increased by leaps and bounds. Minneapolis became the flour manufacturing center of the world. When power machinery came into common use, hundreds of millions of bushels of wheat came out of Minnesota to feed the mouths of a fair share of the civilized world.

Wheat raising, here as elsewhere, proved to be a pioneer industry however. Sometimes the market was glutted and the wheat was burned for fuel.

Some years rust destroyed it or grasshoppers ate it before it could be harvested. Other farm products began to prove more profitable.

As a result, during the past half century Minnesota has ceased to be a wheat producer of consequence and has become an area of mixed farming. Livestock and livestock products have become dominant in farm marketing. Corn, rather than wheat, is used for feeding this livestock. Alfalfa has taken the place of the native grass for feed of the dairy and beef cows raised in such quantity by the farmer and his family. Poultry has changed from the housewife's pin money to really big business. Sugar beets, particularly in the Red River Valley, and soybeans almost everywhere have replaced in large part the wheat fields of the later nineteenth century. Vegetable crops, small fruit, and nursery stock, particularly near the cities, have become substantial means of agricultural income.

Most influential in affecting the lives of our farm people has been the advent of power equipment. Gasoline and diesel fuel has taken the place of horses and oxen. Less human labor is required to produce the food supplies the land affords with a consequent trend toward reducing the size and number of farm families and increasing the size of the farms themselves. This appears to be the continuing trend of the times in which we live.

Agriculture will continue to be one of Minnesota's major economic elements for as long as we can see. That is due to a number of factors. The principal one is the fertility of our farm acres. Only one or two states have a larger number of acres of good and excellent soil than does our own. Another controlling factor is that our location in the mid-point of the continent with the center of population moving toward us, gives us a market advantage which will grow with time. Not least important is that the Minnesota farmer continues to possess many of the qualities of character and competence possessed by his forebears. Added to these, he now has the advantages offered by better seed, fertilizers and chemicals of varied application, and all the findings of science research and technology. The best days of Minnesota agriculture are still to be lived. Total farm income has for some years reached a total of approximately

$1,300,000,000, fifth highest among the states of the nation. As the demand for food and fibre increases, together with our capacity for production, that sum will increase. Even more rapidly, it can be anticipated the capacity for living and enjoying healthful and happy lives on these farms will be achieved, with standards of economic and social well-being far beyond the dreams of those early pioneer farmers who first created those farms.

Elevators for storing grain

254

Combining grain near Crookston in Red River Valley

Grain Exchange trading hall, 1900

Grain sampling at grain exchange

FORESTRY

When the panorama of Minnesota history shifts to our forest lands and those who labored in them, a varied scene is presented.

That scene has its romantic elements. The log drives of the turn of the century when the spring thaws brought downriver the accumulated harvest of timber along Minnesota's uncounted streams created a spectacle which should be permanently imprinted on the pages of Minnesota history.

Those logs were floated by the swiftly flowing waters of recently melted snow. They were guided and directed by as rugged and colorful a crew of men as ever drew breath on this or any other continent. Truly, Minnesota's lumberjacks were a picked lot. None but those possessing in high degree, great physical strength and hardihood, could endure the dangers and difficulties which were unavoidably associated with their trade.

The logging camp of lumber days in Minnesota held no appeal to the dilettante. It was rough. It was rough both as to physical construction and as to the life of those who spent the better part of each year in it.

There were several structures, all made of roughly hewn logs. There was a cook shack where food was prepared and eaten; one or several bunkhouses where the jacks slept and, occasion permitting, loafed and played; the horse barn, the blacksmith shop, and perhaps more. They provided only

Lumberjack sleeping quarters

Lumber camp cook house

the most elementary shelter, were used for a few years at the most, and abandoned when the area had been denuded of all timber of value.

The men who made up the camp were a mixed lot. The first to come were the Mainites, lumbermen who originally came from the lumber camps of the State of Maine and possessed of the skills which had been developed there from pre-Revolutionary days. They were followed by Scandinavians and other northern European immigrants with always a large element of French Canadians and the Yankee farmers who needed the cash wages paid to get their more southern farms into successful operation.

It was a crew of specialists—specialists with the ax, the saw, the piling and hauling of logs, of preparing food and mending tools, care of horses and oxen and all the varied trades associated with a lumber camp. To many a young Minnesotan this was about the only industrial school which was available to him. It was a hard school, one in which there was a large element of danger and sweat and pain, but where the reward for successful attainment was the respect of his fellow men. It was a well-attended school from 1850-1925 and those who graduated from it would prefer no other.

The working day began early, long before sun-

rise. The bull cook (cook in training) would pound the steel triangle to wake the men while the stars were still shining. A breakfast to stagger the imagination was quickly but silently eaten, then off to the woods in the early dawn to chop, saw, pile, drive team, ice trails or whatever until darkness came.

The evening meal, as huge as the appetites of those who ate it, would follow, a few games perhaps, then the deep sleep of physical exhaustion until the breakfast call was again sounded. There was neither time for sickness nor a place for weakness. Accidents did happen all too frequently and surgical and hospital care was either absent or Spartan in nature. The men who were hardened by several winters in lumber camps were those who felt that pioneer farmers had a life of comparative ease.

Not that it was all drudgery and hard work. Sundays were different. Then the men washed their soiled clothes, sang songs, danced with each other (those with red handkerchief tied on their arms were the "women") and, best of all, told stories. It was in the bunkhouses on Sunday nights when Paul Bunyan came into being and the bug-eyed downy-chinned youths in the camps heard tall tales of Babe the Blue Ox and all the varied members of

Paul's remarkable crew. The argot of the lumberjack has now gone the way of his camp, but a few of his tales still have a deserved place in the folklore of our state and nation.

The highlight of the lumberjack's year was the log drive which brought it to a conclusion. With the beginning of the spring freshets, the logs(previously marked with the brand of the camp and piled on the ice of some stream) would start their journey toward the mill situated at Winona, Red Wing, Stillwater, Minneapolis, Brainerd, Grand Rapids or any of scores of others points appropriate for the location of sawmills.

Following the drive would be the lumberjacks with their peevees, steel-pointed poles, breaking up incipient log jams, poking alone straggling logs, keeping the drive in motion. Now their cook shack was the wannigan, the house on a raft where they would occasionally return for hot coffee, beans, beef, and repairs. They often slept on the cold bank, their boot-clad feet in the chill water to keep the leather from shrinking while it dried.

No words can describe the day they landed in "port." They were paid off. Their cash went in some part at least for whiskey, women, gambling games and all the excitement they had been missing during the past months. Their sharp-calked boots chewed up the wooden sidewalks and floors of the village folk who awaited their coming with the mingled emotions of expectation of business stimulation and fear of disorder. Then relative quiet would come as some went to summer employment on distant farms and others translated the logs into finished lumber in the throbbing, ear-piercing sawmills.

The Minnesota lumbermen were very important in the development of the state and the whole area surrounding it.

It is true that they were exceedingly wasteful. They cut any tree big enough to make a ten-foot "two by four." They left the waste timber and slashings where they fell as food for the destructive fires which followed them. Property lines were generally disregarded by the "timber barons" who managed the operations and sometimes made considerable fortunes in denuding acres to which they had but tenuous claims. It was "cut and get out" with little thought for those to come after. The white pine, which originally stood on a large part of all northeastern Minnesota, paid but a fraction of what it could and should have paid our people had it been considered the natural resource of value we now know it to have been.

There is, however, much to be said by way of explanation and excuse for those who treated this timber in such a manner. At that time there was but little realization of the future need which would be felt for that which was so recklessly squandered. There always seemed to be another forest waiting to be cut just a few miles ahead.

Also, there was a hungry market waiting. Those who were erecting farm buildings, villages, and cities, not only in Minnesota, but in the prairie states south and west, were calling in a loud voice for that most easily and cheaply attainable from Minnesota's forest lands. Then there was but little thought of dry kilning lumber, of shaping and planing. The wagons and freight cars were waiting at the sawmill, ready to take the boards and rafters still hot and moist from the saw, eager to make grain elevators, office buildings, stores, homes and furniture and fixtures from what had, but months before, been green and growing trees. Also, it was mistakenly felt that land which grew such trees would quite certainly grow bountiful farm crops as soon as the fires had gone over the cutting and the stumps had rotted or been removed. We know better now and are acting on that knowledge.

Lumbering in Minnesota began as early as 1820 when Franklin Steele, attached to Fort Snelling, built the first sawmill at the Falls of St. Anthony. It continues to the present time, but fell off markedly after passing its peak at the turn of the century. About 1900 it reached proportions of some two billion board feet a year and was correctly considered one of the major enterprises of the state at that time; nothing like it seems probable in the future.

This does not mean, however, that forests and forest products are of little value to us now. While most of our citizens are unaware such is the case, our tree-clad acres now bring us more in the way of both economic and social benefit than was ever true in the days of Paul Bunyan and his crew.

Old mill erected 1822

Material for construction of railroad

While Minnesota has now become an importer rather than exporter of lumber, the millions of acres of forest lands of Minnesota are now proving their worth to us, in terms of dollars, in amounts varying from 150 to 200 millions of dollars a year, substantially more than the returns from the lumber previously sold. The spruce, balsam, fir, birch and poplar trees, scorned by the lumberjack, are now being harvested as crops. Through the magic of the scientist's test tubes and chemicals, paper, insulation, matches, and an ever-increasing range of new products are bringing employment, increased capital investment, and general economic growth to our state as a whole and many communities such as International Falls and Cloquet in particular.

Their advantage to us is by no means measured in direct dollar benefit. Without our forests, our lakes would be of short duration with all the recreational and economic benefit they possess. Wildlife would become largely extinct, floods would desolate the land, beauty would fade, and vast areas we now proudly proclaim as scenic wonders would become gravel-strewn waste.

It is in partial realization of what our forests mean to us that we now spend some millions of dollars of public and private funds each year to keep that which we have and increase its size and productivity. "Keep Minnesota Green" is more than a volunteer organization and a commonly expressed slogan. It is a growing conviction and program of action on the part of our citizens. Uncounted millions of seedling evergreens are planted each year, fire wardens perch in towers wherever trees grow, conservation practices are employed by the major forest industries, and favorable tax laws all combine to assure the generations which follow that they, too, shall know Minnesota as a land of the living green.

We have many reminders that this must be a continuing program. Monuments erected by survivors of the Hinckley and Moose Lake-Cloquet fires of previous generations testify to the hundreds of lives needlessly lost because of previous carelessness. Fortunately, nothing like these holocausts have occurred of late. Like flu epidemics and economic depressions, they could come again if planned and purposeful preventive measures are not consistently taken. Long periods of drouth are unavoidable, no machine has yet been invented to quench a big forest fire; they can come from a single unattended spark. The laws enacted to prevent such catastrophes and the men who enforce those laws should have their injunctions meticulously observed. Our forests are among our most priceless possessions, more for what they keep and preserve for use than for the immediate though substantial income they bring.

Present day lumberjacks

Northern Minnesota forest

Making printing paper

Pulpwood being hauled to paper company in northern lake area

MINING

Few Americans think of Minnesota as a mining state or as an area containing minerals of value. The picture that comes to the mind of the average citizen when he thinks of this state, is that of the illustration in the geography textbook he studied some years ago. It showed a giant steam-driven tractor pulling a gang of twenty plows on a Red River Valley bonanza farm. As has been noted, this is as far removed from today's reality as iron mining of 1958 is removed from that of its original methods of operation.

When the Minnesota panorama swings to iron mining, for iron is the dominant mineral resource of the state up to the present, it brings a setting of large proportions. Iron in itself has very limited use but as an essential constituent of steel, iron ore is more vital to the works of man than is any other mineral. This is the Age of Steel. Wars are won or lost, prosperity gained or missed, society thrives or stagnates, in a large degree upon the availability of that metal. The recent unprecedented growth and world leadership of the United States is more closely associated with some deep holes dug from the surface of the Mesabi Range than is often understood or appreciated by the people of this nation.

Almost from the days of the earliest explorers there was a belief, founded upon some evidence, that there was iron ore in northern Minnesota. Nobody got excited about it. It was much like reports of mineral deposits being found now in the polar regions or northern Alaska. It might be of value some day.

Two forces combined to bring Minnesota's iron ore to market. One was the rapidly expanding demand for iron ore which resulted from the industrial expansion of the nation in the latter part of the nineteenth century. The sources of iron ore up to that time, located near the steel mills in the east, were inadequate. So geologists went out to find new sources and in Minnesota they found much more than they ever dreamed they would or could.

At about the same time the ore bodies were being charted, means of transportation by water through the Great Lakes and by rail to and from the harbors were going through the improvements to make the long trip east economically feasible.

Of course, what helped so much was that from mine to Lake Superior harbor it was a downhill pull, and, when loaded on boats, the ore moved much more cheaply than it could over land.

There are many men whose names are contained in the chronicle of Minnesota mining. Many of them are the names of men who never made their homes in this state. This has had much to do with the general impression felt here that iron mining was a foreign industry in that its origin and management is due in major degree to individuals we do not know.

Among these names are those of Charlemagne Tower who had a large influence in the establishment of mines in the early 1880s near the town named after him and who was a Pennsylvanian. Then there were two of the great financial geniuses of all time, John D. Rockefeller and J. P. Morgan, who instituted some of the early developments and provided the essential transportation facilities. The dominant corporation in the iron mining industry has its offices in Pittsburg and New York City just as most of the smaller, so-called independent mining companies with their headquarters in the cities named Cleveland, Youngstown, and other eastern points.

Any summary of this area of interest in the state's economy must, however, be highlighted with two names bearing Minnesota identification. Those two names are Merritt and Davis. The Merritt name is associated closely with the early period of Minnesota iron, the Davis name is contemporary in point of time.

Lewis Merritt brought his family to Duluth before the Civil War when it was but a struggling village. He reared a numerous brood, among whom were seven sons destined to become the notable Seven Iron Men. Chief of the clan was Leonidas, as dynamic a personality—physically and temperamentally—as the state has ever known.

The Merritts were not miners or geologists, but hard-working and successful lumbermen. Father and sons produced their million feet of lumber over the years, but whether cruising the forests for next year's cut or hauling out that now in process of production, they kept always in mind that somewhere about was the iron ore which would make the area far more rich than did the timber it produced.

What fooled the Merritts and, even more, the scientifically trained geologists who also were looking for ore in the Mesabi region, was that the deposits were not in rocklike layers between greenstone and slate as they were in the Vermilion Range, already opened. That is where iron ore is supposed to be. That is where it is in other portions of the earth. When they could not find greenstone, they were certain there was not any iron ore. Not even when they were walking on it.

In 1890, however, the Merritts found some ore in the wheel ruts of their lumber cuts which, when assayed, proved to be some sixty percent iron. That was at Mountain Iron. A similar deposit was located months later at Biwabik in the roots of a windblown tree. The rush to the Mesabi was on.

While it took some decades to prove the nature of the fabulous Mesabi deposits, experience has proved that there is a low ridge running from Grand Rapids to Aurora where ore is found in higher concentration and larger amount than was ever known previously. Overly simplified, this giant ore body might be compared to a long, twisted loaf of raisin rye bread. All of the bread was, and is, rich in iron ore; rich, that is, in comparison with the earth surface generally, which usually has some iron in it. What makes the Mesabi so valuable however, is not the bread, but the raisins. Scattered through the ore body in hit and miss fashion are pockets of varying size where nature has leached out other elements and provided soft iron ore of exceeding value for its concentration of ferrous oxide and its ease of removal.

The Merritts found some of those pockets. They

Iron mining, Northern Minnesota

stretched their credit to the limit to build a railway, erect docks, and open mines. The Panic of 1893 brought their dreams of quick wealth to quick ruin. The Rockefeller and other financial interests took over, but not before the Seven Iron Men had been able to prove that their father, Lewis Merritt, was right when he insisted there was much iron ore in those parts and it was up to his boys to find it and start it toward the mills.

Turning several pages quickly in the Minnesota panorama, we come to the second Minnesota name of special significance in the history of mining. It is that of Ernest Davis.

Professor Davis was a member of the faculty of the University of Minnesota for over thirty years. He was director of the Mines Experiment Station for much of that time. Unlike the Merritt brothers, he never aspired to be a millionaire or a big operator in any industrial operation. His thinking was in larger and less personal terms.

Noting that iron ore was leaving Minnesota in steadily rising volume with little in the way of replacement being discovered, Dr. Davis concentrated his efforts at finding means to catalyze taconite. Taconite is the name given to the granite-hard rock which makes up the rye bread in which the iron ore raisins were found. There is no conceivable end to the taconite; the rich iron ore is quite definitely approaching exhaustion. What perturbed Dr. Davis was, what if another world war comes along, or even the present peaceday demand continues, the Mesabi goes the way of the white pine it at one time bore, and the nation becomes dependent upon foreign sources for iron. It could mean the strangulation of the economic life of the nation.

It seems a simple matter to learn how to improve the quality of an ore so that the merchantable content would go up from 25 per cent to twice or more that amount. Now that Dr. Davis has proved it can be done and that it is being done in gigantic fashion, it is perhaps easy to overlook or forget the arduous effort, patient persistence and scientific intelligence Dr. Davis applied over the years to make the nation's steel supply certain of attainment.

Now it is possible to visit more than one taconite processing plant in Minnesota, plants to which some one billion dollars have been committed,

plants which turn out millions of tons a year of high grade iron ore, preferred by the steel mills and protecting the nation from any future starvation of the sinews of war and the essential elements for the progress of peace. It is gratifying to know that the good scientist has lived to see much of that for which he aspired, that he now lives in a home looking over Lake Superior, the Ernest C. Davis works of the Reserve Mining Company, and from his window can see the mammoth deposits of concentrated iron ore to which his mind and spirit have given birth.

It is not difficult to quote figures and statistical data as applied to Minnesota's iron mining. Approximately 60 per cent of the nation's steel owes its origin to Minnesota earth. It totals something like 70 million tons a year valued at some $400,-000,000. It provides employment for over 10,000 of our people. The taxes paid by the industry, relatively heavy in comparison with other forms of property, have provided excellent governmental services for the Iron Range regions and aided state institutions, particularly educational, as a whole.

It is the future in iron mining which takes on the most attractive colors in the Minnesota panorama being viewed. The past contained some of the dramatic element but most of the mining operations, like the villages in which the miners lived, were somewhat drab other than for the public buildings the iron ore taxes provided. The miners themselves have been in large part, immigrants from Italy, Poland, Finland, Yugoslavia and other Balkan nations. Their assimilation has not been as rapid as was that of the Germans, Swedes, and Norwegians who settled the farms of the state. In more ways than one the Range has seemed something of a place apart.

The future of iron mining, and much that is going on at present, will tend to change this. The machines, the skills and techniques, homes and social conditions associated with mining of today and tomorrow, will call for craftsmanship of high order, considerable education, and justification for advanced pay scales. Also it will provide, on an average, at least two jobs for each one afforded by the removal of high grade, direct shipping, iron ore.

There is a strong probability that Minnesota

will not much longer produce the greater share of the raw material called for by the nation's steel mills. As South America, Labrador, Africa, and other sources provide half or more of what these mills require, Minnesota can feel no sense of loss. Here will reside in that long low "loaf of bread" which constitutes the Mesabi, a reserve so mighty that the hundred million or more tons taken from it from year to year is comparable to the diet of a single sparrow in a grain elevator. Mighty, strong, and durable is the iron arm of Minnesota.

While iron ore is unquestionably the major mineral product of this state, it is by no means the only one.

Gravel which formed in layers and large deposits by the glacial lakes described in an earlier chapter, has always had large value for our people. It was prefered by those who laid out our early road beds as it is now used by the contractors who construct our hard-surfaced highways and all our cement structures.

The granite found in the St. Cloud, Morton, Ortonville, and Duluth areas has also found frequent application in the history of the state. Even with the stern competition supplied by modern concrete and steel, this rock finds frequent use for monumental and decorative application. So, too, has the travertine limestone of the Winona region and the limestone supplied by the quarries of Kasota and Mankato.

Most historic of all Minnesota minerals is the soft catlinite rock at Pipestone. For ages immemorial this quarry was sacred ground to the Indian tribes of the continent. To it came those from all tribes to fashion the pipes of peace which were smoked about the campfires of the real first settlers of the nation. Quarrying this rock is restricted to those who are Indians. A few remain who are skilled in the sculpture of that unique formation to the traditional use to which it is put.

Ore Locks, Lake Superior

MANUFACTURING

The first factory building in Minnesota or any portion of it was the first home built therein. The early settlers were, of necessity, in large part self-sufficient. What they were unable to make for themselves or trade for with some neighbor they went without. There was no place to buy most of what are now considered necessities of life. As a result, necessity became the mother of invention and the home workshop produced commodities which, while frequently lacking in style, possessed considerable durability as is attested in their being proudly claimed heirlooms a century later.

The Minnesota panorama, therefore, when presenting the story of the processing of goods to make them more useful or more marketable, turns back to the pioneer housewife and her industrious husband—he working over his homemade cobbler's bench to fashion out something in the way of a shoe while she splashed cream about to make butter, hand knit a sock, or make sauerkraut out of the fall crop of cabbage.

Even when the railways were built and the cars they carried gave a market for lumber and wheat and the importation of ready-made clothing, varied food products, and home furnishings, it was a poor housewife who did not fashion with her own hands much that her great granddaughter buys as a matter of course, and her husband would no more think of buying a milk stool or a bedstead than his great grandson would think of making one.

There were some forms of industry which came into being early. One was, of course, the grist mill which ground wheat and corn to make it more nourishing and palatable to both man and beast. Associated with that was often the sorghum mill which ground the maize-like stalks to make a thick dark syrup. Then, of course, there were the brick kilns. There must have been a hundred or more in various localities in the state, especially where the Germans settled, because the Germans liked brick for their homes. And, of course, there was the ubiquitious sawmill which early took over the job of replacing the cold and drafty log house and sod cottage.

One of the more interesting developments of industry in this state is that provided by the famous Red Wing Pottery. This originated about 100 years ago to make the pots and jars in which dairy products and sauerkraut were kept. As time went on the demand for this rough ware declined so dishes were made. Now gift ware, fashioned out of various clays, imported far from the original clay banks, became the product of the plant which was operated through the passing generations.

So, too, have other expressions of man's inventive genious provided the answer to man's changing needs and wants. The world-famous flour mills of Minneapolis and Washburn Crosby Mills, grew up to replace the early sawmills beside the swiftly flowing waters of St. Anthony Falls. The proprietors of those mills learned of scientists and inventors abroad who had discovered techniques and equipment which would make a superior quality of flour, separating the germ of the wheat and the rough outer shell and producing a quality of white flour which became the favorite of both the baker and the housewife. So the mills, close to giant suppliers of "Red River No. 1 hard" from northwestern Minnesota and North Dakota, grew to a capacity of 40,000 barrels a day and the Minnesota brands on the sacks and barrels they shipped became recognized all over the civilized world.

For the period extending from early pioneer days to the recent past, Minnesota manufacturing

Wheat field—Red River Valley

Grain elevator near downtown St. Paul

was largely associated with what the economist terms primary production. Wheat was made into flour, pork into bacon, milk into butter, logs into lumber and the like. It was all a relatively simple operation. It reduced Minnesota's native natural resources in terms of bulk and made them more acceptable to the markets in which they were entered. It dealt more in volume than in value. The employment of labor was not large nor particularly remunerative either to management or to the workmen. By and large, that which came out of the plants, rather few in number, although the flour and sawmills were sometimes large, was small in value in relation to the imports of the finished goods which were purchased by the citizens of the state as a whole. Minnesota has been, until recent years, a producer of raw materials or semi-finished goods rather than a truly industrial state.

When the panorama shifts from the rather distant and the recent past, a marked trend toward change is noted. The breaking point comes during and immediately after World War II. During that conflict, problems associated with labor supply became acute. Firms which had contracts which they could not fulfill unless they were able to secure

additional labor and set up branch plants in Minnesota. Plants already operating here secured contracts of size and discovered that the productivity of Minnesota labor was such that they could overcome the handicap of added transportation costs, their distance from market imposed upon them, and still match profits with their competitors. Industry in Minnesota took on new color and size and began to thrive.

It was time that it did. The application of power machinery on the farms had reduced the demand for labor there. The automobile and the truck and the hard-surfaced roads on which they traveled had eliminated the need for many of the small villages which had sprinkled the map. Young men and women had found jobs easy to get in business and industry a thousand miles and more away. They were leaving in droves to the economic and social loss of our people. Most of them would much prefer to live in or near the community they had always called home, but if there was no good paying job there they went where there was one.

The leading citizens of the state, public leaders such as Governor Harold Stassen and Governor Orville Freeman, business leaders such as James

F. Bell of General Mills and J. Cameron Thomson of Northwest Bancorporation, have noted these trends and sounded a call to arms which has echoed all through the commonwealth. Laws have been enacted to stimulate industrial growth, departments of government have been established, chambers of commerce alerted to create industrial development corporations, and banks, utilities, railways and newspapers have joined in a common effort to prove that Minnesota can provide jobs for its own people.

Most effective in the promotion of their program of business and industrial development has been the proof of profit on the part of industry already in production here. These have not been limited to those engaged in primary production. General Mills has entered such fields as tool making, electronics, chemicals and many others. Minneapolis Honeywell has gained a position of world leadership in electronic controls expressed in literally thousands of different items. Minnesota Mining and Manufacturing Co. pours many millions into its research laboratories each year from which it garners patents, ideas and inventions leading to uncounted numbers of new employment opportunities and ever-increasing profits and production.

So the story could go on and on, listing Brown and Bigelow's dominance in the calendar and specialty printing field, Josten Jewelry in college and school jewelry, Fairmont Motors in railroad equipment, Toro in lawnmowers, and more recently, Remington Rand and International Business Machines in mechanical office equipment.

After the Centennial Year, it is evident that a bright new page is being painted on the Minnesota panorama. The exodus of youth from Minnesota has come to a halt. As of 1958 the in-migration experienced by Minnesota equals or exceeds the out-migration. Men and women, skilled in the assembly of finely made products or willing to become so skilled, are now in demand. Employment rolls grow in length and trade and commerce thrives because of the new jobs offered and the wages paid by those jobs.

Nor is this growth and expansion of industry limited to our larger municipalities. Even small villages seek out the inventor like the land agent

Flour on its way to waiting homemakers

formerly sought out the farm prospect. Branch plant location is being promoted with all the enthusiasm railways earlier promoted immigration from Sweden. Communities which a decade ago were reconciled to stagnation are building new schools, hospitals, parks, sewage disposal units, and residential additions in assured confidence the new job opportunities they are acquiring will warrant such improvements.

A few figures are in order. In 1947, when this new industrial growth was first being felt, the "value added by industry" was proudly acclaimed as having at long last passed the billion dollar mark. By 1955 it had gained some 60 per cent and reached the $1,600,000,000 mark, well over and rapidly exceeding the $1,300,000,000 of farm income of the state. With confidence and assurance, the people of Minnesota note the long line of cars going and coming to these manufacturing plants with each shift, knowing that only a national cataclysm of some nature can prevent the further growth and acceleration of such generators of economic well-being.

Final checkout of Honeywell thermostats

Finished insulating board emerges from the insulite machine

Auto assembly at Twin City plant

Electronic computers used for analyzing new flight control and guidance systems

Minneapolis Brewing Company canning beer

Sandpaper passing through drying and curing oven

Huge rolls of Scotch tape are converted into smaller rolls

Oil industry South St. Paul

An organic chemical synthesis promoted
by ultra violet light studied by scientist

Welding pipe

Backing tractor into freight car for shipment to local or distant points

273

Mississippi River Power Project

Butter plant

Car being unloaded at a terminal elevator

Linemen at work on a power project

TRADE AND COMMERCE

One historic scene on Minnesota's business panorama does not require any demand upon the imagination of the citizen of today. On the shores of Gull Lake near Brainerd there has been re-created from out of the past an almost literal reproduction of the pioneer village main street of seventy-five years ago. Here in "Lumbertown" as it is called, the visitor finds the general store, the barber shop, the theatre, the drugstore, the blacksmith shop, the saloon—all the realistic settings of a previous day and age. They are authentic, too, since in major part, they are the originals which in some manner escaped the wrecker's tools and have been transported from various parts of the state to this last assembly point.

The contrast between 1890 and 1959 generates many a chuckle and some good laughs. So much progress and improvement has taken place during the intervening years that the present generation can be excused for some feeling of superiority. The more sober-minded and historically-informed realize, however, that Lumbertown of 1890 was as much of an advance over 1859 as 2000 probably will be over 1959. If he who laughs last laughs loudest, what giant haw-haws are going to come from later spectators of the Minnesota panorama!

The first of the commercial men of the area were, of course, the French-Canadian fur traders of our earliest recorded years. As has already been told, they were a colorful lot who made up an assiduity and perseverance what they lacked in capital and business equipment.

None of them had a cash register, knew much about bookkeeping, or studied sales psychology. Many of them went bankrupt, sometimes several times. Some of them became quite wealthy. Some, like Kittson and Renville, did much to earn their place on the map of the state. Their accomplishments in preventing some of the bloodshed which would have occurred had they not succeeded, in part, in placating the Indians for the ruthless manner in which the white men appropriated their red brothers' lands and hunting grounds, were in themselves, of warrant for continued appreciation and recognition.

The size of their operations was limited by the number of their customers. More Minnesota furs are bought and sold currently than there were when the American Fur Company records for the area were kept by Henry Hastings Sibley. Of course, there are many more trapping animals now than there were then.

Another sidelight on our early trade is the appearance on the steamboat freight records of the barrels of cranberries which went downriver, principally to St. Louis. There are still cranberries in Minnesota and many more in Wisconsin, but most of our cranberries, different from our mink and muskrats, appear to have been lost. Since these cranberries appear to have been sold at one dollar a barrel, whatever removed them from the trade list of products probably caused little economic loss.

By and large, Minnesota towns came into being from two major causes. Either they were fortuitously located for water transportation and power, as was the case with Stillwater and Minneapolis, or because of railroad advantages, especially at junction points of railroads. When both water and land transportation favored a community, as was the case with both Duluth and St. Paul, they were quite sure to grow because of the commerce which came to them.

When the railway lines were laid out, it was customary for something in the way of a railroad station to be erected about every seven miles. At this station there would be side tracks built to handle freight which might come in the form of livestock, grain or timber. Then a few stores would spring up—something in the way of a hostelry, with perhaps the addition of a land office, a barber shop, a saloon, a furniture and undertaking establishment and even a printing office.

At about every thirty or forty miles there would be a county seat town. Some quality of location or capacity for leadership on the part of its citizens would make this community a center of trade and professional services much larger than the smaller communities on each side of it.

It was not accidental that towns grew up during the later years of the nineteenth century at the distances noted. It took about an hour of travel by

Shopping area in Minneapolis

horse-drawn rig to get from farm to the smaller villages. That was about the time that a farmer would wish to spend to pull in a load of wheat or cordwood or go to buy flour, sugar, and salt. If he had to see a doctor, go to court, or buy an expensive machine or a suit of clothes, he would be willing to spend a whole day going back and forth to the county seat town.

Minnesota's trade and commerce map was changed, as it was elsewhere, with the coming of the automobile, the truck, and the hard-surfaced highway. Now the farmer could get to the county seat-sized community as quickly and more easily than he previously traveled to the neighboring small village. This has tended to reduce the trade of the smaller communities, many of which have become ghost towns, and increased the growth of the larger communities.

While the villages and smaller cities of Minnesota have been experiencing these many changes,

so briefly summarized above, the larger metropolitan centers have gone through corresponding periods. The facilities they afforded for the marketing of large shipments of farm produce, their wholesale establishments, the varied professional services afforded, and such trade as came from hospitals, conventions, and big department stores, caused them to grow more rapidly during the past hundred years than did the smaller municipalities of the state.

Recent years have seen a new trend develop, which again is associated with the automobile. The suburbs have offered the type of healthful recreation, the space for gracious living which many city dwellers craved. Uncounted thousands have left city homes and apartments and secured more in the way of living space in adjoining suburbs. This has resulted, not in reduced population, but a decline in the rate of growth and a sensational increase in the size of the communities which are ten and

277

twenty miles from the city post office. There would appear to be no reason to expect a reversal of this trend in the near future.

Not only the buildings and the communities in which trade has taken place has gone through an evolutionary process; equally marked has been the volume of trade. Due in part to inflation, this increase in dollar volume has been most evident in recent years. In 1929 the state's wholesale sales were less than two billion. In 1949, twenty years later, they were five billion, while present estimates place them above seven billion. During the same period, retail sales have risen form one billion to three billion to nearly six billion. It will be noted that at all times the wholesale sales far exceed the retail sales. This is due to the fact that our three major cities house wholesale operations extending far outside the borders of the state.

These commercial operations are as important to the people of today as the trading post was to the trapper and early settler of a century ago. They are expressed through some 6,000 wholesale establishments, 40,000 retail stores, and furnish employment to hundreds of thousands of our people.

Shopping area in early Minneapolis

St. Paul, Minnesota, skyline

TRANSPORTATION

What a wonderful panorama is provided by the shifting scenes in the development and expansion of transportation in Minnesota. No other area of interest on the pages of history possesses more in the way of varied adaptation to changing situations or impact upon the life of those affected.

It all began with the birch bark canoe. How interesting it is to note that canoes are still popular and that many more of them are made each year in the present than were made a century ago. They are now made out of plastics and aluminum, however, rather than of birch bark.

Water transportation has always been natural with us because of the abundance of water. A century ago and before, when there were few if any horses, few if any roads, and of course, no machines, the canoe which could be portaged from one body to another was the only known answer to the problem of getting from one point to another.

The canoe has, to a large extent at least, ceased to be a "beast of burden" and become a pleasure boat. The waters of Minnesota are, however, still vital to us for transportation purposes because upon them floats much of our freight.

When the early river boats brought people and livestock and finished foods to our pioneer villages and took back grain and furs and cranberries, they served a very useful function for the period from 1820 to 1870. For that half century, in fact, they were about the most important means of transportation we possessed. They stimulated a lot of boys along the Mississippi, the Minnesota, and even the Red River, to dream of piloting such craft even as did Mark Twain. Their number and movements were considerable, too, as many as a thousand a year docking at the wharves in St. Paul.

Of course, the railways changed all that and after 1870, when Chicago was reached by the locomotive, river traffic fell off to a mere dribble. But it was not lost forever.

In the '30s the Federal Government established a series of dams all up the Mississippi to supply a minimum of nine-foot depth from St. Louis to St. Paul. As a consequence, river traffic again began to flow. The boats were far different from the bulging stern-wheelers of an earlier day. Now they were towboats being pushed along by a relatively small tug. The freight they move now is again considerable in quantity, something like four million tons a year. The up-bound traffic, which is much the larger, is made up mostly of petroleum and coal. The down-bound traffic, if any, is usually grain. This traffic on the river is slowly gaining in amount, and Minneapolis, through improvements made at St. Anthony Falls, hopes soon to be the head of navigation, adding substantially to that volume.

The really vital and important portion of transportation using water is, however, that part which stems from the Great Lakes. It was from this point of origin which brought Du Luth and other explorers to us. It is the Great Lakes which move gigantic quantities of Minnesota earth each year from our Lake Superior harbors.

The discovery of immense quantities of high-grade iron ore on the Mesabi was closely associated with the building of docks, locks, and connecting channels on the Great Lakes, like those at Sault Ste. Marie. As the hungry maws of the steel mills reached out to swallow the ore brought to them, the shipping industry of the area employed all the science and skill at its command to reduce the cost of such shipping and improve speed and efficient handling. There is quite a story in the change from sails to whaleback vessels to the giant lake freighters of today. There is not time in which to tell it.

What should be known to all is that the engineers in their various branches have been able to devise loading and unloading mechanism and vessels of carrying capacity which are so designed and operated that they can make a round trip between Duluth-Superior or Two Harbors to lower Lake ports in a very few days. Even more marvelous, they can deliver a ton of iron ore or a ton of coal, after carrying it nearly 1,000 miles, at much less cost than a householder can have a ton of black dirt brought a few blocks from a pit to his garden.

The story and picture of water transportation is by no means all told. The most astonishing scene on the panorama is now being painted, that of so deepening the upper channels of the St. Lawrence River and the connecting channels of the Great Lakes that deep draft ocean vessels, not the largest,

Mississippi River barge

but of really substantial size, will in a few years be docking at Minnesota harbors.

Here is truly a dream come true. It was first dreamt by the early explorers. One generation after another caught the vision and kept it alive. North America was, they felt, the most fortunate of all the continents because it is the only one which possessed a natural seaway, so easily developed, from ocean to mid-continent.

That the dream is so soon to be a reality is due to many factors and many men. Of the men, no one has done more or devoted more years of his life to the project than has Julius Barnes of Duluth, the grand old man of the St. Lawrence Seaway. There are others also deserving of note such as Lewis Castle, also of Duluth, who has been chosen to serve as administrator of the project, and Congressman John Blatnik of the Eighth District, who has so effectively guided the required legislation in congressional hearings.

Transportation over land has also had its dramatic phases, its past, its present, and its future.

One of the more frequently presented pictures of early Minnesota is that of the Red River Trail oxcarts. These were the crudely constructed two-wheel vehicles used by those living far in the northwest to bring their furs and other products to St. Paul and St. Anthony. There they would barter that which they brought for the bacon, salt, tea, traps, and the like which they needed back in the hinterland. Sometimes these oxcarts came in long caravans of eighty or ninety units. Always their coming was known, for the shrieking of their ungreased hubs made their movement more noisy than that of a modern twenty-ton truck.

Like the Mississippi River steamboat, they gave way to the railroad in the late '60s and early '70s. Dependent as we are on the railways today, it is impossible for us to imagine what a difference the "iron horse" made in the life of the pioneer.

280

Without the railway somewhere near his farm or shop, everything he bought was either impossible to buy or very expensive. Everything he had to sell was either unsalable or had to be sold so cheaply as to provide little opportunity for profit.

Because they were so essential, and because the rates they could charge for their services made railroad construction profitable, their miles increased in number rapidly after 1862 when the William Crooks first moved by rail between St. Paul and Minneapolis. That first Minnesota locomotive, incidentally, stands all shiny and bright in the Union Station in St. Paul and is quite capable of making its memorable first trip all over again any number of times.

Bringing a railroad into a town in 1870 to 1890, the period when most of the 9,000 miles of rails were laid in the state, was like wafting a magic wand over the village. Prince Charming, in the guise of business growth, came to life and married Cinderella, who was the sleeping princess of social life and recreation. It was not in the least unusual for villages to double or triple in size in a year. Baseball games could be played with rival villages as much as forty miles away. Fruit could be brought from afar and grace the table of ordinary citizens. Mail came every day and the accompanying telegraph lines made possible a feeling of being part of a fast-moving world.

One feature of life associated with early railway operations is difficult to explain to those of the present generation. It was the appeal of the passenger train as a source of community interest. If there were 1,000 people living in town, as many as 100 or 200 might, on an ordinary weekday, wander down to the depot at 4:14 p.m. or whatever time the daily passenger train was due.

Why not? Perhaps there would be an Uncle Tom troupe getting off or a fellow citizen who had traveled all the way to the World Fair in Chicago, or a bridal couple might be getting on for their honeymoon, all splattered with rice, or a young fellow so ambitious he was going to an academy a hundred miles or more away and planning to come back a lawyer some day. Events and personages just as exciting may take place today. They don't take place in one point as they did at the village before the coming of the automobile.

Who was responsible for all these changes? No one man, to be sure, and of the many who had

Railroad pioneers

Early steam locomotive

a part, most lived in other states. Minnesota was but a small fraction of the railroad enterprise as a whole. There were, for example, names like Jay Gould and Henry Villard associated with the northern Pacific but they never became popular because they were not one of us. One who was very much one of us, one of the big names for all time in Minnesota history, was that of Jim Hill.

Hill came to Minnesota from eastern Canada in 1856. He did not intend to stay here but he missed the last oxcart caravan to what is now Winnipeg and being the kind of young fellow he was, it was not long before he was immersed in river traffic. That led to an interest in the extension of traffic north and west beyond the river terminus of St. Paul. It became an obsession with him. There had to be a railroad! Eventually it must reach to the Pacific. He, Jim Hill, was going to build that railroad. And he did.

The road he built went through various names; he was often threatened with complete failure; he borrowed and invested with apparent reckless energy, but he built his railroad—the Great Northern. And in so building it, he did more than make a fortune for himself and his associates. He made and earned the title of Empire Builder. Others who followed would probably have built that railroad and that empire to the north and west if Jim Hill had not. Something very big and vital in our land would have been missing though, had there been no Jim Hill. There was a man!

Even before Jim Hill died and railroads became commonplace in the land, the internal combustion engine applied to trucks and passenger-carrying automobiles began to make itself felt in the economic and social fabric of the commonwealth. Here, too, it is possible to personify progress through its association with an individual.

Charles Babcock is a name as significant in Minnesota in association with motor cars as Jim Hill in association with locomotives. Babcock was a small town general store operator at Elk River. His home and store were on the edge of the highway carrying traffic north and west of the Twin

Modern railroad

Cities. He watched that traffic move over the rutty road early provided and conceived the idea, quite revolutionary at the time, of having the owners of cars using the highways pay for their improvements. He conceived of a great state highway system, even hard surfaced, which auto licenses and gasoline taxes would finance. First, he sold that idea to Governor Christenson, who made him highway commissioner, and then he sold it to the people of the state. Babcock was not an engineer, but he gave Minnesota leadership in highway construction because he possessed imagination and public leadership, which made him one to remember.

Putting wheels on a gasoline-driven motor has changed Minnesota life in many ways. Most pronounced of its effects may·be that of making us more alike. Travel now being easy, the ordinary Minnesotan sees much of the world and becomes very familiar with those parts of it which are not many miles away.

So the farmer's son and daughter attend the same school, incline to wear the same kind of clothes, attend the same social affairs as does the son and daughter of the city executive. Much the same thing is happening to the parents. Present-

day youth reading Whittier's "Maud Muller" or "Snowbound" do not know what it is all about. Neither are grandfather's stories relating to the difficulties of getting to a doctor or the excursion he took as a child to visit the state fair. The automobile has made what once was so very difficult seem quite matter of course.

The business associated with automobiles has as completely overshadowed that previously associated with the horse as the bus station overshadows the former livery stable. At least one out of ten of us has a job directly connected with the automobile. The Minnesota business enterprise which came into largest national significance in association with the automobile was the Greyhound Corporation. That company had its origin in Hibbing back in 1914 when Carl Wickman and Andrew Anderson started jitney bus operations. There is only one Greyhound bus system. That it was able to grow as it did, absorbing one competitor after another, creating a whole new pattern of moving people from place to place, is a tribute to these Hibbing pioneers and their associates. They recently held a board of directors anniversary business meeting in that Iron Range city. Some of the origi-

283

nal incorporators were present. They noticed quite a change in Hibbing. The bus system they devised has made a comparable change in the face of America.

The automobile in its various applications has made a mighty mark on the picture of Minnesota life. Its benefits in bringing color and variety and a feeling of freedom of movement are impossible to measure. Like every good gift, it carries a price tag. Sometimes when noting the accident reports, its seems quite high.

The scene shifts again in this panoramic presentation of Minnesota life. This time it is to the most dramatic spectacle relating to aerial transportation, the arrival in Paris of the boy from Little Falls, Minnesota, Charles A. Lindbergh.

Charles came from a typical Minnesota background. His grandfather was a Swedish emigrant who homesteaded near Melrose. His father became a successful attorney and farmer. Charles became an airplane fan at an early age and as all the world knows, has made his name synonomous with air flight.

Commercial aviation had hardly begun when Lindbergh made his famous solo flight to Paris. Subsequent years have recorded ever-increasing utilization of airways for transportation.

The first of the commercial airlines to become established in the area and one of the first in the nation was the Northwest, which came to St. Paul in 1927, where it has been growing ever since. A half dozen competitors now seek some portion of the rapidly expanding air traffic while private planes, varying in size from single motored two-passenger hedge hoppers to a plush and elaborate executive plane, claim increasing portions of the sky. Over a hundred landing trips and airports of varying acreage make flying comparatively safe as a means of transport and new uses constantly are being found for flying service gives promise of ever greater expansion of this most recent means of transport.

Modern city transportation

284

Stratocruiser at Wold Chamberlain field

Beginning of Northwest Airlines

Northwest airplane over Waikiki

RECREATION

Recreation is usually considered to be a social attribute of man. It is the means he employs to make his life more wholesome and enjoyable. Some forms of simple recreation, such as lying in a hammock on a summer day, are largely limited to the purely social.

Usually, however, the recreation in which people participate has an economic aspect as well. When a fellow goes fishing, there is more involved than baiting a hook and dropping it in the water. There is a license to buy, fishing tackle to accumulate, a trip of some distance to take, a boat to rent, and perhaps other expenses such as cottage rental, guide services, special clothes, and a score of additional costs.

It is the economic aspects of recreation, the business of getting and giving a good time, which constitutes the next turn of the panoramic screen. There appears to be literally hundreds of ways which have been selected by some of our citizens at all periods in our history which have supplied recreation for them. As a result, the screen is not nearly large enough to hold all of the scenes of the past which would be worth recording. Some which will be briefly noted are common for all times, others are dated present or past.

Because of the difficulties of travel and the lack of communication facilities which we of this day take for granted, pioneer homes and communities were much more self-sufficient, or at least self-dependent, for their recreation than we of today. Also, they had much less money with which to purchase pleasure and change. The community debating society, the spelling party or contest, the church social, skating parties, and the town hall dance were all examples of what was done when groups got together, particularly on a winter's evening. There was a craving for culture which was somewhat satisfied with lyceums, which brought speakers, ministers, authors and musicians from distant cities to elevate the moral tone and educational level. Also, a traveling troupe playing "Uncle Tom's Cabin" or "Ten Nights in a Barroom" could be expected at least once a year. There was some doubt in the minds of the elders as to whether even these performances were suitable to youth, but the small fry were attracted to them almost as much as to the weary little circus performances which were frequently presented during summer months. Mostly it was a matter of staying at home, for then, quite literally, there was no place to go.

To youth of today this may sound quite dreary. It did not seem so to those who lived in this earlier period. One reason was that there was no invidious comparison with others more fortunate. All rural and village life was much the same. Also, because there were books and magazines to read, not so many as now, but those which were in circulation were kept in motion. Periodicals such as "Boys Life" and "The Youths Companion," now only historical terms, were read from cover to cover by every member of the family, passed from home to home until worn away by handling. They brought a degree of vicarious travel and experience which did much to eliminate the barriers of space, as well, perhaps, as stimulating ambitions to see the world, which many of them satisfied in later life.

Women certainly lived a much more sheltered life than they do today. They were presumed to be ladies, and most of them were, with all the connotations which went with that term. The boys and men were not so inhibited. The saloon was the men's club, and while not all the men congregated in them, most of them did. It is questionable if there was more drunkenness in the latter part of the nineteenth century than there is now, but what there was became known to all. The village "drunk" furnished something in the way of entertainment to at least the masculine element of youth, but also an awful example frequently quoted by mother and the Sunday School teacher.

Life in the cities had much more in the way of glamour and appeal. Here the audiences assembled in large theatres could, and did, see plays and actors of high caliber and with considerable frequency. Professional sports, cotillions, balls, and giant political rallies were some of the group activities which attracted not only the city folk, but also drew the more financially competent and interested leaders from out in the more rural areas.

Always there was the great out-of-doors; at least for the men and boys. They were pioneers, or the sons of pioneers. They shunned being in any

Midway—
State Fair, 1904

Lake Minnetonka in 1912

287

Thrill of a lifetime

Duck hunting in Minnesota slough

type or degree of confinement. All about them was the expanse of land and water offering recreation in multiple form.

It is probable that the tales which have come down through the years, of lakes so full of hungry fish that catching them was no sport, are stories which contain more fiction than fact. So, too, of the other forms of wildlife, be it game birds or deer reputed to have blackened the sky and crowded the forest. Generally speaking, wildlife probably was more plentiful, with the exception of the rabbit, which seems like the robin, to thrive in contact with man. Certainly there was much less competition in the killing of game.

The pictures in our historical societies files showing the proud hunters or fishemen standing beside the gigantic display of their kill or catch are factual. Like the lumberjack of the same day and age, the sportsmen felt there was a lot of game and he took pride in being able to count a larger bag than any of his fellows. He may have had something to do with the reduction of wildlife we know today, but the probabilities are that it was the changes in land culture affecting the prairie chicken and alteration of lake waters affecting the fish life in them which do more to explaining the decreases noted than grandfather's gun and rod. Certainly grandfather had a lot of fun with his gun and rod. His grandchildren looking back at 1878 and 1908 from the perspective of 1959 need not feel sorry for him. He lived a pretty good life withal, and one in no sense lacking in recreation, even though most of that recreation was different from our own. He did not take much of it sitting down.

The automobile, radio and television, illustrated magazines, the frequency of family movements from community to community are only some of the factors of change which have altered the rather simple recreational pattern of the past. The giant crowds which attend a University of Minnesota football game have little relation to the sports assembly of an earlier day. That crowd will contain representations from every community in the state. There probably are as many who now fly from Minnesota in their private planes to watch a world series ball game as came from out the Twin Cities to watch a university football game in 1900. In no human activity has change been more fully expressed than in the way our people go about having a good time in comparison with the manner of their forefathers.

Distance has been largely eliminated, or at least reduced, by the powered wheels which carry our bodies, or the instruments of communication, such as television, which carry our imagination and senses. As we tend to participate in large, rather than small groups, so too, we tend to become spectators rather than taking part in the recreational activity which interests us. The brightly lighted village ball field may draw the crowd, but it doesn't afford much physical exercise to most of those who go there.

One thing we have in common with our forebears. That is the out-of-doors. That it still possesses its appeal is testified by the youth who jam the swimming beaches and take Red Cross instruction, by the increasing number of oft-played golf courses which are becoming an accepted part of community life, and, perhaps most important, by the enjoyment of our lakes.

No spectacle of today would more amaze those of some such date as 1898 than to see the mass movement from out of our cities on·a summer Friday evening. More people than lived in the Twin Cities sixty years ago are darting with impatient speed toward a lake home or rented summer cottage. It is not fishing or golf or painting a picture or writing a book which pulls them, although all of these activities and scores of others are engaged in. It is cool spring-fed waters, the shade of green trees on uncut grass, the proximity with nature rather than with man. They find all this and they enjoy it so fully that they spend more dollars in their summer vacation fun than their grandparents did all year for all purposes.

It is worthy of note that each winter brings a clearer recognition that the first ice and snow need not bring the enjoyment of the out-of-doors to an end. The heated body of the automobile, the warm clothes which provide protection from winter chill, the increased provision for assured enjoyment of good roads, smooth skating rinks, and safe ski slides all make for winter as a time when Minne-

The one that didn't get away

Minneapolis Aquatennial parade

sota offers most, rather than least, in the way of healthful recreation.

All of this is important to the Minnesota businessman. He is finding that, contrary to national trends, his business volume goes up when folks go on vacation. Some of Minnesota's vacation centers have bank-clearings nearly twice as high when their recreation-seeking guests are with them than when they are not. The state as a whole profits largely, much more largely than is commonly appreciated, for a million out-of-state people now come to us each year, bringing and leaving with us an average of at least $300 apiece as payment for the fun they have. More and more expensive and substantial summer homes are being erected by those who travel 500 to 1,000 miles or more to have, on a Minnesota lake, their home away from home.

The future of Minnesota in the recreational field is even more promising than the present is cause for gratification. The reasons for such optimism are not alone the 10,000 lakes, the increased ease of travel, the geographical location in mid-continent, and the ever-rising tide of national wealth and hours of leisure. Largest asset of all, perhaps, is the availability of space. Many of the nation's pleasure seekers prefer the racetrack crowds, the noisy pits of pleasure of crowded vacation areas, and the excitement of crowds. An inevitably growing proportion of those who live in our nation seek the peace, quiet, and space which a large portion of Minnesota supplies in such abundance.

Skiing through the forest in deep powder

Making the portage around Basswood Falls

CONCLUSION

In the foregoing pages a few scattered pages of Minnesota business development and the social changes associated with them have been presented. They are as inadequate for the purposes of the chapter as a fading maple leaf picked from the floor of the forest is inadequate to present the color and life of all the trees which abound in their fall glory. They must suffice.

It is hoped that they will possess one value, that of informing those who read and believe that the continuously turning, changing panorama of Minnesota history can know that what has gone before has been, on the whole, good for those who come after. The men and women who came to Minnesota were, in the main, good men and women. They wanted to make more money and acquire a better income for themselves and their families than they felt they could elsewhere or in the land of their origin. In that, they in a large part succeeded.

The reasons for their success were many; one being that they possessed and bequeathed as a heritage to those who followed, those qualities of character, those attributes of health, that faith in the future which made them a truly chosen people.

Another reason for their success was that they here found a good land. It was a land rich in fertility, productive of food, of minerals, of wood fiber. It was also rich in beauty, a quality they themselves appreciated and one which becomes more valuable both commercially and esthetically to those of us who follow them, each passing year.

As has been told in other chapters, the real first settlers of Minnesota—the Sioux and the Chippewa—also appreciated this land of sky blue waters, of virgin forest, of abundant wildlife, and of changing seasons. In contemplating our part in the shaping of the next one hundred years and the painting of the panorama which will record them, the admonition of the Indian chief should be borne ever in mind.

He said, "I conceive that the land belongs to a vast family of which many are dead, a few are living, and countless numbers are still unborn."

The population of Minnesota will soon reach a total of 4,000,000. They will be better fed, better clothed, better housed than the millions who preceded them. That such is true, that the wealth and prosperity of our people continues and increases, is due to a very considerable degree to the fact that those who preceded us willed that it be so. We can all profit by their example.

Gooseberry Falls

fun at Minnesota resort

CHAPTER TEN

Communications

Part 1 Smoke Signals to Telephone

By WILLOUGHBY M. BABCOCK

Tens of thousands of years ago, when primitive men were just beginning to emerge from the brute stage of existence, they learned to communicate with each other, first by signs, then by grunts, and then, as their brain powers gradually developed, by spoken words. Such contacts at first were with members of their own family group, for all others were enemies, in the fierce struggles for the food and shelter necessary for survival. Gradually the family groups expanded into kinship and religious clans, working together for their common protection and welfare. Further expansion of such groups produced tribes, speaking the same basic language, although with local variations, and often spread out over a great expanse of territory. Members of the Algonquian linguistic group, for instance, to which the Minnesota Ojibwa or Chippewa belong, were found all the way from the Atlantic seaboard to western Canada and the Rocky Mountains, and people of Siouan linguistic stock, including the Minnesota Dakota, were scattered over almost as much territory. There was much visiting back and forth, and peoples of the same basic stocks could communicate through the same fundamental language, or at least by signs.

Even today the tradition of sign talking is carried on by the men of the army, the navy, and the Boy Scouts, in the arm and flag signals regularly used for visual communication over considerable distances. A variation of this type of signalling is found in the chain of so-called "telegraphs" or semaphore towers used extensively in Europe and America during the Eighteenth and Nineteenth centuries. By using adjustable arms that spelled out letters and codes, messages could be sent from place to place over long distances. Such signal stations, for example, placed at strategic points along the Atlantic and Pacific seacoasts, signalled the arrival of vessels from overseas.

With the discovery of fire, far back in the history of man's development, it was learned that the glow of light from a fire, or a column of smoke arising therefrom could be seen for long distances, and the practice of communication by light and smoke signals came into being. As far back as early Grecian days, huge bonfires, lighted on mountain tops gave warning of attack from enemies, and conveyed news of victories. Throughout the Middle Ages such signalling was common. Sunlight, reflected from a polished steel shield, or from a mirror, could be used over even longer distances to convey messages from place to place. Today flashing lighthouses and fixed buoys warn vessels at sea and on rivers of dangerous reefs and sandbars, land beacons guide airplanes on their courses, and ships communicate with each other by means of lamps with movable shutters.

In America the Indians early learned that messages could be sent in a sort of pre-arranged code by alternately blocking off and releasing bursts from the heavy smoke of a campfire through the use of skins or blankets. Such signals were very useful in rough country where direct light signalling was not possible. Many a body of troops on the frontiers during the Indian wars was kept on the alert by puffs of smoke signals sent up around them by unseen but watchful enemy Indian scouts. American frontiersmen, too, soon learned—often at the cost of their lives and scalps—that smoky campfires could reveal their positions to hostile savages, and they therefore built their cooking fire of dry non-smoke producing wood in sheltered places.

Today, in the northern forests of Minnesota, fire watchers and forest rangers, stationed on high lookout towers, keep constant vigil during the dry seasons for the telltale wisp of smoke which tells of an embryo forest fire. In the old river steamboat days, too, the black columns of smoke, pouring out from the stacks of an approaching boat, still out of sight around a bend, spelled creature comforts and contact with the outside world to many a hungry and depressed Minnesota pioneer whose town had been isolated from the outside for four or five months by ice and snow.

James M. Goodhue, in the first issue of Minnesota's first newspaper, the *Minnesota Pioneer* of April 28, 1849, reports the joy of the citizens of St. Paul over the arrival of the first steamboat of that year. On the night of April 9, 1849, during a heavy thunderstorm, "in a momentary lull of the wind, the silence was broken by the never-to-be-mistaken groan of a steam engine. In another moment the shrill whistle of a steamboat thrilled through the air, cutting through and dividing as it

were, the heavy booming of heaven's artillery. Another moment and a bright flash of lightning revealed the welcome shape of a steamboat just rounding the bluff, less than a mile below St. Paul.

"In an instant, the welcome news flashed like electricity throughout the town. All were on the *qui vive* and regardless of the pelting rain, the raging wind, and the pealing thunder, almost the entire male population rushed to the landing—hundreds clustered on the shore unmindful of the storm, as the fine steamboat, *Dr. Franklin No. 2*, dashed gallantly up to the landing.

"Before she was made fast to the moorings, she was boarded by the excited throng—without waiting for the shore planks to be laid, numbers sprang on her boiler deck." The captain and the clerk were bombarded with demands for news and newspapers about persons and events in the outside world. "During five months," continued the article, "the communications between this part of the country and our brethren in the United States has been difficult and infrequent. A mail now and then from Prairie du Chien, brought up on the ice in 'train' drawn sometimes by horses and sometimes by dogs, containing news so old that the good people in the country below had forgotten all about it," had been all. News indeed there was by that boat, for Minnesota had become a Territory, but word of the passage of the act on March 3, 1849, had not reached her citizens until that stormy April night five weeks later!

And it was the Mississippi River, of course, that had provided the route by which the news of territoriality had come, for in those days the rivers and lakes furnished the most practicable routes of communication. A glance at a map of Minnesota will show how readily practically all parts of that area can be reached by water. Successive glaciations and recessions of the icecaps over a period of hundreds of thousands of years during the Ice Age, as related earlier in this book, had carved out the great river valleys of the Red, the Minnesota, the Mississippi, the St. Croix, and the Lake of the Woods—Rainy River—Pigeon River systems, and had left thousands of pocket lakes and lesser streams draining into these major river systems. Primitive men, the remote ancestors of the American Indians, in their

Dog team from Fort Gary at St. Paul, 1859

Early Minnesota stagecoach

Lake voyageurs

search for food, learned to make use of these water highways, and worked out well-defined routes from place to place. "Minnesota Man," actually a woman, as told in Chapter Two, is believed to have been drowned in one of these post glacial lakes, perhaps while fishing, some thousands of years ago. "Brown's Valley Man," too, found a resting place on an island or ridge formed by the waters pouring down the Red River—Bois des Sioux Valley into the Minnesota River from Glacial Lake Agassiz.

Our Minnesota Indians of the proto-historic and historic periods, because of the ease of communication by water, and the abundance of fish, turtles, and water fowl for food, were basically canoe Indians, and they established their settlements along the lakes and connecting streams. The vast water highway of the St. Lawrence and the Great Lakes brought the early French explorer-traders to the Minnesota country in their search for the elusive route to the Western Sea, and introduced them to the tremendous opportunities for wealth from the furs and pelts to be secured in the region. Utilizing the knowledge, gleaned from the Indians,

of the possibilities of the bark canoe, and the routes of water travel, these whites developed a most lucrative traffic in furs, and set up their trading posts at strategic points along the water highways.

As this commerce developed, powerful companies, first French, then British-Canadian, and finally American emerged, such as the Hudson's Bay Company, the North West Company, and the American Fur Company. Whole brigades of canoes, heavily laden with furs and trade goods, moved back and forth along the rivers and lakes. As many as a thousand men assembled annually for the great summer rendezvous at Grand Portage on Lake Superior near the mouth of the Pigeon River in the seventeen nineties. Light express canoes sped from one trading post to another, bearing the packets of company mail, and important personages on official business.

Towards the close of the Eighteenth Century, keelboats, capable of carrying many tons of cargo began to appear on the upper Mississippi and the Minnesota rivers. These bargelike boats were laboriously poled and dragged upstream by sheer man-

Keel boat

Grand portage on Lake Superior

power. Though slow and clumsy, their carrying capacity was far greater than that of the birchbark trading canoes.

As the tide of settlement moved steadily westward with the emergence of the new United States at the close of the American Revolution, the volume of traffic up and down the Mississippi to and from New Orleans became increasingly heavy. The Louisiana Purchase of 1803 added the area west of the Mississippi as far as the Rocky Mountains to the new nation, and the United States began to plan for military posts on the upper river. John Jacob Astor's American Fur Company began to move into the upper Mississippi country in opposition to the British-Canadian companies, and it

adopted the Green Bay-Fox-Wisconsin river route as a major supply line.

The War of 1812, coupled with the law of 1816 prohibiting non-American citizens from engaging in the American fur trade, virtually eliminated the foreign companies from the trade south of the international boundary; and Astor's company inherited most of the business, together with the trading locations, and many of the former opposition traders. The same war emphasized the necessity for American military control of the upper Mississippi and Minnesota regions, with their warlike Sioux and Chippewa, who had almost uniformly supported the British in that struggle. Lieutenant Zebulon Pike's tiny expedition to the Minnesota country in the fall and winter of 1805-6 had begun the military movement, by proclaiming American authority over the Northwest, and by selecting a site for a military post at the mouth of the Minnesota River, but nothing further was accomplished until after the close of the war.

Following approval of the Minnesota River fort site by Major Stephen H. Long of the U.S. Topographical Engineers, who had made an unusually rapid trip in a six-oared boat from Prairie du Chien in 1817, Lieutenant Colonel Henry Leavenworth in the summer of 1819 under War Department orders, moved troops of the Fifth Infantry by keelboat to the mouth of the Minnesota and began the work of establishing the post. From 1825 on, the fort was named Fort Snelling. Coincident with the building of the fort came the creation of an Indian agency, designated as the St. Peters Agency, for the control of the Minnesota Indians, and the enforcement of the laws governing the contacts of whites and Indians, with particular reference to the fur trade.

By the early twenties the fur trading post at Mendota on the south bank of the Minnesota River across from Fort Snelling had become a key point of the American Fur Company for the rich trade of southern and western Minnesota. Soldiers, fur traders, and the Indian agency required ever-increasing shipments of trade goods, furs, and military supplies of all sorts, and the keelboat and canoe traffic to and from the mouth of the Minnesota River grew by leaps and bounds. Troops must be moved up and down the Mississippi between St. Louis, Prairie du Chien, and Fort Snelling, and official orders and mail must get through between Washington and its military and civil officials.

Mail communication of a sort was maintained with the outside world by the use of the keelboats of the traders and the supply boats of the military via Prairie du Chien, the nearest point of settlement some two hundred miles to the south. Such service, however, was irregular and uncertain at best, for often the eastern mails had not reached the Prairie in time to be sent off by these boats, or the postmaster at that point failed to forward the packets. The journals kept by Major Lawrence Taliaferro, the Indian agent near Fort Snelling,

are full of complaints over his failure to receive his mail and instructions. When he wrote to Washington for directions as to how to handle an important matter of Indian relations, it was something like four to six months before he could receive a reply, and the answer was frequently unsatisfactory.

Such boat service, too, could only be carried on during the months from April to November when the Mississippi was free from ice. During the winter months, attempts were made to maintain a monthly mail service with Prairie du Chien by dispatching soldier carriers or mixed bloods under contract up and down the river on the ice. Snowstorms and airholes made such travel hazardous. It was particularly bad during the freezing and thawing periods of early and late winter, when the ice was either too slightly frozen or too water-soaked to make travel feasible. On one occasion the downbound mail carrier was caught by the spring breakup of the river, and marooned on a small island, only to find that the upbound mailman had had to take refuge on the same island.

A change in methods of river transportation, however, was in the making. In 1815 Henry Shreve mounted a horizontal steam engine upon a modified version of the keelboat, propelling the boat by paddlewheels instead of by manpower, and the shallow draft Mississippi River steamboat came into being. His idea spread very rapidly and within a few years the river was alive with such vessels. Happy indeed was the day for the occupants of isolated, stonewalled Fort Snelling when they heard the whistle of the first steamboat to brave the unmarked channels of the Upper Mississippi. On May 10, 1823, the "Virginia" nosed into the landing below the fort, and thus established steamboat connections with the outside world. From that time onward, steamboats began to come to the mouth of the Minnesota River with increasing frequency, as cargoes of goods for the trading posts at Mendota and military supplies for Fort Snelling became available. There were occasional delegations of Indians to be taken to Washington to see the Great White Father, and bodies of troops to be moved from post to post, all of which meant revenues for the steamboat captains. Occasional travelers and

Fort Snelling

tourists, as well as military officials, began to make the trip, such as Giacomo Beltrami and Major Stephen H. Long; and they published descriptions of their journeys through the Minnesota Indian country.

Into the northern lake country of Minnesota came Governor Lewis Cass of Michigan Territory with his antiquarian companion, Henry R. Schoolcraft, on an inspection trip in 1820. The party had followed the fur trade canoe route up the Great Lakes to Fond du Lac, and thence via the St. Louis and Sandy Lake rivers to the lake soon named Cass Lake in the governor's honor. En route homeward the official party came down the Mississippi and found Colonel Leavenworth's troops already putting in crops at the new Minnesota River cantonment. Some ninety acres had been planted with Indian corn, potatoes, garden vegetables, and wheat. The account of this expedition was published by Schoolcraft in connection with the report of his later expedition which resulted in the discovery and naming of Itasca Lake as the source of the Mississippi River. The book, like many others of the period, served to disseminate information

about the Minnesota country. Today thousands of people annually visit Itasca State Park, step across the infant Mississippi, and hear the story of the discovery.

Meanwhile, far to the northwest, on the western bank of the Red River of the North, supposedly north of the international boundary, a Scottish nobleman, the Earl of Selkirk, had secured a huge grant of land from the Hudson's Bay Company in 1811, and had begun to send over settlers for his colony. Some of these people were Swiss, largely mechanics and tradesmen, ill-suited to a frontier farming life in a northern latitude, and there was little work for persons in such lines. Conflicts between the Hudson's Bay Company and the North West Company, both having major trading posts in the Pembina-Fort Garry region, too, spelled trouble for the arriving colonists. These factors, coupled with losses from floods and grasshoppers, led many of these settlers to desert the Red River settlement. Between 1821 and 1826 some hundreds of them drifted down to the Fort Snelling area in unique Red River carts, over the earliest of the Red River trails, along the Red River, the Bois des

Sioux, and Minnesota rivers, despite the menace of hostile Sioux Indians. One orphaned victim of such an attack lived at the fort for a time in the household of Colonel Snelling. While most of these refugees passed on down the Mississippi, some of them squatted on the Fort Snelling Reservation, and eventually were found among the earliest settlers of St. Paul.

The Pembina colony gradually overcame its major problems, however, and became a prosperous agricultural and hunting settlement, extending for some fifty miles along the lower Red River, on both sides of the international boundary. Its polyglot population included many mixed-blood hunters whose chief employment was the pursuit of the buffalo on the plains of the Dakotas. Buffalo robes, dried buffalo tongues, and pemmican (dried and pounded buffalo meat over which melted tallow had been poured) became important products for the fur trade. To get a share of this trade, the American Fur Company under Henry H. Sibley and Norman W. Kittson in 1843-'44 established a new trading post at Pembina on the American side of the line, and began to ship the fur products overland to the mouth of the Minnesota River in "trains" or convoys of the clumsy but sturdy two-wheeled wooden carts, each drawn by a single ox or Indian pony. Kittson succeeded in draining off considerable of the output from the Canadian side of the line, to the great annoyance of the Hudson's Bay Company. By the late 1850s hundreds of these carts were making the nine-hundred-mile round trip annually over three principal Red River trails, via the Bois des Sioux-Minnesota route, a second via the Sauk River Valley, and a third via the Crow Wing River. As evidence of the practicability of these routes, it may be noted that three major railroad lines and several trunk highways today follow, in part at least, the general lines of the old Red River trails. During the winter months swift dog teams brought occasional mails and fur trade correspondence down from Pembina to St. Paul.

With the growth of towns in the Mississippi—St. Croix River triangle following the Indian treaties of 1837, roads, often not much more than rude dirt trails, were opened up, and stages began to bump their way along them to link up the scattered communities with each other. The tiny "Pigseye" settlement of 1839-'41 on the west bank of the Mississippi near the head of major steamboat

Red River oxcarts in St. Paul, 1859

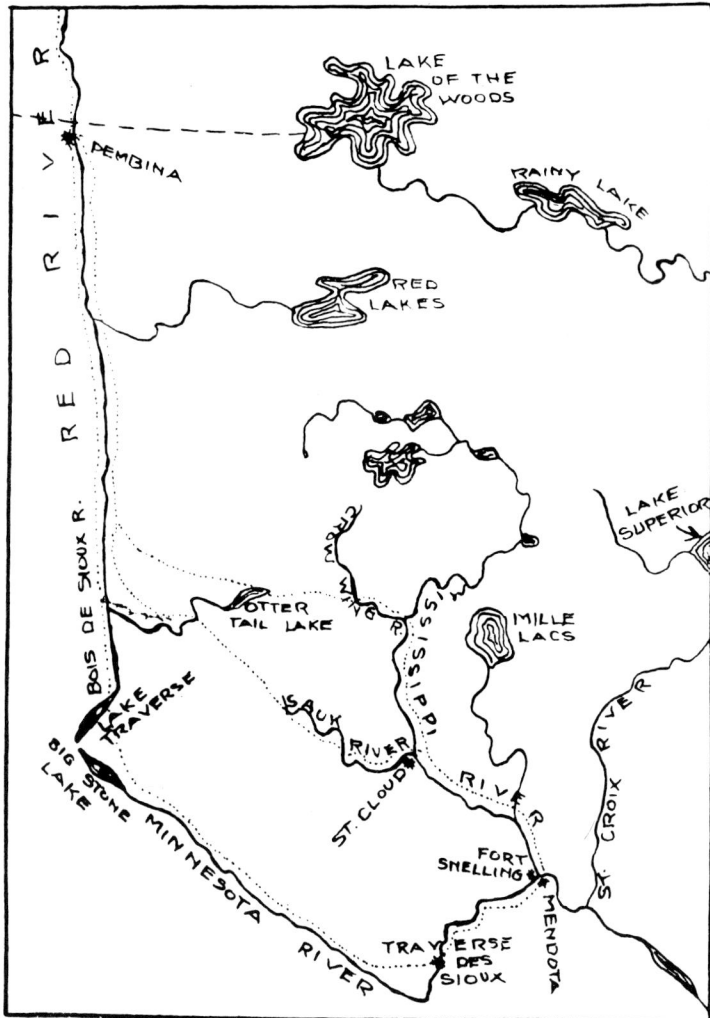

Red River trails

up the hills, and to put their shoulders to the wheels when the vehicles got stuck in the mud. Meals and sleeping accommodations were as good "as could be expected on a new line." By 1851 Burbank and Persons were advertising express messenger service for money and valuables to and from Galena, Illinois, with outside connections with the American Express Company.

Reference was made above to the more or less casual mail service between Minnesota and the outside world. A postoffice was established at Fort Snelling as early as 1827, but carrier service with down-river points left much to be desired. Postage rates, moreover, were high, the costs usually being paid by the sender, and depending upon the distance the letter had to travel. Twenty-five cents for a one-page letter going four hundred miles was normal. When St. Paul was established as a postoffice in 1846, with Henry Jackson, a storekeeper, as its first postmaster, a rude box with twelve cubbyholes was nailed together for service, and that original postbox is still preserved in the museum of the Minnesota Historical Society. As regular steamboat lines came into existence, the river boats contracted for the carrying of the mails during the

navigation, emerged as the village of St. Paul, a thriving commercial place, busily engaged as a major supply base and transshipping point for cargoes from the river steamboats to the oxcarts and freight wagons bound for the interior. The designation of St. Paul as the capital of Minnesota Territory by the act of March 3, 1849, brought federal officials to the community as well as a swarm of settlers, and government money for the construction of buildings, roads, salaries, etc. About the same time a regular line of steamboats began to ply the Upper Mississippi to connect St. Paul, Stillwater, and other river towns with Galena and St. Louis. A stage line went into operation from St. Paul down the east bank of the Mississippi to Prairie du Chien, but the four-horse teams found the going mighty heavy, and male passengers were expected to walk

St. Paul's first post office

months of navigation, and "mail packets," operating on regular schedules were favored by travelers. Stages carried the mails during the winter months on the river routes. Fogs, low water, wrecks, fires and accidents, however, hindered the steamboat service, and the mail stages encountered flooded streams, storms, and endless mud. On one occasion the bottom of a mail stage dropped out in the crossing of a stream, and all the mail sacks were lost. The driver narrowly escaped with his life.

With the steady expansion of settlement up the east bank of the Mississippi, and the growth of such busy lumbering and trading towns as St. Anthony, Sauk Rapids, Stillwater, and Taylor's Falls, roads began to be laid out in earnest. The Sauk River route of the Red River Trail by the middle fifties had become a major artery of overland commerce. The military exploring expedition of Major Samuel Woods and Captain John Pope in 1849, followed in 1853 by the great Isaac Stevens Pacific Railroad Survey, blocked out a practicable road to the Red River of the North which was but a variant of the older Red River Trail. A lumberman's wagon route to supply the camps along the upper St. Croix led up the western bank of that stream from Stillwater, and a county road linked that community with the capital. Military roads to connect St. Paul with Fort Ripley near the mouth of the Crow Wing

St. Paul, 1856

Stillwater, Minnesota

303

River steamboat

St. Paul levee, 1860's

River, and Dubuque to the south, came into existence in the early fifties. By 1851 there was regular light draft steamboat service on the upper Mississippi between St. Anthony and Sauk Rapids.

The rush to the gold fields of California, following the Sutter discovery of 1848-49, followed in 1858 by the opening of the Fraser River mines in British Columbia, aroused the people of St. Paul to the possibilities for a northern overland route to the Pacific via the Sauk River trail to the Red River and Pembina, and thence up the Saskatchewan Valley to the Rockies and the Kootenais Pass. Much of the northern part of this route had been used for years by the Hudson's Bay Company, and its trading posts would furnish convenient supply points for travelers. The opening of such a route, especially if steamboats could be successfully navigated on the Red and the Saskatchewan, would likewise divert the valuable commerce of the Northwest to St. Paul. In January, 1859, after a series of public meetings, the newly organized St. Paul Chamber of Commerce offered a bonus of $1,000

for the first steamboat on Red River. Anson Northup thereupon hauled the boilers and machinery of a small upper Mississippi boat across country from the Crow Wing River very early that spring, built a hull, and on May 28, 1859, successfully navigated his "Anson Northup" from the mouth of the Sheyenne River to Fort Garry.

A road of sorts, too, was cut through to the newly established Fort Abercrombie on the Red River, and on June 21, 1859, the first two stages of a projected thrice-weekly line left St. Cloud as part of a through service via the steamboat, to Fort Garry. About the same time a party of some twenty men under Colonel William H. Nobles, some of them headed for the Fraser River gold fields, traveled from St. Paul to St. Cloud, and thence over the new road and the Red River Trail to Pembina and the Saskatchewan country. The Hudson's Bay Company, appreciating the advantages of the St. Paul route over the old supply line via Hudson Bay, bought the steamboat and contracted for heavy freight shipments via St. Paul, the goods coming

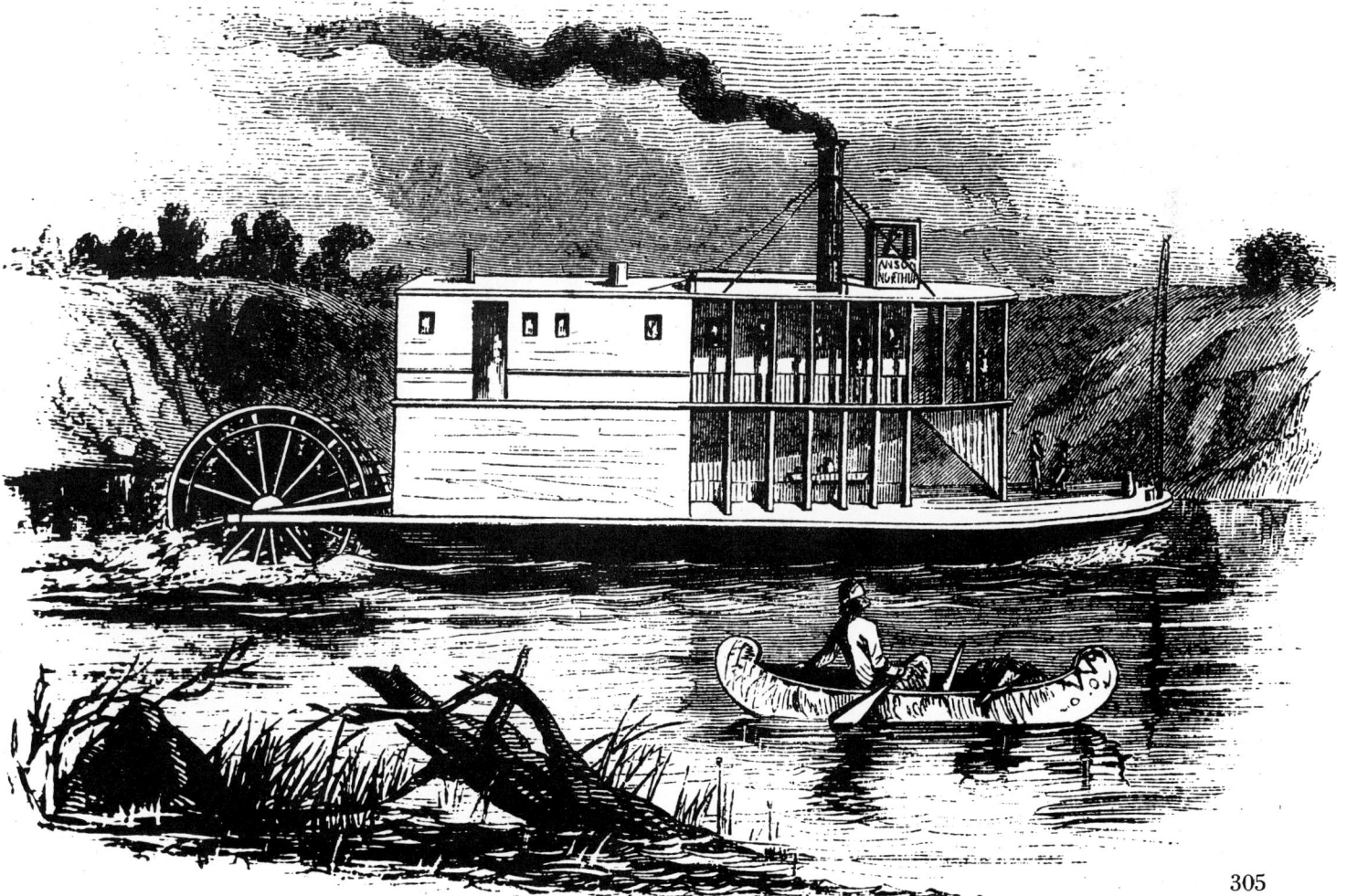

The "Anson Northup"

305

sealed in bond and therefore not having to pay American import duties. The Company, too, began to make substantial purchases of American goods for its Canadian posts.

With the ratification of the Sioux treaties made at Traverse des Sioux and Mendota in 1851 that opened up the Minnesota Valley and the southern part of Minnesota to settlement, people poured into the region by the thousands, and towns sprang up like magic. Fort Ridgely was built on the north bank of the Minnesota River in the extreme corner of Nicollet County in 1853, and work was begun upon a military road up that river valley to effect connections with army posts on the Missouri River. Light draft steamboats based on St. Paul began to operate on the Minnesota River as far as the mouth of the Redwood River to supply the newly established Indian agency there, as well as the mushroom river towns lower downstream. Territorial delegates to Congress pressed constantly for federal money for roads, better mail service, and improved communications generally. The territorial legislatures and county commissioners were bombarded with demands for public improvements. People began to talk of railroads, not only those linking up Minnesota with the rapidly expanding networks in southern Wisconsin and Illinois, but also on a local level between St. Paul and St. Anthony. The great Rock Island Railroad Excursion of 1854, celebrating the arrival of the railroad at the Mississippi, of course, stimulated the demands, but despite numerous legislative charters for Minnesota railroads on paper, no construction work was done for several years.

Meanwhile, Minnesota had acquired on a large scale, that great vehicle of publicity, the newspaper. No sooner had word of the passage of the Minnesota Territory act become noised abroad, than an enterprising young Wisconsin newspaper man, James Madison Goodhue, suspended the publication of his Lancaster *Herald*, packed up his Washington hand press, fonts ˙of worn type, and equipment, and headed for St. Paul, Minnesota Territory. On April 28, 1849, just eight days after his arrival in the new town, he put out volume 1 number 1 of Minnesota's first newspaper, the *Minnesota Pioneer*, which he had originally planned

First office of Pioneer Press

to name "The Epistle of St. Paul." The paper is still running today as the St. Paul *Pioneer Press*. "We print and issue this number of the Pioneer," wrote Goodhue, "in a building through which the out-of-doors is visible by more than five hundred apertures; and as for our type, it is not safe from being pied on the galleys by the wind." A file of this rare weekly newspaper, in surprisingly good condition, is one of the prized possessions of the Minnesota Historical Society in St. Paul. The news-hungry citizens of the tiny capital fairly snatched away the pages as they rolled off the press.

James Madison Goodhue

Another editor, Andrew Randall, had likewise caught the Minnesota fever, and had issued a paper, the *Minnesota Register,* with a St. Paul dateline of April 27, 1849, but which was actually printed in Cincinnati, Ohio, before his departure for the West. Randall never got to Minnesota, but sold out en route, and the second issue of the *Register* did not appear until July 14, 1849, with John P. Owens and Nathaniel McLean as publishers. Still a third weekly, the *Minnesota Chronicle,* made its appearance in St. Paul on May 31, 1849, at the hands of James Hughes. Shortly afterwards these two latter papers combined, and ran as the *Minnesota Chronicle and Register* until 1851. Three newspapers for one small frontier town!

St. Anthony got its first newspaper in 1851 when Elmer Tyler and Isaac Atwater began the publication of the St. Anthony *Express* on May 31. Weekly after weekly rolled off the little hand presses with their worn type, as the vigorous new towns sprang up overnight. Jeremiah Russell's Sauk Rapids *Frontierman* made its appearance in 1854 to chronicle development at this important crossing point on the Sauk River route of the Red River Trail; to be followed late in 1857 by the St. Cloud *Visiter,* the brainchild of that irrepressible advocate of women's rights, Mrs. Jane Grey Swisshelm. The Winona *Republican,* Mantorville *Express,* Red Wing *Republican, Wabashaw County Herald* of Read's Landing and Wabasha, the Chatfield *Democrat,* and a flock of others made their appearance, told the story of their communities, spread abroad news about Minnesota, and then more frequently than not, died in the struggle for existence. Some seventy-five weeklies alone were started during the territorial period, but few have survived to this day, either as weeklies or as dailies. By the late spring of 1854 St. Paul had no less than four dailies, the *Pioneer,* the *Democrat,* the *Minnesotian,* and the *Times.*

"The most important purpose of the newspaper press, especially on the frontier," wrote Goodhue in the *Minnesota Pioneer* of April 17, 1851, "is to mirror back to the world the events, the peculiarities and the whole features of the new world by which it is surrounded. It necessarily has, or should have, a provincial character. Its radius of observa-

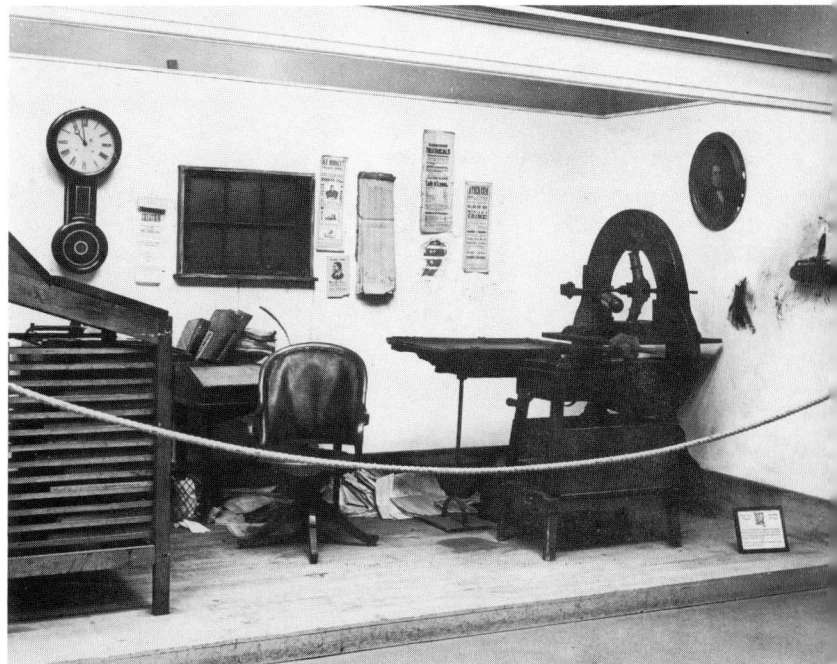

James Goodhue's office

tion is rather confined to the sphere around it. The great news centers, the mammoth presses of the Atlantic cities, derive intelligence from all quarters and radiate news over the whole continent. They are the great reflectors of intelligence. The frontier press is more influential indirectly than directly; by being copied and multiplied in the enormous city papers, which penetrate every corner of the world. . . . For general intelligence, the news of the world at large, we expect our readers to look into the journals of the great cities. An important or interesting item of intelligence from Minnesota, copied into the N.Y. Tribune, or the Herald, or the Sun, or the North American, or Pennsylvanian, will do more to make our Territory known abroad, than the issue of a whole edition of the press from which the article emanated."

Thus wrote Goodhue in 1851, and the principles which he enunciated were followed pretty uniformly by the flock of Minnesota newspapers, both weeklies and dailies which sprang into being in the fifties. Local news they covered in detail, although largely in paragraphic form without headings, to the despair of modern researchers. There are numerous accounts of travels in Minnesota; apparently almost everyone who went anywhere wrote to the editor about his experiences. The editors themselves traveled extensively and they devoted many columns to the happenings in the places they visited. There are reports of experiments in agriculture, and helpful hints culled from outside papers. D. A. Robertson of the *Minnesota*

Democrat, St. Paul, in particular devoted much space to such material. The papers gave lengthy accounts of the proceedings of the territorial legislatures and the courts, the messages and reports of the governors, officials, and public and semi-public groups, published the laws, and spread presidential messages and congressional debates over many columns.

Local politics were handled with great vigor, and editorial rivalries evoked language that today would give ample ground for criminal and civil libel suits. In many towns barely able to support one paper, preceding a political campaign, there would be a Republican and a Democratic paper, each appealing for support from dutiful party members, and frequently the defeat of a party candidate meant the demise of the corresponding party paper, amid the rapturous outbursts of the successful rival editor. The cultural side was not neglected, for practically every issue contained literary efforts good or bad, original or clipped, and bits of poetry, usually submitted by a local "contrib."

These pioneer editors encountered endless difficulties in getting their supplies of paper, and their columns contained frequent references to this problem. As a consequence, there were occasional failures to print for a week or two, and often there were but single sheets of varying sizes. The paper used was made from rags, and as a result, the issues preserved in the collections of the Minnesota Historical Society, dating back seventy-five and even a hundred years, are in surprisingly good condition as compared with those printed on the wood pulp paper of the period from 1880 onward.

Townsite operators, of course, were quick to take advantage of that new medium of publicity, the newspaper, and they filled any amount of newspaper space with their glowing advertisements of new towns, many of which were simply on paper. Unhampered by Better Business Bureaus and the penalties for false advertising, they transferred the rosy prospects of a distant future to the present in their prospectuses. One of the Breckenridge townsite operators, whose development consisted of a sawmill without machinery, a hotel under construction, and a few shacks, promoted a great buffalo hunt, including numerous important person-

Ignatius Donnelly

ages as invited guests, in the summer of 1858, to be based upon his town. Ignatius Donnelly spread the wonders of his town of Nininger, just above Hastings, over the pages of his *Emigrant Aid Journal* in 1856-57, but the town and the paper soon disappeared in the debris of the Panic of 1857. Today that townsite is little more than a wooded pasture. Newly established towns and their promoters strove to get newspapers into operation as soon as possi-

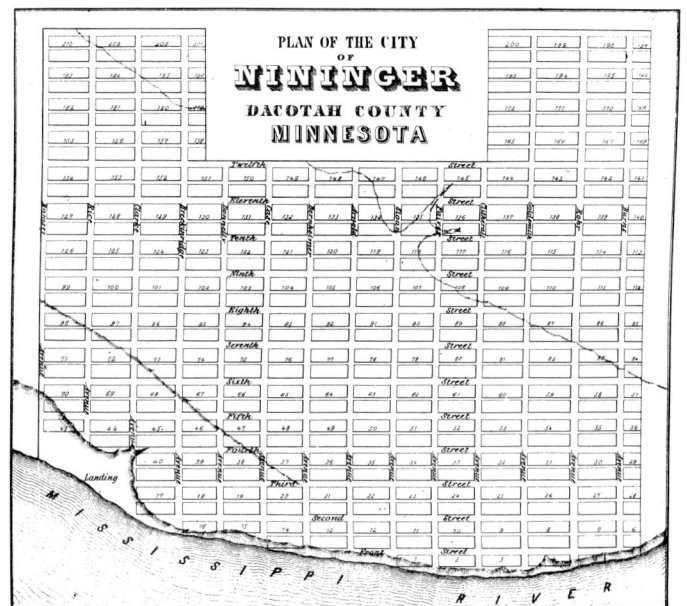

Plan of the city of Nininger, Minn., 1856

ble, and editors were often subsidized for that purpose. In many cases the editors such as Jeremiah Russell of the Sauk Rapids *Frontierman* were themselves of the townsite owner group.

As the fifties rolled along, and the flood of settlers continued to pour into the region, Minnesota Territory came to be less and less remote from the outside, world. Hundreds of steamboat arrivals were recorded in St. Paul in a single year. That marvel of rapid communication, the electric or "magnetic" telegraph, patented by Samuel F. B. Morse in 1837, came into general use after long years of struggle, and its lines of iron wire were reaching to the Mississippi. News dispatches were being carried over the wires to the river towns, and then the newspapers of these communities were rushed onto the steamboats for delivery upstream. Word of the admission of Minnesota as a state on May 11, 1858, came by telegraph to Prairie du Chien. The citizens of the newly admitted state learned the glad news upon May 13, upon the arrival of the first upbound steamboat. Another telegraph line was gradually working its way up the west bank of the Mississippi through Iowa from St. Louis, but both east and west side routes involved the difficult problem of carrying and maintaining the heavy iron wires across the wide river. Underwater cables were still in the experimental stage. How would a Minnesota telegraph line be linked up with the outside connections, and with what company or group of companies?

Telegraph companies had sprung up almost by magic throughout the states east of the Mississippi amid interminable legal complications, bitter competition, and lack of coordination. Local groups set up stock companies to run telegraph lines in various areas, and then solicited the towns along the proposed routes for subscriptions so as to insure their being serviced by the wires. In Minnesota, coincidental with a series of meetings in Winona, Red Wing, Hastings, and St. Paul, the Minnesota Telegraph Company was organized in the latter town on February 21, 1860, to run a line between St. Paul and La Crosse, and businessmen in the river towns en route were urged to contribute liberally by taking stock at $20 per share. The editor of the *Wabashaw County Herald* at Read's Landing

BRING OUT THE BIG GUN

GLORIOUS NEWS!!

MINNESOTA A STATE!!!

100 GUNS FIRED AT WINONA:

GENERAL REJOICING,

bitterly castigated the citizens of his town for their sluggishness in failing to respond, and the line when first strung up actually by-passed that place while going to nearby Wabasha, a subscriber. A spur line was subsequently cut in to Read's Landing a little later, on condition that the citizens provide and set the tamarack poles. It was not until August 28, 1860, that the first round-trip message was handled over the Minnesota line, and then only because, as the St. Paul *Daily Pioneer and Democrat* wrote, "the wires not being strung over the Mississippi at Winona, the operator at that place crossed the river in a skiff and recorded his dispatches on the Wisconsin side, and wrote them off by moonlight with the paper on his knees, and then crossed to the Minnesota side and forwarded them to St. Paul." Minneapolis and St. Anthony were so slow with their subscriptions that they did not

309

get service until November 14 and December 4, 1860, respectively.

Thereafter the newspapers carried dispatches by "Magnetic Telegraph," or by "Electric Telegraph," but there were constant complaints about the service, due to breaks in the line, storms, and other mechanical difficulties, to say nothing of operator "coffee breaks" and deliberate holdups in transmission. In the midst of dispatches concerning exciting events such as major battles of the Civil War, the line would go dead and Minnesotans would realize how out of touch they were with the outside world. Even so it is today when our newspapers fail to be delivered, and the radio and television sets refuse to function.

Perhaps one of the greatest advances in the field of comunications as well as in safety resulting from the introduction of the telegraph came about 1851, when the Erie Railroad in New York State began to experiment with telegraphic train dispatching. Hitherto, operations had been conducted on a calculated timing basis, and the newspapers of the day were full of accounts of frightful collisions and accidents due to such error in this system. Other railroads adopted the idea, and thereafter the click of the telegraph key was heard at every station in the country for almost a century. Railroad wires, too, came into use for commercial messages, and gradually, through a process of consolidation, the great Western Union company of today emerged.

Meanwhile, as was mentioned above, the people of Minnesota Territory had been growing more and more vociferous in their demands for railroads, and one company, the St. Paul and St. Anthony Railroad Company had been chartered as early as 1853. More and more charters were granted by succeeding territorial legislatures, until by 1857 no less than twenty-seven had gone on the statute books, many of them in connection with land grants engineered through Congress and territorial legislatures, but building did not follow in the footsteps of the numerous alleged surveyors. The Panic of 1857 destroyed any chance of actual construction, even if the companies had been more than promoters' dreams, and all of them collapsed.

It is impossible here to pilot the reader through the maze of legal and legislative proceedings rela-

tive to railroads during 1857 and 1858, including approval by popular referendum of what is known as the "Five Million Dollar Loan," which authorized the substitution of state bonds for company issues on the basis of land grants for mileage constructed. Suffice it to say that not until the fall of 1861 had a single foot of railroad track been completed, and then only a strip about fourteen hundred feet long from the St. Paul levee to a storage shed where a single locomotive of the Minnesota and Pacific was housed for the winter of 1861-62. The following spring the St. Paul and Pacific, successor of the Minnesota and Pacific and ancestor of the Great Northern managed to build as far as St. Anthony, ten miles, and on June 28, 1862, the first experimental run was made with great ceremony. Several other companies then got into action, and by the end of 1865 the total rail mileage in Minnesota had risen to 210. The St. Paul and Pacific finally reached Breckenridge on the Bois des Sioux-Red River in 1871. Another line of the same railroad was built by stages up to St. Cloud. About the same time other lines built by various companies were constructed to link up St. Paul with Chicago and Duluth. Relatively fast and reliable rail service along the Mississippi virtually cut the heart out of the passenger and freight revenue traffic of the steamboats, although the Diamond Jo and its successor the Streckfus line continued to operate passenger boats on the upper Mississippi until 1918 for tourists who wanted to enjoy the scenery and the delights of summertime Minnesota. Ever decreasing revenues and increased operating costs finally spelled their end. The heyday of the river steamboat as the passenger and freight connection of Minnesota with the outside world had passed.

Freight steamboating of a different type was lively during the eighties and nineties, because of the tremendous amount of business in the towing of log and lumber rafts, but by 1900 this work had practically come to an end, and the Father of Waters lay empty for a time.

Revival of interest in the utilization of America's inland waterways for the transport of heavy, bulky freight began about 1910. Today after the expenditure of hundreds of millions of dollars for

Officials of the St. Paul and Pacific Railroad, Breckenridge, Minn., 1873

Laying steel in the late 80's

Mammoth raft of logs towed by Steamer "Buckeye"

dams, dredging, channel marking, and other improvements, huge tows of barges propelled by powerful if unromantic towboats handle far more freight on the Upper Mississippi than the steamboats ever carried in the palmiest days of pioneer Minnesota.

Steamboats, railroads, and telegraph lines had all been advances in rapidity of communication, but people could still not talk directly and instantaneously with each other when physically separated by a few yards, let alone hundreds and thousands of miles. Could the human voice, basically a series of vibrations and impulses, be transmitted by corresponding electrical impulses?

Experimentation in this general field had been going on from about the beginning of the Nineteenth Century, but it was not until the night of March 10, 1876, that Alexander Graham Bell in Boston actually transmitted his voice over a wire to his assistant in an adjoining room. Bell's application for a patent had been filed on February 14, of that year, and after amendment had been turned over to him approved, on March 7. The new invention was publicly exhibited at the Philadelphia Centennial Exposition in June, 1876, where on June 25 Dom Pedro, Emperor of Brazil, and other scientists saw the telephone successfully demonstrated. Years of legal battles with other claimants followed, but the Bell patent was finally upheld, and is today the foundation of the nationwide

American Telephone and Telegraph Company.

Curiously enough, Minneapolis and St. Paul, far to the west, and only a few hundred miles from the wild Indian frontier, were among the leaders in setting up a telephone system. Private experimental lines were run in both cities in 1877, and the following year, 1878, found the Northwestern Telephone Company in operation in Minneapolis, with its exchange, for about a dozen subscribers, in the old Minneapolis City Hall. Numerous independent companies sprang up, some of them using the constantly improving Bell equipment under license, and some adopting independently developed devices utilizing early types of dial phones. As late as the first decade of the Twentieth Century there were two major telephone systems operating in the Twin Cities, and it was necessary for business and professional men to have phones of both companies to transact their business. Eventually the two were consolidated into the Northwestern Bell Telephone Company, a subsidiary of the American Telephone and Telegraph Company. Today one can pick up a telephone, and in a matter of seconds talk directly with a specific person on the Atlantic or Pacific seaboard, and even with a little delay converse with friends in trans-oceanic countries, via the wonders of electricity. In two hundred years Minnesota has come, communication-wise, from the Indian smoke and fire signal to radio and television.

312

Part 2 *Communications*

The Mass Media Mature: Newspapers, Magazines, Graphic Arts, Radio and Television

By EDWIN EMERY

The story of the growth of the mass media in Minnesota is a part of the story of their growth in the United States as social agencies vitally important in a democratic society. The printing press and the airwaves have given men the opportunity to communicate through the columns of weekly and daily newspapers, the pages of magazines and other publications, and radio and television programs—especially the opportunity to dig out and interpret news, to offer intelligent opinion, and to help shape the political, economic, and social progress of their times. Minnesota's publishers, editors, printers, broadcasters, and newsmen of the past century have played a significant role in the maturing of a state, and have shared in the maturing of a nation and the development of its communications.

Minnesota's first newspapers of pre-Civil War days appeared at a time when the concept of a "press for the masses" was being developed successfully by such noted American journalists as James Gordon Bennett of the New York *Herald,* Horace Greeley of the New York *Tribune,* and Henry J. Raymond of the New York *Times.* Through the remainder of the 19th century this new movement in newspaper journalism placed ever-increasing concentration of effort upon impartial gathering and reporting of the news as the basic function of the press, and upon growing independence of editorial opinion from partisan pressures. Gradually fading from the scene were the older mercantile press devoted mainly to the interests of a single class, and the partisan political press openly tied to the wishes of political parties and

factions. Minnesota's journalism history reflects this movement in its first decades.

The forces of industrialization, mechanization, and urbanization which transformed American society between the Civil War and World War I brought further extensions of these changes. The modern daily newspaper emerged through the leadership of such famous publisher-editors as Joseph Pulitzer, Edward Wyllis Scripps, William Randolph Hearst, and Adolph S. Ochs. Circulation and advertising revenues of mass-read papers in growing cities and towns provided the means for using new mechanical developments and format techniques—typesetting machines, automatic printing presses, illustrations, better typography. Newspapers were popularized in content, both in style of writing and in choice of subject matter. Their editors often were more responsive to socio-political pressures affecting the country as it adjusted to the growing interdependence of an industrialized society, and were spokesmen for the larger public interest.

The same forces brought other changes in newspaper journalism. First in the metropolitan centers, and then in the growing towns, newspapers became less personal journalistic enterprises and more good-sized business institutions. Economic and social pressures, combined with the effects of mass-circulation competition, brought widespread consolidation of newspaper publishing enterprises. As a consequence, no Minnesota city today has competing daily newspapers under separate ownerships, and the number of smaller communities

Early newspaper printing press

supporting more than one weekly paper has declined steadily. The standard has become the all-purpose community newspaper, flourishing in some 9,000 cities, towns, and villages across the nation. Minnesota's 29 dailies and 393 weeklies of 1958 include strong metropolitan papers, vigorous community dailies in smaller cities, and one of the foremost weekly newspaper networks serving the people of a state at the most intimate local level. Developing alongside them, in Minnesota as in the nation, have been magazines and other publications, the graphic arts industry, and in recent decades, 77 radio and television stations.

St. Paul's newspaper history provides an excellent example of the changing character of metropolitan journalism over a century. James M. Goodhue's *Minnesota Pioneer* of 1849, the territory's first weekly, had four competitors during its first two years of publication. Goodhue cast his lot with the Democratic party faction led by Henry H. Sibley; their rivals led by Henry M. Rice supported the *Minnesota Democrat*, founded in 1850 by Daniel A. Robertson. The *Minnesota Register* and *Minnesota Chronicle*, begun in 1849 and combined the same year as the *Chronicle and Register*, were

Whig in sympathy. The new paper died in 1851, when John P. Owens' *Minnesotian* became the Whig spokesman.

Growing population and newspaper rivalry brought daily newspaper publication to St. Paul in a rush on May 1, 1854. The *Pioneer*, the *Democrat*, and the *Minnesotian* made the change. Challenging them was the St. Paul *Daily Times*, founded May 15 by Thomas M. Newson. With the addition of the *Free Press* in 1855 St. Paul had five dailies, one for each 1,000 of population, and had seen a dozen printer-editors attempt weekly or daily publication. Contraction was in order.

On the Democratic party side, the *Pioneer* emerged the winner. Goodhue, its founder, had died in 1852, worn out at the age of 42 by the demands of frontier life. His successor was Joseph R. Brown, a colorful adventurer who later founded Brown's Valley. In 1854 a trained New York newspaperman, Earle S. Goodrich, guided the paper into daily publication and gave it sufficient vigor to win dominance. The publishers of the *Democrat* agreed to a merger in October, 1855, and the paper became known as the *Pioneer and Democrat* until 1862, when the name reverted to *Daily Pioneer*.

In 1858 Goodrich absorbed the *Advertiser*, edited by a young New Englander who soon was to achieve success in Minnesota journalism, Joseph A. Wheelock.

Turbulence in national politics, which brought an end to the Whig party in the 1850s and the rise of the Republican party, was reflected in Minnesota. Young Wheelock, biding his time as a secondary personage in St. Paul journalism, watched the energetic Dr. Thomas Foster turn the *Minnesotian* into a Republican organ. Newson's *Daily Times* followed the same path; the *Free Press*, begun during a political quarrel, died within six months. By the fall of 1860, Wheelock was ready to make his move to provide Minnesota with a single, strong pro-Republican newspaper.

Joseph A. Wheelock

With William R. Marshall, Wheelock obtained control of telegraphic reports of national and foreign news provided by the Associated Press over wires stretching up across Wisconsin from Chicago. They began publication of the St. Paul *Daily Press* on January 1, 1861, absorbing both the *Daily Times* and the *Minnesotian* in the process. But factionalism on the Republican side brought competition the next year in the form of the *Daily Union*, published by business-minded Frederick Driscoll. Common sense prevailed and on March 1, 1863, the *Union* disappeared into the *Press*. Wheelock

became editor and Driscoll business manager—a combination which was to win continued success until 1900.

St. Paul thus was left with two major newspapers. The *Pioneer* passed from the hands of the Goodrich family in 1865 and was controlled in turn by Harlan P. Hall, William S. King, and David Blakely during the next ten years. All three names bob up more than once in the story of journalism in St. Paul and the growing rival community of Minneapolis; uncertain business conditions brought rapid shifts in ownership of the struggling papers, and in the fortunes of editors and publishers. On April 11, 1875, St. Paul found its morning dailies combined as the *Pioneer Press*, under the Wheelock-Driscoll banner. Competition of a major

Frederick Driscoll

nature now was provided by the evening *Dispatch*, launched on February 29, 1868, by Hall and David Ramaley. In post-Civil War politics, the *Dispatch* was "liberal Republican" or Democratic and the *Pioneer Press* orthodox Republican.

Gradually Wheelock's voice became the most influential journalistic one in his region, and one commanding national notice. His biographer, Quintus C. Wilson, classes him as a "middle-of-the-road conservative" who was sympathetic to the views of the dominant post-Civil War Republican party but who was well aware of his obligations to

315

Office of the St. Peter Herald

instruct and enlighten public opinion. He was for sound money and orthodox economic solutions, and fought the Greenback, Populist, and Democratic movements led by such midwesterners as Minnesota's editor-politician Ignatius Donnelly, Nebraska's William Jennings Bryan, and Wisconsin's Robert La Follette. But he opposed high tariffs, corruptness in railroad expansion, and high freight rates. He worked for the improvement of his state and city, and in particular was responsible for the system of parks, playgrounds, and public boulevards developed in St. Paul.

Driscoll left the *Pioneer Press* team in 1900 to become a nationally-known labor relations expert for the American Newspaper Publishers Association. Wheelock died in 1906. The city's once-dominant morning paper found itself out-maneuvered in a circulation war with the evening *Dispatch*, owned since 1885 by George Thompson. On May 21, 1909, Thompson won control of the *Pioneer Press*, achieving a morning and evening ownership.

The combined *Pioneer Press* and *Dispatch* had only evening competition, from L. V. Ashbaugh's *Daily News*, founded March 31, 1900. The *Globe*, begun in 1878 by Harlan P. Hall as a morning Democratic paper and successfully edited by him until 1885, had been discontinued in 1905 by its final owners, including railroad builder James J. Hill. Out of the competition with the aggressive *Daily News*, and their own reinvigorated ownership and editorial direction, the *Pioneer Press* and *Dispatch* again advanced.

Thompson installed Herbert L. Galt as editor in 1909 and found a vigorous writer who championed individual liberties, fought the prohibition movement, and sought a balance between the interests of agriculture, business, and labor. Galt's publishers stood by him in episodes involving the papers' integrity and fairness. After Thompson's death in 1917 his able widow, Abigail Wheeler Thompson, and Charles K. Blandin shared control; Blandin became owner in 1923. This era ended with Galt's death in 1926 and Blandin's sale of

316

Saint Paul Sunday Pioneer-Press.

VOL. XXI.

SAINT PAUL, MINN., SUNDAY, APRIL 11, 1875.

NO. 86.

CRIMES—CALAMITIES.

A Farmington, Minn., Man of Forty-Five, Elopes with a Girl of Twelve.

Bloody Fight with a Band of Robbers in Arkansas—Three Men Killed.

The Gibson County, Tenn., Ku-Klux Discharged for Want of Evidence.

Another Robbers' Raid in Texas—Murders and Various Lesser Crimes.

Bad Fire at Greenville, Tenn.—Other Calamities Elsewhere.

FOREIGN NEWS.

Paul Boynton Crosses the English Channel in His Life Preserving Dress—Alfonso's University Troubles.

ENGLAND.

SPAIN.

THE DOMINION.

MANITOBA.

FROM MORMONDOM.

TO THE BLACK HILLS.

THE POSTAL FRAUDS.

BOOTS AND SHOES.

H. A. SCHLIEK,

No. 61 East Third-St. and No. 23 Wabasha-St.,

BOOTS & SHOES.

E. C. BURT'S
Ladies' & Misses'
FINE SHOES.

H. A. SCHLIEK,

AUCTION.

FINE

Bedroom Furniture

AND

CARPETS

At Auction.

WE WILL SELL ON

Wednesday, the 14th inst.,

R. & J. M. WARNER,
Auctioneers.

Real Estate Sales

HOUSE AND LOT IN ST. PAUL.
4 Lots in West St. Paul.

HOUSE AND LOT

4 Lots in West St. Paul,

H. A. FAIRCHILD.

CHAIR FACTORY.

J. F. ATKINSON,
APPLETON, WIS.

PAINTERS.

Judson & Brack,
House and Sign
PAINTERS
No. 9 W. Fourth-St.

STOCKHOLDER'S MEETING.

NOTICE TO TAX PAYERS

DRY GOODS.

CLARK'S
O. N. T.
SPOOL COTTON.

Milward's Needles!

Auerbach, Finch & Scheffer,
AND
WILLIAM LEE,
ST. PAUL, MINN.

SILK.

BELDING BROTHERS & CO.'S
MACHINE TWIST
SEWING SILK.

Auerbach, Finch & Scheffer
ST. PAUL, MINN.

AMUSEMENTS.

48TH CONCERT

OF THE
Saint Paul
Musical Society,

ASSISTED BY
MISS JULIA WOOD,
AND THE
GREAT WESTERN BAND
AT THE
OPERA HOUSE.

ON
Tuesday Ev'g, April 13th, 1875,

OPERA HOUSE.

HENRY E. ABBEY......Manager.

HAMLET!

Enoch Arden.

WILD OATS.

NIAGARA

FIRE
INSURANCE COMP'Y OF N. Y.,

N. S. EATON, AGENT.

FIRE INSURANCE

$6,000,000 REPRESENTED!

CHARLES SHANDREW, Agent.

NEWARK

LAND COMPANY

San Francisco Bay, Alameda Co., California.

GEO. A. HAMILTON, Secretary.

MUSICAL HEADQUARTERS!

LEADING MUSIC HOUSE
OF MINNESOTA.

GENERAL AGENCY FOR
Chickering Pianos!
AND
ESTEY ORGANS!

CHAS. H. PETERS, Manager.

W. H. LEIB,

117 Wabasha-st., opp. Capitol, St. Paul.
TENOR CONCERT VOCALIST.

ARTISTIC SINGING.

NOTICE TO CREDITORS.

NOTICE

To the Creditors of Stewart & Co.

April 22d, 1875.

Homeopathic Pharmacy

MINNEAPOLIS.

BOOTS AND SHOES.

C. S. GOODWIN & CO.,

Boots, Shoes and Rubbers
MINNEAPOLIS

SALE OF TOWN LOTS.

WHO WILL INVEST?

$150,000 Worth of Real Estate Offered at Great Bargains!

1,800 Lots for Sale in the Village of Langdon, at Low Rates and on Long Time.

DRY GOODS.

Spring Season, 1875.

AUERBACH, FINCH & SCHEFFER

Have now ready for Inspection a Full Stock of

Dry Goods

AND

NOTIONS.

Complete in Every Department.

OPENING OF SPRING TRADE!

Powers Brothers,

NO. 59 EAST THIRD STREET

WILL OFFER

On Monday, April 12th.

And Invite Comparison With Prices of Any Market!

1875. SPRING 1875.

MILLINERY AND FANCY GOODS,
NOTIONS AND HOSIERY.

I. OPPENHEIM & CO.,

69 East Third-st., St. Paul.

INSURANCE.

HUGHSON, HEMENWAY & PASSAVANT,
Insurance Agents.
REPRESENT OVER $35,000,000 CAPITAL.
Ingersoll Block, St. Paul, Minn.

GENTS' GARMENTS.

1875. PALMES' 1875.

Superb Stock of Fine Woolens for the
Spring and Summer Trade

Gentlemen's Garments.

58 East Third-st., St. Paul, Minn.
ESTABLISHED 1856.

ASSIGNEE'S NOTICE.

NOTICE TO CREDITORS.

R. MARVIN & SON.

FURS.

MERRELL RYDER,
Commission Merchant.
FURS, HIDES, SKINS, HIDES, WOOL, GAME,

GENTS' FURNISHING GOODS.

R. A. LANPHER & CO.

Hatters
AND
GENTS'
FURNISHERS.

DUNLAP'S
Silk Hats.

109 Third Street, Three Doors Above Merchants

PIANOS, ORGANS, ETC.

NOW IS THE TIME!

CHICKERING PIANO for $2
ON EASY TERMS OF PAYMEN
GREAT REDUCTION
DYER BROS. & HOWARD
GENERAL AGENTS FOR STEINWAY PIANOS

SHOW CASES.

Wm. Strueder

249 & 251 Lake-st., South Side, Milwaukee, Wisconsin.

FIRE ENGINES.

Gould Steam Fire Engines,

FOUNDRY.

NORTHWESTERN FOUND

G. MENZEL & CO.,
CAR WHEELS AND CASTIN
MINNEAPOLIS, MINNESOT

IRON WORK.

BAYLEY & GREENSLAD
UNION IRON WORK

STEAM HEATING.

Steam Heating

PLUMBING,
GAS FIXTURES
AND FITTINGS,
WOOD AND IRON WORKING
MACHINERY
SUPPLIES FOR
Mills, Railroads and Brewer

MATCHES.

NORTH MATCHES.

J. R. MAYNARD,
ST. PAUL, MINN.

MERCHANT TAILORS.

T. B. DUNCAN,

TAILOR
48 East Third Street.

CARPETS, WALL PAPER, ETC.

JOHN MATHEIS'

CARPET HOUS

Oil Cloth Mattings, Window Shad
Curtains, Wall Paper.

H. F. E. VITT,
CARPETS
No. 77 Jackson St., St. Paul.

DOORS, SASH & MOULDING

Johnson & Copeland, Minneapolis, Minn.

LUMBER

LUMBER

HERSEY, BEAN & BROWN
MANUFACTURERS AND WHOLESALE DEALE
Stillwater, Minnesota.

Full Line of Dry Lumber Always on Ha

BRIDGE TIMBERS A SPECIAL

CARS LOADED FREE OF CHAR

the papers on October 4, 1927, to the Ridder family of New York City. The Ridders won control of the *Daily News* in 1933 and ended its publication in 1938, leaving St. Paul a morning-evening single ownership city.

Bernard H. Ridder, one of three brothers in a publishing family which got its start with the *Staats-Zeitung* in New York City, became St. Paul's newspaper publisher. Herbert L. Lewis, who served his editorial apprenticeship under Galt, emerged

Bernard H. Ridder

as editor. The papers were strongly internationalist in outlook, and closely concerned with civic progress. The elder Ridder's sons all became newspaper publishers—Daniel in St. Paul; Bernard H., Jr., in Duluth; and Herman and Joseph in California, where the Ridders bought newspapers in Long Beach, San Jose, and Pasadena in the 1950s. With these and other publishing and radio-television interests, the Ridders within 30 years of their arrival in St. Paul had become nationally-known. Victor F. Ridder, another of the original trio of brothers, became active in the life of Duluth, where the family bought newspaper control in 1936; of his sons, Walter headed the Ridders' Washington news coverage and Robert the family's radio-TV interests.

In Minneapolis the story of a century's journalism involves different newspaper names and different actors in the drama, but the pattern of change essentially is the same: struggling beginnings, vigorous competition, the emergence of dominant papers and editors, and a final consolidation in one nationally-recognized ownership.

The up-river settlers at St. Anthony's Falls had their *Express* dating from May 31, 1851. The *Northwestern Democrat*, established in 1854, was the first weekly to be printed on the west bank of the river in what was to be the Minneapolis loop area. This unstable venture became the *Gazette* in 1857, the *Journal* in 1858, and the *State Atlas* in 1859. The vigorous, 31-year-old editor of the *State Atlas* was William S. King, key figure in early Minneapolis journalism. King's support of Abraham Lincoln and the Union cause in hard-hitting editorials won him friends, and in 1863 he was able to absorb the *Falls Evening News*, Minneapolis' first daily dating from 1857.

But King also made enemies, and they started a rival daily, the *Chronicle*, in 1866. In a town of 7,000 population still overshadowed by the capital city of St. Paul, neither paper prospered. A group of Minneapolis leaders—headed by King, W. D. Washburn, and Dorilus Morrison, newly-elected as the first mayor of Minneapolis—arranged a merger. The new daily, named the Minneapolis *Tribune*, appeared on May 25, 1867.

The *Tribune* went through six ownership changes in the first 24 years of its history. One, in 1876, saw it purchased by the St. Paul *Pioneer Press*; for six months the citizens of Minneapolis suffered the indignity of a "Twin Cities newspaper" controlled by Wheelock and Driscoll. Dissatisfaction caused the sale of the *Tribune* and evening *Mail* properties in Minneapolis to David Blakely, and after a period of publication solely as an evening paper, the *Tribune* regained its morning edition status. It survived a disastrous fire in 1889 and was rebuilt by A. J. Blethen.

Then, on March 14, 1891, the *Tribune* gained its most famous owner, William J. Murphy. Murphy, born in Hudson, Wisconsin, in 1859, had attended Notre Dame University and won a law degree before he was 21. He practiced law, ran a newspaper, and began investing in the rapidly growing electric power plant business in Grand Forks, North Dakota, during the 1880s. With Senator Gilbert A. Pierce of North Dakota he purchased the *Tribune* for $450,000. It claimed about 45,000 daily circulation for its combined morning and evening editions in 1891. The original 4-page daily had grown to 8, with 24 on Sunday. Minneapolis, now the state's largest city, had a population of 165,000.

The new *Tribune* owners promised their paper would become the voice of the Northwest. Pierce assumed editorial direction while Murphy ran the business side. During the panic of 1893 Murphy became sole owner and publisher, a position he held until his death in 1918. Murphy installed new Mergenthaler typesetting machines and improved his paper's appearance and news coverage. A second great fire at the *Tribune* plant in 1899 failed to deter him; that year the *Tribune's* circulation was greater than that of the *Pioneer Press*. By 1918, the *Tribune* had twice as many readers as the other major morning paper in the state. Murphy, who continued to invest in electric power plants and land in the Red River Valley, left an estate valued at $1,250,000.

Murphy's greatest skill lay in business management, but his dedication to the newspaper profession was exhibited by a provision in his will establishing the "W. J. Murphy Endowment Fund for a School of Journalism . . . for the establishing and maintaining . . . of instruction in journalism" at the University of Minnesota. The original $350,000 sum—second largest gift to American journalism education—helped provide Murphy Hall as the home of the School of Journalism and by 1958 had grown into an endowment fund dedicated to support of journalism teaching and research totaling nearly $800,000. Minnesota's School of Journalism became a nationally recognized leader in teaching, research, and service to communications media of the state and nation.

The *Tribune* of this period was essentially conservative in its outlook, and pro-Republican in its editorial policy. As in St. Paul, a rival morning Democratic paper failed to survive; the Minneapolis *Morning Times* founded in the 1880s sold out

to the *Tribune* in 1905. The *Tribune's* most vigorous rival was the equally conservative Minneapolis *Journal*, founded in 1878 as an evening paper. Herschel V. Jones worked up through the business side of the paper to become publisher in 1908. His

Herschel V. Jones

son, Carl W. Jones, succeeded him upon his death in 1928. Winthrop B. Chamberlain was editorial director of the *Journal* from 1908 to 1936.

At the *Tribune*, Frederick E. Murphy, brother of William J. Murphy, served as publisher from 1918 until his death in 1940. His famous managing editor was Thomas J. Dillon, who took that post in 1920 after a colorful early career on western newspapers, and who served as editor of the *Tribune* from 1929 to 1945.

The two powerful papers had still other rivals. One was the Minneapolis *Daily News*, an evening paper begun in 1903 by L. V. Ashbaugh as a companion to the St. Paul *Daily News*, and like it, the home of many competent newspapermen. But the *Daily News* faded away in 1923 after Ashbaugh's death. Apparently dying, too, was the *Minnesota Daily Star*, a cooperative evening paper founded by supporters of the Nonpartisan League and labor groups. Inadequate financing and advertising support sent the original *Star* into receivership in 1924; it survived as a conventional daily ranking well behind the *Tribune* and the *Journal* in circulation.

Minneapolis' publishing situation attracted the attention of the Cowles family of Des Moines in 1935. Gardner Cowles, Sr., and his sons, John and Gardner, Jr., had won control of newspaper publishing in Des Moines and wide circulation throughout Iowa for their *Register* and *Tribune*. Buying the *Star* from publisher John Thompson, they set out to achieve the same position in Minneapolis and Minnesota. By 1939, the *Star's* aggressive policies and splashy news techniques had brought it to a competitive position which endangered the rival evening *Journal*. August, 1939, saw a merger under the name *Star-Journal*. The Cowles paper now had a Sunday edition, which quickly challenged that of the *Tribune*. Despite its renaming of its evening edition as the *Times*, in an effort to attract former *Journal* readers, the *Tribune* found the going difficult. In May, 1941, the *Tribune* stockholders agreed to a merger in which publisher John Cowles won control of all three Minneapolis papers. The evening *Times* continued until 1948; the *Star-Journal* shortened its name to the *Star*; and the surviving *Star* and *Tribune* became a morning-evening single ownership.

John Cowles

Under John Cowles' direction, the papers won national position as a part of the Cowles group, including the Des Moines dailies, *Look* magazine,

and radio and television interests. Among their influential editors have been Gideon Seymour, editorial page editor of the *Star* from 1939 to 1944 and executive editor of both newspapers from 1944 until his death in 1954, and Carroll Binder, editorial page editor of the *Tribune* from 1946 until his death in 1956. Their leadership helped to establish editorial policies strongly internationalist in outlook, and influential in community affairs.

Journalism at the "Head of the Lakes" dates from April 24, 1869, when Dr. Thomas Foster of St. Paul established the Duluth *Minnesotian*. The next year saw two competing papers, the Superior *Weekly Tribune* and the Duluth *Weekly Tribune*. In Duluth, the *Tribune* absorbed the *Minnesotian* and Robert D'Unger's early *Herald*, and became a daily in 1881 under the aggressive editorial leadership of Robert C. Mitchell. But by 1892 the *Tribune* had been bought out by the owners of the *Lake Superior News*, founded in 1878. The new paper was named the *News-Tribune*.

A second Duluth *Herald* was begun in 1883 by Milie Bunnell, a longtime major figure in Duluth journalism. It passed into the hands of Anton C. Weiss in 1891, and was sympathetic to Democratic political tenets. The Weiss ownership ended in 1921 when Paul Block, nationally known newspaper broker, and M. F. Hanson purchased the *Herald*. The morning *News-Tribune*, which was under the control of the Superior *Telegram* from 1925 to 1929, fell to the Block-Hanson team in 1929 and Duluth found itself a one-ownership newspaper city. The Ridder family purchased the two newspapers in July, 1936.

Minnesota in 1958 had 23 other daily newspapers in smaller cities. Oldest are the Winona *Daily News*, dating from the original *Republican* of 1855 (the Winona paper dropped its name of *Republican-Herald* in its 99th year), and the Red Wing *Republican Eagle*, which traces its history back to the *Republican* of 1857. In each of these 23 daily newspaper publishing cities the same forces for consolidation that existed in the metropolitan areas brought an eventual merger into a single paper of what had been sometimes scores of publishing enterprises. Typically, each community saw weekly papers come and go, several attempts at

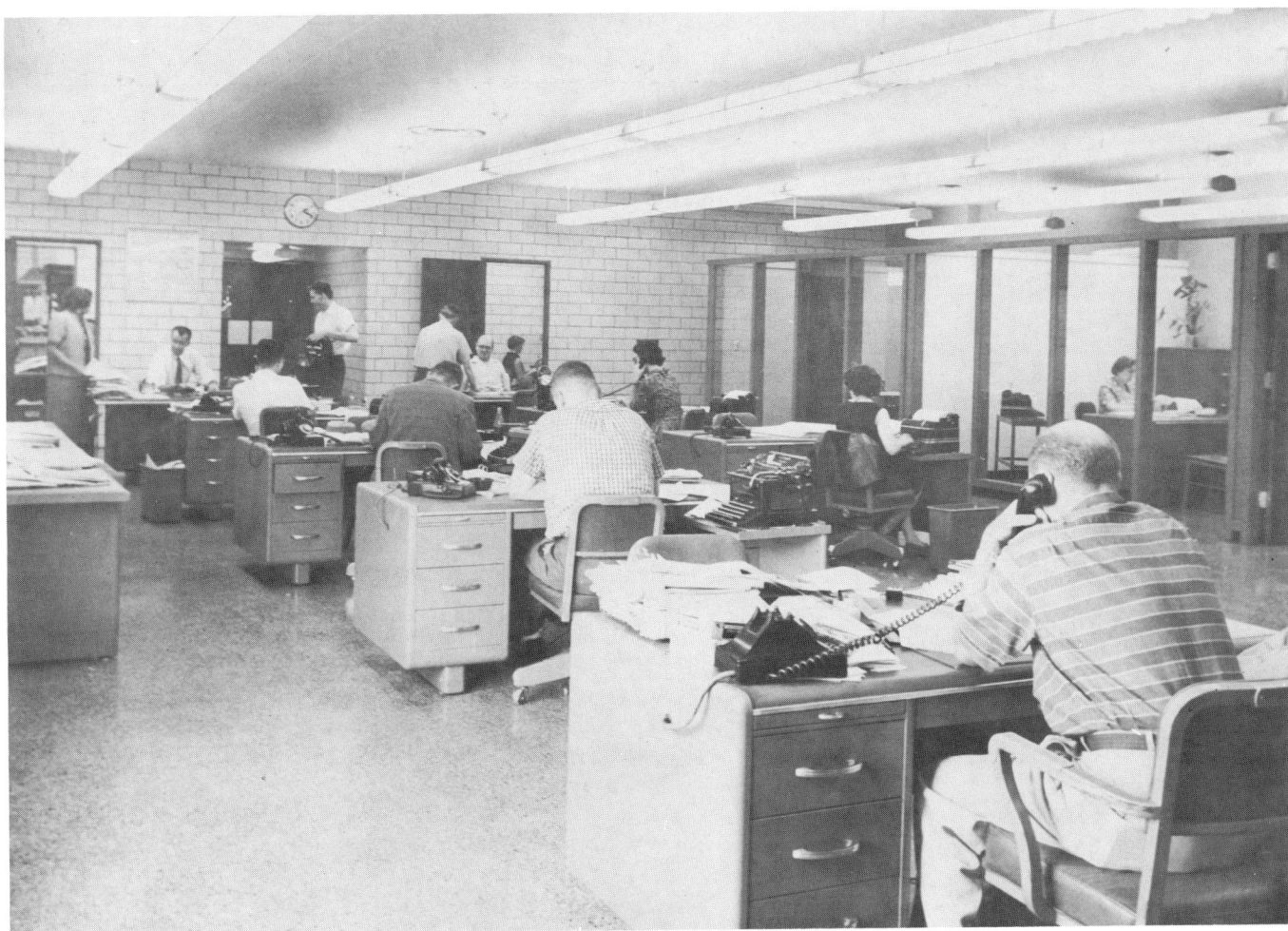

City room of the Winona Daily News

Looking over yesterday's work

Pulling proofs of type

Presses of large metropolitan newspaper

Making up newspaper pages

daily publication, elimination of the weeklies by the dailies, and a final merging of the dailies. In some smaller towns, a daily grew out of weekly or semi-weekly publications during relatively recent times.

The surviving community dailies, in Minnesota's centennial year, are the Albert Lea *Tribune*, Austin *Herald*, Bemidji *Pioneer*, Brainerd *Dispatch*, Crookston *Times*, Fairmont *Sentinel*, Faribault *News*, Fergus Falls *Journal*, Hibbing *Tribune*, International Falls *Journal*, Little Falls *Transcript*, Mankato *Free Press*, Marshall *Messenger*, New Ulm *Journal*, Owatonna *People's Press* (the only morning daily in the group), Red Wing *Republican Eagle*, Rochester *Post-Bulletin*, St. Cloud *Times*, Stillwater *Gazette*, Virginia's *Mesabi Daily News*, Willmar's *West Central Minnesota Tribune*, Winona *News*, and Worthington *Globe*.

Some family names have become synonymous with Minnesota's daily journalism: Rasmussen, in Austin; White, in Winona; Withers, in Rochester; Hitchcock, in Hibbing; Mickelson, in New Ulm and Fairmont; McKenzie, in Crookston; Schilplin, in St. Cloud; Darby, in Owatonna; Vance, in Worthington. Second, and even third, generation continuity has been established.

Through the years influential voices have been heard in these and others of Minnesota's smaller cities, carrying beyond the community limits. The elder Frederick Schilplin of the St. Cloud *Times* long spoke energetically in his editorial columns as an interpreter of Democratic party principles. Victor Lawson of the Willmar *Tribune* represented the radical-minded thinking of western Minnesota from the days of the Farmers' Alliance. Clifford H. Russell of the Mankato *Free Press*, Major Arthur M. Nelson of the Fairmont *Sentinel*, and J. H. Skinner of the Austin *Herald* were others who during lengthy careers won prominence as state editors.

Virtually all Minnesota dailies are members of the Minnesota Associated Press, a part of the worldwide cooperative news service. The AP editors conduct a continuing study of the effectiveness of their state news service. Among longtime leaders of the group are editors Harold Schoelkopf, St. Cloud *Times;* George M. Fisher, Hibbing *Tribune;* and Burt D. Pearson, *Mesabi Daily News.* Together

with dailies in the two Dakotas and portions of Iowa and Wisconsin, the Minnesota smaller dailies belong to the Northwest Daily Press Association, responsible for promoting the economic interests of community newspapers. At the metropolitan level almost entirely, working newsmen are members of the American Newspaper Guild, which had the Twin Cities and Duluth-Superior units as two of its earliest when the national organization was formed in 1934.

Almost as old as the state is the Minnesota Editorial Association, founded in 1867. Its membership includes all the state's newspapers, but primarily it is the voice of the weekly press. Minnesota's "country weeklies" long have been recognized as being among the most vigorous and influential of any state, and Minnesota has stood close to the top of the list of states in numbers of weeklies. In 1958 there were 359 country weeklies and semi-weeklies and 34 other weekly newspaper publications, including 15 in metropolitan areas, 4 Negro, 4 religious, 4 foreign language, 4 labor, and 3 business papers.

The roll call of Minnesota weekly newspaper editors virtually is unending. It begins with James M. Goodhue and his *Minnesota Pioneer* of 1849. Ignatius Donnelly, gifted radical leader of Minnesota politics who edited the *Emigrant Aid Journal* of Nininger, and Jane Grey Swisshelm, fiery abolitionist who founded the St. Cloud *Visitor*, joined the list in the 1850s. John A. Johnson, first three-time governor of Minnesota and Democratic party leader of the turn of the century, was an early president of the Minnesota Editorial Association while editor of the St. Peter *Herald*. Scores of other weekly editors have served in state offices and the legislature, in Congress, and in other public service.

Benjamin B. Herbert of the Red Wing *Republican* sparked the founding of the National Editorial Association in 1885 while serving as MEA president. Since then five Minnesotans have headed the national organization of weeklies: P. V. Collins, Minneapolis *Agriculturist*, 1903; Herbert C. Hotaling, Mapleton *Enterprise*, 1917; Will Wilke, Grey Eagle *Gazette*, 1920; Herman Roe, Northfield *News*, 1927; Alan C. McIntosh, *Rock County*

Famous headlines of yesteryear

Star-Herald, Luverne, 1953. Roe was field secretary of the national association and one of its most influential leaders in the early 1920s.

Family names are as imbedded in the history of Minnesota weeklies as its dailies. Three father-and-son teams from weeklies have served as MEA presidents: James C. and Edward J. Morrison, Morris *Sun* and *Tribune*; John P. and D. M. Coughlin, Waseca *Herald*; L. A. and George A. Rossman, Grand Rapids *Herald-Review*. A unique record has been set by the Frederick E. DuToits, father and son, who have edited the Chaska *Herald* without interruption since 1865. The Bjornsons of Minneota, the McGowans of Appleton, the Caseys of Jordan, the Peases of Anoka, the Clays of Farmington, and the brothers of the Roe, Mills, and Mattson families are still more examples.

The editorial association, whose central office in Minneapolis handles a half-million dollar annual business, has had Ralph W. Keller as executive secretary and field manager since 1941. Its annual meetings in February have grown in attendance from 38 in 1867 to 744 in 1957. MEA members have attended 40 annual short courses sponsored for them by the University of Minnesota's School of Journalism and Department of Agriculture in the interests of maintaining and expanding the state's community press.

Preserved in the priceless newspaper collection of the Minnesota Historical Society is the story of the first hundred years of the state as chronicled by its editors and newsmen—the evidence of changing social fabrics, of political growth, of economic expansion. No one can doubt but that the press, as a social institution expressing the goals of a democratic society, has played a key role in the development of the Minnesota of 1958.

The printing presses of Minnesota turn out many other products in addition to weekly and daily newspapers. Among them are approximately 150 magazines. Oldest is the *Northwestern Miller,* spokesman of the great grain industry. Founded at La Crosse, Wisconsin, in 1873, the magazine was moved to Minneapolis in 1879. There it became the leading publication of the Miller Publishing Company. Serving agricultural readers of the area is *The Farmer*, published in St. Paul since 1890 by the Webb Publishing Company. Biggest in circulation among magazines published in the state, with a million readers, is the *Catholic Digest,* edited in St. Paul. Other major magazines include *Modern Medicine* and its affiliated publications, the *Mississippi Valley Lumberman*, and the Lutheran publications of the Augsburg Publishing House, all of Minneapolis; and the trade journals of the Davidson Publishing Company, Duluth. More than 100 publications, mainly magazines edited for employes, are produced by Minnesota businesses; their editors are members of the Northwestern Industrial Editors Association.

The graphic arts industry is one of the state's most important businesses, and the Twin Cities ranks sixth among metropolitan areas of the country in number of employes and wages paid in printing and publishing. The graphic arts industry includes some 450 firms operating in the Twin Cities area alone, including printing houses, typesetters, photo engravers, electrotypers, lithographers, bookbinders, direct mail letter services, print paper makers, envelope manufacturers, and suppliers of printing machinery, ink, paper, and other products. The 450 firms employ some 17,000 workers and have total sales of more than $230 million a year. Their products are shipped to every state in the union and many foreign countries. The Dunwoody Institute in Minneapolis helps supply skilled workers for the graphic arts industry.

Several of the leading printing houses publish books, including those of the University of Minnesota Press, one of the country's leading university presses. Its best seller has been *The Doctors Mayo,* by Helen Clapesattle, former director of the Press. Like other university presses, the Minnesota Press specializes in books of scholarly importance which add to men's knowledge in a variety of fields of human interest. The West Publishing Co. of St. Paul has achieved distinction as publishers of law books. Another old established book publishing company is T. S. Denison & Co., Inc., founded in 1876 in Chicago and later moved to Minneapolis.

One of the most exciting ways of communicating is by radio and television. In the panorama of Minnesota, the early settlers would have looked upon these modern devices—permitting the fullest possible mass audience—as magic extensions of the clicking telegraph key of the 1860s and the first crude telephones of the 1870s. Voice broadcasting, possible after 1906, did not begin in earnest in the United States until 1919 and 1920, when private transmission began again after a wartime ban on amateur wireless stations. The University of Minnesota began plucking sound out of the air in 1912, and was offering concerts of finer music by 1921 over its radio-telephone broadcasting station, 9x1-WLB, the country's oldest station of its type to be in constant operation since its founding. WCAL, operated at Northfield by St. Olaf College, was licensed in 1921 and WLB in 1922, sharing the same wave length. Thus two educational institutions pioneered in bringing radio broadcasting to the state. WLB was renamed KUOM in 1931.

Commercial broadcasting began in 1922 nationally, as the number of radio stations jumped from 30 to more than 500 and the number of receiving sets from some 50,000 to more than 600,000. In Minnesota, the pioneers included WLAG (forerunner of WCCO), busily broadcasting market reports, Swedish and German band music from the Oak Grove Hotel in Minneapolis in 1922; WAAL, begun by the Minneapolis *Tribune* in November, 1922; WAMD (forerunner of KSTP), and WDGY, Minneapolis, 1923; WEBC, Duluth-Superior, 1924; WRHM (forerunner of WTCN), Minneapolis, 1925; and KGDE, Fergus Falls, 1926 (oldest surviving commercial station outside the Twin Cities and Duluth areas).

Network broadcasting came to Minnesota in 1925. WLAG had been reorganized in 1924 as WCCO by the Washburn Crosby Company (later to become General Mills) and Minneapolis and St. Paul businessmen. It began broadcasting network programs coming to it from the East over telephone wires on March 4, 1925. The Columbia Broadcasting System acquired a part interest in WCCO in 1928 and became sole owner in 1939.

The same year, 1925, Stanley E. Hubbard organized a network link with Chicago for WAMD. In 1928 the station was combined with KFOY, St. Paul, and was renamed KSTP—the National Broadcasting Company's Twin Cities affiliate.

Stanley E. Hubbard

KSTP and WCCO, as outlets of the two leading national networks and as 50,000-watt clear channel stations, led in providing entertainment and information for Minnesota and its surrounding area, and in establishing station news bureaus and special events departments for public service broadcasting.

Among other surviving radio stations in the state, KROC, Rochester, and WMFG, Hibbing, were founded in 1935; KDAL, Duluth, and WHLB, Virginia, in 1936; KATE, Albert Lea, and KVOX, Moorhead, 1937; KFAM, St. Cloud, KWNO, Winona, and KYSM, Mankato, 1938. Other Twin Cities stations still on the air in 1958 were WMIN, 1938; WLOL, 1940; KEVE, 1948; KTIS and WPBC, 1949; and WISK, 1951.

By 1958 there were 62 AM radio stations broadcasting from 48 Minnesota cities and towns. Eleven were in the Twin Cities and three in Duluth-Superior. Three other cities had two stations each — Mankato, St. Cloud, and Winona. The same three smaller cities also had FM stations, all founded in 1948, and the Twin Cities had three, for a total of six.

Television, meanwhile, had become a competitor. KSTP began experimenting with TV cameras in 1939 and brought telecasting to the state on April 27, 1948, using Channel 5 and NBC programs. WTCN-TV began operating on Channel 4 with CBS programs July 1, 1949. WMIN-TV opened Channel 11 in 1952 and KEYD-TV began telecasting on Channel 9 in 1955. KTCA-TV, the state's first educational television station, opened on Channel 2 in 1957. KDAL-TV and WDSM-TV went on the air in Duluth-Superior in March, 1954 (Duluth's first station, WFTV, opened in July, 1953, but later suspended operations). KMMT-TV, Austin, and KROC-TV, Rochester, have been telecasting since July, 1953, giving the state nine television stations.

A reshuffling of ownerships of some of the stations now occurred. WRHM, which had been founded to broadcast music to hospital patients, had been purchased by stockholders of the Minneapolis *Tribune* and St. Paul *Pioneer Press* and *Dispatch* in 1934, and renamed WTCN. In 1952 the WTCN owners, known as Mid-Continent Radio-Television, Inc., purchased WCCO from CBS. Channel 4 was renamed WCCO-TV. Controlling interest of 53% in WCCO and WCCO-TV now was

Behind the scene of a television program

Studios of WCCO Radio and Television

Offices of KSTP radio and television

View of control room of radio station KSTP

held by Mid-Continent, in turn operated by Robert B. Ridder for the Ridder family, publishers of the St. Paul newspapers. The Minneapolis *Star* and *Tribune* held the remaining 47% interest in the stations. WTCN-TV, under new ownership, took over Channel 11 and absorbed WMIN-TV; in 1957 the WTCN properties were purchased by Time, Inc. Channel 9 was renamed KMGM-TV with Loews, Inc. as leading stockholders. WTCN became the Twin Cities ABC outlet and WISK affiliated with MBS. WDGY became a 50,000-watt station for daytime operation and 25,000 watts at night, to lead the independents.

In the Duluth and Superior area, the Superior *Telegram* established WEBC in 1924 as the NBC station. WDSM radio (ABC, MBS) and WDSM-TV (NBC) are owned by the Ridder family. KDAL (CBS) and KDAL-TV (CBS, ABC) are owned by the Red River Broadcasting Company.

The tradition of broadcasting news and special events is strong in Minnesota. WCCO and KSTP have won national awards for their radio-TV news

and public service operations. University of Minnesota's KUOM has been honored for its educational programming, including the Minnesota School of the Air. KTCA-TV, telecasting programs sponsored by the University and the state's independent colleges and the Twin Cities public school systems, promised a further expansion of the use of the new medium for the welfare of the state of Minnesota. The Northwest Radio-Television News Directors Association has helped to promote effective use of both media in the best tradition of the journalistic craft.

Pioneer editor James M. Goodhue came to Minnesota in 1849 to help tell the news and create an informed public opinion. Were he to see his successors in the weekly and daily newspapers, magazine and book publishing, radio and television broadcasting, he would be amazed by the new facilities they possess to do their jobs, but he would not be surprised by their achievements in continuing the tradition of service he and other journalists have believed in—"the people's right to know."

328

CHAPTER ELEVEN

Mighty Men in Minnesota

The Republican Party in Minnesota

By VAL BJORNSON

Despite the fact that Republicans have held the executive reins for 78 out of Minnesota's first hundred years, voters of the state have long been described as "political mavericks." It is likely true that no state equals Minnesota's consistent record of inconsistent voting. Firmly professed "independents" equal in number the partisans on either side of the political fence.

Election of legislators on a nonpartisan basis ever since 1914, with institution of the "blanket ballot" in primaries beginning in 1934, has helped bring about a gradual decline in vigorous partisanship among the rank and file of voters.

Minnesota's first territorial governor, Alexander Ramsey, was a Republican. Although the first governor under statehood, Henry H. Sibley, was a Democrat, Ramsey on succeeding him in 1860 became the first Republican governor and ushered in the early era of unbroken Republican incumbency for almost forty years. Yet the stubborn independence today so typical of Minnesotans was evident even in that long span.

Successive farm protest movements challenged Republican legislative control time and again, even though voters entrusted every state office to Republicans. The "criss-cross" voting pattern was evident in the heydey of the Grange, first so politically vigorous on its birth in this state in 1868. It was revealed further as agrarian protest re-formed its ranks in closing decades of the last century, through

Alexander Ramsey

the Farmers Alliance, the Anti-Monopolists and the People's Party.

John Lind, the first Democratic governor after Sibley, a one-termer elected in 1898, faced a Republican-dominated legislature, as did the distinguished John A. Johnson, Democratic governor from 1905 to his death in 1909. The same was true of Winfield Scott Hammond, claimed by death after just a scant year's service in the governor's chair, in 1915. In the latter two instances, Republican

329

lieutenant governors succeeded their party rivals, for while Minnesotans had picked Democrats in the top executive positions, they had entrusted every other berth on the state's slate to Republicans.

When Republicans lost the governorship again in 1930 through Floyd B. Olson's election as a Farmer-Laborite, beginning what was an eight-year incumbency for that party, voters refused to dislodge Republicans from three of the major constitutional posts. They kept at least two on the job through all of the 1931-1939 period, and never yielded the three-man Railroad and Warehouse commission wholly to the Farmer-Laborites. In our fictional maintenance of nonpartisanship for the legislative body, conservatives—mainly Republicans—have never lost control of the state Senate.

The presidential election of 1912 was the first one in which Minnesota's vote did not go to the Republican nominee. "Bull Mooser" Theodore Roosevelt carried the state, with Democrat Woodrow Wilson in second place and the incumbent Republican President William Howard Taft, trailing. Pursuing the theme of stubborn independence and almost unpredictable voting patterns, it is interesting to note what happened after Republican presidential nominees began to lose the state regularly. Franklin D. Roosevelt swept Minnesota as the victorious Democratic nominee in 1932. He did so again in 1936, and '40 and '44, Harry Truman taking it in 1948. Yet in fourteen of those twenty years, Republicans were elected and re-elected to every major state position.

Even in days of greatest adversity politically, there has been a hardy persistence about Republican strength in Minnesota. When a 1954 defeat ended sixteen years of unbroken incumbency at the state level, margins for the merged Democratic-Farmer Labor party were small, and one veteran Republican office-holder survived, against the current. In 1956, DFL vote margins were smaller despite the bigger poll a presidential year always brings, and one Republican regained state office.

What accounts for this peculiar pattern — or lack of it—in Minnesota's political behavior? Even when voters have been disposed to "punish" Republicans through political banishment, they have tempered the blow. When Democrats or their DFL

successors have been riding high, the victorious phalanx has always turned up with some members missing. The situation simply re-emphasizes the looseness of party lines, the ease with which they are crossed by the state's inordinately large number of independent, uncommitted voters. And it shows an elasticity in the Republican party, a capacity to adapt to changing needs, a survival of the questful pioneering spirit which had to be the party's role in building so much of the state's whole structure through the opening half of our first century.

When the "Grangers," the Farmers Alliance and the Populists made challenging demands in the 60's, the 70's and the 90's, Republican leadership did not ignore them. Making some of those demands part of their own platform, they "delivered" when it came to performance. When the Nonpartisan League embodied the resurgence of farm revolt in the 20's of the present century, Republicans did not stand idly by. Under Governors Preus and Burnquist, in 1919 and 1921, they laid the legal groundwork for the farmer-owned producers' co-operatives, and in doing so they set a pace unequalled nationally.

The Republican record in Minnesota's first century has embodied something of "perpetual pioneering," meeting and anticipating demands made under constantly and rapidly changing conditions. The obvious, initial spadework was well-accomplished in launching needed services and bringing about their gradual expansion.

Framers of the 1857 constitution had agreed that proceeds from the sale of federal land grants would go into an inviolate permanent trust fund structure, its earnings dedicated mainly to education. In the backwash of nationwide financial crisis which immediately preceded statehood, even when a start had just been made, there were those who wanted to imitate the example of some other states in selling off trust fund land grants, using the money for immediate needs. The first Republican governor, Alexander Ramsey, insisted that lands be held at prices that were high in view of the period's trend, and that a substantial fund begin to accumulate to help support education. Republicans have, thus, from the start sought to maintain the essential character of the permanent trust funds as a heritage for posterity.

Republicans corrected some of their own early errors in handling the state's ore and timber assets. They not only began school and highway systems, but initiated state aid to support both. They provided the first regulation of railroads, public utilities and the grain trade. They brought earliest controls over the liquor traffic. They instituted factory inspection and protective measures for labor, put workmen's compensation on the statutes and provided for its enforcement. They instituted child welfare legislation, cared for the needy, the aged and the mentally ill. They installed the secret ballot and legislated to curb corrupt campaign practices.

All the while, there was maintenance of a basic conservatism in fiscal matters — an emphasis on financial soundness and on caution as to contracting public debt.

As to indebtedness, it was Republican Governor William R. Marshall who said, in 1866: "Money comes so easily when it is borrowed and paydays seem so distant, that it is quickly and often unprofitably expended." His statesmanlike successor, Governor Horace Austin, said in his 1871 message to the legislature: "Loans and other methods of anticipating the public revenues are seductive and defective, and, in practice, extravagant and oppressive." Austin, by the way, urged a more realistic debt limitation than the $250,000 maximum, which still stands in the constitution, with its readily heeded invitation to evasion. John S. Pillsbury, the first businessman in the governor's chair and the first three-term governor, in 1878 decried borrowing "for the immediate satisfaction of . . . real or fancied necessities." Governor William R. Merriam echoed him in a narrower particular when, in 1890, he deplored "the growing practice of anticipating tax receipts by borrowing from the trust funds and other state funds."

Republicans have both instituted and expanded numerous state services, keeping, meanwhile, a cautious eye on their costs. Without question, they have made their share of mistakes, and when they may have lagged in the corrective process, they have been punished for that by reverses at the polls.

Viewed from the centenary vantage point, the record of Minnesota Republicanism bespeaks public confidence, bestowed as that confidence has been by the voters for more than three-quarters of the state's first hundred years.

John S. Pillsbury

William R. Merriam

The Democratic Farmer-Labor Party in Minnesota's History

By KARL F. ROLVAAG

The Democratic Farmer-Labor party is both a very old and a very new political party. Despite the fact that it was formed as recently as 1944, it has strong roots that date it back over 150 years to the day of Thomas Jefferson. To give this complex organization added strength, it draws much of its vitality and personality from the spirit and movement of protest and dissent so typical of the expanding west and the transition from a frontier society to a highly developed and complex modern-day culture.

The Grange, the Farmers Alliance, the Greenbackers, the Peoples' party and the Populist movement, the Anti-Monopolists, the Progressives, the Knights of Labor and more recently, the Federation of Labor, the Nonpartisan League, the Farmer-Labor party, the C.I.O. and the Farmers Union have all left their impact on the Democratic Farmer-Labor party. These separate movements of dissent that often sprang up almost with the spontaneity of a prairie fire, were rebellious of nature, and all sought to correct social or economic injustices that existed or were believed to exist. Born in adversity, from these movements, the Democratic Farmer-Labor party has received the tradition of daring to strike against conformity when such action becomes a necessity in a changing world pattern.

In these movements there have been many outspoken leaders and strong personalities. The character of the dissent has tended to produce strong individuals and one of the ever-constant core problems has been to harness the individualism produced by protest. The roster reads from Ignatius Donnelly to John A. Johnson, and from Floyd Olson to Orville Freeman. These men and their colleagues helped to vocalize and give form to the liberal and progressive spirit that has marked the history of Minnesota.

There have been in the last century almost countless objects and subjects towards which these movements have directed their wrath and attention: the railroads, Wall Street, the trusts and combines, monetary policies, the Minneapolis Grain Exchange, tight farm credit, land speculation, war profits, the steel trusts, long work days and low wages, safety laws for workers, workmen's compensation and unemployment insurance, taxes, education and farm-to-market roads, conservation and iron ore.

In addition to specific legislative goals, there are, of course, other over-powering factors in the third party movement. For example, the aspirations of the recent immigrant for opportunity, recognition and status in his community.

The immigrant brought with him the spirit of democracy, nationalism and social justice which was part and parcel of the revolutions sweeping

Ignatius Donnelly

across the face of Europe during the Nineteenth and early years of the Twentieth Century. In his arsenal of knowledge was the Declaration of Independence and the Bill of Rights. He sought freedom and equality. He was often conditioned for liberal action programs.

The waves of immigrants brought much of the raw material for these movements, but they brought with them also added problems of integration into the liberal political scene. The natural and understandable tendency of the Swedes, the Norwegians, Danes, Germans, Finns, and more recently of the Poles and immigrants from the Central and Balkan countries—in fact, the non-English speaking countries—to retain their own languages, their own press and their own cultural institutions served to delay the day when their great strength, vitality and interest would be brought into play on the political horizon in joint effort.

The problems in forming the farmer-labor-liberal political alliance were many, intense, and extremely difficult aside from the integration of the immigrant. There were basic antagonisms and distrusts between the city worker and his rural counterpart.

Still another reason for the delay in the secure establishment of an effective, long-range political movement in Minnesota of the liberal forces was the failure to stress the necessity of building precinct, ward, and county organization to implement their program and philosophy. All too often the leadership was a personal, individual type that could not and did not last when the leader was stricken or weakened for one reason or another.

By 1918, the forces of urban liberalism and agrarian revolt had pretty well centered around the founders of the Farmer-Labor party. Motivated to a large degree by the Nonpartisan League of North Dakota, they sought to first employ the technique of capturing the Minnesota Republican party in the elections of 1918 and 1920, only to meet failure in both years.

As a result of these failures, the Farmer-Labor party was officially formed prior to the 1922 elections and instantaneously met with a degree of success. Dr. Henrik Shipstead was elected to the United States Senate and O. J. Kvale, from the Seventh District, and Knud Wefald, from the Ninth

John A. Johnson

District, were elected to the U. S. House of Representatives.

In election after election, the Farmer-Labor party continued to grow in strength. In 1930, the hyphenated party elected Floyd Bjørnstjerne Olson as Governor of Minnesota. Olson was the dynamic

333

leader with a magnetic personality and tremendous ability, who gave to the Farmer-Labor party its golden era.

Quite apart from the increased improvement in the Farmer-Labor party organization and the personality of Olson, the turbulent and terrifying depression of the Thirties aided the success of the F-L party. The Republican party on both the national and state levels failed completely to grasp the significance, depth and meaning of the depression. The Farmer-Laborites with their organization in the making and with their history of protest and dissent in their background, stood quite ready and able to point up the short-comings of their Republican foes.

As candidate and Governor, Olson took personal and dramatic charge of the campaign against reaction and conservatism, and developed programs in the state to work with the New Deal of Franklin Roosevelt, designed to alleviate suffering and distress.

Floyd B. Olson

Olson became a national figure who, many believed, had he lived, would have become a possible presidential candidate. Death cut short his meteoric career in 1936, in the midst of his campaign for a seat in the United States Senate.

With the death of Olson and after the fall elections in 1936, the forces of internal confusion, disorganization and collapse soon set in within the framework of the Farmer-Labor party and the succeeding administration. To further compound and speed the dissolution of a recently once-proud and effective political organization, certain elements of the extreme left-wing of the political spectrum began a steady and effective infiltration of the party apparatus. This period ended sadly for the Farmer-Laborites in the enormous reversal experienced between 1936 and 1938. Where in 1936, it had scored the largest majority ever accorded a state party, two years later it was defeated by the largest majority ever suffered by a losing party, representing a reversal of more than a half-million votes.

The elections of 1938 closed one definite chapter and began another in the background of the Democratic Farmer-Labor party.

The period from 1938 to 1944, was marked by a state of quiescence and deterioration in the organized political activity of the liberal forces in the state. During this period, the remnants and fragments of the once great Farmer-Labor party struggled amongst themselves for party control, while the Democrats continued to enjoy the fruits—as well as the thorns—of national patronage. At the same time the Republican party enjoyed a virtual monopoly in both state and congressional offices.

The relatively short life of the Farmer-Labor party established once again that a local party, state-wide only in scope and nature, cannot long successfully exist in the American body politic.

In an era of Hitler and Mussolini, of Stalin and Chamberlain, of marching legions and open warfare in Ethiopia and Finland, in Czechoslovakia and China, a political party—even in the Midwest—must have a window to the world.

By 1944, it had become clear to the state's liberals and progressives that political action not based upon the united efforts of the Democrats and Farmer Laborites were doomed to failure. Into this picture came Hubert H. Humphrey.

Humphrey, who had run unsuccessfully for Mayor of Minneapolis in 1943, had made such a strong impact upon state liberals and the Democratic National Committee that he was generally accepted as the leader and spokesman for the liberal movement in the state.

With the official blessings of President Franklin Roosevelt and the Democratic National Committee—both of which had more than a passing interest—Hubert H. Humphrey became the guiding genius which directed the amalgamation of the two long-time liberal forces in the state. There were many who objected strenuously and predicted dire results. They failed, however, to take into account the character, ability and personality of Mr. Humphrey.

In the early and formative years of the Democratic Farmer-Labor party, its greatest asset was Hubert Humphrey. A druggist and college professor trained in the field of political science, with a genius for practical politics, he is an orator with an uncanny ability to educate his audiences. Endowed with a sensitive and perceptive mind, and tireless energy, he has attracted to the young party a host of aggressive labor and farm leaders and was able to merge their efforts with those of the students, professors, intellectuals, as well as the veteran campaigners of the Democratic and Farmer-Labor parties.

With the election of 1944, the break-up of the liberal forces in Minnesota was brought to an end. The new party elected two congressmen, William Gallagher in the Third District, and the veteran liberal, and distinguished labor leader, Frank Starkey, in the Fourth District. It also carried the state for President Roosevelt, seeking his fourth term in office.

Despite the national trend towards Republicanism and the defeat of both Starkey and Gallagher in the 1946 elections, there were some bright spots for the budding young party. John A. Blatnik, of the Eighth District, was elected to the U.S. House of Representatives, a victory which represented not only a gain for the DFL, but one of the very few Democratic victories north of the Mason-Dixon line. At the party's convention, in that year Orville Freeman, just fresh out of the Marine Corps and on the staff of Mayor Hubert Humphrey, was elected Secretary of the DFL State Central Committee. The critical years of building a precinct,

ward, and county organization lay just ahead and Freeman was to play a major role in that effort.

In the course of the 1944 merger, the party had inherited the dissident, disruptive and left-wing elements which had aided in the destruction of the old Farmer-Labor party. It was Freeman, as Secretary of the State Central Committee, who planned, led and directed the building of a responsible party organization, dedicated to the basic principles of a democracy at home and abroad. Freeman and Humphrey and a whole host of others met the challenge of an alien philosophy head-on. In winning their internal battles, they clarified and enunciated more specifically the democratic principles of the party and set the stage for bigger victories in the future.

In 1948, Freeman was elected to a two-year term as State Chairman of the Central Committee, and became, as well, campaign manager for Mayor Humphrey in his bid for the U. S. Senate.

1948 was as successful as 1946 was dismal. Mayor Humphrey won the Senate seat. Blatnik was re-elected. Roy Wier, Eugene McCarthy, and Fred Marshall were elected to the U. S. House of Representatives. And the state was once again delivered to a Democratic President — Harry S. Truman. Liberalism seemed to be on the ascendancy in the North Star State.

The great victory of 1948 was due, of course, to many men and women who have since become prominent in the affairs of Minnesota and the nation. (Ironically enough, the Republican party contributed its share with its Republican-controlled Eightieth Congress.) But certainly much of the credit must go to the then young but able Minneapolis attorney—Orville L. Freeman.

Freeman soon became marked for his courage, decisiveness and administrative ability. Like Humphrey, he was possessed of a restless energy and a remarkably well-developed ability in debate and public speaking. The Governor-to-be had a steadfast will, coupled with a preciseness of mind which made for planned and determined action. Freeman's years as Secretary and Chairman of the state party organization were hard and tough years. From them, he came out battle-scarred, but definitely a leader.

In the ten-year period from 1948 to the close of Minnesota's first century, the DFL continues to grow and develop. The farmer-labor-liberal coalition seems to have become cemented into a solid framework.

Governor Freeman has not only been elected but he has been re-elected. The majority of the state constitutional officers are now of DFL persuasion, and the state House of Representatives is for the second succeeding session under the gavel of a liberal Speaker. Various and sundry other offices have been won by the merged party. Hubert Humphrey has won his second election to the United States Senate, and the congressional delegation numbers four of the state's nine seats.

This rather amazing record of growth and achievement is due to many factors. Insofar as the broad scope of the party is concerned, it has meant a meticulous attention to the detail of the party organization; the development of new organizational techniques designed to expand the base of the party; an emerging attention to platforms and resolutions adopted at party conventions; the refinement to a high degree of the pre-primary endorsement; and a constant and watchful demand by the party that its candidates practice not only a personal integrity, but an integrity of liberal philosophy as well.

Governor Freeman and Senator Hubert H. Humphrey, as the two ranking DFL public officials, have gained for themselves and their colleagues and their party a high degree of respect among the public at large. They have proved to be responsible men of high integrity, capable of vision, imagination, and daring.

In perspective, the great task of the liberal movement in this state has been to build a broadly based organization reaching into a wide diversity of interest groups without constructing an irresponsible machine.

The DFL is a new political party combining the enthusiasm of young intellectuals with the wisdom of an older generation and the great movements of protest and dissent in the Midwest. It is a new party combining elements of Nineteenth Century Populism with Twentieth Century New Dealism. It is a party which has turned its back on isolationism to acknowledge the need for a world-wide view.

It is a party of program, vitality and optimism.

It is a party which has much to offer Minnesotans as they step into their second century—a transition from arrows to atoms.

The Military History of Minnesota

By EUGENE T. NEWHALL

Col. George E. Leach

Minnesota's military history, though rich, varied and studded with action, is inseparable from the political, economic and sociological development of the state.

One of the brightest threads in the fabric of Minnesota history is the fact that many military leaders went on to become leaders of the governmental and business life of the area. Or perhaps it was the system of selecting military leaders in those early days (the company commanders were "elected" by their men, the men having been pretty much recruited by their officers) which caused natural leaders to appear on the military scene.

The first written chapter of Minnesota military history, if credence is put in the controversial Kensington runestone, was chiseled in a rock by a beached band of Scandinavian explorers in the year 1362.

The dispute as to the Kensington runestone authenticity rages since the stone itself was uncovered in Douglas County in 1898, but Minnesotans are determined to recognize America's discoverer. Leif Erickson's statue, west of the state capitol building, records the Viking explorer as "Discoverer of America, A.D. 1000." East of the Capitol, fronting the Historical Society building, the statue of Christopher Columbus is inscribed: "Discoverer of America, 1492."

In fact, the unwritten military history of Minnesota may well have begun not some few centuries ago, but several thousand years before that, as the last mile-thick ice cap receded and vegetation and animal life moved in to support sparse Indian populations in a state of savage competition with nature and with each other.

The Chippewa and the Sioux tribes were already at war with each other for Minnesota's hunting grounds when the first French voyageurs paddled onto the scene more than three centuries ago in search of furs.

Though these early explorations were both religiously and economically inspired, with seekers of skins and of souls riding in the same canoes through the wilderness of lakes and streams, the trading posts, mission stations and forts were one and the same installation.

Military and missionary zeal served parallel needs in the pacification of the heathen frontier.

The one unfortified mission post, located at Mendota at the confluence of the Minnesota and Mississippi rivers, was within the shadow of protection of Ft. Snelling across the river.

In fact, the whole modern-day opening up of Minnesota to peaceful settlement of a large agricultural and industrial population hinged on Ft. Snelling. There, soon after the War of 1812 established the power of the young American republic to stand on its own against Britain, were stationed the garrisons from which army escorts for exploring parties were furnished.

Past Ft. Snelling would float the boatloads of pioneers heading out into the rich "blue earth" country of southern Minnesota via the Minnesota River waterway.

From Ft. Snelling went troops to help suppress the greatest Indian uprising of the state's history—the Sioux ravages in 1862—plus the companies of patriotic frontiersmen who were the first to answer President Lincoln's call for volunteers to preserve the union in 1861. Then followed the surge of enlistments in what was still pretty much a volunteer army for the war with Spain in 1898, and the volunteers and conscripts for World War I, then the draftees for America's greatest military effort, World War II.

Ft. Snelling ceased, in fact, to be an active military post only in 1946, after the dictator regimes in Germany, Italy and Japan were toppled.

The union of the military with other civilizing influences in the development of the state is perhaps nowhere more eloquently exemplified than in the story of a relatively quiet but nonetheless strategic establishment at the geographic center of the state—Ft. Ripley.

The whole concept of that fort was pacification and protection, not conquest or exploitation. First manned in 1849 by Company A of the Sixth Infantry Regiment from Ft. Snelling, Ft. Ripley on the west bank of the Mississippi River between Little Falls and Brainerd served to protect one tribe of Indians—the Winnebago—from the long-warring Sioux to the south and west and the Chippewa to the north and east.

Minnesota's adjutant general, Maj. Gen. Joseph E. Nelson, in a history of Ft. Ripley written when he was a lieutenant colonel, describes the mission of the garrison which "conciliated the constant threats of Indian uprisings in northern Minnesota and enabled civilization to push its frontiers into the rich agricultural regions of the northwest and expansive timber regions of the north.

"The history of Ft. Ripley," the general goes on, "is devoid of any reference to extensive campaigns against the Indians, massacres, or great war between Indian nations. . . .

"The absence of these uprisings is indicative of the important part this military outpost played in the pacification of the redmen within its territory."

The tiny (mile-square) Ft. Ripley has since been absorbed into the nation's largest (43,000-acre) state-owned military reservation, Camp Ripley. Here each summer, national guard troops from several Midwest states take their field training as part of the continuing concept of a trained and ready citizen reserve to give the nation maximum protection in peace and war at least cost in dollars or liberties.

The merging of military and governing forces in Minnesota history is embodied dramatically in the person of one of the earliest governors, Henry Sibley. Though a Democrat, of the opposite party from Republican Gov. Alexander Ramsey, in 1862 when the Sioux uprising broke out, Sibley was appointed a colonel by Ramsey, and given the job of raising a state force to quell the Indians.

Tenseness of the situation is clear in two terse letters of the time between Governor Ramsey and President Lincoln:

Asking a one-month extension of the Civil War draft, Ramsey wrote: "The Indian outbreak has come upon us suddenly. Half the population of the state are fugitives. It is absolutely impossible that we should proceed. The Secretary of War denies our request. I appeal to you, and ask for an immediate answer. No one not there can conceive the panic in the state."

The President, harried by mammoth concerns for the whole survival of the union, replied: "Yours received. Attend to the Indians. If the draft cannot proceed, of course it will not proceed. Necessity knows no law. The Government cannot extend the time. A. Lincoln."

This statement was from a President who himself had served in earlier frontier actions against the Indians, and who remembered that the same Minnesota governor who was asking for a month's relief from the Civil War draft had volunteered the first 1,000 troops from the scantily populated state the day after Ft. Sumter fell to the Confederate "rebel" forces in 1861.

The personal-devotion history of Minnesota military forces is poignantly illustrated in the titles

Alexander Ramsey

tended to perpetuate some of this personal-loyalty type of military life into modern times.

But the last time Minnesota's 47th Infantry (Viking) division was called to federal duty, for the Korean emergency in 1951, the division of near 9,000 Minnesota and North Dakota men found itself training some 13,000 draftees from all 48 states and three territories, and Minnesotans and North Dakotans themselves were reassigned in many cases to posts in the Orient and in Europe, breaking up traditional home town military units.

The old recruiting slogan, "Join the Guard and serve with your buddies," couldn't always be followed under the complex pressures of organizing, training and deploying armed forces all over the globe to fulfill America's modern-day commitments.

* * *

And now for some graphic details of how Minnesotans have answered the call to arms in various conflicts and crises during the state's first 100 years:

Minnesota was just four years out of territorial status in 1862 when the Sioux, under provocations real or assumed, led by the able and zealous Chief Little Crow and triggered by hot-scalped renegades of the tribe, attacked white settlements at New Ulm and elsewhere in southern Minnesota.

Hundreds were massacred, hundreds more fled with only the clothes on their backs. Militia volunteered in small companies, named for their captains, at St. Peter. Colonel Sibley got together some 1,400 men, and relief for Fort Ridgely, crowded with refugees, was provided. From the fort, Sibley took eight companies for the decisive battle of Birch Coulee a few miles away, where Little Crow's offensive power was blunted. From this battle on, settlers gained confidence and tended to stay in their own areas under protection of local stockades.

The day after Christmas, 1862, at what is now the downtown corner of Front and Main streets in Mankato, 38 Sioux were hanged for their direct part in killings. President Lincoln, after studying the grievances of the Indians, including stories of cheating by some whites, commuted the sentences of the rest of the more than 300 Indians found

of old outfits of soldiers, named after their organizers and commanders rather than by numbers and nicknames as today.

The famous 151st Field Artillery battalion, which fired almost continuously during four months of World War I's heaviest fighting, can trace its lineage to "Emmet's light artillery battery," organized in St. Paul soon after the Civil War, and to "Bennet's battery of light artillery" across the river in Minneapolis. (No, competition between units did not extend to exchange of artillery barrages across the Mississippi River.)

The National Guard system, organizing troops by companies and batteries around home town armories on call by the governor for state emergencies or by the federal government in war, has

339

H. H. Sibley

guilty by a military tribunal. But he did order removal of the remaining Sioux and Winnebago to a reservation west of Minnesota up the Missouri River.

In the Civil War a regiment called the 1st Minnesota Volunteers was credited with turning the tide at the battle of Gettysburg. Thinned by long months of earlier campaigning, the 262 men and officers of the regiment carried out emergency orders to charge a much larger Confederate force and

gain the few minutes needed by Union forces to come up. The Minnesotans suffered 82 per cent casualties, 215 men killed or wounded, in this sacrificial action.

These were among the men of the Leif Erickson and Paul Bunyan legend, who served for $11 a month, marched on salt pork and hardtack, and suffered more losses from typhoid water, malarial swamps and exposure than from rebel bullets.

Civil War days at Fort Snelling

Company E of the Minnesota Infantry U.S.V. taken November 1862 at Fort Snelling

In the 1898 war with Spain, Minnesotans again volunteered in the cause of freedom for men other than themselves. And some stayed on after the end of that brief conflict, for the pacification of the Philippines and establishment of the decisive American principle of eventual self-government for the liberated former possessions of colonial Spain.

The American concept of civil-government supremacy in policy matters, with military forces derived from the populace and subject to orders from elected commanders-in-chief, lent a moral as well as a military support to movements for self-government.

In World War I, though Minnesota by then contained a large proportion of residents of German extraction, added to Scandinavian, Irish, Welsh, English and other nationalities, the response in the war to halt conquests by Imperial Germany, in what President Wilson called the war to "make the world safe for democracy," was as generous as in earlier tests of national unity.

One outfit alone, the 151st Field artillery, won World War I battle streamers on the battlegrounds of Lorraine, Champaigne, Champagne - Marne, Aisne-Marne, St. Mihiel and Meuse-Argonne.

In World War II, which broke out scarcely 21 years after the 1918 Armistice, Minnesota put the

342

Minnesota Pioneer Guard, 1858

Last detail leaving for camp, World War 1

first American soldier ashore in Europe, fired the first artillery shell against the Nazis in North Africa, helped make the early Japanese victory at Bataan in the Philippines as costly as possible while the nation re-gathered its forces from the shattering blow at Pearl Harbor in 1941.

The temper of Minnesota was exemplified when voters of the state re-elected to a third term as governor a man who declared before election that he would resign to join the navy. Into his job as governor went a World War I aviator who after the second World War became a United States senator.

As the state turned its Centennial mark the Governor was a World War II combat marine. The first Minnesota civil defense director was Col. E. B. (Ernie) Miller, commander of Brainerd's 194th tankers in the time-winning defense of Bataan peninsula which slowed Japanese gains in the Pacific while America armed and deployed for eventual victory.

In the Korean conflict, to which the United States gave troops, supplies and major leadership in history's first example of a worldwide international organization (the United Nations) going to

the aid of a small attacked nation, Minnesotans served from reserve, national guard, regular army and drafted units.

Minnesota National Guardsmen first trained thousands of inductees from their own and other states, then themselves sailed overseas for service in the conflict which showed the Communist world the determination of the free world to defend itself against armed aggression.

As the state started its second century of history, the nation was at peace, but the world was gripped in a cold war race for the allegiance of developing nations throughout the world, for supremacy not only in military might but also in science, technology, education and service to peoples everywhere.

Minnesota, which in draft examinations had enjoyed among the lowest rates of exemption for physical or mental defects among its hardy inhabitants, continued to train men, from jet pilots to infantry, against any possible future military challenge, while expanding educational facilities to provide men and women skilled in the crafts of peace.

343

CHAPTER TWELVE

In the Interests of Humanity

By JOHN C. KIDNEIGH

Nothing is so interesting as a study of people. A number of ways of life, various nationality backgrounds, many different skills, and a wide range of interests found among the people of Minnesota combine to make them as interesting to know about as any people anywhere. Withal, however, there are many common values and characteristics which make our people relatively homogeneous. A full description of all the people of Minnesota would occupy much more space than is possible in this volume. Such a description would call for an exhaustive sociological presentation.

Generally when we think of being interested in humanity we refer to those qualities thought to be uniquely human. In another sense we tend to think of persons or groups of persons who show some unusual human qualities. In a broader sense we think of persons or groups of persons who are in need of understanding and help.

This chapter is designed to introduce the reader to certain groups of Minnesotans who, for one reason or another, suffer from some need or handicap. And because it is characteristic of Minnesotans to have an interest in humanity, the people of this State have erected—and are in the process of providing—certain agencies and social institutions calculated to meet the need, reduce the handicap or prevent the seriousness of problems which some of our fellow citizens endure. Some of these agencies will be mentioned as we present the sketch of certain groups. Several service professions have come into being to skillfully assist needy people. The principal profession involved in this kind of

work is the profession of social work, so something will be said about that profession. But it must be remembered that all professions play an important role in human welfare.

Life for individuals, groups of individuals and communities is a continuous, never ending series of problem solving events. A problem may be described as a particular combination of factors and circumstances in time which brings discomfort, unhappiness or frustration. A solution consists of a re-arrangement of factors and circumstances with an addition or a subtraction of some factors or environmental change which will result in greater comfort, satisfaction, or achievement. If an individual, group of individuals or community is able to perceive the factors that make up a problem, a solution often can be found independently without the help of a professional or technical specialist. Most of the problems each of us face are solved in this way. If, however, the problem is very complex and is made up of factors which cannot easily be perceived and if there is lack of knowledge about what to do in such difficult straits, it is logical that the individual, the group of individuals, or the community should seek the expert help of a professional or technical specialist. For example, whenever we have a legal problem we turn to the profession of attorneys. Whenever we have a physical health or disease problem we turn to the professions of medicine and nursing. Whenever we have an educational problem we turn to the profession of teaching. Whenever we have a problem involving economic adjustment, social re-

that workers with adequate and special skills be available in sufficient numbers to man the farms, machines, and positions of service. Hence there is a vital role for schools, colleges, and apprenticeships to give the training needed to provide technicians, skilled and semi-skilled workers, farmers, teachers, professional persons, and the like. At the same time there is the need for employment services that will aid in getting the worker connected to the job he can do, or conversely, that will aid the business or industrial establishment find the worker it needs.

Most of our citizens are able to solve the problem of finding and keeping a job by the use of our established resources of training and employment services. Thence, through the earned pay check the necessities of food, clothing, and shelter, among others, may be purchased and provided for themselves and their families. But many of our citizens find it difficult, if not impossible, to qualify for jobs in our society, or may be temporarily or permanently unable to enter the labor market. Hence such a person is unable to procure the pay check through which the basic essentials for survival may be provided. At the same time many of our citizens are unable to secure jobs at high enough pay to fully provide the basic necessities for themselves and their families. Although these marginal earners can do certain kinds of work, they are handicapped by age, lack of training, or by deficiencies in physical or mental abilities. Sometimes individuals try to find work in occupations for which they have very little aptitude, but if given training for other work suited to their special or strongest aptitude they could become successful workers able to fully provide for themselves in jobs matching their abilities. After all, none of us is capable of being expert in everything. For example, one may have abilities to become a scientist but not a carpenter. One may have ability to become a plumber but not a teacher. One may have ability to become a printer but not a salesman. One may have ability to become a scholar but not a mechanic. One may have the ability to become a homemaker but not a businesswoman or a politician.

On the other hand we should not forget that many times lack of income through employment is not necessarily primarily associated with the worker's lack of ability or his handicap. In times of depression, business recession, or other economic dislocation many of the most able of our citizens find it impossible to find jobs. In an industrial economy like ours, it is possible that all may be seriously handicapped by a mal-functioning of the economy as a whole. The most serious of this kind of event in modern history was the great depression of the 1930's. Capable workers of all kinds were deprived of a livelihood by the economic catastrophe. And, from time to time, the closing of a plant, the drop in prices of particular commodities, or other economic changes may throw significant number of workers out of jobs and without income. Hence the operation of our total economy at maximum efficiency is of vital importance to all. From one point of view it may be said that all our farming, mining, manufacturing, business, production and distribution of goods and services exist for the purpose of increasing human welfare.

Even though our economy operates at its best there remains significant groups in our population unable to provide fully for themselves within the economic system. Let us look at a few of these and mention some of the agencies created by the community to serve their needs.

One group which includes nearly all who have recently entered, or are about to enter the labor market, is composed of individuals who need vocational assessment and guidance. Maximum productivity, success and happiness can be achieved if each individual becomes aware of his basic aptitudes and seeks employment where these aptitudes may be used. Often failure and inadequate earning power may result when one tries to do work for which he is not fitted. On the other hand, all but a relatively small number possess adequate endowments for some kind of work. Each needs to discover that for which he has aptitude, then select and complete the education and training logically related to his ability. In such a way the opportunity for work, success, adequate earning and independence is maximized.

Scientific tools for the measurement of intelligence, personality, and vocational aptitude have been created to make possible the discovery and assessment of vocational abilities. Many of the tools, known as psychological and vocational tests, have been developed by our Minnesota psychologists at our own University of Minnesota. Vocational counselling services have been established in many of our schools, colleges, and universities as well as in certain public agencies, particularly the State Office of Vocational Rehabilitation, the U.S. Veterans Administration, and Minneapolis Department of Public Relief. Through these resources a considerable portion of our population may secure vocational testing and guidance services. Unfortunately the resources have not developed to the extent that would make this important service available to all who need it and ought to have it. Because of this many individuals make mistakes in selecting their life work or occupation. Out of these mistakes failure and economic inadequacy result. Hence some people are unable to support themselves adequately because they are not in the field related to their ability. Or the mistake may not be discovered until they have reached an age which makes retraining and relocation difficult.

Some of our citizens are forcibly ejected from their jobs because of sickness or industrial accidents. Fortunately most of these recover and return to employment. In the interim, however, they are unable to support themselves or their families and concomitantly the medical and hospital expenses incurred add a double burden. When this tragedy strikes something must be done to help. A social insurance program, known as Workmen's Compensation has been established to pay some benefits to industrial workers who are off the job due to industrial accidents. These benefits help to provide some money to meet the costs associated with the temporary disability. Often, however, these benefits are not sufficient to cover all the costs. The worker then must use his savings until they are exhausted. Subsequently he must look to the county or township relief department for financial aid for himself and his family until such a time as he can re-enter employment.

In some cases a worker becomes permanently disabled through sickness or accident. If he is over fifty years of age and had been employed under the coverage of another social insurance program, Old-Age and Survivors Insurance (commonly called Social Security), he may secure benefits as though he were 65 years old and retired from the labor market. If under 50 years of age and in need he must turn to his county department of public welfare where, under a public assistance program known as Aid to the Permanently and Totally Disabled (financed under federal-state grants in aid), he may secure assistance for minimum basic subsistence payments.

Some of our citizens find the range of jobs for which they may qualify is sharply limited because of their own physical handicap, such as blindness, epilepsy, crippling conditions, or because of their own limited abilities, such as in the case of mental retardation. A solution to the problem in these cases depends upon adequate medical services to halt or cure the causative disease, and upon adequate medical, social work and rehabilitative services to assist the individual to use his remaining powers to the maximum. A variety of medical and hospital resources has been created by the community to provide medical, social work and rehabilitative service of this sort. The University Hospitals, the Kenny Institute, the Wilder Rehabilitation Center, the Curative Workshop, the U.S. Veterans Administration are representative of these resources. In addition, for those patients who have received the essential medical services, other social agencies play an important role in helping to get the patient back into the normal channels of living, education and employment. These agencies include the State Office of Vocational Rehabilitation, the sheltered workshops, and both public and private social welfare agencies. The state also operates institutions at Owatonna for the educable mentally retarded, at Faribault for the feeble minded, and at Cambridge for the epileptic, providing institutional care for those who have no family able to care for them in any other way.

In times of economic readjustment many of our workers are temporarily deprived of employment through no fault of their own. To help meet the loss of income resulting from such unemployment the community has established another social insurance program known as Unemployment Compensation. Under this program a worker thrown out of employment who consistently seeks employment through the State Employment Service, but who is unable to find suitable employment, may receive, for a limited number of weeks, unemployment benefit checks. Thus he can provide the minimum essentials for himself and his family. When the unemployment insurance benefits are exhausted, if he is in need he can turn to his local county or township for relief. This local public assistance, known as general relief, is designed to provide at least a minimum subsistence for those in need and without resources for self support. Often the payments are inadequate for an unemployed worker to maintain himself at any but the lowest level.

Sometimes the grim hand of death strikes down the breadwinner in the family. In such a case the survivors, the wife and children, are often left without means of support. In earlier days when such a tragedy occurred the family was often broken up, the children placed with relatives or put into an orphanage, the mother had to seek employment or refuge with her relatives. The harsh dislocation had its serious repercussions on all the victims. In order to preserve as much as possible the human and societal values that can come from keeping the family together and providing for their livelihood the community has established a social insurance program, Old-Age and *Survivors* Insurance, and a public assistance program known as Aid to Dependent Children, under which income is provided until the youngest child reaches eighteen years of age. For the widows and children of deceased workers who during their work life were employed in work covered by social security, benefits are paid providing enough to purchase the minimum essentials of life. Nearly two percent of all our Minnesota children under 18 years of age are being supported by these benefits. For those mothers with children whose husband was not covered by Social Security, or where he still lives but is absent from the home or permanently disabled, public assistance payments from the Aid to Dependent Children program may be secured from the local County Welfare Board in an amount determined by budgetary need (and in accordance with certain standards of assistance which define

"need") to provide economic support for the mother and child. Nearly two percent of all Minnesota children under 18 years of age are being supported by these payments.

There are many Minnesotans unable to support themselves for one reason or another. We have mentioned some of these: the disabled, the handicapped, the blind, the crippled, and those too young to enter the labor market. Another and larger group should be mentioned here, although we will say more about this group later. This is the group too old to work. We do not know how many of our 319,000 fellow Minnesotans age 65 or over are out of the labor market. Many have undoubtedly retired and are living on their savings or pensions, or are living with relatives who provide their support. We do know, however, that over 85,000 Minnesotans age 65 or over (382 in every thousand over age 65) are drawing benefits from Old-Age and Survivors Insurance and that an additional number of more than 49,000 are receiving payments under the public assistance program known as Old-Age Assistance. Hence of the 319,000 Minnesotans age 65 or over approximately 130,000 are beneficiaries of our two large public economic security programs. It is fortunate that the community has erected social insurance and public assistance programs to provide at least minimum essentials of food, clothing and shelter for our senior citizens.

As was mentioned earlier, many of our Minnesota families, while having an employed breadwinner, secure such low income as to make it very difficult if not impossible for the family to be supported even at minimum levels. One of the research studies completed at the University of Minnesota School of Social Work seems to suggest that marginal income in some families can be accounted for by lack of education, and that lack of education of the father and breadwinner of this generation resulted from penurious relief administration in the previous generation causing the young man to leave school before he should have in order to help support his father's family. A more generous financial support in the previous generation would have made it possible to keep the child in school long enough so that in this generation his earning power would be sufficient to keep him off relief rolls. It is logical, therefore, to provide an adequate financial support to families in this generation in order to reduce relief costs in the future generations to say nothing of the increased value to society through assuring a more productive member through better and more education than would be acquired if a youngster had to leave school to work in order to barely survive.

As another essential to providing a better generation of adults from among the under privileged children of today, it is generally recognized that housing is a fundamental. Even average housing is beyond the means of the low income family, hence such families tend to be pushed into substandard housing and slum-like conditions. To break this vicious cycle of slum conditions handicapping children so that they cannot ever extricate themselves, plans for public housing have been developed. Under these plans decent housing is built by public money to be rented to low income families at rental rates they are able to pay—usually about the same they would have paid for slum-like housing. Ultimately the cost of building and maintaining these public housing units is liquidated through the rentals paid over a long period. The families raised in such surroundings should have a better chance for normal development and integration into the normal community. The problems usually associated with slum living, such as delinquency, sickness, fire hazards, social disorganization and the like, would be reduced if not eliminated.

In Minnesota some public housing has been erected in St. Paul and Minneapolis. Unfortunately not enough units have been built there to meet the need. Outside the Twin Cities there are many places where public housing is needed but none exists yet.

We can say that no one in Minnesota need starve, nor be completely shelterless. A good many programs are in existence to combat the most extreme handicaps of poverty. On the other hand, poverty has not been completely eliminated. Malnutrition and sub-standard housing continues to exist. Much remains to be done in eliminating the handicapping horror of poverty if we are to have a society truly expressing its dedication to the interests of humanity.

Section 3 — We All Need Friends

Human beings do not live alone. Each person grows up in a family in a neighborhood within the context of groups of fellow beings. Each individual needs relationships with others. He needs the assurance and conviction that he is part of a whole, of a collective that unites him with other persons, and that accepts him as a part. He measures himself by his peers. The social relationship he acquires and maintains are as important to him as the elemental essentials of food, clothing, and shelter. From ancient times the philosophy has been maintained that the whole is stronger and more important than the mere sum of its parts. The whole of society and the group as a distinct collection of people has corporate needs which are not identical with those of the individual members but which are created by the interaction of the individuals who are the parts of this entity. Any individual must experience to some degree this involvement with others to acquire human culture, to find life maximally satisfying, and to be able to live successfully. The essential ingredient in establishing a bond with others is an acquired skill in social relationships usually developed through friendship.

Most of our Minnesota citizens find resources accessible to them so that social relationships with other humans can be developed easily and naturally. The home, the church, the school and a variety of organized clubs and groups furnish a structure and an on-going set of associations into which a new-comer may be assimilated. Every club or group, formal or informal, provides the essential opportunities for developing skill in social relationships within each person who belongs. The importance of these associations cannot be over emphasized because they furnish an essential dimension to life for everyone of us. Restrictions which prohibit participation in group life deprive an individual of a basic necessity as surely as if he were deprived of food. Furthermore, a lack of a variety of kinds of group experience deprives an individual of the opportunity to develop a maturity and rounded personality essential to normality and happiness.

Unfortunately many of our fellow Minnesotans do not have ample unrestricted opportunity for friendship and group associations of a wholesome quality in the volume for each that would be desirable. Individuals in this category would include some, but not all, of members of minority groups (such as Negroes, Indians, Spanish-American, Jews, and others who are excluded from membership in many organizations); individuals from marginal income or poverty-stricken families lacking money for dues, appropriate clothing or equipment required for membership in some groups; individuals recently migrated to this country who suffer from language or cultural handicaps making it difficult to be accepted easily into group memberships; individuals with underdeveloped social skills often socially maladjusted to such a degree as to be not easily accepted by any but an anti-social group; individuals isolated from organized groups by reason of physical distance; and individuals with physical or mental handicaps which limit their ability to participate, plus others who for one reason or another cannot or fail to take advantage of group life experience to a desirable degree.

Fortunately the people of Minnesota have long recognized the importance of group life and recreation as an essential for themselves and their children. Informal groups of people, particularly of young persons, have gathered together for religious services, sportive entertainment, dances, singing, festivities and other activities for many years. More recently formal organizations and agencies have been established to provide continuous access to group life for all. Public recreation departments, public parks and recreational facilities provide one basic framework giving opportunity for recreational group experiences. Other agencies and organizations, such as the Y.M.C.A., Y.W.C.A., Boy Scouts, Girl Scouts, Recreational Associations, Four-H Clubs, Camp Fire Girls, etc., provide another net-work of membership groups giving opportunity for wholesome activity and social relationships for a considerable proportion of our youth. In addition to a wide range of group activ-

ities, physical sports and games, each of these organizations conducts summer camps which make possible an unusually valuable experience for children and youth.

For those whose opportunity or inclination to participate in group life is restricted, another kind of social agency has come into being. A prime example of this kind of social agency is the settlement or neighborhood house. A considerable number of settlement houses have been established in the Twin Cities. Here were to be found many groups, who, for one reason or another were under-privileged. Here also were groups who had less opportunity for meaningful group experiences. The settlement houses were established in the area of residence of such groups adopting as their essential purpose to serve as "good neighbors" to the people of that sub-community. The aims of the settlement houses were to improve the physical and health conditions of the neighborhood, and to utilize the religious and educational capacities of the underprivileged, of ignorant exploited people, and of immigrants and unskilled workers who came to industrial centers and large cities. They attempted to develop among the poor and low-paid working class a feeling of self-respect. Hospitality, friendliness, education, information, and getting acquainted with one another in the neighborhood was and is a chief pattern of their activities.

The settlement houses through their staff leadership and in cooperation with the people of the neighborhood pioneered in slums and congested areas in an endeavor to demonstrate by life experience the firm belief of their members in democracy, human equality, and dignity, and by concerted action how improvements could be achieved. They fight for equal opportunities for the poor and handicapped and for abolition of prejudice and discrimination against people because of skin color, religion, race and foreign birth. In order to achieve these valuable goals of human welfare, education, and cultural development of all persons in the neighborhood, the settlement houses have provided a wide range of activities, such as, boys and girls clubs, playgrounds, gymnasiums, kindergartens, adult education classes in a variety of timely subjects, discussion groups, day-nurseries, therapeutic groups, informal groups devoted to cultural and civic affairs, to discussion of economic and health problems, and to the development of creative abilities in art classes and workshops, dramatic and literary groups. In time it became increasingly evident that programs of various kinds were to be fitted from time to time to the current needs of people in the neighborhood. For example, as the volume of newly arrived immigrants declined Americanization classes were no longer needed. Simultaneously, however, other problems emerged such as the need for an aggressive and out-reaching program to involve pre-delinquent or delinquent youths in rehabilitative or preventive programs providing for development of healthy and socially acceptable behavior. Although program content changed to meet changing needs, the constant throughout was the need for developing a skill in social relationships. Hence, the settlement worker concentrated upon developing a professional skill which would be effective in helping people to acquire attitudes and skills in relating to others. In time this process became identified and defined as social group work. Now it is considered essential to the education of every social worker that he be introduced systematically to social group work methods.

Settlement houses, neighborhood houses, and community centers continue to serve their several neighborhoods or communities in traditional activities and programs, but each is constantly re-assessing itself and its community to make such modifications as may be demanded by the changing times. Although no new settlement house has been established for some time—many having been on their present sites for decades (as for example, Pillsbury House, Northeast Neighborhood House, or Elliot Park Neighborhood House in Minneapolis and Neighborhood House or Hallie Q. Brown House in St. Paul)—nevertheless, each has modified its program over the years to serve as consistently as possible the social needs of its neighborhood. One, Wells Memorial Community Center, has abandoned a house-centered program and instituted a group work program reaching out to natural groups or forming groups for specific purposes

using for meeting places various community facilities such as schools and churches.

A federation of settlement houses provides an area-wide organization providing for interchange of information between the staffs of the various settlements. The impact of the whole of the settlement program and activity is considerable in the urban area.

Many of the several organizations which offer programs of recreation and informal education also operate camping programs. These camping programs serve youth primarily. The typical experience provides a boy or girl a summer week or more of life, recreation and wholesome activity in an organized camp, usually located on or near the shores of one of our more than ten thousand lakes. Here the freshness of out-of-doors, the excitement and fun of living and playing with others and under the helpful leadership of experienced adults, and participation in an organized program of activities give an incomparable opportunity for learning new dimensions of inter-personal relationships. Fortunately thousands of our Minnesota youth enjoy this experience. Unhappily many of our boys and girls are unable to have this important experience, often because of lack of money, but also because some are handicapped physically or mentally. As a consequence a few camps have developed a camping period or two during a camping season to serve a particular youth population, such as crippled or mentally retarded children.

It is safe to say that nearly half the youth of our urban areas participate in one way or another in one or more of the many recreation and informal educational activities provided by our privately supported youth serving agencies, that is, those agencies supported in part by Community Chests. It is also probable that a larger percentage of our youth take advantage of facilities and programs offered by our public parks and recreation departments.

Many of these organizations, publicly and privately supported, see recreation and informal education as primarily an enjoyable and constructive use of leisure time, that is, "leisure time activity engaged in for its own sake." Valuable by-products of recreation are recognized, such as development of creativity, self-expression, self-discovery, mental and physical health, experience in democratic living, and provision of constructive activities. On the other hand, some of these organizations see their program activities as a means to an end, the end being primarily the development in the participants of certain desirable attitudes, values, and skills in inter-personal relationships. When this is the aim a highly trained professional social group worker is usually charged with program responsibility and group leadership.

In any case we can be proud of a relatively well developed network of recreation and informal education agencies in this State providing opportunities for making friends, participating in enjoyable activities, and developing skills in relating to others.

The maintenance and extension of opportunities for wholesome social interaction provides a challenge for anyone who will put time, effort or money into services established in the interest of humanity.

Section 4 — Some of Us Get Sick

The possession of health is a most desirable state. But health is a relative matter because everyone experiences sickness in one form or another at one time or another. Health is hard to define because it is an ideal state not perfectly nor permanently enjoyed by any given individual. It may be thought of as a state of relative equilibrium. Sickness or disease (note this word *dis*-ease) may be considered as being a condition which temporarily or permanently upsets the equilibrium of the organism. To many health and sickness seem to be restricted to the physical or biological make-up of the human. But with increasing recognition of the inter-dependence of physical, psychological and social dimensions of man the concepts of health and sickness have been extended to include the relative state of equilibrium—disequilibrium (*dis*-ease) in physical, psychological *and* social functioning of any given individual. Hence we not only recognize biological disequilibrium (such as a rise in temperature, debility, etc., arising from a

bacterial invasion of the human body) as sickness, but also recognize mental illness (including the so-called *functional* illness, i.e., those that seem to appear without biological reasons), and social pathology (such as chronic truancy, delinquency, or promiscuity) as sickness. It is also recognized that while a given disease may be primarily a state of biological disequilibrium (such as is tuberculosis, for example) it has its psychological and social dimensions as well. Or, on the other hand, while a given illness may be primarily a state of social disequilibrium (such as is delinquency, for example) it has its psychological and physical dimensions as well. Furthermore, we recognize that sickness or disease may range from states of very little disequilibrium (such as a slight cold, or a momentary feeling of depression or a brief period of rudeness in social relationships) to very serious states of disequilibrium (such as pneumonia, mental illness, or cruel behavior).

In another dimension we are wont to classify some other conditions as "not-fully-healthy." These are conditions where the individual lacks or has failed to develop physical, mental or social functioning relatively equal to that possessed by most persons or the average of the population. For example, the individuals classified as mentally retarded, those born with physical deformities, or those whose personality and social functioning has been warped to an unusual degree are thought of as failing to possess a desirable level of health. Here again this "not-fully-healthy" state may range from slight to extreme deviations from the normal.

Attempts to cope with the problems of sickness and disease, or with the problems associated with the "not-fully-healthy" states may take several forms. We may classify these approaches broadly into the following: (a) prevention, (b) treatment, (c) research, and (d) the activities of implementation involving community organization, social action and financing. Broadly speaking effective prevention, treatment or the implementation of either rests upon research.

In the limited space available it is not possible to explicate fully all the extra-ordinary developments in health facilities which are to be found in

Minnesota. It is sufficient for our purpose here to mention but a few.

The range of public health and preventive programs is considerable. Laws to regulate food production and distribution, purity of water supply and hazards of life in housing contribute to the prevention of many diseases. Programs of inoculation and vaccination prevent the occurrence or severity of many diseases. Programs of education in health, social functioning and personal care contribute to the avoidance of sickness and social pathology. Early case finding with early treatment reduces the severity of illness or social mal-functioning. Early recognition of illness depends upon the capacity of parents and associates to recognize the symptoms of physical, psychological or social disequilibrium early enough to seek and secure the professional services of medical doctor, psychologist or social worker for the ailing one. The capacity for recognizing physical illness symptoms is better developed and more widely possessed than the capacity to recognize psychological or social malfunctioning, hence early case finding and treatment of illnesses primarily of a social or psychological nature is not as efficient as it should be. The teacher in primary and secondary schools is in a strategic position to perform a vital role in early case finding among that segment of our population attending schools but frequently the teacher is handicapped in this function because the school system fails to provide the central professional worker that can facilitate the service, namely the school social worker (sometimes called the visiting teacher).

Because of sanitation measures, inoculation programs, and the like, we have virtually conquered or eliminated the threat of the major contagious diseases. The remaining principal public health problem is that group of illnesses (as yet not fully understood) which can be classified as social and mental primarily. Much remains to be done to establish effective measures of prevention for these illnesses.

The range and quality of resources in Minnesota for the treatment of physical illness and disease is outstanding. The volume and quality of facilities and personnel (that is, the hospitals, clinics, medical doctors, nurses, dentists and paramedical personnel) for the treatment of physical illness is as good as can be found anywhere. The ratio of doctors and nurses per thousand of population is relatively high. The number and quality of hospitals makes Minnesota a leader in the field. Such internationally famous medical centers as the Mayo Clinics with their associated hospitals at Rochester, and the great University of Minnesota medical center with its associated hospitals and clinics in the Twin Cities give Minnesota almost unparalleled status in the medical world.

At the same time it can be said that programs and resources for the treatment of mental and social illnesses have lagged in their development. Mainly what facilities and personnel we have are of good quality but the volume of such programs and services falls short of meeting the need that exists. In recent years rapid strides have been taken to try to overcome this deficiency, but much remains to be done.

For many years the University of Minnesota has been a major center for the production of high quality psychiatrists, psychologists and social workers. Most of these highly trained professional experts have found their way into Minnesota agencies, schools, hospitals, clinics and service organizations. Some have also gone to other states and countries to give vital leadership there. But the fact remains that the supply is currently insufficient for the demand.

One of the features of many of the treatment facilities established in this State is the use of medical doctors, (including psychiatrists), clinical psychologists and social workers in joint or teamwork practice. In this pattern the full ramifications of the illness of the patient can be studied, diagnosed more accurately and treated more adequately. In this context the medical social worker, working in a responsible relationship to medicine, and the psychiatric social worker, working in a responsible relationship to psychiatry and psychology, can and does play a vital role in bringing into focus an often overlooked dimension of illness, namely the social functioning dimension. Both social case workers and social group workers function in this role. The classic example of this kind

358

of treatment facility is the child guidance clinic where typically a psychiatrist, a clinical psychologist and several social workers work jointly to treat the emotionally disturbed child and his family. One of the best known of these clinics on the American scene is the Amherst Wilder Child Guidance Clinic in St. Paul. Several other mental hygiene clinics are to be found in the state, some serving children primarily, some primarily serving adults and some serving both children and adults. In each instance there is medical direction of the treatment program.

On the other hand, there are many agencies and facilities in the State which operate with an almost total absence of doctors of medicine, where the social worker must take primary responsibility for the treatment regimen. These are the agencies rendering treatment for illnesses which are primarily characterized by social mal-functioning or disequilibrium. Some of the agencies dealing with social mal-functioning or social pathology may be illustrated by the following:

(a) The Youth Conservation Commission which deals with problems of social pathology expressed by delinquency. It maintains diagnostic centers, treatment programs of institutional care and probation or parole service, and community organization services calculated to assist in prevention of social pathology.

(b) Court service agencies in certain of our larger counties which deal with problems of social pathology expressed by delinquency. Each usually operates in conjunction with a court of record or a juvenile court for legal adjutication of cases, and provide treatment services through institutional facilities and social case work services rendered by a social worker (often called a probation officer).

(c) Family Service agencies which deal with problems of social mal-functioning (such as marital discord, family break up, inability to perform an expected social role, such as to get and keep a job, parent-child conflict, inability to manage economic or relationship problems, or tem-

porary emergencies in physical or mental health which impair the social functioning of the family) and provide treatment services through a skilled case work service rendered by a social worker (often called a family counsellor or sometimes called a child welfare worker).

(d) Public Welfare agencies which, in addition to dealing with problems of economic need, deal with problems of social mal-functioning in family disorganization, personal incapacitation, social dystrophy arising from long term economic dependency and the like. These agencies provide treatment services primarily through a case work service performed by a social worker (often called a public welfare worker or a child welfare worker).

(e) The school social work (sometimes called visiting teacher) departments of some of our larger school systems which deal with problems of social mal-functioning of pupils which has reached such a stage of seriousness as to impair the students' learning or to have become an upsetting influence in the classroom and the school. These departments render a treatment service through a case work service, (often involving the use of community agency resources) rendered by a social worker (often called a visiting teacher).

(f) Neighborhood agencies, such as settlement houses, which deal with a variety of problems of social mal-functioning, sometimes to a rather extreme degree, which impair individual capacities to such a degree as to result in delinquency or mental ill health. These agencies render a treatment service through the use of group process (sometimes in what is known as therapeutic groups because of the intensity of treatment) performed by a social worker (usually called a social group-worker, but sometimes called a program worker or community worker.)

The listing of the types of agencies included above is intended to be illustrative rather than exhaustive of the many social agencies primarily manned by social workers but working in the general field of treatment of illnesses which are primarily of the nature of social mal-functioning or social disequilibrium.

What has been said about prevention and treatment can be paralleled by similar statements about research. In research bearing upon physical and biological aspects of health and disease, the research scientists of Minnesota have produced a magnificent record. The findings arising from research in physiology, anatomy, chemistry, and other basic biological sciences have made possible additional research in applied fields of medicine so as to provide unexcelled progress in treatment techniques in surgery, internal medicine, physical medicine and the like. The mass of new knowledge through research and the burgeoning development of advanced techniques in the treatment of physical illness has made Minnesota one of the principal medical centers of the world.

At the same time it can be said that research bearing upon mental and social illnesses has lagged behind the research bearing upon physical and biological aspects of health and disease. The volume and quality of research in psychological and social sciences carried forward in Minnesota ranks high in the United States, nevertheless. Some of the most distinguished research work in psychological and behavioral science has come from Minnesota social scientists. Not the least of these contributions is the creation of psychological measurement tests and instruments, one of the most widely known of which is the Minnesota Multiphasic Test of Personality. The volume and variety of research efforts of Minnesota social scientists and social workers, plus the increasing volume of research by psychiatry give promise to yield significant advance in knowledge and thence in treatment in the years that lie immediately ahead. As knowledge through research is gained programs of prevention and treatment of physical, psychological and social aspects of disease will improve even more.

A word can now be added about some of the implementing resources which enhance the effectiveness or availability of prevention and treatment

programs. A state department of health, a state department of public welfare, and the associated local health and welfare departments provide a network of public agency structures through which preventive and therapeutic efforts are provided, stimulated or coordinated. Concurrently privately financed health agencies (such as the several tuberculosis associations, the heart association, the muscular dystrophy association, etc.), the privately financed welfare agencies and community welfare councils, plus the professionals in private practice provide a network of effort to stimulate public interest and support for health programs. In another dimension the presence of medical and hospitalization insurance programs, including Blue Cross, Blue Shield and Group Health, make possible, in part, the prepayment of illness expense for a sizable proportion of our population.

As can be observed there exists something of an imbalance in our resources and services for those of us who may get sick. This imbalance is geographical and functional. Urban dwellers have easier access to a variety of treatment resources for physical, psychological or social illness than do those who live in rural areas. The volume and variety of treatment resources of physical illnesses exceed those for psychological or social illnesses. In the interest of humanity these imbalances should be rectified.

Section 5 — Many of Us Grow Old

Every person begins to grow old immediately after birth. What is considered old age is defined differently among various people or societies, and is defined differently within one society from time to time. More than one hundred years ago the people who lived in what is now the State of Minnesota would have declared a person over 45 or 50 years as belonging in the old age class. Now we would be likely to consider such a person as middle-aged. Because of the widespread twentieth century custom of fixing age 65 as the retirement age we tend to define old age as including those above 60 or 65 years. In the final analysis we must recognize it is a relative matter. Some people are older, in the sense of showing significantly declining physical or mental powers, at age 50 than others are at age 70. There is no strict dividing line between youth and middle age, nor between middle age and old age. Despite this, unless death should strike us down prematurely, each of us must inevitably enter the old age class.

Significant advances in measures that control or eliminate causes of death, particularly those associated with infant mortality, have resulted in raising the average age of our population. More people now survive long enough to reach old age than was so a hundred years ago. Life expectancy at birth is now approximately 70 years whereas life expectancy at birth less than a hundred years ago was a mere 34 years. At the same time the chances of surviving from birth to age 65 has risen from 40 to 66 per cent for males, and from 44 to 80 per cent for females within the past fifty years. Significantly, however, the *length* of life has not been extended. This is illustrated by the fact that for those who had or have reached age 60 the expected additional years of life was 15.6 years one hundred years ago and is 15.8 years today.

The survival of a higher percentage of the people born and improved health conditions reducing the number of deaths in subsequent years of life has resulted in a changed age composition of our population. Today 9.5% of the population of Minnesota is age 65 or over. Only ten other states in the United States have higher proportion of their total population in the age 65 and over class. (New Hampshire 11.1%, Iowa 10.8%, Missouri 10.7%, Massachusetts 10.6%, Nebraska 10.5%, Vermont 10.5%, Kansas 10.4%, Maine 10.4%, Washington 9.7%, and Rhode Island 9.6%). While the total population of our country has increased approximately 15% in the last decade, the size of the group age 65 and over has increased more than 20%. Quite obviously it can be said that more of us are in the old age class viewed either from the standpoint of absolute numbers or from the standpoint of the proportionate number who are age 65 and older.

In general, aging persons seek to find security and influence, broadly speaking. The interests of the aged might be summed up in a five-fold way:[1]

1. To live as long as possible; or at least until life's satisfactions no longer compensate for its privations, or until the advantages of death seem to outweigh the burdens of life. Life is, indeed, precious to the old.

2. To get more rest; or release from the necessity of wearisome exertion at humdrum tasks and to get protection from too great exposure to physical hazards. Opportunities, in other words, to safeguard and preserve waning physical energies. Old people have to learn to hoard their energies.

3. To remain active participants in group affairs in either operational or supervisory roles; any participation being preferable to idleness and indifference. "Something to do, and nothing be done," is perhaps the main idea.

4. To safeguard or even strengthen any prerogatives acquired; i.e., skills, possessions, rights, authority, prestige, etc. The aged want to hold on to whatever they have. Seniority rights are zealously guarded.

5. Finally, to withdraw from life, when necessity requires it, as honorably and comfortably as possible and with maximal prospects for an attractive hereafter.

[1]This formulation is that of Dr. Leo W. Simmons of Yale University.

Many older persons are deprived to some degree of certain rights and privileges accorded to people generally. Let us look at a few of these and to note for each how much is being done or left undone that affects the welfare of our Minnesota aged.

1. Equal opportunity to work. Our society recognizes the value of work to the person and to the community. The older person should have equal opportunity, if physically and mentally able, to be gainfully employed. Our rapidly growing population demands more goods and services. In fact by 1965 we will require a volume of goods and services 40% larger than that of 1955. To achieve this we will need ten million additional workers. We can expect to have these additional workers but this increased work force will come principally from the mature work force aged 45 or over, a con-

siderable proportion including the older worker. What research we have seems to indicate that age restrictions on job openings bar many older workers. In the twin cities area 54 of every 75 job openings one month in 1956 were limited to applicants age 45 or less. The restrictions appear despite the fact that it has been demonstrated that many older workers exceed the average output of younger workers, show greater employment stability, possess considerable flexibility in accepting change in assignment, occupation and earnings, possess no significant vocational handicaps for jobs for which they are qualified, and present no significant increase in costs to employers for new hires associated with the funding of insurance and pension plans. Much remains to be done by business and industry in Minnesota, as well as in the nation, to fully exploit the manpower resource found in the older worker group to say nothing of the value to the person and to society when the older worker is gainfully employed.

2. Adequate minimum income. In addition to the right to work when qualified, older persons should have a retirement income sufficient for health and for participation in community life as self respecting citizens. A large number of private, industrial or business pension and retirement systems exist in Minnesota. Undoubtedly these contribute substantially to the maintenance of retirement income for a considerable proportion of our senior citizens. However, the system which serves the largest number, providing a minimum but basic retirement payment, is the governmentally operated system known as Old-Age and Survivors Insurance (often called Social Security). Most of the work force in Minnesota is covered under this system and approximately 26% of the 319,000 persons age 65 and over in Minnesota are drawing retirement benefit checks. Another 16%, approximately, whose income from whatever source

is insufficient to keep them from being classed as "in need" as defined by public assistance laws and rules, are receiving payments under the provisions of the federal-state-local public assistance program of Old Age Assistance. While it is comforting to know we have these two major social programs providing economic support and income for approximately one-third of our aged population, we need to be reminded that the individual requirements of many of our aged (particularly the need for payment of medical care) exceed their economic resources.

3. Housing and living conditions. Older persons are entitled to the satisfactions of living in their own homes and, when this is not feasible, in suitable substitute housing. For older persons who need care that cannot be given them in their own or other private homes, they have a right to expect the institutions that serve them to be as home-like as possible and have high standards of care. The relatively high rate of home ownership in the population of Minnesota possibly means that a considerable proportion of our older citizens are living in their own homes. Many who are recipients of old age assistance payments under our public welfare system are living in their own household and caring for themselves. Several hundred older citizens are living in the homes or institutions provided for the aged by the several agencies, some church-sponsored, that have been established in the State. Mainly these are commercial rest homes for the convalescent care of homeless aged persons. A few aged who are temporarily ill or incapacitated are able to be maintained in their own homes through the ministrations provided by the home-maker services of some of our social agencies. Despite these resources for the housing and care of aged persons in Minnesota there exists critical problems of housing shortage. It is extremely difficult to find adequate housing with reasonably adequate care for

the feeble or physically impaired old person. Because of the increasing numbers of the aged in the population a major housing problem lies ahead in the immediate future.

4. Physical and mental health. Older adults should have adequate nutrition, preventive medicine and medical care adapted to the conditions of their years. Older persons who are chronically ill, physically disabled, mentally disturbed, or unemployable for other reasons, have a right, to the fullest extent possible, to be restored to independent, useful lives in their homes and communities. Doubtless most of our older citizens are able to provide for themselves or they have family which can take responsibility for their care. There are many, however, beset with illness, mental disturbance, inadequate cash income, or declining abilities due to age that die slowly from malnutrition, inactivity and degenerative disease. Despite the resources for medical care many fail to or cannot take advantage of the resources. A considerable number of our senior citizens become inmates of our state mental hospitals because of incroaching senility and mental confusion. But there is another side to the gloomy picture. Many of our older adults possess adequate powers, physical and mental, to make valid and important contributions to the community through self support, productive employment, valuable leadership, and devoted service in one capacity or another. The problems of sickness and disablement among our aged are serious and are being met only in part. The resource in manpower and talent among our aged is considerable and is being utilized only in part.

5. Participation in Community activities. Older persons who wish to continue working encounter almost insuperable obstacles. After 40 years of age workers have increasing difficulties in getting new jobs. At 65, or another fixed age, many are arbitrarily retired. They receive little or no assistance, such as vocational retraining and counselling, in

Repairing toaster at Goodwill Agency

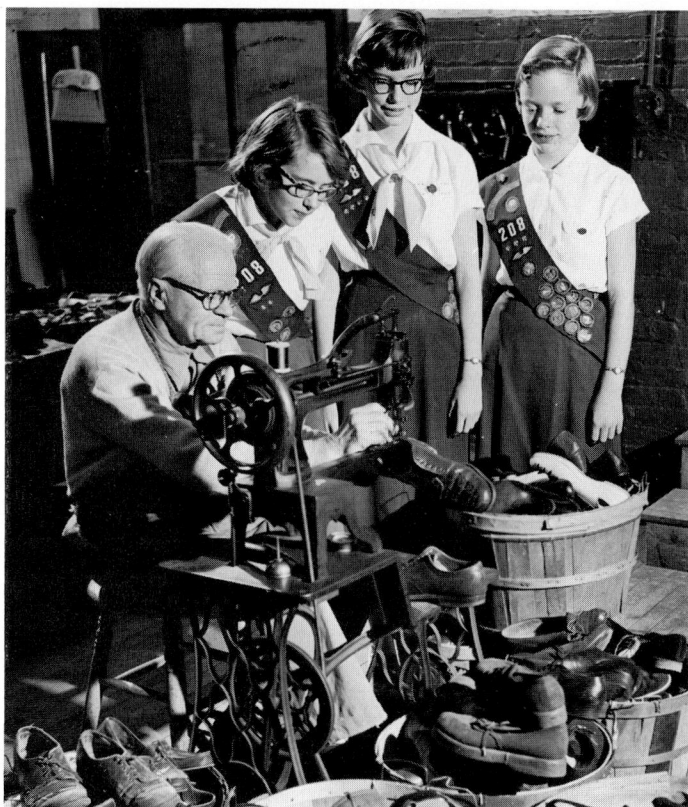

Repairing shoes for resale at Goodwill Agency

363

Experienced workmen make furniture serviceable again

Upholstering chair
Sewing and darning machines are kept busy

meeting special problems of re-employment. Relatively few part-time or full-time jobs are reserved for older workers. This failure to utilize the productive capacity of older persons constitutes a waste of manpower and a loss to the national economy. Tragically this removal of older persons from the work force also brings to the older person a feeling of rejection and depression which adds to the adjustmental burden he inevitably must carry. Likewise he is cut off from accustomed roles in participating in community life. Luckily there is developing in Minnesota a conviction that older citizens should be active as long as their physical and mental powers permit. Encouragement is being given to older citizens to form social groups and to participate with those of other ages in recreational, educational, religious and civic activities in their communities. The State Department of Public Welfare has appointed a special officer to stimulate and coordinate programs for the aged. The Hennepin County Department of Public Welfare has had for several years a social group work consultant to stimulate the formation of golden age clubs and encourage broad consideration of the problems of the aging. Private social agencies and denominational groups are becoming seriously concerned with plans and programs that should contribute significantly to improved resources and facilities.

6. Social Services. In planning for retirement and in meeting the crises of their later years, older persons should have the benefit of such social services as social casework and social group work can provide. Counselling, information, referral to community resources, vocational re-training, informal education, recreation and opportunities for social intercourse are some of the services being provided for some of our aged. A considerable responsibility falls upon the public welfare agencies to give such service to those more than 49,000 recipients of public assistance. Less than a fully desirable program of social service is provided because the public welfare agencies are under-staffed and under-budgeted for the heavy responsibilities placed upon them. Some portion of providing social services to the aged is carried by private social agencies. Here again, however, less than a fully desirable program is possible because of staff and budget limitations. Considerable expansion of social services for the aged is indicated. In securing objectives of human welfare for the aged increased emphasis on the right and obligation of older citizens to free choice, self help and planning of their own futures should be fostered. In the interest of humanity we must give more consideration to the needs of our older citizens.

Section 6 — It Takes Planning to be Truly Humane

Philanthropic giving to needy persons is a humane expression of man's concern for his fellow man. In the earlier years of the first century of the statehood of Minnesota there was considerable attention given to the care of the poor. Early legislation provided for public responsibility for persons found in destitute circumstances. Help through these public resources was meagre at best. Concurrently there was an attitude that it was a degrading experience to have to "go on the county" or to receive poor relief. Consequently it was thought that those who had a bit more of material goods or resources had a responsibility for giving to the poor. In those earlier days there was a widespread practice of giving alms to the "worthy" poor, not so much for the benefit of the recipient as for the salvation of the giver's soul. To some extent, this relatively unenlightened attitude toward giving persists to this day. As people began to take responsibility for the welfare of their neighbors through activities which were called "charity," "poor relief," "philanthropy" and "social reform," and particularly after there appeared a body of paid personnel who served as agents for groups of philanthropists, it began to be apparent that the welfare and rehabilitation of the recipient of aid should take precedence over the salvation of the soul of the almsgiver.

At this point earnest students of the problem of philanthropy began to clarify a dilemma. On the one hand, it was contended that the objects of charity were inferior human beings, that their poverty resulted from their own lack of intelligence or morals. On the other hand, it was contended that poverty and maladjustment arose from society itself and from forces beyond the control of the individual, such as the dislocations arising from industrial revolution, depressions, wars, and similar phenomena of social disorganization or reorganization. The paid personnel who served as agents for groups of philanthropists came to the conclusion that neither of these views was wholly tenable. Sometimes personal inadequacy could largely account for the suffering and unhappy state of the individual. Sometimes societal conditions could be blamed for the individual's plight. More often both forces seemed to be at work. Hence, human problems could best be solved by working with the unfortunate on a case-by-case basis, helping individuals marshal their own and the community resources toward a solution of their individual and family problems. Simultaneously effort had to be made in social reform which would assist the community to take such steps in community organization and to adopt such social policy and programs as would tend to reduce or eliminate the hazards of poverty, sickness, unemployment, delinquency, discrimination against minorities, and the like. Consequently many agencies were founded to assist needy persons. Most of these agencies were established in our urban centers.

Social work programs began to appear in various forms, some primarily adopting the case-by-case method for the solution of human problems— from which the modern method of social casework evolved, and some primarily adopting group action methods—from which the modern methods of social group work and community organization evolved. Later as the agencies became large in size, and particularly as social work programs under

Blighted area of large city

Dejected men

Mission lunch counter

Some Missions are capable of feeding many men

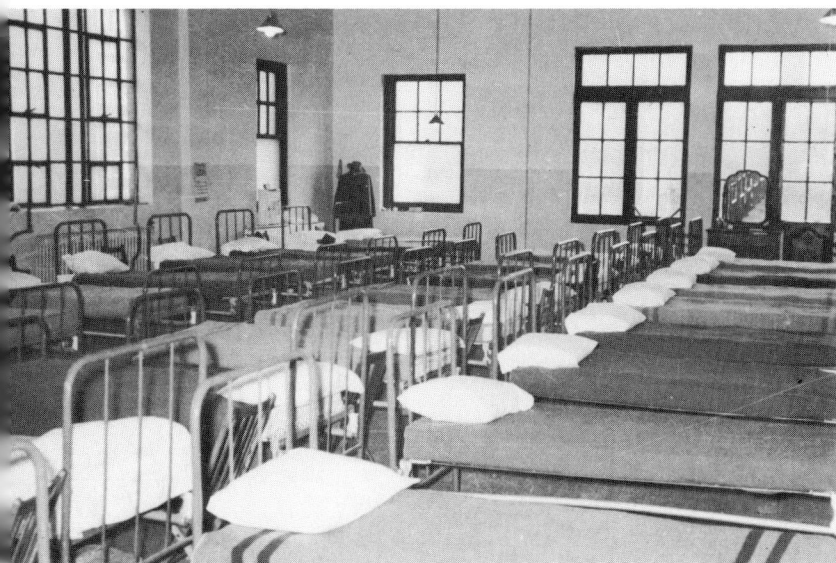

Sleeping rooms are kept clean at Mission

governmental auspices developed, the modern methods of social work administration evolved. Throughout these developments, as social agency leaders sought to understand the problems with which they grappled, there was a development of social work research methods.

The multiplication of philanthropic endeavors, usually expressed in the establishment of various social agencies, brought some confusion, overlapping of programs, and fragmentation of community resources and interests in human welfare. The variety and extent of these services gave rise to demands for coordination and guidance toward orderly development. The demand was met in part before the beginning of the twentieth century by charity organization societies (sometimes these were called United Charities, as was the case in Minneapolis) and social service exchanges (a central registry of all relief receiving clients through which social agencies could exchange information on a given case and effect joint planning for the client). From these earlier efforts at coordination the modern Community Welfare Council has evolved. There are now more than fifteen of these Councils in the cities of Minnesota —three, Duluth, Minneapolis and St. Paul, have established large, modern, and qualitative community welfare councils.

At first the councils were established as a device for cooperative work on the part of the several social and health agencies of the community. One aspect of that joint effort was the establishment of Community Chests which serve to hold a single annual drive or appeal for funds to finance, in part, the several member private agencies. Another aspect of cooperation was to undertake jointly community planning for welfare and health purposes. More recently the Community Welfare Council, while retaining its base of agency membership and its service to that membership, sees itself as a vehicle for citizen action in the promotion of human welfare. As such the Councils are engaged in an established process of social work identified by the term "community organization."

Through the community organization process the Community Welfare Councils survey the whole range of human welfare and health needs in the community, assist social agencies to coordinate their efforts toward meeting those needs, stimulate the development of new programs to meet newly emerging needs, encourage the development of quality of service, help the community to reduce or eliminate instrumentalities when a particular service or program is no longer needed, and provide a means through which the community can express its policy in social and health matters. The process by which these goals are achieved is social planning which in its broadest sense aims to bring about a more effective adjustment between social welfare needs and resources. Simultaneously the Community Chests which are organically joined to the Community Welfare Councils provide a means through which financial support for the recognized qualitative agencies of social welfare may be secured in the most efficient way known. This modern vehicle of financing guarantees the donor that his money will be used in the best way that responsible lay and professional leadership of the community can devise.

Planning for health and welfare on a state-wide basis has become largely a responsibility of the State government. Several state agencies each concerned with particular aspects of human welfare engage in planning and administering the several state administered programs of health, mental health, education, employment security, correctional and welfare. Many of these governmental state agencies are influenced to a considerable degree by federal agencies of the United States government through expert consultative service and financial grants-in-aid. Coordination between state agencies is achieved by inter-departmental committees, by special committees appointed by the Governor, and, when legislative action seems indicated, by interim committees of the state legislature.

At the national level planning for health and welfare is carried forward in three ways:

(1) The U.S. Department of Health, Education and Welfare through its several offices and bureaus, in Washington, D. C. and regional offices, gives consultation to state and local health and welfare agencies.

(2) National associations in the several functional fields, such as the Child Welfare League, the Family Service Association, the American Public Welfare Association, the American Public Health Association, the American Hospital Association, etc., provide consultation and standard setting functions to local and state agencies, governmental as well as private, to assist them and the communities they serve to do a qualitative job in their respective programs. A national community organization instrumentally known as the Social Welfare Assembly serves these national associations in a way similar to the role played by local Community Welfare Councils to local social and health agencies.

(3) National Conferences, the principal one being the National Conference on Social Welfare, provide forums for the interchange of ideas, the formulation of policy and the dissemination of ideas.

The whole complex of social planning organizations exist to improve the quality of service by the community to its needy citizens. Without such planning philanthropic efforts and resources would be fragmented and comparatively ineffectual. Through planning and coordination, the financial and personal resources of the country devoted to human welfare become more truly humane.

The success of health and welfare programs in our modern complex society rests upon public understanding, adequate financial support, but most importantly on the personnel whose full time services are spent in health and welfare activities. Through these workers the community's interest in humanity is implemented. Many kinds of workers and professionals are engaged—clerical workers, bookkeepers, institutional aids, fund raisers, and the like in non-professional tasks—but most importantly, doctors, nurses, educators, public health workers, psychologists, lawyers and social workers in the essential professional tasks. The contribution of the several service professions to human welfare is of considerable magnitude, but because the profession of social work is the principal profession dedicated to and charged with the responsibility of staffing and administering most of the social welfare programs of our State, it is proper that a brief statement about the social work profession be presented.

Social work as a profession is primarily a product of the twentieth century although its roots are well established in earlier times. The emphasis in social work up to 1900 was on effecting the "moral" behavior of the individual through personal influence and neighborly intercourse with the poor accompanied by limited material assistance. After 1900 attention began to be shifted to the conditions under which the individual lived. Social work swung sharply toward a program of environmental improvement as the new means for reaching a solution to the problems of poverty, dependency and disease. With the expansion of the field through the impetus of social reform, the need for more than enthusiastic and inspirational leadership became apparent if the emerging programs were to be sustained and furthered. Workers with administrative abilities and training in the methods of social work were needed. Professional training within the University of Minnesota for training in "social and civic work" was established in 1917. This early training course has evolved to become the present graduate School of Social Work in the University of Minnesota. A national professional organization, known then as the American Association of Social Workers, was formed in 1921, a local chapter was formed in Minnesota that same year. This, with the publication in 1917 of Mary Richmond's book *Social Diagnosis* dates the beginning of modern social work as a profession in this country. As the profession emerged from its lay past, the focus gradually came to be the welfare of the individual for his own sake in the interest of society rather than the measures to deal with specific social problems, such as poverty, alcoholism or crime. Social work has become more and more a conscious application of democratic principles with an increasing understanding of the dynamics of human behavior and of the social process. It is a disciplined helping process which is aimed at assisting individuals, groups of individuals, and communities in the problem solving continuum which is life for them. It attempts to *work with* the relationship problems of human beings *through* a relationship which is consciously controlled, and marked by warmth, consistency, and respect. Successful work of this nature requires broad education, capped by intensive and extensive professional training.

Education for social work consists of six years of College and University education. The first four of these years is spent in securing a broad liberal education including a concentration in one or more of the social sciences (anthropology, economics, political science, psychology and sociology) with a few courses about the field of social work, eventuating in the B.A. Degree. The remaining two of these years is spent in a graduate professional school of social work studying intensively and extensively social work methods of social casework, social group work, social community organization work, social policies and programs, and human behavior, accompanied by a field work internship under tutorial supervision. The liberal arts colleges in the state, as well as the University, offer the first four years leading to the B.A. degree. The University of Minnesota School of Social Work offers the two graduate years of instruction leading to the Master of Social Work degree, and two additional years leading to the Ph.D. degree in social work. Since education for social work began in the University in 1917 thousands of Minnesota youth have studied social work, several thousand bachelor's degrees and over 600 graduate degrees in social work have been conferred. At present our University School of Social Work is one of the leading schools of the 55 in the United States accredited by the Council on Social Work Education.

There are about 100,000 social work positions in the United States, in Minnesota approximately 2,000. Opportunities for a career in service in the interests of humanity in the profession of social work are bright and challenging.

Conclusion —

In this book you have been introduced to some of the history, the beauty, the accomplishments and the glory of our great State of Minnesota. In this chapter you have been given a glimpse of the range and variety of services which have been established to serve those fellow Minnesotans who, for one reason or another, suffer from some need or handicap. A heart-felt concern for our fellows demands increased effort, money, time and attention if we are to measure up to our goals of human welfare. Wherever there is disease, disorganization or fear, let us prevent it, reduce it and treat it with all the skill and tenderness we have. Wherever there is a spark of hope, let us fan it to a flame of accomplishment. Wherever there is need, let us meet it with sound programs of service. In such ways will we earn the right to be called human. If we are to be whole we must have a primary interest in humanity.

Citizens Club helps keep children off streets

The dreams of the aged are security and freedom from want

Playgrounds are provided for needy children

CHAPTER THIRTEEN

Living Creatively in Minnesota

The Theatre

Consultants: John Harvey, Anna Phelan, Frank Whiting, D. Z. Woods

Introduction by Anna von Helmholtz Phelan

This chapter of "Minnesota Heritage" is to give readers an idea of the wealth of creative art and learning that Minnesota has to offer its people. No attempt is made to go into detail, for the detail is too rich; there are too many facets to do more than give an intimation of the riches the state has to offer. The account of the writers, prose and poetry, the learned men and women who have contributed, how great a share, the artist and the actors and those who have fostered the theatre, is too extensive to give more than a hint. Read and you will see, and you will say "I never knew Minnesota had so much to offer so many people, so many people of significance. I shall more than ever be proud to belong to Minnesota!"

The history of Minnesota is in itself the greatest drama of all. As a panorama unfolding before our eyes, the people who have created our state sparkle brilliantly for a moment before passing from view.

In the field of theatre and the dance, an exciting and varied cast of characters appears. The age-old fervent ecstasy of the Sun-Dance worship of our Dakota or Sioux Indians brings us all the elements of drama as a religious experience: struggle and sacrifice, then catharsis. The electrifying performance given in the University of Minnesota's pageant of the early days of our state, "Rifle, Axe and Plow" by David Thompson and James Aliferis, produced in 1949, vividly re-created the Sun-Dance. Our Ojibway or Chippewa Indians have many dramatic ceremonies connected with the

Grand Medicine Lodge and other religious solemnities. The Indian has great gifts of story-telling; dances were passed down from generation to generation; dances enacted in pantomine the buffalo hunt and other vital experiences. Frances Densmore's studies of Indian music offer many provocative glimpses into the life of our aborigines.

Minnesota drew upon other sister arts of the Theatre besides Music and The Dance. In the Panoramas, which might be called our first moving pictures, artists held audiences enthralled by their paintings on canvases 10 or 12 feet high, which depicted scenes of the Mississippi and surrounding territory. Narrators told in gruesome details of battles between Indians and whites, while the vivid paintings were unrolled. Even before Minnesota became a territory in 1849, pioneers flocked to see this absorbing entertainment. Our Minnesota Historical Society has interesting information on this subject.

An invaluable guide to the Theatre in Minnesota is the study Dr. Frank M. Whiting, director of the University Theatre, has made in "A History of the Theatre in St. Paul, Minnesota, From Its Beginning to 1890." A micro-film of his doctor's dissertation on the subject is in the Historical Society, where also is his article in Minnesota History on "Theatrical Personalities of Old Saint Paul." In the latter, Dr. Whiting quotes the fascinating Joseph R. Brown concerning early theatricals at Fort Snelling. Speaking of the play "Pizarro," Brown said, "The representation of this tragedy . . . caused our mind to wander back to the winters of 1821 and 1822, when a thespian corps used to murder ROLLA in the barracks at the mouth of the St. Peters. We were one of the performers and in the play of PIZARRO we done (sic) Elvira . . ." This date proves that St. Paul had some of the earliest theatre west of the Allegheny Mountains. Brown's admission of his role as a heroine caused much hilarity, because he was a huge man, certainly not feminine in any respect. The practice of having soldiers take both men's and women's parts enrolled Harry Watkins as a leading lady in the late 1830's. Watkins later became a well-known actor, and the subject of a biography by Maude and Otis Skinner. Other interesting records concerning early theatricals are to be found in the Minnesota Historical Society.

It seems agreed that the first professional performance of legitimate drama was that of George Holland, one of the country's leading comedians, and his troupe from Placide's Varieties of New Orleans. "Variety" indeed, for Holland's opening performance at Mazourka Hall, St. Paul, August 12, 1851, found him playing six different characters in "A Day After the Fair."

The St. Louis Varieties were the first company to play Shakespeare in our state, with Miss Charlotte Crampton as the star, in 1854. But the actress who really dazzled Minnesota was the enchanting Sallie St. Clair, blonde and beautiful star of the St. Louis Varieties. Her first season in St. Paul in 1855 was climaxed by a farewell benefit given her by the governor of Minnesota and leading citizens. From "Camille" to "Actress of All Work," her performances brought much attention, both pro and con, but even those who thought she couldn't act admitted her charms. The St. Louis Varieties used a local St. Paul group called the Old Gents Band. Dan Emmett, who later became renowned as a top minstrel man and the composer of "Dixie," often played second violin in this band.

The fascinating story of the world-famous Hutchinson family who founded and named the Minnesota town furnishes a colorful chapter in the touring-family tradition in our state, from 1855 until the 1900's. Originally from New Hampshire, the Hutchinson's abolition, temperance and women's suffrage songs added much to the excitement of theatre in Minnesota. We are engrossed as Dr. Philip Jordan tells of "The Hutchinson Family in the Story of American Music" in Minnesota History of June, 1941 and in his fine book on the family, "Singin' Yankees." Carol Ryrie Brink writes of the Hutchinsons in her stimulating "Harps in the Wind."

By 1857 St. Paul was really humming with all sorts of theatre. If only one might find a copy of a favorite short piece performed around this time "Chloroform, or St. Paul One Hundred Years Hence" to see if the predictions came true! (1) Four acting companies appeared: Besides Sallie St. Clair's charms, the St. Louis Varieties had the tragedian, Charles Couldock, as guest star in 1857. Couldock later gave Minnesota some of its finest Shakespeare. (2) Henry Van Liew had the distinction of operating the first true theatre building in St. Paul in 1857. His company included William S. Forrest, the great Edwin Forrest's brother, and R. E. J. Miles, well-known figures later. (3) D. L. Scott's company in July, 1857 and (4) Langrishe and Atwater's troupe (one-night stand) and a circus, a minstrel show, and an acrobatic tent show promised much excitement. On August 7, 1857 Minneapolis (and St. Anthony) benefited by the surfeit of theatre in St. Paul, when the St. Clair Varieties played for 14 nights at Woodman's Hall with great success. "Uncle Tom's Cabin" was one of the bills. Dr. Donald Wood's doctor's dissertation "A History of The Theatre in Minneapolis, Minnesota from its Beginning to 1883" furnishes

The Athenaeum, St. Paul, built 1859

us with mentions of early theatricals both amateur and professional, including the ever-popular Hutchinson Family and Ole Bull, the great violinist. St. Anthony and Minneapolis, since they were newer communities, had lagged behind St. Paul, depending on their lyceum and musical entertainments for theatre. There was some disapproval expressed among strait-laced Yankee settlers in both St. Anthony Falls and Minneapolis about the encroachments of the legitimate theatre.

At this high peak for the theatre came the panic of 1857, in August, which swept away everything.

But an amazing development of the closing of the English-speaking stages was the result of an upsurge in the life of the amateur German theatre, which had begun in both St. Paul and St. Anthony earlier, even before Minnesota became a state. We are indebted to the Herman E. Rothfuss studies of the Early German Theater in Minnesota in his thesis and articles in Minnesota History, June and Autumn, 1951, for an account of this aspect of our theatre life. Irvine Hall in St. Paul was the setting for the debut of the German theatre on November 14, 1857, with two comedies "Einer muss heiraten" ("One Must Marry") and "Der Sprung durchs Fenster" ("The Jump Through the Window"). The actors were amateurs, but far surpassed expectations. Minnesota can be grateful to the German theatre for keeping alive this art. As Mr. Rothfuss says: "The seed planted during the bitter winter of 1857 grew into a plant that flourished, sometimes more, sometimes less for over 80 years and it died only when the state's legitimate English-language stages also gave up their struggle." (Herman Rothfuss, "The Early German Theatre in Minnesota" in *Minnesota History,* June, 1951) The Germans built a hall of their own, in St. Paul, the Athenaum —"a hall in which science and the arts are honored and fostered," which served for almost 27 years after its dedication December 25, 1859. (That was the year when Van Liew's theatre was destroyed by fire. He had presented the James W. Wallacks in a fine season of drama and tragedy.) March 2, 1859 saw the amateur drama, "Der Reisende Student" presented by the German theatre in St. Anthony, and Minneapolis. The little towns in Minnesota showed an amazing interest in all forms of theatre. The University of Minnesota has fostered studies for M.A. and Ph. D. theses concerning theatrical activity in the state, including the Whiting, Woods and Rothfuss works already mentioned. It is hoped that eventually a complete story of the theatre in Minnesota will evolve. Evelyn Anderson's "A History of the Theater in Saint Peter, Minnesota from the Beginning to 1930" is an example of the theatre outside the cities. The decade in St. Peter was livened by the New Ulm German Brass Band in 1860, (many of the entertainments were held in the Court House) the Hutchinson Family in 1866, as well as by panoramas, scientific programs and minstrels.

In St. Paul the great event was the dedication of the new Opera House on February 22, 1867. Two companies who played there were the Macfarland Dramatic Company (remembered for their vivifying production of the extravaganza "The Black Crook,") and Charles Plunkett and company presenting the first winter season of legitimate drama. Both companies visited Minneapolis that year, where the chief theatres included Harmonia Hall (1865) and the Pence Opera House (1867-1892). Besides legitimate drama in Minnesota, speakers such as the fiery journalist Jane Swisshelm, and the extraordinary Ignatius Donnelly, two of the state's most colorful characters, appeared on various occasions and at different places; opera troupes toured, as did the great violinist Ole Bull, along with such novelties as "velocipede shows."

But in the 1870's Minnesota was bursting with all sorts of exciting manifestations of the theatre; our state could vie with any other in this field. Some of the greatest stars of Europe and America (in both music and drama) visited the Twin Cities and even toured to small towns in Minnesota. Theatre luminaries such as Joseph Jefferson in "Rip Van Winkle," Augustin Daly's Fifth Avenue Company, Lawrence Barrett and Company with "Richelieu" and "Hamlet," E. L. Davenport in "Julius Caesar," Mary Anderson in "Romeo and Juliet," John Dillon and the Wallack Combination, Otis Skinner—the list reads like "Who's Who in the Theatre."

Pence Opera House, Minneapolis, built in 1870

375

The Academy of Music was built in Minneapolis in 1872. Keen competition with the Pence resulted in the Academy snaring a greater share of the stars during the 1870's, such as Joseph Jefferson in "Rip Van Winkle," Lawrence Barrett and Company with "Richelieu," "Hamlet" and other great plays, E. L. Davenport in "Julius Caesar," Augustin Daly's Fifth Avenue Theatre Company, Mary Anderson in "Romeo and Juliet" and many others. The Pence had Laura Keane in "The Rivals" and the excellent scene-painter, Peter Clausen, who contributed much to the success of such bills as "Sea of Ice," even providing an ice-break in the polar region, complete with aurora borealis. The management of the Pence hit upon an ingenious scheme to offset the more spectacular arrivals from the East who were shining at the Academy. The Pence theatre was re-christened The Metropolitan and was re-decorated with a white and gold auditorium and mirror panels, and the Murray-Cartland Stock Company took up residence there as a permanent home company. The Minneapolis Tribune encouraged this as it was felt a permanent company added to the metropolitan aspect of Minneapolis. Frederick Bryton became the matinee idol of the day and the home stock company became so popular that the great tragedienne, Fanny Janauschek, appeared at the rival Academy almost unnoticed. She later appeared in Stillwater, Winona, Red Wing and other smaller towns with great success.

In the 1880's, traveling companies brought the best in both American and European theatre to Minnesota. E. W. Herrick booked companies for his own Academy in Minneapolis and for opera houses in St. Paul and Stillwater. Two important theatres in St. Paul before 1890 were the Grand Opera House and the Metropolitan. Seven new Playhouses were constructed in St. Paul before 1890, as well as remodeling of old ones. In 1883 Minneapolis' Grand Opera House opened and the Academy of Music closed. This meant the downfall of the Pence (its original name restored.) A plucky manageress, Rhosa McAllister, had taken over the Pence and tried to make a go of it with everything from Shakespeare to "Around the World in 80 Days," but she couldn't succeed in keeping a permanent stock company in competition with the

world-famous stars which appeared in the Twin Cities in a steady stream. Besides the return appearance of many of those already mentioned, John McCullough was seen in "Virainius," Denman Thompson in "Joshua Whitcomb," Maggie Mitchell in "Fanchon, the Cricket," the great Edwin Booth, Salvini Clara Morris, Sarah Bernhardt, Ristori, Nat Goodwin and many others, with noted playwrights such as William Gillette and Steele Mackaye appearing in their own plays. Lighter fare was also furnished with Alice Oates' Opera Boufee company, Fay Templeton's Comic Opera Company and innumerable musical shows for every taste. Sparkling American personalities from Buffalo Bill to Lillian Russell appeared on Twin City stages and eminent speakers from abroad such as Bjornstjerne Bjornson and Oscar Wilde. Minnesota, in music and theatre circles, could certainly compare favorably with the East. Shakespeare was presented many times. Indeed, Minnesota was blessed with fine theatre.

There are some fascinating accounts of the early theatre history of our state. One of them is Charles A. Parker's "My Autobiography" in manuscript form in the University Library, which gives "Recollections of Early Minneapolis, Its Personalities, Theaters and Anecdotes." Another most interesting article is in Minnesota History of June, 1946, where Andrew F. Jensen tells of "Two Decades of Trouping in Minnesota, 1865-1885." There are pertinent observations on the various types of theatre in Minnesota during that era. Besides the dramatic troupes, there were operas, operettas, musical companies and minstrel shows. There were tent shows, Uncle Tom and Wild West shows and circuses. And even before vaudeville there were variety and burlesque shows, magicians and sleight-of-hand performers, elaborate tableaux and panoramas. Mr. Jensen mentions opera houses in Duluth, Brainerd, Crookston, Moorhead, St. Cloud, Wadena, Stillwater, Hastings, Winona, Owatonna, and Red Wing. Many of the other small towns had halls which served as theatres. With *Harry Miner's Dramatic Directory for the Season 1885-6*, (pp. 137-142) as reference, Mr. Jensen informs us that there were at least 47 halls or theatres in the state, besides those in St. Paul and Minneapolis, even before 1885. Charles L. Wagner

Interior of Grand Opera House, Minneapolis, built in 1883

Harmonia Hall, Minneapolis

Interior of Metropolitan Theater, St. Paul

records his Minnesota theatre contacts in "Seeing Stars," discussing the Lyceum and Chautauqua influences.

Minnesota can also be proud of its own sons and daughters who contributed to the record of theatre in our state. Besides the world-famous Hutchinson family, mentioned earlier who founded a town here, another touring family group originated in our state itself, near St. Peter. Cornelia Andrews DuBois of the second generation of The Andrews Opera Company tells the story of these "Operatic Pioneers" in the Minnesota History of Winter, 1953. The family nucleus of a vocal and instrumental concert troupe graduated into a full-fledged opera company, with performances in English, an innovation. Beginning with Gilbert and Sullivan, they went on to grand opera in 1890, with "Martha," "Faust" and "Carmen" included in

their repertoire, and summer opera on their stage on Lake Tetonka (Le Sueur County), where they built an elaborate resort hotel. The family toured until 1901, a fascinating chapter in Minnesota theatre and music annals. "The Black Angels" by Maud Hart Lovelace, our renowned Minnesota author, tells of a Minnesota family opera company. A Winona girl, Ita Welch, was known on eastern stages in operettas. Truly Trousdale Latchaw's M.A. thesis, "The Trousdale Brothers Theatrical Companies from 1896 to 1915" tells of this Iowa family's almost yearly tours in Minnesota, with musical programs, minstrels, and plays.

In the history of the St. Peter Theatre both the Hutchinson and Andrews family appear as well as a variety of other players such as Billy Marble's Company, the Plunkett Theatrical Troupe, the great star Fanny Janauschek, and the ubiquitous

John Dillon. Plays followed the general taste with the "Under the Gaslight" type to the realistic later drama of Ibsen, but with a sprinkling of Shakespeare and even Goethe's "Faust," too. Almost unbelievably the Rounseville Theatre in St. Peter, which flourished from 1886 to 1903, gave 319 professional plays in 17 years. There were several road companies organized in the town, such as the Gotham Stock Company and the George Engesser and Carl de Vere Swedish dialect shows. Of course the great contribution was the Andrews Family Opera. Mrs. C. T. Weibezahn was an outstanding civic director of plays in St. Peter. The German Goethe Verein presented 12 plays from 1873 to 1880. Indeed, culture in Minnesota was not confined to the Twin Cities during the 19th century. The Ludcke Theatre in St. Peter brought fine plays in the 20th century, with Florence Roberts and her New York company opening the theatre, and such plays as Moody's "The Great Divide," and "Abie's Irish Rose" following later. It is hoped that studies of the theatre in other Minnesota towns will add to our growing knowledge of the state's exciting past.

The German Theatre in various places in Minnesota showed an astonishing vitality, with German actors going to various places to play with local groups. Theodor Steidel directed in New Ulm, Mankato and Winona. The German theatre in St. Anthony and Minneapolis was closely associated with the St. Paul group. Important names in the St. Paul theatre were that of Gustav Amberg, professional director and the actors, Otto Dreher and Karl Ahrendt (who later toured professionally with Booth, Mayo and Keene). H. Blume's original play "Dedication to Art" was performed when the new Harmonia Hall was dedicated in 1884. In New Ulm the German theatre was a very important force in the community. Even before Minnesota became a state, the Germans had presented two-one-act comedies there. Pure German was kept alive in New Ulm for many years because of the theatre. The distinguished Madame Methus-Scheller starred there in "The Daughter of the Regiment," with over 3000 in attendance. Other traveling German companies had played in New Ulm previously. Then the theatre became devoted strictly to its amateur actors, with the play "Der Raub der Sabinerinnen," their greatest success.

Two generations of the Seiter, Fischer and Pfaender families played on the German-American stage in New Ulm. Truly, the German stage has made a fine contribution to the theatre in Minnesota. It is hoped that studies will be made of the Scandinavian theatre groups and others.

What of the theatre in Minnesota in the 20th century? With the coming of motion pictures, radio and television, the pattern has changed. Two studies of the theatre in Minneapolis and St. Paul will probably be released this year, showing the developments in the 1900's: the Audley M. Grossman thesis on Minneapolis theatre and the T. O. Andrus thesis on the theatre in St. Paul. Great names abounded on the Twin City stages in the 20th century, at both Metropolitan theatres in each city and later at the Lyceum in Minneapolis (now sold for evangelistic purposes), and the Orpheum vaudeville theatre in St. Paul, (torn down for a bank to be erected). There is scarcely a star known to the theatre world who did not appear in our Minnesota: Minnie Maddern Fiske in "Becky Sharpe" and with Chauncey Olcott in "The Rivals," Sothern and Marlowe, Mantell and Hamper, Fritz Leiber's company doing Shakespeare, Alla Nazimova, David Warfield in "The Music Master," George Arliss in "The Merchant of Venice," Ethel Barrymore in "The Corn Is Green," Helen Hayes in "Victoria Regina," Katherine Cornell in "Candida," George M. Cohan in "I'd Rather Be Right," Alfred Lunt and Lynn Fontanne in their starring roles, Eddie Dowling, Julie Haydon, Judith Anderson, Julie Harris, Jose Ferrer, Raymond Massey— the list could go on and on to the final season at the Lyceum which includes, Walter Pidgeon, Joseph Schildkraut. The greatest of plays were presented, written by the finest playwrights since time began —Euripides, Shakespeare, Ben Jonson, Ibsen, Eugene O'Neill, Sean O'Casey, Tennessee Williams and Arthur Miller, to suggest a few. Vaudeville and musical comedy were well represented with such luminaries as W. C. Fields, Fred and Adele Astaire, Victor Moore, Bert Lahr, Burns and Allen, The Marx Brothers, Eddie Cantor, Georgie Jessel, Al Jolson, Ed Wynn—the list is endless. (The St. Paul Auditorium is available for touring productions at the present time.) Stock companies remembered are The Bainbridge Players in Minneapolis and the Arthur Casey Players in St. Paul, and the Aulger Brooks tent show, with headquarters in Stillwater.

What has happened to the stars of "yesteryear?" Why are the theatres closing? Are the mechanical devices of the motion pictures, radio and television going to entirely supplant "live" theatre? The old order is changing, but perhaps the new life in the theatre which has been emerging through university, college (and even high school as early as 1884) productions and through the exciting development in community theatre in Minnesota will prove to be the most creative and satisfying flowering of the art of the theatre.

The University Theatre at the University of Minnesota has had a fascinating history. Robert Gee's thesis tells its story from the beginnings in the late 1800's to 1937. One University Dramatic Club was formed in 1896 and later, others were organized. Mrs. Ariel McNaughton Dingwall was the first dramatics director in the Speech Department. Tours were sponsored by the Extension Department. Dr. Anna von Helmholtz Phelan was the founder of The Players and her interest brought Pi Epsilon Delta (National Collegiate Players). Professor F. M. Rarig kept a steady hand on the theatre from 1908 for 40 years. Theatre became a fully accredited division of Speech. Dr. Richard Burton established Minnesota Masquers as the producing organization of the University Theatre. In 1914 Dr. Anna Phelan founded The Players at the express direction of President Vincent who wanted another Dramatic Club because of his institution of University needs. The Players drew actors from the Masquers, and soon were the leading dramatic club on the campus. Under the direction of Dr. Phelan a brilliant series of plays were given with matinees twice a week. Dr. Phelan in rapid succession produced leading plays by Barrie and Clyde Fitch, as well as others. Dr. Phelan also brought to the campus a chapter of the National Collegiate Players. After Dr. Phelan gave up the direction of the players the two dramatic clubs were amalgamated under a specially appointed Theatrical Director. The University Theatre was

on the way. Through the years, with dedicated leaders such as those mentioned and others in the department, the University Theatre has grown, opening its 29th season in the fall of 1959, a distinguished contributor to culture in Minnesota. Its nationally-known director, Dr. Frank M. Whiting (author of "An Introduction to the Theatre Harpers, 1956), served as president of the American Educational Theatre Association and expressed in his presidential address a desire for increased awareness of the theatre's great literary and cultural heritage in this country, as Theatre Arts reported in its April, 1947 issue. The same magazine also mentions in its August, 1957 issue that "two University of Minnesota Theatre touring companies annually play to more than a hundred thousand persons in the surrounding area." An even more exciting development of the University Theatre touring system has been the international tours of 1957 and 1958. University Theatre toured 20 Army and Air Force defense bases in France and Germany with Shakespeare's "Midsummer Night's Dream," and then the State Department sent them to Brazil, with that play and Thornton Wilder's "Our Town." From January through March in 1958 the University Theatre toured defense bases of the Pacific Command at Okinawa, Japan and Korea, Honolulu, Iwo Jima, Wake and Midway. The University Theatre also conducted a showboat for Minnesota's Centennial summer of 1958, reviving plays given in early Minnesota, such as "The Death of Pizarro," "Uncle Tom's Cabin," "Under the Gaslight," "The Rivals" and "The Taming of the Shrew," playing up and down the Mississippi. At least two books on the theatre have been written by University people, Dr. Whiting's fine "Introduction to the Theatre," used as a text in many schools and colleges, and the late Jack Simos' (B.S. Education, M.S.W. from School of Social Work) thought-provoking "Social Growth through Play Production."

Many of our colleges have fine drama departments, with outstanding work in various manifestations of the theatre by Mary Owen's Verse Choir at Macalester, Ann Simley's long years of excellent work at Hamline, Mabel Frey at St. Catherine's, Harold Hayes at U. of M. Duluth, Dr. Paul

"Our Town" Brazil, 1957

Rehearsal for "Our Town" Germany, Summer 1957

"I Remember Mama" Winter International Tour

Centennial showboat

Paul Bunyan's lumberjacks

at Mankato State Teachers, John Woodward at Carleton and Ralph Haugen at St. Olaf, to mention only a few. There is a unique arrangement at Bemidji State Teacher's College with the Paul Bunyan Playhouse there and the University for a professional staff, Louis V. Marchand, director. The Wenonah Players of Winona State College was one of the first to give arena productions; Dorothy B. Magnus directs. Theatre Arts magazine each summer devotes an issue to "Theatre, U.S.A." informing of the activities of college and Little Theatre groups, with Minnesota always included. We can be very proud of our educational theatre groups.

The Duluth Playhouse claims the distinction of originating the phrase 'Little Theatre,' in 1913 for their group. Their Playhouse has been in existence almost 30 years; over 1000 persons are members. The University of Minnesota's Duluth branch and local public schools have charge of the directing, with the actors and technicians all volunteers. This theatre has contributed much to Minnesota's culture.

There have been many community theatres in the Twin Cities and in the state, some of which have existed for a short time, and then have dis-

appeared, such as the North Star Playhouse in Minneapolis, the Minneapolis Civic Playhouse, one of the finest, with such plays as Giraudoux' "The Enchanted." Betty Girling, Francis Drake, Ebba Nelson and Irv Fink were active in the latter playhouse. The Star Playhouse in Hopkins, headed by Phil Gelb and Robert Corrigan, produced Gelb's original comedy, "The Side Door" before the playhouse burned. In St. Paul, Donald Singerman directed *The Grotto Players* for many successful seasons. Near the Twin Cities, both Anoka and White Bear Lake had community theatre groups; the latter's *Plantation Playhouse* was torn down to make way for a business establishment (their new theatre group will be discussed later).

A sampling of the community theatres which remain, and new theatres recently appearing can indicate the healthy interest of Minnesotans in the liveliest of the "Seven Lively Arts." *Old Log Theatre* in Minneapolis has had a long and interesting history. Mr. Don Stolz is the director and operator. He was formerly actor and director of the Lake Minnetonka theatre before World War II; he has guided the destiny of the Old Log since 1946. One of the features of his career is the production of "The Front Page," the newspaper farce in which he and prominent newspaper men take leading roles (for benefit of Variety Club Heart hospital in 1957). The beautiful *Edyth Bush Little Theatre* in St. Paul, underwritten entirely by Mrs. A. G. Bush, has given the area fine theatre for 19 years, opening in 1940. Mrs. Bush produces 12 productions a year; Mr. Charles Meehan is the full-time professional director. Newer theatre groups in the Twin Cities include *Theatre-in-the Round* (Minneapolis), a fine nonprofit corporation with all services volunteered except for the excellent professional director, Frederick W. Hilgendorf, and a guest director for one show a season. This intimate theatre pleases audiences seated on all four sides of the playing area. They have their own meeting and rehearsal space on Hennepin, with productions at Benton Hall, YWCA and hopes for a theatre. *Lakeshore Players* of White Bear Lake are working toward a building for all civic organizations in their vicinity and have accrued a tidy sum toward this goal by presenting melodramas, directed by Helen Peters, at the Shore Club. Polly Van Arsdell, artist, designed the sets. They have a yearly benefit for the American Field Service; Miss Ebba Nelson is the director. The directors of many of the Lakeshore Players, such as Laurie Peterson who won the Theatre St. Paul best actress award, participate in little theatre plays in other community theatres already mentioned, as well as in radio and television. *Theatre St. Paul, Inc.*, begun in 1956, was stimulated by the St. Paul Council of Arts and Sciences and grew out of a survey by the Junior League and Hill Foundation. The exciting plans for the St. Paul Council of Arts and Sciences include a fine building. Their Annual Report, 1956-7, stated: "It was concluded that Creative Theatre should be the opening wedge to pave the way for the ultimate full-fledged arts program—since theatre is the one form of activity which embraces all the arts—the written word, painting, sculpture, dance, music, etc., and because it is the medium having the most immediate and engaging appeal . . ." Member organizations of the Council include these St. Paul groups: International Institute, Civic Opera Association, Civic Orchestra Association, College Club, Gallery and School of Art, St. Paul Institute, Junior League, Musi-

cians' Association, Painters & Sculptors' Association, Schubert Club, Theatre St. Paul, Inc., and the Women's Institute. Theatre St. Paul now has its own building, a flexible arena-type theatre, with Rex Henriot as director.

There are doubtless many new theatre ventures springing up, such as the Bloomington Civic Theatre near Minneapolis, and others out in the state, about which we hope to hear more as they become established. The Rochester Civic Theatre, for instance, has furnished residents with such fine plays as Lewis O. Coxe's new one, "The Witchfinders" (he was co-author of the New York success, "Billy Budd"). This theatre opened in 1952, participating in the annual Rochester Arts Center Festival. Burr Petit directs at the Rochester Theatre and teaches seminars. William F. Davidson of St. Paul is another Minnesotan who has written successful plays, several of which have been given at the University Theatre.

Minnesotans who have gone on in the professional include: Judy Garland, Richard Arlen, Lenore Ulric, Walter Abel, Charles Nolte, Robert Breen, Joan Davis, Hugh Beaumont, and others.

Local pageants have abounded, such as the yearly "Hiawatha" pageant at Pipestone and many town and country pageants were given during Centennial year. A professional company, Hal Garven Productions of Minneapolis, promotes Centennial and Diamond Jubilee Celebrations in Minnesota and neighboring states. T. S. Denison and Co., Inc. of Minneapolis is one of the largest play distributing companies in the world.

One feels a great deal of pride in the contribution the theatre in Minnesota has made to the culture of our state. It is hoped that a complete history may be written in this field in the following years, when material has been collected concerning all the various manifestations of this fascinating art. This study is only an indication of the various facets of the theatre in Minnesota and will be revised when more material comes in and other histories are uncovered. (The Minnesota Statehood Centennial Commission's booklet on *Music and Theater in Minnesota History* by John K. Sherman is a valuable contribution.) In Minnesota "The Play's the Thing" — "the only possible pause in man's existence."

The Dance

By JOHN HARVEY

Dance, as other than a social activity, is both very old and quite new in Minnesota.

The early explorers found the original inhabitants of the state with a well-developed dance, which, as with most primitive peoples, combined the religious, the expressive and the social. Descriptions of some of these ceremonies witnessed by the early explorers include a particularly good account by Schoolcraft of green corn ceremonies among the Sioux of Kaposia village below what is now St. Paul.

However, among the later inhabitants of the state, dance remained pretty much in the social forms until after World War I.

Marie Rothfuss of St. Paul was the first figure of consequence on the scene. She established a ballet school, trained several dancers who went on to wider fields and for a time provided the ballet group for the St. Paul Civic Opera.

She provided a strong early influence on a young Minnesota dancer, Gertrude Lippincott, now nationally noted as a dancer, teacher, choreographer and writer on dance subjects.

Miss Lippincott (she actually is Mrs. Lippincott, wife of Benjamin Lippincott, distinguished University of Minnesota political scientist) has a background of training under the leading modern dancers and teachers of the era—Leslie Burrowes, Martha Graham, Louis Horst, Doris Humphrey, Charles Weidman and Hanya Holm.

She first established the Modern Dance Center in Minneapolis in 1937 and directed it for five years. After a sojourn in the East as head of modern dance activities at Mount Holyoke college, she returned to the Twin Cities in 1947 to become artist-in-residence at Hamline University for two years.

Gertrude Lippincott and Robert Moulton

From 1949 to 1957 she was head of the modern dance center at the Minneapolis YWCA, directing classes for children and adults, heading the Studio Dance Group and being a member, with Robert Moulton and Eunice Cain, of the Dance Trio. Both groups have given numerous performances.

Andahazy Ballet Borealis Company in "Aurora's Wedding"

Lately Miss Lippincott has been active with Mr. Moulton and the Dance Repertory Group which has presented programs of original works by the two of them. Moulton also has directed dance at the University of Minnesota Theater and staged the dance episode of the University's centennial pageant, "Rifle, Axe and Plow."

In addition, Miss Lippincott has given dance programs, lectures and demonstrations and taught master classes throughout the country.

Ballet did not develop on a full scale in Minnesota until the advent of the Andahazys following World War II. This couple met and were married as members of the Ballet Russe de Monte Carlo in its days under the management of Col. de Basil. Mrs. Andahazy (Shirley Bridge of Rochester, N.Y.) was the first American dancer to become a member of that famed international company in which she danced as Anna Adrianova. Lorand Andahazy of Cleveland, Hungarian by birth but American by upbringing, had his career all but ended by war service. He was wounded seven times, the last time a matter involving fracture of both knees.

Undeterred, the Andahazys settled in St. Paul in 1946, by which time Lorand's constant work had put him well on the way to recovery.

Anna Adrianoua and Lorand Andahazy

They opened a school, teaching the pure classic traditions they had absorbed during their careers with the Ballet Russe. The school flourished, expanded into Minneapolis as well to become the largest school of classical ballet in the country, and finally the Andahazys had developed enough able dancers through their strict and uncompro-

386

mising curriculum to fulfill a cherished dream—
a ballet company of their own.

Ballet Borealis they called it, in tribute to the
Northern land from which it sprang. The group
has presented full evenings of ballet, with orchestra and full decor, for the past six years in Northrop Memorial Auditorium under auspices of the
University of Minnesota's department of concerts
and lectures. Programs have included such staples
of classical ballet as "Les Sylphides" and "Aurora's Wedding," thereby inviting comparison with
major ballet companies. Both the enthusiasm of the
large crowds (4,000 to 5,000 persons) and critical
reaction proved that invitation to be based on justified confidence.

A year ago enthusiastic supporters of the Andahazys and their work formed the Ballet Borealis
Foundation. This organization aims at providing
continuing support of the company and its public
appearances. A national tour of the group is projected. Meanwhile, dancers from the school have
been recruited as soloists into professional companies, among them the Ballet Russe de Monte
Carlo and the Ballet Alonso of Cuba.

Returning to modern dance, a strong contribution has been made by the work of Nancy McKnight
Hauser during the past fifteen years. Mrs. Hauser,
whose principal teacher was Hanya Holm, has
taught at Macalester and Carleton colleges, the St.
Paul Gallery and School of Art, Theatre St. Paul
and elsewhere in the Twin Cities area. With her
students and in solo capacity she has made numerous memorable appearances at Macalester and
with the Northwest Sinfonietta and Civic Orchestra of Minneapolis. Her choreography was an outstanding feature of Macalester's seventy-fifth anniversary pageant "Touch The Familiar Sod" in
1949.

Another group which has made itself felt on
the local scene is the Ballet Concertant of the Academy of The Dance, headed by George Verdak,
William Glenn and Sonia Orlova, another Ballet
Russe alumna. The group has furnished the ballet numbers for the St. Paul Civic Opera for the
past several years and has appeared at the Minneapolis Institute of Arts and with the Minneapolis
Symphony orchestra in support of the noted dancer-
diseuse Zorina.

Sonia Orlova Centennial Ballet, White Bear Pageant

George Verdak Centennial Ballet, St. Paul Civic Opera

William Glenn Centennial Ballet, White Bear Pageant

Art in Minnesota

Painting, Sculpture
and Architecture

Consultants: Dewey Albinson, Phyllis Downs, Frances Cranmer Greenman, Clement Haupers, Harriet Hanley, Robert Kilbride, Ruth Lawrence, Peter Lupori, Maggie Morgan, Helen Nebelthau, Gerald Stanwell

SAMOTHRACE

Ascending step by step the louvered stairs,
I suddenly beheld the Samothrace,
The Winged Victory . . .
I paused to let its noble majesty
Sweep through my heart and soul.
And in that golden moment there
I felt as if forever now I was immune
To ugliness and evil in the world.
As if misfortune, yes, or baseness never again
Could cross my path.
And almost then I wept for joy
Redeemed as if from dark ancestral curse.
                    By Anna von Helmholtz Phelan

Minnesota could become one of the leading art centers. There has been steady growth in all forms of art since before we became a state. We can look forward to great advances in the years to come, with our fine museums, art departments in our schools, colleges and universities, and the flowering of art in many communities.

EARLY HISTORY. The early artists in this section of the country left us invaluable paintings of Minnesota, even before we became a state. Unfortunately, the ancient Sioux and Chippewa Indian art was not fostered by the settlers, who were trying desperately to become established on the new frontier. The Indians ornamented their clothing, moccasins (with dyed porcupine quills) and their tepees. Their woven baskets and grass mats and their carved wooden utensils, decorated birch-bark ma-

terials and pipestone peace pipes evidenced their love of beauty. Our Indians were always on the move—the climate was not as conducive to their art development as in some of the warmer spots. With the coming of the French, the Indians were influenced by the ornamental material brought by the traders. Many of the early beaded bags are fine works of art.

Artists who visited our state in the early 1800's included the well-known artist, George Catlin, to whom we are indebted for some of our best Indian scenes. Seth Eastman painted many water colors and handsomely illustrated the explorations of Henry Schoolcraft. Between 1845-1850 a Swiss artist toured up the Mississippi River and spent some time along the Missouri River. His book, "The Journal of Rudolf Kurtz," revealed the conditions of the time and the beauty of the country remarkably well.

Minnesota had recently become a Territory (1849) when Frank B. Mayer, a Baltimore artist, came to Minnesota (1851) with the treaty-makers of the Traverse des Sioux and Mendota treaties. Mayer's fascinating account of his journey is called "With Pen and Pencil on the Frontier" and is illustrated by many sketches of that historic time. The artist's greatest ambition was to paint the signing of the Treaty of Traverse des Sioux for the State Capitol. He tried for years to obtain the commission, but, ten years after his death another artist, Francis D. Millet, painted the picture for the Capitol, using Frank Mayer's sketch as a basis. The oil sketch Mayer made is now in the Minnesota Historical Society. Edwin Whitefield came to our land with the Exploration Association bearing his name, and painted water-colors depicting scenes of his explorations. Other early painters connected with our state were Thomas Holland Howe and Homer Dodge Martin, a painter from Albany, N.Y., who spent his last and most productive years in St. Paul and died there in 1897.

Several painters depicted on canvases twelve feet high, called "panoramas," the beauties of the Mississippi and this territory. These panoramas might be called our first moving pictures, for a narrator discussed the paintings as they were rolled in front of the eyes of an audience. Some of these early panorama painters were Henry Lewis, who wrote and illustrated *Das illustrirte Mississippithal* with colored lithographs, John Rowson Smith, who insisted his canvases were four miles long, and John Banvard, who toured both the United States and England with his canvases.

Every school child in Minnesota looks at the portrait of the explorer Beltrami (by an Italian artist) in the Minnesota Historical Society and at Douglas Volk's painting, "Father Hennepin Discovering the Falls of Saint Anthony" in our state capitol building.

Even before the large galleries arose, small exhibitions, sales and even auctions of local paintings were held in the John S. Bradstreet Co. galleries and the Wm. A. French Co., educating the community.

The love of art had been brought from the East and from their home countries by the settlers who came to Minnesota. Eugene and Elbert Carpenter, civic leaders, devoted their interest and money to art and music. Not too long after Minnesota became a state, art societies began to be formed. In

1870, an Athenaeum Society was founded in Minneapolis. Art books were brought from the society's fund. The Society of Live Arts had William W. Folwell as president. From these beginnings came great developments.

The Minneapolis Society of Fine Arts, governing body of the Minneapolis Institute of Arts, was incorporated in 1883 for the purpose of "promoting a knowledge and love of art in the community." As a first expression of this purpose, the Minneapolis School of Art was founded in 1886, under the direction of Douglas Volk.

From its inception, however, the members of The Society of Fine Arts had purposed to establish, in addition to the Art School, a museum of art. This hope began to be realized when, in January 1911, Clinton Morrison offered as a gift to the Society the ten-acre tract of land at Twenty-fourth Street between Stevens and Third Avenues, valued at $250,000, as a site for the museum and school buildings, provided that $500,000 should be raised for the erection of the museum. Immediately, William Hood Dunwoody, who was then president of the Society, pledged $100,000 to the building fund. By the end of January the entire amount had been raised. In addition to Mr. Dunwoody's generous contribution to the building fund, the Society received a bequest of $1,000,000 for the purchase of works of art, at the time of his death in 1914. The building opened in January, 1915 and in November, 1916, the Art School building, made possible through a fund given by Angus W. Morrison and Ethel Morrison VanDerlip, was opened.

As their bulletin states: "The Institute of Arts is a public museum, chiefly supported by private funds and dedicated to the collection and exhibition of works of art of high quality regardless of place or time of origin." The first direction of the Minneapolis Institute of Arts was Joseph Breck and Russell A. Plimpton, Director of the Minneapolis Institute of Arts for 35 years, made great contributions toward this aim. Richard S. Davis, who succeeded him in 1956, continued the purpose. In addition to a justly famous collection of European painting and sculpture, the Institute owns distinguished collections of more specialized nature in the fields of decorative and Oriental arts, including the world famous Alfred F. Pillsbury

389

Minneapolis Institute of Arts

collection of Chinese bronzes. To interpret these collections it conducts an active program of loan exhibitions and educational services designed to make art an integral and vital part of the community's life. The Museum has also presented 41 annual exhibitions of the work of local artists. Each year several works have been purchased from these exhibitions for the permanent collection. The School of Art, now under the direction of Dr. W. B. Bryan, conducts a comprehensive program of courses in the fine arts, graphic arts, and design. This is integrated with a program of instruction in the liberal arts designed to cultivate the students' general awareness as a necessary base for development of artistic skills and leads to a degree of B.F.A. A handsome new addition to the school building is in the process of construction. Teachers at the school have included: Mary Moulton Cheney, who became director of the Minneapolis School of Art in 1916. Due to her its Design Courses gained a name in the East. Edmund Kopietz followed as director for many years. Instructors and guest instructors included B. J. O. Nordfeldt, Alexander Brook, Arnold Blanch, Vaclav Vytlacil, Cameron Booth, Frances Cranmer Greenman, Anthony Augarolo, Oskar Kokoshka, Robert Brackman, Gustave Krollman, Glen Mitchell, Bimey Quick, Bernard Arnest. At present there are almost forty instructors in the day and evening schools.

THE WALKER ART CENTER

As far back as the 1870's Thomas B. Walker, pioneer lumberman of Minnesota, opened his home in Minneapolis where he began his art collection with chromos and engravings. Quoting from material prepared at the Center: "From the first his dream was to gather and establish an art and science collection for the benefit and use of the public. Around 1881 he began buying pottery, porcelains and jades. His jade collection is hailed by Oriental experts as one of the finest private collections. Gem glass, necklaces and other jewelry from Syria, Egypt and Babylonia, bronze and gold idols from ancient temples of China were added to the collection. In 1918 the Lowry Hill property was purchased; Mr. Walker hoped the city would erect a library with space for his art collection. This plan did not materialize, so he built the Walker Art Galleries, which in 1939 were renamed The Walker Art Center, since there are educational programs there, and contemporary American works." In recent years, the installation of the Design Art Gallery and the publication of the Design Quarterly, which now has international circulation, started the first continuous museum program in that field. Temporary exhibits and even the permanent collection have emphasized contemporary art, under the direction of H. Harvard Arnason, appointed as

Walker Art Center, Minneapolis

Informal atmosphere of Walker Art Center

director in 1951. Active interest in regional and national and representative contemporary European artists has also been stimulated. "A greatly accelerated program of correlated 20th century arts including music, drama, theatre and the dance was instituted several years ago with the organization of the Center Arts Council, a volunteer group of local business and professional men and women." The Center Arts Council sponsors sales and rentals of original art to aid contemporary artists of the area and to encourage local collectors in the purchase of works of art for their homes. Miss Huldah Curl is director of the sales and rentals.

THE SAINT PAUL SCHOOL OF ART

St. Paul has an active school of art. The eminent St. Paulite, Grace Flandrau, wrote of the opening of the St. Paul School of Art, telling of its inception. Paul Manship had studied there. Dewey Albinson was the first head of the school. Classes

in drawing, painting, sculpture, design of all kinds, interior decorating, advertising, and other forms of commercial art were offered. Teaching and a series of great exhibitions met with unexpected success and when Dewey Albinson retired in 1929, Cameron Booth became director. In 1939 Mr. and Mrs. Robert B. Shepard gave the Summit Avenue mansion to house the St. Paul Gallery. The Art Mart in 1955 was, as the brochure states: "an expansion of the Gallery program of support and encouragement of the growing number of capable artists in the area." There is an auxiliary organization, the "Gallenteers," who donate time and money to further the program and purpose of the gallery. Some of the Minnesota artists and sculptors who have been connected with the Gallery (besides those mentioned) are Lowell Bobletter, Montfort Dunn, Foster Kienholtz, S. Chatwood Burton, William F. Ryan, V. Vytlacil, Alice Hugy, Eugene Larkin, Warren and Alix MacKenzie, Kyle Morris,

391

Walter Quirt, Art Kerrick, Walter Kuhlman, Merle Hoesly, Alonzo Hauser, Roy Turney, Ramsey Wieland, John Talleur. The present faculty is composed of Clement Haupers, Paul Kramer, Edna Imm, Mac LeSueur, Louis Safer, Christian Schmidt, Virginia Nagle and Delmar Kolb. Malcolm Lein is the present director of the St. Paul School of Art.

THE AMERICAN SWEDISH INSTITUTE

With the era of Big Mansions and "Castles," one castle will remain—the gift of Swan J. Turnblad, who, with his daughter, in 1929 donated their home on Park Avenue and the Posten building in Minneapolis, and the newspaper and equipment of *Svenska Amerikanska Posten*, so the American Swedish Institute might emerge. As its bulletin states, the aims are: "To preserve the Swedish heritage and culture brought to the United States by our pioneers and later immigrants; to awaken and maintain the interest of all Americans in Sweden as an outstanding member in the free and democratic family of nations; to develop and promote close relations, cultural and otherwise, between the United States and Sweden." Loans of the works of contemporary Scandinavian artists and the Vasa Bridal Crown and the Varmland Bridal crown are features of the Institute. Instruction in the Swedish language is given. "Since 1949 the Institute in cooperation with the University of Minnesota has promoted the interchange of fellow-trainees in Agriculture between the United States and Sweden. The plan provides for six months of practical work on a farm, then six months at a school of agriculture." The Institute sponsors a Male Chorus (with a Women's Auxiliary) and a Woman's Club. The American Swedish Institute has been in the fore with the recent active directorship of Elmer Albinson. Minnesota sculptors and artists who have been connected with the Institute include: Einer Dahl, Ernst J. Dahle, Paul Granlund, Daniel Soderlind, Margreth Brewer, Robert W. Peterson, Dorothy Berge, June Peterson Dille, George A. and Albin Beyer, Marjorie Doht Pinkham, Theodore Sohner, Evelyn Raymond, John K. Daniels, Dewey Albenson, Elof Wedin, Peter Wedin, Esther Edberg Dovre.

392

"The Scandinavian Roots of Our State" exhibit

Grand Hall

"The Scandinavian Roots of Our State" permanent ex[...]

American Swedish Institute

THE UNIVERSITY OF MINNESOTA ART GALLERY

The University Gallery was established by the University of Minnesota in the spring of 1934. For its home, a space over the portico of Northrop Memorial Auditorium was pressed into service, with Hudson Walker as curator. Mrs. Ruth Lawrence was brought that fall to direct the program and has carried it on through 23 years of growth and development. The exhibits have changed every three weeks all through the years; ticket holders to the Symphony, and other concerts and lectures have been enthusiastic. Many artists who have subsequently become famous had their initial showing here.

"The Gallery began early to operate in five areas: namely, exhibition programs; loan of framed color reproductions of art masterpieces to students for their rooms; aid to classes in the form of special materials and exhibits and visual aids in the form of photographs and color reproductions useful in teaching; and finally the beginning and development of a permanent collection of original works of art. This Gallery program was tremendously implemented by a large W.P.A. and N.Y.A. Art project, operating with 62 people at maximum. A fine program was begun, statewide—traveling into areas where possibly an art exhibit had never previously been shown." A fine clipping file, with all types of art information, was instituted. "The permanent collections of paintings, drawings, prints and decorative objects were growing at this period and W.P.A. aided in putting this into exhibitable form." All over the University campuses paintings, etc. were exhibited. When W.P.A. and N.Y.A. were discontinued, changes occurred. An integration of the Art Department at the University was effected, with Harvard H. Arnason at the helm. The Gallery's program expanded in certain aspects and altered in others, when it began to be more closely geared to the art classes' requirements. One most interesting exhibit, "Hand-done Handsome Things," of folk art used in Minnesota's first hundred years commemorated the state's Territorial Centennial (1949). A photographic and slide record of these objects is available. The Gallery, through the generosity of interested friends such as Ione and Hudson Walker and others, has many fine works of art placed on loan. The University Gallery desires not only to serve the campus and the Twin Cities, but all of Minnesota. The George P. Tweed Memorial Art Collection in Duluth is a most important benefaction to the University.

The University of Minnesota includes in its present faculty of the Department of Art, the chairman, H. H. Arnason, Dimitri T. Tselos, Lorenz E. A. Eitner, Donald R. Torbert, Hylton A. Thomas, Melvin Waldfogel, Cameron Booth, Bernard Arnest, Walter Quirt, Josephine Rollins, E. Edwin Young, Malcolm Myers, Warren MacKenzie; in Sculpture, John Rood and Philip G. Morton. The University of Minnesota is one of the few in the country which includes Photography in the Fine Arts: George Amberg, Allen Downs and Jerome Liebling. Allen Downs won a Hollywood award for his film, "Swamp," and three films (one with Bernard Arnest and one with Jerome Leibling) were exhibited at the Brussels World Fair, (1958.)

THE FEDERAL ART PROJECTS

With the depression the first aid given to artists by the Government Projects was through the Adult Education Program which opened two schools—one in Minneapolis and one in St. Paul. Inasmuch as the purpose of W.P.A. was to maintain and develop skills, all phases of arts and crafts were carried on: creative painting and sculpture, map-making and design, instruction in botanical and medical drawing. State institutions and state schools benefitted by gifts of this work. Funds came from Washington and many fine murals were created for post offices during this time, and sculptures enhanced high schools, town halls, hospitals and libraries all over the state. Handcraft projects,

under the technical direction of F.A.P. increased Minnesota lists to about 500 people under the direction of artist Clement Haupers. Dewey Albinson was another artist connected with this project.

HARRIET HANLEY GALLERY

Since the beginning of our state, there have been public spirited men and women who have furthered the interest in art. A rare artist's gallery existed in Minneapolis—Mrs. Harriet Clark Hanley, a fine sculptor herself, for years devoted herself to exhibiting and selling the works of Minnesota artists in her gallery on upper Nicollet. Visiting artists claimed nothing else like this gallery existed elsewhere. Mrs. Hanley's influence and "plugging" for the artists meant much to the development of the area. One artist with the pen has been the devoted champion of art from the early 20's and should not be forgotten, Mr. John K. Sherman of the *Minneapolis Star-Tribune*.

KILBRIDE-BRADLEY ART GALLERY

Located on 10th and Nicollet in Minneapolis, this gallery was founded in 1951 by Byron Bradley and Robert Kilbride. Starting with a sales and rental program of paintings in 1951, the gallery has added art books, framing, pottery and art materials to its activities. These painters and sculptors have been connected with the gallery: Eric Austen Erickson, David Ratner, William Dietrickson, George Letness, John Anderson, Robert Barber, Milton Skoog, Bernard Arnest, Glen Ranney, Urban Couch, Phyllis Downs, Rob Kelly, Paul Olsen, Elof Wedin, Tom Mikkelson, Syd Fossum, Richard Randell, Paul Granlund and others. The gallery publishes a monthly brochure called "The Pot Boiler" of information and news about the art world and hilarious comments and whimsey.

ROCHESTER ART CENTER

Directed by William Saltzman, a fine new building has just been built.

ART ASSOCIATIONS

Approved by the state legistlature in 1903, the Minnesota State Art Society is the second oldest organization of its kind in the country; its

"Sixth and Hennepin" oil painting by Robert Kilbride

purpose to encourage and promote the arts in the state. The eleven man board is appointed for a four-year term by the governor. The current officers and members are Robert Kilbride, Walter Fricke, Clark Dean, Rudolph Johnson, Huldah Curl, William Saltzman, Robert Bliss, John K. Sherman, Bernard Arnest, Philip Gelb, Stanton Catlin. The St. Paul Council of Arts and Sciences includes the International Institute (which sponsors the Festival of Nations, where many objects d'art are displayed in the homelands exhibit) the St. Paul Gallery and School of Art, St. Paul Painters' and Sculptors' Assn., and other St. Paul fine arts institutions: the Civic Opera Assn., Civic Orchestra Assn., Institute (Science Museum) Schubert Club, Theatre St. Paul, Inc., College Club, Junior League, Musicians' Assn. and Women's Institute of St. Paul. Artists' Equity is another art association with a chapter in our state. The Minnesota State Fair has put on exhibitions for many years, selected by outstanding juries. Among State art groups who have been represented are those from Owatonna, Winona, Steele County Art Group and the Wells Art Club.

Erle Loran's article "Artists from Minnesota" in the American Magazine of Art and in Minnesota History (see Historical Society) is a provocative one; he mentions some of our best-known Minnesota artists: Adolf Dehn, Arnold Blanch, Lucile Blanch, Wanda Gag, John B. Flannagan, Harry Gotlieb, Dewey Albinson, Clement Haupers, Frances Cranmer Greenman, Paul Manship, Cameron Booth and others. Frances Cranmer Greenman, the nationally-known portrait painter, has a delightful autobiography, "Higher Than The Sky." Both educational and art magazines have mentioned that it is to the midwest that our nation is looking for virile painting. These are dozens of artists who have come to paint awhile or teach, and we have been able to keep some of them in our state. These include (not mentioned in other connections): Clara Mairs, Elsa Jemne, Charles S. Wells, Floyd Brewer, Bob Brown, Ben Swanson, Elizabeth Olds, Will Norman, Alexander Masley,

Sam Sabean, Stanford Fenell, Josehine Lutz Rollins, Arnold Flagstad, Rob Roy Kelly, Bill Bartsch, Harvey Meline, John Dahl, Malcolm Myers, Virginia Opstad, Marilyn Showley, Ernst Dahle, Robert Reiff, Cyrus Running, Bruce Showbaken, Richard Sussman, Bonnie Harris, Eleanor Harris, Mary Gale Hobbs, Carol Hoorn, Roger Lundquist, Hazel Moore, George Morrison, Birney Quick and others.

SCULPTURE IN MINNESOTA

Minnesota sculpture has come a long way from the bronze figures in our parts to the inspired sculpture of Paul Manship. One of the early contributors to the field was Jacob Fjelde, whose bust of *Henrik Ibsen* (In Como Park) was modeled from the great playwright, himself. *Hiawatha* and *Minnehaha,* near Minnehaha Falls is another of his works, and he has works on various Minneapolis libraries. His son, Paul, is also a sculptor.

The State Capitol is enhanced by Daniel Chester French's sculpture. Originally from Winona, James Earle Fraser, created the equestrian statue, *The End of the Trail,* and figures for Washington government buildings, as well as the Indian head on the buffalo nickel.

Not until the latter part of the 19th century did Minnesota produce a truly great sculptor. He is so esteemed that, in the foreword to a fine book, *Paul Manship,* by Edwin Murtha, this tribute to our Minnesota sculptor was given by David E. Finley, Director of the National Gallery in Washington: ". . . For more than forty years he has been a pervasive force in American Art and has helped, as much as any man, keep alive in this country the great tradition of Western sculpture, as derived from its finest period in Greece and Italy." His *Indian Hunter and His Dog* is in Cochran Memorial Park in St. Paul.

Another fine early sculptor listed in Germany's "Who's Who" was Knute Akerberg, who taught in the Twin Cities. John Flannagan, a student at the Minneapolis School of Art in 1915, was established in the East by the early 20's. He was a sculptor of rare sensibility. His work appears in major museums throughout the country. John K. Daniels' early exhibitions of wood carvings were much admired. Still active, many of his prominent

396

"Jesus Meets His Mother," Sculptor Peter Lupori

"Our Lady," Sculptor Peter Lupori

statues are seen around the state, including the Knute Nelson statue on the capitol grounds.

In 1943 the Society of Minnesota Sculptors was organized with these seven as charter members: Katherine Nash, Jean Laurie, Evelyn Raymond, Charlotte Millis, Graham McGuire, Harriet Maas and Mrs. James Bennett, Jr. Katherine Nash is acting director of the University of Minnesota Art Gallery. Evelyn Raymond has just completed the statue of Maria Sanford, the beloved Minnesota educator, which is placed in the U. S. Capitol. Other Minnesota sculptors include: Alonzo Hauser, Paul Granlund, John Rood, Charles B. Wells, Peter Lupori, Walter Portermain, Dorothy Berge, Daniel Soderlind, Anthony Caponi, Ann Wolfe, Richard Randell and others.

There have been many exciting exhibits of Minnesota sculptors throughout the years. John Rood's sculpture had shows in Milan and Rome.

ARCHITECTURE

Minnesota is not without its gems of historic beauty which are here to delight us.

From the Sioux gabled dwellings at their Mille center to our present ultra-modern designs in architecture, our State has offered an interesting variety to suit every taste. Sod houses and log houses offered shelter in the pioneer days. The immigrants from the east built houses like those they remembered — chiefly colonial in character, or houses like Henry Hastings Sibley's, in stone, built in 1835, reminiscent of the Pennsylvania and Maryland farm houses; this house is lathed with willow wands. (It has been restored by the Daughters of the American Revolution.) Another early home, of much different type, is the William Gates LeDuc Gothic Revival House, built in 1864.

Early stockades were built for the military in the 17th and 18th centuries in Minnesota. We still have the Round tower at Ft. Snelling, made of limestone. As the cities began to be laid out, away from the protective forts, certain styles developed. St. Paul in the development of its streets, reminds one of the East, with Summit Avenue as a boulevard on the stone terraces above the city. James J. Hill's red stone mansion (of 1887) dominates

this section. In contrast with this, the Irvine Park section of St. Paul showed Greek influences with colonnades much like temples. Sherman street in St. Paul shows examples of the four-columned houses, around 1850. Minneapolis shows an entirely different type of street pattern, with a gridiron effect. The lovely parks add to the general picture.

Although the Victorian era influenced the architecture of Minnesota, immigrants from various countries added interesting notes in Eastern Orthodox churches, the French influence with chateau type dwellings, the Romanesque influence as well as Byzantine. Gothic influences have already been mentioned. Minnesota employed its various stones to good advantage with granite, limestone and sandstone used.

In the latter part of the 19th century, the Minneapolis architect, Leroy S. Buffington designed buildings for the University of Minnesota, such as Pillsbury Hall, red sandstone in Romanesque style. Buffington claimed he was the first to patent skyscrapers—the Rand Tower in Minneapolis is an example of this type of skeleton construction.

Cass Gilbert of St. Paul is probably the name Minnesotans know best. He won the 1893 competition for a new state capitol, of Rennaisance influence in white marble. Mr. Gilbert won the competition to design the master plan of the University of Minnesota, also.

Frank Lloyd Wright, the grand master of architects, from our neighboring Wisconsin has designed several Minnesota houses, such as the Lake Minneatonka residence in 1914 for F. W. Little (now the R. V. Stevenson home) and in Minneapolis homes for the Malcolm Willeys (1934) and the H. J. Neils (1941). The Richard S. Davis home at Lake Minnetonka (by Philip C. Johnson), the Ray Lindholm residence at Cloquet, and the Don and Virginia Lovness (the artist) White Bear Lake home (1957).

Another impressive contemporary style is exemplified by the city hall and Ramsey County courthouse in St. Paul (Ellerbe & Co., architects). Carl Milles, the sculptor's Peace Memorial of white onyx, surrounded by dark blue walls of marble, has become quite celebrated. Our grain

Indian statue, Courthouse, St. Paul

elevators are designed with such purity of style that many find them starkly beautiful.

The best example of communal shopping center in our midst, acknowledged as one of the best in the Nation, is Southdale with its almost lyrical freedom of movement, its refreshing color contrasts, its changing forms and witty designs on every side. Dayton the Patron (among others) and Victor Gruen the Architect, have done the Twin Cities, indeed, our entire Minnesotan heritage, an invaluable service with this center.

"Let Minnesotans rejoice, (especially those in the Twin Cities) that their heritage of domestic architecture is (says our architect from England, Gerald Stanwell) almost, with a few exceptions of course, its crowning glory. In the Twin Cities with the delightful proximity of their lakes and the noble Mississippi, the richness and variety of their houses continually delight me. This variety of design and expression of individual character is the very essence of the American scene, even when we are confronted by the perennial and belligerent billboard."

We have considered briefly the relaxed and pleasing variety of the suburban scene. In equally inspiring contrast to this, we have the formal examples of public architecture.

Strictly in the classic form, but none the less pleasing, we have a good example of this in two distinctly great buildings, the State Capitol in Saint Paul (already mentioned) and the equally noble proportions of the Minneapolis Institute of Arts.

On still another phase of the communal life, we find (also with satisfaction) that schools and churches in Minnesota offer nearly every variety of design, and with the encouraging and inspiring co-ordination of both painting and sculpture.

We have already touched on the inspiration lent by well known architects lending their skill to shop and store design.

In connection with this, a fascinating booklet prepared by Harlan E. McClure called "Twin Cities Architecture" has listed many of our prominent forms of architecture with illustrations of each; also to be noted is "A Century of Minnesota Architecture" by Donald R. Torbert and his "A Century of Art and Architecture in Minnesota" (University of Minnesota Press).

On one final and concluding note on this subject, be it remembered that the lack in all our cities is not so much individual genius but of communal *simplicity*, by which is meant the *beautiful* from which has been removed everything redundant and outmoded. There is nothing discordant in this highest of all aims in communal effort, the striving towards the inspiring simplicity of perfection. The ultimate of this essential and much needed aspiration will be found in the gradual improvement of our cities and this will be fast or slow according to the interest and enthusiasm of its collective citizens without which no artist (least of all the architect) can function or make a living at all.

Writers and Poets
of Minnesota

By ANNA A.
VON HELMHOLTZ PHELAN
Consultant

"Minnesota has always been a writing state," said John Sherman in the 1949 Territorial Centennial issue of the *Minneapolis Tribune*.

Every home in Minnesota can have in its library a Minnesota section to which one may point with pride. In reading the fascinating stories of Minnesota one might begin with *Aborigines of Minnesota* and Dr. A. E. Jenks and Dr. Lloyd Wilford's studies on prehistoric man in this state. A companion book would be Dr. G. M. Schwartz and Thiel's *Minnesota's Rocks and Waters*, an absorbing picture of the topography of the land of the sky-tinted waters.

Innumerable books on Indians of Minnesota hold both young and old enthralled. Books on the arts and crafts of our first Minnesotans, with a detailed description of their songs by Frances Densmore add to our understanding of the culture the white man so nearly destroyed. Charles Eastman's (Ohiyesa's) story of his *Indian Boyhood* has a special charm.

If exploration intrigues you, one can read first-hand accounts of Radisson's entry into Minnesota, and Father Hennepin's highly-colored *A Description of Louisiana*, which includes the story of his discovery of our St. Anthony Falls. Dean Theodore C. Blegen and Dr. Philip Jordan of the University have compiled a book of excerpts from writers such as these, and later ones: *With Various*

Voices is the apt title. There is a new book on *La Vérendrye* that holds one's interest, also.

When the English followed the French as explorers in Minnesota, Jonathan Carver's story of his travels aroused much interest; his reproduction of the funeral address given by a Sioux chief caused the great Schiller to write the poem *Song of a Nadowessee Chief*, considered by Goethe to be one of Schiller's best. Two translations of this poem can be found in Dr. E. O'Neill's *Concise History of the State of Minnesota*, one of the earliest of histories of our state.

Other intriguing accounts by early writers include Pike's Journal, the dashing Italian explorer's (Beltrami's) tale of his searching for the source of the Mississippi, Henry Hasting Sibley's *Unfinished Autobiography*, and the engrossing books by Henry R. Schoolcraft. Dr. Grace Lee Nute's books on the romantic voyageur are captivating.

Other early writings of the first half of the 19th century in Minnesota brought translations of the Bible into Sioux. The Pond brothers had made a dictionary of the Sioux language with Stephen Riggs, then they and Dr. T. S. Williamson and Joseph Renville translated the Bible. A Chippewa spelling book had been written by Protestant Ayers, while Catholic Father Baraga compiled a Chippewa dictionary.

Newspapers by Gideon Pond in Sioux, *The Dakota Friend*, and *The Minnesota Pioneer*, with James M. Goodhue as its first editor, appeared. Goodhue extolled our fair state, "Minnesota cannot be excelled for beauty of scenery—for pure and wholesome climate—for everything that makes an earthly paradise."

Two books which give flavor to this period are W. J. Snellings *Tales of the Northwest* and Mary H. Eastman's *Dakotah: or, Life and Legends of the Sioux around Fort Snelling*. Henry W. Longfellow was inspired to write *Hiawatha* by Mrs. Eastman's book and Schoolcraft's writings. (All quotations following are from John Sherman's article in the 1949 Territorial Centennial Issue of the Minneapolis Star & Tribune.)

"Pioneers and early settlers broke into print almost before they had laid the last beams on their log huts. Early editors were highly articulate, even verbose, and not long after them came the early educators, who were handy with a pen and a verb.

"Perhaps the state's high literacy rate has had much to do with its productivity in writing. Whatever the cause, Minnesota, from its territorial days, has bred and attracted scriveners of all degrees of competence and professionalism. The state's recent ascendancy as a literary source and scene has been merely a payoff of its long preoccupation with writing.

"The earliest names—Gideon Pond, John H. Stevens, James M. Goodhue, Isaac Atwater — go back to territorial days, and while their pens contributed little to the mainstream of American letters, they at least represent the first of Minnesota's regional writers.

"Through the last half of the 19th century, Minnesota had little literary identity. If we except the many reminiscences written by pioneers and founders, who made no claim to literary craft, the days of Minnesota's youth and early struggle were not to provide major themes for major writers until after the era had come to a close.

"Hamlin Garland was one of the first nationally important writers to picture this part of the country, writing realistically of his boyhood on homestead claims. Edward Eggleston, author of *The Hoosier Schoolmaster* and well-known in his day, spent some time in Minnesota. Besides the stories for children which he wrote about Minnesota Indians, one of his novels, *Mystery of Metropolisville*, has a Minnesota setting. Eggleston was "well aware of a certain undefined strength, a deep-seated faith in the future, and a character-building influence that together spell Minnesota's contribution to American life." *(Minnesota Fiction* in Minnesota History, Spring, 1958, Vol. 33, No. 5 by William Pierce Randel).

Ignatius Donnelly's strange genius has made him the object of much study. His books, *Atlantis, The Great Cryptogram* and *Caesar's Column* show great originality.

"It was on the University of Minnesota campus —and the fact still holds true—that writing, usually linked with scholarship, attained high status. Two educators, William Watts Folwell, university president and author of the authoritative history of Minnesota, and Maria Sanford, were distinguished and gifted writers.

"Others associated with the university were to exert considerable influence on the literary 'maturing' of the state. They included two scholars, and a poet—Oscar Firkins, Richard Burton and Arthur Upson." William Stearns Davis' historical novels are considered among the best; *A Friend to Caesar* is one. Ruth Phelps taught at the University, also; she and her French husband write under the pen-name of Phelps-Morand.

"Another scholar of world repute, Elmer E. Stoll, is one of the recognized authorities on Shakespeare." Martin Ruud achieved international recognition as an authority on medieval culture.

"Through the years the University, particularly its English department which was under the chairmanship of Joseph Warren Beach, has exerted great stimulus on critical writing. Dr. Anna Phelan had charge of all of the creative writing, drawing students from far and near.

"Beach himself became one of the nation's most acute and perceptive literary analysts, in addition to being a poet and novelist in his own right. Under the direction of the English department there were enrolled writer-teachers of national and international repute, chief among them being Eric Bentley, author of *A Century of Hero Worship* and *The Playwright as Thinker*, and Robert Penn Warren, author of the Pulitzer-prize winning novel, *All the King's Men*." Other Minnesota writers have been connected with the University at one time or another.

"Before leaving the campus group, we must mention Tremaine McDowell *America in Literature*, Theodore Blegen's *Grass Roots History* and many other books on Minnesota history, Dr. Philip Jordan's *Singin' Yankees* and *The National Road*, Helen Clapesattle's of the University Press *The Doctors Mayo*, Donald Ferguson of the music department *A History of Musical Thought*, Dr. Anna von Helmholtz Phelan *The Crystal Cup* and *The Social Philosophy of William Morris*, and Thomas S. Roberts *Birds of Minnesota*.

James Gray includes in his career a professorship in the English department. He is an author and critic, for many years book and drama reviewer for the *St. Paul Dispatch & Pioneer Press*, author of a history of the University of Minnesota, and of several sensitive, well wrought novels, all of them with a Minnesota background, and he is also author of *Pine, Stream and Prairie*, a regional study of Minnesota and Wisconsin.

Other St. Paul authors are also of "major reputation—F. Scott Fitzgerald became one of the important figures of the post-World War I literary generation. A literary craftsman of great skill and sophistication was the late Charles M. Flandrau, whose *Viva Mexico!* is still one of the gems of travel literature. His sister-in-law, Grace Flandrau, has written travel books *Then I Saw the Congo* and novels about Summit Avenue families. Kay Boyle, noted short story writer and novelist, was born in St. Paul. Thomas Boyd *(Through the Wheat)* was once literary editor of the old *St. Paul Daily News*.

"Minnesota's most famous literary native son, of course, is Sinclair Lewis, Nobel prize winner, who started out with stories of Minnesota background in *Main Street* and *Babbitt* and returned to his native state as locale for his novels *Kingsblood Royal* and *The God Seeker*.

"The line of Minnesota writers who have gained national readership has continued fairly steadily since the early novels of Lewis and Fitzgerald. Martha Ostenso became a best-selling novelist with her *Wild Geese,* and she wrote a vivid story of the Red River valley on *O River, Remember!*

"Two important and highly-readable novels which used the social-historical Minnesota background were written by William J. McNally, former Minneapolis newspaperman—*House of Vanished Splendor* and *The Roofs of Elm Street*. Maud Hart Lovelace, with her "colorful and historically accurate chronicle of early days at Fort Snelling, *Early Candlelight*," combined with her husband, Delos, for another interesting Minnesota novel, *Gentlemen From England*.

"Certainly one of the finest novels in immigrant pioneer life in this region was penned by a Norwegian—O. E. Rolvaag—who came here relatively late in life to write *Giants in the Earth*, which might be termed the 'Growth of the Soil' of our region." Another great Norwegian in Minnesota, Thorstein Veblen, wrote many outstanding books on the social and economic system.

"Of the newest generation of Minnesota writers, several of them have already made niches for themselves in the national literary gallery. The tragically premature death of Tom Heggen cut short a career that already was bright with present achievement and future promise. His *Mister Roberts*, an ironic chronicle of tedium aboard a navy cargo vessel in the South Pacific was one of the country's reigning hits in the stage version prepared by Heggen and Joshua Logan.

"Two young writers of markedly contrasting gifts—Feike Feikema or Fred Manfred, and Max Shulman—are fast reaching stardom in their respective fields. Earthy Feikema has written many novels, *The Golden Bowl*, his first, in 1944;" others include a trilogy, *Lord Grizzly* in 1954, *Morning Red* in 1956 and *Riders of Judgment*, 1957. "Shulman has tickled the funnybone of the younger generation with three zany novels, and has also had his hand in Broadway, Hollywood and nightclub productions.

"Two women writers—Mabel Seeley of Minneapolis and Ann Chidester of Stillwater—have established their places in the sun.

"Miss Chidester has dealt with problems of her generation and set some of her stories in her native town on the St. Croix. Mrs. Seely is one of the proud assets of Doubleday's Crime Club, with several quality whodunits to her credit as well as a serious novel about a woman's downfall through greed, *Woman of Property*, laid in Northfield and Minneapolis.

"The roster of Minnesota woman writers is a long one, and constantly growing longer. Margaret Culkin Banning of Duluth is one of the country's best known magazine contributors, writing novels and discussing social problems with equal facility and penetration.

"Among others on the distaff side who have made worthy contributions are Eileen Davis, Thelma Jones, Brenda Ueland, the Chute sisters, Marchette, B. J. and Mary Grace, Borghild Dahl, the Hoffman twins, Sheilah Alexander, Dagmar Doneghy, Darragh Aldrich, Laura Krey and Gladys Hasty Carroll." Others are Cornelia Meigs, Frances Sterrett, Elizabeth Atkins, Evelyn Voss Wise and Lorna Beers.

"Norman Katkov of St. Paul is a newspaperman, novelist and a regular magazine contributor. His controversial novel, *Eagle At My Eyes*, first brought him into the spotlight, and a second one, *A Little Sleep, A Little Slumber,* was published. (1949). A writer of great distinction and originality is James F. Powers, who won a Guggenheim fellowship. His first book was a volume of short stories, *The Prince of Darkness.*

"Meridel Le Sueur's *North Star Country* is undoubtedly the best of the American Folkways series of books, dealing with various regions of the U.S.A." Many Minnesota authors have written books dealing with specific regions, or special fields, such as Dr. Grace Lee Nute. Florence Page Jaques collaborates with her artist husband on books about the out-of-doors. Neil Swanson's *The Forbidden Ground* deals with the fur trade; novels on lumber and the forests include Walter O'Meara's *The Trees Went Forth,* and Kenneth S. Davis' *In the Forests of the Night.* Edward Havill's *Big Ember* tells of the Sioux uprising, and the iron ranges have been featured in novels such as Phil Strong's *Iron Mountain* and George Ryland Bailey's *The Red Mesabi,* with *Iron Land* by Ogley and Cleland adding some concerning the subject.

Many novelists have used the land as basis for their plots: Cornelia James Cannon's *Red Rust,* and Ostenso, Rolvaag, Krause, Beers, Frederick and other writers before mentioned have added to the picture of Minnesota. The railroad tells its story in Benson's *Hill Country* and Sullivan's *Empire Builder* and Meigs' *Railroad West.*

Besides the historians before noted are the Bucks, M. V. Carney, O'Farrell, Burnquist, Christianson, Willard, Ford, Brezler and Painter, Lindquist and Clark for their books on Minnesota history. Other books on Minnesota are constantly being compiled and written.

Nonfiction writers deal with nearly every subject. Some of the best are David Bryn-Jones with his biography of Frank Kellogg, Mitchell Vaughn Charnley with his biographies for boys of the Wright Brothers, Hoover, etc., Theodore Jorgensen with his biography of Rolvaag, (with Nora Solum) and Martin Odland with his biographies of Knute Nelson and Alexander Ramsey. Travelers to unusual places have contributed books like William Carlson's *Gleenland Lies North,* Carroll K. Michener's *Heirs of the Incas* and Glanville Smith's *Many A Green Isle,* and Borghild Dahl's *Glimpses of Norway.* The list could go on and on. Marjorie Edgar is outstanding in her collections of folk songs and folklore, as is of course Dean Theodore C. Blegen, in many fields. Histories of Minneapolis and St. Paul and other towns in the state make fascinating reading; Alfred Hoyt Bill has written much on Minneapolis, and John Sherman has contributed his book on the Minneapolis Symphony Orchestra, *Music and Maestros.*

Other writers with notable books to their credit are Dan Brennan *Never So Young Again,* Charles Lindbergh, co-author of *We,* and *Spirit of St. Louis,* which won the Pulitzer Prize, 1956. Herbert Krause *The Threshers,* Eric Sevareid *Not So Wild A Dream,* Margaret Snyder *The Chosen Valley,* Dorothy Davis Willette *The Spear Penny,* Neil Boardman *The Long Home,* and Martin Quigley *A Tent On Corsica.* In special fields are Martin Bovey *Whistling Wings,* Russell Bennett *The Compleat Rancher,* Howard Haycraft *Life and Times of the Detective Story,* and Theodore Finney *Hearing Music.*

Religion and social problems both in fiction and nonfiction are becoming more and more prevalent. Dr. Glenn Clark's works are well known; Dr.

Arnold Lowe's books, such as *The Importance of Being Ourselves* have been a source of inspiration to many. Gladys Zehnpfennig's religious novels, *The Rock and the Sand* and *Search for Eden* and *Son of Nazareth* transport one to Bible times.

Books on Minnesota abound. *Minnesota Writes* by Carmen Nelson Richards and Genevieve Rose Breen, "reveals in all its facets the really unique status Minnesota holds in American letters."

Juvenile books are almost too numerous to mention, but authors such as these have brought to our children a wealth of reading material: Carol Ryrie Brink, Mildred Houghton Comfort, Ethel Brill, Emma Brock, Helen Acker, Edward Cheyney, Caroline Fuller, Marguerite Murphy, Elizabeth Palmer, Miriam Potter, Rose McLaughlin Sackett, Annette Turngren, W. J. Wilwerding, Laura Ingalls Wilder, and many others. Several of the novelists have written children's stories also; such as Maud Hart Lovelace, with her Betsy-Tracy stories.

The problems of boys in a city revealed by John K. Donohue, chief probation officer of Ramsey County, make a stirring book called *Baffling Eyes of Youth*, which everyone should read.

Centennial year has brought forth many new books on Minnesota, of which one of the first was *Pioneer Panorama* by Mabel Otis Robison who later wrote *Minnesota Pioneers*.

Poets of Minnesota

By MARGARETTE BALL DICKSON

Early verse-writing groups were sponsored by the English Departments of our Colleges and Universities: Maria Sanford, Richard Burton, Joseph Warren Beach and Dr. Anna von Helmholtz-Phelan of the University of Minnesota; Glenn Clark of Macalester, Sister Maris Stella of St. Catherine's, Sister Mary Pierre Boucher of St. Teresa's; Sister Marvella of St. Benedict's, Sister Brigetta of Villa Scholastica and at St. Olaf, Concordia and the Teachers Colleges. Minneapolis Public Library began night classes under Mrs. Oren which spread into the High Schools.

The Bellman used poetry and columns were started, 1935, in *Minnesota Farmer*, Journal of *Education*, Brainerd *Dispatch*, *Hokah Chief* and Twin City papers. The St. Cloud *Times* used daily verse columns.

Started by Robert Cary and Irl Morse (editor New Verse, St. Paul) and plow-work done by Marie Gerry, Clara Clausen, Sister Mary Boucher, Maude Schilpin, Margarette Ball Dickson and others, the League of Minnesota Poets was organized, February 10, 1934, with 30 charter members. Its presidents have been Marie Gerry, Duluth; Margarette Dickson, Staples; Nan Fitz-Patrick, Minneapolis; Louise Leighton, Virginia; and Carmen Richards, Lillian Osborn, Leslie Code, Victoria Janda and De Ette Genung all of the Twin Cities. Its magazine, *The Moccasin*, was first mimeographed, now of fine format and content.

The *St. Paul Seminar* (now *St. Paul Poets*) was organized in 1935, as was the *Minneapolis Poetry Society* and the *Arrowhead Poets*—all still very active. Books sponsored by League or one of its branches: Year books of 1935, '36 and *Moccasin Annual*; (2) Poems of the Arrowhead, Meadows of the Moon, Minneapolis *Skylines* and Minnesota *Skylines* ('11) which sold copies in the thousands. Maude C. Schilpin, League Historian, edited inclusive volumes of *Minnesota Verse* covering 100 years, with Biography and Bibliography, 1934, 1938. Both Territorial and State editions of the *Moccasin* were printed.

A booth for Poetry was set up in Fine Arts Building, State Fair, 1935-38, exhibiting books, award poems, autographs, anthologies and verse volumes from the Historical Society Library. Over 6,000 registered from many states. Governor Youngdahl proclaimed Poetry Day, October 15, 1950. Governor Floyd B. Olson appointed Margarette Ball Dickson, Poet Laureate, April 25, 1934 and Governor Orville Freeman sent congratulations, 1958, when she was recrowned.

The League of *American Penwomen* (Minn.) lists poets: Darragh Aldrich, Elizabeth Bridgeman, Eloise Hackett, Victoria Janda, Florence Jepson, Rose Muckley, Anna Phelan and Hazel B. Selby.

Martha Ostenso's first book was verse, "*A Far Land.*"

Midwest Chaparrals was founded in Minneapolis, 1941 and now has 1,112 members in 11 Midwest States. Its anthology is *From the Valleys to the Mountains,* profusely illustrated. Regents have been Myrta Albertson Wells, A. Phil Londroche, Reba Ward, Laurene Tibbetts. It is making the Midwest poetry conscious and gets out *Chaparral Chats,* (mimeographed) and a magazine of fine format, *Midwest Chaparral Magazine.*

Among noted poets of Minnesota origin or residence are: Henry Adams Bellows, Col. Paul Southworth Bliss, the four Byrnes sisters, Robert Cary, Frank Brooks Cowgill, Grace Noll Crowell, Chester Firkins, Jules Grendron, Grace Farrington Gray *(Farmer's Wife,* editor.); John Allison Haining, Gertrude Hanson, Albert Henrikson *(Bert of the Back Woods,* in The Minnesota *Farmer),* Larry Ho, Deborah Kilmer, Stafford King, Herbert Krause *(Wind Without Rain);* Erwin I. McElroy, James Oppenheim, Ruth Shepard Phelps, Edith Thompson *(Gypsy Poems);* Arthur Upson, Grant Utley, Gertrude Thomas, Alice Ames Winter. Mrs.

Lorena Thomas Witham is our oldest living poet.

Writers' Conferences: Irl Morse established Cabin in the Pines, Akeley, 1934, Margarette Ball Dickson continued it 1936-1944; The Silver Lake Writers' Conference was founded by Maria and Paul Coleman, Poet Haven, Rt. 3, Fairmont, Minnesota, 1950, and has had on its faculty Meridel Le Sueur, Dr. John Neihardt, Margarette Ball Dickson, Margaret Durant, Allan Tate and others.

Notable among recent books of verse is Phil Londroche's *I am Mississippi.* There are hundreds of other poets, past and present who have contributed to a fuller creative expression in poetic form. Margarette Ball Dickson (Mrs. Christan Jenson) is preparing a book in this field, *Minnesota Poets, Then and Now.* She prepared and foreworded the Minnesota section of the five Volume set of *North American Poets,* Harrison; and edited with Gill and Butler *The Book of Father Verse.* Her three volumes on Poetry Technique *Patterns for Poems* was her Ph.D. thesis.

CHAPTER FOURTEEN

Music In Minnesota

By JOHANNES RIEDEL

As large segments of this topic have already been well covered by others, we have decided to emphasize two areas about which less has been said: the history of music education in Minnesota and a discussion of contemporary composition in the state. Some background comments will be made about Indian, folk, and urban music or jazz.

Historical surveys of music in the state of Minnesota have already been handled by others. A history of musical activities between 1850 and 1900 has been compiled reliably and presented in chronological fashion by Louise Chapman for the *Minneapolis Tribune*. A general survey of musical activities during the first hundred years of Minnesota's statehood has been issued recently by John K. Sherman in his *Music and Theater in Minnesota History*. An earlier publication by the same author, entitled *Music and Maestros*, deals elaborately with the history of the Minneapolis Symphony Orchestra. A Master of Arts thesis, entitled "Minnesota Music in the Nineteenth Century, A Guide to Sources and Resources," by Frank Gillis gives additional information. Tribute must be paid to Dean Theodore C. Blegen for his numerous publications on basic Minnesota history and folklore.

Indian Music

From the unexciting but basic studies of the late Frances Densmore on Sioux and Chippewa music, we discover that both used music to cele-brate all the important events of their lives. The Sioux had their songs of war, ceremonial songs, songs of societies (such as the Buffalo Dance Society), songs for chiefs, songs of praise, of love, and of legends. The Buffalo song, as witnessed at Fort Snelling by the eminent painter, George Catlin, found the dancers with buffalo headdresses, imitating the motions of the buffalo.

Among the Chippewa, the several hundred healing and other songs of the *Mide* were ceremonial. Magic and mysterious results were hoped for in these songs; the power of the *Mide* was effected through music and medicine. Love charms were also obtained through music. Songs of hunting, war, peace, powwow dances, the scalp dance, hypnotic juggler songs of animals, trees, and fire, games and social songs commemorated every important event in Chippewa life.

As the Indian was prevented for a long time from becoming an integral member of our society, and as his general position remained for a long time that of a "neophyte" Christian, his music has been of little inspiration to later American composers. The primitivism of Chippewa and Sioux music, its monotonous rhythm, its complex style of vibrato and falsetto singing, and its distinctive instrumentation have had little impact, in spite of "Darwinistic" tendencies of composers who are ever anxious to incorporate new themes into the fabric of their musical language.

Nevertheless, rather sentimental adaptations of Indian music did at times appear. The tone-picture-poem approach of the fin-de-siècle American art song composer is present in Charles Wakefield Cadman's "Land of Sky Blue Waters" which is said to be based on a tribal melody of the Omaha Indians. "By weeping waters" (Minnehaha Falls), a song by Thurlow Lieurance, is based upon both Indian melody and legend. "By the waters of Minnetonka" by the same composer, is an idealized abstraction of a Sioux air in the same vein as Louis Moreau Gottschalk's "Danza de los Gibaros" which gives a salon variant of an aboriginal melody from Costa Rica. The "Indianist," Alberto Bimboni, composed the opera, *Winona* (1926). Carl Busch wrote a symphonic poem, *Minnehaha's Vision.*

The study of Indian music was a primary concern of the St. Paul composer, Arthur Farwell (1872-1951). In his attempt to formulate a national foundation for American music, he established the *Wa-Wan* press in honor of the Indians who inspired the music which formed its basic repertoire. Besides Indian songs for mixed voices such as "The Mother's Vow" (an Omaha melody) and "A Navajo War Dance," he composed many works for piano, string quartet, string and full orchestra which used Indian themes.

Folk and Urban Music

Equated with the Colonial and Territorial history of Minnesota, the occupational songs of the North-West Company's French traders have come down to us as half myth, half fact: a myth of fresh water Argonauts who paddled down the rivers and across the lakes of the sky-tinted waters singing "gracefully" in unison and marking time with their paddles. In order to accelerate the tempo of his oarsmen, the steersman would sing in shanty manner, the others would perform the choral refrain. The idyllic description of their own music by these "gentlemen of French descent" can be contrasted with their descriptions of the music of their "savage" neighbors. Many writers have recorded their impressions when listening to Indian songs, but only a few thought it worthwhile to notate the text or music of these songs. According to these descriptions, the music of the "half-breed" voyagers rivalled closely in noise, wildness, and falsetto singing the war cries of the Indians.

During the first hundred years of Minnesota statehood, folk music consisted of songs of the lumberjacks and of the immigrant groups. The music of the Northwoodsmen, like that of the voyageurs, was frequently described in a "picturesque" language which would befit the era of the "idyllic" water mill rather than that of the industrial steam mill.

Franz Rickaby, however, gives in his *Ballads and Songs of the Shanty Boy* a sense of the shanty man in his proper environment, the rising American lumber industry. Songs were sung on Saturday evenings, according to Rickaby, after six gruelling days of hard work. The singing was usually preceded by card playing, gossiping, or fighting. The purpose of the songs was to provide a release from the malaise and tedium of labor conditions. Music served better than any of the other pastimes to make life bearable. Songs were usually spur-of-the-moment affairs with a shanty taking the lead and other voices joining in on refrained choruses. Some songs referred to specific local situations; for example, the first stanza of the song of the loggers on the Rum River or the song entitled "The Crow Wing Drive" which deals with the era when railroading was young.

The immigrants brought with them folk, popular, and dance music as it was performed in the old country in the nineteenth century. *Turnverein* mid-century favorites such as "Ach du lieber Augustin" for instance were sung by German immigrants in the New Ulm area. On the other hand the dialect songs of the immigrants illustrate their efforts to assimilate themselves in their new surroundings.

Music from the countryside, the music of the pre-union lumberjacks, loggers and railroad men found no corporal expression in the urban communities of the state. Urban music has had its most vivid representative in the twentieth century miracle of jazz. Minneapolis has been for many years a rather active center for jazz. Jazz made an immediate impression on local musicians when the famous New Orleans Rhythm Kings played their first engagement here. Jazz bands on the Strekfuss Line steamboats moving up the river to St. Paul were also influential in spreading this New Orleans music to Minnesota. Another jazz pioneer who did much to enliven local interest in jazz was Ben Pollack whose Dixieland band performed in St. Paul in the early thirties. As early as 1929, the Nankin Cafe had a Dixieland band under Norvy Mulligan, while at the same time jazz was beginning to be heard from campus combos and bands. The now famous Mitch's Club was opened in Mendota in 1939 under Red Dougherty's leadership with Doc Evans and Harry Blons (now well-known leaders of their own jazz bands) among its members.

Doc Evans, Miss Albers and Wilber de Paris

Summer jazz concert held outdoors featuring Doc Evans and his Dixieland Jazz Band

A revived interest in traditional jazz probably began with — or was reflected by — the series of concerts sponsored by the Walker Art Center. These concerts, now in their fifth season, have featured the Doc Evans Band with commentary by Evans and have presented jazz as an art form. Concerts of contemporary jazz under Herb Pilhofer have also been featured at Walker. In 1957, "Jazz at the Institute" presented three types of jazz bands: Doc Evans and his Dixieland band, the Bob Davis quartet playing "progressive" jazz, and the Herb Pilhofer Octet featuring "cool" arrangements of popular and original compositions.

Music Education

The story of music education in this state begins with nineteenth century singing schools. Much of private music teaching during the fifties and sixties of the past century was associated with them. The chief function of country or parish singing schools was to bring a simple, practical form of music to the parishioners and to teach them to participate in it to the best of their abilities. As early as 1851, a singing school was organized in St. Paul by a Professor Bennett who gave an entertaining recital with the assistance of the St. Paul Glee Club. Inside of a year, there were three such singing schools in town.

The advent of public education marked the decline and eventual death of these institutions. Ever since the Civil War, music has been taught in the public schools. Early music supervisors to whom credit should be given for establishing the system of public music education in the Twin Cities were Charles Marsh, O. E. McFadon, Mrs. J. S. Findley, Ruth Anderson, Styles Raymond, Miss Helen Trask of Minneapolis Public Schools and C. H. Congdon of St. Paul Public Schools.

Music was originally taught only in grammar schools. In St. Paul, Elsie M. Shawe, who succeeded C. H. Congdon as supervisor, was one of the founders of the Music Educators National Conference in the early 1900's. The first music in St. Paul high schools came in the middle 1900's when E. C. Hartwell was Superintendent of Schools. Five choruses from these schools gave programs all over the city for civic activities such as Christmas and Memorial Day celebrations, State Fairs, and M.E.A. meetings. Instrumental music was begun early, at first as an extracurricular activity after school.

In 1933, upon Miss Shawe's retirement, Mathilda Heck became supervisor of the St. Paul Public Schools. Under her influence, full-time instrumental teachers were secured for the lower grades. Musical festivals were sponsored in the city; bands and orchestras were encouraged. Miss Heck has for fifteen years given a Music Appreciation lesson once a week over the University Station, KUOM, entitled "Adventures in Music."

In Minneapolis until 1910 one supervisor had charge of all the schools with no assistants. There were some orchestras and glee clubs in high schools, but singing in grade schools was the main feature of the educational program. By 1925, the Minneapolis music program had greatly expanded. It emphasized sight reading and the singing of choral classics, instrumental training and, later, the formation of orchestras. Glee clubs of all kinds and bands were encouraged in the upper grades and high schools. An applied music course in which harmony and original composition were stressed was. pioneered. Under P. T. Giddings, Peter Tkach, and now Charles Wesley Anderson as supervisors in Minneapolis, a cappella choirs and glee clubs as well as bands and orchestras have increased in number and size.

The formative years of Minnesota history, especially the last half of the nineteenth century, saw a significant rise in the number of educational institutions of higher learning. This was largely the result of an eagerness on the part of religious denominations to give their young constituents a formal education while at the same time training them for the clergy.

The first university to offer music instruction was Hamline University at Red Wing. In 1854, Mrs. Frances L. Dunning was the first member of the music faculty—although she was also responsible for a course in ornamental art. In 1857, Miss Densmore was appointed to succeed Mrs. Dunning. Almost immediately the faculty was increased to three with the additions of Miss Eliza Isabell in 1857 and John Lerbeck in 1859.

St. John's University began music instruction in 1862 when it appointed Wolfgang Northman to the faculty. Toward the end of the century, excellent instruction in instrumental performance was offered. Musical organizations consisted of a student choir, an orchestra, and a University cornet band. Among required subjects in the Ecclesiastical course were three years of Gregorian chant.

At Winona, the musical interests of the State Normal School and of the community have been closely identified since the foundation of the school in 1864. O. D. Adams, the first music teacher, was likewise prominent in the St. Cecilia Society, one of Winona's earliest musical organizations.

The first musical instruction at Gustavus Adolphus was given by a Mr. Lindstrom in 1867. Toward the end of the century, a Bachelor of Music degree with a major in piano was offered after five years of study. Swedish in addition to English was a language requirement for this degree. A great number of musical organizations, quartets, sextets, octets, a conservatory orchestra, and chorus created a musical atmosphere of animated performances.

Music at Macalester has been taught as a part of a liberal arts education ever since the college opened in 1885. At Carleton College during the nineties a five-year program was inaugurated for a B.A. with a major in music. In 1903, a music department was established at St. Olaf College under the direction of the famous F. Melius Christiansen. In 1917, the college granted its first Bachelor of Music degree.

The early years of the University of Minnesota (1873-1891) were years of little or no musical instruction. The only musical activities were at commencement time when the musical menu consisted of works by Mozart, Verdi, von Suppe, Rossini and others. In the last decade of the nineteenth century, Northwestern Conservatory instructors under the supervision of Professor Marshall were recognized by the University as qualified to instruct its students in music courses. University catalogs from 1891 to 1902 list music taught at this conservatory. Although music, academically speaking, was not yet taught at the Uni-

versity, there seems to have been considerable musical activity. Many musical organizations were established such as the *Mandolin Club* under the direction of the Italian consul in Minneapolis, Signor Perera, the *Glee Club* under the initiative of president "Billy" Folwell, the *Choral-Union* under the direction of Anna Schoen-René. The band started with the purchase of a trumpet, next a drum, and finally, after a full component of instruments, a director, C. L. Graves from Fort Snelling. He was followed in 1897 by B. A. Rose.

Around the turn of the century, Howard Stearns Gale, then an instructor of psychology at the University, was in a large measure responsible for the musical interest and activity at the University. During the season of 1894-1895, he arranged a series of chamber music concerts to which he gave introductory lectures. Several articles in the "Minnesota Magazine" show his keen interest in the establishment of a music department at the University.

In 1902, at almost the same time that the St. Olaf School of Music was getting under way, a music department was finally organized at the University with a faculty of two: Emil Oberhoffer, Professor of Music, and John Parsons Beach, a talented nephew of the University president, as Assistant Professor. Four courses were offered: two theory courses, a course in "choral culture," and one in "advanced" pianoforte. Carlyle Scott followed Mr. Beach in 1904 as teacher of harmony and pianoforte which he shared with Oberhoffer. In the following years Scott taught additional courses in "Musical form and free composition" and "History of Music." In 1908, the first music education course taught during the regular year was added. In 1909, music could be elected as an academic minor for the first time. In the same year, Laura Frances Kendall was added to the staff. Five years later, Donald Ferguson, "Instructor of pianoforte" and Minnesota's most important contributor to music history, was added. In the same year the first music major was graduated from the University and the music department announced a four year curriculum leading to a degree of bachelor of arts in music. By 1915 more staff personnel were added. In 1916, the University Extension Division and the University Lyceum Series offered a great many vocal and instrumental concert attractions: the Apollo Male Quartet, the Chicago Musical Club, the Chicago Operatic Company, the Faust Opera Singers, groups from MacPhail School, the Metropolitan Male Trio, and many, many others. 1917 saw the first courses offered for graduate credit. In 1919, the University Concert Course under the leadership of Mrs. Carlyle Scott came into being with outstanding performances by artists of world-wide reputation. In 1921, a new building, Scott Hall, was erected. The department had found a permanent home.

Carlyle Scott

The new building, although badly outdated today, fulfilled splendidly the needs of the music faculty in the twenties and thirties.

Paul M. Oberg followed Scott in 1942 as chairman of the combined music and music education departments. As Executive Secretary-Treasurer of the Minneapolis Public School Music League, he has been instrumental in the operation of the high school music contests which take place on the University campus each year. For many years he has been president of the Minnesota Music Teacher's National Association. He has also been very active with the National Association for Schools of Music for which he has been regional vice-president and is now a member of the Asso-

ciation's Commission on Curriculum. Dr. Oberg has been instrumental in bringing musical activity to the St. Paul Campus of the University. He has also spent much effort organizing classical music programs for radio and TV.

Paul M. Oberg

Under Dr. Oberg's leadership the number of graduate courses in the fields of music history and literature, theory and composition, applied music, and music education has increased considerably. Appointments of new staff members were realized in such a way as to bring the course offerings of the music department to the level of course offerings of the University in general and also to bring them into agreement with the offerings of other Big Ten University music departments. A doctoral program in the fields of musicology, theory and composition, and music education was established. The increase of courses and studies in the music department is illustrated best by the increase of books, records, and scores of the Music Library which, by the way, was only opened on December 1, 1947. While the library showed in 1948, 750 scores or books, 2,110 recordings, and 429 choral publications, by 1958 it had

12,850 scores and books, 8,080 recordings, and 67,140 choral publications in circulation.

Choral Music

Ever since the establishment of the singing schools, the practice of choral singing has spread rapidly across the state. Singing societies were formed on many bases. Some were civic groups such as the *Orpheon* from Hastings, the *Mozart Verein* from Watertown, the *Philharmonia* from Winona, and still today the *Apollo Club* in Minneapolis. Others were musical societies drawn from specific nationalities. Most common were the many choirs associated with churches.

In addition, the curricula of the religious colleges and the University showed a great display of choral activities culminated by the phenomenal success of their choral organizations. Well-known choral groups in this area are the St. Olaf Choir, the Concordia Choir, the Augsburg College Choir, the Hamline University a cappella choir, the Macalester Chorus and the University Chorus.

This magnificent array of choral groups has found its echo in the choral writing of a great many composers who wrote for specific church or college choirs. Among the names associated with a late nineteenth and early twentieth century style of choral writing are F. Melius and Olaf C. Chris-

F. Melius Christiansen

tiansen, Oscar R. Overby, Hermann Munson, Rupert Sircom, Arthur B. Jennings, Ralph Williams, Peter Tkach, and others.

This style of writing has left its mark on the choral compositions of the contemporary generation. Some of the composers in this group are: Paul

Augsburg College Choir

J. Christiansen, Leland B. Sateren, G. Winston Cassler, Paul J. Manz, and Frank J. Pooler. These men, like their predecessors, are associated with colleges sponsored by church denominations. Choral compositions of both generations have been encouraged by the far-seeing promotional policies of two nationally famous Minneapolis publishing houses: Augsburg Publishing House (established 1845) and Schmitt, Hall & McCreary.

Sacred choral music of the contemporary generation takes into consideration the aesthetic and theological demands of both college and church choir. The musical language of these compositions fluctuates between a "F. Melius Christiansen traditionalism" and a middle-of-the-road modernism infused with neo-liturgical considerations.

The conflict between the St. Olaf heritage and neo-liturgical modernism can be seen in the choral works of G. Winston Cassler. While most of his choral works employ traditional harmony, neo-liturgical, chant-like effects in his "All laud to God the Father" and "The Godly Stranger" are employed. A refreshingly simple manifestation in sound of liturgical worship is obtained by Paul Manz. His "Let us ever walk with Jesus," his "Psalm 130," and "On my heart imprint thine image" are written in *alternatim* fashion between unison and mixed choirs, and use modal sonorities. Frank Pooler demonstrates in his "Song of Praise" and "Cry out and shout" a beautiful modal lyricism and a good feeling for contrapuntal "chant" lines.

The two major composers of religious choral music residing in Minnesota who experiment with the modern idiom are Leland B. Sateren and Paul J. Christiansen. Leland B. Sateren in his choral output strongly considers the immediate past while moderately utilizing modern devices. To choral compositions reflecting traditional writing belong such pieces as his "A great and mighty wonder," "When Christ as morn is dawning," and "The King is knocking." The last named work is a *lied*-cantata combination of two melodies, presented within an extended three-part song form. To the best of his choral compositions written in a style referring to the immediate past belongs his "Hosanna, Son of David." More modern devices are coined in his

Leland B. Sateren

"Cycle for Christmas." Particularly noteworthy is the expressive use of parallel sixth chords in the three upper voices of "Adoration" (No. 3) over a sustained bass drone at the words, "With bleating lambs and stupid sheep, but how could we whose lives were drawn."

Sateren's choral cycle "The Redeemer" makes use of conventional and moderately contemporary devices. Written to a poem by Pastor Thomas W. Wersell, it is made up of six short choral pieces which are cyclical in form. The first piece, "Promise" (Advent) presents a sparse, declamatory, choral invocation which precedes a lyric, modal "chorale." The second piece, "Birth" (Christmas) uses essentially traditional, harmonic effects, remindful of the St. Olaf school. "Death" (Passion) speaks the rhapsodic language of No. 1. "Resurrection" (Easter) builds big choral effects through frequent changes of the time signature, punctuated by chromatic progressions. "Ascension" proves to be an ingenuous work making use of a "soprano" part accompanied by a closely ranged terzet of low pitched voices. "Return" is a motivic resume of the foregoing sections.

Invocation and Chorale

HALLGRIM PETURSSON

PAUL CHRISTIANSEN

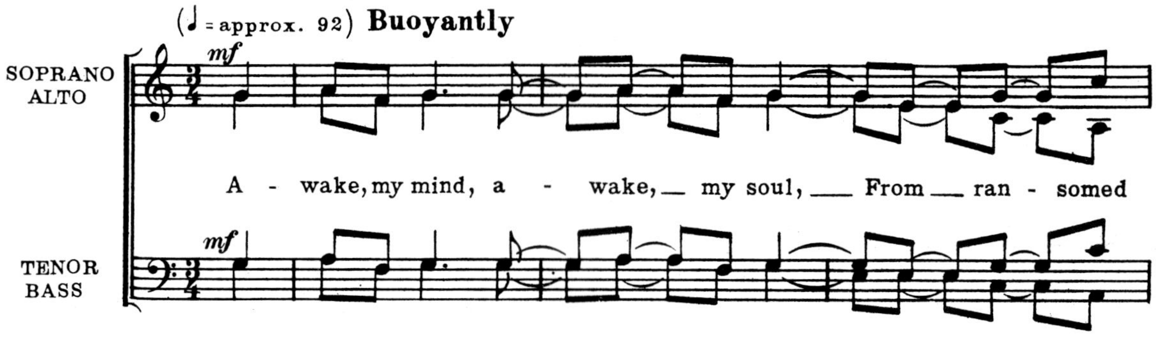

(♩ = approx. 92) **Buoyantly**

SOPRANO
ALTO

mf

A - wake, my mind, a - wake,__ my soul,__ From __ ran - somed

TENOR
BASS

mf

lips __ let __ praise __ forth roll, While __ heart __ and tongue __ as __ one__

f cresc.

Patapan

Bernard de la Monnoye, 1641-1728
Tr., Percy Dearmer, 1867-1936

French Carol
Arr., Paul Christiansen

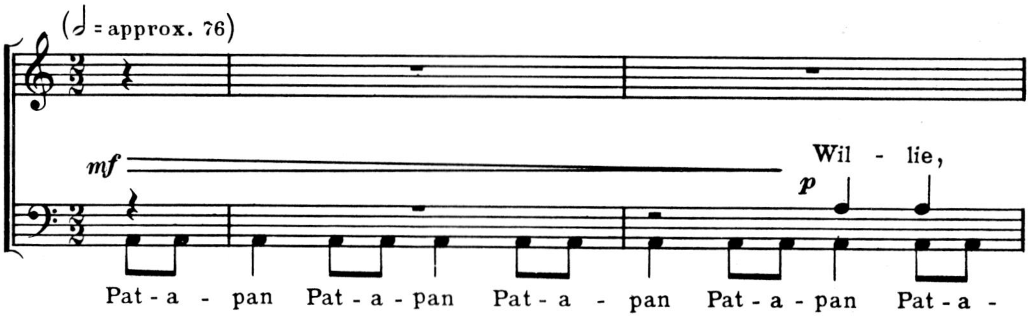

(♩ = approx. 76)

SOPRANO
ALTO

TENOR
BASS

mf

Wil - lie,

p

Pat - a - pan Pat - a - pan Pat - a - pan Pat - a - pan Pat - a -

take your lit - tle drum, With your whist-le, Rob - - - in

pan Pat - a - pan Pat - a - pan Pat - a - pan Pat - a - pan Pat - a - pat - a - pan

414

Bred in the tradition of foremost choral music, Paul J. Christiansen has been devoted to a search for a contrapuntally rhythmic style which adequately expresses his religious beliefs. His choral compositions are of two types: arrangements of secular and sacred folk songs and original compositions. His choral folk song paraphrases are based on traditional melodies from Europe, America, and Mexico. These settings served as a source of inspiration and a musical laboratory for his numerous compositions in the modern idiom. A characteristic example of an effective combination of a percussive ostinato *canzona* motif with the simple *cantus firmus* of a French Noel can be seen in his popular "Patapan."

His father's "Northfield" style of a cappella writing shines through in compositions with *chori spezzati* effects such as "Unto the Lord," "O Thou most high," and "Magnificat." Text-related chromaticism and modulations are frequent. Even the four pieces of his highly convincing choral cycle, "Sketches from Revelation" practice the always effective alternation between scanty solo parts with a hummed accompaniment and chordal sections of imposing resonance. Still propelled by deep-rooted functional harmonicism, is his "Bread of Tears." A soprano duet refrain alternating with full chordal sections reveals most ostensibly the message of the text from psalm 80: "Turn us again to Thee."

From the same psalm another text segment, "Look down from Heaven" allows him to write one of his most impressive modal pieces. A contrapuntal flavor of past ages emerges from a beseeching neo-Gregorian motif. Similarly his "Invocation and Choral" grows from a devotional motif, "Awake my mind" to a powerful climax. First this motif, distinctly derived from the musical vocabulary of the American Lutheran Church, is presented in syncopated chant-like articulations. These are subseded by imitative sections on varying pitch levels. An extensively altered reprise of the syncopated section leads us to the chorale finale.

More contemporary in design, "The solitary City," first number of his cycle, "Four Prophecies," proceeds by means of an *ostinato* motif in open harmonies which are slightly sharpened by expressive declamation dissonances. A similar initial motif has been used by his concert favorite, "This is the Day."

5. Ascension
The Redeemer
A Choral Cycle
Sacred Chorus for Mixed Voices, A Cappella
(S. A. T. B.)

THOMAS W. WERSELL

LELAND B. SATEREN

415

Instrumental Music

Composition and performance of instrumental music in the Twin Cities area have grown from their original status, that of entertaining the inhabitants of a rapidly growing frontier location, to a very complex and cosmopolitan level of a highly polished musical culture.

Instrumental activities in the Cities in the second half of the nineteenth century consisted of concerts by local or visiting conductors and orchestras. The weekly and the special event recitals of such local groups as the Seibert and Danz, Sr. and Jr. orchestras programmed selections typical of the musical taste of any American "main-street" town of the time, i.e. paraphrased selections and overtures from operas, suites, and symphonic poems. Due to the persistent and often ungratifying work of these organizations, the Twin Cities gradually became one of the potentially desirable orchestral locations in the Upper Midwest. In addition, conductors of world-wide reputation such as Theodore Thomas and Arthur Nikisch established a fetish here for "great" orchestral festival performances. Their programs contained mostly symphonic selections from the pens of the most "playable" composers of their time.

Instrumental activities in the Cities during the first half of the twentieth century were centered primarily around the performances of the newly founded Minneapolis Symphony Orchestra. It is interesting to note that from its inception this orchestra had many close connections with the University and its department of music. The orchestra is a department of the University. It is engaged by the University for every season, although it does not receive any funds from the University and is not on its budget. The first director of the orchestra, Emil Oberhoffer, was also the first professor of the music department. Dimitri Mitropoulos taught an advanced piano class and Antal Dorati is now an honorary professor of composition and orchestration. Mrs. Carlyle Scott was for many years the manager of the orchestra. The close liaison between the University, the music department, and the orchestra has shown fruitful results for composers resident at the University. Through performances of the Minneapolis Symphony Orchestra, Minnesota's instrumental composers have begun to gain national attention.

The second quarter of the twentieth century has seen the gradual addition of contemporary compositions to the traditional repertory of the Minneapolis Symphony. Although the majority of those financially able to contribute to the continuance

Minneapolis Symphony Orchestra

fund of the orchestra were of an older generation to whom Tschaikowsky, Brahms, and Richard Strauss represented the ultimate in beauty, they began to recognize in the works of certain modern composers a grandeur and poise similar to that which they found in their beloved nineteenth century music. Gradually, American compositions were also incorporated. However, the change was slow. The absence of American works until the Mitropoulos regime can be explained by the fact that not too many "great" orchestral compositions were as yet available. Music in America up to the end of the First World War was "still an unformed art" as Arthur Farwell has pointed out. Under the leadership of Eugene Ormandy (1932-1937) for example, the works of only six American composers were performed (Ernest Schelling, Edward MacDowell, Leo Sowerby, Paul Nordoff, Aaron Copland, Philip James).

Under the direction of Dimitri Mitropoulos (1937-1949), a considerable increase in the performance of music by American composers can be noticed. Approximately six or seven American composers were represented during each season. However, this number is still small when compared to a total number of approximately sixty-five composers listed for each season. The following works of resident composers were played:

Aliferis, James	Symphony No. 1
	"Minnesota 1849," Fantasy for Orchestra
Erickson, Robert	Introduction and Allegro
Finney, Ross Lee	Slow Piece for Strings
Cordero, Roque	Panamanian Overture, No. 2
Verall, John	Portrait of Man
	Symphony No. 1 in E

Antal Dorati's carefully balanced programming incorporates a moderate number of American and Latin American composers into the repertory. Preference is given with local composers, some of whom are connected to the University of Minnesota and Macalester College. These works performed were:

Carpenter, Vincent	Summer Overture
Fetler, Paul	Gothic Variations
	Symphony No. 3
	Contrasts for Orchestra
George, Earl	Introduction and Allegro
	Violin Concerto
Helm, Everett	Divertimento for String Orchestra
Monhardt, Maurice	Overture: "The Trumpet shall sound"
Peterson, Wayne	Free Variations for Orchestra

Dorati himself demonstrated his capacity as a serious composer in his oratorio, "The Way of the Cross" and a violincello concerto, both to be performed this season. His oratorio is based on a translation from Paul Claudel's poem, *Le Chemin de la Croix*. Its fourteen divisions—or short movements—reflect the fourteen stations of the Cross. The work is written for chorus, orchestra, soprano and baritone soloists, and narrator. Unlike a Bach passion, the soloists play no specific role (as for example, the Evangelist). The narrator is, of course, the poet speaking while the chorus sometimes reflects the passions of the people of Jerusalem, sometimes comments on the action, and sometimes speaks the thoughts of the narrator or the contemporary Christian. This is a highly dramatic and moving work. Particularly exciting is the choral speaking or rhythmic chanting at such points in the text as "Crucify Him!" The first and last movements of the work present clearly a tone row. Motives from this row are developed throughout the other movements. Its first statement can be heard in the opening bars of the orchestra; its last statement comes at the very end of the piece, quietly and with great feeling, when the à cappella chorus sings in unison "Our Lord, Our Lord, O look at your creation. How all profound it is. How it is eternal!"

For the last five years the Civic Orchestra of Minneapolis has met with the enthusiastic support of the community. This is due primarily to the dynamic direction of Thomas Nee who has contributed greatly to the contemporary escenario in the Twin Cities. Not only beloved classics of today's Musical Americana such as Barber's "Knoxville: Summer of 1915" were performed but works were commissioned from local and Latin American composers.

1956-1957 season	Erickson, Robert	Variations for Orchestra
1957-1958 season	Fetler, Paul	Cantata: Of Earth's Image
1958-1959 season	Cordero, Roque	Five Messages for Orchestra
	Harris, Russel G.	Centennial Prelude (not commissioned but specially written on request for Centennial year celebrations).

As for ensemble groups, in the last five years a remarkable increase in varied chamber music concerts has taken place, performed by semi-professional and professional groups in Minneapolis and St. Paul. The best known groups are: The First Unitarian Chamber Orchestra and Chorus, and the

Twin Cities Brass Ensemble (both directed by Tom Nee), the New Friends of Chamber Music, The Minneapolis Variation Chamber Music Players, The Flor String Quartet, the Trio da Camara, and the Hamline Trio in St. Paul. Chamber music of

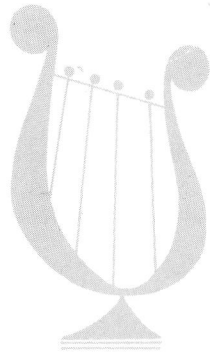

Gene Gutsche

Gene Gutsche: Third Movement from Third String Quartet Opus 27, No. 2

local composers has been acknowledged by local performances. Vincent Carpenter's string quartet was performed at a Centennial recital prepared by the Thursday Musicale, Gene Gutsche's Third String Quartet, Opus 12, No. 3, by the Variation Chamber Music Players, and Lothar Klein's Partita for harp, flute, and clarinet, and his quintet for piano and strings at the Walker Art Center. It has been the program policy of the Trio da Camara (established 1953) to include one contemporary work per program. A piano trio by Glen Glasow, St. Catherine faculty member, was performed by this ensemble on January 27th, 1957. Electronic chamber music made its Twin Cities debut with the performance of a suite for string quartet by L. A. Hiller, Jr. and L. M. Isaacson. The work is written for the Illiac, an automatic high speed digital computer. Ian Morton (Macalester) and Anthony Schultz have for many years pioneered work in the field of electronics and music.

The local chapter of the International Society for Contemporary Music was, during its lifetime, inspired by the dedicated efforts of the famous twelve-tone composer, Ernst Krenek. From 1942 to 1947, Krenek was at Hamline University in St. Paul, first as chairman of the department of music and later as Dean of the School of Fine Arts. While at Hamline, he completed many compositions and edited *The Hamline Studies in Musicology* (2 volumes). Ernst Krenek was not only an influential composition teacher, he also created a general interest in Minnesota for twelve-tone music.

As a genuine expression of the permissive shelter which contemporary music has found in the Twin Cities, the *Composer's Forum* under the chairmanship of Tom Nee, has reopened its activities in the fall of this year. The major purpose of this organization is to perform compositions of local composers and give the composers an opportunity to discuss problems related to their works.

Following Mr. Sherman's example, we may distinguish two categories of Minnesota composers: those who left for either the East or West Coast and those who have remained in Minnesota. To the former group belong John Verall, Ross Lee Finney, Everett Helm, Marge Richter, James Aliferis, Earl George, Fred Goossen, Wilbur Ogden, and Robert Erickson. The latter consists of Gene Gutsche, Paul Fetler, Lothar Klein (at the moment studying with Boris Blacher and Rufer in Berlin) and Wayne Peterson at the University of Minnesota, Vincent Carpenter at Macalester, Russell G. Harris at Hamline, and Glen Glasow at St. Catherine.

I will discuss briefly only the works of one of the representatives of the first group: Ross Lee Finney, one of the most distinguished and successful composers Minnesota has ever produced. His numerous works are distinguished by their directly musical nature, spontaneity, and freshness. In all his compositions, whether tonal, polytonal, or atonal, sophistication and simplicity create unproblematic, adroit melodic lines, harmonies which can be understood tonally, a musical texture which is translucent and exuberantly light, and musical form which is adapted to the individuality of the composition.

In accordance with his contrapuntal simplicity and melodic lyricism, Finney's interest in folk expression is revealed in his Third String Quartet, his Violin Concerto, and his Fiddle-Doodle-Ad. His solo songs to Three Seventeenth Century Lyrics and his Poor Richard, a cycle of Seven Songs to texts by Benjamin Franklin, are brief and concise, expressing one main thought mood. Voice and piano parts are interrelated and blended to a composite whole. Linear, not chordal, quality is characteristic for his piano sonatas Op. 3 and 4. His careful abstention from overloading the texture (he employs large chords only at the end of sections when no other voices are moving) is admirable. This linear writing is an indication of his tendency to employ the sonorities and qualities of chamber music.

According to information obtained from the composer himself, Ross Lee Finney began to work in 1951 with the problem of the twelve tone row. His first work of this kind, his Sixth String Quartet, was well accepted by critics and audiences alike. Its use of three different orders, each with its special function in relation to tonal logic, makes it rather unique. The Second Violin Sonata uses a single order for all movements and has an almost variational solidity. The Piano Quintet uses a single order with two permutations. The Third Sonata for Violin and Piano is primarily concerned with lyricism. It is based upon a single order with two permutations.

I will discuss briefly a few works of three composers who belong to the second group: that which stayed in Minneapolis, Gene Gutsche, Wayne Peterson and Paul Fetler. Gene Gutsche's compositions are dedicated to the exploitation of the twelve tone row. His third string quartet, opus 12, No. 3, was composed in 1950-1951. From the point of view of growth in the composer, it is interesting to this extent: while the first two movements still adopt the use of tonality, the *Allegro Furioso* (third movement) utilizes twelve tone techniques. The final movement in a cyclic sense, brings together not only all principal motives of the preceding movements, but by combining both tonality and row, an interesting feeling for harmony is achieved. Although it resembles the sonata, the structure in the first, second and last movements is only freely adhered to. The movements are loosely connected in spite of the cyclic first movement. The *Allegro Furioso* stands independently as a climax of atmosphere and expression.

While the Third String Quartet is still connected with techniques of the past, in Judith, opus 27, No. 2, an opera in one act and two scenes, Gutsche employs exclusively the Twelve Tone series, adding to it the use of the split interval, namely, the quarter tone which is relegated exclusively to the strings. The actual use of them is achieved by dividing the entire string section in half. The first half of the string body is tuned to "A-Pitch 440" while the remaining half is tuned to "A-Pitch 425." The opera takes the biblical story of Judith (which is narrated by the "biblical" Judith in the prologue of the opera) and transforms it into a present-day situation: the plight of a Negress, Yodi, in a Southern community.

In Wayne Peterson's Free Variations for Orchestra, the variation form is treated in a slightly unorthodox manner. Each variation, a complete movement in itself, adds fresh material to that supplied by the slow theme. Four sections combine to form the second variation, a "song without words," movement. In the *Adagio* variation, can-

onic devices drawn from the main motives of the original theme are used very effectively. In Variation IV, pointillistic fragments combine to form a furious new theme fugally exposed by the strings. A climax is soon reached and a more relaxed diatonic theme patterned after the main theme appears first in the woodwinds, then in the strings and horns. A long contrapuntal treatment of the two leads to the recapitulation of the fugue theme with which the coda begins. The emotional intensity increases with the addition of more instruments until syncopations bring the piece to a violent close.

As to Paul Fetler's impressive writing, it is diametrically opposed to the twelve-tone school. The model flavor of his works reminds us of his kinship with Hindemith and Bartok rather than with Schoenberg. The composer is primarily concerned with an economic exploitation of a restricted number of musical thoughts seeking concentrated

Paul Fetler

unification within his tonal speech rather than experimental diversification of an "ars ultima et novissima." He believes in the importance of a feeling of firmness within *tonal* centers. The musical texture in his composition depends on the principles of tension and repose as exposed by movement from one tonal center to the next. This relationship between energy and release of energy can also be seen in his handling of rhythm and in his brilliant orchestration.

The first movement of Fetler's Symphony No. 3 presents three themes in sonata allegro fashion. The recapitulation, however, uses the unusual device of repeating these themes in inverse order. The main theme of the 2nd movement is a lovely song performed gently by the violins accompanied by pizzicato bass violins. The brilliant orchestral colors and energetic rhythms of the last movement are an exciting conclusion to the symphony.

Paul Fetler describes his Contrasts for Orchestra as a "nontraditional" symphony. The entire work is permeated by a germ idea which is varied and developed throughout the composition. In the 2nd movement (Adagio) this germ idea, or "shape" as Donald Ferguson calls it, recurrs as a choral-phrase in a modified rondo fashion. In the 3rd movement, an ABA form, the "shape" appears

in sprightly melodies played here and there by flute, violin, and piano. In the last movement, a modification of the germ idea appears as the theme in a Theme and Variations structure.

The preceding information has described Minnesota's past and present accomplishments in the field of music education, composition, and performance. It is interesting that this contribution has been made despite the fact that in this area there is no professional school of music of university caliber. Through our discussion we have tried to point out that Minnesota is a state in which great opportunities await the performing and instructing musician as well as the composer. Many vital factors have contributed to this musical atmosphere: increased though sometimes bewildered interest of a growing public for music and contemporary music in particular, exuberantly varied activities in the field of church music, and the persistently interesting symphonic offerings of the Minneapolis Symphony Orchestra, just to name a few.

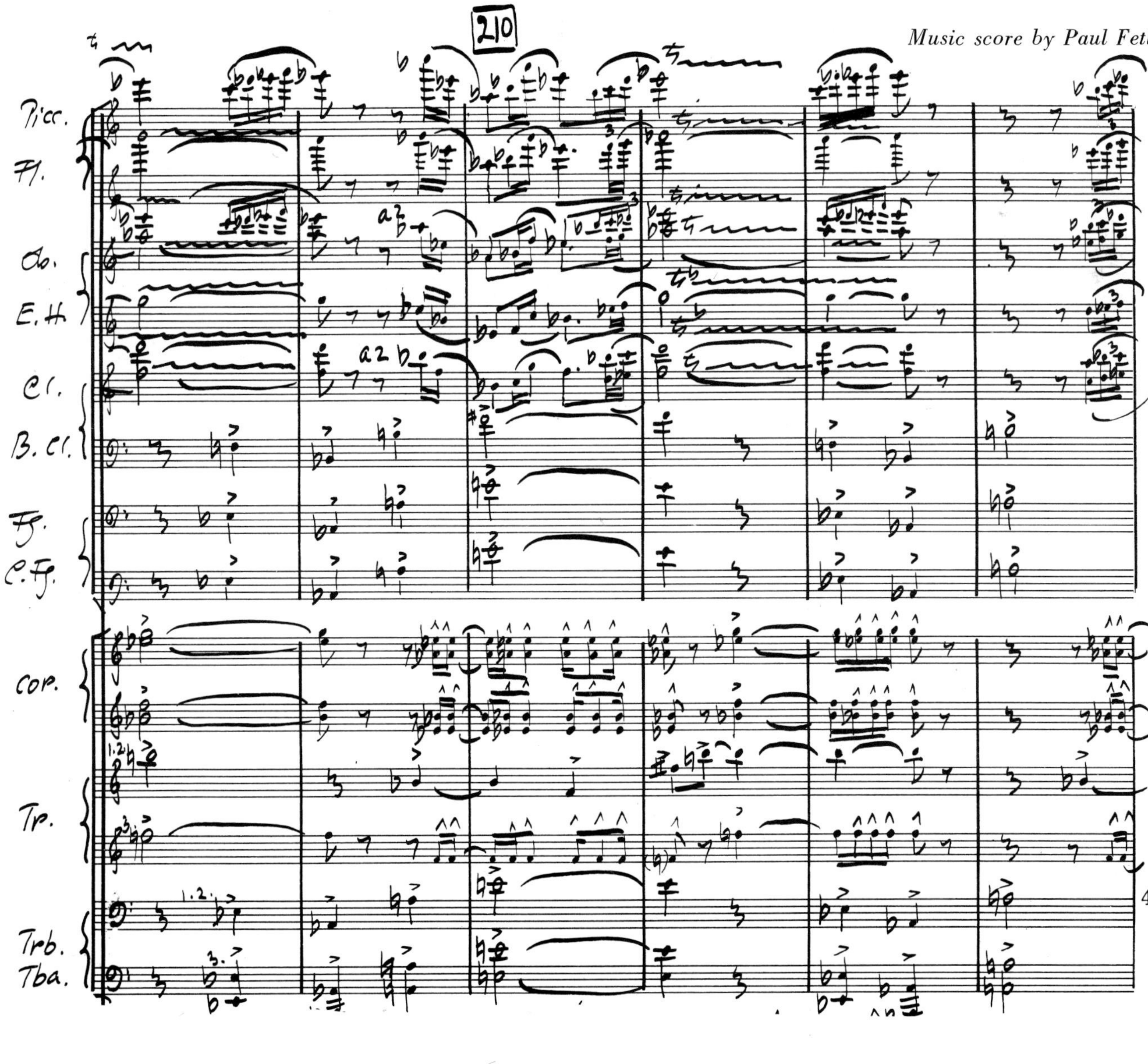

Music score by Paul Fetler

421

EPILOGUE:

Minnesota
Of The Future

By Former Governor Orville L. Freeman

Minnesota, as we enjoy it today, has been built by its people. The diversity of national backgrounds from which they came is one of our great assets. Today Minnesota counts as its citizens people whose national origins represent nearly every country in the world.

Minnesota owes its greatness to its people, to the personal qualities and the cultural heritage they brought with them. They came with a dream of better things, and a burning desire for freedom. They came with a willingness to work hard. And, because they came from many different lands with varying traditions, we in Minnesota have developed a mutual respect for differences, and a conviction that individual qualities and character alone are the factors that count. We have learned from our own experience that there are no inherent differences among human beings that should prevent their living together in cooperation, harmony, and peace.

Minnesota's pioneers faced hardships with great courage. They turned a wilderness into one of the world's greatest and most productive agricultural areas. With steady determination they overcame obstacles of loneliness and distance from friends. They harnessed the forces of nature that often seemed hostile, by hard work, great skill, and steadfast devotion. They did it by working with

and helping each other, in a spirit of cooperation that has become characteristic of our state.

Minnesota's pioneers laid the foundation for the building of great cities and great industries. They built churches and synagogues, giving us a heritage of deep spiritual values and basic religious freedom. They established a system of education dedicated to the principle that educational opportunity must be available to all. They provided for a great university, and for many other public and private institutions of higher education; and gave abundant evidence of their recognition of the importance of research, of experimentation, of scientific progress, and of cultural advance.

As we review Minnesota's heritage we pay sincere and grateful tribute to the pioneers of the past, whose achievements have provided our state with its values of today and its promise for tomorrow. But we must do more than this. For unless we gain from the accomplishments of the past a compelling determination to go forward to greater progress in the future our tribute will lose its greatest value.

For we have only begun to pioneer, here in Minnesota, and in the United States, and in the rest of the world. There lie ahead new frontiers of adventure, exploration, discovery, and achieve-

Modern farm methods increase productivity.

Checking progress of silicon crystal at Minneapolis Honeywell's research center.

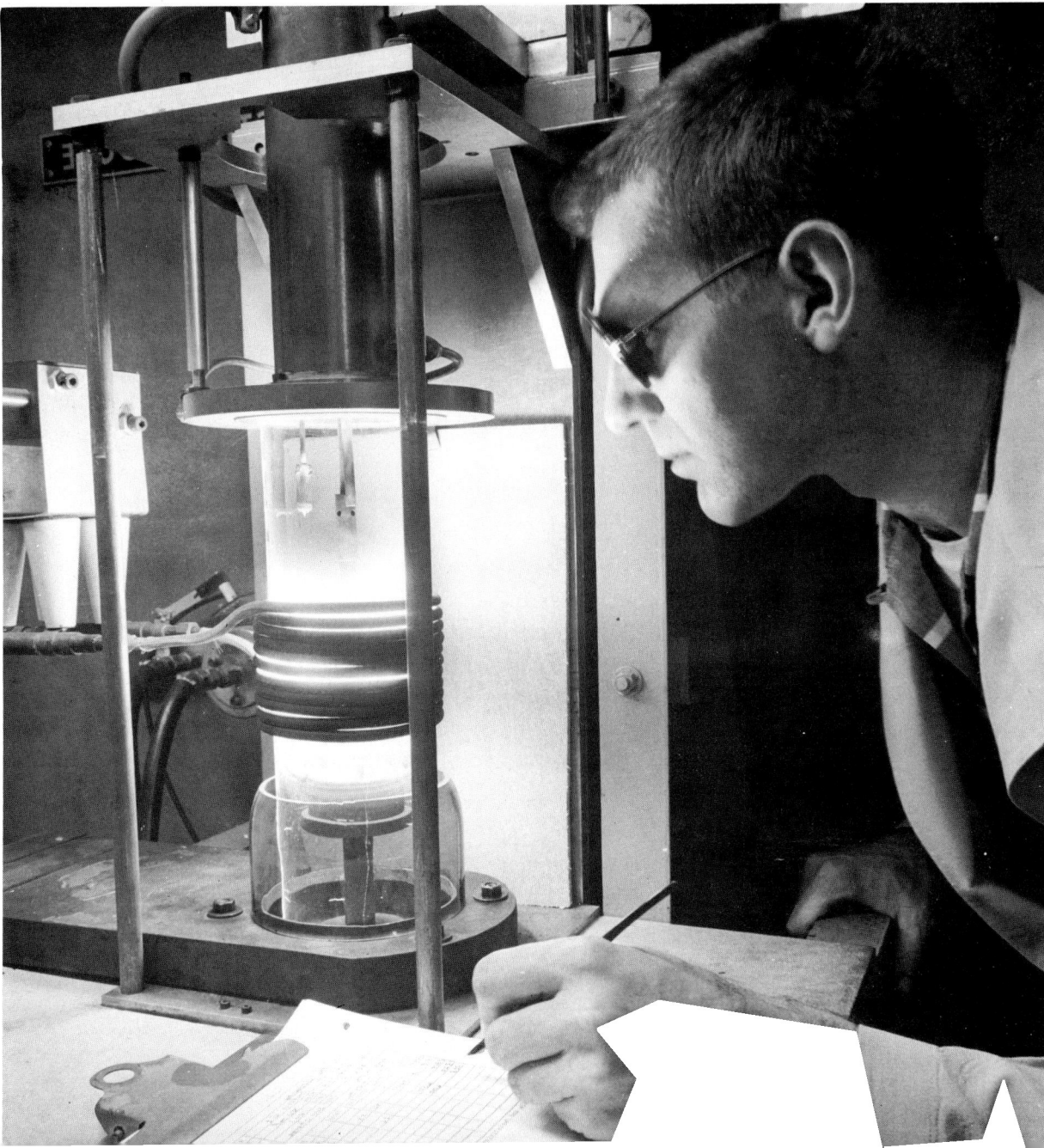

ment that are far more exciting, far more challenging, and far more important to the future of mankind than any in our history.

The pioneering that needs to be done in the present and in the future is in some ways different from that of the past. Instead of the old wilderness of great plains, western forests and mountains, the new frontiers involve discoveries in science, the development of new technology, and—most important of all—progress in the art of human relations.

Let us look, for a moment, at these new frontiers, and compare them with the old.

In agriculture we need to continue the scientific progress that eliminates human drudgery, that minimizes natural hazards, and that produces more and better food and fiber. We have already come a long way from the oxen and the primitive machinery of Minnesota pioneers.

We have come so far along in the mechanization of agriculture that we face the economic and social problems that arise from the high cost of mechanized methods, and the challenge of finding a way to use them efficiently and still maintain the traditional values of the family farm.

We have progressed so far in scientific agriculture that we see the possibility of producing enough food for all the people on earth. There is confidence that we can conquer this physical frontier that stands in the way of victory over hunger. But we face an even more difficult human frontier. We must meet the challenge in the field of human relations—the challenge of arranging the relationships among peoples so that, in this one world, we no longer have millions of hungry people and millions of tons of surplus food.

In industry, too, new frontiers present great challenges. Mechanization, automation, and other technological changes are minimizing toil and monotony. We are optimistic that continued progress will make it possible to increase productive capacity sufficiently to supply all the goods we need. But here, again, we face a critically serious lag along the frontier of economic organization. We in the United States today are not using the productive capacity we have. We have not yet organized our economy for full production. We must recognize this as a frontier to conquer. It is critically important, for us and for the world, that we meet this challenge—that we utilize our productive capacity to the full—and that we make sure that the benefits of our greatly increased productivity are distributed fairly and equitably to contribute to the well-being of all.

Limitless frontiers await development in the field of harnessing new sources of power—the energy of the atom and the energy of the sun. Here, too, physical science has progressed so far toward the conquest of its frontier that we foresee, in the relatively near future, almost unbelievable possibilities. But we are afraid of this new power. We know that the power that can light a million homes can destroy a city. We fear this power because we seem so far away from victory in our search for a way to a peaceful world.

New methods and techniques of communication and transportation, in common use today, would have seemed more impossible to Minnesotans a hundred years ago than a trip to the moon does to us now. We have conquered the physical problems of communication. But this conquest has presented us with the problem of preventing the misuse of the new media to foster misunderstanding, prejudice, and hate. We are challenged with the task of using these media to advance truth and tolerance, friendship and understanding.

As we review these new frontiers, and compare them with the frontiers of the past, one element of contrast seems to me to be of greatest significance. The hardships, struggles, and achievements in our history have led to great and almost incredible success in our conquest of the physical forces of nature. In this field we have progressed so far during the century just past that we are now confident of continued success. For the first time in human history we can foresee the physical possibility of providing food, clothing and shelter enough to meet the needs of every man, woman, and child on earth. But we do not feel the same confidence today in our ability to control the use of this great new power for the benefit—rather than the destruction—of mankind.

Jet airliners are now being used on northwest routes.

Port of Duluth, one of the most modern and efficient marine terminals in the United States.

Proposed redevelopment of Minneapolis' lower loop gives a look of the city of the future.

The new seaway port of Duluth opens northwest area to ships of the world.

The great challenge of the century ahead is, therefore, the conquest of the frontiers of human relations. Success in this field is all the more critically urgent because of the great scientific progress we have made. A man travelling by horseback in 1858 could make an error in directing his mount off the road without risking much injury, even to himself; but a man with his foot on the accelerator controlling a 300 horse-power motor cannot afford that mistake. During most of the past century it was possible to suffer a depression—yes, even to go through a war—and when it was over we could pick up the pieces, repair the damage, and go on. This may no longer be possible today.

Progress toward conquering the frontiers of human relations is therefore our greatest task in the years ahead, here in Minnesota as well as elsewhere in the nation and in the world. The challenge must be met both on the home front and in the field of international relations. And the two fields are closely interrelated.

Basic to victory on the home front will be our progress toward making available, to all people, the higher standards of living that increased productivity will make possible. We will need to insure that the increased proportion of older people—whose lives are being lengthened by the amazing progress of medical and related sciences—can live useful and happy lives during their later years. We will need to provide the kind of educational and cultural opportunities for the young that will enable each individual to develop his maximum potential and contribute his best to society. We will need to progress ever closer to our ideal of equality of opportunity for all.

And, in view of the crisis of our day, the most critically urgent challenge is to preserve and extend the principles of democracy and freedom as we work toward a program of international relations that will insure a peaceful world.

We in Minnesota are increasingly conscious of our responsibility for sharing in the conquest of this frontier. There is much in Minnesota's tradition, there is much in our heritage from the nations from which our people came, that enables us to see clearly that in the century ahead our future is tied to that of the rest of the world.

Three flags floated over this land of ours before the Stars and Stripes. In the early days when the land that is now Minnesota was in the hands of Spain, and France, and Britain, this territory and its future were tied to international events taking place in an old world far away. There were few people in Minnesota to know or care.

During the long years of pioneering, settlement, and rapid development, this part of America became known as isolationist. We were located in the interior, and we lacked international trade. We were so absorbed in conquering the frontiers close at hand that we felt no need for keeping up with problems abroad.

But this old kind of isolationism is rapidly passing from the scene. We are no longer a hinterland. We are now a heartland at the crossroads of a continent. International trade is becoming more important to Minnesotans every year. And we are aware of the fact that distances have shortened, so that in a matter of hours friendly visitors—or deadly missiles—can reach us across the North Pole.

We are no longer as self-sufficient as we thought we were a hundred years ago. And just as we know today that our economic prospertiy is tied to that of the rest of the nation, we know that our prospects for peace are tied to those of the rest of the world. We are therefore ready and eager to join our efforts with those of free men everywhere to work toward that goal of peace.

In our efforts to meet the challenge of this critical new frontier we can gain inspiration, courage, and determination from the best of the principles, ideals, and experiences that have contributed so much to our progress during the past hundred years.

We have learned, for example, from the diversity of backgrounds of the people of Minnesota that there is validity in the idea of the United Nations. We have become deeply appreciative of the common needs, hopes and aspirations that lie in the hearts of all men, regardless of nation, color or creed.

We have learned the value of study and research, of education and understanding, in our efforts to surmount the difficulties and to solve the

Modern residence hall on Gustavus Adolphus campus.

problems that were met on the frontiers of the past. We know that these methods are just as essential in working toward the goals of international peace and better human relations as they are when applied to the conquest of the physical world.

And we have learned from experience the supreme importance of two invaluable traits inherent in the character of the pioneers who built our state: the desire for something better, and the willingness to work hard. Immigrants to Minnesota came from scores of different backgrounds and for many specific reasons. But they all had these two traits in common. They wanted something better than they had, and were willing to work hard to achieve it. No one who was content with the status quo would face the hardships of a new country. No matter how they may have cherished the values of the past, their eyes were on a vision of the future. Their dream was for a better life. This is still our goal.

The future that lies ahead, with all its dangers, offers more promise for a better life than man has ever before been able to glimpse across the frontiers of the past. These new horizons demand new concepts, and to reach these new horizons we must be as ready to cast off outmoded shackles of the past as our pioneer forefathers were in their determination to make their dreams a reality. And we must be as ready and willing to assume our responsibility for the hard work involved as they were when they broke the sod of a new land. For the task is more difficult than any we have ever faced. The penalty for error will be greater. And the penalty for apathy and indifference, for inability or unwillingness to see the possibilities, could be permanent failure.

I believe that we will succeed; that we have the resources, the ability, and the will to overcome the obstacles that lie on the frontier of human relations, so that we may gain full benefit from continued progress on the physical frontier. I am confident that, in our second century, we in Minnesota will contribute our share in the effort to reach the goal beyond the frontier. I believe that we can achieve it, not as Minnesotans alone, not even as Americans alone, but in cooperation with free men, and with men who aspire to freedom, everywhere.

428

PHOTO CREDITS

We gratefully acknowledge credit to the following organizations, companies and individuals who so generously supplied photographs to make a better presentation of our Minnesota history possible.

PHOTO CREDITS (*Continued*)

Associated Press

Augsburg College

Carleton College

Chicago Natural History Museum

Cold Springs Granite Co.

College of Saint Benedict

College of Saint Catherine

College of Saint Scholastica

College of Saint Teresa

College of Saint Thomas

Community Chest

Concordia College

Don Berg Photography

Erling Larsen

Ford Motor Company

Furness Sisters

General Mills, Inc.

George Miles Ryan Studios

Great Northern Railroad

Gustavus Adolphus College

Hamline University

Hare Photographs, Inc.

Keith Brings and Karen Petersen

Kenneth Wright Studios, St. Paul

Leo Simmer Photography

Macalester College

Minneapolis Brewing Co.

Minneapolis Chamber of Commerce

Minneapolis Grain Exchange

Minneapolis Honeywell Co.

Minneapolis Moline

Minneapolis Star and Tribune

Minneapolis Symphony Orchestra

Minnesota and Ontario Paper Co.

Minnesota Dept. of Business Development

Minnesota Division of Publicity

Minnesota Mining & Manufacturing Co.

Mr. William Madison

Northern Pacific Railroad

Northern States Power Co.

Northwest Orient Airlines

Norton & Peel Studios

Novak Studio, Mpls.

Peter Marcus Photography

Photomatic

Phototech

Radio Station KSTP

Radio Station WCCO

Riehle Studios

Robert R. Blanch Photography

Ronald Anderson

Saint John's University

Saint Mary's College

Saint Olaf College

Saint Paul Chamber of Commerce

St. Paul Dispatch and Pioneer Press

Swedish Institute

T. S. Denison & Company, Inc.

University of Minnesota

Walker Art Center